Constitutional Law

for

Criminal Justice Professionals

Second Edition

Irving J. Klein, B.S., J.D.

Professor of Law and Police Science
John Jay College of Criminal Justice
City University of New York

Constitutional Law

for

Criminal Justice Professionals

Second Edition

CORAL GABLES PUBLISHING CO. INC.
5065 S.W. 107 Ave. Unit 123
Miami, Florida, 33173

Coral Gables Publishing Co.

Interior design was provided by Amato Prudente.

Library of Congress Catalog Card Number: 86–71450

Klein, Irving J.
Constitutional Law For Criminal Justice Professionals
Second Edition

Includes indexes.
1. United States—Constitutional Law. 2. Criminal justice, Administration of—United States. 3. Criminal justice personnel—United States. I. Title.
KF4550.K58 1986 345.' 73' 05 86–71450
ISBN First Edition 0–87872–219X
ISBN 0–938993–00–3

Printed in the United States of America
1 2 3 4 5 6 7 8 9—90 89 88 87 86

Dedicated to my dear wife, Dr. Marta Arias-Klein, whose encouragement and help were largely responsible for the completion of this work.

Contents

Preface to the Second Edition

The major problem with a textbook containing cases and principles of law that include United States Supreme Court decisions is that some of the material is out of date when the book is initially printed. Second and third printings only exacerbate the deficiency. This is particularly a problem when the book is focused on constitutional law dealing with criminal law problems because this area of law changes more rapidly than any other legal topic.

To correct this condition, I have adopted the much used device of providing for a pocket part at the end cover of the book. Annual supplements of more recent noteworthy decisions or trends will be available at moderate costs. The main volume has been brought up to date to include prominent decisions of the United States Supreme Court up to and including May 1986. Parallel citations have been provided where available. Some cases were so recent when the book went to press that not all of the citations were available at that time. The pocket part supplements will contain the full citations as they become available.

State courts throughout the country are citing state constitutions to increase the protection of individual rights beyond the minimum requirements that recently have been set by the United States Supreme Court. This new trend promises to create variations of individual constitutional rights depending upon the state that the individual is located in when the alleged violation of rights occurs.

It is obviously impractical for a book of this type to differentiate between the decisions of one state as compared with another. For that reason the emphasis has been placed on minimum constitutional rights afforded individuals by the United States Supreme Court. If a student is interested in ascertaining whether any particular state affords greater protection for a specified right, that student is advised to consult the state or regional law digest to find and read cases dealing with the topic of interest. It is always a good idea when doing this to consult the pocket part of the digest before going to the main volume, if the main volume contains a pocket part.

I have collaborated with my wife, Marta Arias-Klein, M.A., Ed.D., in the preparation of a teacher's manual. Her expertise in criminal justice as well as in pedagogy is a welcome addition to assist teachers to help students master the contents of the book.

The objectives of the second edition are similar to those expressed in the preface of the first edition which follows this preface. It is suggested that the reader consult the preface to the first edition to assist in the comprehension of the material.

I would be remiss if I failed to bring attention to the fact that many of the professors throughout the country who have adopted the first edition of this book have communicated with me and have given me their valuable constructive criticism. I have corrected the errors that were brought to my attention and I thank them for their interest.

I welcome hearing from readers. I may be reached at John Jay College of Criminal Justice, C.U.N.Y., 444 West 56th Street, New York, New York 10019.

The other persons who assisted in the preparation of this book are too numerous to be mentioned. Therefore, I will omit the usual ending to a preface. I thank them collectively.

Irving J. Klein

New York City, New York
July 1, 1986

Preface to First Edition

It is no longer practical or economical for a government to employ a person in the criminal justice system without first requiring that the new employee be thoroughly familiar with the day-to-day standard operating procedures of that agency. The law enforcement officer must also be given a thorough understanding of the constitutional requirements of the position. At one time, the deprivation of a constitutional right carried a sanction of the exclusion of certain tainted evidence. Today, in addition to the exclusionary rule, money judgments against the employee and/or the governmental employer are an ever present threat as well.

To minimize this risk, many progressive governmental units now require that entering personnel have a minimum of an associate degree from an accredited institution of higher learning. Others require a minimum of a baccalaureate degree. There are some states, counties, and cities that grant extra compensation to in-service and entrance level personnel who have acquired a formal degree from an accredited institution. Considering the present economic climate, it is good business practice for a government to have highly qualified professional employees in its criminal justice agencies.

I have designed this book for use in classes in constitutional law with an emphasis on the criminal aspects of this law. It can provide both in-service students and pre-service students of criminal law with a greater insight of the reasons why law enforcement officers are limited in their responsibilities and powers. Although the officer may initially believe that the courts inhibit and prevent convictions of perpetrators of crime, after reading and studying this book, the student should understand that there is an overriding reason for the exclusionary rule which is very important to the survival of our country as a free democratic state.

My hope is that *Constitutional Law for Criminal Justice Professionals* will teach those persons charged with the responsibility of enforcing our criminal laws methods to apprehend, supervise, adjudicate, and convict accused persons within the framework of constitutional procedure.

The text begins with the history of the constitutional development of the United States. The first two chapters are introductory in nature, dealing with both this development and the judicial system. Subsequent chapters deal with topics that concern many criminal justice employees in their daily work. The sections are numbered first by chapter number, followed by a period, and then the consecutive number of the section. Beginning with Chapter 3, I have included a selection of edited landmark cases which should highlight the chapter material. An instructor may wish the student to read these cases and submit written or oral student's briefs to demonstrate proficiency in course content and analytical ability.

I have drawn on my experience as a police officer, social worker, county prosecutor, defense counsel, and college professor in an effort to make this text interesting and readable. I hope my intentions have been realized.

One reading this book is exposed to the evolutionary process of constitutional guarantees afforded to those who are accused of crime. Some United States Supreme Court decisions included in the text are no longer considered as binding law. Later cases, which have modified or changed the principle of law of the older cases, are included to bring the content up to date as of April 1979. This pedagogical approach was used to enable the student to observe the evolutionary changes in our law.

The book does not treat civil or sociological aspects of constitutional law. Such material is properly included in other texts and courses dealing with those subjects. The student will be studying material extracted primarily from decisions of the United States Supreme Court. Some lower court decisions are also included where no higher authority was located by your author, so that a lower court might have some persuasive argument for a particular position which might be before the court.

There are two basic methods to study law. The first is the "case method" and the second is the "text method." Some students and professors have indicated that they prefer to use both methods simultaneously. It is for this reason that beginning with Chapter 3, each chapter is followed by several cases that illustrate a principle of law that has been discussed in that chapter.

The "case method" is designed to help the student remember the principle of law of the case relating to a factual pattern which occurred in the case. Thus the student learns to understand the law by inductive reasoning, and then is able to apply this principle of law to other cases having similar facts.

The procedure under the "case method" requires a student to read the decision, summarize it in writing pursuant to directions received from the teacher, and recite in class the results of the summary, emphasizing the primary principle of law. This is a student brief.

case may be found in the volume and page number indicated in the citation. For example, the case of Stone v. Powell, 428 U.S. 465, 96 S.Ct. 3037, 49 L.Ed.2d 1067 (1976), has been cited. This means that the decision of Stone v. Powell may be found in three parallel places, viz., Volume 428 of the *United States Reports* at page 465, Volume 96 of the *Supreme Court Reporter* at page 3037, and Volume 49 of the *Lawyers' Edition of the United States Supreme Court Reports*, second series, at page 1067. This case was reported by the Court during the 1976 Term and hence (1976) at the end of the citation denotes that fact. Reports of the United States Supreme Court are first published as "slip decisions." The official edition is published by the United States Government Printing Office. Three unofficial editions are published. They are *United States Law Week, Commerce Clearing House Supreme Court Bulletin*, and the *Criminal Law Reporter*. Slip decisions are published shortly after the decision is handed down and hence they are subject to revision. The citation of the "slip decision" is indicated by docket number, court, and date of decision (not Term of Court), e.g., Holloway et al. v. Arkansas, No.76-5856, U.S.Sup.Ct., April 3, 1978. The unofficial decisions have a wide circulation. This case would be cited as Holloway et al. v. Arkansas, No.76-5856, U.S.Sup.Ct., April 3, 1978 (46 L.W. 4289), or C.C.H., Sup.Ct.Bull. or Cr.L. citations may be used.

Limited repetition will be observed as one reads through the pages of this book. This design was intentionally adopted to conform with the pedagogical method that first tells the student what is going to be discussed, next tells it, and finally, tells what has been told.

This book has resulted from the combined efforts of many people. Among them are my wife, Professor Marta A. Klein, Long Island University, C.W. Post Center; my son, Professor Michael R. Klein, Nassau Community College; Professor John J. Sullivan, Mercy College; Vice-Chancellor Richard H. Ward, University of Chicago, Chicago Circle; Professor Eileen Rowland, Chief Librarian, John Jay College of Criminal Justice; Professor Bernard Braverman, Biscayne College, Miami; William J. Kittridge; Boston State College; Edwin C. Pearson, Department Chairman, Division of Criminal Justice, University of New Haven; Judith A. Hails, J.D., California State University, Long Beach; Professor Frederick G. Barry, Jr., Massasoit Community College; Doctor Thomas A. Reppetto, President of Citizen's Crime Commission of New York City; Irwin R. Berenson, former Director Peninsula Public Library; Edward L. Francis, former Managing Editor at Duxbury Press; Pat Fitzgerald, present Editor at Duxbury Press; and my secretary, Marion Berenson, who deserves much credit for the endless job of typing the manuscript.

Irving J. Klein

New York City, N.Y.
November 15, 1979

Table of Edited Decisions and Applicable Chapters

CHAPTER 13

CHAPTER 14

CHAPTER 1

Contents

The Constitutional Process

§ 1.1 Introduction

In the pages that follow, constitutional concepts are expressed citing United States Supreme Court decisions close to the heart and interest of police officers and other law enforcement personnel. The purpose of this book is to enable the law enforcement officer to read, discuss, and brief these cases in a manner which will expose the student to the "why" of the court's thinking rather than merely to the end result. Often the end result of a decision which is considered abstractly imparts a negative response from the law enforcement officer. However, when the decision is explained and understood, the officer is better able by training, intellect, and temperament to perform more efficiently.

The law enforcer who is honestly attempting to do a conscientious job can work effectively within the framework of the United States Constitution if properly trained and properly motivated. The converse of this works to the advantage of the offender who is arrested and walks out of the courtroom a free person shortly after being apprehended by the police. If our society is to prevail, special instruction, special care, and special motivation must find their way into the more than forty thousand law enforcement entities in the United States of America.

§ 1.2 Constitutional Law Defined

Constitutional law is defined very loosely because it escapes a precise definition. In its broadest sense, the term *constitutional law* designates that branch of jurisprudence which deals with the formation, construction, and interpretation of the Constitution by the President, Congress, court decisions, rulings of public officials, as well as governmental practices and customs.

§ 1.3 Common Law Defined

In order to understand the concept of constitutional law, the student must have an understanding of the phrase *common law*. This has been defined by case law as follows:

As distinguished from law created by the enactment of legislatures, the common law comprises the body of those principles and rules of action, relating to the government and security of persons and property which derive their authority solely from usages and customs of immemorial antiquity, or from the judgments and decrees of the courts recognizing, affirming, and enforcing such usages and customs; and, in this sense, particularly the ancient unwritten law of England. 1 Kent, Comm. 492; Western Union Tel. Co. v. Call Pub. Co., 181 U.S. 92, 21 S.Ct. 561, 45 L.Ed. 765; State v. Buchanan, 5 Har. & J. (Md.) 365, 9 Am.Dec. 534; Lux v. Haggin, 69 Cal. 255, 10 P. 674; Barry v. Port Jervis, 64 App. Div. 268, 72 N.Y.S. 104; U.S. v. Miller 236 F. 798, 800 (D.C.).

As concerns its force and authority in the United States, the phrase designates that portion of the common law of England (including such acts of parliament as were applicable) which had been adopted and was in force here at the time of the Revolution. This, so far as it has not since been expressly abrogated, is recognized as an organic part of the jurisprudence of most of the United States. Browning v. Browning, 3 N.M. 371, 9 P. 677; Guardians of Poor v. Greene, 5 Bin. (Pa.) 557; U.S. v. New Bedford Bridge, 27 Fed.Cas. 107; Hageman v. Vanderdoes, 15 Ariz. 312, 138 P. 1053, 1056, L.R.A. 1915A, 491, Ann.Cas. 1915D, 1197; Industrial Acceptance Corporation v. Webb Mo. App. 287 S.W. 657, 660.

It has also been said that the common law is that body of law and juristic theory which was originated, developed and formulated and is administered in England, and has obtained among most of the states and peoples of Anglo-Saxon stock. Lux v. Haggin, 69 Cal. 255, 10 P. 674.

§ 1.4 Changes in Law

Law may be changed in three basic ways. One is by legislative enactment. This occurs when the legislature, be it Congress, a state legislature, or a local legislative body, presents a bill that is passed and enacted into law. Another method is by constitutional amendment, the procedure for which is included in the document itself. The third method is by interpretations given to the Constitution by courts, legislative bodies, executive departments of government, and administrative agencies of government. The third method of changing the law is the one which we will be largely concerned with in the pages which follow in this text.

§ 1.5 Citations Explained

Throughout the text are references to and quotations from cases. For example, you might see Lux v. Haggin, 69 Cal. 255, 10 P. 674. In law, the numbers and letters following the name of a case are known as *citations*. They refer to a designated book in which can be found the full text of the named case. Lux v. Haggin can be found in volume 69 of the California Reports, page 255. It is also available in volume 10 of the Pacific Reporter, page 674. The City of Topeka v. Robert Moodberry, 191 Kan. 304, 380 P.2d 371, can be found in volume 191 of the Kansas Reports, page 304 and in volume 380 of the Pacific Reporter, second series, page 371.

§ 1.6 Federal Cases

Most of the cases considered in this text are cases that have been decided in federal courts. These sometimes are referred to as *federal cases*. Some have their origin in state courts, having gone through the state court system and then finding their way to the United States Supreme Court. For example, Betts v. Brady is cited 316 U.S. 455, 62 S.Ct. 1252, 86 L.Ed. 1595 (1942). The case may be found in volume 316 of the United States Reports, page 455; in volume 62 of the Supreme Court Reporter, page 1252; and in volume 86 of the Lawyers' Edition, Supreme Court Reports, page 1595, for the year 1942.

§ 1.7 United States Supreme Court Cases

Cases appear in the United States Supreme Court in four basic ways. The first and most common method is by a writ of certiorari. This is a common law writ in which a petitioner asks for a writ from a higher court, and if issued, the writ directs the lower court to send the whole record of the case up to the higher court for review. The petition for the writ is made in the first instance to the higher court.

Another method to get the United States Supreme Court to review a case is by means of an appeal from a lower court decision. Appeals may be made as a right only in designated cases.

The third and least used method is a certification of a question of law. This type of review occurs when a lower appellate court believes that they should not decide a question of law and they certify the question of law, send it on to the United States Supreme Court, and ask that court for guidance to decide a case pending before the lower court.

The fourth method is indicated in Article III of the Constitution. "In all cases affecting ambassadors, other public ministers and consuls, and those in which a state shall be a party, the Supreme Court shall have original jurisdiction."

§ 1.8 Article III, the Judicial Article

There are provisions in Article III of the United States Constitution providing for original jurisdiction of the United States Supreme Court, but these are not pertinent to the law enforcer's role and hence will be omitted in this discussion.

It is interesting to note that at present, the United States Supreme Court does not have to consider every case that comes before it except those where appellant has a right of appeal. A minimum of four justices of the Court must conclude that a substantial federal question of law exists before the Court is required to review a decision of a lower court when the case comes before the Court on a writ of certiorari.

Article III of the Constitution concerns itself with the judicial power of the United States. This is the article of the Constitution from which the United States Supreme Court derives its power and authority.

§ 1.9 Checks and Balances

We are all familiar with the system of checks and balances that was built into the structure of the Constitution. The framers were largely young and practical men. They knew well the principle that power begets power, and they were determined to do all they could to prevent one branch of the government from being more powerful than the other two branches. Accordingly they established the executive power (Article II), wherein the executive branch of the government was charged with the responsibility of implementing the laws as promulgated by the legislative power (Article I) and as interpreted by the judicial power (Article III). In this way each power acts as a check and balance on the others. We need look no further than the Watergate scandal to see how efficiently the concept of checks and balances operates. When the executive branch took too much power unto itself, it was impeded and checked by the legislative and judicial branches.

I could think of no greater example of the greatness of the American Constitution and how it has worked than when I compared it with an incident which occurred to me when I engaged in a conversation with a Portuguese youth in the Lisbon, Portugal, airport in 1972. My wife and I were in a lounge free of all other persons except this youth. After exchanging pleasantries in his obvious attempt to be friendly and practice the English language, he furtively looked about the terminal and said in a scarcely audible voice, "Is it true that you have free speech in the United States?" I replied that we have free speech and that I was a professor of constitutional law and we often studied cases in class where the courts have granted persons the right to freely express their opinions. I advised him, however, that the right of free speech did not include the right to incite a riot or falsely alarm persons in a crowded theater that there was a fire in progress when in fact that was not the case.

The youth appeared to be overwhelmed because he looked around again in the same furtive manner and exclaimed, "We have the right of free speech in our constitution, but if people say anything against the government, they are put in jail."

This short conversation with this young man increased my understanding of the constitutional process of our government more than all that I had previously learned through reading United States history.

We can verbalize about individual rights in the United States, but the Constitution might be a worthless document similar to that of the 1972 Portugal Constitution if it were not for the important division of governmental power and authority—the system of checks and balances—coupled with the desire of our military officers for an ordered society based upon the rule of law as opposed to the rule of man.

We, in the United States of America, are most fortunate to have a governmental structure that is subject to the will of the majority of the people, which over the years has represented a middle-of-the-road doctrine.

The Prime Minister of England, William E. Gladstone (1809–1888), once said, when speaking about the American Constitution, that it is "the most wonderful work ever struck off at a given time by the brain and purpose of man."

§ 1.10 The Constitution, a Living Document

The Constitution has been able to survive and is a living thing because it contains so many vague words and phrases which need to be interpreted by human beings of future generations. Examples of these terms are "full faith and credit," "necessary and proper," "general welfare," and "unreasonable search and seizure."

For example, the reasonableness of a search in 1960 might be different from that in 1975 or the year 2000. Certainly in 1950 it would have been considered unreasonable for commercial airline passengers to be searched and their luggage searched and x-rayed prior to boarding. Who among us who use the commercial airlines is not comforted when a thorough search of all passengers is conducted before they are permitted to board the flight?

§ 1.11 Vague Words in the Constitution

We can consider the vague word concept a little further if we examine the word "commerce" as it is used in Section 8, Article I, where the Constitution in delineating the powers of Congress reads: "... To regulate Commerce with foreign Nations and among the several States, and with Indian Tribes." While much credit may be accorded to the foresight of the framers of the document, no person at that time in their wildest imagination could foresee that we would be using the airways for travel or for sending messages or transmitting photographs. However it has been possible, under the interstate commerce clause, to bring order into these industries when without it we might have had complete chaos. The Constitution is a living instrument—ever changing to meet new problems confronting the American people, their way of life, and their well-being.

§ 1.12 Power Granted and Limited by the Constitution

The Constitution contains a preamble followed by seven articles and twenty-six amendments. It has three major objectives.

1. It establishes the framework or structure of government.
2. It delegates or assigns the powers of government.
3. It restrains the exercise of these powers by governmental officials in order that certain individual rights may be preserved.

In summary, one might say that the Constitution establishes the framework of government by granting and limiting its powers.

§ 1.13 Power to Government from the People

Since the time of King John and the Magna Carta of 1215, the Anglo-Saxon concept of government was established as flowing from the people. Accordingly the preamble of the United States Constitution reads: "We, the People of the United States, in Order to form a more perfect Union, establish Justice, insure domestic Tranquility, provide for the common defence, promote the general Welfare, and secure the Blessings of Liberty to ourselves and our Posterity, do ordain and establish this Constitution for the United States of America." The signatories to the document were representing the states and in that position they represented the people of their respective states.

Note that the framers of the Constitution were influenced by Anglo-Saxon tradition and common law but went one step further in the democratization process by providing that no one person or group of persons would have unlimited and unending power.

From the viewpoint of hindsight, one may not give too much importance to this revolutionary idea, but to fully appreciate its significance it is necessary to consider the conditions which existed in England and the American colonies before the Revolution.

§ 1.14 Historical Background of the Constitution

While it is not the intention of this text to deal extensively with the historical events leading to the establishment of Anglo-Saxon law and the conflict between the colonies of America with England, it is however felt that it is necessary to understand certain historical fundamentals from which grew the establishment of our system of government under the Constitution of the United States of America.

The reader is no doubt aware that colonies were established along the eastern seaboard as a result of several different reasons. Some settlers came for what they called "Religious Freedom." Others came because they were deported because of criminal activity in England. Others came to seek their fortunes in the New World. Others were pirates who established home ports from which they could attack and plunder ships on the high seas.

§ 1.15 Colonists' Desire for "Religious Freedom"

I particularly emphasized the phrase that some came for what they called "Religious Freedom" because the Plymouth Colony was established for this reason. The leaders of the colony, however, would not permit any deviation from their religion, and many other colonies were established because of this intolerance. Providence and Newport were colonies established in this manner.

§ 1.16 Procedural Rights for the Accused

The development of procedural safeguards for persons accused of crime is a fascinating chronicle in the annals of Anglo-American law. The safeguards are based upon two underlying assumptions of democracy:

1. The sanctity of the individual against the government;
2. Government by law rather than by man.

These rights were obtained at a very high price, through the blood, sweat, and tears of many generations of men and women. Fair trial as we know it today took centuries to evolve. It was an outgrowth of the Magna Carta (1215), the Petition of Rights (1628), and the Bill of Rights (1689).

§ 1.17 Bill of Rights

The first ten amendments to the United States Constitution are called the Bill of Rights. The rights enumerated therein were not new to the colonies. Eight state constitutions gathered these rights into separate provisions called a Declaration of Rights, or a Bill of Rights. Connecticut and Rhode Island, for example, had these rights in their original charter from England. The most influential of the states' Bills of Rights was the Virginia Bill of Rights of 1776. It greatly influenced the final document that was ratified by the thirteen new states.

§ 1.18 Articles of Confederation

It is interesting to note that the Articles of Confederation (1777) preceding the Constitution of the United States of America did not grant important legislative power to the central government, and therefore there was no Bill of Rights incorporated in the document.

§ 1.19 Constitutional Convention and the Bill of Rights

The Constitutional Convention of 1787 did not deal with the concept of a Bill of Rights. It appears that the delegates to the convention were persuaded to avoid the issue, thinking the limited powers of Congress made a Bill of Rights unnecessary.[1]

A Bill of Rights was suggested in the closing days of the convention by George Mason. Apparently most of the delegates agreed with Roger Sherman when he said that a Bill of Rights was unnecessary because those guarantees already existed in state constitutions. Many states refused to ratify the Constitution without a Bill of Rights included. They questioned the absence of a guarantee of freedom of religion, speech, security against

[1]Annals of Congress 438–439 (1834).

unreasonable searches and seizures, jury trials, a guarantee to life, liberty, and property through due process of law, and a guarantee against excessive bail.

The struggle for ratification by the states was lengthy. The convention was in session from May 25 through September 17, 1787. The delegates agreed that after nine state conventions had ratified the Constitution, the government of the United States of America would be established. It was not until May of 1790 that Rhode Island, the last of the thirteen states, made its decision to enter the Union and this was accomplished by a narrow margin. Rhode Island, along with North Carolina, was probably influenced by the spectre of being charged import duties on products that it sent to the states of the United States of America, along with other travel restrictions.

Many states were brought to ratify the original document based upon a promise that a bill of rights would be included at the first opportunity. In fulfillment of this promise, James Madison arose in the First Congress to introduce the proposals of the first ten amendments. These were quickly passed by Congress on September 25, 1789 and ratified by three-fourths of the states on December 15, 1791. They became known as the Bill of Rights.

§ 1.20 Offenders' Rights under Early Common Law

There were no procedural safeguards in early English history for those accused of crimes. There was a procedure known as the hue and cry. In some respects it was similar to programs being used in some cities and rural areas today. In essence, victims of crimes would raise a hue and cry. Then all the inhabitants of the community would arm themselves to seek the felon. We would call this a vigilante system today. At this juncture, the present-day vigilante system and the ancient hue and cry procedure take separate paths. In the hue and cry, the felon had a precarious existence. If captured, there would be a hastily convened court. If capture was resisted, a member of the community could legally kill the fugitive. Usually, there was little chance of exoneration or even for an impartial jury. Accused persons could say nothing before the court in their defense. They were usually executed by being hanged, beheaded, or thrown from a cliff by the aggrieved or a relative of the aggrieved. If they were caught, they were almost certain to endure severe sanctions. If the accused escaped, s/he would be declared an outlaw and therefore not entitled to the protection of the law. There was no right to appeal and the suspect could be executed without first being indicted. Outlaws who were captured with stolen goods on them could be executed summarily by a member of the community. Under the above conditions it was understandable that many state conventions balked at entering a government without fundamental safeguards of a bill of rights.

§ 1.21 Administration of Criminal Justice

The courts in interpreting the Tenth Amendment to the Constitution have held consistently that the administration of criminal justice is principally the function of the states, unless in so doing they offend some fundamental principle of justice, thereby violating a constitutional right.

§ 1.22 Rule of Law

The rule of law was most eloquently expressed by Prof. Albert V. Dicey when he wrote:

> No man is punishable or can be lawfully made to suffer in body or goods except for a distinct breach of law established in the ordinary legal manner before the ordinary courts of the land. In this sense the rule of law is contrasted with every system of government based on the exercise by persons in authority of wide arbitrary or discretionary powers of constraint.
>
> ... We mean in the second place, when we speak of the "rule of law" as a characteristic of our country not only that with us no man is above the law but ... that here every man, whatever be his rank or condition, is subject to the ordinary law of the realm and amenable to the jurisdiction of the ordinary tribunal.
>
> ... There remains yet a third and a different sense in which the "rule of law" or the predominance of the legal spirit may be described as a special attribute of English institutions. We may say that the constitution is pervaded by the rule of law on the ground that the general principles of the constitution (as for example the right to personal liberty, or the right of public meetings) are with us the result of judicial decisions determining the rights of private persons in particular cases brought before the courts. Campbell v. Hall (1774) Leefe 655; K.&L. 487. It should be noted, however, that the origin of parliament may not be traced to judicial decision and the independence of judges has rested on statute since the Act of Settlement (1701).

The English constitution, from which the Constitution of the United States of America evolved, was an unwritten constitution and body of laws that developed from treaties, agreements, statutes, and court decisions.

It is difficult for an American to comprehend that as the English were developing a constitution raising the status and individual liberty of its inhabitants, the converse was true in much of the civilized world. It is said that when Voltaire came to England, his feeling was that he had passed out of the realm of despotism to a land where the laws might be harsh but where men were ruled by law and not by caprice.

To point up his despair, Voltaire was sent to the Bastille for a poem which he had not written, nor did he know who had written it, nor did he agree with its message. Voltaire had other experiences in his struggle against arbitrary power. He finally saved his life and property by accepting exile from France.

Prof. Dicey's third rule of law is not applicable to the study of the American Constitution. Even though the Constitution of the United States of America specifically declares certain rights to its inhabitants, it has remained for the courts to guarantee these rights through judicial interpretation.

In summary, the rule of law as we know it in the United States dictates an absolute supremacy of regular law in contrast to arbitrary power. It even excludes wide discretionary authority on the part of government. People may be punished for a breach of law, but they shall not be punished for anything else. It further means that there shall be equality before the law regardless of the influence that the litigants may possess through wealth or politics.

§ 1.23 Right to Personal Freedom

The English theory was and is that the freedom of a person is not a special privilege but is the result of the ordinary law of the land, which is enforced by the courts.

The Star Chamber Abolition Act of 1641 guaranteed to the English subject that a writ of habeas corpus was available against the King and the Council. In England and in the United States the right of personal liberty means essentially that a person shall not be subjected to arrest, imprisonment, or other physical or mental coercion unless there is a legal reason for such action. The law provides a remedy for those whose liberty has been taken away sans legal justification. As indicated above, the Star Chamber Abolition Act of 1641 provided for a writ of habeas corpus, which made the King and the Council accountable to the court.

§ 1.24 Writ of Habeas Corpus

One of the fundamental guarantees afforded the inhabitants of the United States is the writ of habeas corpus. The United States Constitution reinforces this guarantee by providing in Article I, Section 9, subdivision (2), "The privilege of the Writ of Habeas Corpus shall not be suspended, unless when in Cases of Rebellion or Invasion the public Safety may require it." A writ of habeas corpus may be defined as an order from a court to a named person or official to produce the body of a confined person before the court. The court then hears evidence to determine the legality of the detention of the incarcerated person. This right is so basic to our system of government that various states have provided statutory sanctions against jurists who fail to comply with a petition for a writ of habeas corpus. New York State provides by statute that if a judge refuses to issue a writ of habeas corpus, with respect to an incarcerated person who has not had the legality of his detention previously determined by habeas corpus proceedings, the judge forfeits to the person detained $1000 to be recovered by an action in his name or in the name of the petitioner to his use. (N.Y.) C.P.L.R. 7003. New York further provides by statute that any officer who shall deliver to a demanding state in an extradition case the person in custody, in disobedience of a writ of habeas corpus, commits a felony. (N.Y.) C.P.L. 570.26. Florida provides in Section 79.01, Florida Statutes, as interpreted by Chase v. State, 93 Fla. 963, 113 So. 103, 54 A.L.R. 271, where the court held that this is a writ of a person's right not subject to the court's discretion. It is also found in Section 13, Article I, of the Florida Constitution as follows:

> The writ of habeas corpus shall be grantable of right, freely and without cost. It shall be returnable without delay, and shall never be suspended unless, in case of rebellion or invasion, or suspension is essential to public safety.

Section 79.05, Florida Statutes, provides for a civil liability of $300 against a person who fails to bring a prisoner before the court within three days of his being served with a writ of habeas corpus. The writ of habeas corpus has general recognition in all states.

§ 1.25 Bills of Attainder and Impeachment

A bill of attainder pertains to a right of personal freedom. Such a bill is crucial to the preservation of the English and American concept of due process of law. Article I, Section 9, subdivision (3), of the United States Constitution notes, "No Bill of Attainder or ex post facto Law shall be passed." It also appears in Article I, Section 10, as a limitation on state power.

The English experience with bills of attainder was disastrous. *Bills of attainder* can be defined as legislative acts, no matter what their form, that apply to named individuals or to easily ascertainable members of a group in such a way as to inflict punishment on them without a judicial trial. United States v. Brown, 381 U.S. 437, 448 (1965).

A bill of attainder was a Tudor weapon whereby Parliament could vote a person to death without a regular trial. It was not uncommon to still the voice of a political enemy by passing a bill of attainder. This type of action was supplanted with the device known as impeachment, which was far less ghastly. Apparently impeachment was first used in the Good Parliament of 1376. This was done by Parliament, presuming the idea that it was the highest court in the land and still retaining the concept that the King can do no wrong. The House of Commons acted as a sort of grand jury in presenting offending ministers to the Upper House for trials of high offenses. Even though the King could do no wrong, it was still an offense to give the King bad advice or even obey bad orders given by him. In this way, Parliament had complete control over finances, reasonable control over legislation, and a little control over policies.

The framers of the United States Constitution, armed with the knowledge of what had occurred in England, provided for the remedy of impeachment as a method of keeping control over the executive. U.S.Const., Art. II, Sec. 4. Executions were no longer necessary.

§ 1.26 Ex Post Facto Law

Article I, Section 9, subdivision (3), and Section 10, of the United States Constitution, previously indicated, prohibits the enactment of an ex post facto law. An *ex post facto law* has been defined as "every law that makes an action done before the passing of the law which was innocent when done, to be criminal and punishable as (a crime); every law that aggravates a crime or makes it greater than when it was committed; every law that alters the legal rules of evidence and requires less or different testimony than the law required at the time of the commission of the offense in order to convict the offender." Hill v. State of Texas 171 S.W.2d 880 (1943). The courts have construed ex post facto laws to be applicable only to criminal statutes that work to the disadvantage of the defendant. Calder et Wife v. Bull et Wife, 3 U.S. 386, 1 L.Ed. 648 (1798).

§ 1.27 Writ of Assistance

A writ of assistance was an ancient writ issuing from the court of exchequer to the sheriff commanding him to aid the king's tenants by knights' service or to the king's collectors, debtors, or accountants to enforce payment of their own dues so that they in turn could pay their dues to the kings. In effect, it put the creditor in possession of lands owned by the debtor when the sheriff could not execute against any other property. For a detailed discussion of this writ see Marbelhead Land Co. v. Los Angeles County, (D.C. 276 F. 305).

§ 1.28 Early Function of the United States Government

The government conceived by the framers of the Constitution was to maintain law and order and to protect life, liberty, and property from both internal and external threats. The state government was to protect the health, morals, and welfare of its inhabitants. Individuals were to be left free to follow their own interests in competition with other individuals without interference from government.

At the time of the ratification of the Constitution, approximately 75% of the American people were farmers, while the rest were small craftsmen, tradesmen, merchants, professional men, or seamen.

Around 1900 this composition of the people came to an end as a result of the Industrial Revolution, the growth in population, and the rise of giant industrial corporations. The immigrants from Europe came in droves as they flocked to the cities and industrialized centers looking for work and living accommodations. The economic life of the country changed as rural populations moved to the cities and the attitude toward government changed. The industrialized society caused the individual to be less and less self-sufficient and the people looked to the government for help.

§ 1.29 Supreme Court Supervisory Powers

The United States Supreme Court has supervisory powers over federal criminal justice by virtue of Article III of the United States Constitution. While Article III established and defined the judicial power of the United States in one Supreme Court, it delegated to Congress the power to create lower federal courts. The supervisory powers are inherent in interpretation of the Constitution, a role the Supreme Court has assumed since Chief Justice

Marshall's decision in Marbury v. Madison, 1 Cranch 137, 5 U.S. 368, 2 L.Ed. 60 (1803), where Chief Justice Marshall elevated a court of law into an important organ of government. Although judicial review was not expressly granted by the Constitution, it was first asserted in Marbury v. Madison (supra). In that case, Marshall, who was an ardent Federalist, favored a strong national government and distrusted the people's capacity for self-government.

The Federalists were defeated in the election of 1800, but they tried to maintain their influence by finding positions for loyal followers between the time of the election of 1800 and the inauguration on March 4, 1801. In January 1801, President Adams, a Federalist, named his Secretary of State, John Marshall, as Chief Justice of the United States. The lame-duck Congress passed the Judiciary Act of 1801, which created many new judgeships in lower courts and also provided that the next vacancy of the Supreme Court should not be filled. This act reduced the number of justices of the Court from six to five, making the appointment of a justice by the new Democratic-Republican President, Thomas Jefferson, all but impossible. A number of commissions for justices of the peace for the District of Columbia were not signed by midnight on March 3, 1801, by the outgoing Secretary of State, John Marshall, and were in the Secretary of State's office waiting delivery when Jefferson became President. Jefferson ordered his new Secretary of State, James Madison, not to deliver some of the commissions to the "midnight appointees."

William Marbury was one of the "midnight appointees" whose commission as justice of the peace for the District of Columbia had not been delivered. He and three other appointees petitioned the Supreme Court for a writ of mandamus to compel Secretary of State Madison to deliver the commissions. This had been a common law writ that had English origin.

It was thought that Marshall, being a Federalist, would order Madison to deliver the commissions and thereby initiate a struggle between the Court and the executive branch of government. To most people's surprise, he did not order this. Although he found fault with Madison for failing to deliver the commissions, Marshall held that the Court could not compel Madison to act because the statute cited by Marbury and the other petitioner was unconstitutional. They had relied on Section 13 of the Judiciary Act of 1789, which stated that the Supreme Court could issue writs of mandamus in "cases warranted by the principles and usages of law, to any courts appointed, or persons holding office under authority of the United States." Marshall stated that this act enlarged the original jurisdiction of the Supreme Court beyond that stated in Article III of the Constitution. In that Article, original jurisdiction was conferred on the Supreme Court in only two types of cases; those "affecting ambassadors, other public ministers and consuls, and those in which a state shall be a party." Since Marbury's suit did not fall into either of these categories, Marshall ruled that the suit should not have been brought initially to the Supreme Court. Further, since there was a contradiction between the law of Congress and that of the Constitution, the Supreme Court had a clear duty to maintain the higher law of the Constitution and to declare the legislative act unconstitutional.

Thus, we see the principle of the supervisory power of the Supreme Court developed. To use the words of Howard L. McBain as he expressed them in the Bacon Lectures on the Constitution of the United States, "Some Aspects of Judicial Review," published by Boston University, Heffernan Press, 1939:

> The concept of judicial review rests upon an extraordinarily simple foundation. Stripped to its essence, it is almost too plain for stating. The Constitution is the supreme law. It was ordained by the people, for ultimate source of all political authority. It confers limited powers on the national government. These limitations derive partly from the mere fact that these powers are enumerated—the government cannot exercise powers not granted to it—and partly from certain express prohibitions upon its powers or upon the manner of their exercise. If the government consciously or unconsciously oversteps these limitations there must be some authority competent to hold it in control, to thwart its unconstitutional attempt, and thus to vindicate and preserve inviolate the will of the people as expressed in the Constitution. This power the courts exercise. This is the beginning and the end of the theory of judicial review.[2]

[2]McBain, *Some Aspects of Judicial Review,* BACON LECTURES ON THE CONSTITUTION (1939).

CHAPTER 2

Contents

History of the Adoption of the Constitution

§ 2.1 Events Preceding the Articles of Confederation

To properly understand how the United States Constitution came about, it is necessary to retrace a little into the history of the United States before the Constitutional Convention of 1787.

George III was King of England and had been at war with France in what came to be known as the Seven Years' War (1756–1763). It is said that Montcalm, while in Quebec, predicted that while France would lose Canada, England would lose her more populous colonies to the south. The French and Indian raids on the northern English colonies begun by Count Frontenac in 1689 caused these colonists living on the frontier to be constantly in terror. They were comforted somewhat by the fact that British regulars were available to assist them in emergencies. Experiences such as Braddock's defeat, however, had demonstrated to the colonial troops that in many respects they themselves were superior fighting men to the British regulars. With the removal of the threat from the north and the steadily increasing population, the colonists were beginning to feel self-assured.

The continental colonies had become thirteen in number with the founding of Georgia in 1733. These colonies were models of self-government for the era. Each colony had an assembly based on the principle of representative democracy in that their members were elected by popular vote. The assembly raised taxes for local purposes and exercised the police power of protecting the health, welfare, and morals of its inhabitants. Most of the colonies, however, had a governor appointed by the king who could override the acts of the assembly by exercising a veto. In practice, governors used their veto power very seldom because their salaries were paid by the colonies and were voted upon by the assembly. A council appointed by the governor also could override the acts of the assembly. Hence the derivation of the bicameral type of legislature. The acts of the colonial legislature, including the governor's councils, were subject to review by the Privy Council in England.

It is not the intention of this text to comprehensively treat the historical development of the American colonies from independent colonies to a federal state. This is left to the historians. However, it is thought that the student of constitutional law should have some insight into the reasons for the joining of the colonies into one nation.

The mercantile theory of colonialism was changing to that of the imperialistic theory. The mercantile theory regarded the colonies as places for the sale of goods from the mother country and as sources of raw materials. The imperialistic theory, on the other hand, which was the new policy, considered colonies primarily as a means to greater financial, political, and military power. The imperialistic doctrine could only be achieved through greater military and political control and direct taxation.

The imperialistic system adversely affected the economic interests of most of the Americans. Americans were becoming aware that there were cultural and economic differences between Britain and the colonists. The large merchants and landed gentry were the first to lead the attack against the British taxes, but as the matter became more heated, most of them, except for those in Virginia, became Tories and supported Britain in the Revolutionary War.

§ 2.2 Sugar Act

During the Seven Years' War, colonial assemblies had not cooperated fully with Britain because they practically discontinued voluntary appropriations for the war effort. Accordingly, there were a Proclamation of 1763, the Sugar Act of 1764, and the Stamp Act of 1765. The Proclamation of 1763 closed the frontier west of the Alleghenies to further settlement and forbade further land purchases in that region. The Sugar Act levied a threepence per gallon duty on molasses imported into the colonies and also levied small duties on other imports. The preamble of this act read, ". . . defraying the expenses of defending, protecting and securing the colonies." It was therefore a revenue act which raised the question of the power of Britain to tax the colonies.

§ 2.3 Stamp Act

In 1764, Lord Grenville concluded that because the Seven Years' War had increased the national debt by approximately £130 million, and since part of the expense had been incurred by the English defense of the American colonists, the colonists should raise revenue for the mother country. England already had reimbursed the colonies for their military expenses during the war. However, there still remained a serious possibility of raids by the Indians in the west, and a large force of British regulars had to be maintained in the colonies to combat that threat. Lord Grenville reasoned that the colonists should at least pay for their own protection in time of peace.

§ 2.6 *Common Sense*

Thomas Paine, in January 1776, published a pamphlet entitled *Common Sense*. Pamphlets were the principal means of disseminating information at that time. *Common Sense* espoused the theme that the palaces of kings are built on the ruins of bowers of paradise; that the only proper sphere of government is to provide freedom and security to its inhabitants; that the survival of monarchy hopelessly corrupted the English political system; that the first king had been nothing better than "the principal ruffian of some restless gang." His cryptic remark—"The blood of the slain, the weeping voice of nature cries, 'tis time to part' "—had a great impact on the hastening of an inevitable separation.

§ 2.7 First Resolution of Independence

On June 7, 1776, Richard Henry Lee, acting pursuant to instructions from the then state of Virginia, placed the following before Congress:

> RESOLVED, that these United Colonies are, and of right ought to be free and independent States, and that they are absolved from all allegiance to the British Crown, and that all connection between them and the State of Great Britain is, and ought to be, totally dissolved.

On June 11, the resolution was referred to a committee, which was assigned the task of drafting a declaration to the effect of the resolution. On July 2, the congress approved Lee's resolution and, strictly speaking, this act was the official declaration of independence.

§ 2.8 Declaration of Independence

History has subordinated that congressional declaration to the declaration agreed to by twelve of the colonies on July 4, 1776. This document is entitled as a unanimous declaration, but in truth it was not unanimous until July 19 when the New York delegation, which had not voted on July 4, reported that it was in favor of the declaration. The final document, which is on display in the National Archives Building in Washington, D.C., was not signed until August 2, 1776. It was largely the creation of Thomas Jefferson. It is said that Franklin and John Adams helped somewhat, but only with respect to minor changes. The document consists of five parts:

1. Introduction—set forth the intent;
2. A brief statement of American political philosophy;
3. An indictment against George III;
4. Resolution of independence;
5. Signatures, which are omitted here.

As you read the document it is suggested that you try to break it down into its components.

The Declaration of Independence

WHEN in the Course of human events, it becomes necessary for one people to dissolve the political bands which have connected them with another, and to assume among the powers of the earth, the separate and equal station to which the Laws of Nature and of Nature's God entitle them, a decent respect to the opinions of mankind requires that they should declare the causes which impel them to the separation.—We hold these truths to be self-evident, that all men are created equal, that they are endowed by their Creator with certain unalienable Rights, that among these are Life, Liberty and the pursuit of Happiness.—That to secure these rights, Governments are instituted among Men, deriving their just powers from the consent of the governed.—That whenever any Form of Government becomes destructive of these ends, it is the Right of the People to alter or to abolish it, and to institute new Government, laying its foundation on such principles and organizing its powers in such form, as to them shall seem most likely to effect their Safety and Happiness. Prudence, indeed, will dictate that Governments long established should not be changed for light and transient causes; and accordingly all experience hath shewn, that mankind are more disposed to suffer, while evils are sufferable, than to right themselves by abolishing the forms to which they are accustomed. But when a long train of abuses and usurpations, pursuing invariably the same Object evinces a design to reduce them under absolute Despotism, it is their right, it is their duty, to throw off such Government, and to provide new Guards for their future security.—Such has been the patient sufferance of these Colonies; and such is now the necessity which constrains them to alter their former Systems of Government. The history of the present King of Great Britain is a history of repeated injuries and usurpations, all having in direct object the establishment of an absolute Tyranny over these States. To prove this, let Facts be submitted to a candid world.—He has refused his Assent to Laws, the most wholesome and necessary for the public good.—He has forbidden his Governors to pass Laws of immediate and pressing importance, unless suspended in their operation till his Assent should be obtained; and when so suspended, he has utterly neglected to attend to them.—He has refused to pass other Laws for the accommodation of large districts of people, unless those people would relinquish the right of Representation in the Legislature, a right inestimable to them and formidable to tyrants only.—

He has called together legislative bodies at places unusual, uncomfortable, and distant from the depository of their public Records, for the sole purpose of fatiguing them into compliance with his measures.—He has dissolved Representative Houses repeatedly, for opposing with manly firmness his invasions on the rights of the people.—He has refused for a long time, after such dissolutions, to cause others to be elected; whereby the Legislative powers, incapable of Annihilation, have returned to the People at large for their exercise; the State remaining in the meantime exposed to all the dangers of invasion from without, and convulsions within.—He has endeavoured to prevent the population of these States; for that purpose obstructing the Laws for Naturalization of Foreigners; refusing to pass others to encourage their migrations hither, and raising the conditions of new Appropriations of Lands.—He has obstructed the Administration of Justice, by refusing his Assent to Laws for establishing Judiciary powers.—He has made Judges dependent on his Will alone, for the tenure of their offices, and the amount and payment of their salaries.—He has erected a multitude of New Offices, and sent hither swarms of Officers to harass our people, and eat out their substance. He has kept among us, in times of peace, Standing Armies without the Consent of our legislatures.—He has affected to render the Military independent of and superior to the Civil power.—He has combined with others to subject us to a jurisdiction foreign to our constitution, and unacknowledged by our laws; giving his Assent to their Acts of pretended Legislation:—For quartering large bodies of armed troops among us:—For protecting them, by a mock Trial, from punishment for any Murders which they should commit on the Inhabitants of these States:—For cutting off our Trade with all parts of the world:—For imposing Taxes on us without our Consent:—For depriving us in many cases, of the benefits of Trial by Jury:—For transporting us beyond Seas to be tried for pretended offences:—For abolishing the free System of English Laws in a neighbouring Province, establishing therein an Arbitrary government, and enlarging its Boundaries so as to render it at once an example and fit instrument for introducing the same absolute rule into these Colonies:—For taking away our Charters, abolishing our most valuable Laws and altering fundamentally the Forms of our Governments:—For suspending our own Legislatures, and declaring themselves invested with power to legislate for us in all cases whatsoever.—He has abdicated Government here, by declaring us out of his Protection and waging War against us.—He has plundered our seas, ravaged our Coasts, burnt our towns, and destroyed the lives of our people.—He is at this time transporting large Armies of foreign Mercenaries to compleat the works of death, desolation and tyranny, already begun with circumstances of Cruelty & perfidy scarcely paralleled in the most barbarous ages, and totally unworthy the Head of a civilized nation.—He has constrained our fellow Citizens taken Captive on the high Seas to bear Arms against their Country, to become the executioners of their friends and Brethren, or to fall themselves by their Hands.—He has excited domestic insurrections amongst us, and has endeavoured to bring on the inhabitants of our frontiers, the merciless Indian Savages, whose known rule of warfare, is an undistinguished destruction of all ages, sexes and conditions. In every stage of these Oppressions We have Petitioned for Redress in the most humble terms: Our repeated Petitions have been answered only by repeated injury. A Prince, whose character is thus marked by every act which may define a Tyrant, is unfit to be the ruler of a free people. Nor have We been wanting in attentions to our British brethren. We have warned them from time to time of attempts by their legislature to extend an unwarrantable jurisdiction over us. We have reminded them of the circumstances of our emigration and settlement here. We have appealed to their native justice and magnanimity, and we have conjured them by the ties of our common kindred to disavow these usurpations, which would inevitably interrupt our connections and correspondence. They too have been deaf to the voice of justice and of consanguinity. We must, therefore, acquiesce in the necessity, which denounces our Separation, and hold them, as we hold the rest of mankind, Enemies in War, in Peace Friends.—

We, therefore, the Representatives of the United States of America, in General Congress, Assembled, appealing to the Supreme Judge of the world for the rectitude of our intentions, do, in the Name, and by Authority of the good People of these Colonies, solemnly publish and declare, That these United Colonies are, and of Right ought to be Free and Independent States; that they are Absolved from all Allegiance to the British Crown, and that all political connection between them and the State of Great Britain, is and ought to be totally dissolved; and that as Free and Independent States, they have full Power to levy War, conclude Peace, contract Alliances, establish Commerce, and to do all other Acts and Things which Independent States may of right do.—And for the support of this Declaration, with a firm reliance on the protection of divine Providence, we mutually pledge to each other our Lives, our Fortunes and our sacred Honor.

[signatures omitted]

§ 2.9 State Constitutions

The custom of establishing a written constitution was an outgrowth of trading-company royal or proprietary charters. It was a means of establishing fundamental written law. Vattel, who wrote a pamphlet on the *Laws of Nations* which had some popularity in America, insisted that the fundamental law ought to be a fixed and written document. It is interesting to note that none of the state conventions during 1776 and 1777 submitted their results to the people for approval. Each merely proclaimed a new constitution to be in operation. The early state constitutions were not democratic in nature according to present-day standards. Most constitutions required a property qualification in order to have voting privileges. In order to be a governor or legislator the aspirant had to have considerable wealth. All of the constitutions guaranteed religious liberty and equal political rights for all Protestants; several extended these guarantees to all Christians, including Catholics. Sephardic Jews, fleeing the Spanish Inquisition, were permitted to live and practice their religion in Newport, Rhode Island. One of these was Aaron Lopez. He was among the leading merchants in the town and he, along with other Sephardic Jews, helped to make that seaport a thriving community.

§ 2.10 Concept of Judicial Review

Judicial review was an outgrowth of the revolutionary philosophy. Its basis was that the legislature should have limited power with an independent judiciary combined with a separation of powers. James Otis had argued in the Writs of Assistance case that an act against the supreme Constitution was void and that it was the duty of the *courts* to "pass the law into disuse."

§ 2.11 Articles of Confederation

The Articles of Confederation were a legalization of the ad hoc government which had already developed prior to 1781. They placed the full authority of the confederation government in Congress, along with the retention of state equality in that body wherein each state was allowed one vote. Congress was given authority to coin money, establish a post office, enter into treaties and alliances, to make war or peace, etc. The Congress had no power, however, to tax or to regulate commerce. This resulted in financial difficulties. The Articles had no provision for an executive but had a direction that a President of Congress be elected to preside over Congress who could serve one term of one year in any three years. Consequently, there was no cohesive force to implement the dictates of the Congress acting through a multiplicity of committees.

The government was akin to a league of friendship or loose confederation among independent states. Many of the provisions were designed as modes of international comity. Many of the same provisions were adopted in the Constitution of 1787 and have served well under a tightly controlled federal state. For example, the provisions for extradition, equal privileges and immunities, and equal protection of life and property were all products of interstate or international comity.

The states failed to meet their economic requisitions for the central government thereby putting the federal government into bankruptcy. The federal government had no judiciary and the state courts, upon whom the people relied, refused to recognize any rights other than those of their own respective states. Amendments required unanimous vote of all members. It soon became obvious that the Articles of Confederation were not a viable instrument of government.

§ 2.12 Constitutional Convention

James Madison provided careful notes on the convention's proceedings. His notes were published more than fifty years later but they provided far more insight into the proceedings than the official journal of the convention's business.

The convention had been scheduled to convene on the second Monday in May but insufficient delegates arrived until the end of June when eleven states were represented. There was a tug of interests between the strong federal government advocates and the weak federation delegates. There was additional strain because the small states had different problems vis-à-vis the larger states. Many times it appeared that the convention would be torn apart. In early September the convention had agreed on all consequential aspects of the new Constitution and a Committee of Style was appointed. Gouverneur Morris is given most of the credit for drafting the document. A few of the delegates refused to sign it and others not supporting it had left the convention in disgust. Accordingly, at the suggestion of Franklin, the proposal was endorsed "Done in Convention by the Unanimous Consent of the states present."

§ 2.13 Ratification of Constitution

There were economic and class divisions which divided proponents and antagonists of the adoption of the Constitution. For example, New York's government was supported by the taxes the state levied on interstate commerce. If the Constitution were adopted, this source of revenue would be lost. Land taxes might become necessary. The landed aristocracy objected to this. The American propensity for translating economic conflicts into legalistic and constitutional issues was apparent in the debates over ratification. However by late July 1788, only North Carolina and Rhode Island had not yet ratified the Constitution. Many states adopted it by very narrow margins, and it is almost miraculous that a government such as that of the

United States has endured so long, given the divisions of the thinking of the leaders of the time of its adoption and all through its history. To give a few examples of the closeness of the vote, New York ratified by a vote of 30 to 27, Virginia by 89 to 79, and Rhode Island by 34 to 32.

North Carolina finally came on board in November of 1789 when the new government had already been functioning and Rhode Island adopted it in May of 1790. Some historians believe that these latter two states were economically forced to ratify the Constitution because of the spectre of isolation which hung over their commerce.

§ 2.14 Bill of Rights

There was much infighting within the state conventions and olive branches were offered in the form of a Bill of Rights which would be attached to the document at the first opportunity.

James Madison had at first proposed that the content of the original document be altered to include the provisions of the Bill of Rights. After much debate in both houses, a compromise resulted in the passage by Congress of the Bill of Rights which was followed by the adoption of the first ten amendments to the Constitution.

It should be noted that James Madison did not initially agree with the Tenth Amendment in that he believed that "powers must necessarily be admitted by implication." The ten amendments were finally adopted by Congress in 1789 and by the states within two years of the establishment of the government.

With this historical insight into the development of the Constitution of the United States of America, the student is brought to the realization that it was not created overnight; that it was the result of trial and error worked on by the best minds of the time; that it was fraught with economic implications; and that it was accomplished by the blood, sweat, tears, and dedication of many persons with opposing viewpoints. It is said that a compromise exists where no one is completely satisfied and no one is completely dissatisfied. This is the nature of the Constitution of the United States. Its general terms have left to future generations the job of interpreting its clauses in the light of contemporary thinking.

§ 2.15 Distribution of Powers and Reservation of Powers

Hence we now have a legacy of a document which derives its power from the people to the government. Where the government is one of enumerated powers with a legislature to make the laws, an executive to implement the laws, and a judiciary to interpret the laws. Concomitant with this, we have in the Tenth Amendment provision that if the enumerated power of government is not expressly given to the United States government, it is therefore reserved to the states to exercise this power. One of the basic powers not specifically given to the government of the United States was the power over the health, welfare, and morals of the state inhabitants. This is commonly referred to as the police power. However, through the concept of implied power as construed by the United States Supreme Court, there has been a gradual incursion into the police power of the states.

It is the judicial and police power which we will be concerned with in the following chapters of this book.

§ 2.16 Constitutional Judicial Review

Article VI of the Constitution reads:

> *This Constitution, and the Laws of the United States which shall be made in Pursuance thereof; and all Treaties made, or which shall be made, under the Authority of the United States, shall be the supreme Law of the Land; and the Judges in every State shall be bound thereby; any Thing in the Constitution or Laws of any State to the Contrary notwithstanding....*

This Article was the source of much controversy initially. State judges went along their own merry way in deciding cases contrary to the intent of the Constitution. The first Chief Justice of the United States Supreme Court was John Jay. He thought so little of the office that he sought and won the "higher" office of Governor of the State of New York.

It was not until John Marshall, the fourth Chief Justice, took the position that the office came to be one of the most influential forces in government. A case decided by his court within two years after he began his service in the Court caused the Constitution to assume significant new directions. This was accomplished through his leadership.

The case was Marbury v. Madison, 5 U.S. 368, 2 L.Ed. 60, decided in 1803, and it provided for judicial review to examine the language of the Constitution, to invalidate any lower form of law found by the courts to be in violation of the Constitution which is the "supreme Law of the Land." John Marshall implemented what he and his associate judges believed the framers of the Constitution had in mind. They were perhaps buttressed in this opinion by the writings of James Otis.

§ 2.17 Limitations on Judicial Power

There is a proclivity for a person who has ascended the bench to think that God has died and the judge assumes the role of God. The Constitution has guarded against this phenomenon by the system of checks and balances previously described. Notwithstanding this system, we often find cases wherein the judicial power is abused. The Constitution as interpreted by the Marshall decisions ultimately protects the litigant from this human frailty.

A famous example of overbearing judicial temperament occurred in Sheppard v. Maxwell, 384 U.S. 333, 86 S.Ct. 1507 (1966), where the presiding judge was more interested in his image with the media than he was with the concept of fundamental fairness of a trial.[1] Unfortunately, not every litigant has the resources to take cases to the United States Supreme Court, and admittedly there are still judges who abuse the powers of their office.

It is, however, interesting to note that one by one each of the states is enacting legislation to review the judicial temperament of judges, their competence, and their right to remain in office or to be reappointed.

Your attention is directed to the following sentences in the Marbury v. Madison case (supra):

> From these, and many other selections which might be made, it is apparent, that the framers of the constitution contemplated that instrument as a rule for the government of courts, as well as legislature. Why otherwise does it direct the judges to take an oath to support it? ... Why does a judge swear to discharge his duties agreeably to the constitution of the United States if that constitution forms no rule for his government? ... and that courts as well as other departments, are bound by that instrument.

In Martin v. Hunter's Lessee, 14 U.S. 562, 4 L.Ed. 97 (1816), and Cohens v. Virginia, 19 U.S. 82, 5 L.Ed. 257 (1821), the United States Supreme Court applied the theory of judicial review to decisions of state courts.

§ 2.18 Means by Which Cases Reach the United States Supreme Court

Any lawyer who has been in general private practice can tell you of experiences which he has had where an irate client comes to his office and says substantially, "I don't care what it costs, I want to take this case to the

[1]Chapter 5 infra.

United States Supreme Court." Little does the client know that the probability of the United States Supreme Court's deciding his case is very small because appeal, as a right, exists only in a small number of designated cases. Even if a constitutional issue is involved, the workload of the Court is so large that, of necessity, the Court must screen its case load to consist of those matters where a substantial federal question is involved. The word "substantial," being nebulous, creates problems, but the Justices of the Court have the final word in this area. The largest number of cases reaching the Court are by way of writ of certiorari.

§ 2.19 Federal Court Structure

Section 1, Article III, provides that "the judicial power of the United States shall be vested in one Supreme Court, and in such inferior courts as the Congress from time to time, ordain and establish."

To implement this provision, Congress passed the First Judiciary Act in 1789. By the terms of the Act, a federal court system was established which was substantially unchanged for almost a century. It set up the power of the Supreme Court to supervise state courts dealing with federal constitutional issues and set up a system of federal courts operating throughout the nation instead of only in the nation's capital.

§ 2.20 District Courts

The court of original jurisdiction in federal matters is called a United States District Court. It might be called the United States District Court for the Eastern District of New York or the United States District Court for the Southern District of Florida.

The district courts are scattered throughout the fifty states and their number is set by Congress. The number of courts varies from time to time depending on legislation, log rolling in Congress, and need. There is at least one district court in each of the states. United States District Courts, as their name implies, have jurisdiction over all federal matters, both criminal and civil, except a few disputes which start in the specialized legislative courts or the Supreme Court.

§ 2.21 Courts of Appeal

The United States Courts of Appeal are the next higher court in the federal system. At one time they were referred to as the Circuit Court of Appeals.

The older cases refer to them as such. The name was changed by Congress in 1948.

These courts hear appeals from District Courts and from important independent regulatory commissions. These courts usually represent the end of the appellate procedure because the case seldom goes to the United States Supreme Court for reasons which will be explained later.

There are eleven circuits for these courts plus one for the District of Columbia. Each has a designated number except the court in the District of Columbia which is designated as United States Court of Appeals for the District of Columbia. It is therefore obvious that territory of a United States Court of Appeals includes more than one state's boundaries. A panel of three judges usually reviews cases in that court.

§ 2.22 United States Supreme Court

This is the highest court of the federal system. It presently consists of a Chief Justice and eight Associate Justices. I emphasize the word "presently" in the preceding sentence because Congress has the power to change that number through legislation and, in fact, it has on several occasions.

However, it has not been changed by Congress since 1869. There was a great possibility of a change during the Franklin Roosevelt administration with his "packing the court" idea but the reason for the legislation disappeared and with it went the legislation. The legislation proposed that the number of justices be increased. In this way, Roosevelt hoped to appoint persons to the Court who would find social legislation passed by Congress to be constitutional.

The United States Supreme Court has original as well as appellate jurisdiction. Article III, Section 2, reads as follows:

> *In all Cases affecting Ambassadors, other public Ministers, and Consuls, and those in which a State shall be a Party, the supreme Court shall have original Jurisdiction. In all other Cases before mentioned, the supreme Court shall have appellate Jurisdiction, both as to Law and Fact, with such Exceptions, and under such Regulations, as the Congress shall make.*

For all practical purposes, however, the Supreme Court is an appellate court.

The Supreme Court hears the following appeals where federal questions are involved:

1. From the highest state court;
2. Directly from United States District Courts in some cases (explained more fully later in this chapter);

3. From United States Courts of Appeal;
4. From legislative courts (e.g., Court of Military Appeals).

The Supreme Court and lower courts in the federal system are called constitutional courts if they are legislated into being by virtue of Article III of the Constitution. On the other hand, if Congress legislates a court into being under the implied powers given to it in other than Article III of the Constitution, the court is then known as a legislative court. The basic difference is the requirement of appointment to Article III judges in that they be appointed for life or good behavior and can only be removed by impeachment, whereas the legislative judicial appointments need not carry these qualifications.

Congress has legislated the procedure by which a case may be entertained by the United States Supreme Court. There are three basic methods. One is by a writ of certiorari, another is by certification, and the third is by appeal. Some of the older cases appeared by the common law writ of error but that was discontinued in 1928 and the substitute is generally an appeal.

§ 2.23 Writ of Certiorari

A writ of certiorari in Supreme Court practice is obtained by an unsuccessful litigant in a lower court by presenting a petition to the Supreme Court to review a lower court's decision. The opposing litigant may file answering briefs showing reasons why the writ should not be granted. Should the court decide that a substantial federal question is involved, it issues a writ to the lower court to send the entire record of the case in the court below to the United States Supreme Court for review. A very small percentage of the petitions for the writ are granted. That is why you will often see in a citation cert. denied.

§ 2.24 Certification

The better nomenclature for this type of review might be certification of a question of law. This review is not controlled by the litigants. It occurs when a United States Court of Appeals or the Court of Claims is looking for guidance in deciding a case that is presently before that tribunal. The court will send certified questions of law to the United States Supreme Court with the hope that the Supreme Court will render a decision so that the lower court will, in effect, render a decision in the case before it, which it will believe will not be reversed by the United States Supreme Court if it should reach that body. This method of review, however, is seldom used.

§ 2.25 Appeal

This is the method most laymen have heard about but know very little about. The term "appeal" as used in United States Supreme Court procedure refers to a method of review, which is a matter of right of a party to an action. Therefore the Supreme Court is obligated to review cases emanating from state courts in two situations as follows:

1. Where the validity of a treaty or statute of the United States is questioned and the state court has held it to be invalid;
2. Where the validity of a state law has been questioned on the ground that it contravenes the Constitution, treaties, or laws of the United States and the state court sustains its validity.

In addition to the above mandatory reconsiderations, the Supreme Court may review by appeal a decision of a United States Court of Appeals when a federal statute is held to be unconstitutional in a suit where the United States is a party or where a state statute is held by this court to be unconstitutional or repugnant to the laws of the United States or treaties of the United States. Some cases of the United States District Courts are reviewed directly by the United States Supreme Court on appeal if they are deemed by the court to be of sufficient importance and that they must be settled by the Supreme Court as quickly as possible.

Direct appeals from the United States District Court to the Supreme Court are allowed as follows:

1. Where the district court has held an act of Congress unconstitutional;
2. Where either a one-judge or three-judge district court has rendered a judgment in a suit brought by the United States to enforce:
   (a) the Interstate Commerce Act;
   (b) the Antitrust Laws;
   (c) the Federal Communications Act;
3. Suits brought by private parties in district court to restrain the enforcement of state or federal statutes because of unconstitutionality;
4. Suits brought in district courts before a three-judge bench where the court grants or denies an injunction setting aside orders of the Interstate Commerce Commission.

It should be noted with great emphasis, however, that even though an appeal may be a matter of right to a litigant, a minimum of four justices have to decide that a substantial federal question exists before the entire Court will review a case on appeal. Accordingly, while every litigant who has a right to appeal does get judicial review of a sort in the United States Supreme Court, the full Court may never render a decision as to the merits of the case.

§ 2.26 Decision-Making Method of the United States Supreme Court

Few people are privy to the inner workings of how a case is decided in the United States Supreme Court.

The machinations at the Supreme Court are similar to a secret society. Little is known by the general public or bar as to how a case is decided by that Court. The justices do not speak about a case other than the written decisions. Of all the other branches of government, the Supreme Court is the least accountable. This is so because of the cardinal principle of our government that we shall have an independent judiciary.

Behind the robed figures that one sees on the bench of the court, however, are people, each with his own foibles, prejudices, and experiences of life. Given such a group, it is natural to assume that these jurists have differences of opinion which cause personal irritations between them.

There is a weekly conference usually scheduled for Wednesday afternoon and all day Friday. At these conferences cases are discussed. The Justices arrive punctually at 9:30 AM. In the center of the oak-paneled room is a massive mahogany table which is surrounded by nine high-backed chairs and many carts. These carts are wheeled in to the room before the conference, and they contain information on cases that each Justice thinks he may need to intelligently discuss a pending case. They pour themselves coffee from a silver urn and shake hands. This apparently has been the custom since 1888. Following this, they sit down to argue their points.

As has been pointed out earlier in this text, not every case that finds its way to the hallowed chambers of the United States Supreme Court is decided by that Court. Some of the conferences are for the purpose of deciding what cases are worthy of their full consideration.

Copies of each case go to every Justice. Some of the Justices delegate the function of reading the petitions for review to their clerks and then rely on the clerks' summarizing memos. Mr. Justice Brennan has the reputation of personally reading virtually all of the petitions which ask for review.

Each Justice then makes his own decision as to whether the case presents a substantial federal question requiring a decision by the United States Supreme Court. If one Justice believes that such a substantial federal question exists, he asks that it be placed on the conference list for discussion. Most of the petitions for review, however, do not arouse a Justice's interest and are placed on "the dead list." If a case is placed on "the dead list," that case is not decided by the Court.

When a case is placed on the conference list, it requires the vote of at least four Justices to grant it review. The results of this voting are usually kept secret. On occasion, if a Justice believes very strongly that a case should be considered by the Court for review and the vote, after it has been placed on the conference list, is negative, the Justice who felt so strongly about it writes a dissenting opinion with respect to the Court's refusal to hear and decide the case. There have been times when such a dissenting opinion resulted in a reconsideration at a subsequent conference list and because of the persuasiveness of the dissenting Justice's opinion, other Justices have changed their votes to place the matter on the Court's calendar.

After the Court agrees to hear the case, it is scheduled for oral argument some months later. Meanwhile, lawyers for opposing sides file written briefs usually consisting of sixty to eighty pages. Often friends of the Court also supply the Court with their briefs. When the appointed day arrives, each side has one-half hour for oral argument. The Justices often ask questions of the attorneys who are arguing their cases.

At the following Friday conference, these cases are again considered by the Justices. Beginning with the Chief Justice and then the Associate Justices in the order of their seniority, each expresses his view. At length a vote is taken but this time the junior Justice votes first. Presumably, this method is used so that the junior Justice's vote will not be influenced by the vote of the senior Justices.

No one, except the Justices, is permitted in the conference room. All notes are taken by the Justices themselves. If the Chief Justice is on the majority side, he will assign an Associate Justice to write the decision or may elect to write it himself. The dissenters decide among themselves who is going to write the decision.

There is a rule that up until the moment that an opinion is announced in public, each Justice may change his mind. It appears that this frequently happens. The shifts in their votes are a result of changes in the Justices' minds based upon their efforts to apply their knowledge and experience to their understanding of the facts of the case.

Each Justice has three law clerks to assist him. Naturally, each Justice has his own method in writing opinions. Some write initial opinions after extended research. They then give these opinions to their clerks to add.

delete, or check out the veracity of the reasoning and citations. Then a conference is held which might extend to the early hours of the morning, whereby each comma, period, or phrase is checked out between the clerks and the Justice. Finally, a completed document is submitted to the other Justices. Following this, "joint memos" are sent, hopefully, to the Justice who wrote the opinion. Sometimes other Justices recommend additional or different language to the authoring Justice, and he must decide whether or not to change his original opinion to meet the requirements of the other Justices. When minor differences occur, the point may be omitted entirely. When this occurs, scholars may have difficulty understanding what the Court had in mind because of a step being missed in the Court's reasoning process.

Each time a new draft of an opinion is circulated, any change is indicated in the margin by means of a black line. Many decisions require many draft corrections before they are finally agreed upon and announced.

United States Supreme Court Justices are reported to be working six or seven days a week. If one computes the overtime, they may be said to work eight or ten days a week.

From the above, it becomes quite apparent that the law of the land as interpreted by the United States Supreme Court is not created without serious deliberation and compromise.

CHAPTER 3

Contents

States' Right to Arrest, Detain, and Punish

§ 3.1 Introduction

We have discussed the Anglo-Saxon and American concept of freedom of the individual. Now we shall treat the other side of the coin. As has been shown, the framers of the Constitution, recognizing the will of the people for protection from enemies from within, provided that the states have an obligation to provide for the arrest of malefactors.

There was no organized police force until 1829 when Sir Robert Peel persuaded the English Parliament to pass an act creating a police force for the City of London. He, therefore, is sometimes referred to as the father of the concept of an organized police force to keep the peace; hence, the affectionate name of "Bobbies" which the London police still bear.

Prior to 1829, the Crown appointed sheriffs and constables. They were the only peace officers and they had the authority to call upon the citizens to form a posse comitatus which would assist in making an arrest of a suspect. From this idea we have evolved the concept of a citizen's arrest. It had been the duty of the citizen to make an arrest and this has continued to this day with a modification of the word "duty" to that of a "right" of a private citizen to make an arrest. He is no longer under any duty unless he is called upon to assist a peace officer. In that case, many states today provide by statute that a refusal to assist a peace officer in making an arrest when requested to do so by the peace officer results in the commission of a criminal offense by the refusing citizen.

At common law, most arrests were made after the issuance of a warrant. There was a distinction between less grievous and more grievous crimes and they were given the nomenclatures of misdemeanors and felonies respectively.

In misdemeanor cases, both the peace officer and the private citizen could not lawfully effect an arrest without a warrant unless the crime was a breach of the peace committed in their presence. Felonies, however, being far more serious, and the possibility of flight by the perpetrator being greater because of the severity of the punishment, called for more drastic action. Accordingly, in the case of a felony, a peace officer or a private person, acting without a warrant, could make an arrest for a felony actually committed, if it were committed in his presence or if he had reasonable grounds to believe that the person to be arrested had committed the felony. Thus we see developed through common law, an obligation by the executive branch of government to maintain the peace and to arrest, detain, and punish violators.

Most states have by statute adopted the original common law concept of arrest but have enlarged it to give greater authority of arrest to peace officers. Some states have further divided the duties of a peace officer to add that of a police officer with added power and responsibilities. (N.Y.) Criminal Procedure Law 140.10; 140.25.

(Tenn.) Tennessee Code, Section 40.803, reads as follows:

> Grounds for arrest by officer without warrant—An officer may, without a warrant, arrest a person:
> (1) For a public offense committed or a breach of the peace threatened in his presence.
> (2) When the person has committed a felony, though not in his presence.
> (3) When a felony has in fact been committed, and he has reasonable cause for believing the person arrested to have committed it.
> (4) On a charge made, upon reasonable cause, of the commission of a felony by the person arrested.

However, Section 40.816 of the Tennessee Code is as follows:

> Grounds for arrest by private persons—No fee allowed—A private person may arrest another:
> (1) For a public offense committed in his presence.
> (2) When the person arrested has committed a felony, although not in his presence.
> (3) When a felony has been committed, and he has reasonable cause to believe that the person arrested committed it.
> Provided, That a private person who makes an arrest of another pursuant to the provisions of Sections 40.816—40.823, shall receive no arrest fee or compensation therefor.

A close reading of the powers of arrest of a private person as compared to those of an officer in Tennessee reveals that the private person has almost as much power to arrest as that of an officer, but there are civil restraints available in the nature of an action for false imprisonment, seeking money damages where a private person unlawfully arrests another.

§ 3.2 Constitutional Basis of Arrest

The Constitution of the United States has provisions regarding arrest, search, and seizure. As had been indicated previously, the framers of the Constitution were fearful of creating another monarchy with omnipotent powers. Accordingly, the Fourth Amendment, along with the remaining Bill of Rights, was proposed during the first Congress by James Madison.

The Fourth Amendment adopted in 1791 reads as follows:

The right of the people to be secure in their persons, houses, papers, and effects, against unreasonable searches and seizures, shall not be violated, and no Warrants shall issue, but upon probable cause, supported by Oath or affirmation, and particularly describing the place to be searched, and the person or things to be seized.

History has demonstrated that there was extensive litigation relating to the construction the United States Supreme Court would give to this amendment. Between 1914 and 1962, federal law enforcement officers were strickly bound by its direction while state law enforcement officers in some states were not bound by it. Weeks v. United States, 232 U.S. 383, 34 S.Ct. 341, 58 L.Ed. 652 (1962). Colorado was one state which had previously had its own interpretation of reasonable search which was different from the federal rule. The United States Supreme Court sustained Colorado's right to arrest and convict persons whose Fourth Amendment rights had been violated. In Wolf v. Colorado, 338 U.S. 25, 698 S.Ct. 1359, 93 L.Ed. 1782 (1949), Mr. Justice Frankfurter, speaking for a majority of the court, said in a 5–4 decision,

> ... the security of one's privacy against arbitrary intrusion by the police—which is the core of the Fourth Amendment—is basic to a free society. It is therefore implicit in "the concept of ordered liberty" and as such enforceable against the states... Accordingly, we have no hesitation in saying that were a State affirmatively to sanction such police incursion into privacy, it would run counter to the guarantee of the Fourteenth Amendment. But the ways of enforcing such a basic right raise questions of a different order.

The court continued by discussing the exclusionary rule which forbade the introduction of such unreasonably seized evidence and the use of the exclusionary rule in federal prosecutions as well as some State jurisdictions. The court then went on to say:

> We cannot, therefore, regard it as a departure from basic standards to remand such persons, together with those who emerge scatheless from a search, to the remedies of private action and such protection as the internal discipline of its police, under the eyes of an alert public opinion may afford.
>
> Granting that in practice the exclusion of evidence may be an effective way of deterring unreasonable searches, it is not for this Court to condemn as falling below the minimal standards assured by the Due Process Clause a State's reliance upon other methods which, if consistently enforced would be equally effective... The public opinion of a community can far more effectively be exerted against oppressive conduct on the part of the police directly responsible to the community itself than can local opinion, spo-

> radically aroused, be brought to bear upon remote authority pervasively exerted throughout the country.

In essence, the court said that if a state violated a person's Fourth Amendment rights, the person could not take advantage of an exclusionary rule but could sue the officer and bring public opinion to bear to have the officer disciplined. However, the evidence was admissible and the conviction will not be disturbed.

In 1963, Ker v. California, 374 U.S. 23, 24 Ohio Op.2d 201, 10 L.Ed.2d 726, 83 S.Ct. 1623, the court held that legality of arrests by state and local police officers are to be judged by the same constitutional standards as those of the federal government.

For some time there was a question as to whether the Fourth Amendment applied to mere arrests of persons. This was laid to rest in Henry v. United States, 361 U.S. 98, 80 S.Ct. 168, 4 L.Ed.2d 134 (1959), where the court said the statute states the constitutional standard, for it is the command of the Fourth Amendment that no warrants for either searches or arrests shall issue except upon probable cause, supported by oath or affirmation, and particularly describing the place to be searched, and the persons or things to be seized. Note that the court included the words "searches and arrests" in its determination.

§ 3.3 Arrest Defined

The reader is no doubt conversant with the layman's concept of the meaning of arrest. Many times the courts are called upon to distinguish between an arrest and the taking of a person into custody for the purpose of investigation. It is frequently said that the officer invited the suspect to come to the police station to answer some questions and the suspect complied with the invitation. Defense attorneys frequently ask the officers what the officer would have done had the suspect refused. This question is based upon probabilities and should not be permitted as a legally admissible question.

A legal definition of arrest which has been given much authority contains the following elements:

1. The purpose or intention to effect the arrest under real or pretended authority;
2. Actual or constructive seizure or detention of the person to be arrested by the person having present power to control him;
3. Communication by the arresting officer of intention or purpose then and there to make the arrest;

4. Understanding by the person to be arrested that such is the intention of the arrester. U.S. v. Raidl, 250 F.Supp. 278, 280.

A careful reading of the elements indicated above reveals that an arrest may be effected under pretended authority. If the authority is lacking the officer and/or the governmental agency in which s/he is employed may be liable for money damages as a result of a civil action in unlawful arrest. The officer may also be liable for criminal and civil sanctions for arresting a person in violation of his constitutional rights. (Title 42 U.S.C. 1983, 18 U.S.C. 241, 18 U.S.C. 242.) These will be treated in much greater detail in a later portion of this text. In Miami v. Aronowitz, 141 S.2d 784 (Fla. 1959), the court held that a traffic officer's stopping the movement of vehicular traffic was not an arrest.

No governmental entity is permitted to enact a statute that is vague. If it would be otherwise, "men" would read into a statute what they wished and a possible violator would not have fair warning. An example of this occurred in a California statute that required a person who wanders on the streets to provide "credible" and "reliable" identification when stopped by the police. This statute was declared unconstitutional because it contained no standards on what would satisfy the identification requirement and it was deemed vague on its face. KOLENDER v. LAWSON, 33 Cr.L. 3063 (1983).

§ 3.4 Valid Arrest and Search Warrant Requirements

You will remember that I previously indicated the terms of the Fourth Amendment. You will also remember that a comment was made that this amendment has been the subject of much litigation. We have also discussed how the United States Supreme Court has construed this amendment to be applicable to arrest situations.

We will now direct our attention to some requirements that the courts have construed as being necessary in every warrant of arrest. Foremost among these is the requirement that the warrant be supported by probable cause. Probable cause was defined in Carroll v. United States, 267 U.S. 132, 162, 45 S.Ct. 280, 288, 69 L.Ed. 543, 555 (1925), as "the facts and circumstances within (the officers') knowledge and of which they had reasonable trustworthy information were sufficient in themselves to warrant a man of reasonable caution to believe that a particular offense had been or was being committed." (See §6.19 for further discussion on this topic.) The probable cause must be found in the first instance by the officer who applies for the arrest warrant. However, his basis for probable cause must be reviewed by a detached magistrate or other judicial officer. If probable cause is found by the detached magistrate or other judicial officer, the order for the arrest is issued.

In practice, the general format for applying for either a search warrant or an arrest warrant is that the officer will prepare and execute an affidavit detailing all facts which either s/he or a police informant has observed. If an informant is used, the officer must indicate the past reliability of the informant. The officer must buttress the information of the informant by his/her own personal observations or the observations of a fellow officer who, in the line of duty, imparted the information to the officer who is executing the affidavit. The detached magistrate or judicial officer then makes an individual appraisal based upon the information in the affidavit. If s/he feels that probable cause exists based upon an evaluation of the facts and the credibility of the fact observer, s/he will issue a warrant to the officer to arrest the named person or search the premises particularly described in the warrant for the particular evidence sought.

Jurisdictions may vary with respect to the times of the day that the warrant may be executed and how long the warrant is effective.

After the warrant is issued, the officer then executes the warrant by either arresting the named person or making the seizure of the particularly described evidence and place to be searched. The next court appearance is sometimes called a "Return." In effect, the officer returns to the court and makes a report to the court as to what s/he has found as a result of executing the warrant.

The foregoing procedure is only a general analysis of how a warrant is obtained, executed, and returned. Local practices may vary but generally the above procedure is used and has met with favor in the courts. See Coolidge v. New Hampshire, 403 U.S. 443, 91 S.Ct. 2022, 29 L.Ed.2d 564 (1971). In this case the United States Supreme Court treats the requirement for an independent magistrate or judicial officer. In Shadwick v. City of Tampa, 407 U.S. 345, 92 S.Ct. 2119, 32 L.Ed.2d 783 (1972), the court held that a court clerk who was not a lawyer could fulfill the requirement of a judicial officer establishing probable cause to issue a warrant for a violation of a city ordinance.

§ 3.5 Uniform Arrest Act

As indicated previously, the police officer who invites a suspect to come to the police station is not deemed to be arresting that person. There has been much confusion in this area for many years. Accordingly, a Uniform Arrest Act was adopted by the Interstate Commission on Crime. It contains the following provisions concerning detention:

1. A peace officer may stop any person abroad whom he has reasonable ground to suspect is committing, has committed or is about to commit

a crime, and may demand of him his name, address, business abroad and whither he is going.

2. Any person so questioned who fails to identify himself or explain his actions to the satisfaction of the officer stopping him, may be detained and further questioned and investigated.
3. The total period of detention provided for by this section shall not exceed two hours. Such detention is not an arrest and shall not be recorded as an arrest in any official record. At the end of the detention period, the person so detained shall be released unless arrested and charged with a crime.

The statute has been adopted by several states and has been upheld as constitutional. The United States Supreme Court has not yet decided the constitutionality of this statute. However, suppose the subject of the detention stands mute when he is accosted by the police officer. Does this give the officer sufficient grounds to detain him for up to two hours? On the other hand, suppose the subject makes incriminating statements at the time of his first contact with the officer. The officer asks him a question without giving the subject Miranda warnings, and the subject makes incriminating statements. Can these statements be used at the later trial? Was the subject compelled to identify himself and explain his actions to the satisfaction of the officer or face a detention of up to two hours? Were his Fifth Amendment self-incrimination rights violated? These and other interesting constitutional questions have been answered and will be discussed further by the United States Supreme Court in the future.

§ 3.6 Stop and Frisk

The right of an officer to stop and frisk a suspect for weapons has been firmly established through a landmark decision in the case of Terry v. Ohio, 392 U.S. 1, 440 Ohio Op.2d 383, 88 S.Ct. 1868, 20 L.Ed.2d 889 (1968). This case is edited and included at the end of this chapter.

New York State, Florida, Ohio, and other states have codified what had been apparent through common law decisions. New York Section 140.50 of the Criminal Procedure Law reads as follows:

Temporary questioning of persons in public places; search for weapons—

1. In addition to the authority provided by this article for making an arrest without a warrant, a police officer may stop a person in a public place located within the geographical area of such officer's employment when he reasonably suspects that such person is committing, has committed or is about to commit either (a) a felony or (b) a Class A misdemeanor defined in the penal law and may demand of him his name, address and an explanation of his conduct.

Florida's similar statute is:

901.151 Stop and frisk law

(1) This section may be known and cited as the "Florida stop and frisk law."

(2) Whenever any law enforcement officer of this state encounters any person under circumstances which reasonably indicate that such person has committed, is committing, or is about to commit a violation of the criminal laws of this state or the criminal ordinances of any municipality or county, he may temporarily detain such person for the purpose of ascertaining the identity of the person temporarily detained and the circumstances surrounding his presence abroad which led the officer to believe that he had committed, was committing, or was about to commit a criminal offense.

(3) No person shall be temporarily detained under the provisions of subsection (2) of this section longer than is reasonably necessary to effect the purposes of that subsection. Such temporary detention shall not extend beyond the place where it was first effected or the immediate vicinity thereof.

(4) If at any time after the onset of the temporary detention authorized by subsection (2) of this section, probable cause for arrest of person shall appear, the person shall be arrested. If, after an inquiry into the circumstances which prompted the temporary detention, no probable cause for the arrest of the person shall appear, he shall be released.

(5) Whenever any law enforcement officer authorized to detain temporarily any person under the provisions of subsection (2) of this section has probable cause to believe that any person whom he has temporarily detained, or is about to detain temporarily, is armed with a dangerous weapon and therefore offers a threat to the safety of the officer or any other person, he may search such person so temporarily detained only to the extent necessary to disclose, and for the purpose of disclosing, the presence of such weapon. If such a search discloses such a weapon or any evidence of a criminal offense it may be seized.

(6) No evidence seized by a law enforcement officer in any search under this section shall be admissible against any person in any court of this state or political subdivision thereof unless the search which disclosed its existence was authorized by and conducted in compliance with the provisions of subsections (2)–(5).

A case decided with the Terry case was the Sibron v. New York case, 392 U.S. 40, 44 Ohio Op.2d 402, 88 S.Ct. 1889, 20 L.Ed.2d 917. The officer had plenty of time in this case to secure a warrant and the stop and frisk was for the purpose of finding narcotics, not weapons. Therefore the Court invalidated the search.

§ 3.7 The Moving Motor Vehicle Problem

The right of a police officer to stop a driver of a moving motor vehicle because of suspicious actions by the driver of the automobile has been a particularly troublesome area of constitutional law. The problem arises because of the possible abuse of this privilege by law enforcement personnel. Frequently if a driver is driving a new shiny car and the driver is young, or if the driver is apparently of a different ethnic group or color of skin from the dominant population in a particular community, or if the driver is driving slowly accompanied by others in the vehicle and they are in a ghetto area, or if the driver violates a traffic law, the suspicions of the police are aroused. Many excellent arrests have been made under these conditions. On the other hand, many persons have been stopped and questioned under the same conditions who were doing nothing illegal. They resent the intrusion into their privacy by the police and get the impression that they are living in a police state. Obviously, there must be some balance between these opposing views.

The United States Supreme Court has met this problem on a case-by-case basis. In Carpenter v. Sigler, 419 F.2d 169, the United States Court of Appeals for the Eighth Circuit held that suspicious actions by a driver of an automobile occurring at about 3:30 AM warranted the officer to stop the car and ask one of the occupants to step out. As the occupant got out of the car, a noise of metal hitting metal was heard by the officer and this noise was apparently caused by the exiting offender as he labored to get out of the car. The officer beamed his light on the floor of the car and found two crowbars there. The court held that the prior activity of the driver raised sufficient justification for the officers to stop the car. However, in Harris v. U.S., 390 U.S. 234, 88 S.Ct. 992, 19 L.Ed.2d 1067 (1968), the court held that FBI agents who had received information regarding interstate shipment of stolen property and seeing two persons drive to a residence on two occasions and load cartons into a car and drive away, did not have probable cause for a warrantless search. The issues presented in the arrest and search of the occupants of an automobile and a search of the parties and the automobile are more extensively discussed in § 6.23 infra.

§ 3.8 Statutory Authority to Stop Vehicles

All states have statutes which authorize law enforcement officers to stop vehicles to inspect these vehicles. When one gets a license to drive a vehicle, it is a license and nothing more. It is revocable for cause and one does not have a constitutional right to drive an automobile. He does, however, have a constitutional right to equal protection under the law and equal privileges and immunities. If he complies with the statutes as others do, he must be treated as others are treated. Reasoning thusly, if driving is a privilege and not a right, and if a condition of the privilege of driving a vehicle is that the driver subject himself and his vehicle to inspections by designated law enforcers, then the statute authorizing law enforcement personnel in the line of their duty to inspect drivers and their vehicles is constitutional. The question remains, however, does this statute give authority to law enforcement officers to stop and question passengers in the automobile?

§ 3.9 Detention for Fingerprints

The right to take fingerprints from a person who has been lawfully arrested has been held to be elementary by the courts. In Smith v. U.S., 324 F.2d 879 (D.C.Circ 1963), the court said, "We find no error in the admission of the palm print of Smith, taken the day before trial for purposes of comparison with the palm print on the victim's credit card. Unlike the situation in Bynum v. United States, appellant here was in lawful custody at the time the prints were recorded... and it is elementary that a person in lawful custody may be required to submit to photographing and fingerprinting as part of routine identification processes."

However, the problem arises when the police take the fingerprints of suspects who are not in lawful custody and whose prints are taken for the purpose of connecting the suspect to the commission of a crime. This type of case arose in Davis v. Mississippi, 394 U.S. 721, 89 S.Ct. 1394, 22 L.Ed.2d 676 (1969).

In the Davis case, the defendant and several other black youths were taken to police headquarters where they were questioned in connection with an alleged rape of an eighty-six-year-old white woman. They were questioned briefly and fingerprinted. Several days later the defendant was jailed and fingerprinted again. His fingerprints were found to match those on the window of the victim's home. The United States Supreme Court in an opinion by Brennan, J., expressed the view of six members of the Court in holding that since the defendant's detention by the police was unlawful, his fingerprints were obtained in violation of the Fourth and Fourteenth Amendments, so as to be inadmissible at his trial.

§ 3.10 Doctrine of Close Pursuit

The nations of the world, as well as the states of the union, have had to protect themselves from the lawbreaker who would commit a crime in one jurisdiction and then flee to freedom in another jurisdiction. We are all acquainted with the western films of yore where the bad man (usually wearing a mustache or beard and with black horse and clothing) would race for the border to gain his freedom. To counteract this situation, many nations have entered into treaties to extradite persons accused of crimes. The states have also entered into agreements called compacts.

Interstate compacts are authorized by Article I, Section 10, of the United States Constitution. As the text of this section reads, it is necessary for Congress to consent to an agreement or compact between states. It has been found that this device has been very useful for the solution of regional problems which require continuing administration and regulation. One of these problems particularly of interest to law enforcement has been the case of the fleeing offender.

For this reason, a uniform close pursuit act has been promulgated and has been adopted by many states. The Massachusetts statute reads as follows:

> *10A. Authority of officer of another state to arrest felon*
> Any member of a duly organized state, county or municipal peace unit of another state of the United States the laws of which contain provisions substantially equivalent to the provisions of this and the following sections, who enters this commonwealth in fresh pursuit, and continues herein in such fresh pursuit, of a person in order to arrest him on the ground that he has committed a felony in such other state shall have the same authority to arrest and hold in custody such person as members of a duly organized state, county or municipal peace unit of this commonwealth have to arrest and hold in custody a person on the ground that he has committed a felony in this commonwealth. This section shall not be construed so as to make unlawful any arrest in this commonwealth which would otherwise be lawful.
>
> *10B. Proceedings after arrest*
> If an arrest is made in this commonwealth by an officer of another state in accordance with the provisions of the preceding section he shall without unnecessary delay take the person arrested before a justice, associate justice or special justice of a court of record in the county in which the arrest was made, who shall conduct a hearing for the purpose of determining the lawfulness of the arrest. If such justice, associate justice or special justice determines that the arrest was lawful he shall commit the person arrested to await for a reasonable time the issuance of a rendition warrant by the governor of the state from which he fled. If such justice, associate justice or special justice determines that the arrest was unlawful he shall discharge the person arrested.
>
> *10C. Partial invalidity*
> If any part of sections ten A and ten B is for any reason declared void, it is declared to be the intent of said sections that such invalidity shall not affect the validity of the remaining portions of said sections.

10D. Citation of law; uniform construction

Sections ten A to ten C, inclusive, may be cited as the uniform extraterritorial arrest or fresh pursuit law, and shall be so interpreted and construed as to effectuate their general purpose to make uniform the law of the states which enact similar laws.

Judicial Decisions Relating to Chapter 3

Weeks *v.* United States

232 U.S. 383, 34 S.Ct. 341, 58 L.Ed. 652 (1914)

ERROR TO THE DISTRICT COURT OF THE UNITED STATES FOR THE WESTERN DISTRICT OF MISSOURI

Argued December 2, 3, 1913.—Decided February 24, 1914.

. . .

MR. JUSTICE DAY delivered the opinion of the court.

An indictment was returned against the plaintiff in error, defendant below, and herein so designated, in the District Court of the United States for the Western District of Missouri, containing nine counts. The seventh count, upon which a conviction was had, charged the use of the mails for the purpose of transporting certain coupons or tickets representing chances or shares in a lottery or gift enterprise, in violation of § 213 of the Criminal Code. Sentence of fine and imprisonment was imposed. This writ of error is to review that judgment.

The defendant was arrested by a police officer, so far as the record shows, without warrant, at the Union Station in Kansas City, Missouri, where he was employed by an express company. Other police officers had gone to the house of the defendant and being told by a neighbor where the key was kept, found it and entered the house. They searched the defendant's room and took possession of various papers and articles found there, which were afterwards turned over to the United States Marshal. Later in the same day police officers returned with the Marshal, who thought he might find additional evidence, and, being admitted by someone in the house, probably a boarder, in response to a rap, the marshal searched the defendant's room and carried away certain letters and envelopes found in the drawer of a chiffonier. Neither the marshal nor the police officers had a search warrant.

The defendant filed in the cause before the time for trial the following petition:

Petition to Return Private Papers, Books and Other Property.

"Now comes defendant and states that he is a citizen and resident of Kansas City, Missouri, and that he resides, owns and occupies a home at 1834 Penn Street in said City;

"That on the 21st day of December, 1911, while plaintiff was absent at his daily vocation certain officers of the government whose names are to plaintiff unknown, unlawfully and without warrant or authority so to do, broke open the door to plaintiff's said home and seized all of his books, letters, money, papers, notes, evidences of indebtedness, stock, certificates, insurance policies, deeds, abstracts, and other muniments of title, bonds, candies, clothes and other property in said home, and this in violation of Sections 11 and 23 of the Constitution of Missouri and of the 4th and 5th Amendments to the Constitution of the United States:

> "That the District Attorney, Marshal and Clerk of the United States Court for the Western District of Missouri took the above described property so seized into their possession and have failed and refused to return to defendant portion of same, to-wit:
>
> "One (1) leather grip, value about $7.00; one (1) tin box valued at $3.00; one (1) Pettis County, Missouri, bond, value $500.00; three (3) Mining stock certificates which defendant is unable to more particularly describe valued at $12,000.00, and certain stock certificates in addition thereto issued by the San Domingo Mining Loan and Investment Company, about $75.00 in currency; one (1) newspaper published about 1790, an heirloom; and certain other property which plaintiff is now unable to describe:
>
> "That said property is being unlawfully and improperly held by said District Attorney, Marshal and Clerk in violation of defendant's rights under the Constitution of the United States and the State of Missouri:
>
> "That said District Attorney purposes to use said books, letters, papers, certificates of stock, etc., at the trial of the above entitled cause and that by reason therefore and of the facts above set forth defendant's rights under the amendments aforesaid to the Constitution of Missouri, and the United States have been and will be violated unless the Court order the return prayed for:
>
> "Wherefore, defendant prays that said District Attorney, Marshal and Clerk be notified, and that the Court direct and order said District Attorney, Marshal and Clerk to return said property to said defendant."

Upon consideration of the petition the court entered in the cause an order directing the return of such property as was not pertinent to the charge against the defendant, but denied the petition as to pertinent matter, reserving the right to pass upon the pertinency at a later time. In obedience to the order the District Attorney returned part of the property taken and retained the remainder, concluding a list of the latter with the statement that, "all of which last above described property is to be used in evidence in the trial of the above entitled cause, and pertains to the alleged sale of lottery tickets of the company above named."

After the jury had been sworn and before any evidence had been given, the defendant again urged his petition for the return of his property, which was denied by the court. Upon the introduction of such papers during the trial, the defendant objected on the ground that the papers had been obtained without a search warrant and by breaking open his home, in violation of the Fourth and Fifth Amendments to the Constitution of the United States, which objection was overruled by the court. Among the papers retained and put in evidence were a number of lottery tickets and statements with reference to the lottery, taken at the first visit of the police to the defendant's room, and a number of letters written to the defendant in respect to the lottery, taken by the Marshal upon his search of defendant's room.

The defendant assigns error, among other things, in the court's refusal to grant his petition for the return of his property and in permitting the papers to be used at the trial.

It is thus apparent that the question presented involves the determination of the duty of the court with reference to the motion made by the defendant for the return of certain letters, as well as other papers, taken from his room by the United States Marshal, who, without authority of process, if any such could have been legally issued, visited the room of the defendant for the declared purpose of obtaining additional testimony to support the charge against the accused, and having gained admission to the house took from the drawer of a chiffonier there found certain letters written to the defendant, tending to show his guilt. These letters were placed in the control of the District Attorney and were subsequently produced by him and offered in evidence against the accused at the trial. The defendant contends that such appropriation of his private correspondence was in violation of rights secured to him by the Fourth and Fifth Amendments to the Constitution of the United States. We shall deal with the Fourth Amendment, which provides:

> "The right of the people to be secure in their persons, houses, papers, and effects, against unreasonable searches and seizures, shall not be violated, and no warrants shall issue, but upon probable cause, supported by oath or affirmation and particularly describing the place to be searched, and the persons or things to be seized."

The history of this Amendment is given with particularity in the opinion of MR. JUSTICE BRADLEY, speaking for the court in Boyd v. United States, 116 U.S. 616. As was there shown, it took its origin in the determination of the framers of the Amendments to the Federal Constitution to provide for that instrument a Bill of Rights, securing to the American people, among other things, those safeguards which had grown up in England to protect the people from unreasonable searches and seizures, such as were permitted under the general warrants issued under authority of the Government by which there had been invasions of the home and privacy of the citizens and the seizure of their private papers in support of charges, real or imaginary made against them. Such practices had also received sanction under warrants and seizures under the so called writs of assistance, issued in the American colonies. See 2 Watson on the Constitution, 1414 et seq. Resistance to these practices had established the principle which was enacted into the fundamental law in the Fourth Amendment, that a man's house was his castle and not to be invaded by any general authority to search and seize his goods and papers. Judge Cooley, in his Constitutional Limitations, pp. 425, 426, in treating of this feature of our Constitution, said: "The maxim that 'every man's house is his castle,' is made a part of our constitutional law in the clauses prohibiting unreasonable searches and seizures, and has always been looked upon as of high value to the citizen." "Accordingly," says Lieber in his work on Civil Liberty and Self-Government, 62, in speaking of the English law in this respect, "no man's house can be forcibly opened, or he or his goods be carried away after it has thus been forced, except in cases of felony, and then the sheriff must be furnished with a warrant, and take great care lest he commit a trespass. This principle is jealously insisted upon." In Ex parte Jackson, 96 U.S. 727, 733, this court recognized the principle of protection as applicable to letters and sealed packages in the mail; and held that consistently with this guaranty of the right of the people to be secure in their papers against unreasonable searches and seizures such matter could only be opened and examined upon warrants issued on oath or affirmation particularly describing the thing to be seized, "as is required when papers are subjected to search in one's own household."

In the Boyd case, supra, after citing Lord Camden's judgment in Entick v. Carrington, 19 Howell's State Trials, 1029, MR. JUSTICE BRADLEY said (630):

> "The principles laid down in this opinion affect the very essence of constitutional liberty and security. They reach farther than the concrete form of the case then before the court, with its adventitious circumstances; they apply to all invasions on the part of the government and its employés of the sanctity of a man's home and the privacies of life. It is not the breaking of his doors, and the rummaging of his drawers, that constitutes the essence of the offence; but it is the invasion of his indefeasible right of personal security, personal liberty and private property, where that right has never been forfeited by his conviction of some public offence,—it is the invasion of this sacred right which underlies and constitutes the essence of Lord Camden's judgment."

In Bram v. United States, 168 U.S. 532, this court in speaking by the present Chief Justice of Boyd's case, dealing with the Fourth and Fifth Amendments, said (544):

> "It was in that case demonstrated that both of these Amendments contemplated perpetuating, in their full efficacy, by means of a constitutional provision, principles of humanity and civil liberty, which had been secured in the mother country only after years of struggle, so as to implant them in our institutions in the fullness of their integrity, free from the possibilities of future legislative change."

The effect of the Fourth Amendment is to put the courts of the United States and Federal officials, in the exercise of their power and authority, under limitations and restraints as to the exercise of such power and authority, and to forever secure the people, their persons, houses, papers and effects against all unreasonable searches and seizures under the guise of law. This protection reaches all alike, whether accused of crime or not, and the duty of giving to it force and effect is obligatory upon all entrusted under our Federal system with the enforcement of the laws. The tendency of those who execute the criminal laws of the country to obtain conviction by means of unlawful seizures and enforced confessions, the latter often obtained after subjecting accused persons to unwarranted practices destructive of rights secured by the Federal Constitution, should find no sanction in the judgments of the courts which are charged at all times with the support of the Constitution and to which people of all conditions have a right to appeal for the maintenance of such fundamental rights.

What then is the present case? Before answering that inquiry specifically, it may be well by a process of exclusion to state what it is not. It is not an assertion of the right on the part of the Government, always recognized under English and American law, to search the person of the accused when legally arrested to discover and seize the fruits or evidences of crime. This right has been uniformly maintained in many cases. 1 Bishop on Criminal Procedure, § 211; Wharton, Crim. Plead. and Practice, 8th ed., § 60; Dillon v. O'Brien and Davis, 16 Cox C.C. 245. Nor is it the case of testimony offered at a trial where the court is asked to stop and consider the illegal means by which proofs, otherwise competent, were obtained—of which we shall have occasion to treat later in this opinion. Nor is it the case of burglar's tools or other proofs of guilt found upon his arrest within the control of the accused.

The case in the aspect in which we are dealing with it involves the right of the court in a criminal prosecution to retain for the purposes of evidence the letters and correspondence of the accused, seized in his house in his absence and without his authority, by a United States Marshal holding no warrant for his arrest and none for the search of his premises. The accused, without awaiting his trial, made timely application to the court for an order for the return of these letters, as well as other property. This application was denied, the letters retained and put in evidence, after a further application at the beginning of the trial, both applications asserting the rights of the accused under the Fourth and Fifth Amendments to the Constitution. If letters and private documents can thus be seized and held and used in evidence against a citizen accused of an offense, the protection of the Fourth Amendment declaring his right to be secure against such searches and seizures is of no value, and, so far as those thus placed are concerned, might as well be stricken from the Constitution. The efforts of the courts and their officials to bring the guilty to punishment, praiseworthy as they are, are not to be aided by the sacrifice of those great principles established by years of endeavor and suffering which have resulted in their embodiment in the fundamental law of the land. The United States Marshal could only have invaded the house of the accused when armed with a warrant issued as required by the Constitution, upon sworn information and describing with reasonable particularity the thing for which the search was to be made. Instead, he acted without sanction of law, doubtless prompted by the desire to bring further proof to the aid of the Government, and under color of his office undertook to make a seizure of private papers in direct violation of the constitutional prohibition against such action. Under such circumstances, without sworn information and particular description, not even an order of court would have justified such procedure, much less was it within the authority of the United States Marshal to thus invade the house and privacy of the accused. In Adams v. New York, 192 U.S. 585, this court said that the Fourth Amendment was intended to secure the citizen in person and property against unlawful invasion of the sanctity of his home by officers of the law acting under legislative or judicial sanction. This protection is equally extended to the action of the Government and officers of the law acting under it. (Boyd case, supra.) To sanction such proceedings would be to affirm by judicial decision a manifest neglect if not an open defiance of the prohibitions of the Constitution, intended for the protection of the people against such unauthorized action.

The court before which the application was made in this case recognized the illegal character of the seizure and ordered the return of property not in its judgment competent to be offered at the trial, but refused the application of the accused to turn over the letters, which were afterwards put in evidence on behalf of the Government. While there is no opinion in the case, the court in this proceeding doubtless relied upon what is now contended by the Government to be the correct rule of law under such circumstances, that the letters having come into the control of the court, it would not inquire into the manner in which they were obtained, but if competent would keep them and permit their use in evidence. Such proposition, the Government asserts, is conclusively established by certain decisions of this court, the first of which is Adams v. New York, supra. In that case the plaintiff in error had been convicted in the Supreme Court of the State of New York for having in his possession certain gambling paraphernalia used in the game known as policy, in violation of the Penal Code of New York. At the trial certain papers, which had been seized by police officers executing a search warrant for the discovery and seizure of policy slips and which had been found in addition to the policy slips, were offered in evidence over his objection. The conviction was affirmed by the Court of Appeals of New York (176 N.Y. 351), and the case was brought here for alleged violation of the Fourth and Fifth Amendments to the Constitution of the United States. Pretermitting the question whether these amendments applied to the action of the States, this court proceeded to examine the alleged violations of the Fourth and Fifth Amendments, and put its decision upon the ground that the papers found in the execution of the search warrant, which warrant had a legal purpose in the attempt to find gambling paraphernalia, were competent evidence against the accused, and their offer in testimony did not violate his constitutional privilege against unlawful search or seizure, for it was held that such incriminatory documents thus discovered were not the subject of an unreasonable search and seizure, and in effect that the same were incidentally seized in the lawful execution of a warrant and not in the wrongful invasion of the home of the citizen and the unwarranted seizure of his papers and property. It was further held, approving in that respect the doctrine laid down in 1 Greenleaf, § 254a, that it was no valid objection to the use of the papers that they had been thus seized, and that the courts in the course of a trial would not make an issue to determine that question, and many state cases were cited supporting that doctrine.

The same point had been ruled in People v. Adams, 176 N.Y. 351, from which decision the case was brought to this court, where it was held that if the papers seized in addition to the policy slips were competent evidence in the case, as the court held they were, they were admissible in evidence at the trial, the court saying (p. 358): "The underlying principle obviously is that the court, when engaged in trying a criminal cause, will not take notice of the manner in which witnesses have possessed themselves of papers, or other articles of personal property, which are material and properly offered in evidence." This doctrine thus laid down by the New York Court of Appeals and approved by this court, that a court will not in trying a criminal cause permit a collateral issue to be raised as to the source of competent testimony, has the sanction of so many state cases that it would be impracticable to cite or refer to them in detail. Many of them are collected in the note to State v. Turner, 136 Am. St. Rep. 129, 135 et seq. After citing numerous cases the editor says: "The underlying principle of all these decisions obviously is, that the court, when engaged in the trial of a criminal action, will not take notice of the manner in which a witness has possessed himself of papers or other chattels, subjects of evidence, which are material and properly offered in evidence: People v. Adams, 176 N.Y. 351, 98 Am. St. Rep. 675, 68 N.E. 636, 63 L.R.A. 406. Such an investigation is not involved necessarily in the litigation in chief, and to pursue it would be to halt in the orderly progress of a cause, and consider incidentally a question which has happened to cross the path of such litigation, and which is wholly independent thereof."

It is therefore evident that the Adams case affords no authority for the action of the court in this case, when applied to in due season for the return of papers seized in violation of the Constitutional Amendment. The decision in that case rests upon incidental seizure made in the execution of a legal warrant and in the application of the doctrine that a collateral issue will not be raised to ascertain the source from which testimony, competent in a criminal case, comes.

The Government also relies upon Hale v. Henkel, 201 U.S. 43, in which the previous cases of Boyd v. United States, supra, Adams v. New York, supra, Interstate Commerce Commission v. Brimson, 154 U.S. 447, and Interstate Commerce Commission v. Baird, 194 U.S. 25, are reviewed, and wherein it was held that a subpoena duces tecum requiring a corporation to produce all its contracts and correspondence with no less than six other companies, as well as all letters received by the corporation from thirteen other companies located in different parts of the United States, was an unreasonable search and seizure within the Fourth Amendment, and it was there stated that (201 U.S. p. 76) "an order for the production of books and papers may constitute an unreasonable search and seizure within the Fourth Amendment. While a search ordinarily implies a quest by an officer of the law, and a seizure contemplates a forcible dispossession of the owner, still, as was held in the Boyd case, the substance of the offense is the compulsory production of private papers, whether under a search warrant or a subpoena duces tecum, against which the person, be he individual or corporation, is entitled to protection." If such a seizure under the authority of a warrant supposed to be legal, constitutes a violation of the constitutional protection, a fortiori does the attempt of an officer of the United States, the United States Marshal, acting under color of his office, without even the sanction of a warrant, constitute an invasion of the rights within the protection afforded by the Fourth Amendment.

. . .

The right of the court to deal with papers and documents in the possession of the District Attorney and other officers of the court and subject to its authority was recognized in Wise v. Henkel, 220 U.S. 556. That papers wrongfully seized should be turned over to the accused has been frequently recognized in the early as well as later decisions of the courts. 1 Bishop on Criminal Procedure, § 210; Rex v. Barnett, 3 C. & P. 600; Rex v. Kinsey, 7 C. & P. 447; United States v. Mills, 185 Fed. Rep. 318; United States v. McHie, 194 Fed. Rep. 894, 898.

We therefore reach the conclusion that the letters in question were taken from the house of the accused by an official of the United States acting under color of his office in direct violation of the constitutional rights of the defendant; that having made a seasonable application for their return, which was heard and passed upon by the court, there was involved in the order refusing the application a denial of the constitutional rights of the accused, and that the court should have restored these letters to the accused. In holding them and permitting their use upon the trial, we think prejudicial error was committed. As to the papers and property seized by the policemen, it does not appear that they acted under any claim of Federal authority such as would make the Amendment applicable to such unauthorized seizures.

The record shows that what they did by way of arrest and search and seizure was done before the finding of the indictment in the Federal Court, under what supposed right or authority does not appear. What remedies the defendant may have against them we need not inquire, as the Fourth Amendment is not directed to individual misconduct of such officials. Its limitations reach the Federal Government and its agencies. Boyd Case, 116 U.S., supra, and see Twining v. New Jersey, 211 U.S. 78.

It results that the judgment of the court below must be reversed, and the case remanded for further proceedings in accordance with this opinion.

Reversed.

Terry *v.* Ohio

392 U.S. 1, 88 S.Ct. 1868, 20 L.Ed. 2d. 889 (1968)

CERTIORARI TO THE SUPREME COURT OF OHIO

Argued December 12, 1967.—Decided June 10, 1968.

. . .

MR. CHIEF JUSTICE WARREN delivered the opinion of the Court.

This case presents serious questions concerning the role of the Fourth Amendment in the confrontation on the street between the citizen and the policeman investigating suspicious circumstances.

Petitioner Terry was convicted of carrying a concealed weapon and sentenced to the statutorily prescribed term of one to three years in the penitentiary. Following the denial of a pretrial motion to suppress, the prosecution introduced in evidence two revolvers and a number of bullets seized from Terry and a codefendant, Richard Chilton, by Cleveland Police Detective Martin McFadden. At the hearing on the motion to suppress this evidence, Officer McFadden testified that while he was patrolling in plain clothes in downtown Cleveland at approximately 2:30 in the afternoon of October 31, 1963, his attention was attracted by two men, Chilton and Terry, standing on the corner of Huron Road and Euclid Avenue. He had never seen the two men before, and he was unable to say precisely what first drew his eye to them. However, he testified that he had been a policeman for 39 years and a detective for 35 and that he had been assigned to patrol this vicinity of downtown Cleveland for shoplifters and pickpockets for 30 years. He explained that he had developed routine habits of observation over the years and that he would "stand and watch people or walk and watch people at many intervals of the day." He added: "Now, in this case when I looked over they didn't look right to me at the time."

His interest aroused, Officer McFadden took up a post of observation in the entrance to a store 300 to 400 feet away from the two men. "I get more purpose to watch them when I seen their movements," he testified. He saw one of the men leave the other one and walk southwest on Huron Road, past some stores. The man paused for a moment and looked in a store window, then walked on a short distance, turned around and walked back toward the corner, pausing once again to look in the same store window. He rejoined his companion at the corner, and the two conferred briefly. Then the second man went through the same series of motions, strolling down Huron Road, looking in the same window, walking on a short distance, turning back, peering in the store window again, and returning to confer with the first man at the corner. The two men repeated this ritual alternately between five and six times apiece—in all, roughly a dozen trips. At one point, while the two were standing together on the corner, a third man approached them and engaged them briefly in conversation. This man then left the two others and walked west on Euclid Avenue. Chilton and Terry resumed their measured pacing, peering, and conferring. After this had gone on for 10 to 12 minutes, the two men walked off together, heading west on Euclid Avenue, following the path taken earlier by the third man.

By this time Officer McFadden had become thoroughly suspicious. He testified that after observing their elaborately casual and oft-repeated reconnaissance of the store window on Huron Road, he suspected the two men of "casing a job, a stick-up," and that he considered it his duty as a police officer to investigate further. He added that he feared "they may have a gun." Thus, Officer McFadden followed Chilton and Terry and saw them stop in front of Zucker's store to talk to the same man who had conferred with them earlier on the street corner. Deciding that the situation was ripe for direct action, Officer McFadden approached the three men, identified himself as a police officer and asked for their names. At this point his knowledge was confined to what he had observed. He was not acquainted with any of the three men by name or by sight, and he had received no information concerning them from any other source. When the men "mumbled something" in response to his inquiries, Officer McFadden grabbed petitioner Terry, spun him around so that they were facing the other two, with Terry between McFadden and the others, and patted down the outside of his clothing. In the left breast pocket of Terry's overcoat Officer McFadden felt a pistol. He reached inside the overcoat pocket, but was unable to remove the gun. At this point, keeping Terry between himself and the others, the officer ordered all three men to enter Zucker's store. As they went in, he removed Terry's overcoat completely, removed a .38-caliber revolver from the pocket and ordered all three men to face the wall with their hands raised. Officer McFadden proceeded to pat down the outer clothing of Chilton and the third man, Katz. He discovered another revolver in the outer pocket of Chilton's overcoat, but no weapons were found on Katz. The officer testified that he only patted the men down to see whether they had weapons, and that he did not put his hands beneath the outer garments of either Terry or Chilton until he felt their guns. So far as appears from the record, he never placed his hands beneath Katz' outer garments. Officer McFadden seized Chilton's gun, asked the proprietor of the store to call a police wagon, and took all three men to the station, where Chilton and Terry were formally charged with carrying concealed weapons.

On the motion to suppress the guns the prosecution took the position that they had been seized following a search incident to a lawful arrest. The trial court rejected this theory, stating that it "would be stretching the facts beyond reasonable comprehension" to find that Officer McFadden had had probable cause to arrest the men before he patted them down for weapons. However, the court denied the defendants' motion on the ground that Officer McFadden, on the basis of his experience, "had reasonable cause to believe . . . that the defendants were conducting themselves suspiciously, and some interrogation should be made of their action." Purely for his own protection, the court held, the officer had the right to pat down the outer clothing of these men, who he had reasonable cause to believe might be armed. The court distinguished between an investigatory "stop" and an arrest, and between a "frisk" of the outer clothing for weapons and a full-blown search for evidence of crime. The frisk, it held, was essential to the proper performance of the officer's investigatory duties, for without it "the answer to the police officer may be a bullet, and a loaded pistol discovered during the frisk is admissible."

After the court denied their motion to suppress, Chilton and Terry waived jury trial and pleaded not guilty. The court adjudged them guilty, and the Court of Appeals for the Eighth Judicial District, Cuyahoga County, affirmed. State v. Terry, 5 Ohio App. 2d 122, 214 N.E. 2d 114 (1966). The Supreme Court of Ohio dismissed their appeal on the ground that no "substantial constitutional question" was involved. We granted certiorari, 387 U.S. 929 (1967), to determine whether the admission of the revolvers in evidence violated petitioner's rights under the Fourth Amendment, made applicable to the States by the Fourteenth. Mapp v. Ohio, 367 U.S. 643 (1961). We affirm the conviction.

I

The Fourth Amendment provides that "the right of the people to be secure in their persons, houses, papers, and effects, against unreasonable searches and seizures, shall not be violated. . . ." This inestimable right of personal security belongs as much to the citizen on the streets of our cities as to the homeowner closeted in his study to dispose of his secret affairs. For, as this Court has always recognized,

> "No right is held more sacred, or is more carefully guarded, by the common law, than the right of every individual to the possession and control of his own person, free from all restraint or interference of others, unless by clear and unquestionable authority of law." Union Pac. R. Co. v. Botsford, 141 U.S. 250, 251 (1891).

We have recently held that "the Fourth Amendment protects people, not places," Katz v. United States, 389 U.S. 347, 351 (1967), and wherever an individual may harbor a reasonable "expectation of privacy," id., at 361 (Mr. Justice Harlan, concurring), he is entitled to be free from unreasonable governmental intrusion. Of course, the specific content and incidents of this right must be shaped by the context in which it is asserted. For "what the Constitution forbids is not all searches and seizures, but unreasonable searches and seizures," Elkins v. United States, 364 U.S. 206, 222 (1960). Unquestionably petitioner was entitled to the protection of the Fourth Amendment as he walked down the street in Cleveland. Beck v. Ohio, 379 U.S. 89 (1964); Rios v. United States, 364 U.S. 253 (1960); Henry v. United States, 361 U.S. 98 (1959); United States v. Di Re, 332 U.S. 581 (1948); Carroll v. United

States, 267 U.S. 132 (1925). The question is whether in all the circumstances of this on-the-street encounter, his right to personal security was violated by an unreasonable search and seizure.

We would be less than candid if we did not acknowledge that this question thrusts to the fore difficult and troublesome issues regarding a sensitive area of police activity—issues which have never before been squarely presented to this Court. Reflective of the tensions involved are the practical and constitutional arguments pressed with great vigor on both sides of the public debate over the power of the police to "stop and frisk"—as it is sometimes euphemistically termed—suspicious persons.

On the one hand, it is frequently argued that in dealing with the rapidly unfolding and often dangerous situations on city streets the police are in need of an escalating set of flexible responses, graduated in relation to the amount of information they possess. For this purpose it is urged that distinctions should be made between a "stop" and an "arrest" (or a "seizure" of a person), and between a "frisk" and a "search." Thus, it is argued, the police should be allowed to "stop" a person and detain him briefly for questioning upon suspicion that he may be connected with criminal activity. Upon suspicion that the person may be armed, the police should have the power to "frisk" him for weapons. If the "stop" and the "frisk" give rise to probable cause to believe that the suspect has committed a crime, then the police should be empowered to make a formal "arrest," and a full incident "search" of the person. This scheme is justified in part upon the notion that a "stop" and a "frisk" amount to a mere "minor inconvenience and petty indignity," which can properly be imposed upon the citizen in the interest of effective law enforcement on the basis of a police officer's suspicion.

On the other side the argument is made that the authority of the police must be strictly circumscribed by the law of arrest and search as it has developed to date in the traditional jurisprudence of the Fourth Amendment. It is contended with some force that there is not—and cannot be—a variety of police activity which does not depend solely upon the voluntary cooperation of the citizen and yet which stops short of an arrest based upon probable cause to make such an arrest. The heart of the Fourth Amendment, the argument runs, is a severe requirement of specific justification for any intrusion upon protected personal security, coupled with a highly developed system of judicial controls to enforce upon the agents of the State the commands of the Constitution. Acquiescence by the courts in the compulsion inherent in the field interrogation practices at issue here, it is urged, would constitute an abdication of judicial control over, and indeed an encouragement of, substantial interference with liberty and personal security by police officers whose judgment is necessarily colored by their primary involvement in "the often competitive enterprise of ferreting out crime." Johnson v. United States, 333 U.S. 10, 14 (1948). This, it is argued, can only serve to exacerbate police-community tensions in the crowded centers of our Nation's cities.

In this context we approach the issues in this case mindful of the limitations of the judicial function in controlling the myriad daily situations in which policemen and citizens confront each other on the street. The State has characterized the issue here as "the right of a police officer . . . to make an on-the-street stop, interrogate and pat down for weapons (known in street vernacular as 'stop and frisk')." But this is only partly accurate. For the issue is not the abstract propriety of the police conduct, but the admissibility against petitioner of the evidence uncovered by the search and seizure. Ever since its inception, the rule excluding evidence seized in violation of the Fourth Amendment has been recognized as a principal mode of discouraging lawless police conduct. See Weeks v. United States, 232 U.S. 383, 391–393 (1914). Thus its major thrust is a deterrent one, see Linkletter v. Walker, 381 U.S. 618, 629–635 (1965), and experience has taught that it is the only effective deterrent to police misconduct in the criminal context, and that without it the constitutional guarantee against unreasonable searches and seizures would be a mere "form of words." Mapp v. Ohio, 367 U.S. 643, 655 (1961). The rule also serves another vital function—"the imperative of judicial integrity." Elkins v. United States, 364 U.S. 206, 222 (1960). Courts which sit under our Constitution cannot and will not be made party to lawless invasions of the constitutional rights of citizens by permitting unhindered governmental use of the fruits of such invasions. Thus in our system evidentiary rulings provide the context in which the judicial process of inclusion and exclusion approves some conduct as comporting with constitutional guarantees and disapproves other actions by state agents. A ruling admitting evidence in a criminal trial, we recognize has the necessary effect of legitimizing the conduct which produced the evidence, while an application of the exclusionary rule withholds the constitutional imprimatur.

The exclusionary rule has its limitations, however, as a tool of judicial control. It cannot properly be invoked to exclude the products of legitimate police investigative techniques on the ground that much conduct which is closely similar involves unwarranted intrusions upon constitutional protections. Moreover, in some contexts the rule is ineffective as a deterrent. Street encounters between citizens and police officers are incredibly rich in diversity. They range from wholly friendly exchanges of pleasantries or mutually useful information to hostile confrontations of armed men involving arrests, or injuries, or loss of life. Moreover, hostile confrontations are not all of a piece. Some of them begin in a friendly enough manner, only to take a different turn upon the injection of some unexpected element into the conversation. Encounters are initiated by the police for a wide variety of purposes, some of which are wholly unrelated to a desire to prosecute for crime. Doubtless some police "field interrogation" conduct violates the Fourth Amendment. But a stern refusal by this Court to condone such activity does not necessarily render it responsive to the exclusionary rule. Regardless of how effective the rule may be where obtaining convictions is an important objective of the police, it is powerless to deter invasions of constitutionally guaranteed rights where the police either have no interest in prosecuting or are willing to forgo successful prosecution in the interest of serving some other goal.

Proper adjudication of cases in which the exclusionary rule is invoked demands a constant awareness of these limitations. The wholesale harassment by certain elements of the police community, of which minority groups, particularly Negroes, frequently complain, will not be stopped by the exclusion of any evidence from any criminal trial. Yet a rigid and unthinking application of the exclusionary rule, in futile protest against practices which it can never be used effectively to control, may exact a high toll in human injury and frustration of efforts to prevent crime. No judicial opinion can comprehend the protean variety of the street encounter, and we can only judge the facts of the case before us. Nothing we say today is to be taken as indicating approval of police conduct outside the legitimate investigative sphere. Under our decision, courts still retain their traditional responsibility to guard against police conduct which is overbearing or harassing, or which trenches upon personal security without the objective evidentiary justification which the Constitution requires. When such conduct is identified, it must be condemned by the judiciary and its fruits must be excluded from evidence in criminal trials. And, of course, our approval of legitimate and restrained investigative conduct undertaken on the basis of ample factual justification should in no way discourage the employment of other remedies than the exclusionary rule to curtail abuses for which that sanction may prove inappropriate.

Having thus roughly sketched the perimeters of the constitutional debate over the limits on police investigative conduct in general and the background against which this case presents itself, we turn our attention to the quite narrow question posed by the facts before us: whether it is always unreasonable for a policeman to seize a person and subject him to a limited search for weapons unless there is probable cause for an arrest. Given the narrowness of this question, we have no occasion to canvass in detail the constitutional limitations upon the scope of a policeman's power when he confronts a citizen without probable cause to arrest him.

II

Our first task is to establish at what point in this encounter the Fourth Amendment becomes relevant. That is, we must decide whether and when Officer McFadden "seized" Terry and whether and when he conducted a "search." There is some suggestion in the use of such terms as "stop" and "frisk" that such police conduct is outside the purview of the Fourth Amendment because neither action rises to the level of a "search" or "seizure" within the meaning of the Constitution. We emphatically reject this notion. It is quite plain that the Fourth Amendment governs "seizures" of the person which do not eventuate in a trip to the station house and prosecution for crime—"arrests" in traditional terminology. It must be recognized that whenever a police officer accosts an individual and restrains his freedom to walk away, he has "seized" that person. And it is nothing less than sheer torture of the English language to suggest that a careful exploration of the outer surfaces of a person's clothing all over his or her body in an attempt to find weapons is not a "search." Moreover, it is simply fantastic to urge that such a procedure performed in public by a policeman while the citizen stands helpless, perhaps facing a wall with his hands raised, is a "petty indignity." It is a serious intrusion upon the sanctity of the person, which may inflict great indignity and arouse strong resentment, and it is not to be undertaken lightly.

The danger in the logic which proceeds upon distinctions between a "stop" and an "arrest," or "seizure" of the person, and between a "frisk" and a "search" is twofold. It seeks to isolate from constitutional scrutiny the initial stages of the contact between the policeman and the citizen. And by suggesting a rigid all-or-nothing model of justification and regulation under the Amendment, it obscures the utility of limitations upon the scope, as well as the initiation, of police action as a means of constitutional regulation. This Court has held in the past that a search which is reasonable at its inception may violate the Fourth Amendment by virtue of its intolerable intensity and scope. Kremen v. United States, 353 U.S. 346 (1957); Go-Bart Importing Co. v. United States, 282 U.S. 344, 356–358 (1931); see United States v. Di Re, 332 U.S. 581, 586–587 (1948). The scope of the search must be "strictly tied to and justified by" the circumstances which rendered its initiation permissible. Warden v. Hayden, 387 U.S. 294, 310 (1967) (MR. JUSTICE FORTAS, concurring); see, e.g., Preston v. United States, 376 U.S. 364, 367–368 (1964); Agnello v. United States, 269 U.S. 20, 30–31 (1925).

The distinctions of classical "stop-and-frisk" theory thus serve to divert attention from the central inquiry under the Fourth Amendment—the reasonableness in all the circumstances of the particular governmental invasion of a citizen's personal security. "Search" and "seizure" are not talismans. We therefore reject the notions that the Fourth Amendment does not come into play at all as a limitation upon police conduct if the officers stop short of something called a "technical arrest" or a "full-blown search."

In this case there can be no question, then, that Officer McFadden "seized" petitioner and subjected him to a "search" when he took hold of him and patted down the outer surfaces of his clothing. We must decide whether at that point it was reasonable for Officer McFadden to have interfered with petitioner's personal security as he did. And in determining whether the seizure and search were "unreasonable" our inquiry is a dual one—whether the officer's action was justified at its inception, and whether it was reasonably related in scope to the circumstances which justified the interference in the first place.

III

If this case involved police conduct subject to the Warrant Clause of the Fourth Amendment, we would have to ascertain whether "probable cause" existed to justify the search and seizure which took place. However, that is not the case. We do not retreat from our holdings that the police must, whenever practicable, obtain advance judicial approval of searches and seizures through the warrant procedure, see, e.g., Katz v. United States, 389 U.S. 347 (1967); Beck v. Ohio, 379 U.S. 89, 96 (1964); Chapman v. United States, 365 U.S. 610 (1961), or that in most instances failure to comply with the warrant requirement can only be excused by exigent circumstances, see, e.g., Warden v. Hayden, 387 U.S. 294 (1967) (hot pursuit); cf. Preston v. United States, 376 U.S. 364, 367–368 (1964). But we deal here with an entire rubric of police conduct—necessarily swift action predicated upon the on-the-spot observations of the officer on the beat—which historically has not been, and as a practical matter could not be, subjected to the warrant procedure. Instead, the conduct involved in this case must be tested by the Fourth Amendment's general proscription against unreasonable searches and seizures.

Nonetheless, the notions which underlie both the warrant procedure and the requirement of probable cause remain fully relevant in this context. In order to assess the reasonableness of Officer McFadden's conduct as a general proposition, it is necessary "first to focus upon the governmental interest which allegedly justifies official intrusion upon the constitutionally protected interests of the private citizen," for there is "no ready test for determining reasonableness other than by balancing the need to search [or seize] against the invasion which the search [or seizure] entails." Camara v. Municipal Court, 387 U.S. 523, 534–535, 536–537 (1967). And in justifying the particular intrusion the police officer must be able to point to specific and articulable facts which, taken together with rational inferences from those facts, reasonably warrant that intrusion. The scheme of the Fourth Amendment becomes meaningful only when it is assured that at some point the conduct of those charged with enforcing the laws can be subjected to the more detached, neutral scrutiny of a judge who must evaluate the reasonableness of a particular search or seizure in light of the particular circumstances. And in making that assessment it is imperative that the facts be judged against an objective standard: would the facts available to the officer at the moment of the seizure or the search "warrant a man of reasonable caution in the belief" that the action taken was appropriate? Cf. Carroll v. United States, 267 U.S. 132 (1925); Beck v. Ohio, 379 U.S. 89, 96–97 (1964). Anything less would invite intrusions upon constitutionally guaranteed rights based on nothing more substantial than inarticulate hunches, a result this Court has consistently refused to sanction. See, e.g., Beck v. Ohio, supra; Rios v. United States, 364 U.S. 253 (1960); Henry v. United States, 361 U.S. 98 (1959). And simple "'good faith on the part of the arresting officer is not enough.'... If subjective good faith alone were the test, the protections of the Fourth Amendment would evaporate, and the people would be 'secure in their persons, houses, papers, and effects,' only in the discretion of the police." Beck v. Ohio, supra, at 97.

Applying these principles to this case, we consider first the nature and extent of the governmental interests involved. One general interest is of course that of effective crime prevention and detection; it is this interest which underlies the recognition that a police officer may in appropriate circumstances and in an appropriate manner approach a person for purposes of investigating possibly criminal behavior even though there is no probable cause to make an arrest. It was this legitimate investigative function Officer McFadden was discharging when he decided to approach petitioner and his companions. He had observed Terry, Chilton, and Katz go through a series of acts, each of them perhaps innocent in itself, but which taken together warranted further investigation. There is nothing unusual in two men standing together on a street corner, perhaps waiting for someone. Nor is there anything suspicious about people in such circumstances strolling up and down the street, singly or in pairs. Store windows, moreover, are made to be looked in. But the story is quite different where, as here, two men hover about a street corner for an extended period of time, at the end of which it becomes apparent that they are not waiting for anyone or anything; where these men pace alternately along an identical route, pausing to stare in the same store window roughly 24 times; where each completion of this route is followed immediately by a conference between the two men on the corner; where they are joined in one of these conferences by a third man who leaves swiftly; and where the two men finally follow the third and rejoin him a couple of blocks away. It would have been poor police work indeed for an officer of 30 years' experience in the detection of thievery from stores in this same neighborhood to have failed to investigate this behavior further.

The crux of this case, however, is not the propriety of Officer McFadden's taking steps to investigate petitioner's suspicious behavior, but rather, whether there was justification for McFadden's invasion of Terry's personal security by searching him for weapons in the course of that investigation. We are now concerned with more than the governmental interest in investigating crime; in addition, there is the more immediate interest of the police officer in taking steps to assure himself that the person with whom he is dealing is not armed with a weapon that could unexpectedly and fatally be used against him. Certainly it would be unreasonable to require that police officers take unnecessary risks in the performance of their duties. American criminals have a long tradition of armed violence, and every year in this country many law enforcement officers are killed in the line of duty, and thousands more are wounded. Virtually all of these deaths and a substantial portion of the injuries are inflicted with guns and knives.

In view of these facts, we cannot blind ourselves to the need for law enforcement officers to protect themselves and other prospective victims of violence in situations where they may lack probable cause for an arrest. When an officer is justified in believing that the individual whose suspicious behavior he is investigating at close range is armed and presently dangerous to the officer or to others, it would appear to be clearly unreasonable to deny the officer the power to take necessary measures to determine whether the person is in fact carrying a weapon and to neutralize the threat of physical harm.

We must still consider, however, the nature and quality of the intrusion on individual rights which must be accepted if police officers are to be conceded the right to search for weapons in situations where probable cause to arrest for crime is lacking. Even a limited search of the outer clothing for weapons constitutes a severe, though brief, intrusion upon cherished personal security, and it must surely be an annoying, frightening, and perhaps humiliating experience. Petitioner contends that such an intrusion is permissible only incident to a lawful arrest, either for a crime involving the possession of weapons or for a crime the commission of which led the officer to investigate in the first place. However, this argument must be closely examined.

Petitioner does not argue that a police officer should refrain from making any investigation of suspicious circumstances until such time as he has probable cause to make an arrest; nor does he deny that police officers in properly discharging their investigative function may find themselves confronting persons who might well be armed and dangerous. Moreover, he does not say that an officer is always unjustified in searching a suspect to discover weapons. Rather, he says, it is unreasonable for the policeman to take that step until such time as the situation evolves to a point where there is probable cause to make an arrest. When that point has been reached, petitioner would concede the officer's right to conduct a search of the suspect for weapons, fruits or instrumentalities of the crime, or "mere" evidence, incident to the arrest.

There are two weaknesses in this line of reasoning, however. First, it fails to take account of traditional limitations upon the scope of searches, and thus recognizes no distinction in purpose, character, and extent between a search incident to an arrest and a limited search for weapons. The former, although justified in part by the acknowledged necessity to protect the arresting officer from assault with a concealed weapon, Preston v. United States, 376 U.S. 364, 367 (1964), is also justified on other grounds, ibid., and can therefore involve a relatively extensive exploration of the person. A search for weapons in the absence of probable cause to arrest, however, must, like any other search, be strictly circumscribed by the exigencies which justify its initiation. Warden v. Hayden, 387 U.S. 294, 310 (1967) (MR. JUSTICE FORTAS, concurring). Thus it must be limited to that which is necessary for the discovery of weapons which might be used to harm the officer or others nearby, and may realistically be characterized as something less than a "full" search, even though it remains a serious intrusion.

A second, and related, objection to petitioner's argument is that it assumes that the law of arrest has already worked out the balance between the particular interests involved here—the neutralization of danger to the policeman in the investigative circumstance and the sanctity of the individual. But this is not so. An arrest is a wholly different kind of intrusion upon individual freedom from a limited search for weapons, and the interests each is designed to serve are likewise quite different. An arrest is the initial stage of a criminal prosecution. It is intended to vindicate society's interest in having its laws obeyed, and it is inevitably accompanied by future interference with the individual's freedom of movement, whether or not trial or conviction ultimately follows. The protective search for weapons, on the other hand, constitutes a brief, though far from inconsiderable, intrusion upon the sanctity of the person. It does not follow that because an officer may lawfully arrest a person only when he is apprised of facts sufficient to warrant a belief that the person has committed or is committing a crime, the officer is equally unjustified, absent that kind of evidence, in making any intrusions short of an arrest. Moreover, a perfectly reasonable apprehension of danger may arise long before the officer is possessed of adequate information to justify taking a person into custody for the purpose of prosecuting him for a crime. Petitioner's reliance on cases which have worked out standards of reasonableness with regard to "seizures" constituting arrests and searches incident thereto is thus misplaced. It assumes that the interests sought to be vindicated and the invasions of personal security may be equated in the two cases, and thereby ignores a vital aspect of the analysis of the reasonableness of particular types of conduct under the Fourth Amendment. See Camara v. Municipal Court, supra.

Our evaluation of the proper balance that has to be struck in this type of case leads us to conclude that there must be a narrowly drawn authority to permit a reasonable search for weapons for the protection of the police officer, where he has reason to believe that he is dealing with an armed and dangerous individual, regardless of whether he has probable cause to arrest the individual for a crime. The officer need not be absolutely certain that the individual is armed; the issue is whether a reasonably prudent man in the circumstances would be warranted in the belief that his safety or that of others was in danger. Cf. Beck v. Ohio, 379 U.S. 89, 91 (1964); Brinegar v. United States, 338 U.S. 160, 174–176 (1949); Stacey v. Emery,

97 U.S. 642, 645 (1878). And in determining whether the officer acted reasonably in such circumstances, due weight must be given, not to his inchoate and unparticularized suspicion or "hunch," but to the specific reasonable inferences which he is entitled to draw from the facts in light of his experience. Cf. Brinegar v. United States, supra.

IV

We must now examine the conduct of Officer McFadden in this case to determine whether his search and seizure of petitioner were reasonable, both at their inception and as conducted. He had observed Terry, together with Chilton and another man, acting in a manner he took to be preface to a "stick-up." We think on the facts and circumstances Officer McFadden detailed before the trial judge a reasonably prudent man would have been warranted in believing petitioner was armed and thus presented a threat to the officer's safety while he was investigating his suspicious behavior. The actions of Terry and Chilton were consistent with McFadden's hypothesis that these men were contemplating a daylight robbery—which, it is reasonable to assume, would be likely to involve the use of weapons—and nothing in their conduct from the time he first noticed them until the time he confronted them and identified himself as a police officer gave him sufficient reason to negate that hypothesis. Although the trio had departed the original scene, there was nothing to indicate abandonment of an intent to commit a robbery at some point. Thus, when Officer McFadden approached the three men gathered before the display window at Zucker's store he had observed enough to make it quite reasonable to fear that they were armed; and nothing in their response to his hailing them, identifying himself as a police officer, and asking their names served to dispel that reasonable belief. We cannot say his decision at that point to seize Terry and pat his clothing for weapons was the product of a volatile or inventive imagination, or was undertaken simply as an act of harassment; the record evidences the tempered act of a policeman who in the course of an investigation had to make a quick decision as to how to protect himself and others from possible danger, and took limited steps to do so.

The manner in which the seizure and search were conducted is, of course, as vital a part of the inquiry as whether they were warranted at all. The Fourth Amendment proceeds as much by limitations upon the scope of governmental action as by imposing preconditions upon its initiation. Compare Katz v. United States, 389 U.S. 347, 354–356 (1967). The entire deterrent purpose of the rule excluding evidence seized in violation of the Fourth Amendment rests on the assumption that "limitations upon the fruit to be gathered tend to limit the quest itself." United States v. Poller, 43 F. 2d 911, 914 (C.A. 2d Cir. 1930); see, e.g., Linkletter v. Walker, 381 U.S. 618, 629–635 (1965); Mapp v. Ohio, 367 U.S. 643 (1961); Elkins v. United States, 364 U.S. 206, 216–221 (1960). Thus, evidence may not be introduced if it was discovered by means of a seizure and search which were not reasonably related in scope to the justification for their initiation. Warden v. Hayden, 387 U.S. 294, 310 (1967) (Mr. Justice Fortas, concurring).

We need not develop at length in this case, however, the limitations which the Fourth Amendment places upon a protective seizure and search for weapons. These limitations will have to be developed in the concrete factual circumstances of individual cases. See Sibron v. New York, post, p. 40 decided today. Suffice it to note that such a search, unlike a search without a warrant incident to a lawful arrest, is not justified by any need to prevent the disappearance or destruction of evidence of crime. See Preston v. United States, 376 U.S. 364, 367 (1964). The sole justification of the search in the present situation is the protection of the police officer and others nearby, and it must therefore be confined in scope to an intrusion reasonably designed to discover guns, knives, clubs, or other hidden instruments for the assault of the police officer.

The scope of the search in this case presents no serious problem in light of these standards. Officer McFadden patted down the outer clothing of petitioner and his two companions. He did not place his hands in their pockets or under the outer surface of their garments until he had felt weapons, and then he merely reached for and removed the guns. He never did invade Katz' person beyond the outer surfaces of his clothes, since he discovered nothing in his pat-down which might have been a weapon. Officer McFadden confined his search strictly to what was minimally necessary to learn whether the men were armed and to disarm them once he discovered the weapons. He did not conduct a general exploratory search for whatever evidence of criminal activity he might find.

V

We conclude that the revolver seized from Terry was properly admitted in evidence against him. At the time he seized petitioner and searched him for weapons, Officer McFadden had reasonable grounds to believe that petitioner was armed and dangerous, and it was necessary for the protection of himself and others to take swift measures to discover the true facts and neutralize the threat of harm if it materialized. The policeman carefully restricted his search to what was appropriate to the discovery of the particular items which he sought. Each case of this sort will, of course, have to be decided on its own facts. We merely hold today that where a police officer observes unusual conduct which leads him reasonably to conclude in light of his experience that criminal activity may be afoot and that the persons with whom he is dealing may be armed and presently dangerous, where in the course of investigating this behavior he identifies himself as a policeman and makes reasonable inquiries, and where nothing in the initial stages of the encounter serves to dispel his reasonable fear for his own or others' safety, he is entitled for the protection of himself and others in the area to conduct a carefully limited search of the outer clothing of such persons in an attempt to discover weapons which might be used to assault him. Such a search is a reasonable search under the Fourth Amendment, and any weapons seized may properly be introduced in evidence against the person from whom they were taken.

Affirmed.

Coolidge *v.* New Hampshire

403 U.S. 443, 91 S.Ct. 2022, 29 L.Ed. 2d. 564 (1971)

CERTIORARI TO THE SUPREME COURT OF NEW HAMPSHIRE

Argued January 12, 1971.—Decided June 21, 1971.

. . .

MR. JUSTICE STEWART delivered the opinion of the Court.

We are called upon in this case to decide issues under the Fourth and Fourteenth Amendments arising in the context of a state criminal trial for the commission of a particularly brutal murder. As in every case, our single duty is to determine the issues presented in accord with the Constitution and the law.

Pamela Mason, a 14-year-old girl, left her home in Manchester, New Hampshire, on the evening of January 13, 1964, during a heavy snowstorm, apparently in response to a man's telephone call for a babysitter. Eight days later, after a thaw, her body was found by the side of a major north-south highway several miles away. She had been murdered. The event created great alarm in the area, and the police immediately began a massive investigation.

On January 28, having learned from a neighbor that the petitioner, Edward Coolidge, had been away from home on the evening of the girl's disappearance, the police went to his house to question him. They asked him, among other things, if he owned any guns, and he produced three, two shotguns and a rifle. They also asked whether he would take a lie-detector test concerning his account of his activities on the night of the disappearance. He agreed to do so on the following Sunday, his day off. The police later described his attitude on the occasion of this visit as fully "cooperative." His wife was in the house throughout the interview.

On the following Sunday, a policeman called Coolidge early in the morning and asked him to come down to the police station for the trip to Concord, New Hampshire, where the lie-detector test was to be administered. That evening, two plainclothes policemen arrived at the Coolidge house, where Mrs. Coolidge was waiting with her mother-in-law for her husband's return. These two policemen were not the two who had visited the house earlier in the week, and they apparently did not know that Coolidge had displayed three guns for inspection during the earlier visit. The plainclothesmen told Mrs. Coolidge that her husband was in "serious trouble" and probably would not be home that night. They asked Coolidge's mother to leave, and proceeded to question Mrs. Coolidge. During the course of the interview they obtained from her four guns belonging to Coolidge, and some clothes that Mrs. Coolidge thought her husband might have been wearing on the evening of Pamela Mason's disappearance.

Coolidge was held in jail on an unrelated charge that night, but he was released the next day. During the ensuing two and a half weeks, the State accumulated a quantity of evidence to support the theory that it was he who had killed Pamela Mason. On February 19, the results of the investigation were presented at a meeting between the police officers working on the case and the State Attorney General, who had personally taken charge of all police activities relating to the murder, and was later to serve as chief prosecutor at the trial. At this meeting, it was decided that there was enough evidence to justify the arrest of Coolidge on the murder charge and a search of his house and two cars. At the conclusion of the meeting, the Manchester police chief made formal application, under oath, for the arrest and search warrants. The complaint supporting the warrant for a search of Coolidge's Pontiac automobile, the only warrant that concerns us here, stated that the affiant "has probable cause to suspect and believe, and does suspect and believe, and herewith offers satisfactory evidence, that there are certain objects and things used in the Commission of said offense, now kept, and concealed in or upon a certain vehicle, to wit: 1951 Pontiac two-door sedan . . . ." The warrants were then signed and issued by the Attorney General himself, acting as a justice of the peace. Under New Hampshire law in force at that time, all justices of the peace were authorized to issue search warrants. N.H. Rev. Stat. Ann. § 595:1 (repealed 1969).

The police arrested Coolidge in his house on the day the warrant issued. Mrs. Coolidge asked whether she might remain in the house with her small child, but was told that she must stay elsewhere, apparently in part because the police believed that she would be harassed by reporters if she were accessible to them. When she asked whether she might take her car, she was told that both cars had been "impounded," and that the police would provide transportation for her. Some time later, the police called a towing company, and about two and a half hours after Coolidge had been taken into custody the cars were towed to the police station. It appears that at the time of the arrest the cars were parked in the Coolidge driveway, and that although dark had fallen they were plainly visible both from the street and from inside the house where Coolidge was actually arrested. The 1951 Pontiac was searched and vacuumed on February 21, two days after it was seized, again a year later, in January 1965, and a third time in April 1965.

At Coolidge's subsequent jury trial on the charge of murder, vacuum sweepings, including particles of gun powder, taken from the Pontiac were introduced in evidence against him, as part of an attempt by the State to show by microscopic analysis that it was highly probable that Pamela Mason had been in Coolidge's car. Also introduced in evidence was one of the guns taken by the police on their Sunday evening visit to the Coolidge house—a .22-caliber Mossberg rifle, which the prosecution claimed was the murder weapon. Conflicting ballistics testimony was offered on the question whether the bullets found in Pamela Mason's body had been fired from this rifle. Finally, the prosecution introduced vacuum sweepings of the clothes taken from the Coolidge house that same Sunday evening, and attempted to show through microscopic analysis that there was a high probability that the clothes had been in contact with Pamela Mason's body. Pretrial motions to suppress all this evidence were referred by the trial judge to the New Hampshire Supreme Court, which ruled the evidence admissible. 106 N.H. 186, 208 A. 2d 322. The jury found Coolidge guilty and he was sentenced to life imprisonment. The New Hampshire Supreme Court affirmed the judgment of conviction, 109 N.H. 403, 206 A. 2d 547, and we granted certiorari to consider the constitutional questions raised by the admission of this evidence against Coolidge at his trial. 399 U.S. 926.

I

The petitioner's first claim is that the warrant authorizing the seizure and subsequent search of his 1951 Pontiac automobile was invalid because not issued by a "neutral and detached magistrate." Since we agree with the petitioner that the warrant was invalid for this reason, we need not consider his further argument that the allegations under oath supporting the issuance of the warrant were so conclusory as to violate relevant constitutional standards. Cf. Giordenello v. United States, 357 U.S. 480; Aguilar v. Texas, 378 U.S. 108.

The classic statement of the policy underlying the warrant requirement of the Fourth Amendment is that of MR. JUSTICE JACKSON, writing for the Court in Johnson v. United States, 333 U.S. 10, 13–14:

> "The point of the Fourth Amendment, which often is not grasped by zealous officers, is not that it denies law enforcement the support of the usual inferences which reasonable men draw from evidence. Its protection consists in requiring that those inferences be drawn by a neutral and detached magistrate instead of being judged by the officer engaged in the often competitive enterprise of ferreting out crime. Any assumption that evidence sufficient to support a magistrate's disinterested determination to issue a search warrant will justify the officers in making a search without a warrant would reduce the Amendment to a nullity and leave the people's homes secure only in the discretion of police officers.... When the right of privacy must reasonably yield to the right of search is, as a rule, to be decided by a judicial officer, not by a policeman or government enforcement agent."

Cf. United States v. Lefkowitz, 285 U.S. 452, 464; Giordenello v. United States, supra, at 486; Wong Sun v. United States, 371 U.S. 471, 481–482; Katz v. United States, 389 U.S. 347, 356–357.

In this case, the determination of probable cause was made by the chief "government enforcement agent" of the State—the Attorney General—who was actively in charge of the investigation and later was to be chief prosecutor at the trial. To be sure, the determination was formalized here by a writing bearing the title "Search Warrant," whereas in Johnson there was no piece of paper involved, but the State has not attempted to uphold the warrant on any such artificial basis. Rather, the State argues that the Attorney General, who was unquestionably authorized as a justice of the peace to issue warrants under then-existing state law, did in fact act as a "neutral and detached magistrate." Further, the State claims that *any* magistrate, confronted with the showing of probable cause made by the Manchester chief of police, would have issued the warrant in question. To the first proposition it is enough to answer that there could hardly be a more appropriate setting than this for a per se rule of disqualification rather than a case-by-case evaluation of all the circumstances. Without disrespect to the state law enforcement agent here involved, the whole point of the basic rule so well expressed by MR. JUSTICE JACKSON is that prosecutors and policemen simply cannot be asked to maintain the requisite neutrality with regard to their own investigations—the "competitive enterprise" that must rightly engage their single-minded attention. Cf. Mancusi v. DeForte, 392 U.S. 364, 371. As for the proposition that the existence of probable cause renders noncompliance with the warrant procedure an irrelevance, it is enough to cite Agnello v. United States, 269 U.S. 20, 33, decided in 1925:

> "Belief, however well founded, that an article sought is concealed in a dwelling house furnishes no justification for a search of that place without a warrant. And such searches are held unlawful notwithstanding facts unquestionably showing probable cause."

See also Jones v. United States, 357 U.S. 493, 497–498; Silverthorne Lumber Co. v. United States, 251 U.S. 385, 392. ("[T]he rights... against unlawful search and seizure are to be protected even if the same result might have been achieved in a lawful way.")

But the New Hampshire Supreme Court, in upholding the conviction, relied upon the theory that even if the warrant procedure here in issue would clearly violate the standards imposed on the Federal Government by the Fourth Amendment, it is not forbidden the States under the Fourteenth. This position was premised on a passage from the opinion of this Court in Ker v. California, 374 U.S. 23, 31:

> "Preliminary to our examination of the search and seizures involved here, it might be helpful for us to indicate what was not decided in Mapp [v. Ohio, 367 U.S. 643]. First, it must be recognized that the 'principles governing the admissibility of evidence in federal criminal trials have not been restricted... to those derived solely from the Constitution. In the exercise of its supervisory authority over the administration of criminal justice in the federal courts... this Court has... formulated rules of evidence to be applied in federal criminal prosecutions.' McNabb v. United States, 318 U.S. 332, 341... Mapp, however, established no assumption by this Court of supervisory authority over state courts... and, consequently, it implied no total obliteration of state laws relating to arrests and searches in favor of federal law. Mapp sounded no death knell for our federalism; rather, it echoed the sentiment of Elkins v. United States, supra, at 221, that 'a healthy federalism depends upon the avoidance of needless conflict between state and federal courts' by itself urging that '[f]ederal-state cooperation in the solution of crime under constitutional standards will be promoted, if only by recognition of their now mutual obligation to respect *the same fundamental criteria* in their approaches.' 367 U.S., at 658." (Emphasis in Ker.)

It is urged that the New Hampshire statutes which at the time of the searches here involved permitted a law enforcement officer himself to issue a warrant was one of those "workable rules governing arrests, searches and seizures to meet 'the practical demands of effective criminal investigation and law enforcement' in the States," id., at 34, authorized by Ker.

That such a procedure was indeed workable from the point of view of the police is evident from testimony at the trial in this case:

"*The Court:* You mean that another police officer issues these [search warrants]?
"*The Witness:* Yes. Captain Couture and Captain Shea and Captain Loveren are J.P.'s.

"*The Court:* Well, let me ask you, Chief, your answer is to the effect that you never go out of the department for the Justice of the Peace?

"*The Witness:* It hasn't been our—policy to go out of the department.

"*Question:* Right. Your policy and experience, is to have a fellow police officer take the warrant in the capacity of Justice of the Peace?

"*Answer:* That has been our practice."

But it is too plain for extensive discussion that this now abandoned New Hampshire method of issuing "search warrants" violated a fundamental premise of both the Fourth and Fourteenth Amendments—a premise fully developed and articulated long before this Court's decisions in Ker v. California, supra, and Mapp v. Ohio, 367 U.S. 643. As Mr. Justice Frankfurter put it in Wolf v. Colorado, 338 U.S. 25, 27–28:

> "The security of one's privacy against arbitrary intrusion by the police—which is at the core of the Fourth Amendment—is basic to a free society. It is therefore implicit in 'the concept of ordered liberty' and as such enforceable against the States through the Due Process Clause. The knock at the door, whether by day or by night, as a prelude to a search, without authority of law but solely on the authority of the police, did not need the commentary of recent history to be condemned...."

We find no escape from the conclusion that the seizure and search of the Pontiac automobile cannot constitutionally rest upon the warrant issued by the state official who was the chief investigator and prosecutor in this case. Since he was not the neutral and detached magistrate required by the Constitution, the search stands on no firmer ground than if there had been no warrant at all. If the seizure and search are to be justified, they must, therefore, be justified on some other theory.

II

The State proposes three distinct theories to bring the facts of this case within one or another of the exceptions to the warrant requirement. In considering them, we must not lose sight of the Fourth Amendment's fundamental guarantee. Mr. Justice Bradley's admonition in his opinion for the Court almost a century ago in Boyd v. United States, 116 U.S. 616, 635, is worth repeating here:

> "It may be that it is the obnoxious thing in its mildest and least repulsive form; but illegitimate and unconstitutional practices get their first footing in that way, namely, by silent approaches and slight deviations from legal modes of procedure. This can only be obviated by adhering to the rule that constitutional provisions for the security of person and property should be liberally construed. A close and literal construction deprives them of half their efficacy, and leads to gradual depreciation of the right, as if it consisted more in sound than in substance. It is the duty of courts to be watchful for the constitutional rights of the citizen, and against any stealthy encroachments thereon."

Thus the most basic constitutional rule in this area is that "searches conducted outside the judicial process, without prior approval by judge or magistrate, are per se unreasonable under the Fourth Amendment—subject only to a few specifically established and well-delineated exceptions." The exceptions are "jealously and carefully drawn," and there must be "a showing by those who seek exemption . . . that the exigencies of the situation made that course imperative." "[T]he burden is on those seeking the exemption to show the need for it." In times of unrest, whether caused by crime or racial conflict or fear of internal subversion, this basic law and the values that it represents may appear unrealistic or "extravagant" to some. But the values were those of the authors of our fundamental constitutional concepts. In times not altogether unlike our own they won—by legal and constitutional means in England, and by revolution on this continent—a right of personal security against arbitrary intrusions by official power. If times have changed, reducing everyman's scope to do as he pleases in an urban and industrial world, the changes have made the values served by the Fourth Amendment more, not less, important.

A

The State's first theory is that the seizure on February 19 and subsequent search of Coolidge's Pontiac were "incident" to a valid arrest. We assume that the arrest of Coolidge inside his house was valid, so that the first condition of a warrantless "search incident" is met. Whiteley v. Warden, 401 U.S. 560, 567 n. 11. And since the events in issue took place in 1964, we assess the State's argument in terms of the law as it existed before Chimel v. California, 395 U.S. 752, which substantially restricted the "search incident" exception to the warrant requirement, but did so only prospectively. Williams v. United States, 401 U.S. 646. But even under pre-Chimel law, the State's position is untenable.

The leading case in the area before Chimel was United States v. Rabinowitz, 339 U.S. 56, which was taken to stand "for the proposition, inter alia, that a warrantless search 'incident to a lawful arrest' may generally extend to the area that is considered to be in the 'possession' or under the 'control' of the person arrested." Chimel, supra, at 760. In this case, Coolidge was arrested inside his house; his car was outside in the driveway. The car was not touched until Coolidge had been removed from the scene. It was then seized and taken to the station, but it was not actually searched until two days later.

First, it is doubtful whether the police could have carried out a contemporaneous search of the car under Rabinowitz standards. For this Court has repeatedly held that, even under Rabinowitz, "[a] search may be incident to an arrest '"only if it is substantially contemporaneous with the arrest and is confined to the *immediate* vicinity of the arrest. . . ."'" Vale v. Louisiana, 399 U.S. 30, 33, quoting from Shipley v. California, 395 U.S. 818, 819, quoting from Stoner v. California, 376 U.S. 483, 486. (Emphasis in Shipley.) Cf. Agnello v. United States, 269 U.S., at 30–31; James v. Louisiana, 382 U.S. 36. These cases make it clear beyond any question that a lawful pre-Chimel arrest of a suspect outside his house could never by itself justify a warrantless search inside the house. There is nothing in search-incident doctrine (as opposed to the special rules for automobiles and evidence in "plain view," to be considered below) that suggests a different result where the arrest is made inside the house and the search outside and at some distance away.

Even assuming, *arguendo,* that the police might have searched the Pontiac in the driveway when they arrested Coolidge in the house, Preston v. United States, 376 U.S. 364, makes plain that they could not legally seize the car, remove it, and search it at their leisure without a warrant. In circumstances virtually identical to those here, MR. JUSTICE BLACK's opinion for a unanimous Court held that "[o]nce an accused is under arrest and in custody, then a search [of his car] made at another place, without a warrant, is simply not incident to the arrest." Id., at 367. Dyke v. Taylor Implement Mfg. Co., 391 U.S. 216. Cf. Chambers v. Maroney, 399 U.S. 42, 47. Search-incident doctrine, in short, has no applicability to this case.

B

The second theory put forward by the State to justify a warrantless seizure and search of the Pontiac car is that under Carroll v. United States, 267 U.S. 132, the police may make a warrantless search of an automobile whenever they have probable cause to do so, and, under our decision last Term in Chambers v. Maroney, 399 U.S. 42, whenever the police may make a legal contemporaneous search under Carroll, they may also seize the car, take it to the police station, and search it there. But even granting that the police had probable cause to search the car, the application of the Carroll case to these facts would extend it far beyond its original rationale.

Carroll did indeed hold that "contraband goods concealed and illegally transported in an automobile or other vehicle may be searched for without a warrant," provided that "the seizing officer shall have reasonable or probable cause for believing that the automobile which he stops and seizes has contraband liquor therein which is being illegally transported." Such searches had been explicitly authorized by Congress, and, as we have pointed out elsewhere, in the conditions of the time "[a]n automobile . . . was an almost indispensable instrumentality in large-scale violation of the National Prohibition Act, and the car itself therefore was treated somewhat as an offender and became contraband." In two later cases, each involving an occupied automobile stopped on the open highway and searched for contraband liquor, the Court followed and reaffirmed Carroll. And last Term in Chambers, supra, we did so again.

The underlying rationale of Carroll and of all the cases that have followed it is that there is

> "a necessary difference between a search of a store, dwelling house or other structure in respect of which a proper official warrant readily may be obtained, and a search of a ship, motor boat, wagon or automobile, for contraband goods, where *it is not practicable to secure a warrant* because the vehicle can be quickly moved out of the locality or jurisdiction in which the warrant must be sought." 267 U.S., at 153. (Emphasis supplied.)

As we said in Chambers, supra, at 51, "exigent circumstances" justify the warrantless search of "an automobile *stopped on the highway,*" where there is probable cause, because the car is "movable, the occupants are alerted, and the car's contents may never be found again if a warrant must be obtained." "[T]he opportunity to search is fleeting...." (Emphasis supplied.)

In this case, the police had known for some time of the probable role of the Pontiac car in the crime. Coolidge was aware that he was a suspect in the Mason murder, but he had been extremely cooperative throughout the investigation, and there was no indication that he meant to flee. He had already had ample opportunity to destroy any evidence he thought incriminating. There is no suggestion that, on the night in question, the car was being used for any illegal purpose, and it was regularly parked in the driveway of his house. The opportunity for search was thus hardly "fleeting." The objects that the police are assumed to have had probable cause to search for in the car were neither stolen nor contraband nor dangerous.

When the police arrived at the Coolidge house to arrest him, two officers were sent to guard the back door while the main party approached from the front. Coolidge was arrested inside the house, without resistance of any kind on his part, after he had voluntarily admitted the officers at both front and back doors. There was no way in which he could conceivably have gained access to the automobile after the police arrived on his property. When Coolidge had been taken away, the police informed Mrs. Coolidge, the only other adult occupant of the house, that she and her baby had to spend the night elsewhere and that she could not use either of the Coolidge cars. Two police officers then drove her in a police car to the house of a relative in another town, and they stayed with her there until around midnight, long after the police had had the Pontiac towed to the station house. The Coolidge premises were guarded throughout the night by two policemen.

The word "automobile" is not a talisman in whose presence the Fourth Amendment fades away and disappears. And surely there is nothing in this case to invoke the meaning and purpose of the rule of Carroll v. United States—no alerted criminal bent on flight, no fleeting opportunity on an open highway after a hazardous chase, no contraband or stolen goods or weapons, no confederates waiting to move the evidence, not even the inconvenience of a special police detail to guard the immobilized automobile. In short, by no possible stretch of the legal imagination can this be made into a case where "it is not practicable to secure a warrant," Carroll, supra, at 153, and the "automobile exception," despite its label, is simply irrelevant.

Since Carroll would not have justified a warrantless search of the Pontiac at the time Coolidge was arrested, the later search at the station house was plainly illegal, at least so far as the automobile exception is concerned. Chambers, supra, is of no help to the State, since that case held only that, where the police may stop and search an automobile under Carroll, they may also seize it and search it later at the police station. Rather, this case is controlled by Dyke v. Taylor Implement Mfg. Co., supra. There the police lacked probable cause to seize or search the defendant's automobile at the time of his arrest, and this was enough by itself to condemn the subsequent search at the station house. Here there was probable cause, but no exigent circumstances justified the police in proceeding without a warrant. As in Dyke, the later search at the station house was therefore illegal.

C

The State's third theory in support of the warrantless seizure and search of the Pontiac car is that the car itself was an "instrumentality of the crime," and as such might be seized by the police on Coolidge's property because it was in plain view. Supposing the seizure to be thus lawful, the case of Cooper v. California, 386 U.S. 58, is said to support a subsequent warrantless search at the station house, with or without probable cause. Of course, the distinction between an "instrumentality of crime" and "mere evidence" was done away with by Warden v. Hayden, 387 U.S. 294, and we may assume that the police had probable cause to seize the automobile. But, for the reasons that follow, we hold that the "plain view" exception to the warrant requirement is inapplicable to this case. Since the seizure was therefore illegal, it is unnecessary to consider the applicability of Cooper, supra, to the subsequent search.

It is well established that under certain circumstances the police may seize evidence in plain view without a warrant. But it is important to keep in mind that, in the vast majority of cases, *any* evidence seized by the police will be in plain view, at least at the moment of seizure. The problem with the "plain view" doctrine has been to identify the circumstances in which plain view has legal significance rather than being simply the normal concomitant of any search, legal or illegal.

An example of the applicability of the "plain view" doctrine is the situation in which the police have a warrant to search a given area for specified objects, and in the course of the search come across some other article of incriminating character. Cf. Go-Bart Importing Co. v. United States, 282 U.S. 344, 358; United States v. Lefkowitz, 285 U.S. 452, 465; Steele v. United States, 267 U.S. 498; Stanley v. Georgia, 394 U.S. 557, 571 (STEWART, J., concurring in result). Where the initial intrusion that brings the police within plain view of such an article is supported, not by a warrant, but by one of the recognized exceptions to the warrant requirement, the seizure is also legitimate. Thus the police may inadvertently come across evidence while in "hot pursuit" of a fleeing suspect; Warden v. Hayden, supra; cf. Hester v. United States, 265 U.S. 57. And an object that comes into view during a search incident to arrest that is appropriately limited in scope under existing law may be seized without a warrant. Chimel v. California, 395 U.S., at 762–763. Finally, the "plain view" doctrine has been applied where a police officer is not searching for evidence against the accused, but nonetheless inadvertently comes across an incriminating object. Harris v. United States, 390 U.S. 234; Frazier v. Cupp, 394 U.S. 731; Ker v. California, 374 U.S., at 43. Cf. Lewis v. United States, 385 U.S. 206.

What the "plain view" cases have in common is that the police officer in each of them had a prior justification for an intrusion in the course of which he came inadvertently across a piece of evidence incriminating the accused. The doctrine serves to supplement the prior justification—whether it be a warrant for another object, hot pursuit, search incident to lawful arrest, or some other legitimate reason for being present unconnected with a search directed against the accused—and permits the warrantless seizure. Of course, the extension of the original justification is legitimate only where it is immediately apparent to the police that they have evidence before them; the "plain view" doctrine may not be used to extend a general exploratory search from one object to another until something incriminating at last emerges. Cf. Stanley v. Georgia, supra, at 571–572 (STEWART, J., concurring in result).

The rationale for the "plain view" exception is evident if we keep in mind the two distinct constitutional protections served by the warrant requirement. First, the magistrate's scrutiny is intended to eliminate altogether searches not based on probable cause. The premise here is that *any* intrusion in the way of search or seizure is an evil, so that no intrusion at all is justified without a careful prior determination of necessity. See, e.g., McDonald v. United States, 335 U.S. 451; Warden v. Hayden, 387 U.S. 294; Katz v. United States, 389 U.S. 347; Chimel v. California, 395 U.S., at 761–762. The second, distinct objective is that those searches deemed necessary should be as limited as possible. Here, the specific evil is the "general warrant" abhorred by the colonists, and the problem is not that of intrusion per se, but of a general, exploratory rummaging in a person's belongings. See, e.g., Boyd v. United States, 116 U.S., at 624-630; Marron v. United States, 275 U.S. 192, 195–196; Stanford v. Texas, 379 U.S. 476. The warrant accomplishes this second objective by requiring a "particular description" of the things to be seized.

The "plain view" doctrine is not in conflict with the first objective because plain view does not occur until a search is in progress. In each case, this initial intrusion is justified by a warrant or by an exception such as "hot pursuit" or search incident to a lawful arrest, or by an extraneous valid reason for the officer's presence. And, given the initial intrusion, the seizure of an object in plain view is consistent with the second objective, since it does not convert the search into a general or exploratory one. As against the minor peril to Fourth Amendment protections, there is a major gain in effective law enforcement. Where, once an otherwise lawful search is in progress, the police inadvertently come upon a piece of evidence, it would often be a needless inconvenience, and sometimes dangerous—to the evidence or to the police themselves—to require them to ignore it until they have obtained a warrant particularly describing it.

The limits on the doctrine are implicit in the statement of its rationale. The first of these is that plain view *alone* is never enough to justify the warrantless seizure of evidence. This is simply a corollary of the familiar principle discussed above, that no amount of probable cause can justify a warrantless search or seizure absent "exigent circumstances." Incontrovertible testimony of the senses that an incriminating object is on premises belonging to a criminal suspect may establish the fullest possible measure of probable cause. But even where the object is contraband, this Court has repeatedly stated and enforced the basic rule that the police may not enter and make a warrantless seizure. Taylor v. United States, 286 U.S. 1; Johnson v. United States, 333 U.S. 10; McDonald v. United States, 335 U.S. 451; Jones v. United States, 357 U.S. 493, 497–498; Chapman v. United States, 365 U.S. 610; Trupiano v. United States, 334 U.S. 699.

The second limitation is that the discovery of evidence in plain view must be inadvertent. The rationale of the exception to the warrant requirement, as just stated, is that a plain-view seizure will not turn an initially valid (and therefore limited) search into a "general" one, while the inconvenience of procuring a warrant to cover an inadvertent discovery is great. But where the discovery is anticipated, where the police know in advance the location of the evidence and intend to seize it, the situation is altogether different. The requirement of a warrant to seize imposes no inconvenience whatever, or at least none which is constitutionally cognizable in a legal system that regards warrantless searches as "per se unreasonable" in the absence of "exigent circumstances."

If the initial intrusion is bottomed upon a warrant that fails to mention a particular object, though the police know its location and intend to seize it, then there is a violation of the express constitutional requirement of "Warrants . . . particularly describing . . . [the] things to be seized." The initial intrusion may, of course, be legitimated not by a warrant but by one of the exceptions to the warrant requirement, such as hot pursuit or search incident to lawful arrest. But to extend the scope of such an intrusion to the seizure of objects—not contraband nor stolen nor dangerous in themselves—which the police know in advance they will find in plain view and intend to seize, would fly in the face of the basic rule that no amount of probable cause can justify a warrantless seizure.

In the light of what has been said, it is apparent that the "plain view" exception cannot justify the police seizure of the Pontiac car in this case. The police had ample opportunity to obtain a valid warrant; they knew the automobile's exact description and location well in advance; they intended to seize it when they came upon Coolidge's property. And this is not a case involving contraband or stolen goods or objects dangerous in themselves.

The seizure was therefore unconstitutional, and so was the subsequent search at the station house. Since evidence obtained in the course of the search was admitted at Coolidge's trial, the judgment must be reversed and the case remanded to the New Hampshire Supreme Court. Mapp v. Ohio, 367 U.S. 643.

. . .

Both sides to the controversy appear to recognize a distinction between searches and seizures that take place on a man's property—his home or office—and those carried out elsewhere. It is accepted, at least as a matter of principle, that a search or seizure carried out on a suspect's premises without a warrant is per se unreasonable, unless the police can show that it falls within one of a carefully defined set of exceptions based on the presence of "exigent circumstances." As to other kinds of intrusions, however, there has been disagreement about the basic rules to be applied, as our cases concerning automobile searches, electronic surveillance, street searches, and administrative searches make clear.

With respect to searches and seizures carried out on a suspect's premises, the conflict has been over the question of what qualifies as an "exigent circumstance." It might appear that the difficult inquiry would be when it is that the police can enter upon a person's property to seize his "person . . . papers, and effects," without prior judicial approval. The question of the scope of search and seizure once the police are on the premises would appear to be subsidiary to the basic issue of when intrusion is permissible. But the law has not developed in this fashion.

The most common situation in which Fourth Amendment issues have arisen has been that in which the police enter the suspect's premises, arrest him, and then carry out a warrantless search and seizure of evidence. Where there is a warrant for the suspect's arrest, the evidence seized may later be challenged either on the ground that the warrant was improperly issued because there was not probable cause, or on the ground that the police search and seizure went beyond that which they could carry out as an incident to the execution of the arrest warrant. Where the police act without an arrest warrant, the suspect may argue that an arrest warrant was necessary, that there was no probable cause to arrest, or that even if the arrest was valid, the search and seizure went beyond permissible limits. Perhaps because each of these lines of attack offers a plethora of litigable issues, the more fundamental question of when the police may arrest a man in his house without a warrant has been little considered in the federal courts. This Court has chosen on a number of occasions to assume the validity of an arrest and decide the case before it on the issue of the scope of permissible warrantless search. E.g., Chimel v. California, supra. The more common inquiry has therefore been: "Assuming a valid police entry for purposes of arrest, what searches and seizures may the police carry out without prior authorization by a magistrate?"

Two very broad, and sharply contrasting answers to this question have been assayed by this Court in the past. The answer of Trupiano v. United States, supra, was that *no* searches and seizures could be legitimated by the mere fact of valid entry for purposes of arrest, so long as there was no showing of special difficulties in obtaining a warrant for search and seizure. The contrasting answer in Harris v. United States, 331 U.S. 145, and United States v. Rabinowitz, supra, was that a valid entry for purposes of arrest served to legitimate warrantless searches and seizures throughout the premises where the arrest occurred, however spacious those premises might be.

The approach taken in Harris and Rabinowitz was open to the criticism that it made it so easy for the police to arrange to search a man's premises without a warrant that the Constitution's protection of a man's "effects" became a dead letter. The approach taken in Trupiano, on the other hand, was open to the criticism that it was absurd to permit the police to make an entry in the dead of night for purposes of seizing the "person" by main force, and then refuse them permission to seize objects lying around in plain sight. It is arguable that if the very substantial intrusion implied in the entry and arrest are "reasonable" in Fourth Amendment terms, then the less intrusive search incident to arrest must also be reasonable.

This argument against the Trupiano approach is of little force so long as it is assumed that the police must, in the absence of one of a number of defined exceptions based on "exigent circumstances," obtain an arrest warrant before entering a man's house to seize his person. If the Fourth Amendment requires a warrant to enter and seize the person, then it makes sense as well to require a warrant to seize other items that may be on the premises. The situation is different, however, if the police are under no circumstances required to obtain an arrest warrant before entering to arrest a person they have probable cause to believe has committed a felony. If no warrant is ever required to legitimate the extremely serious intrusion of a midnight entry to seize the person, then it can be argued plausibly that a warrant should never be required to legitimate a very sweeping search incident to such an entry and arrest. If the arrest without a warrant is per se reasonable under the Fourth Amendment, then it is difficult to perceive why a search incident in the style of Harris and Rabinowitz is not per se reasonable as well.

It is clear, then, that the notion that the warrantless entry of a man's house in order to arrest him on probable cause is per se legitimate is in fundamental conflict with the basic principle of Fourth Amendment law that searches and seizures inside a man's house without warrant are per se unreasonable in the absence of some one of a number of well defined "exigent circumstances." This conflict came to the fore in Chimel v. California, supra. The Court there applied the basic rule that the "search incident to arrest" is an exception to the warrant requirement and that its scope must therefore be strictly defined in terms of the justifying "exigent circumstances." The exigency in question arises from the dangers of harm to the arresting officer and of destruction of evidence within the reach of the arrestee. Neither exigency can conceivably justify the far-ranging searches authorized under Harris and Rabinowitz. The answer of the dissenting opinion of MR. JUSTICE WHITE in Chimel supported by no decision of this Court, was that a warrantless entry for the purpose of arrest on probable cause is legitimate and reasonable no matter what the circumstances. 395 U.S., at 776–780. From this it was said to follow that the full-scale search incident to arrest was also reasonable since it was a lesser intrusion. 395 U.S., at 772–775.

The same conflict arises in this case. Since the police knew of the presence of the automobile and planned all along to seize it, there was no "exigent circumstance" to justify their failure to obtain a warrant. The application of the basic rule of Fourth Amendment law therefore requires that the fruits of the warrantless seizure be suppressed. MR. JUSTICE WHITE's dissenting opinion, however, argues once again that so long as the police could reasonably make a warrantless nighttime entry onto Coolidge's property in order to arrest him, with no showing at all of an emergency, then it is absurd to prevent them from seizing his automobile as evidence of the crime.

MR. JUSTICE WHITE takes a basically similar approach to the question whether the search of the automobile in this case can be justified under Carroll v. United States, supra, and Chambers v. Maroney, supra. Carroll, on its face, appears to be a classic example of the doctrine that warrantless searches are per se unreasonable in the absence of exigent circumstances. Every word in the opinion indicates the Court's adherence to the underlying rule and its care in delineating a limited exception. Read thus, the case quite evidently does not extend to the situation at bar. Yet if we take the viewpoint of a judge called on only to decide in the abstract, after the fact, whether the police have behaved "reasonably" under all the circumstances—in short if we simply ignore the warrant requirement—Carroll comes to stand for something more. The stopping of a vehicle on the open highway and a subsequent search amount to a major interference in the lives of the occupants. Carroll held such an interference to be reasonable without a warrant, given probable cause. It may be thought to follow a fortiori that the seizure and search here—where there was no stopping and the vehicle was unoccupied—were also reasonable, since the intrusion was less substantial, although there were no exigent circumstances whatever. Using reasoning of this sort, it is but a short step to the position that it is *never* necessary for the police to obtain a warrant before searching and seizing an automobile, provided that they have probable cause.... The warrant requirement has been a valued part of our constitutional law for decades, and it has determined the result in scores and scores of cases in courts all over this country. It is not an inconvenience to be somehow "weighed" against the claims of police efficiency. It is, or should be, an important working part of our machinery of government, operating as a matter of course to check the "well-intentioned but mistakenly over-zealous executive officers" who are a part of any system of law enforcement. If it is to be a true guide to constitutional police action, rather than just a pious phrase, then "[t]he exceptions cannot be enthroned into the rule." United States v. Rabinowitz, supra, at 80 (FRANKFURTER, J., dissenting). The confinement of the exceptions to their appropriate scope was the function of Chimel v. California, supra, where we dealt with the assumption that a search "incident" to a lawful arrest may encompass all of the premises where the arrest occurs, however spacious. The "plain view" exception is intimately linked with the search-incident exception, as the cases discussed in Part C above have repeatedly shown. To permit warrantless plain-view seizures without limit would be to undo much of what was decided in Chimel, as the similar arguments put forward in dissent in the two cases indicate clearly enough.

Finally, a word about Trupiano v. United States, supra. Our discussion of "plain view" in Part C above corresponds with that given in Trupiano. Here, as in Trupiano, the determining factors are advance police knowledge of the existence and location of the evidence, police intention to seize it, and the ample opportunity for obtaining a warrant. See 334 U.S., at 707–708 and n. 27, supra. However, we do not "reinstate" Trupiano, since we cannot adopt all its implications. To begin with, in Chimel v. California, supra, we held that a search of the person of an arrestee and of the area under his immediate control could be carried out without a warrant. We did not indicate there, and do not suggest here, that the police must obtain a warrant if they anticipate that they will find specific evidence during the course of such a search. See n. 24, supra. And as to the automobile exception, we do not question the decisions of the Court in Cooper v. California, 386 U.S. 58, and Chambers v. Maroney, supra, although both are arguably inconsistent with Trupiano.

. . .

Of course, it would be nonsense to pretend that our decision today reduces Fourth Amendment law to complete order and harmony. The decisions of the Court over the years point in differing directions and differ in emphasis. No trick of logic will make them all perfectly consistent. But it is no less nonsense to suggest, as does MR. JUSTICE WHITE, post, at 521, 520, that we cease today "to strive for clarity and consistency of analysis," or that we have "abandoned any attempt" to find reasoned distinctions in this area. The time is long past when men believed that development of the law must always proceed by the smooth incorporation of new situations into a single coherent analytical framework. We need accept neither the "clarity and certainty" of a Fourth Amendment without a warrant requirement nor the facile consistency obtained by wholesale overruling of recently decided cases.... We are convinced that the result reached in this case is correct, and that the principle it reflects—that the police must obtain a warrant when they intend to seize an object outside the scope of a valid search incident to arrest—can be easily understood and applied by courts and law enforcement officers alike. It is a principle that should work to protect the citizen without overburdening the police, and a principle that preserves and protects the guarantees of the Fourth Amendment.

III

Because of the prospect of a new trial, the efficient administration of justice counsels consideration of the second substantial question under the Fourth and Fourteenth Amendments presented by this case. The petitioner contends that when the police obtained a rifle and articles of his clothing from his home on the night of Sunday, February 2, 1964, while he was being interrogated at the police station, they engaged in a search and seizure violative of the Constitution. In order to understand this contention, it is necessary to review in some detail the circumstances of the February 2 episode.

A

The lie-detector test administered to Coolidge in Concord on the afternoon of the 2d was inconclusive as to his activities on the night of Pamela Mason's disappearance, but during the course of the test Coolidge confessed to stealing $375 from his employer. After the group returned from Concord to Manchester, the interrogation about Coolidge's movements on the night of the disappearance continued, and Coolidge apparently made a number of statements which the police immediately checked out as best they could. The decision to send two officers to the Coolidge house to speak with Mrs. Coolidge was apparently motivated in part by a desire to check his story against whatever she might say, and in part by the need for some corroboration of his admission to the theft from his employer. The trial judge found as a fact, and the record supports him, that at the time of the visit the police knew very little about the weapon that had killed Pamela Mason. The bullet that had been retrieved was of small caliber, but the police were unsure whether the weapon was a rifle or a pistol. During the extensive investigation following the discovery of the body, the police had made it a practice to ask all those questioned whether they owned any guns, and to ask the owners for permission to run tests on those that met the very general description of the murder weapon. The trial judge found as a fact that when the police visited Mrs. Coolidge on the night of the 2d, they were unaware of the previous visit during which Coolidge had shown other officers three guns, and that they were not motivated by a desire to find the murder weapon.

The two plainclothesmen asked Mrs. Coolidge whether her husband had been at home on the night of the murder victim's disappearance, and she replied that he had not. They then asked her if her husband owned any guns. According to her testimony at the pretrial suppression hearing, she replied, "Yes, I will get them in the bedroom." One of the officers replied, "We will come with you." The three went into the bedroom where Mrs. Coolidge took all four guns out of the closet. Her account continued:

"*Answer:* I believe I asked if they wanted the guns. One gentleman said, 'No'; then the other gentleman turned around and said, 'We might as well take them.' I said, 'If you would like them, you may take them.'
"*Question:* Did you go further and say, 'We have nothing to hide.'?
"*Answer:* I can't recall if I said that then or before. I don't recall.
"*Question:* But at some time you indicated to them that as far as you were concerned you had nothing to hide, and they might take what they wanted?
"*Answer:* That was it.

. . .

"*Question:* Did you feel at that time that you had something to hide?
"*Answer:* No."

The two policemen also asked Mrs. Coolidge what her husband had been wearing on the night of the disappearance. She then produced four pairs of trousers and indicated that her husband had probably worn either of two of them on that evening. She also brought out a hunting jacket. The police gave her a receipt for the guns and the clothing, and, after a search of the Coolidge cars not here in issue, took the various articles to the police station.

B

The first branch of the petitioner's argument is that when Mrs. Coolidge brought out the guns and clothing, and then handed them over to the police, she was acting as an "instrument" of the officials, complying with a "demand" made by them. Consequently, it is argued, Coolidge was the victim of a search and seizure within the constitutional meaning of those terms. Since we cannot accept this interpretation of the facts, we need not consider the petitioner's further argument that Mrs. Coolidge could not or did not "waive" her husband's constitutional protection against unreasonable searches and seizures.

Had Mrs. Coolidge, wholly on her own initiative, sought out her husband's guns and clothing and then taken them to the police station to be used as evidence against him, there can be no doubt under existing law that the articles would later have been admissible in evidence. Cf. Burdeau v. McDowell, 256 U.S. 465. The question presented here is whether the conduct of the police officers at the Coolidge house was such as to make her actions their actions for purposes of the Fourth and Fourteenth Amendments and their attendant exclusionary rules. The test, as the petitioner's argument suggests, is whether Mrs. Coolidge, in light of all the circumstances of the case, must be regarded as having acted as an "instrument" or agent of the state when she produced her husband's belongings. Cf. United States v. Goldberg, 330 F. 2d 30 (CA3), cert. denied, 377 U.S. 953 (1964); People v. Tarantino, 45 Cal. 2d 590, 290 P. 2d 505 (1955); see Byars v. United States, 273 U.S. 28; Gambino v. United States, 275 U.S. 310.

In a situation like the one before us there no doubt always exist forces pushing the spouse to cooperate with the police. Among these are the simple but often powerful convention of openness and honesty, the fear that secretive behavior will intensify suspicion, and uncertainty as to what course is most likely to be helpful to the absent spouse. But there is nothing constitutionally suspect in the existence, without more, of these incentives to full disclosure or active cooperation with the police. The exclusionary rules were fashioned "to prevent, not to repair," and their target is official misconduct. They are "to compel respect for the constitutional guaranty in the only effectively available way—by removing the incentive to disregard it." Elkins v. United States, 364 U.S. 206, 217. But it is no part of the policy underlying the Fourth and Fourteenth Amendments to discourage citizens from aiding to the utmost of their ability in the apprehension of criminals. If, then, the exclusionary rule is properly applicable to the evidence taken from the Coolidge house on the night of February 2, it must be upon the basis that some type of unconstitutional police conduct occurred.

Yet it cannot be said that the police should have obtained a warrant for the guns and clothing before they set out to visit Mrs. Coolidge, since they had no intention of rummaging around among Coolidge's effects or of dispossessing him of any of his property. Nor can it be said that they should have obtained Coolidge's permission for a seizure they did not intend to make. There was nothing to compel them to announce to the suspect that they intended to question his wife about his movements on the night of the disappearance or about the theft from his employer. Once Mrs. Coolidge had admitted them, the policemen were surely acting normally and properly when they asked her, as they had asked those questioned earlier in the investigation, including Coolidge himself, about any guns there might be in the house. The question concerning the clothes Coolidge had been wearing on the night of the disappearance was logical and in no way coercive. Indeed, one might doubt the competence of the officers involved had they not asked exactly the questions they did ask. And surely when Mrs. Coolidge of her own accord produced the guns and clothes for inspection, rather than simply describing them, it was not incumbent on the police to stop her or avert their eyes.

The crux of the petitioner's argument must be that when Mrs. Coolidge asked the policemen whether they wanted the guns, they should have replied that they could not take them, or have first telephoned Coolidge at the police station and asked his permission to take them, or have asked her whether she had been authorized by her husband to release them. Instead, after one policeman had declined the offer, the other turned and said, "We might as well take them," to which Mrs. Coolidge replied, "If you would like them, you may take them."

In assessing the claim that this course of conduct amounted to a search and seizure, it is well to keep in mind that Mrs. Coolidge described her own motive as that of clearing her husband, and that she believed that she had nothing to hide. She had seen her husband himself produce his guns for two other policemen earlier in the week, and there is nothing to indicate that she realized that he had offered only three of them for inspection on that occasion. The two officers who questioned her behaved, as her own testimony shows, with perfect courtesy. There is not the slightest implication of an attempt on their part to coerce or dominate her, or, for that matter, to direct her actions by the more subtle techniques of suggestion that are available to officials in circumstances like these. To hold that the conduct of the police here was a search and seizure would be to hold, in effect, that a criminal suspect has constitutional protection against the adverse consequences of a spontaneous, good-faith effort by his wife to clear him of suspicion.

The judgment is reversed and the case is remanded to the Supreme Court of New Hampshire for further proceedings not inconsistent with this opinion.

It is so ordered.

CHAPTER 4

Contents

Absorption of Bill of Rights

§ 4.1 Absorption Defined

*Absorption is a term that has been commonly applied to a rule of constitutional law that when the United States Supreme Court declares that a right given to United States citizens as provided for in the Bill of Rights of the Constitution is applicable to the action of state and local government, the right is thus absorbed and the inhabitant may not be lawfully denied that right by the actions of any governmental authority within the jurisdiction of the federal or state governments.

§ 4.2 Fourteenth Amendment

The Fourteenth Amendment to the United States Constitution came about as a response to the turmoil following the War between the States. The black people of the southern states were, to a large extent, homeless and unemployed. Many of the communities in which they and their white masters had lived were devastated. Southern legislatures enacted laws compelling the former slaves to return to the service of their former masters as employees. They were not permitted to own or rent their own land nor to engage in their own business. Vigilante groups of white people terrorized the blacks.

Congress, meeting at the close of the Civil War, set up military governments in the former Confederate States and three new constitutional amendments were added, as well as many statutes applying to civil rights in an effort to protect the black.

The Thirteenth, Fourteenth, and Fifteenth Amendments which read as follows, were the nation's effort to find a solution to the problems of reconstruction:

Amendment 13 *Section 1—Neither slavery nor involuntary servitude, except as a punishment for crime whereof the party shall have been duly convicted, shall exist within the United States, or any place subject to their jurisdiction.*

Section 2—Congress shall have power to enforce this article by appropriate legislation.

Amendment 14 *Section 1—All persons born or naturalized in the United States, and subject to the jurisdiction thereof, are citizens of the United States and of the State wherein they reside.*

No State shall make or enforce any law which shall abridge the privileges or immunities of citizens of the United States; nor shall any State deprive any person of life, liberty, or property, without due process of law; nor deny to any person within its jurisdiction the equal protection of the laws. . . .

. . .

Section 5—The Congress shall have power to enforce, by appropriate legislation, the provisions of this article.

Amendment 15 *Section 1—The right of citizens of the United States to vote shall not be denied or abridged by the United States or by any State on account of race, color, or previous condition of servitude.*

Section 2—The Congress shall have power to enforce this article by appropriate legislation.

During the 1865–66 session of Congress, a Joint Congressional Committee on Reconstruction was set up to conduct an investigation into reports of racial violence in the South (United States Commission on Civil Rights—Law Enforcement: A Report on Equal Protection in the South, 6–10, 1865). The results of this investigation culminated in the adoption of the first of many federal civil rights laws in 1866.

The statutes were designed to punish by fines and imprisonment, or both, those persons who under color of any law, statute, ordinance, regulation, or custom subjected any inhabitants of any State, Territory, or District to a deprivation of any rights, privileges, or immunities secured or protected by the laws of the United States or to different punishment, pains, or penalties because the person was an alien or by reason of his color or race.

A statute passed during this period which passed into oblivion but has been resurrected in recent years is now embodied in 42 U.S.C. 1983. It has become known to law enforcement officers as Section 1983. It was originally known as the Klu Klux Klan Act of 1871. It creates a civil cause of action, enforceable in the federal courts against any person, acting under color of state law, who deprives another of rights, privileges, or immunities secured by the Constitution or laws of the United States. There have been recent actions resulting in judgments against law enforcement personnel where the allegations were that these persons conspired against the plaintiff to deny the plaintiff the enumerated rights. More will be said about this in Chapter 14, infra.

The Fourteenth Amendment created questions concerning the extent to which the provisions of the Bill of Rights would be made applicable to state action. The first cases dealing with the problem which were decided by the United States Supreme Court were the Slaughterhouse cases, 83 U.S. 36,

16 Wall 36, 21 L.Ed. 394 (1873). In these cases butchers challenged a state law which granted a monopoly to slaughter all animals in the New Orleans vicinity for a period of twenty-five years. The challenges to the statute relied upon the due process and equal protection clause and privilege and immunities clause of the Fourteenth Amendment. The court rejected the petitioners claims but in so doing did not rule on anything other than the privileges and immunities clauses. The Court said that the right to follow a trade or profession without state interference in the form of a monopoly was not a "privilege or immunity" of citizens of the United States. The Court contended that the equal privilege and immunity clauses would give equal rights to seek the protection of government, to assert claims against the government, the right to hold office, etc., but not the unfettered right to engage in a trade or profession.

You will remember that the Bill of Rights was included in the Constitution at the behest of several states who would not ratify the document unless it was amended in short order to include these rights. Some made it a condition of their ratification. The fear, at that time, was that a strong national government might take away the individual's right to personal liberty. There was no comparable fear that the states might accomplish the same ends. It was thought that the Bill of Rights, as contained in the first ten amendments of the United States Constitution, was applicable only to the federal government. That view, held by many, was reinforced when in 1833, Justice Marshall speaking for the Court in Barron v. Baltimore, 32 U.S. 243, 8 L.Ed. 672, held that the Fifth Amendment's requirement that private property not be taken for public use, without just compensation did not apply as a protection against a local government which had diverted a stream in such a manner so as to damage the plaintiff's property. Marshall contended that the limitations in the Constitution's First Amendment, "Congress shall make no law . . . ," indicated a limitation on the national government and by implication a limitation on the amendments which followed the First Amendment. In effect, the court was adhering to the principle of dual citizenship, i.e., citizen of the United States and citizen of the state of his domicile.

In the Slaughterhouse cases (supra), the Court, speaking through Mr. Justice Samuel F. Miller, said that "... there is a citizenship of the United States and a citizenship of a State which are distinct from each other... We think this distinction and its explicit recognition in this amendment (Fourteenth Amendment) of great weight in this argument, because the next paragraph of this same section which is the one mainly relied on by the plaintiffs in error (old method of describing appellant), speaks only of privileges and immunities of citizens of the United States and does not speak of those citizens of the several states... The language is, 'No State shall make or enforce any law which shall abridge the privileges or immunities of citizens of the United States.'" In practical effect, the majority of the Court held that if a citizen of a state is denied equal privileges and immunities by state action, his recourse is only to the state courts and to the state legislature. The Court contended that the Fourteenth Amendment was adopted for the protection of discrimination against blacks as a class or on account of their race or a denial of equal justice in state courts. There were, however, three strong dissents in this case by Mr. Justice Stephen J. Field and concurred in by Mr. Justice Noah H. Swayne and Mr. Justice Joseph P. Bradley.

The student should take note that often when a strong dissent is written, as the personnel of the court changes over the years, the dissenting minority is joined by others of like mind and the previous dissent becomes the holding of the Court. This is the slow deliberate changing of our laws which makes revolution unnecessary, for if the argument for change has merit, there is a great likelihood that a change will take place. This is precisely what happened in the development of the court construction of the Fourteenth Amendment.

The Fourteenth Amendment has been a much litigated one but the later Supreme Court decisions have dealt very sparingly with the privileges and immunities aspect and have broadened the scope of the amendment by enlarging on the meaning of the due process and equal protection clauses. Lochner v. New York, 198 U.S. 45, 25 S.Ct. 539, 49 L.Ed. 937 (1905), was such a case. In this case the court struck down a state statute which limited the number of hours an employee in a bakery or confectionery establishment could work. It limited the amount to a maximum of sixty hours in one week or an average of ten hours a day. The statute was included in the Labor Law of New York State, and it made it unlawful for an employer to require an employee to work in excess of the prescribed hours. Ostensibly, the legislature enacted this statute in the belief that it was properly exercising its rights under the police power to protect the health, welfare, and morals of its people.

Lochner was convicted and lost all New York State appeals. He then brought the case to the United States Supreme Court. Mr. Justice Rufus W. Peckham delivered the opinion of the Court. He stated that "such a statute interferes with the right of contract between an employer and an employee . . . The general right to make a contract in relation to his business is part of the liberty of the individual protected by the Fourteenth Amendment of the Federal Constitution . . . Under the provision no State can deprive any person of life, liberty or property without due process of law. The right to sell labor is part of the liberty protected by this amendment unless there are circumstances which exclude the right." The Justice went on to explain that the State does retain police powers which relate to the safety, health, morals, and general welfare of the public and if a statute is a legitimate exercise of its police powers, it has the right to enact such a statute. However there is a limit to the police power. He said "the question necessarily arises: Is this a fair, reasonable and appropriate exercise of the police power of the State, or is it unreasonable, unnecessary and arbitrary interference with the right of the individual to his personal liberty or to enter into those contracts in relation to labor which may seem to him appropriate or necessary for the support of himself and his family? . . . It seems to us that the real object and purpose were simply to regulate the hours of labor between master and his employees (all being men, sui juris) in a private business not dangerous in any degree to morals or in any real and substantial degree to the health of the employees. Under such circumstances the freedom of master and employee to contract with each other in relation to their employment, and in defining the same, cannot be prohibited or interfered with without violating the Federal Constitution . . . ."

Here, too, there was a strong dissent by Mr. Justice Harlan with whom Mr. Justice White and Mr. Justice Day concurred. Mr. Justice Holmes wrote a strong dissent on his own.

We therefore find a slim majority of one writing the law for that day. This, as every student knows, has changed so that today there are many state statutes limiting the hours of work. The reason that they are now not a violation of the Fourteenth Amendment is that after the Lochner case, the Supreme Court continued the same construction of the due process and equal protection clauses in Adkins v. Children's Hospital, 261 U.S. 525, 43 S.Ct. 394, 67 L.Ed. 785 (1923), but in West Coast Hotel Co. v. Parrish, 300 U.S. 379, 57 S.Ct. 578, 81 L.Ed. 703 (1937), the Court specifically overruled the Adkins case. In the West Coast Hotel Co. case the court sustained a state statute which set up minimum wages and conditions of labor for women and minors. The court in substance said that the community may direct its lawmaking power to correct an abuse which springs from employers' selfish disregard of the public interest.

The Fourteenth Amendment has been construed in the criminal branch of the law also. The due process and equal protection clauses were discussed in Palko v. Conn., 302 U.S. 319, 58 S.Ct. 149, 82 L.Ed. 288 (1937). Palko was indicted and tried for murder in the first degree. A jury found him guilty of second degree murder. A Connecticut statute permitted the state to appeal rulings and decisions "upon all questions of law arising on the trial of criminal cases." The state appealed and was successful. A new trial was ordered and after trial, Palko was found guilty of First Degree Murder and was sentenced to death. He appealed to the Supreme Court on the grounds of his being placed in double jeopardy in violation of the Fifth and Fourteenth Amendments.

The Court in an opinion by Mr. Justice Benjamin N. Cardoza discussed the relationship of the Fifth Amendment provision that no person shall be held to answer for a capital or otherwise infamous crime unless on presentment or indictment of a grand jury and that no person shall be compelled in any criminal case to be a witness against himself, and spoke of DeJonge v. Oregon, 299 U.S. 353, 57 S.Ct. 255, 81 L.Ed. 279 (1937), and Herndon v. Lowry, 301 U.S. 242, 57 S.Ct. 732, 81 L.Ed. 1066 (1937), and other cases which had made the Fourteenth Amendment applicable to the States with respect to freedom of speech, freedom of the press, the free exercise of religion, the right to peaceable assembly, or the right of counsel to one accused of crime. Mr. Justice Cardoza said, "In these and other situations immunities that are valid as against the federal government by force of the specific pledges of particular amendments have been found to be implicit in the concept of ordered liberty, and thus through the Fourteenth Amendment become valid as against the states... The right to a trial by jury and immunity from prosecution except as the result of an indictment may have value and importance. Even so, they are not of the very essence of a scheme of ordered liberty. To abolish them is not to violate a 'principle of justice' so rooted in the traditions and conscience of our people as to be ranked as fundamental... Few would be so narrow or provincial as to maintain that fair and enlightened system of justice would be impossible without them. What is true of jury trials and indictments is true also, as the cases show, of the immunity from self incrimination... This too might be lost and justice still be done... If the Fourteenth Amendment has absorbed them (privileges and immunities) the process of absorption has had its source in the belief that neither liberty nor justice would exist if they were sacrificed... On which side of the line the case made out by the appellant has appropriate location must be the next inquiry and final one. Is that kind of double jeopardy to which the statute has subjected him a hardship so acute and shocking that our policy will not endure it? Does it violate those 'fundamental principles of liberty and justice which lie at the base of all our civil and political institutions?'... The answer surely must be 'no.'"

In this case the state successfully based its argument on the premise that the first trial was not free from substantial error and it should be permitted a trial without a substantial error. The court held that the appellant was not deprived of any privileges or immunities that were granted him as a citizen of the United States.

This case stands for the proposition, however, that if a state denies a state citizen of a fundamental principle of liberty and justice which lies at the base of all of our civil and political institutions, the citizen will be protected against state action by invoking the Fourteenth Amendment due process clause and for such a transgression by a state, the Fourteenth Amendment had absorbed the Bill of Rights given to federal citizens against federal action.

The Palko case was followed by others among which we find Snyder v. Massachusetts, 291 U.S. 97, 54 S.Ct. 330, 78 L.Ed. 674 (1941), which held that the Fourteenth Amendment was applicable against state action when it violated principles of justice so rooted in the traditions and conscience of our people as to be ranked as fundamental and Lisenba v. California, 314 U.S. 291, 62 S.Ct. 280, 86 L.Ed. 166 (1941), where the court held a state liable for the administration of fundamental fairness essential to the very concept of justice.

For example, the student will find that the due process clause of the Fourteenth Amendment and the equal protection clause of the amendment brought about the absorption of many of the rights of the Bill of Rights into state action. Chicago, B & Q R Co. v. City of Chicago, 166 U.S. 226, 17 S.Ct. 581, 41 L.Ed. 979 (1897); Lochner v. New York, 198 U.S. 45, 25 S.Ct. 539, 49 L.Ed. 937 (1905). Other cases will be explained and cited to show the development of the Fourteenth Amendment in chapters which follow.

§ 4.3 First Amendment

You will remember that the First Amendment reads as follows:

> *Congress shall make no law respecting an establishment of religion, or prohibiting the free exercise thereof; or abridging the freedom of speech, or of the press; or the right of the people peaceably to assemble, and to petition the Government for a redress of grievances.*

You will also remember that the limitation of power is directly related to Congress. Apparently the framers of the Constitution did not believe that this should be a limitation of power of the States and local governments.

However, the freedom of speech, press, peaceful assembly, and petition for a redress of grievances as enunciated in the First Amendment to the United States Constitution have been construed by the Supreme Court to be so rooted in the traditions and conscience of our people as to be ranked high on the list of rights. The First Amendment rights were so fundamental that any encroachment on these rights by state sovereignties was quickly eliminated. The courts have held that any governmental authority which seeks to infringe in the slightest degree on First Amendment rights of any person has a special burden because of the preferred status of these rights when compared to other individual rights found in the United States Constitution. The due process clause of the Fourteenth Amendment to the United States Constitution protects freedom of speech and of the press against infringement by state action. Winters v. People of the State of New York, 333 U.S. 507, 68 S.Ct. 665, 92 L.Ed. 840; Bowden v. City of Ft. Smith, Ark., 316 U.S. 584, 62 S.Ct. 1231, 86 L.Ed. 1691, 141 A.L.R. 514. While this concept is so well rooted in our law, we still have had cases decided by courts in recent years dealing with the same point. Wash.—Adam v. Hinkle, 51 Wash.2d 763, 322 P.2d 844. Therefore, there was no problem in the absorption of the First Amendment rights when they are considered in conjunction with the Fourteenth Amendment.

§ 4.4 Fourth Amendment

> *The right of the people to be secure in their persons, houses, papers, and effects, against unreasonable searches and seizures, shall not be violated, and no Warrants shall issue, but upon probable cause, supported by Oath or affirmation, and particularly describing the place to be searched, and the persons or things to be seized.*

The Fourth Amendment to the United States Constitution was construed by the United States Supreme Court for many years as a protection against unreasonable searches by federal law enforcement officers. The lawyers of our nation, however, pounded at the door of the courts until the door finally gave way. A fuller explanation of the evolution of the theory of the Fourth Amendment application to state action as well as federal action appears later in this book.

An overview would not be complete, however, without referring to the case of Mapp v. Ohio, 367 U.S. 643, 81 S.Ct. 1680, 6 L.Ed.2d 108 (1961). This was the case that opened the door to a new body of state law dealing with unreasonable search and seizure by state law enforcement officers. Prior to this decision, there were basically two sets of rules governing unreasonable search and seizure by governmental authority. They were the Federal Rule and the State Rule. The Federal Rule was much more restrictive on governmental agents than the State Rule. Much will be said about the development of these rules in Chapter 6, infra.

§ 4.5 Fifth Amendment

No person shall be held to answer for a capital, or otherwise infamous crime, unless on a presentment or indictment of a Grand Jury, except in cases arising in the land or naval forces, or in the Militia, when in actual service in time of War or public danger; nor shall any person be subject for the same offence to be twice put in jeopardy of life or limb; nor shall be compelled in any criminal case to be a witness against himself, nor be deprived of life, liberty, or property, without due process of law; nor shall private property be taken for public use, without just compensation.

One must have at the very least, a slight acquaintance with the history of the rights protected in the Fifth Amendment to understand its significance. The public condemnation that is aroused when one hears that a witness "took the Fifth" is wholly unwarranted if those who chastise the witness for exercising his constitutional right would take a minute to understand why the amendment is in the Constitution.

The inclusion of the Fifth Amendment in the United States Constitution was a reaction against the practice of the Court of Star Chamber, established by Henry VII in 1487 as the Star Chamber Statute. The proceedings of these courts were founded on a system which had prevailed on the continent of Europe for many centuries. It has been given the nomenclature of an inquisitorial system. In England, prior to 1487 and after the Star Chamber was abolished, the accusatorial method was practiced in England.

The Star Chamber proceedings sanctioned the examination of an accused under oath even without a formal charge. It was widely used in sedition and heresy trials. The English judges gradually changed to the accusatorial system because of many abuses. People were tortured into admitting crimes that they did not commit just for a temporary surcease from the pain. By 1700 the privilege against self-incrimination in England was fully recognized.

The history of the absorption of the Fifth Amendment to be effective against state action has been long and arduous. Here too, the unsung heroes of the legal profession pounded on the doors of the courthouse until they gave in. The first United States Supreme Court test of this privilege occurred in Twining v. New Jersey, 211 U.S. 78, 29 S.Ct. 14, 53 L.Ed. 97 (1908), where the issue presented to the court was whether the privilege against self-incrimination was a right protected against state action by the Privileges and Immunities Clause of the Fourteenth Amendment where the state had no statute or constitutional provision of its own prohibiting self-incrimination.

In that case, the Supreme Court held by an 8–1 decision, that neither the Privileges and Immunities Clause of the Fourteenth Amendment nor the Due Process Clause of the Fourteenth Amendment required states to extend the protections of the Fifth Amendment Self-Incrimination Clause. The court said:

> In order to bring themselves within the protection of the Constitution it is incumbent upon the defendants to prove two propositions: first, that the exemption from compulsory self incrimination is guaranteed against impairment by the states; and second, if it be so guaranteed, that the exemption was in fact impaired in the case at bar.

After discussing the history of the need for the Fifth Amendment, the court went on to say:

> The privilege was not included in the Federal Constitution as originally adopted... Since then all the states of the Union have from time to time, with varying form, but uniform meaning included the privilege in their Constitutions except the states of New Jersey and Iowa, and in those states it is held to be part of existing law... We have to consider whether the right is so fundamental in due process that a refusal is a denial of due process... we find nothing to show that it was then thought to be other than a just and useful principle of law. None of the great instruments in which we are accustomed to look for the declaration of fundamental rights made reference to it... The inference that it has been the opinion of constitution makers that the privilege, if fundamental in any sense, is not fundamental in due process of law... We conclude, therefore, that the exemption of compulsory self incrimination is not a privilege or immunity of national citizenship guaranteed by this clause of the Fourteenth Amendment against abridgement by the states.

In Adamson v. California, 332 U.S. 46, 67 S.Ct. 1672, 91 L.Ed. 1903 (1947), the Twining case was reaffirmed where, as in Twining, the court commented on the failure of the defendant to take the stand and testify at the trial.

The further development of the self-incrimination application to state action showing a complete reversal of Twining and Adamson will be treated in depth in Chapter 7, infra.

§ 4.6 Sixth Amendment

> *In all criminal prosecutions, the accused shall enjoy the right to a speedy and public trial, by an impartial jury of the State and district wherein the crime shall have been committed, which district*

shall have been previously ascertained by law, and to be informed of the nature and cause of the accusation; to be confronted with the witnesses against him; to have compulsory process for obtaining witnesses in his favor, and to have the Assistance of Counsel for his defence.

Too many of us fail to appreciate the protections given to each of us through the United States Constitution. We cannot conceive of a state or federal government in the United States where we could be placed in jail for an indeterminate period of time at the pleasure of the jailer; where we could be tried in a secluded place in the middle of the night; where the jury would have made up its mind as to our innocence or guilt, prior to hearing the evidence; where we could be tried in a jurisdiction other than prescribed by written law prior to the commission of the offense and whisked away to a community having prejudices against us; where we were not informed of the nature and cause of the accusation; where we were not able to cross-examine witnesses against us; where we could get no compulsory process of witnesses who would testify in our favor; and where we could not have the assistance of an attorney.

Knowing the nature of man when given power, the thought of being denied any of the preceding rights of the Sixth Amendment is a horrifying one. Yet we take these rights as a matter of course.

Before 1688, a person in England charged with treason or a felony had no right to demand assistance of counsel for his defense. However, civil litigants and persons charged with misdemeanors during this period had a right of counsel. The argument was advanced that in more serious offenses, the judge would provide sufficient protection for the accused. The English Revolution of 1688 caused the rule to be changed with respect to the right of counsel in cases of treason but the denial of counsel in felony cases persisted to 1836 when Parliament granted a corresponding right with respect to felony cases in general. Powell v. Alabama, 287 U.S. 45, 53 S.Ct. 55, 77 L.Ed. 158 (1932). The right to counsel in criminal cases developed earlier in America. There was some diversity in the colonies and states but the direction was set towards giving this right to defendants.

The United States Constitution specifically mandated it, but it was construed to apply only to federal actions for many years. However, lawyers disagreed as to whether counsel was "required" or only "permitted" and whether it only applied to cases where, upon conviction, the defendant would be executed or if it applied to all felony cases. In 1938 the United States Supreme Court decided Johnson v. Zerbst, 304 U.S. 458, 58 S.Ct. 1019, 82 L.Ed. 1461. The case involved two United States Marines who were arrested in Charleston, South Carolina, and charged with passing counterfeit United States currency. They were arrested, confined, and indicted two months later. They were represented by counsel at the time of the arrest but had no counsel at the trial. They were convicted and sentenced to four and one-half years in the penitentiary. The time to appeal having expired, one of the defendants brought a habeas corpus proceeding in a federal district court. The federal district court denied the writ and he appealed to the Supreme Court of the United States. His conviction was reversed and the case was remanded for a new trial.

The case established two rules of law in federal courts:

1. Unless there is a competent waiver, counsel must be appointed for an indigent defendant.
2. The effective waiver envisages an intelligent and informed choice. If a defendant merely fails to make the request, this is not a waiver and there is, therefore, a duty by the court to inform the defendant of his rights.

The absorption of the right of counsel in state trials and the development of other personal Sixth Amendment rights will be treated in greater detail in the chapters of this book which follow.

§ 4.7 Eighth Amendment

Excessive bail shall not be required, nor excessive fines imposed, nor cruel and unusual punishments inflicted.

As with the other Bill of Rights amendments, abuses perpetrated in the old world, wherein bail was denied, prisoners were left in prison to literally rot, and cruel and inhuman punishments were the rule rather than the exception, led to the inclusion of the Eighth Amendment to the United States Constitution.

There has not been as much litigation involving the Eighth Amendment as might be expected. The provision of excessive bail or excessive fines is so ambiguous that it leaves much for the discretion of the courts and unless the bail or fine is so arbitrary, capricious, and/or unreasonable, the higher courts are not apt to interfere. However, it has been held that the due process clause of the federal constitution affirms the right to bail, U.S.—State of Texas v. Whittingon, C.A.Tex. 391 F.2d 905, but a deprivation of liberty without due process of law may exist where there is a denial of the right to bail to a person charged with a crime which is not a capital offense or is a capital offense but the proof of guilt is not evident nor the presumption great. Ind.—Bozovichar v. State, 230 Ind. 358, 103 N.E.2d 680, 681.

There has been a movement of late to attack certain practices of jailers as being an example of cruel and unusual punishment. One such case involved harsh treatment of a prisoner. The court held that in view of the guarantee of due process and other constitutional guarantees, unreasonably harsh treatment of a prisoner, not necessary to his safe confinement, by the warden or other officer in charge of the prison is a wrong which the courts are open to redress. U.S.—Wilson v. Kelly, D.C.Ga. 294 F.Supp. 1005, affd. 393 U.S. 266, 89 S.Ct. 477. The death penalty cases have arisen under this amendment and are discussed in §9.5 (infra).

§ 4.8 Tenth Amendment

You will recall that the colonies were very jealous of their individual rights and privileges of self-government. They were very wary of giving up their rights of self-determination but also realized that there was greater strength in a combination of states in a central government than in separate independent nations. Accordingly, they delegated specific powers of government to the federal government but did not want to delegate all functions of government. To accomplish this end, the wording of the Tenth Amendment was contrived:

> *The powers not delegated to the United States by the Constitution nor prohibited by it to the States, are reserved to the States respectively, or to the people.*

The police power, being the power of government to prescribe, regulate, and control the health, welfare, and morals of its inhabitants, was not specifically delegated to the central government by the states. This accounts for the presence of state, city, and county law enforcement personnel instead of a central government police force. For many years, therefore, there was complete autonomy among the approximately forty thousand law enforcement agencies throughout the nation. This has been changing, not by constitutional amendment but by the carrot at the end of the stick in the way of federal funds being given to local law enforcement on the condition that certain federal controls be complied with.

Judicial Decisions Relating to Chapter 4

John Barron, survivor of John Craig, for the use of Luke Tiernan, Executor of John Craig *v.* The Mayor and City Council of Baltimore

32 U.S. 243, 7 Peters 243, 8 L.Ed. 672 (1833)

. . .

MR. CHIEF JUSTICE MARSHALL delivered the opinion of the Court.

The judgment brought up by this writ of error having been rendered by the court of a state, this tribunal can exercise no jurisdiction over it, unless it be shown to come within the provisions of the twenty-fifth section of the judicial act.

The plaintiff in error contends that it comes within that clause in the fifth amendment to the constitution, which inhibits the taking of private property for public use, without just compensation. He insists that this amendment, being in favour of the liberty of the citizen, ought to be so construed as to restrain the legislative power of a state, as well as that of the United States. If this proposition be untrue, the court can take no jurisdiction of the cause.

The question thus presented is, we think, of great importance, but not of much difficulty.

The constitution was ordained and established by the people of the United States for themselves, for their own government, and not for the government of the individual states. Each state established a constitution for itself, and, in that constitution, provided such limitations and restrictions on the powers of its particular government as its judgment dictated. The people of the United States framed such a government for the United States as they supposed best adapted to their situation, and best calculated to promote their interests. The powers they conferred on this government were to be exercised by itself; and the limitations on power, if expressed in general terms, are naturally, and, we think, necessarily applicable to the government created by the instrument. They are limitations of power granted in the instrument itself; not of distinct governments, framed by different persons and for different purposes.

If these propositions be correct, the fifth amendment must be understood as restraining the power of the general government, not as applicable to the states. In their several constitutions they have imposed such restrictions on their respective governments as their own wisdom suggested; such as they deemed most proper for themselves. It is a subject on which they judge exclusively, and with which others interfere no farther than they are supposed to have a common interest.

The counsel for the plaintiff in error insists that the constitution was intended to secure the people of the several states against the undue exercise of power by their respective state governments; as well as against that which might be attempted by their general government. In support of this argument he relies on the inhibitions contained in the tenth section of the first article.

We think that section affords a strong if not a conclusive argument in support of the opinion already indicated by the court.

The preceding section contains restrictions which are obviously intended for the exclusive purpose of restraining the exercise of power by the departments of the general government. Some of them use language applicable only to congress: others are expressed in general terms. The third clause, for example, declares that "no bill of attainder or ex post facto law shall be passed." No language can be more general; yet the demonstration is complete that it applies solely to the government of the United States. In addition to the general arguments furnished by the instrument itself, some of which have been already suggested, the succeeding section, the avowed purpose of which is to restrain state legislation, contains in terms the very prohibition. It declares that "no state shall pass any bill of attainder or ex post facto law." This provision, then, of the ninth section, however comprehensive its language, contains no restriction on state legislation.

The ninth section having enumerated, in the nature of a bill of rights, the limitations intended to be imposed on the powers of the general government, the tenth proceeds to enumerate those which were to operate on the state legislatures. These restrictions are brought together in the same section, and are by express words applied to the states. "No state shall enter into any treaty," &c. Perceiving that in a constitution framed by the people of the United States for the government of all, no limitation of the action of government on the people would apply to the state government, unless expressed in terms; the restrictions contained in the tenth section are in direct words so applied to the states.

It is worthy of remark, too, that these inhibitions generally restrain state legislation on subjects entrusted to the general government, or in which the people of all the states feel an interest.

A state is forbidden to enter into any treaty, alliance or confederation. If these compacts are with foreign nations, they interfere with the treaty making power which is conferred entirely on the general government; if with each other, for political purposes, they can scarcely fail to interfere with the general purpose and intent of the constitution. To grant letters of marque and reprisal, would lead directly to war; the power of declaring which is expressly given to congress. To coin money is also the exercise of a power conferred on congress. It would be tedious to recapitulate the several limitations on the powers of the states which are contained in this section. They will be found, generally, to restrain state legislation on subjects entrusted to the government of the union, in which the citizens of all the states are interested. In these alone were the whole people concerned. The question of their application to states is not left to construction. It is averred in positive words.

If the original constitution, in the ninth and tenth sections of the first article, draws this plain and marked line of discrimination between the limitations it imposes on the powers of the general government, and on those of the states; if in every inhibition intended to act on state power, words are employed which directly express that intent; some strong reason must be assigned for departing from this safe and judicious course in framing the amendments, before that departure can be assumed.

We search in vain for that reason.

Had the people of the several states, or any of them, required changes in their constitutions; had they required additional safeguards to liberty from the apprehended encroachments of their particular governments; the remedy was in their own hands, and would have been applied by themselves. A convention would have been assembled by the discontented state, and the required improvements would have been made by itself. The unwieldy and cumbrous machinery of procuring a recommendation from two-thirds of congress, and the assent of three-fourths of their sister states, could never have occurred to any human being as a mode of doing that which might be effected by the state itself. Had the framers of these amendments intended them to be limitations on the powers of the state governments, they would have imitated the framers of the original constitution, and have expressed that intention. Had congress engaged in the extraordinary occupation of improving the constitutions of the several states by affording the people additional protection from the exercise of power by their own governments in matters which concerned themselves alone, they would have declared this purpose in plain and intelligible language.

But it is universally understood, it is a part of the history of the day, that the great revolution which established the constitution of the United States, was not effected without immense opposition. Serious fears were extensively entertained that those powers which the patriot statesmen, who then watched over the interests of our country, deemed essential to union, and to the attainment of those invaluable objects for which union was sought, might be exercised in a manner dangerous to liberty. In almost every convention by which the constitution was adopted, amendments to guard against the abuse of power were recommended. These amendments demanded security against the apprehended encroachments of the general government—not against those of the local governments.

In compliance with a sentiment thus generally expressed, to quiet fears thus extensively entertained, amendments were proposed by the required majority in congress, and adopted by the states. These amendments contain no expression indicating an intention to apply them to the state governments. This court cannot so apply them.

We are of opinion that the provision in the fifth amendment to the constitution, declaring that private property shall not be taken for public use without just compensation, is intended solely as a limitation on the exercise of power by the government of the United States, and is not applicable to the legislation of the states. We are therefore of opinion that there is no repugnancy between the several acts of the general assembly of Maryland, given in evidence by the defendants at the trial of this cause, in the court of that state, and the constitution of the United States. This court, therefore, has no jurisdiction of the cause; and it is dismissed.

This cause came on to be heard on the transcript of the record from the court of appeals for the western shore of the state of Maryland, and was argued by counsel; on consideration whereof, it is the opinion of this court that there is no repugnancy between the several acts of the general assembly of Maryland, given in evidence by the defendants at the trial of this cause in the court of that state, and the constitution of the United States; whereupon, it is ordered and adjudged by this court that this writ of error be, and the same is hereby dismissed for the want of jurisdiction.

Lochner *v.* New York

198 U.S. 45, 25 S.Ct. 539, 49 L.Ed. 937 (1905)

ERROR TO THE COUNTY COURT OF ONEIDA COUNTY, STATE OF NEW YORK

Argued February 23, 24, 1905.—Decided April 17, 1905.

. . .

THIS is a writ of error to the County Court of Oneida County, in the State of New York (to which court the record had been remitted), to review the judgment of the Court of Appeals of that State, affirming the judgment of the Supreme Court, which itself affirmed the judgment of the County Court, convicting the defendant of a misdemeanor on an indictment under a statute of that State, known, by its short title, as the labor health measure or otherwise, the courts should give the construction which sustains the act and makes it applicable in furtherance of the public interests. Bohmer v. Haffen, 161 N.Y. 390, 399.

MR. JUSTICE PECKHAM, after making the foregoing statement of the facts, delivered the opinion of the court.

The indictment, it will be seen, charges that the plaintiff in error violated the one hundred and tenth section of article 8, chapter 415, of the Laws of 1897, known as the labor law of the State of New York, in that he wrongfully and unlawfully required and permitted an employé working for him to work more than sixty hours in one week. There is nothing in any of the opinions delivered in this case, either in the Supreme Court or the Court of Appeals of the State, which construes the section, in using the word "required," as referring to any physical force being used to obtain the labor of an employé. It is assumed that the word means nothing more than the requirement arising from voluntary contract for such labor in excess of the number of hours specified in the statute. There is no pretense in any of the opinions that the statute was intended to meet a case of involuntary labor in any form. All the opinions assume that there is no real distinction, so far as this question is concerned, between the words "required" and "permitted." The mandate of the statute that "no employé shall be required or permitted to work," is the substantial equivalent of an enactment that "no employé shall contract or agree to work," more than ten hours per day, and as there is no provision for special emergencies the statute is mandatory in all cases. It is not an act merely fixing the number of hours which shall constitute a legal day's work, but an absolute prohibition upon the employer, permitting, under any circumstances, more than ten hours work to be done in his establishment. The employé may desire to earn the extra money, which would arise from his working more than the prescribed time, but this statute forbids the employer from permitting the employé to earn it.

The statute necessarily interferes with the right of contract between the employer and the employés, concerning the number of hours in which the latter may labor in the bakery of the employer. The general right to make a contract in relation to his business is part of the liberty of the individual protected by the Fourteenth Amendment of the Federal Constitution. Allgeyer v. Louisiana, 165 U.S. 578. Under that provision no State can deprive any person of life, liberty or property without due process of law. The right to purchase or to sell labor is part of the liberty protected by this amendment, unless there are circumstances which exclude the right. There are, however, certain powers, existing in the sovereignty of each State in the Union, somewhat vaguely termed police powers, the exact description and limitation of which have not been attempted by the courts. Those powers, broadly stated and without, at present, any attempt at a more specific limitation, relate to the safety, health, morals and general welfare of the public. Both property and liberty are held on such reasonable conditions as may be imposed by the governing power of the State in the exercise of those powers, and with such conditions the Fourteenth Amendment was not designed to interfere. Mugler v. Kansas, 123 U.S. 623; In re Kemmler, 136 U.S. 436; Crowley v. Christensen, 137 U.S. 86; In re Converse, 137 U.S. 624.

The State, therefore, has power to prevent the individual from making certain kinds of contracts, and in regard to them the Federal Constitution offers no protection. If the contract be one which the State, in the legitimate exercise of its police power, has the right to prohibit, it is not prevented from prohibiting it by the Fourteenth Amendment. Contracts in violation of a statute, either of the Federal or state government, or a contract to let one's property for immoral purposes, or to do any other unlawful act, could obtain no protection from the Federal Constitution, as coming under the liberty of person or of free contract. Therefore, when the State, by its legislature, in the assumed exercise of its police powers, has passed an act which seriously limits the right to labor or the right of contract in regard to their means of livelihood between persons who are sui juris (both employer and employé), it becomes of great importance to determine which shall prevail—the right of the individual to labor for such time as he may choose, or the right of the State to prevent the individual from laboring or from entering into any contract to labor, beyond a certain time prescribed by the State.

This court has recognized the existence and upheld the exercise of the police powers of the States in many cases which might fairly be considered as border ones, and it has, in the course of its determination of questions regarding the asserted invalidity of such statutes, on the ground of their violation of the rights secured by the Federal Constitution, been guided by rules of a very liberal nature, the application of which has resulted, in numerous instances, in upholding the validity of state statutes thus assailed. Among the later cases where the state law has been upheld by this court is that of Holden v. Hardy, 169 U.S. 366. A provision in the act of the legislature of Utah was there under consideration, the act limiting the employment of workmen in all underground mines or workings, to eight hours per day, "except in cases of emergency, where life or property is in imminent danger." It also limited the hours of labor in smelting and other institutions for the reduction or refining of ores or metals to eight hours per day, except in like cases of emergency. The act was held to be a valid exercise of the police powers of the State. A review of many of the cases on the subject, decided by this and other courts, is given in the opinion. It was held that the kind of employment, mining, smelting, etc., and the character of the employes in such kinds of labor, were such as to make it reasonable and proper for the State to interfere to prevent the employés from being constrained by the rules laid down by the proprietors in regard to labor. The following citation from the observations of the Supreme Court of Utah in that case was made by the judge writing the opinion of this court, and approved: "The law in question is confined to the protection of that class of people engaged in labor in underground mines, and in smelters and other works wherein ores are reduced and refined. This law applies only to the classes subjected by their employment to the peculiar conditions and effects attending underground mining and work in smelters, and other works for the reduction and refining of ores. Therefore it is not necessary to discuss or decide whether the legislature can fix the hours of labor in other employments."

It will be observed that, even with regard to that class of labor, the Utah statute provided for cases of emergency wherein the provisions of the statute would not apply. The statute now before this court has no emergency clause in it, and if the statute is valid, there are no circumstances and no emergencies under which the slightest violation of the provisions of the act would be innocent. There is nothing in Holden v. Hardy which covers the case now before us. Nor does Atkin v. Kansas, 191 U.S. 207, touch the case at bar. The Atkin case was decided upon the right of the State to control its municipal corporations and to prescribe the conditions upon which it will permit work of a public character to be done for a municipality. Knoxville Iron Co. v. Harbison, 183 U.S. 13, is equally far from an authority for this legislation. The employés in that case were held to be at a disadvantage with the employer in matters of wages, they being miners and coal workers, and the act simply provided for the cashing of coal orders when presented by the miner to the employer.

The latest case decided by this court, involving the police power is that of Jacobson v. Massachusetts, decided at this term and reported in 197 U.S. 11. It related to compulsory vaccination, and the law was held valid as a proper exercise of the police powers with reference to the public health. It was stated in the opinion that it was a case "of an adult who, for aught that appears, was himself in perfect health and a fit subject for vaccination, and yet, while remaining in the community, refused to obey the statute and the regulation adopted in execution of its provisions for the protection of the public health and the public safety, confessedly endangered by the presence of a dangerous disease." That case is also far from covering the one now before the court.

Petit v. Minnesota, 177 U.S. 164, was upheld as a proper exercise of the police power relating to the observance of Sunday, and the case held that the legislature had the right to declare that, as matter of law, keeping barber shops open on Sunday was not a work of necessity or charity.

It must, of course, be conceded that there is a limit to the valid exercise of the police power by the State. There is no dispute concerning this general proposition. Otherwise the Fourteenth Amendment would have no efficacy and the legislatures of the States would have unbounded power, and it would be enough to say that any piece of legislation was enacted to conserve the morals, the health or the safety of the people; such legislation would be valid, no matter how absolutely without foundation the claim might be. The claim of the police power would be a mere pretext—become another and delusive name for the supreme sovereignty of the State to be exercised free from constitutional restraint. This is not contended for. In every case that comes before this court, therefore, where legislation of this character is concerned and where the protection of the Federal Constitution is sought, the question necessarily arises: Is this a fair, reasonable and appropriate exercise of the police power of the State, or is it an unreasonable, unnecessary and arbitrary interference with the right of the individual to his personal liberty or to enter into those contracts in relation to labor which may seem to him appropriate or necessary for the support of himself and his family? Of course the liberty of contract relating to labor includes both parties to it. The one has as much right to purchase as the other to sell labor.

This is not a question of substituting the judgment of the court for that of the legislature. If the act be within the power of the State it is valid, although the judgment of the court might be totally opposed to the enactment of such a law. But the question would still remain: Is it within the police power of the State? and that question must be answered by the court.

The question whether this act is valid as a labor law, pure and simple, may be dismissed in a few words. There is no reasonable ground for interfering with the liberty of person or the right of free contract, by determining the hours of labor, in the occupation of a baker. There is no contention that bakers as a class are not equal in intelligence and capacity to men in other trades or manual occupations, or that they are not able to assert their rights and care for themselves without the protecting arm of the State, interfering with their independence of judgment and of action. They are in no sense wards of the State. Viewed in the light of a purely labor law, with no reference whatever to the question of health, we think that a law like the one before us involves neither the safety, the morals nor the welfare of the public, and that the interest of the public is not in the slightest degree affected by such an act. The law must be upheld, if at all, as a law pertaining to the health of the individual engaged in the occupation of a baker. It does not affect any other portion of the public than those who are engaged in that occupation. Clean and wholesome bread does not depend upon whether the baker works but ten hours per day or only sixty hours a week. The limitation of the hours of labor does not come within the police power on that ground.

It is a question of which of two powers or rights shall prevail—the power of the State to legislate or the right of the individual to liberty of person and freedom of contract. The mere assertion that the subject relates though but in a remote degree to the public health does not necessarily render the enactment valid. The act must have a more direct relation, as a means to an end, and the end itself must be appropriate and legitimate, before an act can be held to be valid which interferes with the general right of an individual to be free in his person and in his power to contract in relation to his own labor.

This case has caused much diversity of opinion in the state courts. In the Supreme Court two of the five judges composing the Appellate Division dissented from the judgment affirming the validity of the act. In the Court of Appeals three of the seven judges also dissented from the judgment upholding the statute. Although found in what is called a labor law of the State, the Court of Appeals has upheld the act as one relating to the public health—in other words, as a health law. One of the judges of the Court of Appeals, in upholding the law, stated that, in his opinion, the regulation in question could not be sustained unless they were able to say, from common knowledge, that working in a bakery and candy factory was an unhealthy employment. The judge held that, while the evidence was not uniform, it still led him to the conclusion that the occupation of a baker or confectioner was unhealthy and tended to result in diseases of the respiratory organs. Three of the judges dissented from that view, and they thought the occupation of a baker was not to such an extent unhealthy as to warrant the interference of the legislature with the liberty of the individual.

We think the limit of the police power has been reached and passed in this case. There is, in our judgment, no reasonable foundation for holding this to be necessary or appropriate as a health law to safeguard the public health or the health of the individuals who are following the trade of a baker. If this statute be valid, and if, therefore, a proper case is made out in which to deny the right of an individual, sui juris, as employer or employé, to make contracts for the labor of the latter under the protection of the provisions of the Federal Constitution, there would seem to be no length to which legislation of this nature might not go. The case differs widely, as we have already stated, from the expressions of this court in regard to laws of this nature, as stated in Holden v. Hardy and Jacobson v. Massachusetts, supra.

|We think that there can be no fair doubt that the trade of a baker, in and of itself, is not an unhealthy one to that degree which would authorize the legislature to interfere with the right to labor, and with the right of free contract on the part of the individual, either as employer or employé. In looking through statistics regarding all trades and occupations, it may be true that the trade of a baker does not appear to be as healthy as some other trades, and is also vastly more healthy than still others. To the common understanding the trade of a baker has never been regarded as an unhealthy one. Very likely physicians would not recommend the exercise of that or of any other trade as a remedy for ill health. Some occupations are more healthy than others, but we think there are none which might not come under the power of the legislature to supervise and control the hours of working therein, if the mere fact that the occupation is not absolutely and perfectly healthy is to confer that right upon the legislative department of the Government. It might be safely affirmed that almost all occupations more or less affect the health. There must be more than the mere fact of the possible existence of some small amount of unhealthiness to warrant legislative interference with liberty. It is unfortunately true that labor, even in any department, may possibly carry with it the seeds of unhealthiness. But are we all, on that account, at the mercy of legislative majorities? A printer, a tinsmith, a locksmith, a carpenter, a cabinetmaker, a dry goods clerk, a bank's, a lawyer's or a physician's clerk, or a clerk in almost any kind of business, would all come under the power of the legislature, on this assumption. No trade, no occupation, no mode of earning one's living, could escape this all-pervading power, and the acts of the legislature in limiting the hours of labor in all employments would be valid, although such limitation might seriously cripple the ability

of the laborer to support himself and his family. In our large cities there are many buildings into which the sun penetrates for but a short time in each day, and these buildings are occupied by people carrying on the business of bankers, brokers, lawyers, real estate, and many other kinds of business, aided by many clerks, messengers, and other employés. Upon the assumption of the validity of this act under review, it is not possible to say that an act, prohibiting lawyers' or bank clerks, or others, from contracting to labor for their employers more than eight hours a day, would be invalid. It might be said that it is unhealthy to work more than that number of hours in an apartment lighted by artificial light during the working hours of the day; that the occupation of the bank clerk, the lawyer's clerk, the real estate clerk, or the broker's clerk in such offices is therefore unhealthy, and the legislature in its paternal wisdom must, therefore, have the right to legislate on the subject of and to limit the hours for such labor, and if it exercises that power and its validity be questioned, it is sufficient to say, it has reference to the public health; it has reference to the health of the employés condemned to labor day after day in buildings where the sun never shines; it is a health law, and therefore it is valid, and cannot be questioned by the courts.

It is also urged, pursuing the same line of argument, that it is to the interest of the State that its population should be strong and robust, and therefore any legislation which may be said to tend to make people healthy must be valid as health laws, enacted under the police power. If this be a valid argument and a justification for this kind of legislation, it follows that the protection of the Federal Constitution from undue interference with liberty of person and freedom of contract is visionary, wherever the law is sought to be justified as a valid exercise of the police power. Scarcely any law but might find shelter under such assumptions, and conduct, properly so called, as well as contract, would come under the restrictive sway of the legislature. Not only the hours of employés, but the hours of employers, could be regulated, and doctors, lawyers, scientists, all professional men, as well as athletes and artisans, could be forbidden to fatigue their brains and bodies by prolonged hours of exercise, lest the fighting strength of the State be impaired. We mention these extreme cases because the contention is extreme. We do not believe in the soundness of the views which uphold this law. On the contrary, we think that such a law as this, although passed in the assumed exercise of the police power, and as relating to the public health, or the health of the employés named, is not within that power, and is invalid. The act is not, within any fair meaning of the term, a health law, but is an illegal interference with the rights of individuals, both employers and employés, to make contracts regarding labor upon such terms as they may think best, or which they may agree upon with the other parties to such contracts. Statutes of the nature of that under review, limiting the hours in which grown and intelligent men may labor to earn their living, are mere meddlesome interferences with the rights of the individual, and they are not saved from condemnation by the claim that they are passed in the exercise of the police power and upon the subject of the health of the individual whose rights are interfered with, unless there be some fair ground, reasonable in and of itself, to say that there is material danger to the public health or to the health of the employés, if the hours of labor are not curtailed. If this be not clearly the case the individuals, whose rights are thus made the subject of legislative interference, are under the protection of the Federal Constitution regarding their liberty of contract as well as of person; and the legislature of the State has no power to limit their right as proposed in this statute. All that it could properly do has been done by it with regard to the conduct of bakeries, as provided for in the other sections of the act, above set forth. These several sections provide for the inspection of the premises where the bakery is carried on, with regard to furnishing proper wash-rooms and water-closets, apart from the bake-room, also with regard to providing proper drainage, plumbing and painting; the sections, in addition, provide for the height of the ceiling, the cementing or tiling of floors, where necessary in the opinion of the factory inspector, and for other things of that nature; alterations are also provided for and are to be made where necessary in the opinion of the inspector, in order to comply with the provisions of the statute. These various sections may be wise and valid regulations, and they certainly go to the full extent of providing for the cleanliness and the healthiness, so far as possible, of the quarters in which bakeries are to be conducted. Adding to all these requirements, a prohibition to enter into any contract of labor in a bakery for more than a certain number of hours a week, is, in our judgment, so wholly beside the matter of a proper, reasonable and fair provision, as to run counter to that liberty of person and of free contract provided for in the Federal Constitution.

It was further urged on the argument that restricting the hours of labor in the case of bakers was valid because it tended to cleanliness on the part of the workers, as a man was more apt to be cleanly when not overworked, and if cleanly then his "output" was also more likely to be so. What has already been said applies with equal force to this contention. We do not admit the reasoning to be sufficient to justify the claimed right of such interference. The State in that case would assume the position of a supervisor, or pater familias, over every act of the individual, and its right of governmental interference with his hours of labor, his hours of exercise, the character thereof, and the extent to which it shall be carried would be recognized and upheld. In our judgment it is not possible in fact to discover the connection between the number of hours a baker may work in the bakery and the healthful quality of the bread made by the workman. The connection, if any exists, is too shadowy and thin to build any argument for the interference of the legislature. If the man works ten hours a day it is all right, but if ten and a half or eleven his health is in danger and his bread may be unhealthful, and, therefore, he shall not be permitted to do it. This, we think, is unreasonable and entirely arbitrary. When assertions such as we have adverted to become necessary in order to give, if possible, a plausible foundation for the contention that the law is a "health law," it gives rise to at least a suspicion that there was some other motive dominating the legislature than the purpose to subserve the public health or welfare.

This interference on the part of the legislatures of the several States with the ordinary trades and occupations of the people seems to be on the increase. In the Supreme Court of New York, in the case of People v. Beattie, Appellate Division, First Department, decided in 1904, 89 N.Y. Supp. 193, a statute regulating the trade of horseshoeing, and requiring the person practicing such trade to be examined and to obtain a certificate from a board of examiners and file the same with the clerk of the county wherein the person proposes to practice such trade, was held invalid, as an arbitrary interference with personal liberty and private property without due process of law. The attempt was made, unsuccessfully, to justify it as a health law.

The same kind of a statute was held invalid (In re Aubry) by the Supreme Court of Washington in December, 1904, 78 Pac. Rep. 900. The court held that the act deprived citizens of their liberty and property without due process of law and denied to them the equal protection of the laws. It also held that the trade of a horseshoer is not a subject of regulation under the police power of the State, as a business concerning and directly affecting the health, welfare or comfort of its inhabitants; and that therefore a law which provided for the examination and registration of horseshoers in certain cities was unconstitutional, as an illegitimate exercise of the police power.

The Supreme Court of Illinois in Bessette v. People, 193 Illinois, 334, also held that a law of the same nature, providing for the regulation and licensing of horseshoers, was unconstitutional as an illegal interference with the liberty of the individual in adopting and pursuing such calling as he may choose, subject only to the restraint necessary to secure the common welfare. See also Godcharles v. Wigeman, 113 Pa. St. 431, 437; Low v. Rees Printing Co., 41 Nebraska, 127, 145. In these cases the courts upheld the right of free contract and the right to purchase and sell labor upon such terms as the parties may agree to.

It is impossible for us to shut our eyes to the fact that many of the laws of this character, while passed under what is claimed to be the police power for the purpose of protecting the public health or welfare, are, in reality, passed from other motives. We are justified in saying so when, from the character of the law and the subject upon which it legislates, it is apparent that the public health or welfare bears but the most remote relation to the law. The purpose of a statute must be determined from the natural and legal effect of the language employed; and whether it is or is not repugnant to the Constitution of the United States must be determined from the natural effect of such statutes when put into operation, and not from their proclaimed purpose. Minnesota v. Barber, 136 U.S. 313; Brimmer v. Rebman, 138 U.S. 78. The court looks beyond the mere letter of the law in such cases. Yick Wo v. Hopkins, 118 U.S. 356.

It is manifest to us that the limitation of the hours of labor as provided for in this section of the statute under which the indictment was found, and the plaintiff in error convicted, has no such direct relation to and no such substantial effect upon the health of the employé, as to justify us in regarding the section as really a health law. It seems to us that the real object and purpose were simply to regulate the hours of labor between the master and his employés (all being men, sui juris), in a private business, not dangerous in any degree to morals or in any real and substantial degree, to the health of the employés. Under such circumstances the freedom of master and employé to contract with each other in relation to their employment, and in defining the same, cannot be prohibited or interfered with, without violating the Federal Constitution.

The judgment of the Court of Appeals of New York as well as that of the

Supreme Court and of the County Court of Oneida County must be reversed and the case remanded to the County Court for further proceedings not inconsistent with this opinion.

Reversed.

Adkins et al., Constituting the Minimum Wage Board of the District of Columbia, *v.* Children's Hospital of the District of Columbia

261 U.S. 525, 43 S.Ct. 394, 67 L.Ed. 785 (1923)

APPEALS FROM THE COURT OF APPEALS OF THE DISTRICT OF COLUMBIA.

Argued March 14, 1923.—Decided April 9, 1923.

. . .

APPEALS from decrees of the Court of Appeals of the District of Columbia, affirming two decrees, entered, on mandate from that court, by the Supreme Court of the District, permanently enjoining the appellants from enforcing orders fixing minimum wages under the District of Columbia Minimum Wage Act.

MR. JUSTICE SUTHERLAND delivered the opinion of the Court.

The question presented for determination by these appeals is the constitutionality of the Act of September 19, 1918, providing for the fixing of minimum wages for women and children in the District of Columbia. 40 Stat. 960, c. 174.

The act provides for a board of three members, to be constituted, as far as practicable, so as to be equally representative of employers, employees, and the public. The board is authorized to have public hearings, at which persons interested in the matter being investigated may appear and testify, to administer oaths, issue subpoenas requiring the attendance of witnesses and production of books, etc., and to make rules and regulations for carrying the act into effect.

By § 8 the board is authorized—

> "(1), To investigate and ascertain the wages of women and minors in the different occupations in which they are employed in the District of Columbia; (2), to examine, through any member or authorized representative, any book, pay roll or other record of any employer of women or minors that in any way appertains to or has a bearing upon the question of wages of any such women or minors; and (3), to require from such employer full and true statements of the wages paid to all women and minors in his employment."

And by § 9, "to ascertain and declare, in the manner hereinafter provided, the following things: (a), Standards of minimum wages for women in any occupation within the District of Columbia, and what wages are inadequate to supply the necessary cost of living to any such women workers to maintain them in good health and to protect their morals; and (b), standards of minimum wages for minors in any occupation within the District of Columbia, and what wages are unreasonably low for any such minor workers."

The act then provides (§ 10) that if the board, after investigation, is of opinion that any substantial number of women workers in any occupation are receiving wages inadequate to supply them with the necessary cost of living, maintain them in health and protect their morals, a conference may be called to consider and inquire into and report on the subject investigated, the conference to be equally representative of employers and employees in such occupation and of the public, and to include one or more members of the board.

The conference is required to make and transmit to the board a report including, among other things, "recommendations as to standards of minimum wages for women workers in the occupation under inquiry and as to what wages are inadequate to supply the necessary cost of living to women workers in such occupation and to maintain them in health and to protect their morals." § 11.

The board is authorized (§ 12) to consider and review these recommendations and to approve or disapprove any or all of them. If it approve any recommendations it must give public notice of its intention and hold a public hearing at which the persons interested will be heard. After such hearing, the board is authorized to make such order as to it may appear necessary to carry into effect the recommendations, and to require all employers in the occupation affected to comply therewith. It is made unlawful for any such employer to violate in this regard any provision of the order or to employ any woman worker at lower wages than are thereby permitted.

There is a provision (§ 13) under which the board may issue a special license to a woman whose earning capacity "has been impaired by age or otherwise," authorizing her employment at less than the minimum wages fixed under the act.

All questions of fact (§ 17) are to be determined by the board, from whose decision there is no appeal; but an appeal is allowed on questions of law.

Any violation of the act (§ 18) by an employer or his agent or by corporate agents is declared to be a misdemeanor, punishable by fine and imprisonment.

Finally, after some further provisions not necessary to be stated, it is declared (§ 23) that the purposes of the act are "to protect the women and minors of the District from conditions detrimental to their health and morals, resulting from wages which are inadequate to maintain decent standards of living; and the Act in each of its provisions and in its entirety shall be interpreted to effectuate these purposes."

The appellee in the first case is a corporation maintaining a hospital for children in the District. It employs a large number of women in various capacities, with whom it had agreed upon rates of wages and compensation satisfactory to such employees, but which in some instances were less than the minimum wage fixed by an order of the board made in pursuance of the act. The women with whom appellee had so contracted were all of full age and under no legal disability. The instant suit was brought by the appellee in the Supreme Court of the District to restrain the board from enforcing or attempting to enforce its order on the ground that the same was in contravention of the Constitution, and particularly the due process clause of the Fifth Amendment.

In the second case the appellee, a woman twenty-one years of age, was employed by the Congress Hall Hotel Company as an elevator operator, at a salary of $35 per month and two meals a day. She alleges that the work was light and healthful, the hours short, with surroundings clean and moral, and that she was anxious to continue it for the compensation she was receiving and that she did not earn more. Her services were satisfactory to the Hotel Company and it would have been glad to retain her but was obliged to dispense with her services by reason of the order of the board and on account of the penalties prescribed by the act. The wages received by this appellee were the best she was able to obtain for any work she was capable of performing and the enforcement of the order, she alleges, deprived her of such employment and wages. She further averred that she could not secure any other position at which she could make a living, with as good physical and moral surroundings, and earn as good wages, and that she was desirous of continuing and would continue the employment but for the order of the board. An injunction was prayed as in the other case.

The Supreme Court of the District denied the injunction and dismissed the bill in each case. Upon appeal the Court of Appeals by a majority first affirmed and subsequently, on a rehearing, reversed the trial court. Upon the first argument a justice of the District Supreme Court was called in to take the place of one of the Appellate Court justices, who was ill. Application for rehearing was made and, by the court as thus constituted, was denied. Subsequently, and during the term, a rehearing was granted by an order concurred in by two of the Appellate Court justices, one being the justice whose place on the prior occasion had been filled by the Supreme Court member. Upon the rehearing thus granted, the Court of Appeals, rejecting the first opinion, held the act in question to be unconstitutional and reversed the decrees of the trial court. Thereupon the cases were remanded, and the trial court entered decrees in pursuance of the mandate, declaring the act in question to be unconstitutional and granting permanent injunctions. Appeals to the Court of Appeals followed and the decrees of the trial court were affirmed. It is from these final decrees that the cases come here.

Upon this state of facts the jurisdiction of the lower court to grant a rehearing, after first denying it, is challenged. We do not deem it necessary to consider the matter farther than to say that we are here dealing with the second appeals, while the proceedings complained of occurred upon the first appeals. That the lower court could properly entertain the second appeals and decide the cases does not admit of doubt; and this the appellants virtually conceded by having themselves invoked the jurisdiction. See Rooker v. Fidelity Trust Co., ante, 114.

We come then, at once, to the substantive question involved.

The judicial duty of passing upon the constitutionality of an act of Congress is one of great gravity and delicacy. The statute here in question has successfully borne the scrutiny of the legislative branch of the government, which, by enacting it, has affirmed its validity; and that determination must be given great weight. This Court, by an unbroken line of decisions from CHIEF JUSTICE MARSHALL to the present day, has steadily adhered to the rule that every possible presumption is in favor of the validity of an act of Congress until overcome beyond rational doubt.

But if by clear and indubitable demonstration a statute be opposed to the Constitution we have no choice but to say so. The Constitution, by its own terms, is the supreme law of the land, emanating from the people, the repository of ultimate sovereignty under our form of government. A congressional statute, on the other hand, is the act of an agency of this sovereign authority and if it conflict with the Constitution must fall; for that which is not supreme must yield to that which is. To hold it invalid (if it be invalid) is a plain exercise of the judicial power—that power vested in courts to enable them to administer justice according to law. From the authority to ascertain and determine the law in a given case, there necessarily results, in case of conflict, the duty to declare and enforce the rule of the supreme law and reject that of an inferior act of legislation which, transcending the Constitution, is of no effect and binding on no one. This is not the exercise of a substantive power to review and nullify acts of Congress, for no such substantive power exists. It is simply a necessary concomitant of the power to hear and dispose of a case or controversy properly before the court, to the determination of which must be brought the test and measure of the law.

The statute now under consideration is attacked upon the ground that it authorizes an unconstitutional interference with the freedom of contract included within the guaranties of the due process clause of the Fifth Amendment. That the right to contract about one's affairs is a part of the liberty of the individual protected by this clause, is settled by the decisions of this Court and is no longer open to question. Allgeyer v. Louisiana, 165 U.S. 578, 591; New York Life Insurance Co. v. Dodge, 246 U.S. 357, 373–374; Coppage v. Kansas, 236 U.S. 1, 10, 14; Adair v. United States, 208 U.S. 161; Lochner v. New York, 198 U.S. 45; Butchers' Union Co. v. Crescent City Co., 111 U.S. 746; Muller v. Oregon, 208 U.S. 412, 421. Within this liberty are contracts of employment of labor. In making such contracts, generally speaking, the parties have an equal right to obtain from each other the best terms they can as the result of private bargaining.

In Adair v. United States, supra, MR. JUSTICE HARLAN (pp. 174, 175), speaking for the Court, said:

> "The right of a person to sell his labor upon such terms as he deems proper is, in its essence, the same as the right of the purchaser of labor to prescribe the conditions upon which he will accept such labor from the person offering to sell. . . . In all such particulars the employer and employé have equality of right, and any legislation that disturbs that equality is an arbitrary interference with the liberty of contract which no government can legally justify in a free land."

In Coppage v. Kansas, supra (p. 14), this Court, speaking through MR. JUSTICE PITNEY, said:

> "Included in the right of personal liberty and the right of private property—partaking of the nature of each—is the right to make contracts for the acquisition of property. Chief among such contracts is that of personal employment, by which labor and other services are exchanged for money or other forms of property. If this

right be struck down or arbitrarily interfered with, there is a substantial impairment of liberty in the long-established constitutional sense. The right is as essential to the laborer as to the capitalist, to the poor as to the rich; for the vast majority of persons have no other honest way to begin to acquire property, save by working for money.

"An interference with this liberty so serious as that now under consideration, and so disturbing of equality of right, must be deemed to be arbitrary, unless it be supportable as a reasonable exercise of the police power of the State."

There is, of course, no such thing as absolute freedom of contract. It is subject to a great variety of restraints. But freedom of contract is, nevertheless, the general rule and restraint the exception; and the exercise of legislative authority to abridge it can be justified only by the existence of exceptional circumstances. Whether these circumstances exist in the present case constitutes the question to be answered. It will be helpful to this end to review some of the decisions where the interference has been upheld and consider the grounds upon which they rest.

(1) *Those dealing with statutes fixing rates and charges to be exacted by businesses impressed with a public interest. There are many cases, but it is sufficient to cite* Munn v. Illinois, 94 U.S. 113. The power here rests upon the ground that where property is devoted to a public use the owner thereby, in effect, grants to the public an interest in the use which may be controlled by the public for the common good to the extent of the interest thus created. It is upon this theory that these statutes have been upheld and, it may be noted in passing, so upheld even in respect of their incidental and injurious or destructive effect upon preexisting contracts. See Louisville & Nashville R.R. Co. v. Mottley, 219 U.S. 467. In the case at bar the statute does not depend upon the existence of a public interest in any business to be affected, and this class of cases may be laid aside as inapplicable.

(2) *Statutes relating to contracts for the performance of public work.* Atkin v. Kansas, 191 U.S. 207; Heim v. McCall, 239 U.S. 175; Ellis v. United States, 206 U.S. 246. These cases sustain such statutes as depending, not upon the right to condition private contracts, but upon the right of the government to prescribe the conditions upon which it will permit work of a public character to be done for it, or, in the case of a State, for its municipalities. We may, therefore, in like manner, dismiss these decisions from consideration as inapplicable.

(3) *Statutes prescribing the character, methods and time for payment of wages.* Under this head may be included McLean v. Arkansas, 211 U.S. 539, sustaining a state statute requiring coal to be measured for payment of miners' wages before screening; Knoxville Iron Co. v. Harbison, 183 U.S. 13, sustaining a Tennessee statute requiring the redemption in cash of store orders issued in payment of wages; Erie R.R. Co. v. Williams, 233 U.S. 685, upholding a statute regulating the time within which wages shall be paid to employees in certain specified industries; and other cases sustaining statutes of like import and effect. In none of the statutes thus sustained, was the liberty of employer or employee to fix the amount of wages the one was willing to pay and the other willing to receive interfered with. Their tendency and purpose was to prevent unfair and perhaps fraudulent methods in

the payment of wages and in no sense can they be said to be, or to furnish a precedent for, wage-fixing statutes.

(4) *Statutes fixing hours of labor.* It is upon this class that the greatest emphasis is laid in argument and therefore, and because such cases approach most nearly the line of principle applicable to the statute here involved, we shall consider them more at length. In some instances the statute limited the hours of labor for men in certain occupations and in others it was confined in its application to women. No statute has thus far been brought to the attention of this Court which by its terms, applied to all occupations. In Holden v. Hardy, 169 U.S. 366, the Court considered an act of the Utah legislature, restricting the hours of labor in mines and smelters. This statute was sustained as a legitimate exercise of the police power, on the ground that the legislature had determined that these particular employments, when too long pursued, were injurious to the health of the employees, and that, as there were reasonable grounds for supporting this determination on the part of the legislature, its decision in that respect was beyond the reviewing power of the federal courts.

That this constituted the basis of the decision is emphasized by the subsequent decision in Lochner v. New York, 198 U.S. 45, reviewing a state statute which restricted the employment of all persons in bakeries to ten hours in any one day. The Court referred to Holden v. Hardy, supra, and, declaring it to be inapplicable, held the statute unconstitutional as an unreasonable, unnecessary and arbitrary interference with the liberty of contract and therefore void under the Constitution.

MR. JUSTICE PECKHAM, speaking for the Court (p. 56), said:

> "It must, of course, be conceded that there is a limit to the valid exercise of the police power by the State. There is no dispute concerning this general proposition. Otherwise the Fourteenth Amendment would have no efficacy and the legislatures of the States would have unbounded power, and it would be enough to say that any piece of legislation was enacted to conserve the morals, the health or the safety of the people; such legislation would be valid, no matter how absolutely without foundation the claim might be. The claim of the police power would be a mere pretext—become another and delusive name for the supreme sovereignty of the State to be exercised free from constitutional restraint."

And again (pp. 57–58):

> "It is a question of which of two powers or rights shall prevail—the power of the State to legislate or the right of the individual to liberty of person and freedom of contract. The mere assertion that the subject relates though but in a remote degree to the public health does not necessarily render the enactment valid. The act must have a more direct relation, as a means to an end, and the end itself must be appropriate and legitimate, before an act can be held to be valid which interferes with the general right of an individual to be free in his person and in his power to contract in relation to his own labor."

Coming then directly to the statute (p. 58), the Court said:

> "We think the limit of the police power has been reached and passed in this case. There is, in our judgment, no reasonable foundation for holding this to be necessary or appropriate as a health law to safeguard the public health or the health of the individuals who are following the trade of a baker. If this statute be valid, and if, therefore, a proper case is made out in which to deny the right of an individual, sui juris, as employer or employé, to make contracts for the labor of the latter under the protection of the provisions of the Federal Constitution, there would seem to be no length to which legislation of this nature might not go."

And, after pointing out the unreasonable range to which the principle of the statute might be extended, the Court said (p. 60):

> "It is also urged, pursuing the same line of argument, that it is to the interest of the State that its population should be strong and robust, and therefore any legislation which may be said to tend to make people healthy must be valid as health laws, enacted under the police power. If this be a valid argument and a justification for this kind of legislation, it follows that the protection of the Federal Constitution from undue interference with liberty of person and freedom of contract is visionary, wherever the law is sought to be justified as a valid exercise of the police power. Scarcely any law but might find shelter under such assumptions, and conduct, properly so called, as well as contract, would come under the restrictive sway of the legislature."

And further (p. 61):

> "Statutes of the nature of that under review, limiting the hours in which grown and intelligent men may labor to earn their living, are mere meddlesome interferences with the rights of the individual, and they are not saved from condemnation by the claim that they are passed in the exercise of the police power and upon the subject of the health of the individual whose rights are interfered with, unless there be some fair ground, reasonable in and of itself, to say that there is material danger to the public health or to the health of the employés, if the hours of labor are not curtailed."

Subsequent cases in this Court have been distinguished from that decision, but the principles therein stated have never been disapproved.

In Bunting v. Oregon, 243 U.S. 426, a state statute forbidding the employment of any person in any mill, factory or manufacturing establishment more than ten hours in any one day, and providing payment for overtime not exceeding three hours in any one day at the rate of time and a half of the regular wage, was sustained on the ground that, since the state legislature and State Supreme Court had found such a law necessary for the preservation of the health of employees in these industries, this Court would accept their judgment, in the absence of facts to support the contrary conclusion. The law was attacked on the ground that it constituted an attempt to fix wages, but that contention was rejected and the law sustained as a reasonable regulation of hours of service.

Wilson v. New, 243 U.S. 332, involved the validity of the so-called Adamson Law, which established an eight-hour day for employees of interstate carriers for which it fixed a scale of minimum wages with proportionate increases for overtime, to be enforced, however, only for a limited period. The act was sustained primarily upon the ground that it was a regulation of a business charged with a public interest. The Court, speaking through the Chief Justice, pointed out that regarding "the private right and private interest as contradistinguished from the public interest the power exists between the parties, the employers and employees, to agree as to a standard of wages free from legislative interference" but that this did not affect the power to deal with the matter with a view to protect the public right, and then said (p. 353):

> "And this emphasizes that there is no question here of purely private right since the law is concerned only with those who are engaged in a business charged with a public interest where the subject dealt with as to all the parties is one involved in that business and which we have seen comes under the control of the right to regulate to the extent that the power to do so is appropriate or relevant to the business regulated."

Moreover, in sustaining the wage feature, of the law, emphasis was put upon the fact (p. 345) that it was in this respect temporary "leaving the employers and employees free as to the subject of wages to govern their relations by their own agreements after the specified time." The act was not only temporary in this respect, but it was passed to meet a sudden and great emergency. This feature of the law was sustained principally because the parties, for the time being, could not or would not agree. Here they are forbidden to agree.

The same principle was applied in the Rent Cases (Block v. Hirsh, 256 U.S. 135, and Marcus Brown Holding Co. v. Feldman, 256 U.S. 170), where this Court sustained the legislative power to fix rents as between landlord and tenant upon the ground that the operation of the statutes was temporary to tide over an emergency and that the circumstances were such as to clothe "the letting of buildings . . . with a public interest so great as to justify regulation by law." The Court said (p. 157):

> "The regulation is put and justified only as a temporary measure [citing Wilson v. New, supra]. A limit in time, to tide over a passing trouble, well may justify a law that could not be upheld as a permanent change."

In a subsequent case, Pennsylvania Coal Co. v. Mahon, 260 U.S. 393, 416, this Court, after saying "We are in danger of forgetting that a strong public desire to improve the public condition is not enough to warrant achieving the desire by a shorter cut than the constitutional way of paying for the change," pointed out that the Rent Cases dealt with laws intended to meet a temporary emergency and "went to the verge of the law."

In addition to the cases cited above, there are the decisions of this Court dealing with laws especially relating to hours of labor for women: Muller v.

Oregon, 208 U.S. 412; Riley v. Massachusetts, 232 U.S. 671; Miller v. Wilson, 236 U.S. 373; Bosley v. McLaughlin, 236 U.S. 385.

In the Muller Case the validity of an Oregon statute, forbidding the employment of any female in certain industries more than ten hours during any one day was upheld. The decision proceeded upon the theory that the difference between the sexes may justify a different rule respecting hours of labor in the case of women than in the case of men. It is pointed out that these consist in differences of physical structure, especially in respect of the maternal functions, and also in the fact that historically woman has always been dependent upon man, who has established his control by superior physical strength. The cases of Riley, Miller and Bosley follow in this respect the Muller Case. But the ancient inequality of the sexes, otherwise than physical, as suggested in the Muller Case (p. 421) has continued "with diminishing intensity." In view of the great—not to say revolutionary—changes which have taken place since that utterance, in the contractual, political and civil status of women, culminating in the Nineteenth Amendment, it is not unreasonable to say that these differences have now come almost, if not quite, to the vanishing point. In this aspect of the matter, while the physical differences must be recognized in appropriate cases, and legislation fixing hours or conditions of work may properly take them into account, we cannot accept the doctrine that women of mature age, sui juris, require or may be subjected to restrictions upon their liberty of contract which could not lawfully be imposed in the case of men under similar circumstances. To do so would be to ignore all the implications to be drawn from the present day trend of legislation, as well as that of common thought and usage, by which woman is accorded emancipation from the old doctrine that she must be given special protection or be subjected to special restraint in her contractual and civil relationships. In passing, it may be noted that the instant statute applies in the case of a woman employer contracting with a woman employee as it does when the former is a man.

The essential characteristics of the statute now under consideration, which differentiate it from the laws fixing hours of labor, will be made to appear as we proceed. It is sufficient now to point out that the latter as well as the statutes mentioned under paragraph (3), deal with incidents of the employment having no necessary effect upon the heart of the contract, that is, the amount of wages to be paid and received. A law forbidding work to continue beyond a given number of hours leaves the parties free to contract about wages and thereby equalize whatever additional burdens may be imposed upon the employer as a result of the restrictions as to hours, by an adjustment in respect of the amount of wages. Enough has been said to show that the authority to fix hours of labor cannot be exercised except in respect of those occupations where work of long continued duration is detrimental to health. This Court has been careful in every case where the question has been raised, to place its decision upon this limited authority of the legislature to regulate hours of labor and to disclaim any purpose to uphold the legislation as fixing wages, thus recognizing an essential difference between the two. It seems plain that these decisions afford no real support for any form of law establishing minimum wages.

If now, in the light furnished by the foregoing exceptions to the general rule forbidding legislative interference with freedom of contract, we examine and analyze the statute in question, we shall see that it differs from them in every material respect. It is not a law dealing with any business charged with a public interest or with public work, or to meet and tide over a temporary emergency. It has nothing to do with the character, methods or periods of wage payments. It does not prescribe hours of labor or conditions under which labor is to be done. It is not for the protection of persons under legal disability or for the prevention of fraud. It is simply and exclusively a price-fixing law, confined to adult women (for we are not now considering the provisions relating to minors), who are legally as capable of contracting for themselves as men. It forbids two parties having lawful capacity—under penalties as to the employer—to freely contract with one another in respect of the price for which one shall render service to the other in a purely private employment where both are willing, perhaps anxious, to agree, even though the consequence may be to oblige one to surrender a desirable engagement and the other to dispense with the services of a desirable employee. The price fixed by the board need have no relation to the capacity or earning power of the employee, the number of hours which may happen to constitute the day's work, the character of the place where the work is to be done, or the circumstances or surroundings of the employment; and, while it has no other basis to support its validity than the assumed necessities of the employee, it takes no account of any independent resources she may have. It is based wholly on the opinions of the members of the board and their advisers—perhaps an average of their opinions, if they do not precisely agree—as to what will be necessary to provide a living for a woman, keep her in health and preserve her morals. It applies to any and every occupation in the District, without regard to its nature or the character of the work.

The standard furnished by the statute for the guidance of the board is so vague as to be impossible of practical application with any reasonable degree of accuracy. What is sufficient to supply the necessary cost of living for a woman worker and maintain her in good health and protect her morals is obviously not a precise or unvarying sum—not even approximately so. The amount will depend upon a variety of circumstances: the individual temperament, habits of thrift, care, ability to buy necessaries intelligently, and whether the woman live alone or with her family. To those who practice economy, a given sum will afford comfort, while to those of contrary habit the same sum will be wholly inadequate. The cooperative economies of the family group are not taken into account though they constitute an important consideration in estimating the cost of living, for it is obvious that the individual expense will be less in the case of a member of a family than in the case of one living alone. The relation between earnings and morals is not capable of standardization. It cannot be shown that well-paid women safeguard their morals more carefully than those who are poorly paid. Morality rests upon other considerations than wages; and there is, certainly, no such prevalent connection between the two as to justify a broad attempt to adjust the latter with reference to the former. As a means of safeguarding morals the attempted classification, in our opinion, is without reasonable basis. No distinction can be made between women who work for others and those who do not; nor is there ground for distinction between women and men, for, certainly, if women require a minimum wage to preserve their morals men require it to preserve their honesty. For these reasons, and others which might be stated, the inquiry in respect of the necessary cost of living and of the income necessary to preserve health and morals, presents an individual and not a composite question, and must be answered for each individual considered by herself and not by a general formula prescribed by a statutory bureau.

This uncertainty of the statutory standard is demonstrated by a consideration of certain orders of the board already made. These orders fix the sum to be paid to a woman employed in a place where food is served or in a mercantile establishment, at $16.50 per week; in a printing establishment, at $15.50 per week; and in a laundry, at $15 per week, with a provision reducing this to $9 in the case of a beginner. If a woman employed to serve food requires a minimum of $16.50 per week, it is hard to understand how the same woman working in a printing establishment or in a laundry is to get on with an income lessened by from $1 to $7.50 per week. The board probably found it impossible to follow the indefinite standard of the statute, and brought other and different factors into the problem; and this goes far in the direction of demonstrating the fatal uncertainty of the act, an infirmity which, in our opinion, plainly exists.

The law takes account of the necessities of only one party to the contract. It ignores the necessities of the employer by compelling him to pay not less than a certain sum, not only whether the employee is capable of earning it, but irrespective of the ability of his business to sustain the burden, generously leaving him, of course, the privilege of abandoning his business as an alternative for going on at a loss. Within the limits of the minimum sum, he is precluded, under penalty of fine and imprisonment, from adjusting compensation to the differing merits of his employees. It compels him to pay at least the sum fixed in any event, because the employee needs it, but requires no service of equivalent value from the employee. It therefore undertakes to solve but one-half of the problem. The other half is the establishment of a corresponding standard of efficiency, and this forms no part of the policy of the legislation, although in practice the former half without the latter must lead to ultimate failure, in accordance with the inexorable law that no one can continue indefinitely to take out more than he puts in without ultimately exhausting the supply. The law is not confined to the great and powerful employers but embraces those whose bargaining power may be as weak as that of the employee. It takes no account of periods of stress and business depression, of crippling losses, which may leave the employer himself without adequate means of livelihood. To the extent that the sum fixed exceeds the fair value of the services rendered, it amounts to a compulsory exaction from the employer for the support of a partially indigent person, for whose condition there rests upon him no peculiar responsibility, and therefore, in effect, arbitrarily shifts to his shoulders a burden which, if it belongs to anybody, belongs to society as a whole.

The feature of this statute which, perhaps more than any other, puts upon it the stamp of invalidity is that it exacts from the employer an arbitrary payment for a purpose and upon a basis having no causal connection with his business, or the contract or the work the employee engages to do. The declared basis, as already pointed out, is not the value of the service rendered, but the extraneous circumstance that the employee needs to get a prescribed sum of money to insure her subsistence, health and morals. The ethical right of every worker, man or woman, to a living wage may be conceded. One of the declared and important purposes of trade organizations is to secure it. And with that principle and with every legitimate effort to realize it in fact, no one can quarrel; but the fallacy of the proposed method of attaining it is that it assumes that every employer is bound at all events to furnish it. The moral requirement implicit in every contract of employment, viz, that the amount to be paid and the service to be rendered shall bear to each other some relation of just equivalence, is completely ignored. The necessities of the employee are alone considered and these arise outside of the employment, are the same when there is no employment, and as great in one occupation as in another. Certainly the employer by paying a fair equivalent for the service rendered, though not sufficient to support the employee, has neither caused nor contributed to her poverty. On the contrary, to the extent of what he pays he has relieved it. In principle, there can be no difference between the case of selling labor and the case of selling goods. If one goes to the butcher, the baker or grocer to buy food, he is morally entitled to obtain the worth of his money but he is not entitled to more. If what he gets is worth what he pays he is not justified in demanding more simply because he needs more; and the shopkeeper, having dealt fairly and honestly in that transaction, is not concerned in any peculiar sense with the question of his customer's necessities. Should a statute undertake to vest in a commission power to determine the quantity of food necessary for individual support and require the shopkeeper, if he sell to the individual at all, to furnish that quantity at not more than a fixed maximum, it would undoubtedly fall before the constitutional test. The fallacy of any argument in support of the validity of such a statute would be quickly exposed. The argument in support of that now being considered is equally fallacious, though the weakness of it may not be so plain. A statute requiring an employer to pay in money, to pay at prescribed and regular intervals, to pay the value of the services rendered, even to pay with fair relation to the extent of the benefit obtained from the service, would be understandable. But a statute which prescribes payment without regard to any of these things and solely with relation to circumstances apart from the contract of employment, the business affected by it and the work done under it, is so clearly the product of a naked, arbitrary exercise of power that it cannot be allowed to stand under the Constitution of the United States.

We are asked, upon the one hand, to consider the fact that several States have adopted similar statutes, and we are invited, upon the other hand, to give weight to the fact that three times as many States, presumably as well informed and as anxious to promote the health and morals of their people, have refrained from enacting such legislation. We have also been furnished with a large number of printed opinions approving the policy of the minimum wage, and our own reading has disclosed a large number to the contrary. These are all proper enough for the consideration of the lawmaking bodies, since their tendency is to establish the desirability or undesirability of the legislation; but they reflect no legitimate light upon the question of its validity, and that is what we are called upon to decide. The elucidation of that question cannot be aided by counting heads.

It is said that great benefits have resulted from the operation of such statutes, not alone in the District of Columbia but in the several States, where they have been in force. A mass of reports, opinions of special observers and students of the subject, and the like, has been brought before us in support of this statement, all of which we have found interesting but only mildly persuasive. That the earnings of women now are greater than they were formerly and that conditions affecting women have become better in other respects may be conceded, but convincing indications of the logical relation of these desirable changes to the law in question are significantly lacking. They may be, and quite probably are, due to other causes. We cannot close our eyes to the notorious fact that earnings everywhere in all occupations have greatly increased—not alone in States where the minimum wage law obtains but in the country generally—quite as much or more among men as among women and in occupations outside the reach of the law as in those governed by it. No real test of the economic value of the law can be had during periods of maximum employment, when general causes keep wages up to or above the minimum; that will come in periods of depression and struggle for employment when the efficient will be employed at the minimum rate while the less capable may not be employed at all.

Finally, it may be said that if, in the interest of the public welfare, the police power may be invoked to justify the fixing of a minimum wage, it may, when the public welfare is thought to require it, be invoked to justify a maximum wage. The power to fix high wages connotes, by like course of reasoning, the power to fix low wages. If, in the face of the guaranties of the Fifth Amendment, this form of legislation shall be legally justified, the field for the operation of the police power will have been widened to a great and dangerous degree. If, for example, in the opinion of future lawmakers, wages in the building trades shall become so high as to preclude people of ordinary means from building and owning homes, an authority which sustains the minimum wage will be invoked to support a maximum wage for building laborers and artisans, and the same argument which has been here urged to strip the employer of his constitutional liberty of contract in one direction will be utilized to strip the employee of his constitutional liberty of contract in the opposite direction. A wrong decision does not end with itself: it is a precedent, and, with the swing of sentiment, its bad influence may run from one extremity of the arc to the other.

It has been said that legislation of the kind now under review is required in the interest of social justice, for whose ends freedom of contract may lawfully be subjected to restraint. The liberty of the individual to do as he pleases, even in innocent matters, is not absolute. It must frequently yield to the common good, and the line beyond which the power of interference may not be pressed is neither definite nor unalterable but may be made to move, within limits not well defined, with changing need and circumstance. Any attempt to fix a rigid boundary would be unwise as well as futile. But, nevertheless, there are limits to the power, and when these have been passed, it becomes the plain duty of the courts in the proper exercise of their authority to so declare. To sustain the individual freedom of action contemplated by the Constitution, is not to strike down the common good but to exalt it; for surely the good of society as a whole cannot be better served than by the preservation against arbitrary restraint of the liberties of its constituent members.

It follows from what has been said that the act in question passes the limit prescribed by the Constitution, and, accordingly, the decrees of the court below are

Affirmed.]

CHAPTER 5

Contents

First Amendment

Congress shall make no law respecting the establishment of religion, or prohibiting the free exercise thereof; or abridging the freedom of speech, or of the press; or the right of people peacefully to assemble, and to petition the Government for redress of grievances.

§ 5.1 Introduction

To most knowledgeable people, the First Amendment's prohibition against the denial of freedom of speech is one of the fundamental values of American society. It is a right that is taken for granted.

In its most fundamental sense, it does not give a person the right to incite a riot, or to urge another person to commit a crime, or to unreasonably interfere with pedestrian or vehicular traffic by speaking and causing a crowd to gather, or to establish and practice a religion which causes the death of its believers through religious rituals. In short, we might say that the rights of the First Amendment, given to the people in the United States Constitution, are conditional rights which are to be balanced against the overall good of the orderly administration of government to which we aspire.

There is a conflict with respect to the freedom of the press to publish information and the right of a defendant to a fair and orderly trial. When a particularly newsworthy crime is committed, the newspapers are known to report the details of the crime and the efforts of law enforcement to bring the malefactor to the bar of justice. There have been cases where the reporting was not accurate, or facts which might be allegedly relevant were reported which would not be admissible in evidence in court. When an alleged perpetrator is apprehended and brought to trial, it becomes exceedingly difficult to impanel an impartial jury to try the facts of the case on the evidence to be admitted at the trial. The attorney for the defendant will conduct a "voir dire" in some state courts where he may be permitted to ask questions of the prospective jurors directly or, as in the federal system or some other states, he may recommend questions to the presiding judge to ask the prospective jurors questions relating to their possible prejudices against the defendant or whether they have read or heard anything about the case from the newspapers or other sources. If the case has been widely reported in the news media and the prospective juror indicates that he has heard nothing about the case, one might reasonably question the prospective juror's awareness and intelligence. If, on the other hand, s/he responds that s/he has heard about the case from reports in the news media, the defendant's right to a fair trial may be in jeopardy, depending upon the effect that the news reports would have on the reasoning processes of the prospective jurors. One such case occurred in Murphy v. Florida, 421 U.S. 794, 95 S.Ct. 203, 44 L.Ed.2d 589 (1975), where the Supreme Court of the United States held in an 8–1 decision that the defendant, who received widespread publicity as "Murph, the Surf," was not denied a fair trial even though "members of the jury had learned from news accounts about a prior felony conviction or certain facts about the crime with which he was charged." However, an earlier case, Sheppard v. Maxwell, 384 U.S. 333, 86 S.Ct. 1507, 16 L.Ed.2d 600 (1966), was distinguished by the court in that in the Sheppard case convictions were "obtained in a trial atmosphere that had been utterly corrupted by press coverage," and the court went on to say that this case as well as Rideau v. Louisiana, 373 U.S. 723, 83 S.Ct. 1417 (1963), and Estes v. Texas, 381 U.S. 532, 85 S.Ct. 1628 (1965), cannot be made to stand for the proposition that the juror exposure to information about a state's defendant's prior convictions or to news accounts of the crime with which he is charged alone presumptively deprives the defendant of due process. In the Murphy case, the court found that the defendant failed "to demonstrate" the actual existence of such an opinion in the mind of the juror as will raise the presumption of partiality. The court further found no evidence in the record to suggest that the general atmosphere in the community or the courtroom was sufficiently inflammatory to deprive the defendant of a fair trial.

While this case represents the present law, it would appear that a police department or representative thereof who gives out too much information with respect to the facts of a crime or does what is commonly referred to as "trying the case in the newspapers" is treading on very marshy ground if it is the intent of the department to get a conviction which will be upheld in the appellate courts.

Peaceful demonstrations may be turned into riots when hecklers in the crowd use their "right of free speech" to prevent others from exercising their right to be heard. Implied with the right of free speech is the right to be heard. When this occurs, it is incumbent upon the police to do all in their power to separate the groups into different locations so that all can speak and be heard. By the absorption doctrine, the First Amendment guarantees were extended to state government action through the due process clause of the Fourteenth Amendment. Gitlow v. N.Y., 268 U.S. 652, 45 S.Ct. 625, 69 L.Ed. 1138 (1925). The Fourteenth Amendment will be treated more thoroughly in Chapter 11, infra.

§ 5.2 Police Power

The term "police power" as it relates to governmental authority has been interpreted as the power "to prescribe regulations to promote the health, peace, morals, education and good order of the people, and to legislate so as to increase the industries of the state, develop its resources, and add to its wealth and prosperity." Barbier v. Connolly, 113 U.S. 27, 5 S.Ct. 357, 28 L.Ed. 923 (1885).

It will be noted that the federal government is one of delegated powers which were so delegated by the colonies. Those powers not delegated to the federal government were expressly retained by the states through the Tenth Amendment, which reads:

> *The powers not delegated to the United States by the Constitution, nor prohibited by it to the States, are reserved to the States respectively, or to the people.*

There was no delegation of the police power to the United States and hence the police power is one of those powers retained by the states. Therefore, we have a proliferation of state law enforcement agencies, each originally having autonomous control and direction.

It is said by some that there are over forty thousand independent governmental police departments in the United States. It is quite evident that such a structure for law enforcement is not a practical solution to the criminal justice problems confronting the United States today. Many small departments with their own power structure and their duplication of services with state or county law enforcement make for an almost impossible and wasteful system of law enforcement in this country. The advent of the airplane, the fast automobile equipped with citizens band radio, the fast-moving boat, the increase in white-collar and computer-related crime, and the web of organized crime into legitimate businesses have all made the small police department incapable of properly performing its duty to prevent crime and arrest violators of law.

The Law Enforcement Assistance Administration was Congress's answer to the problem. This agency of the central government was empowered to do research in the criminal justice discipline and to turn over money to local police authorities. In return, on a quid pro quo basis, the police departments receiving this money gave up some of their autonomy to the Law Enforcement Assistance Administration. Since most local communities were hard pressed financially, the communities accepted this money.

§ 5.3 Conduct Intended to Articulate a Belief

While it is most obvious that the First Amendment guarantees of free speech and press are concerned with actually speaking or publishing, the United States Supreme Court has held other modes of expression as within the protection of this amendment. For example, the wearing of a black armband as an antiwar emblem, Tinker v. Des Moines School District, 393 U.S. 503, 89 S.Ct. 733, 21 L.Ed.2d 731 (1969), or the burning of a red flag as a symbol of opposition to organized government, Stromberg v. California, 283 U.S. 359, 51 S.Ct. 532, 75 L.Ed. 1117 (1931), and other similar cases of physical expression have been held to be protected activity under the First Amendment. However, the burning of a draft card as a symbolic form of protest to the war in Vietnam is violation of a federal statute which makes it an offense to knowingly destroy a draft card. The burning of a draft card was held to be a violation of a constitutional statute and was impermissible notwithstanding the fact that the free speech argument was invoked to aid the defendant. The court reasoned here that the government had a substantial interest unrelated to the free speech issue and this substantial issue far outweighed the right of the defendant to exercise his right of free speech in this manner. U.S. v. O'Brien, 391 U.S. 367, 88 S.Ct. 1683, 20 L.Ed.2d 672.

The relative weights of the individual's constitutional rights are thus placed theoretically on a scale of values. The right which the Supreme Court holds to be the most weighty at a given time becomes the law of the land. There is nothing in the Constitution which specifically refers to the scale of values or balancing concept but the Supreme Court has interpreted the document in this way.

There are many policy decisions involving this balancing concept which must be made by police officials in the area of free speech which might later find their way into courtrooms. To mention a few, one can think of the following:

- Who is to decide if there must be a restriction of speech and assembly and what would the proper guidelines be?
- What extent does freedom of the press have in investigating and reporting criminal activity?
- If it is lawful to picket a public building, is it also lawful to bring a large number of people to a private home of a governmental official or business executive to demonstrate in front of his home and through the residential neighborhood twenty-four hours a day?

§ 5.4 Fighting Words

The policeman confronted with free speech problems looks for guidelines to assist him/her in making a policy determination. It is difficult to present these guidelines with any degree of certainty. However, it is widely accepted that the use of "fighting words," which are very likely to cause violence, will not be tolerated. Chaplinsky v. New Hampshire, 315 U.S. 568, 62 S.Ct. 766, 86 L.Ed. 1031 (1942).

A more recent problem which will probably find its way into the United States Supreme Court is the issue of whether the National Socialist Party of America, a small group of Nazis with their office in Chicago, Illinois, should be prohibited from marching in Skokie, Illinois, which is a suburb of the City of Chicago. This group planned to march in this village, whose inhabitants of about seventy thousand people contained approximately forty thousand persons of the Jewish faith. Of these, it is reported that approximately seven thousand were survivors of the World War II Nazi Holocaust, harboring bitter memories of degradation, torture, murder, theft, rape, and systematic extermination of families and persons, young and old, both Jewish and non-Jewish.

It was quite apparent that the Nazis were looking for some inexpensive publicity by picking this locality to demonstrate and they were successful in this because the media publicized the struggle that ensued. Skokie adopted a group of ordinances requiring that no parade or assembly involving more than fifty persons could be held without giving thirty days notice in advance and furnishing a $35,000 bond to cover public liability and property damage. The ordinance also prohibited any demonstrations that would "incite violence, hatred, abuse or hostility toward a person or group of persons by reason or reference to racial, ethnic, national or religious affiliation." The governing body of Skokie was permitted to waive any of the ordinances in its discretion.

An injunction was obtained from the Illinois Circuit Court prohibiting the Nazis from demonstrating. The Nazis obtained the assistance of the American Civil Liberties Union (ACLU) because of what they termed a denial of free speech and appealed the injunction order. The Court, in a 5–4 decision, ordered the Illinois Appellate Court to rule immediately by either lifting the injunction or reviewing the case.

Pursuant to this, the Illinois Appellate Court ruled that the Nazis could march in Skokie but they could not wear or display the swastika, presumably on the grounds that the swastika was unprotected speech because its display could provoke a violent reaction (fighting words), 366 N.E.2d 347 (1977).

The case went to the Supreme Court of Illinois which reversed the Illinois Appellate Court by ruling that the display of the swastika cannot be enjoined under the "fighting words" exception to free speech. The court thought it entirely clear that the wearing of distinctive clothing could be a symbolic expression of a thought or philosophy, and it emphasized that the symbolic expression of thought falls within the free speech clause of the First Amendment and the village had the "heavy burden" of justifying the imposition of a prior restraint. The court said "... when, as here, there had been advance notice by the demonstrators so that their plans had become, as the complaint alleged 'common knowledge' and those to whom sight of the swastika banner or uniforms would be offensive 'are forewarned and need not view them.'... A speaker who gives prior notice of his message has not compelled a confrontation with those who voluntarily listen." Village of Skokie v. National Socialist Party, January 27, 1978, 373 N.E.2d 21.

§ 5.5 Speech Pure

Speech pure is speech without accompanying conduct. In Watts v. United States, 394 U.S. 705, 89 S.Ct. 1399, 22 L.Ed.2d 664 (1969), the court reversed a conviction of a defendant who stated "if they ever make me carry a rifle, the first man I want in my sights is L.B.J." He was originally convicted under a federal law penalizing one who knowingly and willfully makes a threat to the President's person. Since the defendant was not proven to have a personal intent to actually kill President Johnson, the court held that the defendant was exercising his right of free speech. This type of action has been given the name of speech pure. Another example of this form of speech pure is heard frequently at baseball games when we hear the resounding theme of "kill the umpire."

§ 5.6 Speech Plus

"Speech plus" is best exemplified by the activities of a labor picket line where the persons picketing will shout certain statements and then follow up with conduct which might be contrary to a substantial governmental interest. For example, if a picket line physically prevents persons from lawfully entering or leaving a commercial building where a labor strike is in progress, there is a substantial governmental interest to provide ingress and egress to those who wish it. Or.—Greenfield v. Central Labor Council of Portland and Vicinity, 104 Or. 236, 207 P. 168. A state may, without violating the Fourteenth Amendment, authorize its courts to enjoin acts of picketing in themselves peaceful, where such acts are enmeshed with contemporaneously violent conduct which is concededly outlawed. Ill.—Maywood Farms Co. v. Milk Wagon Drivers Union of Chicago, Local 753, 316 Ill.App. 47, 43 N.E.2d 700.

§ 5.7 Newspeople's Privilege of Freedom of Expression

While newsmen or -women have a constitutional right to freedom to print what they wish, they have no constitutional right of access to the scenes of crime or disaster when the general public is excluded. Branzburg v. Hayes, 408 U.S. 665, 92 S.Ct. 2646, 33 L.Ed.2d 626 (1972). However, it is suggested, as a practical matter, that properly qualified and identified news representatives be permitted into the cordoned area of a crime or disaster.

§ 5.8 Commercial Freedom of Expression

There have been cases where a commercial enterprise in an effort to stimulate business employs persons to stand at locations where there is heavy pedestrian traffic to hand out leaflets advertising the wares of this business. An example of this kind of conduct might occur in front of a moving-picture theater showing a pornographic film where men would hand out pamphlets to likely prospects of a nearby body-massage parlor. A police officer armed with the proper statutory authority could validly prohibit the distribution of all advertising matter on the public streets if the statute had as its prime motive that it was being used to keep the streets clean and free of litter. U.S.—Valentine v. Christensen, 316 U.S. 52, 62 S.Ct. 920, 86 L.Ed. 1262 (1942).

A so-called "head shop" contested the right of a local government to enforce an ordinance that provided a license for any establishment if it sells "any item, effect, paraphernalia, accessory or thing which is designed or marketed for use with illegal cannabis or drugs as defined by the Illinois Revised Statutes." The ordinance further required that when a license was granted, the establishment could not sell to minors under eighteen years of age and was obliged to maintain records of the sale of these items, containing, inter alia, the name, date and quantity of the items sold to each purchaser. The record was to be open to inspection by the police during business hours. Furthermore, applicants for the license and each and every employee must submit an affidavit that such person has never been convicted of a drug related offense. The case was VILLAGE OF HOFFMAN ESTATES v. FLIPSIDE, HOFFMAN ESTATES 455 U.S. 489, 102 S.Ct. 1186, 71 L.Ed.2d. 362, 30 Cr.L. 3079 (1982). The challenge was made that it was a denial of the First Amendment free speech rights of either the business or their customers and that the ordinance was facially vague when applied to a store that marketed merchandise such as drug related publications . . . The Court held against the store on both theories saying, inter alia, that the ordinance is not facially overbroad and does not restrict speech as such but simply regulates commercial marketing of items that the labels reveal may be used for an illicit purpose and thus does not embrace non-commercial speech.

§ 5.9 Religious and Political Freedom of Expression

The right of a municipality to enforce a statute against a commercial establishment for littering the streets has not carried over to a similar right against religions. The United States Supreme Court has maintained a balancing of private and public interests in its decisions in this problem. It has been held that a municipality may not prevent the handing out of handbills which are espousing a religious or political cause. Schneider v. Irvington, 308 U.S. 147, 60 S.Ct. 146, 84 L.Ed. 155 (1939). However, soundtrucks exhorting a candidate for political office, or urging persons to vote, or the like may be the subject of reasonable regulation. N.Y.—Crennan v. Patrick, 171 Misc. 705, 14 N.Y.S.2d 249 (1939).

From a consideration of the foregoing, we can readily understand that First Amendment rights are not absolute rights but are conditioned upon reasonable police powers designed to promote the public health, welfare, and morals of the community.

§ 5.10 Parade Regulation

Police officers are often confronted with the problem of supervising parades. Whether the parade occurs in a large city or on the main street of a small town, the problems are basically similar. There is a balancing of the rights of those people interested in participating in the event with the rights of those who wish to pursue their normal routine.

The First Amendment protects those who wish peacefully to assemble and if the people wish to assemble peacefully in a parade for the purpose of celebrating Labor Day, Independence Day, Thanksgiving, New Year's Eve, St. Patrick's Day, Pulaski Day, Italian Day, Jews for Israel Day, Shriners' Convention, Memorial Day and others that I am certain that I unintentionally have omitted, this is the privilege given to them by a free society. However, the courts have held that these demonstrations are subject to reasonable regulation.

Under the police power doctrine, a law enforcement agency may regulate parades. Governmental authorities have the duty and responsibility to keep their streets open and available for movement. A group of demonstrators could not insist upon the right to cordon off a street or entrance to a public or private building and allow no one to pass who did not agree to listen to their exhortations. Poulos v. New Hampshire, 345 U.S. 395, 73 S.Ct. 760, 97 L.Ed. 1105 (1953). It is, of course, undisputed that appropriate, limited discretion, under properly drawn statutes or ordinances, concerning the time, place, duration, or manner of use of the streets for public assemblies may be vested in administrative officials, provided that such limited discretion is "exercised with uniformity of method of treatment upon the facts of each application, free from improper or inappropriate considerations and from unfair discrimination . . . ." Cox v. Louisiana, 379 U.S. 536, 85 S.Ct. 453, 13 L.Ed.2d 471 (1965).

§ 5.11 Clear-and-Present-Danger Doctrine

The clear-and-present-danger doctrine was first enunciated in Schenk v. U.S., 249 U.S. 47, 39 S.Ct. 247, 63 L.Ed. 470 (1919). This concept acts as a guide to determine the constitutionality of governmental restrictions on the right of free speech and free press. In short, it balances the right of the individual to self-expression against the government's right to prevent grave and immediate danger to interests which the government may lawfully protect. In Schenk v. U.S. (supra), the court held, "The most stringent protection of free speech would not protect a man in falsely shouting fire in a theatre causing a panic . . . The question in every case is whether the words used are used in such circumstances and are of such a nature as to create a clear and present danger that they will bring about the substantive evils that Congress has a right to prevent. It is a question of proximity and degree. When a nation is at war many things that might be said in time of peace are such a hindrance to its effort that their utterance will not be endured so long as men fight and that no Court could regard them as protected by any constitutional right . . . ."

§ 5.12 The Sedentary Demonstrator

In recent years a new form of expression has evolved by large numbers of people gathering before an entrance to a building or in the middle of a busy street and sitting down after chaining themselves together to prevent their removal by the police. This, they claim to be their right under the First Amendment. I have heard of one police department's handling this problem by attaching a little extra chain to the demonstrators' chain and attaching the other end of the police chain to a firm part of a police patrol wagon. The police would move the wagon slowly and, of course, after the demonstrators were dragged a little they submitted to arrest. I don't know how a court would consider this type of police action but it appears that it was very effective in removing the obstruction to vehicular and pedestrian traffic. The courts, however, have held that demonstrations of this type are not protected by the First Amendment.

§ 5.13 Labor Dispute Regulation

The police problems involving labor disputes are similar in some respects to that of the Parade Regulation. There are two competing constitutional rights that the police officer is confronted with: those who are on strike who have a constitutional right to peacefully picket and those who may wish to go to work who have a constitutional right to peacefully conduct their business. In this type of problem, the courts have held that the police may reasonably regulate the manner of picketing at a given location so that those who wish to pass through the picket line may do so. Utah—International Union of Operating Engineers Local No. 3 v. Utah Labor Relations Bd., 115 Utah 183, 203 P.2d 404; Texas—International Union of Operating Engineers Local No. 561 v. Cox, 148 Tex. 421, 219 S.W.2d 787. A municipality may require a permit specifying the time and place at which the applicant intends to picket, parade, or demonstrate. Cox v. New Hampshire, 312 U.S. 569, 61 S.Ct. 762, 85 L.Ed. 1049 (1941). However, the constitutional guarantee of freedom of speech has been held to extend to labor matters and the combatants are constitutionally protected to disseminate facts and opinions relating to the dispute. U.S.N.L.R.B. v. Winona Textile Mills, C.C.A. 8 Circ., 160 F.2d 201. A statute which prohibits violence by mass picketing is not unconstitutional. N.Y.—Haber v. Fink, Inc. v. Jones, 277 App.Div. 176, 98 N.Y.S.2d 393; N.J.—Independent Dairy Workers Union of Heightstown v. Milk Drivers & Dairy Emp. Local No. 680, 23 N.J. 85, 127 A.2d 869. A California case permitted peaceful picketing on private property without the owner's permission and approval because it was protected by the National Labor Relations Act, Sec. 7 as amended 29 U.S.C.A. 157. Sears Roebuck & Co. v. San Diego County Dist. Council of Carpenters, 132 Cal.Rptr. 443, 553 P.2d 603 (1976). This case raises questions with respect to the picketing on private premises of shopping centers and was a refinement of Central Hardware Company v. National Labor Relations Board, 407 U.S. 539, 92 S.Ct. 2238, 33 L.Ed.2d 122 (1972), where the Supreme Court denied the right of a union to set up a picket line inside of a separately housed establishment which had its own customer-parking facilities.

An Illinois statute that prohibits picketing of residences but exempted from its prohibition the "peaceful picketing of a place of employment involved in a labor dispute" was held to be an unconstitutional discrimination among speech-related activities in CAREY v. BROWN, 447 U.S. 455, 100 S.Ct. 2286, 65 L.Ed.2d. 263, 27 Cr.L. 3195 (1980).

§ 5.14 Seizure of Public or Private Premises

Another form of protest that is being used of late is for several people to go into a public or private building and demonstrate by taking control of the building and its occupants. The taking over of the building, so they argue, is their way of expressing themselves with respect to an issue which is bothering them. The holding of hostages in the building cannot be logically explained by them. In any event, the taking over of buildings for the purpose of demonstrations has been held not to be protected by the First Amendment. Cameron v. Johnson, 390 U.S. 611, 88 S.Ct. 1335, 20 L.Ed.2d 182 (1968). The taking of hostages, of course, amounts to a kidnapping.

§ 5.15 Right of Public Meeting in Streets, Parks, and Public Buildings

The government may reasonably and without discrimination regulate the use of public streets, parks, or other locations within its control. It may require a permit for such public gatherings but discriminatory regulations are unconstitutional. U.S.—Robinson v. Coopwood, D.C. Miss.—292 F.Supp. 926, affd. C.A. 415 F.2d 1377; Resistance v. Commissioners of Fairmont Park, City of Philadelphia, Pa., 298 F.Supp. 961. The state does not have to make school buildings available for public meetings. U.S.—Grossner v. Trustees of Columbia University in the City of New York, D.C.N.Y.—287 F.Supp. 535; Smith v. Ellington, D.C.Tenn.—334 F.Supp. 90.

The police administrator is often confronted with the problem of maintaining order when groups unlawfully and without applying for a permit take over the streets, parks, or public buildings. Different administrators may take varying views with respect to permitting these gatherings to continue. The prevailing rule now appears to be that so long as the gathering is reasonably orderly, notwithstanding the fact that the police may validly enforce a constitutional limitation, the demonstration is permitted in order to avoid a confrontation which might result in loss of life or injury to persons or property. Many large police departments have had considerable experience with these demonstrations in recent years and their efforts have been to attempt to control the demonstration by reasonable limitations and by having the personnel of the agency cajole the demonstrators, but at the same time, placing certain outside limits on permissiveness beyond which both the demonstrators and the police know that the breach of these limits will not be tolerated. Such a limit might be to set up a cordon of police around a notable personage or a public building for the protection of the person or building.

The National Park Service has a regulation that permits camping in a National Park only in designated areas. It further defines camping as including sleeping activities. A group calling itself "Community for Creative Non-Violence" made a request for a permit to allow demonstrators to call attention to the plight of the homeless to sleep in symbolic tents to be erected in Lafayette Park and the Mall in Washington, D.C.

The Park Service having never designated these areas as camping sights refused to issue the permits. The applicants and other individuals filed an action in Federal District Court alleging, inter alia, that application of the regulation violated the First Amendment.

The Court held that there was no denial of the First Amendment saying, inter alia, that the regulation is neutral and leaves alternate methods of communicating the intended message concerning the plight of the homeless. 468 U.S.—, 104 S.Ct. 3065, 82 L.Ed.2d.221, 35 Cr.L.3214 (1984).

§ 5.16 Freedom of Religion

The First Amendment to the Articles of Amendment of the United States Constitution gives to every individual his natural right to worship as he pleases according to his own conscience. Article 6 of the same Constitution provides that "no religious Test shall ever be required as a Qualification to any Office or public Trust under the United States." The freedom of worship is a right which may not be subject to a vote. Neb.—Hanson v. Union Pacific R.R.Co., 160 Neb. 699, 71 N.W.2d 526, rev. on other grounds. 351 U.S. 225, 76 S.Ct. 714, 100 L.Ed. 1112, reh.den. 76 S.Ct. 22. However, Congress or a state may reasonably limit the free exercise of religion for the protection of society, such as general laws which are enacted for the purpose of restraining and punishing acts which have a tendency to disturb the public peace or corrupt the public morals. U.S.—McGowan v. State of Md., 366 U.S. 420, 81 S.Ct. 1101, 6 L.Ed.2d 393 (1961); N.Y.—Brown v. McGinniss, 10 N.Y.2d 531, 225 N.Y.S.2d 497, 180 N.E.2d 791. The First Amendment to the federal Constitution providing that Congress shall make no law respecting an establishment of a religion, or prohibiting the free exercise thereof, was never intended as a defense to acts inimical to the peace and good order of society. U.S.—Shapiro v. Lyle, D.C.Wash.—30 F.2d 971, appeal dism. C.C.A. 36 F.2d 1021. The right of freedom of conscience does not extend to freedom to meet with others, knowingly and deliberately for discussion of plans to overthrow the government by force or violence. Cal.—First Unitarian Church of Los Angeles v. Los Angeles County, 48 C.2d 419, 311 P.2d 508, rev. on other grounds 357 U.S. 545, 78 S.Ct. 1350, 2 L.Ed.2d 1484. The Constitution does not guarantee the right to anyone to go freely onto private property to preach or disseminate information. N.Y.—On the complaint of DuBois v. Thorpe, 198 Misc. 462, 101 N.Y.S.2d 986. Therefore if a missionary goes door-to-door in a residential neighborhood with intent to spread an interpretation of religious beliefs, the acts might be considered a trespass and the missionary does not have a constitutional right to engage in such activity. The principle of freedom of speech does not sanction incitement to riot nor does religious liberty connote the privilege to exhort others to physical attack upon those belonging to another sect. When clear and present danger of riot, disorder, interference with traffic upon the public streets, or other immediate threat to public safety, peace, or order appears, the power of the state to prevent or punish is obvious. Cantwell v. Conn., 310 U.S. 296, 60 S.Ct. 906, 84 L.Ed. 1213, 128 A.L.R. 1352 (1940).

§ 5.17 Freedom of the Press

While freedom of the press is encompassed in the guarantees of the First Amendment to the United States Constitution, the law enforcement officer rarely encounters problems in this area. For that reason the treatment given to this freedom is minimal.

The police do, however, have contact with freedom of the press problems in connection with the efficient and orderly running of elections for political office. Candidates may distribute ballots outside of the official ballots used in the election to instruct voters to vote for them. A statute forbidding this practice has been held constitutional and was not a denial of freedom of speech. Ark.—Branton v. State, 214 Ark. 861, 218 S.W.2d 690, cert. den. 338 U.S. 878, 70 S.Ct. 155, 94 L.Ed. 538. The probability of this problem arising diminishes year by year as the use of voting machines becomes popular.

A 1978 decision by the Court held that a search warrant based upon probable cause may issue to search the office of a newspaper on the grounds that the newspaper had a photograph in its possession that showed the identity of perpetrators of an assault on police officers. Zurcher v. Stanford Daily, 436 U.S. 547, 98 S.Ct. 1970, 56 L.Ed.2d 525 (1978).

The courts in Massachusetts enforced a law mandating exclusion of the general public from trials of specified sexual offenses involving a victim under the age of 18 years. The Globe Newspaper Co. contested this procedure in GLOBE NEWSPAPER CO. v. SUPERIOR COURT FOR COUNTY OF NORFOLK, 102 S.Ct. 2613, 73 L.Ed.2d. 248, 31 Cr.L. 3111 (1982) and the Court held that the Statute as construed by the Massachusetts Courts violates the 14th Amendment. The United States Supreme Court said that there is a non-absolute right of access to these trials. If, however the State can show that the denial of that right is necessitated by a compelling governmental interest, the public may be excluded.

§ 5.18 Photographing of Demonstrations

One of the most effective police methods to control demonstrations is to photograph the participants with a motion picture or still camera. Some argue that this has a chilling effect and inhibits freedom of expression. Others argue that it does not prevent a person from freedom of his/her expression but makes the participant accountable for his/her actions and this is a lawful and constitutional police tactic in order to protect the public peace. For every attack there seems to be a counterattack. Many demonstrators have avoided somewhat the problem of identification by wearing false noses or other disguises. However, anyone who has walked a patrol beat for any length of time knows that he can recognize a fellow officer wearing a police uniform who is more than a city block away by his peculiar walking pattern. Therefore the mere wearing of a facial disguise may not be the complete answer for those demonstrators who are trying to avoid identification by a photo or movie film.

The United States Supreme Court has not dealt directly with this problem to date but lower courts have approved the police practice of taking pictures of demonstrators. U.S.—Donohum v. Duling, E.D.Va. 1971—330 F.Supp. 308 (1971); N.J.—Anderson v. Sills, 265 A(2d) 678 (1970).

§ 5.19 Pornographic Literature, Movies, and Photos

The right of freedom of expression has come to a head-on collision with those proponents of pornographic literature, movies, and photos. A concomitant of this is the advertising and sale of so-called "sex aids." Rumor has it that the profits from these enterprises are enormous and the legal batteries available to these entrepreneurs are far reaching and well supported. The police are in a dilemma in enforcing statutes designed to inhibit or control this activity. Probably the best way to control it is to make it socially undesirable for customers to patronize these establishments. In a large city this method of control is almost an impossible task in that the customers enjoy the protection of anonymity and care little what their fellow person thinks of their cravings.

The Supreme Court has not been too helpful in offering precise guidelines as to what is constitutional and what is unconstitutional behavior. In United States v. Thirty-Seven Photographs, 402 U.S. 363, 91 S.Ct. 1400, 28 L.Ed.2d 822 (1971), the Supreme Court held that it was permissible to import obscene literary materials from another country where the purpose was to be for the petitioner's personal consumption or enjoyment, but that did not grant him permission to acquire such literature or protection to read it outside the home.

In Miller v. California, 413 U.S. 151, 93 S.Ct. 2607, 37 L.Ed.2d 419

(1973), the court held in a five to four decision, that obscene material was not protected by the First Amendment but the basic guidelines for the trier of fact in questions of regulation of obscene materials must be:

1. Whether the average person, applying contemporary standards, would find that the work, taken as a whole, appeals to the prurient interest;
2. Whether the work depicts or describes, in a patently offensive way, sexual conduct specifically defined by the applicable state law; and
3. Whether the work, taken as a whole, lacks serious literary, artistic, political or scientific value—there being no requirement that the work be "utterly without redeeming social value" or "social importance"; if a state law that regulates obscene material is thus limited, as written or construed, the First Amendment values applicable to the states through the Fourteenth Amendment are adequately protected by the ultimate power of appellate courts to conduct an independent review of constitutional claims when necessary.

Nudity alone is not enough to make material legally obscene under the constitutional obscenity standards formulated in Miller v. California (supra). Jenkins v. Georgia, 418 U.S. 153, 94 S.Ct. 2750, 41 L.Ed.2d 642 (1974). The court held further in the Jenkins case that it is permissible to allow juries to rely on the understanding of the community from which they come as to contemporary community standards of obscenity, and the states have considerable latitude in framing statutes under such element of the case of Miller v. California (supra); a state may choose to define an obscenity offense in terms of "contemporary community standards" without further specification, or it may choose to define the standards in more precise geographic terms.

From a reading of the Miller and Jenkins cases, it becomes obvious that the United States Supreme Court has left the question of what is obscene and subject to state regulations up to state and local option. To put it another way, if the local people want it that way, they can have it.

While the Court has been very liberal in its decision relating to pornographic films and literature, it limited its expansive former interpretations in NEW YORK v. FERBER, 458 U.S. 747, 102 S.Ct. 3348, 73 L.Ed.2d. 1113, 31 Cr.L. 3139 (1982). In that case, the respondent was a book store proprietor who sold books depicting young boys masturbating.

The promotion of a sexual performance by a child was in violation of a state statute. The Court said that this statute was not a violation of the Fourteenth and First Amendment in that a state has greater leeway in the regulation of pornographic depictions of children and it gave several reasons for their holding.

An outgrowth of the pornographic movie situation arose in Camden County, New Jersey. A store selling adult books, magazines and films was established in a commercially zoned area of the BOROUGH OF MOUNT EPHRAIM located in Camden County, New Jersey. Business apparently was flourishing causing the store to add duly licensed coin operated machines where a patron could enter a booth and view an adult film. The operator of the store then introduced another device wherein a customer could, by inserting a coin, watch a live dancer who was usually nude.

This last introduction was the "last straw" for the local citizenry and they moved in to bring charges against the operators of the store as being in violation of an ordinance of the Borough, restricting the use of premises within the Borough to exclude live dancing, whether nude or otherwise. Fines were imposed and after going through the appellate process, it arrived in the United States Supreme Court. The Court held in SCHAB v. BOROUGH OF MOUNT EPHRAIM, 452 U.S. 61, 101 S.Ct. 2176, 68 L.Ed.2d. 671, 29 Cr.L. 3053 (1981) that the ordinance was a violation of the First and Fourteenth Amendments guarantee against the prohibition of freedom of expression.

§ 5.20 Canvassing and Distribution of Literature

Many localities have made it a statutory offense to canvass for new business in the city or town or county without first applying for and obtaining a permit. This is done to prevent potential burglars from ringing doorbells to find whether the occupant is at home. If the occupant does not answer the bell, the potential burglar becomes the burglar. By requiring persons soliciting business to secure a permit, a background check can be made on the applicant before a permit is issued. This has been determined to be a constitutional exercise of the police power. A municipal ordinance prohibiting canvassers or peddlers from calling on private residences unless requested or invited by the occupant to do so does not, as applied to solicitors of magazine subscriptions, unconstitutionally abridge freedom of speech and press. Breard v. Alexandria, 341 U.S. 622, 71 S.Ct. 920, 95 L.Ed. 1233 (1951).

§ 5.21 Soundtruck Regulation

If the municipality issues permits for the use of soundtrucks, the person having the discretion to issue or deny the permits must have standards prescribed or the statute is unconstitutional. See Saia v. New York, 334 U.S. 558, 68 S.Ct. 1148, 92 L.Ed. 1574 (1948).

Judicial Decisions Relating to Chapter 5

Samuel H. Sheppard, Petitioner, *v.* E. L. Maxwell, Warden

384 U.S. 333, 86 S.Ct. 1507, 16 L.Ed. 2d. 600 (1966)

Argued February 28, 1966.—Decided June 6, 1966.

. . .

MR. JUSTICE CLARK delivered the opinion of the Court.

This federal habeas corpus application involves the question whether Sheppard was deprived of a fair trial in his state conviction for the second-degree murder of his wife because of the trial judge's failure to protect Sheppard sufficiently from the massive, pervasive and prejudicial publicity that attended his prosecution. The United States District Court held that he was not afforded a fair trial and granted the writ subject to the State's right to put Sheppard to trial again, 231 F Supp 37 (DCSD Ohio 1964). The Court of Appeals for the Sixth Circuit reversed by a divided vote, 346 F2d 707 (1965). We granted certiorari, 382 US 916, 15 L ed 2d 231, 86 S Ct 289 (1965). We have concluded that Sheppard did not receive a fair trial consistent with the Due Process Clause of the Fourteenth Amendment and, therefore, reversed the judgment.

I

Marilyn Sheppard, petitioner's pregnant wife, was bludgeoned to death in the upstairs bedroom of their lakeshore home in Bay Village, Ohio, a suburb of Cleveland. On the day of the tragedy, July 4, 1954, Sheppard pieced together for several local officials the following story: He and his wife had entertained neighborhood friends, the Aherns, on the previous evening at their home. After dinner they watched television in the living room. Sheppard became drowsy and dozed off to sleep on a couch. Later, Marilyn partially awoke him saying that she was going to bed. The next thing he remembered was hearing his wife cry out in the early morning hours. He hurried upstairs and in the dim light from the hall saw a "form" standing next to his wife's bed. As he struggled with the "form" he was struck on the back of the neck and rendered unconscious. On regaining his senses he found himself on the floor next to his wife's bed. He rose, looked at her, took her pulse and "felt that she was gone." He then went to his son's room and found him unmolested. Hearing a noise he hurried downstairs. He saw a "form" running out the door and pursued it to the lake shore. He grappled with it on the beach and again lost consciousness. Upon his recovery he was lying face down with the lower portion of his body in the water. He returned to his home, checked the pulse on his wife's neck, and "determined or thought that she was gone." He then went downstairs and called a neighbor, Mayor Houk of Bay Village. The Mayor and his wife came over at once, found Sheppard slumped in an easy chair downstairs and asked, "What happened?" Sheppard replied: "I don't know but somebody ought to try to do something for

Marilyn." Mrs. Houk immediately went up to the bedroom. The Mayor told Sheppard, "Get hold of yourself. Can you tell me what happened?" Sheppard then related the above-outlined events. After Mrs. Houk discovered the body, the Mayor called the local police, Dr. Richard Sheppard, petitioner's brother, and the Ahern s. The local police were the first to arrive. They in turn notified the Coroner and Cleveland police. Richard Sheppard then arrived, determined that Marilyn was dead, examined his brother's injuries, and removed him to the nearby clinic operated by the Sheppard family. When the Coroner, the Cleveland police and other officials arrived, the house and surrounding area were thoroughly searched, the rooms of the house were photographed, and many persons, including the Houks and the Aherns, were interrogated. The Sheppard home and premises were taken into "protective custody" and remained so until after the trial.

From the outset officials focused suspicion on Sheppard. After a search of the house and premises on the morning of the tragedy, Dr. Gerber, the Coroner, is reported—and it is undenied—to have told his men, "Well, it is evident the doctor did this, so let's go get the confession out of him." He proceeded to interrogate and examine Sheppard while the latter was under sedation in his hospital room. On the same occasion, the Coroner was given the clothes Sheppard wore at the time of the tragedy together with the personal items in them. Later that afternoon Chief Eaton and two Cleveland police officers interrogated Sheppard at some length, confronting him with evidence and demanding explanations. Asked by Officer Shotke to take a lie detector test, Sheppard said he would if it were reliable. Shotke replied that it was "infallible" and "you might as well tell us all about it now." At the end of the interrogation Shotke told Sheppard: "I think you killed your wife." Still later in the same afternoon a physician sent by the Coroner was permitted to make a detailed examination of Sheppard. Until the Coroner's inquest on July 22, at which time he was subpoenaed, Sheppard made himself available for frequent and extended questioning without the presence of an attorney.

On July 7, the day of Marilyn Sheppard's funeral, a newspaper story appeared in which Assistant County Attorney Mahon—later the chief prosecutor of Sheppard—sharply criticized the refusal of the Sheppard family to permit his immediate questioning. From there on headline stories repeatedly stressed Sheppard's lack of cooperation with the police and other officials. Under the headline "Testify Now In Death, Bay Doctor Is Ordered," one story described a visit by Coroner Gerber and four police officers to the hospital on July 8. When Sheppard insisted that his lawyer be present, the Coroner wrote out a subpoena and served it on him. Sheppard then agreed to submit to questioning without counsel and the subpoena was torn up. The officers questioned him for several hours. On July 9, Sheppard, at the request of the Coroner, reenacted the tragedy at his home before the Coroner, police officers, and a group of newsmen, who apparently were invited by the Coroner. The home was locked so that Sheppard was obliged to wait outside until the Coroner arrived. Sheppard's performance was reported in detail by the news media along with photographs. The newspapers also played up Sheppard's refusal to take a lie detector test and "the protective ring" thrown up by his family. Front-page newspaper headlines announced on the same day that "Doctor Balks At

Lie Test; Retells Story." A column opposite that story contained an "exclusive" interview with Sheppard headlined: "'Loved My Wife, She Loved Me,' Sheppard Tells News Reporter." The next day, another headline story disclosed that Sheppard had "again late yesterday refused to take a lie detector test" and quoted an Assistant County Attorney as saying that "at the end of a nine-hour questioning of Dr. Sheppard, I felt he was now ruling [a test] out completely." But subsequent newspaper articles reported that the Coroner was still pushing Sheppard for a lie detector test. More stories appeared when Sheppard would not allow authorities to inject him with "truth serum."

On the 20th, the "editorial artillery" opened fire with a front-page charge that somebody is "getting away with murder." The editorial attributed the ineptness of the investigation to "friendships, relationships, hired lawyers, a husband who ought to have been subjected instantly to the same third-degree to which any other person under similar circumstances is subjected...." The following day, July 21, another page-one editorial was headed: "Why No Inquest? Do It Now, Dr. Gerber." The Coroner called an inquest the same day and subpoenaed Sheppard. It was staged the next day in a school gymnasium; the Coroner presided with the County Prosecutor as his advisor and two detectives as bailiffs. In the front of the room was a long table occupied by reporters, television and radio personnel, and broadcasting equipment. The hearing was broadcast with live microphones placed at the Coroner's seat and the witness stand. A swarm of reporters and photographers attended. Sheppard was brought into the room by police who searched him in full view of several hundred spectators. Sheppard's counsel were present during the three-day inquest but were not permitted to participate. When Sheppard's chief counsel attempted to place some documents in the record, he was forcibly ejected from the room by the Coroner, who received cheers, hugs, and kisses from ladies in the audience. Sheppard was questioned for five and one-half hours about his actions on the night of the murder, his married life, and a love affair with Susan Hayes. At the end of the hearing the Coroner announced that he "could" order Sheppard held for the grand jury, but did not do so.

Throughout this period the newspapers emphasized evidence that tended to incriminate Sheppard and pointed out discrepancies in his statements to authorities. At the same time, Sheppard made many public statements to the press and wrote feature articles asserting his innocence. During the inquest on July 26, a headline in large type stated: "Kerr [Captain of the Cleveland Police] Urges Sheppard's Arrest." In the story, Detective McArthur "disclosed that scientific tests at the Sheppard home have definitely established that the killer washed off a trail of blood from the murder bedroom to the downstairs section," a circumstance casting doubt on Sheppard's accounts of the murder. No such evidence was produced at trial. The newspapers also delved into Sheppard's personal life. Articles stressed his extramarital love affairs as a motive for the crime. The newspapers portrayed Sheppard as a Lothario, fully explored his relationship with Susan Hayes, and named a number of other women who were allegedly involved with him. The testimony at trial never showed that Sheppard had any illicit relationships besides the one with Susan Hayes.

On July 28, an editorial entitled "Why Don't Police Quiz Top Suspect" demanded that Sheppard be taken to police headquarters. It described him in the following language:

> "Now proved under oath to be a liar, still free to go about his business, shielded by his family, protected by a smart lawyer who has made monkeys of the police and authorities, carrying a gun part of the time, left free to do whatever he pleases...."

A front-page editorial on July 30 asked: "Why Isn't Sam Sheppard in Jail?" It was later titled "Quit Stalling—Bring Him In." After calling Sheppard "the most unusual murder suspect ever seen around these parts" the article said that "[e]xcept for some superficial questioning during Coroner Sam Gerber's inquest he has been scot-free of any official grilling...." It asserted that he was "surrounded by an iron curtain of protection [and] concealment."

That night at 10 o'clock Sheppard was arrested at his father's home on a charge of murder. He was taken to the Bay Village City Hall where hundreds of people, newscasters, photographers and reporters were awaiting his arrival. He was immediately arraigned—having been denied a temporary delay to secure the presence of counsel—and bound over to the grand jury.

The publicity then grew in intensity until his indictment on August 17. Typical of the coverage during this period is a front-page interview entitled: "DR. SAM: 'I Wish There Was Something I Could Get Off My Chest—but There Isn't.'" Unfavorable publicity included items such as a cartoon of the body of a sphinx with Sheppard's head and the legend below: "'I Will Do Everything In My Power to Help Solve This Terrible Murder,'—Dr. Sam Sheppard." Headlines announced, inter alia, that: "Doctor Evidence is Ready for Jury," "Corrigan Tactics Stall Quizzing," "Sheppard 'Gay Set' Is Revealed By Houk," "Blood Is Found In Garage," "New Murder Evidence Is Found, Police Claim," "Dr. Sam Faces Quiz At Jail On Marilyn's Fear Of Him." On August 18, an article appeared under the headline "Dr. Sam Writes His Own Story." And reproduced across the entire front page was a portion of the typed statement signed by Sheppard: "I am not guilty of the murder of my wife, Marilyn. How could I, who have been trained to help people and devoted my life to saving life, commit such a terrible and revolting crime?" We do not detail the coverage further. There are five volumes filled with similar clippings from each of the three Cleveland newspapers covering the period from the murder until Sheppard's conviction in December 1954. The record includes no excerpts from newscasts on radio and television but since space was reserved in the courtroom for these media we assume that their coverage was equally large.

II

With this background the case came on for trial two weeks before the November general election at which the chief prosecutor was a candidate for common pleas judge and the trial judge, Judge Blythin, was a candidate to succeed himself. Twenty-five days before the case was set, 75 veniremen were called as prospective jurors. All three Cleveland newspapers published the names and addresses of the veniremen. As a consequence, anonymous letters and telephone calls, as well as calls from friends, regarding the impending prosecution were received by all of the prospective jurors. The selection of the jury began on October 18, 1954.

The courtroom in which the trial was held measured 26 by 48 feet. A long temporary table was set up inside the bar, in back of the single counsel table. It ran the width of the courtroom, parallel to the bar railing, with one end less than three feet from the jury box. Approximately 20 representatives of newspapers and wire services were assigned seats at this table by the court. Behind the bar railing there were four rows of benches. These seats were likewise assigned by the court for the entire trial. The first row was occupied by representatives of television and radio stations, and the second and third rows by reporters from out-of-town newspapers and magazines. One side of the last row, which accommodated 14 people, was assigned to Sheppard's family and the other to Marilyn's. The public was permitted to fill vacancies in this row on special passes only. Representatives of the news media also used all the rooms on the courtroom floor, including the room where cases were ordinarily called and assigned for trial. Private telephone lines and telegraphic equipment were installed in these rooms so that reports from the trial could be speeded to the papers. Station WSRS was permitted to set up broadcasting facilities on the third floor of the courthouse next door to the jury room, where the jury rested during recesses in the trial and deliberated. Newscasts were made from this room throughout the trial, and while the jury reached its verdict.

On the sidewalk and steps in front of the courthouse, television and newsreel cameras were occasionally used to take motion pictures of the participants in the trial, including the jury and the judge. Indeed, one television broadcast carried a staged interview of the judge as he entered the courthouse. In the corridors outside the courtroom there was a host of photographers and television personnel with flash cameras, portable lights and motion picture cameras. This group photographed the prospective jurors during selection of the jury. After the trial opened, the witnesses, counsel, and jurors were photographed and televised whenever they entered or left the courtroom. Sheppard was brought to the courtroom about 10 minutes before each session began; he was surrounded by reporters and extensively photographed for the newspapers and television. A rule of court prohibited picture-taking in the courtroom during the actual sessions of the court, but no restraints were put on photographers during recesses, which were taken once each morning and afternoon, with a longer period for lunch.

All of these arrangements with the news media and their massive coverage of the trial continued during the entire nine weeks of the trial. The courtroom remained crowded to capacity with representatives of news media. Their movement in and out of the courtroom often caused so much confusion that, despite the loudspeaker system installed in the courtroom, it was difficult for the witnesses and counsel to be heard. Furthermore, the reporters clustered within the bar of the small courtroom made confidential talk among Sheppard and his counsel almost impossible during the proceedings. They frequently had to leave the courtroom to obtain privacy. And many times when counsel wished to raise a point with the judge out of the hearing of the jury it was necessary to move to the judge's chambers. Even then, news media representatives so packed the judge's anteroom that counsel could hardly return from the chambers to the courtroom. The reporters vied with each other to find out what counsel and the judge had discussed, and often these matters later appeared in newspapers accessible to the jury.

The daily record of the proceedings was made available to the newspapers and the testimony of each witness was printed verbatim in the local editions, along with objections of counsel, and rulings by the judge. Pictures of Sheppard, the judge, counsel, pertinent witnesses, and the jury often accompanied the daily newspaper and television accounts. At times the newspapers published photographs of exhibits introduced at the trial, and the rooms of Sheppard's house were featured along with relevant testimony.

The jurors themselves were constantly exposed to the news media. Every juror, except one, testified at voir dire to reading about the case in the Cleveland papers or to having heard broadcasts about it. Seven of the 12 jurors who rendered the verdict had one or more Cleveland papers delivered in their home; the remaining jurors were not interrogated on the point. Nor were there questions as to radios or television sets in the jurors' homes, but we must assume that most of them owned such conveniences. As the selection of the jury progressed, individual pictures of prospective members appeared daily. During the trial, pictures of the jury appeared over 40 times in the Cleveland papers alone. The court permitted photographers to take pictures of the jury in the box, and individual pictures of the members in the jury room. One newspaper ran pictures of the jurors at the Sheppard home when they went there to view the scene of the murder. Another paper featured the home life of an alternate juror. The day before the verdict was rendered—while the jurors were at lunch and sequestered by two bailiffs—the jury was separated into two groups to pose for photographs which appeared in the newspapers.

III

We now reach the conduct of the trial. While the intense publicity continued unabated, it is sufficient to relate only the more flagrant episodes:

1. On October 9, 1954, nine days before the case went to trial, an editorial in one of the newspapers criticized defense counsel's random poll of people on the streets as to their opinion of Sheppard's guilt or innocence in an effort to use the resulting statistics to show the necessity for change of venue. The article said the survey "smacks of mass jury tampering," called on defense counsel to drop it, and stated that the bar association should do something about it. It characterized the poll as "non-judicial, non-legal, and nonsense." The article was called to the attention of the court but no action was taken.

2. On the second day of voir dire examination a debate was staged and broadcast live over WHK radio. The participants, newspaper reporters, accused Sheppard's counsel of throwing roadblocks in the way of the prosecution and asserted

that Sheppard conceded his guilt by hiring a prominent criminal lawyer. Sheppard's counsel objected to this broadcast and requested a continuance, but the judge denied the motion. When counsel asked the court to give some protection from such events, the judge replied that "WHK doesn't have much coverage," and that "[a]fter all, we are not trying this case by radio or in newspapers or any other means. We confine ourselves seriously to it in this courtroom and do the very best we can."

3. While the jury was being selected, a two-inch headline asked: "But Who Will Speak for Marilyn?" The front-page story spoke of the "perfect face" of the accused. "Study that face as long as you want. Never will you get from it a hint of what might be the answer...." The two brothers of the accused were described as "Prosperous, poised. His two sisters-in-law. Smart, chic, well-groomed. His elderly father. Courtly, reserved. A perfect type for the patriarch of a staunch clan." The author then noted Marilyn Sheppard was "still off stage," and that she was an only child whose mother died when she was very young and whose father had no interest in the case. But the author—through quotes from Detective Chief James McArthur—assured readers that the prosecution's exhibits would speak for Marilyn. "Her story," McArthur stated, "will come into this courtroom through our witnesses." The article ends:

> "Then you realize how what and who is missing from the perfect setting will be supplied.
> "How in the Big Case justice will be done.
> "Justice to Sam Sheppard.
> "And to Marilyn Sheppard."

4. As has been mentioned, the jury viewed the scene of the murder on the first day of the trial. Hundreds of reporters, cameramen and onlookers were there, and one representative of the news media was permitted to accompany the jury while it inspected the Sheppard home. The time of the jury's visit was revealed so far in advance that one of the newspapers was able to rent a helicopter and fly over the house taking pictures of the jurors on their tour.

5. On November 19, a Cleveland police officer gave testimony that tended to contradict details in the written statement Sheppard made to the Cleveland police. Two days later, in a broadcast heard over Station WHK in Cleveland, Robert Considine likened Sheppard to a perjurer and compared the episode to Alger Hiss' confrontation with Whittaker Chambers. Though defense counsel asked the judge to question the jury to ascertain how many heard the broadcast, the court refused to do so. The judge also overruled the motion for continuance based on the same ground, saying:

> "Well, I don't know, we can't stop people, in any event, listening to it. It is a matter of free speech, and the court can't control everybody.... We are not going to harass the jury every morning.... It is getting to the point where if we do it every morning, we are suspecting the jury. I have confidence in this jury...."

6. On November 24, a story appeared under an eight-column headline: "Sam Called a 'Jekyll-Hyde' By Marilyn, Cousin To Testify." It related that Marilyn had recently told friends that Sheppard was a "Dr. Jekyll and Mr. Hyde" character. No such testimony was ever produced at the trial. The story went on to announce: "The prosecution has a 'bombshell witness' on tap who will testify to Dr. Sam's display of fiery temper—countering the defense claim that the defendant is a gentle physician with an even disposition." Defense counsel made motions for change of venue, continuance and mistrial, but they were denied. No action was taken by the court.

7. When the trial was in its seventh week, Walter Winchell broadcast over WXEL television and WJW radio that Carole Beasley, who was under arrest in New York City for robbery, had stated that, as Sheppard's mistress, she had borne him a child. The defense asked that the jury be queried on the broadcast. Two jurors admitted in open court that they had heard it. The judge asked each: "Would that have any effect upon your judgment?" Both replied, "No." This was accepted by the judge as sufficient; he merely asked the jury to "pay no attention whatever to that type of scavenging. . . . Let's confine ourselves to this courtroom, if you please." In answer to the motion for mistrial, the judge said:

> "Well, even, so, Mr. Corrigan, how are you ever going to prevent those things, in any event? I don't justify them at all. I think it is outrageous, but in a sense, it is outrageous even if there were no trial here. The trial has nothing to do with it in the Court's mind, as far as its outrage is concerned, but—
>
> "*Mr. Corrigan:* I don't know what effect it had on the mind of any of these jurors, and I can't find out unless inquiry is made.
>
> "*The Court:* How would you ever, in any jury, avoid that kind of a thing?"

8. On December 9, while Sheppard was on the witness stand he testified that he had been mistreated by Cleveland detectives after his arrest. Although he was not at the trial, Captain Kerr of the Homicide Bureau issued a press statement denying Sheppard's allegations which appeared under the headline: "'Bare-faced Liar,' Kerr Says of Sam." Captain Kerr never appeared as a witness at the trial.

9. After the case was submitted to the jury, it was sequestered for its deliberations, which took five days and four nights. After the verdict, defense counsel ascertained that the jurors had been allowed to make telephone calls to their homes every day while they were sequestered at the hotel. Although the telephones had been removed from the jurors' rooms, the jurors were permitted to use the phones in the bailiffs' rooms. The calls were placed by the jurors themselves; no record was kept of the jurors who made calls, the telephone numbers or the parties called. The bailiffs sat in the room where they could hear only the jurors' end of the conversation. The court had not instructed the bailiffs to prevent such calls. By a subsequent motion, defense counsel urged that this ground alone warranted a new trial, but the motion was overruled and no evidence was taken on the question.

IV

The principle that justice cannot survive behind walls of silence has long been reflected in the "Anglo-American distrust for secret trials." In re Oliver, 333 US 257, 268, 92 L ed 682, 691, 68 S Ct 499 (1948). A responsible press has always been regarded as the handmaiden of effective judicial administration, especially in the criminal field. Its function in this regard is documented by an impressive record of service over several centuries. The press does not simply publish information about trials but guards against the miscarriage of justice by subjecting the police, prosecutors, and judicial processes to extensive public scrutiny and criticism. This Court has, therefore, been unwilling to place any direct limitations on the freedom traditionally exercised by the news media for "[w]hat transpires in the court room is public property." Craig v Harney, 331 US 367, 374, 91 L ed 1546, 1551, 67 S Ct 1249 (1947). The "unqualified prohibitions laid down by the framers were intended to give to liberty of the press . . . the broadest scope that could be countenanced in an orderly society." Bridges v California, 314 US 252, 265, 86 L ed 192, 204, 62 S Ct 190, 159 ALR 1346 (1941). And where there was "no threat or menace to the integrity of the trial," Craig v Harney, supra, 331 US at 377, 91 L ed at 1553, we have consistently required that the press have a free hand, even though we sometimes deplored its sensationalism.

But the Court has also pointed out that "[l]egal trials are not like elections, to be won through the use of the meeting-hall, the radio, and the newspaper." Bridges v California, supra, 314 US at 271, 86 L ed at 207, 159 ALR 1346. And the Court has insisted that no one be punished for a crime without "a charge fairly made and fairly tried in a public tribunal free of prejudice, passion, excitement, and tyrannical power." Chambers v Florida, 309 US 227, 236–237, 84 L ed 716, 722, 60 S Ct 472 (1940). "Freedom of discussion should be given the widest range compatible with the essential requirement of the fair and orderly administration of justice." Pennekamp v Florida, 328 US 331, 347, 90 L ed 295, 1303, 66 S Ct 1029 (1946). But it must not be allowed to divert the trial from the "very purpose of a court system . . . to adjudicate controversies, both criminal and civil, in the calmness and solemnity of the courtroom according to legal procedures." Cox v Louisiana, 379 US 559, 583, 13 L ed 2d 487, 503, 85 S Ct 476 (1965) (BLACK, J., dissenting). Among these "legal procedures" is the requirement that the jury's verdict be based on evidence received in open court, not from outside sources. Thus, in Marshall v United States, 360 US 310, 3 L ed 2d 1250, 79 S Ct 1171 (1959), we set aside a federal conviction where the jurors were exposed "through news accounts" to information that was not admitted at trial. We held that the prejudice from such material "may indeed be greater" than when it is part of the prosecution's evidence "for it is then not tempered by protective procedures." At 313, 3 L ed 2d at 1252. At the same time, we did not consider dispositive the statement of each juror "that he would not be influenced by the news articles, that he could decide the case only on the evidence of record, and that he felt no prejudice against petitioner as a result of the articles." At 312, 3 L ed 2d at 1252. Likewise, in Irvin v Dowd, 366 US 717, 6 L ed 2d 751, 81 S Ct 1639 (1961), even though each juror indicated that he could render an impartial verdict despite exposure to prejudicial newspaper articles, we set aside the conviction holding:

> "With his life at stake, it is not requiring too much that petitioner be tried in an atmosphere undisturbed by so huge a wave of public passion . . . ." At 728, 6 L ed 2d at 759.

The undeviating rule of this Court was expressed by MR. JUSTICE HOLMES over half a century ago in Patterson v Colorado, 205 US 454, 462, 51 L ed 879, 881, 27 S Ct 556 (1907):

> "The theory of our system is that the conclusions to be reached in a case will be induced only by evidence and argument in open court, and not by any outside influence, whether of private talk or public print."

Moreover, "the burden of showing essential unfairness . . . as a demonstrable reality," Adams v United States ex rel. McCann, 317 US 269, 281, 87 L ed 268, 276, 63 S Ct 236, 143 ALR 435 (1942), need not be undertaken when television has exposed the community "repeatedly and in depth to the spectacle of [the accused] personally confessing in detail to the crimes with which he was later to be charged." Rideau v Louisiana, 373 US 723, 726, 10 L ed 2d 663, 665, 83 S Ct 1417 (1963). In Turner v Louisiana, 379 US 466, 13 L ed 2d 424, 85 S Ct 546 (1965), two key witnesses were deputy sheriffs who doubled as jury shepherds during the trial. The deputies swore that they had not talked to the jurors about the case, but the Court nonetheless held that, "even if it could be assumed that the deputies never did discuss the case directly with any members of the jury, it would be blinking reality not to recognize the extreme prejudice inherent in this continual association . . . ." At 473, 13 L ed 2d at 429.

Only last Term in Estes v Texas, 381 US 532, 14 L ed 2d 543, 85 S Ct 1628 (1965), we set aside a conviction despite the absence of any showing of prejudice. We said there:

> "It is true that in most cases involving claims of due process deprivations we require a showing of identifiable prejudice to the accused. Nevertheless, at times a procedure employed by the State involves such a probability that prejudice will result that it is deemed inherently lacking in due process." At 542–543, 14 L ed 2d at 550.

And we cited with approval the language of MR. JUSTICE BLACK for the Court in In re Murchison, 349 US 133, 136, 99 L ed 942, 946, 75 S Ct 623 (1955), that "our system of law has always endeavored to prevent even the probability of unfairness."

V

It is clear that the totality of circumstances in this case also warrants such an approach. Unlike Estes, Sheppard was not granted a change of venue to a locale away from where the publicity originated; nor was his jury sequestered. The Estes jury saw none of the television broadcasts from the courtroom. On the contrary, the Sheppard jurors were subjected to newspaper, radio and television coverage of the trial while not taking part in the proceedings. They were allowed to go their separate ways outside of the courtroom, without adequate directions not to read or listen to anything concerning the case. The judge's "admonitions" at the beginning of the trial are representative:

> "I would suggest to you and caution you that you do not read any newspapers during the progress of this trial, that you do not listen to radio comments nor watch or listen to television comments, insofar as this case is concerned. You will feel very much better as the trial proceeds.... I am sure that we shall all feel very much better if we do not indulge in any newspaper reading or listening to any comments whatever about the matter while the case is in progress. After it is all over, you can read it all to your heart's content...."

At intervals during the trial, the judge simply repeated his "suggestions" and "requests" that the jurors not expose themselves to comment upon the case. Moreover, the jurors were thrust into the role of celebrities by the judge's failure to insulate them from reporters and photographers. See Estes v Texas, supra, 381 US at 545–546, 14 L ed 2d at 551, 552. The numerous pictures of the jurors, with their addresses, which appeared in the newspapers before and during the trial itself exposed them to expressions of opinion from both cranks and friends. The fact that anonymous letters had been received by prospective jurors should have made the judge aware that this publicity seriously threatened the jurors' privacy.

The press coverage of the Estes trial was not nearly as massive and pervasive as the attention given by the Cleveland newspapers and broadcasting stations to Sheppard's prosecution. Sheppard stood indicted for the murder of his wife; the State was demanding the death penalty. For months the virulent publicity about Sheppard and the murder had made the case notorious. Charges and countercharges were aired in the news media besides those for which Sheppard was called to trial. In addition, only three months before trial, Sheppard was examined for more than five hours without counsel during a three-day inquest which ended in a public brawl. The inquest was televised live from a high school gymnasium seating hundreds of people. Furthermore, the trial began two weeks before a hotly contested election at which both Chief Prosecutor Mahon and Judge Blythin were candidates for judgeships.

While we cannot say that Sheppard was denied due process by the judge's refusal to take precautions against the influence of pretrial publicity alone, the court's later rulings must be considered against the setting in which the trial was held. In light of this background, we believe that the arrangements made by the judge with the news media caused Sheppard to be deprived of that "judicial serenity and calm to which [he] was entitled." Estes v Texas, supra, 381 US at 536, 14 L ed 2d at 546. The fact is that bedlam reigned at the courthouse during the trial and newsmen took over practically the entire courtroom, hounding most of the participants in the trial, especially Sheppard. At a temporary table within a few feet of the jury box and counsel table sat some 20 reporters staring at Sheppard and taking notes. The erection of a press table for reporters inside the bar is unprecedented. The bar of the court is reserved for counsel, providing them a safe place in which to keep papers and exhibits, and to confer privately with client and co-counsel. It is designed to protect the witness and the jury from any distractions, intrusions or influences, and to permit bench discussions of the judge's rulings away from the hearing of the public and the jury. Having assigned almost all of the available seats in the courtroom to the news media the judge lost his ability to supervise that environment. The movement of the reporters in and out of the courtroom caused frequent confusion and disruption of the trial. And the record reveals constant commotion within the bar. Moreover, the judge gave the throng of newsmen gathered in the corridors of the courthouse absolute free rein. Participants in the trial, including the jury, were forced to run a gantlet of reporters and photographers each time they entered or left the courtroom. The total lack of consideration for the privacy of the jury was demonstrated by the assignment to a broadcasting station of space next to the jury room on the floor above the courtroom, as well as the fact that jurors were allowed to make telephone calls during their five-day deliberation.

VI

There can be no question about the nature of the publicity which surrounded Sheppard's trial. We agree, as did the Court of Appeals, with the findings in Judge Bell's opinion for the Ohio Supreme Court:

> "Murder and mystery, society, sex and suspense were combined in this case in such a manner as to intrigue and captivate the public fancy to a degree perhaps unparalleled in recent annals. Throughout the preindictment investigation, the subsequent legal skirmishes and the nine-week trial, circulation-conscious editors catered to the insatiable interest of the American public in the bizarre. ... In this atmosphere of a 'Roman holiday' for the news media, Sam Sheppard stood trial for his life." 165 Ohio St., at 294, 135 NE2d, at 342.

Indeed, every court that has considered this case, save the court that tried it, has deplored the manner in which the news media inflamed and prejudiced the public.

Much of the material printed or broadcast during the trial was never heard from the witness stand, such as the charges that Sheppard had purposely impeded the murder investigation and must be guilty since he had hired a prominent criminal lawyer; that Sheppard was a perjurer; that he had sexual relations with numerous women; that his slain wife had characterized him as a "Jekyll-Hyde"; that he was "a bare-faced liar" because of his testimony as to police treatment; and, finally, that a woman convict claimed Sheppard to be the father of her illegitimate child. As the trial progressed, the newspapers summarized and interpreted the evidence, devoting particular attention to the material that incriminated Sheppard, and often drew unwarranted inferences from testimony. At one point, a front-page picture of Mrs. Sheppard's blood-stained pillow was published after being "doctored" to show more clearly an alleged imprint of a surgical instrument.

Nor is there doubt that this deluge of publicity reached at least some of the jury. On the only occasion that the jury was queried, two jurors admitted in open court to hearing the highly inflammatory charge that a prison inmate claimed Sheppard as the father of her illegitimate child. Despite the extent and nature of the publicity to which the jury was exposed during trial, the judge refused defense counsel's other requests that the jurors be asked whether they had read or heard specific prejudicial comment about the case, including the incidents we have previously summarized. In these circumstances, we can assume that some of this material reached members of the jury. See Commonwealth v Crehan, 345 Mass 609, 188 NE2d 923 (1963).

VII

The court's fundamental error is compounded by the holding that it lacked power to control the publicity about the trial. From the very inception of the proceedings the judge announced that neither he nor anyone else could restrict prejudicial news accounts. And he reiterated this view on numerous occasions. Since he viewed the news media as his target, the judge never considered other means that are often utilized to reduce the appearance of prejudicial material and to protect the jury from outside influence. We conclude that these procedures would have been sufficient to guarantee Sheppard a fair trial and so do not consider what sanctions might be available against a recalcitrant press nor the charges of bias now made against the state trial judge.

The carnival atmosphere at trial could easily have been avoided since the courtroom and courthouse premises are subject to the control of the court. As we stressed in Estes, the presence of the press at judicial proceedings must be limited when it is apparent that the accused might otherwise be prejudiced or disadvantaged. Bearing in mind the massive pretrial publicity, the judge should have adopted stricter rules governing the use of the courtroom by newsmen, as Sheppard's counsel requested. The number of reporters in the courtroom itself could have been limited at the first sign that their presence would disrupt the trial. They certainly should not have been placed inside the bar. Furthermore, the judge should have more closely regulated the conduct of newsmen in the courtroom. For instance, the judge belatedly asked them not to handle and photograph trial exhibits lying on the counsel table during recesses.

Secondly, the court should have insulated the witnesses. All of the newspapers and radio stations apparently interviewed prospective witnesses at will, and in many instances disclosed their testimony. A typical example was the publication of numerous statements by Susan Hayes, before her appearance in court, regarding her love affair with Sheppard. Although the witnesses were barred from the courtroom during the trial the full verbatim testimony was available to them in the press. This completely nullified the judge's imposition of the rule. See Estes v. Texas, supra, 381 US at 547, 14 L ed 2d at 552.

Thirdly, the court should have made some effort to control the release of leads, information, and gossip to the press by police officers, witnesses, and the counsel for both sides. Much of the information thus disclosed was inaccurate, leading to groundless rumors and confusion. That the judge was aware of his responsibility in this respect may be seen from his warning to Steve Sheppard, the accused's brother, who had apparently made public statements in an attempt to discredit testimony for the prosecution. The judge made this statement in the presence of the jury:

> "Now, the Court wants to say a word. That he was told—he has not read anything about it at all—but he was informed that Dr. Steve Sheppard, who has been granted the privilege of remaining in the court room during the trial, has been trying the case in the newspapers and making rather uncomplimentary comments about the testimony of the witnesses for the State.
>
> "Let it be now understood that if Dr. Steve Sheppard wishes to use the newspapers to try his case while we are trying it here, he will be barred from remaining in the court room during the progress of the trial if he is to be a witness in the case.
>
> "The Court appreciates he cannot deny Steve Sheppard the right of free speech, but he can deny him the . . . privilege of being in the court room, if he wants to avail himself of that method during the progress of the trial."

Defense counsel immediately brought to the court's attention the tremendous amount of publicity in the Cleveland press that "misrepresented entirely the testimony" in the case. Under such circumstances, the judge should have at least warned the newspapers to check the accuracy of their accounts. And it is obvious that the judge should have further sought to alleviate this problem by imposing control over the statements made to the news media by counsel, witnesses, and especially the Coroner and police officers. The prosecution repeatedly made evidence available to the news media which was never offered in the trial. Much of the "evidence" disseminated in this fashion was clearly inadmissible. The exclusion of such evidence in court is rendered meaningless when news media make it available to the public. For example, the publicity about Sheppard's refusal to take a lie detector test came directly from police officers and the Coroner. The story that Sheppard had been called a "Jekyll-Hyde" personality by his wife was attributed to a prosecution witness. No such testimony was given. The further report that there was "a 'bombshell witness' on tap" who would testify as to Sheppard's "fiery temper" could only have emanated from the prosecution. Moreover, the newspapers described in detail clues that had been found by the police, but not put into the record.

The fact that many of the prejudicial news items can be traced to the prosecution, as well as the defense, aggravates the judge's failure to take any action. See Stroble v California, 343 US 181, 201, 96 L ed 872, 886, 72 S Ct 599 (1952) (FRANKFURTER, J., dissenting). Effective control of these sources—concededly within the court's power—might well have prevented the divulgence of inaccurate information, rumors, and accusations that made up much of the inflammatory publicity, at least after Sheppard's indictment.

More specifically, the trial court might well have proscribed extrajudicial statements by any lawyer, party, witness, or court official which divulged prejudicial matters, such as the refusal of Sheppard to submit to interrogation or take any lie detector tests; any statement made by Sheppard to officials; the identity of prospective witnesses or their probable testimony; any belief in guilt or innocence; or like statements concerning the merits of the case. See State v Van Duyne, 43 NJ 369,

389, 204 A 2d 841, 852 (1964), in which the court interpreted Canon 20 of the American Bar Association's Canons of Professional Ethics to prohibit such statements. Being advised of the great public interest in the case, the mass coverage of the press, and the potential prejudicial impact of publicity, the court could also have requested the appropriate city and county officials to promulgate a regulation with respect to dissemination of information about the case by their employees. In addition, reporters who wrote or broadcast prejudicial stories, could have been warned as to the impropriety of publishing material not introduced in the proceedings. The judge was put on notice of such events by defense counsel's complaint about the WHK broadcast on the second day of trial. See p. 611, supra. In this manner, Sheppard's right to a trial free from outside interference would have been given added protection without corresponding curtailment of the news media. Had the judge, the other officers of the court, and the police placed the interest of justice first, the news media would have soon learned to be content with the task of reporting the case as it unfolded in the courtroom—not pieced together from extrajudicial statements.

From the cases coming here we note that unfair and prejudicial news comment on pending trials has become increasingly prevalent. Due process requires that the accused receive a trial by an impartial jury free from outside influences. Given the pervasiveness of modern communications and the difficulty of effacing prejudicial publicity from the minds of the jurors, the trial courts must take strong measures to ensure that the balance is never weighed against the accused. And appellate tribunals have the duty to make an independent evaluation of the circumstances. Of course, there is nothing that proscribes the press from reporting events that transpire in the courtroom. But where there is a reasonable likelihood that prejudicial news prior to trial will prevent a fair trial, the judge should continue the case until the threat abates, or transfer it to another county not so permeated with publicity. In addition, sequestration of the jury was something the judge should have raised sua sponte with counsel. If publicity during the proceedings threatens the fairness of the trial, a new trial should be ordered. But we must remember that reversals are but palliatives; the cure lies in those remedial measures that will prevent the prejudice at its inception. The courts must take such steps by rule and regulation that will protect their processes from prejudicial outside interferences. Neither prosecutors, counsel for defense, the accused, witnesses, court staff nor enforcement officers coming under the jurisdiction of the court should be permitted to frustrate its function. Collaboration between counsel and the press as to information affecting the fairness of a criminal trial is not only subject to regulation, but is highly censurable and worthy of disciplinary measures.

Since the state trial judge did not fulfill his duty to protect Sheppard from the inherently prejudicial publicity which saturated the community and to control disruptive influences in the courtroom, we must reverse the denial of the habeas petition. The case is remanded to the District Court with instructions to issue the writ and order that Sheppard be released from custody unless the State puts him to its charges again within a reasonable time.

It is so ordered.

Tinker et al. *v.* Des Moines Independent Community School District et al.

393 U.S. 503, 89 S.Ct. 733, 21 L.Ed. 2d. 731 (1969)

CERTIORARI TO THE UNITED STATES COURT OF APPEALS FOR THE EIGHTH CIRCUIT.

Argued November 12, 1968.—Decided February 24, 1969.

. . .

MR. JUSTICE FORTAS delivered the opinion of the Court.

Petitioner John F. Tinker, 15 years old, and petitioner Christopher Eckhardt, 16 years old, attended high schools in Des Moines, Iowa. Petitioner Mary Beth Tinker, John's sister, was a 13-year-old student in junior high school.

In December 1965, a group of adults and students in Des Moines held a meeting at the Eckhardt home. The group determined to publicize their objections to the hostilities in Vietnam and their support for a truce by wearing black armbands during the holiday season and by fasting on December 16 and New Year's Eve. Petitioners and their parents had previously engaged in similar activities, and they decided to participate in the program.

The principals of the Des Moines schools became aware of the plan to wear armbands. On December 14, 1965, they met and adopted a policy that any student wearing an armband to school would be asked to remove it, and if he refused he would be suspended until he returned without the armband. Petitioners were aware of the regulation that the school authorities adopted.

On December 16, Mary Beth and Christopher wore black armbands to their schools. John Tinker wore his armband the next day. They were all sent home and suspended from school until they would come back without their armbands. They did not return to school until after the planned period for wearing armbands had expired—that is, until after New Year's Day.

This complaint was filed in the United States District Court by petitioners, through their fathers, under § 1983 of Title 42 of the United States Code. It prayed for an injunction restraining the respondent school officials and the respondent members of the board of directors of the school district from disciplining the petitioners, and it sought nominal damages. After an evidentiary hearing the District Court dismissed the complaint. It upheld the constitutionality of the school authorities' action on the ground that it was reasonable in order to prevent disturbance of school discipline. 258 F. Supp. 971 (1966). The court referred to but expressly declined to follow the Fifth Circuit's holding in a similar case that the wearing of symbols like the armbands cannot be prohibited unless it "materially and substantially interfere[s] with the requirements of appropriate discipline in the operation of the school." Burnside v. Byars, 363 F. 2d 744, 749 (1966).

On appeal, the Court of Appeals for the Eighth Circuit considered the case en banc. The court was equally divided, and the District Court's decision was accordingly affirmed, without opinion. 383 F. 2d 988 (1967). We granted certiorari. 390 U.S. 942 (1968).

I

The District Court recognized that the wearing of an armband for the purpose of expressing certain views is the type of symbolic act that is within the Free Speech Clause of the First Amendment. See West Virginia v. Barnette, 319 U.S. 624 (1943); Stromberg v. California, 283 U.S. 359 (1931). Cf. Thornhill v. Alabama, 310 U.S. 88 (1940); Edwards v. South Carolina, 372 U.S. 229 (1963); Brown v. Louisiana, 383 U.S. 131 (1966). As we shall discuss, the wearing of armbands in the circumstances of this case was entirely divorced from actually or potentially disruptive conduct by those participating in it. It was closely akin to "pure speech" which, we have repeatedly held, is entitled to comprehensive protection under the First Amendment. Cf. Cox v. Louisiana, 379 U.S. 536, 555 (1965); Adderley v. Florida, 385 U.S. 39 (1966).

First Amendment rights, applied in light of the special characteristics of the school environment, are available to teachers and students. It can hardly be argued that either students or teachers shed their constitutional rights to freedom of speech or expression at the schoolhouse gate. This has been the unmistakable holding of this Court for almost 50 years. In Meyer v. Nebraska, 262 U.S. 390 (1923), and Bartels v. Iowa, 262 U.S. 404 (1923), this Court, in opinions by MR. JUSTICE MCREYNOLDS, held that the Due Process Clause of the Fourteenth Amendment prevents States from forbidding the teaching of a foreign language to young students. Statutes to this effect, the Court held, unconstitutionally interfere with the liberty of teacher, student, and parent. See also Pierce v. Society of Sisters, 268 U.S. 510 (1925); West Virginia v. Barnette, 319 U.S. 624 (1943); McCollum v. Board of Education, 333 U.S. 203 (1948); Wieman v. Updegraff, 344 U.S. 183, 195 (1952) (concurring opinion); Sweezy v. New Hampshire, 354 U.S. 234 (1957); Shelton v. Tucker, 364 U.S. 479, 487 (1960); Engel v. Vitale, 370 U.S. 421 (1962); Keyishian v. Board of Regents, 385 U.S. 589, 603 (1967); Epperson v. Arkansas, ante, p. 97 (1968).

In West Virginia v. Barnette, supra, this Court held that under the First Amendment, the student in public school may not be compelled to salute the flag. Speaking through MR. JUSTICE JACKSON, the Court said:

> "The Fourteenth Amendment, as now applied to the States, protects the citizen against the State itself and all of its creatures—Boards of Education not excepted. These have, of course, important, delicate, and highly discretionary functions, but none that they may not perform within the limits of the Bill of Rights. That they are educating the young for citizenship is reason for scrupulous protection of Constitutional freedoms of the individual, if we are not to strangle the free mind at its source and teach youth to discount important principles of our government as mere platitudes." 319 U.S., at 637.

On the other hand, the Court has repeatedly emphasized the need for affirming the comprehensive authority of the States and of school officials, consistent with fundamental constitutional safeguards, to prescribe and control conduct in the schools. See Epperson v. Arkansas, supra, at 104; Meyer v. Nebraska, supra, at 402. Our problem lies in the area where students in the exercise of First Amendment rights collide with the rules of the school authorities.

II

The problem posed by the present case does not relate to regulation of the length of skirts or the type of clothing, to hair style, or deportment. Cf. Ferrell v. Dallas Independent School District, 392 F. 2d 697 (1968); Pugsley v. Sellmeyer, 158 Ark. 247, 250 S. W. 538 (1923). It does not concern aggressive, disruptive action or even group demonstrations. Our problem involves direct, primary First Amendment rights akin to "pure speech."

The school officials banned and sought to punish petitioners for a silent, passive expression of opinion, unaccompanied by any disorder or disturbance on the part of petitioners. There is here no evidence whatever of petitioners' interference, actual or nascent, with the schools' work or of collision with the rights of other students to be secure and to be let alone. Accordingly, this case does not concern speech or action that intrudes upon the work of the schools or the rights of other students.

Only a few of the 18,000 students in the school system wore the black armbands. Only five students were suspended for wearing them. There is no indication that the work of the schools or any class was disrupted. Outside the classrooms, a few students made hostile remarks to the children wearing armbands, but there were no threats or acts of violence on school premises.

The District Court concluded that the action of the school authorities was reasonable because it was based upon their fear of a disturbance from the wearing of the armbands. But, in our system, undifferentiated fear or apprehension of disturbance is not enough to overcome the right to freedom of expression. Any departure from absolute regimentation may cause trouble. Any variation from the majority's opinion may inspire fear. Any word spoken, in class, in the lunchroom, or on the campus, that deviates from the views of another person may start an argument or cause a disturbance. But our Constitution says we must take this risk, Terminiello v. Chicago, 337 U.S. 1 (1949); and our history says that it is this sort of hazardous freedom—this kind of openness—that is the basis of our national strength and of the independence and vigor of Americans who grow up and live in this relatively permissive, often disputatious, society.

In order for the State in the person of school officials to justify prohibition of a particular expression of opinion, it must be able to show that its action was caused by something more than a mere desire to avoid the discomfort and unpleasantness that always accompany an unpopular viewpoint. Certainly where there is no finding and no showing that engaging in the forbidden conduct would "materially and substantially interfere with the requirements of appropriate discipline in the operation of the school," the prohibition cannot be sustained. Burnside v. Byars, supra, at 749.

In the present case, the District Court made no such finding, and our independent examination of the record fails to yield evidence that the school authorities had reason to anticipate that the wearing of the armbands would substantially interfere with the work of the school or impinge upon the rights of other students. Even an official memorandum prepared after the suspension that listed the reasons for the ban on wearing the armbands made no reference to the anticipation of such disruption.

On the contrary, the action of the school authorities appears to have been based upon an urgent wish to avoid the controversy which might result from the expression, even by the silent symbol of armbands, of opposition to this Nation's part in the conflagration in Vietnam. It is revealing, in this respect, that the meeting at which the school principals decided to issue the contested regulation was called in response to a student's statement to the journalism teacher in one of the schools that he wanted to write an article on Vietnam and have it published in the school paper. (The student was dissuaded.)

It is also relevant that the school authorities did not purport to prohibit the wearing of all symbols of political or controversial significance. The record shows that students in some of the schools wore buttons relating to national political campaigns, and some even wore the Iron Cross, traditionally a symbol of Nazism. The order prohibiting the wearing of armbands did not extend to these. Instead, a particular symbol—black armbands worn to exhibit opposition to this Nation's involvement in Vietnam—was singled out for prohibition. Clearly, the prohibition of expression of one particular opinion, at least without evidence that it is necessary to avoid material and substantial interference with schoolwork or discipline, is not constitutionally permissible.

In our system, state-operated schools may not be enclaves of totalitarianism. School officials do not possess absolute authority over their students. Students in school as well as out of school are "persons" under our Constitution. They are possessed of fundamental rights which the State must respect, just as they themselves must respect their obligations to the State. In our system, students may not be regarded as closed-circuit recipients of only that which the State chooses to communicate. They may not be confined to the expression of those sentiments that are officially approved. In the absence of a specific showing of constitutionally valid reasons to regulate their speech, students are entitled to freedom of expression of their views. As Judge Gewin, speaking for the Fifth Circuit, said, school officials cannot suppress "expressions of feelings with which they do not wish to contend." Burnside v. Byars, supra, at 749.

In Meyer v. Nebraska, supra, at 402, Mr. Justice McReynolds expressed this Nation's repudiation of the principle that a State might so conduct its schools as to "foster a homogeneous people." He said:

> "In order to submerge the individual and develop ideal citizens, Sparta assembled the males at seven into barracks and intrusted their subsequent education and training to official guardians. Although such measures have been deliberately approved by men of great genius, their ideas touching the relation between individual and State were wholly different from those upon which our institutions rest; and it hardly will be affirmed that any legislature could impose such restrictions upon the people of a State without doing violence to both letter and spirit of the Constitution."

This principle has been repeated by this Court on numerous occasions during the intervening years. In Keyishian v. Board of Regents, 385 U.S. 589, 603, Mr. Justice Brennan, speaking for the Court, said:

> "'The vigilant protection of constitutional freedoms is nowhere more vital than in the community of American schools.' Shelton v. Tucker, [364 U.S. 479,] at 487. The classroom is peculiarly the 'marketplace of ideas.' The Nation's future depends upon leaders trained through wide exposure to that robust exchange of ideas which discovers truth 'out of a multitude of tongues, [rather] than through any kind of authoritative selection.'"

The principle of these cases is not confined to the supervised and ordained discussion which takes place in the classroom. The principal use to which the schools are dedicated is to accommodate students during prescribed hours for the purpose of certain types of activities. Among those activities is personal intercommunication among the students. This is not only an inevitable part of the process of attending school; it is also an important part of the educational process. A student's rights, therefore, do not embrace merely the classroom hours. When he is in the cafeteria, or on the playing field, or on the campus during the authorized hours, he may express his opinions, even on controversial subjects like the conflict in Vietnam, if he does so without "materially and substantially interfer[ing] with the requirements of appropriate discipline in the operation of the school" and without colliding with the rights of others. Burnside v. Byars, supra, at 749. But conduct by the student, in class or out of it, which for any reason—whether it stems from time, place, or type of behavior—materially disrupts classwork or involves substantial disorder or invasion of the rights of others is, of course, not immunized by the constitutional guarantee of freedom of speech. Cf. Blackwell v. Issaquena County Board of Education, 363 F. 2d 749 (C.A. 5th Cir. 1966).

Under our Constitution, free speech is not a right that is given only to be so circumscribed that it exists in principle but not in fact. Freedom of expression would not truly exist if the right could be exercised only in an area that a benevolent government has provided as a safe haven for crackpots. The Constitution says that Congress (and the States) may not abridge the right to free speech. This provision means what it says. We properly read it to permit reasonable regulation of speech-connected activities in carefully restricted circumstances. But we do not confine the permissible exercise of First Amendment rights to a telephone booth or the four corners of a pamphlet, or to supervised and ordained discussion in a school classroom.

If a regulation were adopted by school officials forbidding discussion of the Vietnam conflict, or the expression by any student of opposition to it anywhere on school property except as part of a prescribed classroom exercise, it would be obvious that the regulation would violate the constitutional rights of students, at least if it could not be justified by a showing that the students' activities would materially and substantially disrupt the work and discipline of the school. Cf. Hammond v. South Carolina State College, 272 F. Supp. 947 (D.C. S.C. 1967) (orderly protest meeting on state college campus); Dickey v. Alabama State Board of Education, 273 F. Supp. 613 (D.C. M.D. Ala. 1967) (expulsion of student editor of college newspaper). In the circumstances of the present case, the prohibition of the silent, passive "witness of the armbands," as one of the children called it, is no less offensive to the Constitution's guarantees.

As we have discussed, the record does not demonstrate any facts which might reasonably have led school authorities to forecast substantial disruption of or material interference with school activities, and no disturbances or disorders on the school premises in fact occurred. These petitioners merely went about their ordained rounds in school. Their deviation consisted only in wearing on their sleeve a band of black cloth, not more than two inches wide. They wore it to exhibit their disapproval of the Vietnam hostilities and their advocacy of a truce, to make their views known, and, by their example, to influence others to adopt them. They neither interrupted school activities nor sought to intrude in the school affairs or the lives of others. They caused discussion outside of the classrooms, but no interference with work and no disorder. In the circumstances, our Constitution does not permit officials of the State to deny their form of expression.

We express no opinion as to the form of relief which should be granted, this being a matter for the lower courts to determine. We reverse and remand for further proceedings consistent with this opinion.

Reversed and remanded.

Murphy *v.* Florida

421 U.S. 794, 95 S.Ct. 203, 44 L.Ed. 2d. 589 (1975)

CERTIORARI TO THE UNITED STATES COURT OF APPEALS FOR THE FIFTH CIRCUIT

Argued April 15, 1975.—Decided June 16, 1975.

. . .

MR. JUSTICE MARSHALL delivered the opinion of the Court.

The question presented by this case is whether the petitioner was denied a fair trial because members of the jury had learned from news accounts about a prior felony conviction or certain facts about the crime with which he was charged. Under the circumstances of this case, we find that petitioner has not been denied due process, and we therefore affirm the judgment below.

I

Petitioner was convicted in the Dade County, Fla., Criminal Court in 1970 of breaking and entering a home, while armed, with intent to commit robbery, and of assault with intent to commit robbery. The charges stemmed from the January 1968 robbery of a Miami Beach home and petitioner's apprehension, with three others, while fleeing from the scene.

The robbery and petitioner's arrest received extensive press coverage because petitioner had been much in the news before. He had first made himself notorious for his part in the 1964 theft of the Star of India sapphire from a museum in New York. His flamboyant lifestyle made him a continuing subject of press interest; he was generally referred to—at least in the media—as "Murph the Surf."

Before the date set for petitioner's trial on the instant charges, he was indicted on two counts of murder in Broward County, Fla. Thereafter the Dade County court declared petitioner mentally incompetent to stand trial; he was committed to a hospital and the prosecutor *nolle prossed* the robbery indictment. In August 1968 he was indicted by a federal grand jury for conspiring to transport stolen securities in interstate commerce. After petitioner was adjudged competent for trial, he was convicted on one count of murder in Broward County (March 1969) and pleaded guilty to one count of the federal indictment involving stolen securities (December 1969). The indictment for robbery was refiled in August 1969 and came to trial one year later.

The events of 1968 and 1969 drew extensive press coverage. Each new case against petitioner was considered newsworthy, not only in Dade County but elsewhere as well. The record in this case contains scores of articles reporting on petitioner's trials and tribulations during this period; many purportedly relate statements that petitioner or his attorney made to reporters.

Jury selection in the present case began in August 1970. Seventy-eight jurors were questioned. Of these, 30 were excused for miscellaneous personal reasons; 20 were excused peremptorily by the defense or prosecution; 20 were excused by the court as having prejudged petitioner; and the remaining eight served as the jury and two alternates. Petitioner's motions to dismiss the chosen jurors, on the ground that they were aware that he had previously been convicted of either the 1964 Star of India theft or the Broward County murder, were denied, as was his renewed motion for a change of venue based on allegedly prejudicial pretrial publicity.

At trial, petitioner did not testify or put in any evidence; assertedly in protest of the selected jury, he did not cross-examine any of the State's witnesses. He was convicted on both counts, and after an unsuccessful appeal he sought habeas corpus relief in the District Court for the Southern District of Florida.

The District Court denied petitioner relief, 363 F. Supp. 1224 (1973), and the Court of Appeals for the Fifth Circuit affirmed. 495 F. 2d 553 (1974). We granted certiorari, 419 U.S. 1088 (1974), in order to resolve the apparent conflict between the decision below and that of the Third Circuit in United States ex rel. Doggett v. Yeager, 472 F. 2d 229 (1973), over the applicability of Marshall v. United States, 360 U.S. 310 (1959), to state criminal proceedings.

II

The defendant in Marshall was convicted of dispensing certain drugs without a prescription. In the course of the trial seven of the jurors were exposed to various news accounts relating that Marshall had previously been convicted of forgery, that he and his wife had been arrested for other narcotics offenses, and that he had for some time practiced medicine without a license. After interviewing the jurors, however, the trial judge denied a motion for a mistrial, relying on the jurors' assurances that they could maintain impartiality in spite of the news articles.

Noting that the jurors had been exposed to information with a high potential for prejudice, this Court reversed the conviction. It did so, however, expressly "[i]n the exercise of [its] supervisory power to formulate and apply proper standards for enforcement of the criminal law in the federal courts," and not as a matter of constitutional compulsion. Id., at 313.

In the face of so clear a statement, it cannot be maintained that Marshall was a constitutional ruling now applicable, through the Fourteenth Amendment, to the States. Petitioner argues, nonetheless, that more recent decisions of this Court have applied to state cases the principle underlying the Marshall decision: that persons who have learned from news sources of a defendant's prior criminal record are presumed to be prejudiced. We cannot agree that Marshall has any application beyond the federal courts.

Petitioner relies principally upon Irvin v. Dowd, 366 U.S. 717 (1961), Rideau v. Louisiana, 373 U.S. 723 (1963), Estes v. Texas, 381 U.S. 532 (1965), and Sheppard v. Maxwell, 384 U.S. 333 (1966). In each of these cases, this Court overturned a state-court conviction obtained in a trial atmosphere that had been utterly corrupted by press coverage.

In Irvin v. Dowd the rural community in which the trial was held had been subjected to a barrage of inflammatory publicity immediately prior to trial, including information on the defendant's prior convictions, his confession to 24 burglaries and six murders including the one for which he was tried, and his unaccepted offer to plead guilty in order to avoid the death sentence. As a result, eight of the 12 jurors had formed an opinion that the defendant was guilty before the trial began; some went "so far as to say that it would take evidence to overcome their belief" in his guilt. 366 U.S., at 728. In these circumstances, the Court readily found actual prejudice against the petitioner to a degree that rendered a fair trial impossible.

Prejudice was presumed in the circumstances under which the trials in Rideau, Estes, and Sheppard were held. In those cases the influence of the news media, either in the community at large or in the courtroom itself, pervaded the proceedings. In Rideau the defendant had "confessed" under police interrogation to the murder of which he stood convicted. A 20-minute film of his confession was broadcast three times by a television station in the community where the crime and the trial took place. In reversing, the Court did not examine the voir dire for evidence of actual prejudice because it considered the trial under review "but a hollow formality"—the real trial had occurred when tens of thousands of people, in a community of 150,000, had seen and heard the defendant admit his guilt before the cameras.

The trial in Estes had been conducted in a circus atmosphere, due in large part to the intrusions of the press, which was allowed to sit within the bar of the court and to overrun it with television equipment. Similarly, Sheppard arose from a trial infected not only by a background of extremely inflammatory publicity but also by a courthouse given over to accommodate the public appetite for carnival. The proceedings in these cases were entirely lacking in the solemnity and sobriety to which a defendant is entitled in a system that subscribes to any notion of fairness and rejects the verdict of a mob. They cannot be made to stand for the proposition that juror exposure to information about a state defendant's prior convictions or to news accounts of the crime with which he is charged alone presumptively deprives the defendant of due process. To resolve this case, we must turn therefore, to any indications in the totality of circumstances that petitioner's trial was not fundamentally fair.

III

The constitutional standard of fairness requires that a defendant have "a panel of impartial, 'indifferent' jurors." Irvin v. Dowd, 366 U.S., at 722. Qualified jurors need not, however, be totally ignorant of the facts and issues involved.

> "To hold that the mere existence of any preconceived notion as to the guilt or innocence of an accused, without more, is sufficient to rebut the presumption of a prospective juror's impartiality would be to establish an impossible standard. It is sufficient if the juror can lay aside his impression or opinion and render a verdict based on the evidence presented in court." Id., at 723.

At the same time, the juror's assurances that he is equal to this task cannot be dispositive of the accused's rights, and it remains open to the defendant to demonstrate "the actual existence of such an opinion in the mind of the juror as will raise the presumption of partiality." Ibid.

The voir dire in this case indicates no such hostility to petitioner by the jurors who served in his trial as to suggest a partiality that could not be laid aside. Some of the jurors had a vague recollection of the robbery with which petitioner was charged and each had some knowledge of petitioner's past crimes, but none betrayed any belief in the relevance of petitioner's past to the present case. Indeed, four of the six jurors volunteered their views of its irrelevance, and one suggested that people who have been in trouble before are too often singled out for suspicion of each new crime—a predisposition that could only operate in petitioner's favor.

In the entire voir dire transcript furnished to us, there is only one colloquy on which petitioner can base even a colorable claim of partiality by a juror. In response to a leading and hypothetical question, presupposing a two- or three-week presentation of evidence against petitioner and his failure to put on any defense, one juror conceded that his prior impression of petitioner would dispose him to convict. We cannot attach great significance to this statement, however, in light of the leading nature of counsel's questions and the juror's other testimony indicating that he had no deep impression of petitioner at all.

The juror testified that he did not keep up with current events and, in fact, had never heard of petitioner until he arrived in the room for prospective jurors where some veniremen were discussing him. He did not know that petitioner was "a convicted jewel thief" even then; it was petitioner's counsel who informed him of this fact. And he volunteered that petitioner's murder conviction, of which he had just heard, would not be relevant to his guilt or innocence in the present case, since "[w]e are not trying him for murder."

Even these indicia of impartiality might be disregarded in a case where the general atmosphere in the community or courtroom is sufficiently inflammatory, but the circumstances surrounding petitioner's trial are not at all of that variety.

Petitioner attempts to portray them as inflammatory by reference to the publicity to which the community was exposed. The District Court found, however, that the news articles concerning petitioner had appeared almost entirely during the period between December 1967 and January 1969, the latter date being seven months before the jury in this case was selected. 363 F. Supp., at 1228. They were, moreover, largely factual in nature. Compare Beck v. Washington, 369 U.S. 541 (1962), with Sheppard v. Maxwell, supra.

The length to which the trial court must go in order to select jurors who appear to be impartial is another factor relevant in evaluating those jurors' assurances of impartiality. In a community where most veniremen will admit to a disqualifying prejudice, the reliability of the others' protestations may be drawn into question; for it is then more probable that they are part of a community deeply hostile to the accused, and more likely that they may unwittingly have been influenced by it. In Irvin v. Dowd, for example, the Court noted that 90% of those examined on the point were inclined to believe in the accused's guilt, and the court had excused for this cause 268 of the 430 veniremen. In the present case, by contrast, 20 of the 78 persons questioned were excused because they indicated an opinion as to petitioner's guilt. This may indeed be 20 more than would occur in the trial of a totally obscure person, but it by no means suggests a community with sentiment so poisoned against petitioner as to impeach the indifference of jurors who displayed no animus of their own.

In sum, we are unable to conclude, in the circumstances presented in this case, that petitioner did not receive a fair trial. Petitioner has failed to show that the setting of the trial was inherently prejudicial or that the jury-selection process of which he complains permits an inference of actual prejudice. The judgment of the Court of Appeals must therefore be

Affirmed.

CHAPTER 6

Contents

Continued

Search and Seizure

The Fourth Amendment to the United States Constitution provides:

> *The right of the people to be secure in their persons, houses, papers, and effects, against unreasonable searches and seizures, shall not be violated and no Warrants shall issue but upon probable cause, supported by Oath or affirmation, and particularly describing the place to be searched, and the persons or things to be seized.*

§ 6.1 History of the Exclusionary Rule

The reader will recall that in an earlier chapter of this text we discussed the theory of checks and balances where each major branch of the government, i.e., the Executive, Legislative, and Judicial, acts as a check and balances the power of the other branches of government. In this way, no one branch is able to have complete authority to administer the governmental processes. Each branch of the government is a complete unit in itself and theoretically is not to be dominated by the others. It sometimes happens, however, that a strong President, acting with a majority of his own political party in the legislative branch, can get legislation passed, but in the final analysis, the Supreme Court, consisting of persons enjoying the highest prestige and having lifetime positions, acts as a leveling influence against unconstitutional legislation.

You will recall that the executive power is exercised by the President of the United States or the Governors of the respective States. You will also remember that the implementation or enforcement of laws is the responsibility of the executive branch of government. Hence the State, City, or County police departments and agencies are arms of the executive branch of government.

The United States Constitution, we say, gives basic fundamental rights to citizens and persons within our geographical borders. If these rights are denied to these people by the legislative or executive branches of government, it then becomes the responsibility of the judicial branch of government to see that this condition is corrected.

The Fourth Amendment to the United States Constitution dealing with unreasonable search and seizure had at first been intended to limit only the central federal government from the infringement of this right of United States citizens. With the passage of the Fourteenth Amendment to the

United States Constitution, lawyers were finding new meaning in that document that one wonders whether the framers and proposers of the original Fourth Amendment and the Fourteenth Amendment had any idea of at the time of adoption.

The United States Supreme Court does not have the power to send an army into the field to enforce a judgment of the court but it must rely upon the integrity of the executive branch to enforce its decisions. Because of the nature of people, if one has some power, inherently s/he grabs more power unless restrained in some manner. The police of the nation, given certain powers, were frequently obsessed with the idea that they could do anything they wanted to do with suspected persons, in the interest of effective law enforcement. The United States Supreme Court devised what has come to be known as the exclusionary rule. In essence the rule provides that if the court finds that the conduct of the police deprived the defendant/petitioner of a substantial constitutional right, all evidence secured as a result of such conduct would not be admissible on the trial of the defendant. Without this evidence in the trial record, no impartial trier of the facts, be it the judge, trying the case without a jury, or the jury, could find that the defendant was guilty. The defendant, however, is required to object to the introduction of this tainted evidence by a procedural device known as a motion to suppress. This is merely an application to the trial court, preceding the actual trial, to conduct a hearing as to whether the defendant has been denied any constitutional right and whether any evidence was obtained as a result of this denial. If the trial judge finds that there was a denial of a constitutional right, the judge will grant the motion to suppress and the prosecutor must find other evidence or move the court for dismissal of the case against the defendant for the reason that s/he has insufficient admissible evidence to convict the defendant.

The concept of the exclusionary rule developed slowly in our legal system. It had been employed to prevent abuses of the privilege of self-incrimination of the Fifth Amendment in Boyd v. U.S., 116 U.S. 616, 6 S.Ct. 524, 29 L.Ed. 746 (1886), where compelled statements were elicited from the defendant by the police. The court, however, had a greater problem in the cases involving Fourth Amendment unreasonable searches. In Weeks v. U.S., 232 U.S. 383, 34 S.Ct. 341, 58 L.Ed. 652 (1914), the court held that any evidence obtained by federal officers in violation of the Fourth Amendment would be barred from a federal prosecution. However, they did permit state officers to secure the evidence in accordance with the state rules of evidence and then hand this evidence over to the federal officers for federal prosecution. This came to be known as the "Silver Platter Doctrine" on the theory that the state officers could engage in practices forbidden to federal officers and then hand over the evidence on a theoretical "Silver Platter" to the federal officers.

At that time many states were operating under the theory enunciated by Mr. Justice Benjamin Cardoza when he was Chief Judge of the Court of Appeals of the State of New York, where in People v. DeFore, 242 N.Y. 13, 150 N.E. 585 (1926), he said at 242 N.Y. 13, 21, "The criminal is to go free because the constable has blundered"; and at page 23, "The pettiest police officer would have it in his power through overzeal or indiscretion to confer immunity upon an offender for crimes the most flagitious. A room is searched against the law, and the body of a murdered man is found.... The privacy of the home has been infringed and the murderer goes free"; and at 242 N.Y. 13, 24, "The question is whether the protection for the individual would not be gained at a disproportionate loss of protection for society. On the one side is the social need that crime shall be repressed. On the other, the social need that law shall not be flouted by the insolence of office."

The Supreme Court decided a similar case in Wolf v. Colorado, 338 U.S. 25, 69 S.Ct. 1359, 93 L.Ed. 1782 (1949), where it held that a state officer, enforcing a state law, was not controllable by the Fourth Amendment in that this amendment was directed towards governmental abuse and the state officer was in the guise of a private person. The concept being that with respect to state officers' actions, he was acting in conformity with a rule of evidence in that state and the state had a reserved right to enact and implement its own rules of evidence. It is apparent that the Supreme Court was stretching to validate state action in Wolf v. Colorado (supra) because the Court also indicated that an unreasonable search and seizure by a state officer violates the federal constitution by violating the due process clause of the Fourteenth Amendment, but it did not require the exclusion of the evidence in state courts.

The "Silver Platter Doctrine" was discontinued as a result of the court's decision in Elkins v. United States, 364 U.S. 206, 80 S.Ct. 1437, 4 L.Ed.2d 1669 (1960), where it held that the evidence seized by state officers by an unreasonable search and seizure could not be admitted into evidence in a federal prosecution.

The court, however, still did not interfere with the admissibility of evidence by state law enforcement officers in state courts except where the evidence was obtained by a search and seizure accomplished by coercion, violence, or brutality to the person such as "shocks the conscience." Rochin v. California, 342 U.S. 165, 72 S.Ct. 205, 96 L.Ed. 183 (1952). This was a case where a stomach pump was employed to regurgitate narcotics swallowed by the defendant/petitioner.

The court continued to deal with the problem in Irvine v. California, 347 U.S. 128, 75 S.Ct. 381, 98 L.Ed. 561 (1954), wherein they limited Rochin to situations involving coercion, violence, or brutality to the person. In Breithaupt v. Abram, 352 U.S. 432, 77 S.Ct. 408, 1 L.Ed.2d 448 (1957), a blood sample was taken under the watchful eye of a physician. The sample was taken from the defendant while he was unconscious and it was determined that he had a high alcoholic content in his blood and this was used against him in connection with a vehicular homicide case. In that case the court upheld the conviction because the court found no coercion, violence, or brutality employed by the police.

The court overruled Wolf v. Colorado (supra) when it decided Mapp v. Ohio, 367 U.S. 643, 81 S.Ct. 1684, 6 L.Ed.2d 1081 (1961), wherein the court stated that:

> . . . The efforts of the courts and their officials to bring the guilty to punishment, praiseworthy as they are, are not to be aided by the sacrifice of those great principles established by years of endeavor and suffering which have resulted in their embodiment in the fundamental law of the land . . . Because there can be no fixed formula, we are admittedly met with recurring questions of the reasonableness of searches, but less is not to be expected when dealing with a Constitution, and, at any rate (r)easonableness is in the first instance for the (trial judge) to determine . . . We hold that all evidence obtained by searches and seizures in violation of the Constitution is, by that same authority, inadmissible in a state court.

The "Burger Court" has been more law-and-order-oriented than the "Warren Court" and recent decisions appear to give greater authority to law enforcement officers to make searches without a warrant. In United States v. Santana, 427 U.S. 38, 96 S.Ct. 2406, 49 L.Ed.2d 300 (1976), the court held that when the police observed petitioner possessing contraband while she was standing in the doorway of her house, her retreat to the interior vestibule of the house, taking the contraband with her, did not give her protection of the unreasonable search provisions of the Fourth and Fourteenth Amendments.

In United States v. Watson, 423 U.S. 411, 96 S.Ct. 820, 46 L.Ed.2d 598 (1976), the court again decided in favor of a warrantless search. This case was based upon 18 U.S.C. 3061(a)(3) which expressly authorized postal inspectors to make arrests without a warrant for a felony when they had probable cause to believe that the person to be arrested had committed or was committing such a felony. The court wrote, ". . . The duty of law enforcement officers to seek a warrant 'where practicable to do so' is merely a rule of 'judicial preference' and not one of constitutional dimensions . . . ."

From a reading of these 1976 cases relating to alleged violations of Fourth and Fourteenth Amendments and from other later cases, it appears that the court is lowering its threshold for exclusion of evidence based upon alleged violations of the Bill of Rights. There are, however, many states whose highest court has required a higher threshold where more rights are granted to an arrestee than those which are required by the federal government. They decide their cases based upon the Bill of Rights as enunciated in their state constitutions. In a text such as this, it would be impractical to indicate the threshold in each state and, hence, if there is any doubt on the part of the reader, s/he is referred to the latest decisions in his/her jurisdiction.

Thus we have the present trend of the law with respect to the exclusionary rule as it applies to unreasonable search and seizure. Its applicability to other fundamental rights of the Bill of Rights of the United States Constitution will be discussed in later chapters of this text.

§ 6.2 Search Warrants

A search warrant is an order in writing in the name of the People signed by a neutral and detached magistrate, directed to a peace officer, commanding him/her to search for personal property and bring it before the court.

A search warrant is obtained by a law enforcement officer by applying to a detached neutral magistrate that s/he issue such a warrant. In order to do this constitutionally and to preserve the record, the officer is required to indicate by way of an affidavit what probable cause exists for the issuance of such a court order. After reading the affidavit setting forth facts which in the officer's opinion give the officer probable cause to make the search to obtain evidence to arrest the defendant for violation of some law, the detached, neutral magistrate makes his/her own conclusion as to whether probable cause exists. If the necessary probable cause exists, the judicial officer will sign an order, which is usually prepared beforehand by the prosecution. This order will direct the law enforcement officer to make a search and if the evidence sought is found, to bring the evidence and the person described in the warrant before the court. The returning of the evidence and/or the named person before the court has come to be known as the "return."

§ 6.3 Probable Cause Regarding Search Warrants

Probable cause and reasonable grounds are almost synonymous. The reason that the court has insisted that a neutral detached magistrate view the circumstances of probable cause is that the court has manifested a preference for arrest under search warrants on the grounds that interposing an orderly procedure whereby a neutral and detached magistrate makes the decision is better than allowing those engaged in the competitive enterprise of ferreting out crime to make hurried decisions which would be reviewable by a magistrate only after the fact and by hindsight judgment. "In a doubtful or marginal case a search warrant may be sustainable where without one it would fall." United States v. Ventresca, 380 U.S. 102, 85 S.Ct. 741, 13 L.Ed.2d 684 (1965). The court treated the problem of judicial determination of probable cause in Aguilar v. Texas, 378 U.S. 108, 84 S.Ct. 1509, 12 L.Ed.2d 723 (1964), where it struck down a state search warrant issued on the basis of an affidavit which recited only that the police "have received reliable information from a credible person" and "do believe" that defendant possesses narcotics at described premises because the affidavit contained "mere conclusions," not enabling the magistrate to "judge for himself the persuasiveness of the facts relied on . . . to show probable cause." The affidavit should have indicated specific facts which led them to their conclusion and did not give proof that the informant was credible or reliable. A magistrate may require the testimony of the informer before he signs the warrant.

The problem of the requirement of a neutral and detached magistrate issuing the warrant was met squarely by the court in Coolidge v. New Hampshire, 403 U.S. 443, 91 S.Ct. 2022, 29 L.Ed.2d 564 (1971), where the Attorney General of the State of New Hampshire, acting as a Justice of the Peace, under New Hampshire Law in force at that time, issued a search warrant. The court held that this action did not satisfy the requirements of the Fourth and Fourteenth Amendments in that the Attorney General was not detached but was interested in the prosecution of the case.

§ 6.4 Identity of Informants Regarding Search Warrants

The government is sometimes confronted with a serious problem in decision making when at a motion to suppress and controvert a warrant hearing, the defendant's counsel asks the affiant of the application for the warrant for the identity of the informant. Anyone who has any familiarity with informers knows that they do not want to be identified. In some cases their very life depends upon their anonymity. At the very least, their future use to law enforcement is extinguished.

Those students who are familiar with the law of evidence will know that in a trial of an action, hearsay evidence is not admissible unless it falls within certain long used and reliable exceptions. However, in a motion to suppress, in most jurisdictions, hearsay evidence is admissible. In this way it is possible for the officer to testify that an informer told him something even though the informer is not available for cross-examination.

The conversation between a law enforcement officer and an informant is privileged, much like that of husband and wife, attorney and client, penitent and clergyman, and other privileged communications. However, where disclosure of an informer's identity or of the contents of his communication is relevant and helpful to the defense of the accused or it is essential to a fair determination of the cause, the privilege must give way. Roviaro v. United States, 353 U.S. 53, 77 S.Ct. 623, 1 L.Ed. 639 (1957); Rugendorf v. United States, 376 U.S. 528, 84 S.Ct. 825, 11 L.Ed.2d 887 (1964). In Roviaro, the defendant was charged in two counts with (1) an illegal sale of heroin to "John Doe" and (2) illegal transportation of heroin. The court reasoned that "John Doe" was a participant in the transportation charge and that "John Doe" was an informer. In this factual pattern, the court said the government should be required to supply the identity of the informant or suffer dismissal.

McCray v. Illinois, 386 U.S. 300, 87 S.Ct. 1056, 18 L.Ed.2d 782 (1967), was another case treating the question of whether an informer need be identified at the insistence of the defendant. In that case petitioner was arrested for possession of narcotics and heroin was found on his person. A preliminary hearing on a motion to suppress was held and the arresting officers testified that an informant who had supplied reliable information on about twenty previous cases told them that he had observed McCray selling narcotics at a certain corner and then accompanied the police to that corner and pointed out McCray. Both officers were asked for the name and address of the informant, but objections to these questions were sustained and petitioner's motion was denied. He was subsequently convicted. The court reasoned that the arresting officers testified in open court fully and in precise detail as to what the informer told them and as to why they had reason to believe his information was trustworthy. Each officer was under oath. Each was subject to a searching cross-examination. The judge was obviously satisfied that each was telling the truth and for that reason he exercised discretion conferred upon him by the established law of Illinois to respect the informer privilege. "Nothing in the Due Process Clause of the Fourteenth Amendment requires a state court judge in every such hearing to assume the arresting officers are committing perjury...."

The court denied the petitioner's right to cross-examine the arresting officers on the identity of the informer reasoning that the claim of the petitioner of violation of his Sixth Amendment right of cross-examination can not be sustained because it would follow from this argument that no witness on cross-examination could ever constitutionally assert a testimonial privilege including the privilege compelling self-incrimination guaranteed by the Constitution itself.

The author believes that to assume that every policeman who testifies is telling the truth is an absurdity. However, the court probably took the right course of action in this case in deciding as it did because if it had decided to the contrary, the law enforcement officer's most valuable asset, the informer, would be destroyed and many serious crimes would not otherwise be solved.

In People v. Verrechihio, 23 N.Y.2d 489, 245 N.E.2d 222 (1969), a New York Court of Appeals case where the officer testified that an informant of past reliability had told him that the defendant "usually had heroin," the court, per Burke, J., held:

> Obviously the information imparted was extremely vague and lacking in specifics and the source of the informer's information is nowhere detailed so that it could as readily be rumor or outright fiction as personal knowledge of fact.... On these facts we are presented with a "rare" case in which identity should be disclosed unless the officer's observations provide objective verification of the details of the information supplied by the informer.

This was not a reversal of McCray (supra) but followed Roviaro (supra) and New York chose to place a higher threshold on the right of confrontation and cross-examination in cases where the information relayed to the officer by the informant was extremely vague. Each state may do this with respect to its own constitution and their courts' interpretation of it. On the other hand, as each right of the Bill of Rights of the Federal Constitution is absorbed by virtue of the Fourteenth Amendment, each state is required to give the basic threshold of rights to its inhabitants as is declared by the United States Supreme Court.

Another case where the state refused to identify the informant referred to in an affidavit supporting the issuance of a search warrant occurred in COLORADO v NUNEZ, 465 U.S. 324, 104 S.Ct. 1257, 79 L.Ed.2d. 338, (1984), where the state court suppressed evidence seized because the state refused to identify the informant who gave the police officer the initial information leading to the issuance of the search warrant. The Court dismissed the writ as improvidently granted saying that it appeared that the judgment of the court below rested on independent and adequate state grounds. This appears to be an extension of MICHIGAN v. LONG, infra, in 6.23. In the Nunez case, three concurring justices joined in a dissenting decision wherein they said that this decision confers on trial courts in Colorado discretion to do far more than the Federal Constitution minimally requires. The Federal cases require disclosure of the identity of the informer when there is a showing of a reasonable basis in fact to question the accuracy of the informant's rentals.

§ 6.5 Particularity in Search Warrants of Place and Person to Be Searched and Seized

The Fourth Amendment proscription respecting the particularity of the description of the place to be searched and the person or things to be seized was inserted to prevent a recurrence of a General Warrant or a Writ of Assistance which had previously existed in England. Accordingly, the courts have required law enforcement officers to be precise in their requests for search warrants. Typographical errors in the descriptive part of the warrant may not prove fatally defective but care should be taken to avoid them. If the address indicated is 2300 S. State Street when it should have been 2310 S. State Street, the warrant can withstand attack if the apartment number is correct. Peo. v. Watson, 26 Ill.2d 203, 186 N.E.2d 326 (1962). Often an address has a deep lot and there is a building adjacent to the street and another building in the rear of the one adjacent to the street. This must be specifically described. So too must a particular apartment number or floor number in a building be particularly described so as to comply with the particularity requirement of the Amendment. In Watson (supra) the Illinois Supreme Court held that a warrant is sufficiently descriptive if it enables the officer, with reasonable effort, to identify the place. If the property is sufficiently recognizable from the description to enable the officer to locate the premises with definiteness and certainty it is adequate. The constitutional safeguard is designed to require a description which particularly points to a definite ascertainable place so as to exclude all others.

Because of freedom afforded to the press under the First Amendment, in obscenity cases, great particularity of the things to be seized is required. A Quantity of Copies of Books v. Kansas, 378 U.S. 205, 84 S.Ct. 1723, 12 L.Ed.2d 809 (1964).

States vary as to the particularity requirement but it is safe to say that if an officer exercises the greatest care in his description of the place to be searched, what he is seeking, and the person to be seized, the warrant will withstand a motion to controvert.

§ 6.6 No Delay in Execution of Search Warrants

A search warrant is a procedural device which is prescribed by both state and federal statute. The statute may vary from state to state in its particular requirements but if there is no time limit for its execution indicated in the statute, the common law rule of reasonable time attaches. Some states require an authorization to that effect if the warrant is to be executed at night. N.Y.—Criminal Procedure Law 690.45(5).

§ 6.7 Search Warrants and Seizure of Nondescribed Contraband

If an officer, pursuant to a search warrant, enters a premises and in searching for the items described on the search warrant in the particularly described location observes a revolver unlawfully possessed or a machine gun or other contraband, it is his/her duty to seize this contraband along with the items described in the warrant and the seizure is valid. Harris v. United States, 331 U.S. 145, 67 S.Ct. 1098, 91 L.Ed. 1399 (1947). Such items are admissible in evidence under the theory that they have been seized as incidental to a lawful arrest. Chimel v. California, 395 U.S. 752, 89 S.Ct. 2034, 23 L.Ed.2d 685 (1969). The difficult problem arises, however, when the items mentioned in the search warrant are not found but other contraband is found. In that case the officer is to seize the contraband anyway but when the defendant moves for a motion to suppress, he may be successful in suppressing the evidence so obtained. Notwithstanding this, the contraband is not returned to the defendant but is confiscated.

§ 6.8 Search Warrants and Seizure of Authorized Objects

A search warrant may not be validly issued to seize objects which are not unlawfully held. It cannot be used in civil actions as a substitute for an action in replevin or a warrant of attachment. The statutes of the various states indicate with specificity the type of items which may be seized. Generally, they are issued upon property which was stolen or embezzled, or when the property was used as a means of committing a felony, or when the property is either in the possession of a person who intends to use it as a means of committing a crime, or if the property is in possession of another to whom such person delivered it for the purpose of concealing it or preventing it from being discovered. It is recommended that the reader consult the criminal procedure statute of his/her state to ascertain local requirements for the authorized objects of a search warrant.

§ 6.8(a) Good Faith Exception

In the year 1980, the courts appeared to begin a trend which appears to represent the thinking of many law enforcement persons with respect to the situation where an arresting officer makes an arrest under conditions which, if it were strictly construed, would result in the dismissal of criminal charges against a defendant who is obviously guilty of the crime charged, when the officer made an effort to comply with constitutional safeguards but made a good-faith error. Such a situation arose in U.S. v. WILLIAMS, 622 F.2d. 830, 27 Cr.L. 3293 (1980) where in the United States Court of Appeals for the Fifth Circuit, the court in an en-banc decision held that evidence obtained by police conduct that is alleged to be unlawful shall not be suppressed if the government establishes that the conduct, if mistaken or unauthorized, was taken in the reasonable good-faith belief that it was proper. The United States Supreme Court denied certiorari in 449 U.S. 961 which leaves this decision to be followed in other circuits. Other circuits and some state courts did just that. As of that time, as known to the author, the 2nd and 4th Circuit as well as California, Florida, Georgia, Montana, New Hampshire, Colorado and Virginia had followed it.

The denial of certiorari by the Supreme Court in the Williams case has been followed by other denials of other cases such as U.S. v. SINDONA 636 F.2d. 792, Cert. den. 451 U.S. 912, 101 S.Ct. 1984, 68 L.Ed.2d. 302 (1980) and U.S. v. ASLOUNY, 629 F.2d. 830 Cert. den. 449 U.S. 1111, 101 S.Ct. 920, 66 L.Ed.2d. 840 (1980).

As of this writing, it has not been adopted as a federal statute but movement is being made in that direction. It therefore appears that the good-faith exception is with us for some time to come.

The Supreme Court delivered a decision in GATES v. ILLINOIS, 462 U.S. 213, 103 S.Ct. 2317, 76 L.Ed.2d. 527, 51 LW 4709 (1983) that appears to skirt the problem of the good-faith exception. In that case, a search warrant was obtained for the auto and residence of a husband and wife drug dealing team. The Illinois courts suppressed the evidence on the ground that the police application for the warrant failed to satisfy a two pronged test announced in AGUILAR v. TEXAS, 387 U.S. 108 and SPINELLI v. UNITED STATES, 393 U.S. 410, i.e. (1) revealing the informant's "basis of knowledge" and (2) providing sufficient facts to establish either the informant's "veracity" or the "reliability" of the informant's report. The Supreme Court wrote that it would not pass on the question of whether or not to exclude evidence obtained in the reasonable belief that the search and seizure was consistent with the Fourth Amendment since it was not presented or decided by the Illinois courts. However they announced a new concept which they called the "totality of the circumstances" approach and abandoned the two pronged test. They explained that the task of the issuing magistrate is simply to make a practical, common sense decision whether, given all the circumstances set forth in the affidavit before him, there is a fair probability that contraband or evidence of a crime will be found in a particular place. And the duty of the reviewing court is simply to ensure that the magistrate had a substantial basis for concluding that probable cause existed. In the instant case, the Court held that the issuing magistrate had a substantial basis for concluding that probable cause to search respondent's home and car existed. The Illinois courts were reversed. This case greatly expands the power of law enforcement agencies to get convictions.

An extension of the "totality of the circumstances" approach was made by the Court in U.S. v LEON, —U.S.—, 104 S.Ct. 3105, 82 L.Ed.2d. 677 (1984). In the Leon case, the police initiated a drug-trafficking investigation by surveillance of the respondent's activities. Based on an affidavit summarizing the police officer's observations, a facially valid search warrant for three residences and automobiles was obtained and executed.

The searches produced large quantities of drugs and other evidence. Respondents were indicted for federal drug offenses, and motions to suppress were filed and granted in part. The District Court concluded that the affidavit was insufficient to establish probable cause, although recognizing that the officer had acted in good faith.

The Supreme Court held that the Fourth Amendment exclusionary rule should not be applied so as to bar the use of the prosecution's case-in-chief of evidence obtained by officers acting in reasonable reliance on a search warrant issued by a detached and neutral magistrate but ultimately found to be invalid.

Hence the good faith exception to the exclusionary rule, long in incubation, finally saw the light of day. A fortiorari, MASSACHUSETTS v. SHEPPARD: 468 U.S.—, 104 S.Ct.3424, 82 L.Ed.2d 737, 35, Cr.L. 3296 (1984).

§ 6.9 Force Necessary for Execution of Search Warrants

During the 1960s few police departments were free from the cry of police brutality. In recent years this complaint has markedly diminished as more police departments become professionalized. Unfortunately, there are still some departments against whom many complaints of police brutality are still made. It is noteworthy at this point, however, that with the Burger Court's decision in Rizzo v. Goode, 423 U.S. 362, 96 S.Ct. 598, 46 L.Ed.2d 561 (1976), the Court held that twenty complaints of incidents in a city of three million residents and seventy-five hundred policemen "established neither a conspiratorial design nor departmental policy actively promulgated by the named petitioners to deprive them of their constitutional rights." In that case petitioners were seeking injunctive relief against the Mayor and City Government to prevent further police brutality. Statutes usually give the police the right to use reasonable force in effecting an arrest. This inferentially includes reasonable force to obtain evidence from one who is attempting to conceal it or destroy it.

To be defensive against complaints of police brutality and 1983 action, a member of the force executing a search warrant should use only such force as is necessary to accomplish the intended purpose and no more.

The statutes usually provide that when an officer executes a warrant he has the authority to break both outer and inner doors if, after giving notice of his authority and purpose and demanding entrance, he is refused admittance. 18 U.S.C. 3109. This sounds wonderful in theory but any experienced officer knows that an experienced potential defendant will have the evidence down the toilet, or in a fire at a fireplace, or swallowed, or thrown out of a window by the time the officer makes his entrance. The statute does not indicate the time between the notice, the refusal of entry, and the right to break the door down and begin the race to the toilet or other places of activities mentioned above. From personal experience, this time interval is little short of a simultaneous action or the evidence is irretrievably gone.

The question of whether law enforcement officers, possessing a valid search warrant, can detain forcefully the occupants of a premises being searched until they had completed the search came on to be heard in MICHIGAN v. SUMMERS, 452 U.S. 692, 101 S.Ct. 2587, 69 L.Ed.2d. 340, 29 Cr.L. 3097 (1981).

In that case, police officers executing a search warrant of a house for narcotics, came upon the respondent, George Summers, as he was descending the front steps. They requested assistance to gain entry and detained him while they searched the premises. After finding narcotics and ascertaining that Summers was the owner of the house, they searched him and found heroin in his possession. He alleged that his personal search was a violation of the Fourth Amendment. The State Courts upheld his theory, but the United States Supreme Court held inter alia that for Fourth Amendment purposes, a warrant to search for contraband founded on probable cause implicitly carries with it the limited authority to detain occupants of the premises while a proper search is conducted.

§ 6.10 Reasonable Searches

The Fourth Amendment prohibits unreasonable searches and seizures by the government. It does not prevent reasonable searches. Naturally, the term "reasonable" has a nebulous meaning but it is subject to court interpretation, much like other terms used in the document. What may be reasonable today may not have been reasonable yesterday.

Whether a search is reasonable or unreasonable within the meaning of the Fourth Amendment is a judicial question and Congress could enact no law declaring reasonable a search which the courts hold to be unreasonable, though it could pass an act prohibiting searches that were unreasonable. U.S. v. Bateman, D.C. Cal., 278 F. 231. In Agnello v. U.S., C.C.A. N.Y. 290 F. 671, affirmed in part and reversed in part on other grounds in 269 U.S. 20, 46 S.Ct. 4, 70 L.Ed. 145 (1925), the court held that it was within the judicial function to determine whether a search is reasonable within the meaning of the Fourth Amendment to the federal Constitution.

The courts have construed searches to be reasonable under the following circumstances:

1. Consent search;
2. Probable cause search;
3. Search incidental to a lawful arrest;
4. Plain-view search;
5. Inventory search;
6. Automobile search under restricted conditions;
7. Administrative search;
8. Close pursuit.
9. Custom and Immigration Officers
10. Reasonable Suspicion

§ 6.11 The Consent Search

The consent search is one which is permissible as a reasonable search in theory. The courts, however, tend to disbelieve the officers' testimony in many of these cases because they reason that a defendant knowing his rights with respect to searches of his person or property would ordinarily not consent to such a search. Notwithstanding this, there have been many cases where evidence has been admitted into the trial based upon a consent search. In this situation the subject of the search is waiving a constitutional right.

§ 6.12 Voluntary Nature of Consent

If a constitutional right is waived, the courts must conduct an inquiry as to the voluntary nature of the waiver and carefully evaluate the evidence with a presumption against waiver which must be rebutted and overcome by the prosecution. This does not mean that a person giving a consent to a search must be advised that he has a right to refuse because any defendant who was the subject of a search authorized solely by his/her consent could effectively frustrate the introduction into evidence of the fruits of that search by simply failing to testify that s/he in fact knew that s/he could refuse to consent. In Schneckloth v. Bustamonte, 412 U.S. 218, 93 S.Ct. 2041, 36 L.Ed.2d 854 (1973), it was held that "... when the subject of a search is not in custody and the State attempts to justify a search on the basis of his consent, the Fourth and Fourteenth Amendments require that it demonstrate that the consent was in fact voluntarily given, and not the result of duress or coercion, express or implied. Voluntariness is a question of fact to be determined from all the circumstances, and while the subject's knowledge of a right to refuse is a factor to be taken into account, the prosecution is not required to demonstrate such knowledge as a prerequisite to establishing a voluntary consent."

In U.S. v. MENDENHALL, 446 U.S. 544, 100 S.Ct. 1870, 64 L.Ed.2d. 497, reh, den, (U.S.) 100 S.Ct. 3051, 65 L.Ed.2d. 1138, 22 Cr.L. 3127 (1980), a young black woman who met a profile of the Drug Enforcement Administration with respect to possibly being a person unlawfully carrying narcotics was stopped in the Detroit Metropolitan Airport upon her arrival on a flight from Los Angeles. Her driver's license and her airline ticket had two different names. After returning both items to her, one Drug Enforcement Agent asked her if she would accompany him to the airport DEA office for further questioning and she agreed. At the office, the agent asked her if she would allow a search of her person and handbag and told her that she had a right to refuse. She agreed and handed her purse to the agent. A female police officer was summoned to conduct the search of her person, and she too asked the respondent whether she consented to the search. Respondent began to disrobe and took two packages from her undergarments and handed them to the policewoman. One of the packages appeared to contain heroin. She was then arrested for possessing heroin. A motion to suppress was denied in the District Court but reversed in the Court of Appeals. The United States Supreme Court reversed the Court of Appeals saying, inter alia, the fact that the respondent was 22 years old and had not been graduated from high school and was a Negro accosted by white officers while not irrelevant were not decisive . . . A person has been "seized" within the meaning of the Fourth Amendment only if, in view of all of the circumstances surrounding the incident, a reasonable person would have believed that he was not free to leave, and as long as the person to whom questions are put remains free to leave, and as long as the person to whom questions are put remains free to disregard the questions and walk away, there has been no intrusion on that person's liberty or privacy as would require some particularized and objective justification.

Another case involving a drug courier occurred in FLORIDA v. ROYER, 460 U.S. 491, 103 S.Ct. 1319, 75 L.Ed.2d. 229, 32 Cr.L. 3095 (1983). In that case the suspect had purchased an airline ticket in Miami under an assumed name. Two detectives decided that the subject fit the "drug courier profile" and upon request, but without consent he produced his driver's license with his correct name. He explained that a friend had made the reservation for the airline ticket for him. Without returning the airline ticket or his driver's license, the detectives identified themselves and asked him to accompany them to a small room adjacent to the concourse. Also without his consent, one detective retrieved his checked luggage and brought it to the room. He procured a key to one bag and opened it. The detectives found that it contained marihuana. The second piece of luggage had a combination lock on it and the suspect said that he did not know the combination, but he did not object to its being pried open by the officers. This too contained marihuana. He was then told that he was under arrest. Motion to suppress was denied in the trial court, reversed in the District Court of Appeal. This case came to the Court on a writ of certiorari to the District Court of Appeal of Florida.

A strong and sarcastic dissent was written by Justice Rehnquist joined by Chief Justice Burger and Justice O'Connor. However the majority held that the defendant was illegally detained in the small room and thus the search of the luggage without his consent was tainted by his illegal detention.

§ 6.13 Capacity of Consenting Person

The person giving the consent must also have the capacity to consent. Consider, if you will, the situation of a uniformed police officer knocking on the door of an apartment to gain entrance because of a noise complaint. Consider also that a young child of approximately ten years of age responds to the officer's knock and seeing the huge man in uniform at the entrance to the apartment, becomes frightened and invites the officer into the apartment. While in the apartment under these circumstances, the officer is told to leave the apartment by the father of the child. Let us assume further that there is no noise or other apparent violation of law observed by the officer. The query in this situation is whether the officer should gracefully leave or engage in a verbal contest with the father? The answer should be that he should leave gracefully because there is a question as to the competency of the child to consent to a search of the apartment or his/her competency to admit the officer under those conditions. The competency of the person authorizing the search also arises when a landlord, spouse, innkeeper, partner, agent, employee, or servant gives the consent.

It has been held that a joint owner or user of property or premises may be effective against another. Frazier v. Cupp, 394 U.S. 731, 89 S.Ct. 1420, 22 L.Ed.2d 684 (1969). A consent to search a rented hotel room violated the constitutional rights of a person who rented the room. Stoner v. California, 376 U.S. 483, 84 S.Ct. 889, 11 L.Ed.2d 856 (1964). A landlord's consent to search a house is not effective against a tenant, otherwise tenants' homes would be "secure only in the discretion of the landlord." Chapman v. U.S., 365 U.S. 610, 81 S.Ct. 776, 5 L.Ed.2d 828 (1961).

§ 6.14 Consent by Spouse

It appears that a spouse may validly consent to a search of property and/or premises which is jointly used by them but not to property or premises which is not jointly occupied and therefore a wife cannot consent to the search of a husband's garage which is used solely by him. Cabey v. Mazurkiewicz, 3 C.C.A. 7/29/70. This is not a uniformly accepted rule and the reader is encouraged to research cases in the subject jurisdiction to ascertain the latest rulings of the court.

§ 6.15 Consent by School Authorities

There is some uncertainty as to whether a teacher or principal can authorize the search of a student's locker. The argument is advanced that the faculty member stands in the position of in loco parentis of the student while the student is at school and thus has the capacity to consent to the search. One such case where the consent search was upheld is in N.Y., Peo. v. Overton, 249 N.E.2d 366 (1969).

In another case, NEW JERSEY v. T.L.O., —U.S.—, 105 S.Ct. 733, 83 L.Ed.2d. 720, 36 Cr.L. 3091, (1985), the Court held that the Fourth Amendment requires that unreasonable searches and seizures applies to searches conducted by public school officials and is not limited to searches carried out by law enforcement personnel. In carrying out searches mandated by state statutes, they act as representatives of the State, not as surrogates of the parents of the students. However, school officials need not obtain a warrant before searching a student who is under their authority. The legality of a search of a student should depend on reasonableness, under all of the circumstances, of the search. Under ordinary circumstances, where there are reasonable grounds to believe that the search will turn up evidence that the student has violated either the law or the rules of the school, the search is valid.

§ 6.16 Consent by Parent

As an extension of Peo. v. Overton (supra), we can assume that a parent may consent to a search on behalf of a minor child. However in Bumper v. North Carolina, 391 U.S. 543, 88 S.Ct. 1788, 20 L.Ed.2d 797 (1968), the grandmother of a defendant who thought that the police had a search warrant acquiesced to the search of the family's house, but when the warrant was a mere piece of paper purporting to be a warrant, it was held that the search was invalid.

§ 6.17 Revocation of Consent

There is uncertainty as to whether a consent search can be withdrawn after the consent was given. Strong v. United States, 1st C.C.A., held that a defendant may revoke his consent while the search is in process.

§ 6.18 Summation of Consent

The courts require the government to rebut a presumption that the defendant did not give his/her consent. It should therefore be evident that great proof by the government is required to sustain this burden. This can be accomplished by written consents signed by the defendant prior to the search, spelling out the terms of the consent, or by the presence of a disinterested witness who will testify as to the oral communication of the defendant's consent. When there is the slightest doubt that the defendant does not comprehend the English language, the law enforcement officer should make certain that the defendant is made fully aware of the request to search in his native tongue or in sign language, if s/he is unable to speak and/or hear.

§ 6.19 Probable Cause Search

The probable cause search is one which is decided almost on an ad hoc basis with certain general rules. As stated previously, the court has the power to determine the reasonableness of a search. Agnello v. U.S. (supra). A judicial definition of probable cause appears in Carroll v. United States, 267 U.S. 132, 162, 45 S.Ct. 280, 288, 69 L.Ed. 543, 555 (1925), where Chief Justice Taft wrote that probable cause was said to exist where "the facts and circumstances within (the officers') knowledge and of which they had reasonably trustworthy information were sufficient in themselves, to warrant a person of reasonable caution" to believe that a particular offense had been or was being committed. Probable cause is not to be confused with mere suspicion on the part of an officer. S/he must set forth in testimony at a suppression hearing and/or trial, evidence which would be sufficient in itself to cause a reasonably prudent person to believe that a particular offense was being committed.

In Terry v. Ohio, 392 U.S. 1, 88 S.Ct. 1868, 20 L.Ed.2d 889 (1968), an experienced officer observed the defendants "casing" a jewelry store and when he stopped them and patted them down he found two revolvers. The Supreme Court said: "It would have been poor police work indeed for an officer of 30 years' experience in the detection of thievery from stores in this same neighborhood to have failed to investigate this behavior further."

Where there is sufficient time to get a warrant, absence of the warrant will cause an exclusion of the evidence. One such case occurred when Federal Narcotics Agents, who had information about persons on an Amtrak train, had dogs sniff for marijuana when the train arrived in Boston, Massachusetts. They found a footlocker containing the contraband and waited until the respondents had claimed the luggage and were loading it into a trunk of a car, whereupon three persons were arrested. The footlocker and the prisoners were taken to the Federal Building in Boston. About one and a half hours after arrival at the Federal Building, the footlocker was opened without respondents' consent and the contraband was discovered. The Court affirmed the suppression of these items, indicating that the agents should have gotten a warrant under these circumstances. U.S. v. Chadwich, 433 U.S. 1, 97 S.Ct. 2476, 53 L.Ed.2d 538, 21 Cr.L. 3169 (1977).

A law enforcement officer whose observations cause him to reasonably believe that a traveler is carrying luggage containing narcotics may briefly detain the luggage pursuant to TERRY v. OHIO, 392 U.S. 1 (1968) but a warrantless detention for one and a half hours of this luggage when the agents had several hours notice of when and where the defendant would arrive was unreasonable. U.S. v. PLACE, 462 U.S. 696, 103 S.Ct. 2637, 77 L.Ed.2d. 110, 33 Cr.L. 3186 (1983).

§ 6.19(a) Open Fields Doctrine

The Fourth Amendment gave special protection to "persons, houses, papers and effects and does not extend to the open fields," HESTER

v. UNITED STATES, 265 U.S. 57 (1924). This rule was litigated and extended in OLIVER v. UNITED STATES, —U.S.—, 104 S.Ct. 1735, 80 L.Ed.2d. 214 (1984) where Kentucky State Police had received information that marihuana was being grown on petitioner's farm. They investigated and found a locked vehicle entrance gate with a "No Trespassing" sign. They walked around a foot path that was on one side of the gate, and continued to walk along the road for several hundred yards. The officers found a field of marihuana over a mile from petitioner's home. A motion to suppress was granted by the District Court, holding, inter alia, that the fields were highly secluded; they are bounded on all sides by woods, fences and embankments and cannot be seen from any point of public access. The court concluded that this was not an "open field." The Court of Appeals for the Sixth Circuit sitting en banc reversed and it came to the United States Supreme Court on certiorari. The Court held that an individual may not legitimately demand privacy for activity conducted out of doors, in fields, except in the area immediately surrounding the home.

§ 6.20 Search Incidental to a Lawful Arrest

Once an arrest takes place, the usual police practice is to "book" the prisoner. This means that s/he is taken to a police building or other location and his/her pedigree is recorded. Prior to detention, certain property should be removed from the prisoner. This will include items which might facilitate escape, might be used to injure him/herself or another, might be used to deface property, or might be valuable property to be held by the police for safekeeping or for the purpose of preventing destruction of evidence. In order to implement these requirements the officer will search the prisoner in the presence of the recording or booking officer. Frequently contraband is uncovered in the prisoner's clothing in this way. This contraband is lawfully seized and may be introduced into evidence at a trial if the original arrest was valid.

The history of the right of police officers to conduct searches incident to a lawful arrest has been somewhat inconsistent. In Weeks v. United States, 232 U.S. 383, 34 S.Ct. 341, 58 L.Ed.2d 652 (1914), the Supreme Court held that if the original arrest was lawful, the officers were at liberty to look throughout the premises where the arrest occurred. Agnello v. United States, 269 U.S. 20, 46 S.Ct. 4, 70 L.Ed. 145 (1925), declined to sustain a search of a house several blocks from the scene of the arrest. This concept was further restricted in Chimel v. California, 395 U.S. 752, 89 S.Ct. 2034, 23 L.Ed.2d 685 (1969), where the court restricted the search incidental to a lawful arrest to the person of the arrestee and the area from within which he might have obtained a weapon or something that could have been used as evidence against him. In U.S. v. Edwards, 415 U.S. 800, 98 S.Ct. 1234, 39 L.Ed.2d 771 (1974), it was held that a search of a prisoner's clothing while he is in custody may be made without a warrant as a search incidental to a lawful arrest. In U.S. v. Robinson, 414 U.S. 218, 94 S.Ct. 467, 38 L.Ed.2d 427 (1973), the defendant was arrested for driving after revocation of his driver's license. The officer searched the defendant and found fourteen capsules of heroin. The Court held that this was admissible evidence as incidental to a lawful arrest. In Gustafson v. Florida, 414 U.S. 260, 94 S.Ct. 488, 38 L.Ed.2d 456 (1973), the Court similarly held that where a search of a person arrested for driving without a valid driver's license occurred and where marijuana was found on the person arrested, the marijuana was admissible in evidence as incidental to a lawful arrest.

§ 6.20(a) Arrest Warrant—No Authority to Search Third Person

An arrest warrant in the possession of a law enforcement officer gives that officer the authority to enter the suspects' own premises to effect his arrest. PAYTON v. NEW YORK, 445 U.S. 602, 603. Further, no warrant is required to apprehend a suspected felon in a public place, U.S. v. WATSON, 423 U.S. 411 (1976), but when law enforcement officers have an arrest warrant for a suspect, the officer has no authority to enter the residence of a third person in search of the suspect and thus any entry made under these circumstances absent a search warrant for the particular premises is an unconstitutional search. Hence any contraband thus seized, even if it was in full view, is subject to suppression. STEAGOLD v. UNITED STATES, 451 U.S. 204, 101 S.Ct. 1642, 68 L.Ed.2d. 38, 29 Cr.L. 3007 (1981).

§ 6.21 Plain-View Search

The plain-view search is another exception to the requirement that a search warrant is necessary to conduct a legally sufficient search and seizure. This concept was best explained by Mr. Justice Potter Stewart in Coolidge v. New Hampshire, 403 U.S. 443, 91 S.Ct. 2022, 29 L.Ed.2d 564 (1971), when he wrote: "It is well established that under certain circumstances the police may seize evidence in plain view without a warrant. But it is important to keep in mind that, in the vast majority of cases, (any) evidence seized by the police will be in plain view, at least at the moment of seizure.... An example of the applicability of the plain view doctrine is the situation in which the police have a warrant to search a given area for specified objects, and in the course of the search come across some other article of incriminating character. Where the initial intrusion that brings the police within plain view of such an article is supported, not by a warrant, but one of the recognized exceptions to the warrant requirement, the seizure is also legitimate. . . ."

In United States v. Santana, 427 U.S. 38, 96 S.Ct. 2406, 49 L.Ed.2d 1300 (1976), the court held for the principle that what is knowingly exposed to the public is not protected.

Under the plain-view doctrine, the following conditions must be present in order to have the evidence admissible:

1. The officer is lawfully present;
2. The discovery is inadvertent;
3. The object is incriminating.
   Coolidge v. New Hampshire (supra).

In TEXAS v. BROWN, 460 U.S. 730, 75, L.Ed. 2d. 502, 103 S.Ct. 1535 (1983) 33 Cr.L. 3001 (1983) the Court upheld a seizure of a tied-off, opaque balloon when an officer had lawfully stopped an automobile in a routine driver's license checkpoint, and based on his knowledge and experience he believed that the balloon contained heroin which in fact it did.

When an officer lawfully arrests a person and then escorts him to his home for the purpose of securing credentials to establish the arrestees identity, any contraband, observed by the officer in plain view in the premises may be lawfully seized by the officer and used as evidence against the arrestee. WASHINGTON v. CHRISMAN, 455 U.S. 1, 102 S.Ct. 812, 70 L.Ed.2d. 778, 30 Cr.L. 3041 (1982).

Another example of this concept was to be found in MARYLAND v. MACON, —U.S.—, 105 S.Ct. 2778, 86 L.Ed.2d. 370, 37 Cr.L. 3111 (1985) where an officer entered an adult book store where he made a purchase of an obscene magazine. After conviction and a denial of a motion to suppress, the case was decided by the United States Supreme Court. The Court held that this premises was open for the public and the transaction was a sale in the ordinary course of business. The money used to make the purchase was retrieved but never introduced in the trial. This money was the only "fruit of the arrest" and was not introduced in evidence.

§ 6.22 Inventory Search

When an officer makes an arrest, the arrestee is "booked" as previously indicated. If the arrestee is in possession of a vehicle, many times the vehicle must be safeguarded by the police. In order to do this, police agencies have devised recording methods to fix responsibility should anything of value be later found to be missing. Therefore an inventory of the vehicle and its contents are noted and recorded. It sometimes occurs that items indicating the commission of a crime are present in such vehicles and the problem arises as to whether such items are admissible in evidence against the arrestee. The courts have decided that this is a normal method of inventory which is necessary for the police to perform their sworn responsibility and all items secured thereby are admissible as an inventory search. There is a close distinction between this concept and that of "incidental to arrest" situations. Usually the term incidental to an arrest applies to the arrestee's person and the area to which he may reach to secure a weapon. Chimel v. California (supra). In South Dakota v. Opperman, 428 U.S. 364, 96 S.Ct. 3092, 49 L.Ed.2d 1000 (1976), it was held that where the police impounded a vehicle for a traffic violation and an inventory search of the unlocked area of the vehicle followed, the contraband seized as a result of this search was admissible in evidence as being according to standard police procedures and the search was reasonable.

A police officer who had lawfully arrested a person was held to be acting properly when he inventoried the contents of a shoulder bag arrestee had been carrying and the amphetamine pills contained therein were admissible as evidence against the arrestee. ILLINOIS v. LAFAYETTE, 462 U.S. 640, 103 S.Ct. 2605, 77 L.Ed.2d. 65, 33 Cr.L. 3183 (1983).

§ 6.23 Automobile Search

As indicated in the preceding section, an automobile may be legally searched for inventory purposes and contraband found therein can be admissible in evidence. There are other situations where probable cause may exist for a police officer to search an automobile. An automobile is capable of being moved quickly from one location to another. In some cases it would be futile to first apply for a search warrant because by the time the warrant is obtained and executed, the evidence would have disappeared.

In Cardwell v. Lewis, 417 U.S. 583, 94 S.Ct. 2464, 41 L.Ed.2d 325 (1974), the court sustained the admissibility of paint scrapings taken from the exterior of a car and an observation of the tread of a tire on an operative wheel. An automobile similar in color and model to defendant's car had been seen leaving the scene of a crime. This similarity was corroborated by comparison of the paint scraping taken from the victim's car with the color and paint of defendant's automobile. The defendant had repair work done on his car immediately after the death of the victim. He also had a nexus with the victim on the day of death. All of this provided reason to believe that the car was used in the commission of the crime for which Lewis was arrested.

The automobile search may also be conducted under the incidental-to-lawful-arrest doctrine if the officer can show that s/he believed s/he was in danger and therefore searched the vehicle to protect him/herself. However, Chimel v. California (supra) limited the area to be searched under this doctrine.

Frequently an automobile is stopped by a police officer for a traffic violation. Upon stopping the automobile, the officer may see contraband in plain view. This contraband is admissible in evidence.

Another situation involving a lawful search of a moving vehicle occurred in Carroll v. U.S., 267 U.S. 132, 45 S.Ct. 280, 69 L.Ed. 543 (1925), where the court permitted evidence to be admitted which had been secured by federal officers after they justified their actions by indicating to the court that they had probable cause to stop the moving vehicle. Another case upholding the right of officers to make this kind of search was Chambers v. Maroney, 399 U.S. 42, 90 S.Ct. 1975, 26 L.Ed.2d 419 (1970).

Mr. Justice Rehnquist writing for the majority in Rakus v. Illinois, 436 U.S. 954, 99 S.Ct. 421, 58 L.Ed.2d 387 (1978), held that passengers in an automobile that they did not own or lease had no standing to object to the lawfulness of a police search of the automobile because the Fourth Amendment rights are personal rights.

A 1979 case involving an automobile search occurred in Prouse v. Delaware, 440 U.S. 648, 99 S.Ct. 1391, 59 L.Ed.2d 660, 24 Cr.L. 4168. In that case the police conducted random stops of motor vehicles without any apparent violation of law taking place. The Court held this to be a Fourth and Fourteenth Amendment violation. This decision does not prevent a roadblock of all vehicles where the officer might ask for identification, as long as all persons and vehicles are treated similarly.

Another 1979 case where the Court reversed a random automobile stop and search was Kretchmar v. Nebraska, 78-558, 25 Cr.L. 4001.

An interesting automobile search by Border Patrol Officers lead to a clarification and expansion of the law enforcement officers' right to search a moving vehicle. In U.S. v. CORTEZ, 449 U.S. 411, 101 S.Ct. 690, 66 L.Ed.2d. 621, 28 Cr.L. 3051 (1981), Border Patrol Officers had discovered distinctive human footprints in the desert. They deduced that on several occasions, groups of between 8 and 20 persons had been guided through the desert from Mexico by the same individual into Arizona and that they were entering the United States illegally. The prints indicated that they stopped at an isolated point on a road and were picked up on clear nights between 2:00 a.m. and 6:00 a.m.

Based on this information, they stationed themselves at a point on the road where they believed the pickup vehicle would pass. Indeed it did pass, once in either direction, within the estimated time that it would take to go to the point of pickup and return with its human cargo. When it returned the officers stopped the vehicle which was being driven by the respondent. Cortez and another respondent, Hernandez-Lorea were found in the vehicle wearing shoes which matched with the suspect desert footprints. There were illegal aliens in the vehicle. The Supreme Court held that the objective facts and circumstantial evidence in this case justified the investigative stop of respondent's vehicle. The Court went further in saying that the totality of the circumstances must be taken into account . . . the evidence must be weighed as understood by those versed in the field of law enforcement. Notice that the Court did not say that the officers were aware of a repeated practice and that they might have secured a search warrant for another occasion. It is the author's view that some earlier Courts would have required a search warrant in this case. We can therefore see that the Berger Court of 1981 is leaning towards enlargement of the search powers of law enforcement officers.

On July 1, 1981, the United States Supreme Court handed down two closely related decisions involving automobile searches. In the first case reported ROBBINS v. CALIFORNIA, 453 U.S. 420, 101 S.Ct. 2841, 69 L.Ed.2d. 744, 29 Cr.L. 3115 (1981), California Highway Patrol officers stopped petitioner's car because it was proceeding erratically. They smelled marihuana smoke as he opened the car door. They then searched the vehicle and found in the luggage compartment two packages wrapped in green opaque plastic. Upon unwrapping the plastic packages, they found that they contained bricks of marihuana. He was charged with various drug offenses, including the possession of the marihuana bricks. His suppression motions were denied and he was convicted. The conviction was affirmed twice by the California Court of Appeal because the United States Supreme Court had remanded it to that court for further consideration in light of ARKANSAS v. SAUNDERS, 442 U.S. 753, 443 U.S. 903.

After granting a writ of certiorari, the United States Supreme Court held that unless a closed container found in an automobile is such that its contents may be said to be in plain view, those contents are fully protected by the Fourth Amendment . . . To fall within such exception, a container must so clearly announce its contents whether by its distinctive configuration, transparency, or otherwise, that its contents are obvious to the observer. The Court held that this was not the situation in the instant case and the opening of the package without a search warrant violated the Fourth Amendment and Fourteenth Amendments.

The second case had a contrary result. In NEW YORK v. BELTON, 453 U.S. 454, 101 S.Ct. 2860, L.Ed.2d. 768, 29 Cr.L. 3124 (1981) the respondent was in a vehicle stopped by a New York State policeman because of an excessive speed violation. Other occupants were in the vehicle but none of the occupants owned the car or were related to the owner. The officer smelled burnt marihuana and had seen on the floor of the car an envelope marked "SUPER GOLD" that he associated with marihuana. He frisked all four occupants of the vehicle after announcing that they were all under arrest and split them up into four separate areas of the Thruway at this time so that they would not be in "physical touching area of each other." He then picked up the envelope marked "SUPER GOLD" and found it contained marihuana. After giving Miranda warnings, he searched each of them. Following this, he searched the passenger compartment of the car. On the back seat he found a black leather jacket belonging to Belton. He unzippered one of the pockets and discovered cocaine. Placing the jacket in his automobile, he drove the four arrestees to a nearby police station. The Court held that the search of the jacket was not a violation of the Fourth Amendment and Fourteenth Amendment under the theory of CHIMEL v. CALIFORNIA, 395 U.S. 752, wherein it was held that a lawful custodial arrest creates a situation justifying the contemporaneous warrantless search of the arrestee and of the immediately surrounding area. Not only may the police search the passenger compartment of the car in such circumstances, they may also examine the contents of any containers found in the passenger compartment. The author believes that the Court was stretching to validate this search because it could be argued that when the search of the passenger compartment occurred, the trooper was not in danger that Belton could have, at that time, reached into his jacket to get a weapon or to destroy evidence as was the theory in CHIMEL v. CALIFORNIA, supra. Nevertheless, this case expands the authority of the police officer to search the passenger compartment of an auto after a lawful arrest has taken place so long as it is reasonably contemporaneous with the arrest.

This holding of ROBBINS v. CALIFORNIA (supra) was short lived when in June of 1982 the Court handed down U.S. v. ROSS, —U.S.—, 102 S.Ct. 2157, 72 L.Ed.2d. 572, 31 Cr.L. 3051 (1982). In that case the Court rejected the holding in ROBBINS v. CALIFORNIA (supra) and held that police who have probable cause for a vehicle search under the "automobile exception" to the Fourth Amendment's warrant requirement may search without a warrant, every part of that vehicle and its contents, including closed containers, that may conceal the object of the search. The Court also rejected that part of ARKANSAS v. SAUNDERS, 442 U.S. 753 (1979) that suggested that a warrantless search of a container found in an automobile could never be sustained as part of a warrantless automobile search. This decision caused much confusion in the final outcome of cases with respect to trials in progress between the Robbins decision, July 1, 1981 and the time of Ross, June 1, 1982.

In MICHIGAN v. LONG, —U.S.—, 103 S.Ct. 3469, 77 L.Ed.2d. 1201 (1983), two police officers patrolling a rural area at night saw a car traveling erratically and at excessive speed. When the car swerved into a ditch, the officers investigated and were met by respondent, the sole occupant of the car, the driver appeared to be under the influence of something. When he opened the door of his vehicle, the officers observed a hunting knife on the floorboard on the driver's side. They patted him down and found no weapons. A flashlight beamed into the car revealed a open pouch containing marihuana under the armrest on the front seat. The trunk of the car was then searched and the officers found some more marihuana. The Michigan State Supreme Court suppressed the marihuana taken from the passenger compartment holding it was an illegal search. The United States Supreme Court remanded the issue of the legality of the trunk search. The Court held further that it would no longer give advisory opinions in state court matters when the state court references to state law constituted adequate and independent state grounds. It will no longer look beyond the opinion under revision. This case came to the United States Supreme Court by a writ of certiorari. In the author's opinion, it was an extension of STONE v. POWELL, 428 U.S. 465, 98 S.Ct. 3037, 49 L.Ed.2d. 1067 (1976) where the court indicated that federal habeas corpus review would no longer be available to state defendants on the issue of unreasonable search and seizure where the state had provided a full and fair litigation of a Fourth Amendment claim.

However in the LONG case (supra), the Court held that the state court decided the case on Federal grounds and the Court would take jurisdiction. It further ruled that the officers' action was reasonable and it reversed the Michigan Supreme Court decision.

A later case involved an investigatory stop of a passenger automobile and a trunk with a camper traveling in tandem on a highway that was under surveillance for suspected drug traffic. Both vehicles appeared to be traveling together. A Drug Enforcement Administration agent, patrolling the highway noticed these vehicles. The pickup truck was apparently overloaded. After following them for about 20 miles, he decided to make an investigative stop and radioed the South Carolina State Highway Patrol for assistance. When the state officer responded, they attempted to stop the two vehicles. The passenger automobile pulled over to the side of the road but the truck continued on pursued by the state officer. The D.E.A. agent identified himself and attempted unsuccessfully to contact the state officer. He then radioed the local police for help. In the meantime, the state officer had stopped the truck and told the driver that he would be held until the D.E.A. agent arrived. The D.E.A. agent, left the passenger automobile driver with the local police and arrived at the location of the detained truck about 15 minutes after the truck had been stopped. Upon smelling marihuana coming from the truck, he opened the rear camper without the driver's permission and found burlap bags containing marihuana therein. He arrested the driver and returned to the passenger vehicle and then arrested the driver of that vehicle. The case came before the United States Supreme Court because motions to suppress had been granted below.

The Court held that the evidence should not be suppressed because in evaluating the reasonableness of an investigative stop, the Court examines "whether the officer's action was justified at its inception and whether it was reasonably related in scope to the circumstances which justified the interference in the first place," citing TERRY v. OHIO (supra). They held further that although brevity is an important factor in determining whether the detention is unreasonable, courts must also consider the purposes to be served by the stop as well as the time reasonably needed to effectuate those purposes. Here the D.E.A. agent diligently pursued his investigation and clearly no delay unnecessary to the investigation was involved. U.S. v. SHARPE, —U.S.—, 105 S.Ct. 1568, 84 L.Ed.2d. 605 (1985).

The automobile exception was extended to include a mobile motor home located in a public parking lot. CALIFORNIA v. CARNEY, —U.S.—, 105 S.Ct. 2066, 85 L.Ed.2d. 406 (1985).

§ 6.24 Administrative Search

Tax assessors, health inspectors, fire inspectors, and building inspectors all belong to that category of persons who, in order to properly do their mandated jobs, must have access to the interior of buildings. When they are denied entrance, a controversy arises. Some persons object to these visits on constitutional grounds. The United States Supreme Court has upheld the right of these inspections as administrative searches where there is an objection but only after a warrant has been secured and properly executed.

Camara v. Municipal Court, 387 U.S. 523, 87 S.Ct. 1727, 18 L.Ed.2d 930 (1967).

In the case of welfare investigators, however, the court had held otherwise. In Wyman v. James, 400 U.S. 309, 91 S.Ct. 381, 27 L.Ed.2d 408 (1971), the court sustained the right of a welfare investigator to visit the home of a client where aid to a dependent child was being received, on the grounds that it was not unreasonable for Fourth Amendment limitations where the requirement served the paramount needs of the child; there was reasonable advance notice given concerning the date of the visit; neither forcible nor surreptitious entry of the home would take place; and visits occurred at reasonable times of the day. The court further held that such a visitation was not a search in the traditional criminal law context of the Fourth Amendment and the consequence of refusal to allow a home visit is not a criminal prosecution but the termination of benefits, thereby allowing a choice to the client.

In MICHIGAN v. CLIFFORD, —U.S.—, 104 S.Ct. 641, 78 L.Ed.2d. 1477 (1984), arson investigators entered a premises five hours after the firefighters had left the premises. They had no administrative warrant, but conducted a search and found objects which in their opinion caused the fire and were deliberately placed there for that purpose. The Court held that the evidence seized in that search was obtained in violation of respondent's rights under the Fourth and Fourteenth Amendments because it was not authorized by consent or exigent circumstances.

§ 6.24(a) Prisoners—Privacy of

A prison inmate has no reasonable expectation of privacy in his prison cell entitling him to protection of the Fourth Amendment against unreasonable searches. HUDSON v. PALMER, —U.S.—, 104 S.Ct. 3194, 82 L.Ed.2d. 393 (1984). In that case a prisoner sustained a shakedown search of his cell and locker by correction officer Hudson, and a fellow officer. The officers discovered a ripped pillow case in a trash can near respondent's cell bunk. Charges against Palmer were instituted for destroying state property and he was found guilty after a hearing. Palmer later brought a pro se action under 42 U.S. 1983 claiming that the shakedown search was instituted solely to harass him and they had brought false charges against him in violation of his Fourteenth Amendment right not to be deprived of property without due process of law and that Hudson intentionally destroyed certain of his non contraband personal items during this search.

The Court further held that there was no Fourteenth Amendment

Due Process Clause violation because respondent had adequate post-deprivation remedies under Virginia law for any loss suffered.

§ 6.25 Hot-Pursuit Searches

Let us assume that a police officer arrives at the scene of a robbery shortly after the perpetrator has left the premises. Let us further assume that the officer gets a good description of the perpetrator and is told that the malefactor was seen entering a premises. Does the police officer have to wait to get a warrant to enter the premises in hot pursuit of the accused? The answer is no. In Warden v. Hayden, 387 U.S. 294, 87 S.Ct. 1642, 18 L.Ed.2d 782 (1967), it was held that this type of search was a reasonable search for items having some evidentiary bearing on the case under investigation.

In another case where officers searched for a defendant where the offense was a non jailable one, the Court held otherwise. In WELSH v. WISCONSIN, —U.S.—, 104 S.Ct. 2091, 80 L.Ed.2d. 732 (1984) the defendant had driven his automobile erratically and swerved off the road into an open field and stopped. No property damage or personal injury occurred. The defendant was observed by a witness who suggested that he wait for assistance. Ignoring the witness' suggestion, he exited from the vehicle and walked away. The police arrived, checked the registered owner and went to the defendant's house. They were permitted to enter by the defendant's stepdaughter and they found the defendant nude in his bed. He was then arrested for driving a motor vehicle while under the influence of an intoxicant in violation of a Wisconsin statute which provided that a first offense was a noncriminal violation subject to a civil forfeiture proceeding for a maximum fine of $200.00.

The United States Supreme Court held that the warrantless, night-time entry of petitioner's home to arrest him for a civil, non jailable traffic offense was prohibited by the Fourth Amendment.

However, in U.S. v. HENSLEY, —U.S.—, 105 S.Ct. 675, 84 L.Ed.2d. 604 (1985) the Court held that where the police had stopped a vehicle because they had received information from another police department that the described vehicle and its occupants were wanted in connection with a robbery, the police did not violate any Fourth Amendment right in that they may briefly stop a person suspected of involvement in a past crime, ask questions, or check identification in the absence of probable cause, because it promotes the strong government interest in solving crimes and bringing offenders to justice.

§ 6.25(a) Custom and Immigration Searches

Customs officers and immigration officers are given greater latitude in searching without a warrant, pursuant to Congressional authorization to the Executive Plenary Authority to search at the border with probable cause or a warrant. In a case involving customs officers, it was held that when a custom officer opened a container as it arrived from Calcutta and observed marihuana in the container, it was not an unreasonable search when the container was closed and shipped to addressee. When the addressee exited from his premises with the container, while an application was being made for a search warrant, the Court held that a D.E.A. was acting lawfully when he arrested the addressee and opened the container while he possessed no search warrant. ILLINOIS v. ANDREAS, 463 U.S. 765, 103 S.Ct. 3319, 77 L.Ed.2d. 1003 (1984).

U.S. Customs agents have been held to have authority to make "suspicionless" boarding of sailboats in a channel leading to the open sea for purpose of examining vessel's documentation pursuant to 19 U.S.C. 158(a). U.S. v. VILLAMONTE-MARQUEZ, 51 L.W. 4812.

§ 6.25(b) Identity Stop

In IMMIGRATION AND NATURALIZATION SERVICE v. DELGADO, —U.S.—, 104 S.Ct. 1758, 80 L.Ed.2d. 247 (1984) agents of the service conducted three surveys of a garment factory seeking illegal aliens. During the surveys, each of them lasting two to three hours, I.N.S. agents positioned themselves near the factory exits, while other agents moved systematically through the factory, approaching employees, and, after identifying themselves, they asked the employees a maximum of three questions relating to their citizenship. If they were satisfied with the reply or credentials of each employee, they would move on to the next. Agents were placed at the exit doors and the employees were permitted to do their work and were free to walk around the factory. The union, citizen employees and those with permanent resident cards brought actions, later consolidated, in Federal District Court seeking declaratory and injunctive relief. The District Court granted summary judgment for the I.N.S., but the Court of Appeals reversed holding that the surveys constituted a search in violation of the Fourth Amendment. It was reviewed by the United States Supreme Court. That Court held that the surveys were not a seizure and the Court further held that interrogation relating to one's identity or a request for identification by the police does not, by itself, constitute a Fourth Amendment seizure. Unless the circumstances of the encounter are so intimidating as to demonstrate that a reasonable person would have believed he was not free to leave if he had not responded, such questioning does not result in a detention under the Fourth Amendment. If one of the respondent employees had in fact been seized or detained there would have been a seizure. However, their disposition indicated that none of them were seized or detained. They therefore had no standing to litigate the issue. The Court of Appeals was thus reversed.

U.S. v. ROSS (supra) was extended in U.S. v. JOHNS, et al, — U.S.—, 105 S.Ct. 881, 83 L.Ed.2d. 890 (1985) when United States Custom officers had probable cause to search lawfully stopped trucks and smelled marihuana. They took packages from the trunks to a D.E.A. warehouse and three days later government agents opened some of the packages and took samples that later proved to be marihuana. No search warrant had ever been obtained. The Court held that the warrantless search of the trucks was not unreasonable because it occurred three days after the packages were unloaded from the trucks. Ross did not establish that the warrantless search of a vehicle need to occur contemporaneously with its lawful seizure. Nor does Ross or other "vehicle search" decisions of this Court suggest that warrantless searches of containers must invariably be conducted "immediately" as part of the vehicle inspection or "soon thereafter."

§ 6.25(c) Reasonable Suspicion Search

An alimentary canal search is one in which the suspect swallows the contraband, much as what happened in ROCHIN v. CALIFORNIA 342 U.S. 165, 72 S.Ct. 205, 96 L.Ed.2d. 183 (1952) where a stomach pump was used to extract the contraband. You will recall that in that case the Court held that this kind of action shocked the conscience and declared it unconstitutional. However, in U.S. v. ELVIRA MONTOYA DE HERNANDEZ, 37 Cr.L. 3175 (1985) a border search case, the Court upheld the search of a woman who had swallowed 88 balloons containing cocaine hydrochloride. The search was initiated after much delay by a customs officer's suspicion that respondent was an alimentary canal smuggler. After giving respondent other options, which could not be implemented, a court order was obtained for an x-ray and a rectal search. A physician conducted the rectal search and retrieved one of the aforementioned balloons. She subsequently defacated the remaining balloons over a 4 day period. The Court announced a new concept to be known as a "reasonable suspicion." The Court held that the detention of a traveler at the border, beyond the scope of a routine customs search and suspicion, is justified at its inception if custom agents, considering all the facts surrounding the traveler is smuggling contraband in her alimentary canal.

§ 6.25d Aerial Search

The aerial search, an old weapon of law enforcement, has been given the approval of the United States Supreme Court in California V. Ciraolo —U.S.—, —S.Ct.—, —L.Ed.2d—, 39 Cr.L. 3106 (1986) where police officers, receiving a tip that Marijuana was growing in respondent's back yard which was enclosed by two fences and could not be observed at ground level, secured a private plane and flew over respondent's land at an altitude of 1,000 feet. The officers, who were trained in marijuana identification, identified plants growing in a 15 by 25 foot plot. They photographed the area with a standard 35 mm camera and then obtained a search warrant and executed it. The Court, in a 5–4 decision, held that it was unreasonable for respondent to expect that his marijuana plants were constitutionally protected from being observed with the naked eye from an altitude of 1,000 feet. No search warrant by the police was required.

§ 6.26 Electronic Surveillance and Wiretapping

The issue of whether the use of electronic surveillance and/or wiretapping was a violation of unreasonable search and seizure has gone full circle in the courts. Naturally, the country's founders had no idea that one day telephones, wireless, radio and electronic devices would be available to infringe on the privacy of the individual in his home, on the street, or in his place of business.

The problem was given attention in Olmstead v. United States, 277 U.S. 438, 48 S.Ct. 564, 72 L.Ed. 944 (1928). That case involved the tapping of telephone wires which led to information leading to the petitioner for the crimes of conspiracy to import, possess, and sell liquor unlawfully. There was no trespass into any real property of the defendant. The wiretaps were made in the basement of an office building and on the streets near the petitioner's house. The court held that pursuant to common law, the admissibility of evidence was not affected by the illegality of the means by which it was obtained. It held further that the tapping of telephone lines, as was done in this case, was not a search and seizure as was contemplated by the Fourth Amendment. The court said that if Congress wanted to protect the secrecy of telephone messages, it could, by direct legislation, make it inadmissible in federal criminal trials.

Mr. Justice Brandeis wrote a strong dissent to this opinion, calling attention to the fact that by the laws of Washington, wiretapping was a crime. Pierce's Code, 1921 Section 8976 (18). He went on to say, "Decency, security and liberty alike demand that government officials shall be subjected to the same rules of conduct that are commanded to the citizen ... If the government becomes a lawbreaker, it breeds contempt for law; it invites every man to become a law unto himself; it invites anarchy." This terminology was later to be heard in many cases that followed where the exclusionary rule was invoked by the court to keep law enforcement practices within the confines of the constitutional limitations.

Congress yielded to the court's direction six years later, when it enacted Section 605 of the Federal Communications Act which provided:

> ... (N)o person not being authorized by the sender shall intercept any communication and divulge or publish the existence, contents, substance, purport, effect or meaning of such intercepted communication to any person.

With the tremendous advances in technology, law enforcement agents are now able to monitor the location of articles and the conversations of persons in buildings, vehicles and practically any private area by means of electronic beepers. A question of a beeper intrusion was considered by the United States Supreme Court in U.S. v. KNOTTS, 400 U.S. 276, 103 S.Ct. 1081, 73 L.Ed.2d. 55, 32 Cr.L. 3069 (1983). In that case the Court held that a warrantless monitoring of an electronic tracking device ("beeper") inside a container of chemicals did not violate the Fourth Amendment when it revealed no information that could have been obtained by visual surveillance. Following the Knotts case, in 1984, the case of U.S. v. KARO, —U.S.—, 104 S.Ct. 3296, 82 L.Ed.2d. 530, came before the Court. Here, an informant permitted a (D.E.A.) agent to place a beeper in a can along with other cans filled with ether. A Court order was obtained allowing the placement. The ether was to be used to extract cocaine from clothing. The ether and the beeper were taken to successive locations. Finally, the agents determined by the use of the beeper, and observations that it was in one of the defendant's houses and they secured a search warrant for the house. Upon executing the warrant, they found cocaine illegally possessed therein and made the arrests. After having reached the United States Supreme Court, the Court held that no Fourth Amendment interest of any respondent was infringed because it was neither a search nor a seizure since it contained no information that Karo wished to keep private. However, the monitoring of a beeper in a private residence, a location not open to surveillance violates the Fourth Amendment rights of those who have a justifiable interest in the privacy of the residence. In this case however, the government had sufficient probable cause for the issuance of the warrant without the use of the beeper, and hence the seizure of the cocaine pursuant to a search with a warrant was not a violation of the Fourth Amendment.

§ 6.27 Fruit of the Poisonous Tree

Section 501 of this act provided a fine not exceeding $10,000 or imprisonment for a term not exceeding one year, or both, for willful violations of Section 605. The section made no mention of the exclusion of evidence seized in violation of the act but the courts have so interpreted it on the grounds that it was obtained in violation of Section 605 on the grounds that such evidence was tainted as fruit of the poisonous tree. To remove all incentive by law enforcement authorities to violate the act, the United States Supreme Court in Nardone v. United States, 302 U.S. 379, 58 S.Ct. 275, 82 L.Ed. 314 (1937), adopted the exclusionary rule to exclude in federal trials all evidence, leads, and other derivative evidence which becomes available as a result of illegal interceptions. This idea was reiterated in Wong Sun v. U.S., 371 U.S. 471, 83 S.Ct. 407, 9 L.Ed.2d 441 (1963). In this case federal narcotic agents made an unlawful entry and an unauthorized arrest. As a result of this action, heroin was found at another location and another defendant was arrested. The Court reversed and remanded, saying that "...verbal evidence which derives so immediately from an unlawful entry and an unauthorized arrest... is no less the 'fruit' of official illegality than the more common tangible fruits of the unwarranted intrusion."

Sometimes it is not an easy matter to detect what is and what is not a poisonous tree case. In TAYLOR v. ALABAMA, —U.S.—, 102 S.Ct. 2664, 73 L.Ed.2d 314, 31 Cr.L. 3118 (1982) the defendant was arrested on the basis of an uncorroborated tip, without a warrant and without probable cause. The crime charged was a robbery of a grocery store. His fingerprints were taken and Miranda warnings were given. After being advised that his fingerprints matched those on some grocery items and after a visit from his girlfriend, he made a confession. HELD: A confession obtained through custodial interrogation after an illegal arrest should be excluded unless intervening events break the original connection between the arrest and the confession.

§ 6.28 Standing to Object

A defendant in a federal criminal trial could only object to the use of evidence secured by violation of Section 605 if s/he was an actual party to the intercepted conversation. Goldstein v. United States, 316 U.S. 114, 86 L.Ed. 1312, 62 S.Ct. 1000 (1942).

In UNITED STATES v. SALUCCI, et. al., 448 U.S. 83, 100 S.Ct. 2547, 65 L.Ed.2d. 619, 27 Cr.L. 3241 (1980), the Court held that defendants charged with possession may only claim the benefits of the exclusionary rule, if their own Fourth Amendment rights have been violated. In this case the police had a search warrant of one of the respondent's mother's apartment where stolen mail was found. The court held the seizure constitutionally valid in that the respondent had sustained no violation of their own Fourth Amendment rights even though the trial court held that the affidavit used to support the warrant did not show probable cause. The Court further held that the respondents in this case did not have "automatic standing" to challenge the legality of the search. A fortiori, in RAWLINGS v. KENTUCKY, 448 U.S. 98, 100 S.Ct. 2556, 65 L.Ed.2d. 633, 27 Cr.L. 3245 (1980) the court did not allow "automobile standing" to challenge Fourth Amendment violation where a defendant had placed drugs in the purse of an acquaintance where she admitted ownership of the drugs to the police at the scene of the arrest in a spontaneous reaction to the discovery of the drugs in the purse.

§ 6.29 Section 605 Violations in State Courts

In 1914, in Weeks v. United States, 232 U.S. 383, 34 S.Ct. 341, 58 L.Ed. 652 (1914), the Court first adopted the exclusionary rule for evidence seized in violation of the Fourteenth Amendment. In 1952 the issue of Section 605 came before the United States Supreme Court as to whether the exclusionary rule applied to state court trials when state officers violated the provisions of Section 605. Wolf v. Colorado, 338 U.S. 25, 69 S.Ct. 1359, 93 L.Ed. 1782 (1949), decided that issue when the Court said that it would not be applicable to state trials in that each state was free to adopt its own rules of evidence.

§ 6.30 Silver-Platter Doctrine Revisited

In view of the fact that the states could have their own rules of evidence, a system of cooperation developed whereby state law enforcement officers would cooperate with federal law enforcement officers in effecting arrests. The procedure was for the state officers to violate Section 605 or any other Fourth Amendment direction, seize the evidence and/or arrest the perpetrator, book and arraign the arrestee before a magistrate who would turn over the evidence and the defendant to federal authorities for prosecution. This came to be known as the "silver platter doctrine."

This doctrine continued until 1937 when in Elkins v. United States, 364 U.S. 206, 80 S.Ct. 1437, 4 L.Ed.2d 1669 (1960), the court held that evidence seized by state agents in violation of standards of the Fourth Amendment could not be used by federal agents in federal prosecutions.

§ 6.31 Electronic Device Intrusion

Silverman v. United States, 365 U.S. 505, 81 S.Ct. 679, 5 L.Ed.2d 734, was to be decided by the court in 1961. In that case an electronic spike mike which penetrated the heating duct system of the suspect's house was a sufficient invasion of a private premises to be an unreasonable search and seizure. Berger v. New York, 388 U.S. 41, 87 S.Ct. 1873, 18 L.Ed.2d 1040 (1967), finally laid the Olmstead decision to rest in a historical grave. The Berger case invalidated a New York statute which permitted application to court, by law enforcement officers, for an ex parte order permitting eavesdropping under prescribed conditions. The court held that the Fourth Amendment right of privacy was enforceable against the states and that the statute was too broad and was a trespassory intrusion.

Katz v. United States, 389 U.S. 347, 88 S.Ct. 507, 19 L.Ed.2d 576 (1967), followed this. Katz was subjected to an electronic listening and recording device which had been attached to the outside of a public telephone booth where he was transmitting wagering calls from Los Angeles to Miami and Boston in violation of a federal statute. No warrant had been issued for this intrusion. The court held that "One who occupies it (telephone booth) shuts the door behind him and pays the toll that permits him to place a call is surely entitled to assume that the words he utters into the mouthpiece will not be broadcast to the world...." The court refused to retroactively validate the conduct of the FBI because they probably could have obtained a warrant for the actions that the agents engaged in.

In United States v. Donovan, 429 U.S. 413, 97 S.Ct. 658, 50 L.Ed.2d 652 (1977), the Court held that the government has a responsibility to inform the judge who issues the wiretap order of the identities of those persons whose conversation is to be overheard, but it is not a constitutional requirement that all those likely to be overheard engaged in incriminating conversations be named.

The Court in another case held that a pen register that records telephone numbers dialed from a monitored telephone does not intercept wire or oral communications within the meaning of the federal electronics eavesdropping statute. It sustained a district court's order to a telephone company to provide reasonable technical assistance for the installation of a pen register and to be compensated for its services was held not to be an abuse of discretion. U.S. v. N.Y. Telephone Co., 434 U.S. 159, 98 S.Ct. 364, 54 L.Ed.2d 376, 22 Cr.L. 3001 (1977).

§ 6.32 Federal and State Fourth Amendment Rights Joined

Mapp v. Ohio, 367 U.S. 643, 160 Ohio Op.(2d) 384, 81 S.Ct. 1680, 6 L.Ed.2d 1081 (1961), in a 5 to 3 decision, finally merged the federal and state exclusionary rules with respect to Fourth Amendment violations. The state was no longer permitted to admit evidence in state trials which violated the dictates of the Fourth Amendment. This was accomplished by the court by reading the Due Process Clause of the Fourteenth Amendment along with the Fourth Amendment so as to make Fourth Amendment rights which were applicable to United States citizens with respect to the federal government applicable to all inhabitants against both federal and state governments.

§ 6.32(a) Bullet—Removal from Suspect's Body

Sometimes the law may appear to work an injustice to society. This conclusion is reached by many layman when a bullet is lodged in a suspect's body who probably committed a crime; the bullet is necessary to connect this person to the alleged crime; and the Court prohibits the surgery necessary to extract the bullet. This situation occurred in WINSTON v. LEE, —U.S.—, 105 S.Ct. 1611, 84 L.Ed.2d. 662 (1985). The Court held that the proposed surgery in this case would violate respondent's right to be secure in his person and the search would be "unreasonable" under the Fourth Amendment. However the Court said further that the reasonableness of surgical intrusions beneath the skin depends on a case-by-case approach in which the individuals' interest in privacy and security are weighed against society's interests in conducting the procedure to obtain evidence for fairly determining guilt or innocence. In this case the bullet was lodged substantially deep in suspect's body.

§ 6.32(b) Deadly Force

The apprehension of a criminal suspect by the use of deadly force has been limited by the Court's decision in TENNESSEE v. GARDNER, —U.S.—, 105 S.Ct. 1694, 85 L.Ed.2d. 1 (1985). That case held a Tennessee statute unconstitutional that permitted police to use deadly force to prevent the escape of suspected felons. The Court said that it violated the Fourth Amendment prohibition against unreasonable seizures because it permits the use of deadly force against an apparently unarmed, nondangerous fleeing suspect; such force may not be used unless necessary to prevent the escape, and the officer has probable cause to believe that the suspect poses a significant threat of death or serious physical injury to the officer or others.

§ 6.33 Omnibus Crime Control and Safe Streets Act

On July 23, 1965, recognizing the urgency of the nation's crime problem and the depth of ignorance about it, President Johnson established the Commission on Law Enforcement and Administration of Justice. This commission conducted extensive studies into the problem and this culminated in a comprehensive report published in 1967 entitled "The Challenge of Crime in a Free Society."

The nation was disturbed at the state of criminal justice and at this writing, it is still disturbed. Much money and man/woman hours have been spent on this problem and the solution has not surfaced to date. In response to the problem, Congress enacted the Criminal Justice Act of 1964, the Narcotic Addict Rehabilitation Act of 1966, the Juvenile Delinquency Prevention and Control Act of 1968, the Gun Control Act of 1968, Title III of the Omnibus Crime Control and Safe Streets Act of 1968 (relating to wiretapping and electronic surveillance), and Title XI of the Organized Crime Control Act of 1970 (relating to regulation of explosives).

The statutes indicated above were designated to be included in the Attorney General's First Annual Report dated September 1, 1972, available from the Superintendent of Documents, United States Printing Office, Washington, D.C. 20402, stock number 2700-0160.

Title III of the Omnibus Crime Control and Safe Streets Act of 1968 (relating to wiretapping and electronic surveillance) is particularly relevant to this chapter of this text and is included below. The student should read it and analyze its provisions keeping in mind the following guidelines:

1. What crimes are involved?
2. Who may authorize surveillance?
3. What specifically is required?
4. What is the time limitation on the authorization?
5. When is no prior judicial authorization permitted?

§ *2510. Definitions*
As used in this chapter—

(1) "wire communication" means any communication made in whole or in part through the use of facilities for the transmission of communications by the aid of wire, cable, or other like connection between the point of origin and the point of reception furnished or operated by any person engaged as a common carrier in providing or operating such facilities for the transmission of interstate or foreign communications;

(2) "oral communication" means any oral communication uttered by a person exhibiting an expectation that such communication is not subject to interception under circumstances justifying such expectation;...

(4) "intercept" means the aural acquisition of the contents of any wire or oral communication through the use of any electronic, mechanical, or other device;

(5) "electronic, mechanical, or other device" means any device or apparatus which can be used to intercept a wire or oral communication other than—

(a) any telephone or telegraph instrument, equipment or facility, or any component thereof, (i) furnished to the subscriber or user by a communications common carrier in the ordinary course of its business and being used by the subscriber or user in the ordinary course of its business; or (ii) being used by a communications common carrier in the ordinary course of its business, or by an investigative or law enforcement officer in the ordinary course of his duties;

(b) a hearing aid or similar device being used to correct subnormal hearing to not better than normal;

(6) "person" means any employee, or agent of the United States or any State or political subdivision thereof, and any individual, partnership, association, joint stock company, trust, or corporation;

(7) "Investigative or law enforcement officer" means any officer of the United States or of a State or political subdivision thereof, who is empowered by law to conduct investigations of or to make arrests for offenses enumerated in this chapter, and any attorney authorized by law to prosecute or participate in the prosecution of such offenses;

(8) "contents" when used with respect to any wire or oral communication, includes any information concerning the identity of the parties to such communication or the existence, substance, purport, or meaning of that communication;

(9) "Judge of competent jurisdiction" means—

(a) a judge of a United States district court or a United States court of appeals; and

(b) a judge of any court of general criminal jurisdiction of a State who is authorized by a statute of that State to enter orders authorizing interceptions or wire or oral communications;

(10) "communication common carrier" shall have the same meaning which is given the term "common carrier" by section 153(h) of title 47 of the United States Code; and

(11) "aggrieved person" means a person who was a party to any intercepted wire or oral communication or a person against whom the interception was directed.

§ *2511. Interception and disclosure of wire or oral communications prohibited*

(1) Except as otherwise specifically provided in this chapter any person who—

(a) willfully intercepts, endeavors to intercept, or procures any other person to intercept or endeavor to intercept, any wire or oral communication;

(b) willfully uses, endeavors to use, or procures any other person to use or endeavor to use any electronic, mechanical, or other device to intercept any oral communication when—

(i) such device is affixed to, or otherwise transmits a signal through, a wire, cable, or other like connection used in wire communication; or

(ii) such device transmits communications by radio, or interferes with the transmission of such communication; or

(iii) such person knows, or has reason to know, that such device or any component thereof has been sent through the mail or transported in interstate or foreign commerce; or

(iv) such use or endeavor to use (A) takes place on the premises of any business or other commercial establishment the operations of which affect interstate or foreign commerce; or (B) obtains or is for the purpose of obtaining information relating to the operations of any business or other commercial establishment the operations of which affect interstate or foreign commerce; or

(v) such person acts in the District of Columbia, the Commonwealth of Puerto Rico, or any territory or possession of the United States;

(c) willfully discloses, or endeavors to disclose, to any other person the contents of any wire or oral communication, knowing or having reason to know that the information was obtained through the interception of a wire or oral communication in violation of this subsection; or

(d) willfully uses, or endeavors to use, the contents of any wire or oral communication, knowing or having reason to know that the information was obtained through the interception of a wire or oral communication in violation of this subsection;

shall be fined not more than $10,000 or imprisoned not more than five years, or both....

(c) It shall not be unlawful under this chapter for a person acting under color of law to intercept a wire or oral communication, where such person is a party to the communication or one of the parties to the communication has given prior consent to such interception.

(d) It shall not be unlawful under this chapter for a person not acting under color of law to intercept a wire or oral communication where such person is a party to the communication or where one of the parties to the communication has given prior consent to such interception unless such communication is intercepted for the purpose of committing any criminal or tortious act in violation of the Constitution or laws of the United States or of any State or for the purpose of committing any other injurious act.

(3) Nothing contained in this chapter or in section 605 of the Communications Act of 1934 (48 Stat. 1143; 47 U.S.C. 605) shall limit the constitutional power of the President to take such measures as he deems necessary to protect the Nation against actual or potential attack or other hostile acts of a foreign power, to obtain foreign intelligence information deemed essential to the security of the United States, or to protect national security information against foreign intelligence activities. Nor shall anything contained in this chapter be deemed to limit the constitutional power of the President to take such measures as he deems necessary to protect the United States against the overthrow of the Government by force or other unlawful means, or against any other clear and present danger to the structure or existence of the Government. The contents of any wire or oral communication intercepted by authority of the President in the exercise of the foregoing powers may be received in evidence in any trial hearing, or other proceeding only where such interception was reasonable, and shall not be otherwise used or disclosed except as is necessary to implement that power....

. . .

§ *2515. Prohibition of use as evidence of intercepted wire or oral communications*

Whenever any wire or oral communication has been intercepted, no part of the contents of such communication and no evidence derived therefrom may be received in evidence in any trial, hearing, or other proceeding in or before any court, grand jury, department, officer, agency, regulatory body, legislative committee, or other authority of the United States, a State, or a political subdivision thereof if the disclosure of that information would be in violation of this chapter.

§2516. Authorization for interception of wire or oral communications

(1) The Attorney General, or any Assistant Attorney General specially designated by the Attorney General, may authorize an application to a Federal judge of competent jurisdiction for, and such judge may grant in conformity with section 2518 of this chapter an order authorizing or approving the interception of wire or oral communications by the Federal Bureau of Investigation, or a Federal agency having responsibility for the investigation of the offense as to which the application is made, when such interception may provide or has provided evidence of—

(a) any offense punishable by death or by imprisonment for more than one year under sections 2274 through 2277 of title 42 of the United States Code (relating to the enforcement of the Atomic Energy Act of 1954), or under the following chapters of this title: chapter 37 (relating to espionage), chapter 105 (relating to sabotage), chapter 115 (relating to treason), or chapter 102 (relating to riots);

(b) a violation of section 186 of section 501(c) of title 29, United States Code (dealing with restrictions on payments and loans to labor organizations), or any offense which involves murder, kidnapping, robbery, or extortion, and which is punishable under this title;

(c) any offense which is punishable under the following sections of this title: section 201 (bribery of public officials and witnesses), section 224 (bribery in sporting contests), section 1084 (transmission of wagering information), section 1503 (influencing or injuring an officer, juror, or witness generally), section 1510 (obstruction of criminal investigations), section 1751 (Presidential assassinations, kidnapping and assault), section 1951 (interference with commerce by threats or violence), section 1952 (interstate and foreign travel or transportation in aid of racketeering enterprises), section 1954 (offer, acceptance, or solicitation to influence operations of employee benefit plan), section 659 (theft from interstate shipment), section 664 (embezzlement from pension and welfare funds), or sections 2314 and 2315 (interstate transportation of stolen property);

(d) any offense involving counterfeiting punishable under section 471, 472 or 473 of this title;

(e) any offense involving bankruptcy fraud or the manufacture, importation, receiving, concealment, buying, selling, or otherwise dealing in narcotic drugs, marihuana, or other dangerous drugs, punishable under any law of the United States;

(f) any offense including extortionate credit transactions under sections 892, 893, or 894 of this title, or

(g) any conspiracy to commit any of the foregoing offenses.

(2) The principal prosecuting attorney of any State, or the principal prosecuting attorney of any political subdivision thereof, if such attorney is authorized by a statute of that State to make application to a State court judge of competent jurisdiction for an order authorizing or approving the interception of wire or oral communications, may apply to such judge for, and such judge may grant in conformity with section 2518 of this chapter and with the applicable State statute an order authorizing or approving the interception of wire or oral communications by investigative or law enforcement officers having responsibility for the investigation of the offense as to which the application is made, when such interception may provide or has provided evidence of the commission of the offense of murder, kidnapping, gambling, robbery, bribery, extortion, or dealing in narcotic drugs, marihuana or other dangerous drugs, or other crime dangerous to life, limb, or property, and punishable by imprisonment for more than one year, designated in any applicable State statute authorizing such interception, or any conspiracy to commit any of the foregoing offenses.

§ *2517. Authorization for disclosure and use of intercepted wire or oral communication*

(1) Any investigative or law enforcement officer who, by any means authorized by this chapter, has obtained knowledge of the contents of any wire or oral communication, or evidence derived therefrom, may disclose such contents to another investigative or law enforcement officer to the extent that such disclosure is appropriate to the proper performance of the official duties of the officer making or receiving the disclosure.

(2) Any investigative or law enforcement officer who, by any means authorized by this chapter, has obtained knowledge of the contents of any wire or oral communication or evidence derived therefrom may use such contents to the extent such use is appropriate to the proper performance of his official duties.

(3) Any person who has received, by any means authorized by this chapter, any information concerning a wire or oral communication, or evidence derived therefrom intercepted in accordance with the provisions of this chapter may disclose the contents of that communication or such derivative evidence while giving testimony under oath or affirmation in any criminal proceeding in any court of the United States or of any State or in any Federal or State grand jury proceeding.

(4) No otherwise privileged wire or oral communication intercepted in accordance with, or in violation of, the provisions of this chapter shall lose its privileged character.

(5) When an investigative or law enforcement officer, while engaged in intercepting wire or oral communications in the manner authorized here-

in, intercepts wire or oral communications relating to offenses other than those specified in the order of authorization or approval, the contents thereof, and evidence derived therefrom, may be disclosed or used as provided in subsections (1) and (2) of this section. Such contents and any evidence derived therefrom may be used under subsection (3) of this section when authorized or approved by a judge of competent jurisdiction where such judge finds on subsequent application that the contents were otherwise intercepted in accordance with the provisions of this chapter. Such application shall be made as soon as practicable.

§*2518. Procedure for interception of wire or oral communications*

(1) Each application for an order authorizing or approving the interception of a wire or oral communication shall be made in writing upon oath or affirmation to a judge of competent jurisdiction and shall state the applicant's authority to make such application. Each application shall include the following information:

(a) the identity of the investigative or law enforcement officer making the application, and the officer authorizing the application;

(b) a full and complete statement of the facts and circumstances relied upon by the applicant, to justify his belief that an order should be issued, including (i) details as to the particular offense that has been, is being, or is about to be committed, (ii) a particular description of the nature and location of the facilities from which or the place where the communication is to be intercepted, (iii) a particular description of the type of communications sought to be intercepted, (iv) the identity of the person, if known, committing the offense and whose communications are to be intercepted;

(c) a full and complete statement as to whether or not other investigative procedures have been tried and failed or why they reasonably appear to be unlikely to succeed if tried or to be too dangerous;

(d) a statement of the period of time for which the interception is required to be maintained. If the nature of the investigation is such that the authorization for interception should not automatically terminate when the described type of communication has been first obtained, a particular description of facts establishing probable cause to believe that additional communications of the same type will occur thereafter;

(e) a full and complete statement of the facts concerning all previous applications known to the individual authorizing and making the application, made to any judge for authorization to intercept, or for approval of interceptions of, wire or oral communications involving any of the same persons, facilities or places specified in the application, and the action taken by the judge on each such application; and

(f) where the application is for the extension of an order, a statement setting forth the results thus far obtained from the interception, or a reasonable explanation of the failure to obtain such results.

(2) The judge may require the applicant to furnish additional testimony or documentary evidence in support of the application.

(3) Upon such application the judge may enter an ex parte order, as requested or as modified, authorizing or approving interception of wire or oral communications within the territorial jurisdiction of the court in which the judge is sitting, if the judge determines on the basis of the facts submitted by the applicant that—

(a) there is probable cause for belief that an individual is committing, has committed, or is about to commit a particular offense enumerated in section 2516 of this chapter;

(b) there is probable cause for belief that particular communications concerning that offense will be obtained through such interception;

(c) normal investigative procedures have been tried and have failed or reasonably appear to be unlikely to succeed if tried or to be too dangerous.

(d) there is probable cause for belief that the facilities from which, or the place where, the wire or oral communications are to be intercepted are being used, or are about to be used, in connection with the commission of such offense, or are leased to, listed in the name of, or commonly used by such person.

(4) Each order authorizing or approving the interception of any wire or oral communication shall specify—

(a) the identity of the person, if known, whose communications are to be intercepted;

(b) the nature and location of the communications facilities as to which, or the place where, authority to intercept is granted;

(c) a particular description of the type of communication sought to be intercepted, and a statement of the particular offense to which it relates;

(d) the identity of the agency authorized to intercept the communications, and of the person authorizing the application; and

(e) the period of time during which such interception is authorized, including a statement as to whether or not the interception shall automatically terminate when the described communication has been first obtained.

(5) No order entered under this section may authorize or approve the interception of any wire or oral communication for any period longer than is

necessary to achieve the objective of the authorization, nor in any event longer than thirty days. Extension of an order may be granted, but only upon application for an extension made in accordance with subsection (1) of this section and the court making the findings required by subsection (3) of this section. The period of extension shall be no longer than the authorizing judge deems necessary to achieve the purposes for which it was granted and in no event for longer than thirty days. Every order and extension thereof shall contain a provision that the authorization to intercept shall be executed as soon as practicable, shall be conducted in such a way as to minimize the interception of communications not otherwise subject to interception under this chapter, and must terminate upon attainment of the authorized objective, or in any event in thirty days.

(6) Whenever an order authorizing interception is entered pursuant to this chapter, the order may require reports to be made to the judge who issued the order showing what progress has been made toward achievement of the authorized objective and the need for continued interception. Such reports shall be made at such intervals as the judge may require.

(7) Notwithstanding any other provision of this chapter, any investigative or law enforcement officer, specially designated by the Attorney General or by the principal prosecuting attorney of any State or subdivision thereof acting pursuant to a statute of that State, who reasonably determines that—

(a) an emergency situation exists with respect to conspiratorial activities threatening the national security interest or to conspiratorial activities characteristic of organized crime that requires a wire or oral communication to be intercepted before an order authorizing such interception can with due diligence be obtained, and

(b) there are grounds upon which an order could be entered under this chapter to authorize such interception,

may intercept such wire or oral communication if the application for an order approving the interception is made in accordance with this section within forty-eight hours after the interception has occurred, or begins to occur. In the absence of an order, such interception shall immediately terminate when the communication sought is obtained or when the application for the order is denied, whichever is earlier. In the event such application for approval is denied, or in any other case where the interception is terminated without an order having been issued, the contents of any wire or oral communication intercepted shall be treated as having been obtained in violation of this chapter, and an inventory shall be served as provided for in subsection (d) of this section on the person named in the application.

(8) (a) The contents of any wire or oral communication intercepted by any means authorized by this chapter shall, if possible, be recorded on tape

or wire or other comparable device. The recording of the contents of any wire or oral communication under this subsection shall be done in such way as will protect the recording from editing or other alterations. Immediately upon the expiration of the period of the order, or extensions thereof, such recordings shall be made available to the judge issuing such order and sealed under his directions. Custody of the recordings shall be wherever the judge orders. They shall not be destroyed except upon an order of the issuing or denying judge and in any event shall be kept for ten years. Duplicate recordings may be made for use or disclosure pursuant to the provisions of subsections (1) and (2) of section 2517 of this chapter for investigations. The presence of the seal provided for by this subsection, or a satisfactory explanation for the absence thereof, shall be a prerequisite for the use or disclosure of the contents of any wire or oral communication or evidence derived therefrom under subsection (3) of section 2517.

(b) Applications made and orders granted under this chapter shall be sealed by the judge. Custody of the applications and orders shall be wherever the judge directs. Such applications and orders shall be disclosed only upon a showing of good cause before a judge of competent jurisdiction and shall not be destroyed except on order of the issuing or denying judge, and in any event shall be kept for ten years.

(c) Any violation of the provisions of this subsection may be punished as contempt of the issuing or denying judge.

(d) Within a reasonable time but not later than ninety days after the filing of an application for an order of approval under section 2518 (7)(b) which is denied or the termination of the period of an order or extensions thereof, the issuing or denying judge shall cause to be served, on the persons named in the order or the application, and such other parties to intercepted communications as the judge may determine in his discretion that is in the interest of justice, an inventory which shall include notice of—

(1) the fact of the entry of the order or the application;

(2) the date of the entry and the period of authorized, approved or disapproved interception, or the denial of the application; and

(3) the fact that during the period wire or oral communications were or were not intercepted.

The judge, upon the filing of a motion, may in his discretion make available to such person or his counsel for inspection such portions of the intercepted communications, applications and orders as the judge determines to be in the interest of justice. On an ex parte showing of good cause to a judge of competent jurisdiction the serving of the inventory required by this subsection may be postponed.

(9) The contents of any intercepted wire or oral communication or evidence derived therefrom shall not be received in evidence or otherwise dis-

closed in any trial, hearing, or other proceeding in a Federal or State court unless each party, not less than ten days before the trial, hearing, or proceeding, has been furnished with a copy of the court order, and accompanying application, under which the interception was authorized or approved. This ten-day period may be waived by the judge if he finds that it was not possible to furnish the party with the above information ten days before the trial, hearing, or proceeding and that the party will not be prejudiced by the delay in receiving such information.

(10)(a) Any aggrieved person in any trial, hearing, or proceeding in or before any court, department, officer, agency, regulatory body, or other authority of the United States, a State, or a political subdivision thereof, may move to suppress the contents of any intercepted wire or oral communication, or evidence derived therefrom, on the grounds that—

(i) the communication was unlawfully intercepted;

(ii) the order of authorization or approval under which it was intercepted is insufficient on its face; or

(iii) the interception was not made in conformity with the order of authorization or approval.

Such motion shall be made before the trial, hearing, or proceeding unless there is no opportunity to make such motion or the person was not aware of the grounds of the motion. If the motion is granted, the contents of the intercepted wire or oral communication, or evidence derived therefrom, shall be treated as having been obtained in violation of this chapter. The judge, upon the filing of such motion by the aggrieved person, may in his discretion make available to the aggrieved person or his counsel for inspection such portions of the intercepted communication or evidence derived therefrom as the judge determines to be in the interests of justice.

(b) In addition to any other right to appeal, the United States shall have the right to appeal from an order granting a motion to suppress made under paragraph (a) of this subsection, or the denial of an application for an order of approval, if the United States attorney shall certify to the judge or other official granting such motion or denying such application that the appeal is not taken for purposes of delay. Such appeal shall be taken within thirty days after the date the order was entered and shall be diligently prosecuted.

§ *2519. Reports concerning intercepted wire or oral communications*

(1) Within thirty days after the expiration of an order (or each extension thereof) entered under section 2518, or the denial of an order approving the interception, the issuing or denying judge shall report to the Administrative Office of the United States Courts—

(a) the fact that an order or extension was applied for;

(b) the kind of order or extension applied for;

(c) the fact that the order or extension was granted as applied for, was modified, or was denied;

(d) the period of interceptions authorized by the order, and the number and duration of any extensions of the order;

(e) the offense specified in the order or application, or extension of an order;

(f) the identity of the applying investigative or law enforcement officer and agency making the application and the person authorizing the application; and

(g) the nature of the facilities from which or the place where communications were to be intercepted.

(2) In January of each year the Attorney General, an Assistant Attorney General specially designated by the Attorney General, or the principal prosecuting attorney of a State, or the principal prosecuting attorney for any political subdivision of a State, shall report to the Administrative Office of the United States Courts—

(a) the information required by paragraphs (a) through (g) of subsection (1) of this section with respect to each application for an order or extension made during the preceding calendar year;

(b) a general description of the interceptions made under such order or extension, including (i) the approximate nature and frequency of incriminating communications intercepted, (ii) the approximate nature and frequency of other communications intercepted, (iii) the approximate number of persons whose communications were intercepted, and (iv) the approximate nature, amount, and cost of the manpower and other resources used in the interceptions;

(c) the number of arrests resulting from interceptions made under such order or extension, and the offenses for which arrests were made;

(d) the number of trials resulting from such interceptions;

(e) the number of motions to suppress made with respect to such interceptions, and the number granted or denied;

(f) the number of convictions resulting from such interceptions and the offenses for which the convictions were obtained and a general assessment of the importance of the interceptions; and

(g) the information required by paragraphs (b) through (f) of this subsection with respect to orders or extensions obtained in preceding calendar year.

(3) In April of each year the Director of the Administrative Office of the United States Courts shall transmit to the Congress a full and complete report concerning the number of applications for orders authorizing or approving the interception of wire or oral communications and the number of orders and extensions granted or denied during the preceding calendar year. Such report shall include a summary and analysis of the data required to be filed with the Administrative Office by subsections (1) and (2) of this section. The Director of the Administrative Office of the United States Courts is authorized to issue binding regulations dealing with the content and form of the reports required to be filed by subsections (1) and (2) of this section.

§ *2520. Recovery of civil damages authorized*

Any person whose wire or oral communication is intercepted, disclosed, or used in violation of this chapter shall (1) have a civil cause of action against any person who intercepts, discloses, or uses, or procures any other person to intercept, disclose, or use such communications, and (2) be entitled to recover from any such person—

(a) actual damages but not less than liquidated damages computed at the rate of $100 a day for each day of violation or $1,000, whichever is higher;

(b) punitive damages; and

(c) a reasonable attorney's fee and other litigation costs reasonably incurred.

A good faith reliance on a court order or on the provisions of section 2518(7) of this chapter shall constitute a complete defense to any civil or criminal action brought under this chapter.

§ 6.34 Use of False Friends

No police agency can be effective unless it utilizes the services of undercover agents. There is an old cliché that a detective is as good as his informant and no more. The courts have recognized this need; however, they have placed certain restrictions on its use where other fundamental rights are infringed upon by undercover agents. If, for example, an undercover agent represents himself to be a physician who is treating the defendant and exacts privileged information as a result of this role, the courts have said that this is a violation of fundamental right. N.Y.—Peo. v. Leyra, 302 N.Y. 353, 98 N.E.2d 553.

There are six leading cases which were decided by the United States Supreme Court. They are On Lee v. United States, 343 U.S. 747, 72 S.Ct. 967, 96 L.Ed. 1270 (1952); Lopez v. United States, 373 U.S. 427, 83 S.Ct. 1381, 10 L.Ed.2d 462 (1963); Hoffa v. United States, 385 U.S. 293, 87 S.Ct. 408, 17 L.Ed.2d 374 (1966); Osborn v. United States, 385 U.S. 323, 87 S.Ct. 429,

17 L.Ed.2d 394 (1966); United States v. Russel, 411 U.S. 423, 93 S.Ct. 1637, 36 L.Ed.2d 366 (1973); and Weatherford v. Bursey, 429 U.S. 545, 97 S.Ct. 837, 53 L.Ed.2d 30, 20 Cr.L. 3059 (1977).

In each of these cases the defendant petitioner relied on and confided in friends who later turned out to be government informers. The Supreme Court in divided decisions upheld the right of law enforcement authorities to use undercover false friends of the accused to get a conviction.

A slight deviation from this false friend doctrine took place in MAINE v. MOULTON, —U.S.—, 106 S.Ct. 477, 88 L.Ed.2d. 481, 38 Cr.L. 3037 (1985). A codefendant who agreed to cooperate with the police was equipped with a body transmitter and then went to meet the other defendant to plan for their upcoming trial. The non-cooperating defendant made incriminating statements during this conference, some of which were used at trial. The United States Supreme Court held that the non-cooperating defendant was denied his right to counsel and affirmed the decision of the Supreme Judicial Court of Maine that held that the statements made by the non-cooperating defendant should be suppressed and remanded for a new trial.

§ 6.35 Privileged Communications

There are certain conversations between persons which, pursuant to common law, are privileged and are not admissible in evidence against an accused. Some states and the federal government have given these privileges further imprimatur by statutory enactment.

The privileges which now exist in many jurisdictions are conversations between spouses in the furtherance of the marriage relation, between attorney and client, physician and patient, clergyman and penitent, and newspaper reporter and his source of information.

It is not the purpose of this text to treat these privileges in great detail because it is thought that such treatment belongs to a course in the law of evidence. However, it should be noted here that if a common law privilege or statutory privilege is invaded by undercover government agents, the courts will suppress the evidence as a violation of due process under the Fourteenth and Fourth Amendments to the United States Constitution. People v. Leyra (supra).

§ 6.36 Conversations Not Protected by Fourth Amendment

There are many types of situations where the Fourth Amendment does not protect the contents of conversations. The Fourth Amendment is only designed to protect secrecy. Therefore if the conversation is not concealed in any way, it would be admissible at trial. If it can be shown that there is a threat to national security and the President proves that it was reasonable and it shall not be otherwise used or disclosed, except as is necessary to implement his/her power to obtain foreign intelligence information deemed essential to the security of the United States or to protect national security, he may eavesdrop without a warrant and the evidence is admissible at trial. Omnibus Crime Control and Safe Streets Act of 1968—Title III, § 2511(3).

In every case where a government undercover agent is used, the speaker bears the risk that his friend is a government agent. If participants to a conversation make no effort to be secret, their conversation thus becomes public. For example, let us assume that two persons are engaged in a conversation in an airplane or train and they are conversing in a loud tone of voice, apparently not concerned that their conversation is being overheard by others. The use of this conversation against them at a trial would not be subject to a suppression order because they are not being deprived of their privacy in any way.

§ 6.37 Access to Federal Courts

The defendant in a state court who had an unlawful search and seizure problem from the time of Mapp v. Ohio had relatively easy access to the Federal Court after s/he had exhausted all state remedies. This was done by a petition for a writ of certiorari to the highest court of the state from the United States Supreme Court or by initiating a new review through the local United States District Court by way of a petition for a writ of habeas corpus. The second remedy has been severely limited since the Court decided Stone v. Powell, 428 U.S. 465, 96 S.Ct. 3037, 49 L.Ed.2d 1067 (1976). In that case the Court said that if a defendant in a state court had a full and fair consideration of their reliance on the exclusionary rule with respect to allegedly unlawfully seized evidence by the state courts at trial and on direct review, the prisoner may not be granted federal habeas corpus relief on the ground that evidence obtained in an unconstitutional search or seizure was introduced at his trial.

Where a state prisoner brings a petition for a writ of habeas corpus to the Federal District Court, based on an alleged violation of a constitutional right, the petition should be denied, if it is shown that the petitioner was barred by a procedural default, from raising a constitutional claim on direct appeal without showing cause for and actual prejudice from the default. ENGLE v. ISAAC, —U.S.—, 102 S.Ct. 1558, L.Ed.2d 783, 31 Cr.L. 3001 (1982). In that case the petitioner had not raised constitutional claims pursuant to an Ohio Rule of Criminal Procedure 30 and the Ohio Supreme Court dismissed his appeal.

If trial errors of a constitutional nature occur and the defendant fails to make a contemporaneous objection, the defendant is not able to get a collateral review by the United States Supreme Court unless it falls within the "cause and actual prejudice" standard under which a convicted defendant must show both "cause" excusing his double procedure default and "actual prejudice" resulting from the errors of which he complains. U.S. v. FRADY, —U.S.—, 102 S.Ct. 2287, 71 L.Ed.2d. 816, 31 Cr.L. 3013 (1982).

§ 6.38 Suppressed Evidence, Impeachment Tool

In U.S. v. HAVENS, 446 U.S. 620, 100 S.Ct. 1912, 64 L.Ed.2d. 559, 27 Cr.L. 3136 (1980) the Court allowed previously suppressed evidence to be used for impeachment purposes where a defendant's statement made in response to proper cross examination reasonably suggested by the defendants direct examination, are subject to otherwise proper impeachment by the government albeit by evidence that had been illegally obtained and is inadmissible as substantive evidence of guilt, citing HARRIS v. NEW YORK, 401 U.S. 222 and OREGON v. HASS, 420 U.S. 714. In the instant case, the respondent arrived at Miami International Airport with another male person from Peru. As a result of a customs search, the other persons T shirt revealed pockets sewn into it containing cocaine. The respondent's luggage was searched and T shirts were found therein that had matching pieces of cloth cut out to that of the sewn pockets. These T shirts were suppressed by the District Court but when respondent took the stand in his trial, he denied knowledge as to the presence of T shirts in his luggage with pieces of the cloth missing. The evidence of the T shirts was admitted, over objection, and the jury was instructed to consider this evidence only with respect to the defendant's credibility. The Court of Appeals reversed but the United States Supreme Court held that it was proper to use this suppressed evidence for impeachment purposes.

In JENKINS v. ANDERSON, WARDEN, petitioner claimed that he acted in self defense in a homicide charge. However, he failed to notify the governmental authorities until two weeks after the killing. On his trial, he testified that he had acted in self defense and the prosecutor questioned him, over objection, about his two weeks silence. The Court held that this was no violation of his constitutional rights saying, inter alia, that while the Fifth Amendment prevents the prosecution from commenting on the silence of a defendant who asserts the right to remain silent during his criminal trial, it is not violated when a defendant who testified in his own defense is impeached by his prior silence. JENKINS v. ANDERSON, WARDEN, 447 U.S. 231, 100 S.Ct. 2124, 65 L.Ed.2d. 86, (1983).

Judicial Decisions Relating to Chapter 6

Rochin *v.* California

342 U.S. 165, 72 S.Ct. 205, 96 L.Ed. 183 (1952)

CERTIORARI TO THE DISTRICT COURT OF APPEAL FOR THE SECOND APPELLATE DISTRICT OF CALIFORNIA

Argued October 16, 1951.—Decided January 2, 1952.

. . .

MR. JUSTICE FRANKFURTER delivered the opinion of the Court.

Having "some information that [the petitioner here] was selling narcotics," three deputy sheriffs of the County of Los Angeles, on the morning of July 1, 1949, made for the two-story dwelling house in which Rochin lived with his mother, common-law wife, brothers and sisters. Finding the outside door open, they entered and then forced open the door to Rochin's room on the second floor. Inside they found petitioner sitting partly dressed on the side of the bed, upon which his wife was lying. On a "night stand" beside the bed the deputies spied two capsules. When asked "Whose stuff is this?" Rochin seized the capsules and put them in his mouth. A struggle ensued, in the course of which the three officers "jumped upon him" and attempted to extract the capsules. The force they applied proved unavailing against Rochin's resistance. He was handcuffed and taken to a hospital. At the direction of one of the officers a doctor forced an emetic solution through a tube into Rochin's stomach against his will. This "stomach pumping" produced vomiting. In the vomited matter were found two capsules which proved to contain morphine.

Rochin was brought to trial before a California Superior Court, sitting without a jury, on the charge of possessing "a preparation of morphine" in violation of the California Health and Safety Code, 1947, § 11,500. Rochin was convicted and sentenced to sixty days' imprisonment. The chief evidence against him was the two capsules. They were admitted over petitioner's objection, although the means of obtaining them was frankly set forth in the testimony by one of the deputies, substantially as here narrated.

On appeal, the District Court of Appeal affirmed the conviction, despite the finding that the officers "were guilty of unlawfully breaking into and entering defendant's room and were guilty of unlawfully assaulting and battering defendant while in the room," and "were guilty of unlawfully assaulting, battering, torturing and falsely imprisoning the defendant at the alleged hospital." 101 Cal. App. 2d 140, 143, 225 P. 2d 1, 3. One of the three judges, while finding that "the record in this case reveals a shocking series of violations of constitutional rights," concurred only because he felt bound by decisions of his Supreme Court. These, he asserted, "have been looked upon by law enforcement officers as an encouragement, if not an invitation, to the commission of such lawless acts." Ibid. The Supreme Court of California denied without opinion Rochin's petition for a hearing. Two justices dissented from this denial, and in doing so expressed themselves thus: "... a conviction which rests upon evidence of incriminating objects obtained from the body of the accused by physical abuse is as invalid as a conviction which rests upon a verbal confession extracted from him by such abuse.... Had the evidence forced from the defendant's lips consisted of an oral confession that he illegally possessed a drug... he would have the protection of the rule of law which excludes coerced confessions from evidence. But because the evidence forced from his lips consisted of real objects the People of this state are permitted to base a conviction upon it. [We] find no valid ground of distinction between a verbal confession extracted by physical abuse and a confession wrested from defendant's body by physical abuse." 101 Cal. App. 2d 143, 149–150, 225 P. 2d 913, 917–918.

This Court granted certiorari, 341 U.S. 939, because a serious question is raised as to the limitations which the Due Process Clause of the Fourteenth Amendment imposes on the conduct of criminal proceedings by the States.

In our federal system the administration of criminal justice is predominantly committed to the care of the States. The power to define crimes belongs to Congress only as an appropriate means of carrying into execution its limited grant of legislative powers. U.S. Const., Art. I, § 8, cl. 18. Broadly speaking, crimes in the United States are what the laws of the individual States make them, subject to the limitations of Art. I, § 10, cl. 1, in the original Constitution, prohibiting bills of attainder and ex post facto laws, and of the Thirteenth and Fourteenth Amendments.

These limitations, in the main, concern not restrictions upon the powers of the States to define crime, except in the restricted area where federal authority has preempted the field, but restrictions upon the manner in which the States may enforce their penal codes. Accordingly, in reviewing a State criminal conviction under a claim of right guaranteed by the Due Process Clause of the Fourteenth Amendment, from which is derived the most far-reaching and most frequent federal basis of challenging State criminal justice, "we must be deeply mindful of the responsibilities of the States for the enforcement of criminal laws, and exercise with due humility our merely negative function in subjecting convictions from state courts to the very narrow scrutiny which the Due Process Clause of the Fourteenth Amendment authorizes." Malinski v. New York, 324 U.S. 401, 412, 418. Due process of law, "itself a historical product," Jackman v. Rosenbaum Co., 260 U.S. 22, 31, is not to be turned into a destructive dogma against the States in the administration of their systems of criminal justice.

However, this Court too has its responsibility. Regard for the requirements of the Due Process Clause "inescapably imposes upon this Court an exercise of judgment upon the whole course of the proceedings [resulting in a conviction] in order to ascertain whether they offend those canons of decency and fairness which express the notions of justice of English-speaking peoples even toward those charged with the most heinous offenses." Malinski v. New York, supra, at 416–417. These standards of justice are not authoritatively formulated anywhere as though they were specifics. Due process of law is a summarized constitutional guarantee of respect for those personal immunities which, as MR. JUSTICE CARDOZO twice wrote for the Court, are "so rooted in the traditions and conscience of our people as to be ranked as fundamental." Snyder v. Massachusetts, 291 U.S. 97, 105, or are "implicit in the concept of ordered liberty." Palko v. Connecticut, 302 U.S. 319, 325.

The Court's function in the observance of this settled conception of the Due Process Clause does not leave us without adequate guides in subjecting State criminal procedures to constitutional judgment. In dealing not with the machinery of government but with human rights, the absence of formal exactitude, or want of fixity of meaning, is not an unusual or even regrettable attribute of constitutional provisions. Words being symbols do not speak without a gloss. On the one hand the gloss may be the deposit of history, whereby a term gains technical content. Thus the requirements of the Sixth and Seventh Amendments for trial by jury in the federal courts have a rigid meaning. No changes or chances can alter the content of the verbal symbol of "jury"—a body of twelve men who must reach a unanimous conclusion if the verdict is to go against the defendant. On the other hand, the gloss of some of the verbal symbols of the Constitution does not give them a fixed technical content. It exacts a continuing process of application.

When the gloss has thus not been fixed but is a function of the process of judgment, the judgment is bound to fall differently at different times and differently at the same time through different judges. Even more specific provisions, such as the guaranty of freedom of speech and the detailed protection against unreasonable searches and seizures, have inevitably evoked as sharp divisions in this Court as the least specific and most comprehensive protection of liberties, the Due Process Clause.

The vague contours of the Due Process Clause do not leave judges at large. We may not draw on our merely personal and private notions and disregard the limits that bind judges in their judicial function. Even though the concept of due process of law is not final and fixed, these limits are derived from considerations that are fused in the whole nature of our judicial process. See Cardozo, The Nature of the Judicial Process; The Growth of the Law; The Paradoxes of Legal Science. These are considerations deeply rooted in reason and in the compelling traditions of the legal profession. The Due Process Clause places upon this Court the duty of exercising a judgment, within the narrow confines of judicial power in reviewing State convictions, upon interests of society pushing in opposite directions.

Due process of law thus conceived is not to be derided as resort to a revival of "natural law." To believe that this judicial exercise of judgment could be avoided by freezing "due process of law" at some fixed stage of time or thought is to suggest that the most important aspect of constitutional adjudication is a function for inanimate machines and not for judges, for whom the independence safeguarded by Article III of the Constitution was designed and who are presumably guided by established standards of judicial behavior. Even cybernetics has not yet made that haughty claim. To practice the requisite detachment and to achieve sufficient objectivity no doubt demands of judges the habit of self-discipline and self-criticism, incertitude that one's own views are incontestable and alert tolerance toward views not shared. But these are precisely the presuppositions of our judicial process. They are precisely the qualities society has a right to expect from those entrusted with ultimate judicial power.

Restraints on our jurisdiction are self-imposed only in the sense that there is from our decisions no immediate appeal short of impeachment or constitutional amendment. But that does not make due process of law a matter of judicial caprice. The faculties of the Due Process Clause may be indefinite and vague, but the mode of their ascertainment is not self-willed. In each case "due process of law" requires an evaluation based on a disinterested inquiry pursued in the spirit of science, on a balanced order of facts exactly and fairly stated, on the detached consideration of conflicting claims, see Hudson County Water Co. v. McCarter, 209 U.S. 349, 355, on a judgment not ad hoc and episodic but duly mindful of reconciling the needs both of continuity and of change in a progressive society.

Applying these general considerations to the circumstances of the present case, we are compelled to conclude that the proceedings by which this conviction was obtained do more than offend some fastidious squeamishness or private sentimentalism about combatting crime too energetically. This is conduct that shocks the conscience. Illegally breaking into the privacy of the petitioner, the struggle to open his mouth and remove what was there, the forcible extraction of his stomach's contents—this course of proceeding by agents of government to obtain evidence is bound to offend even hardened sensibilities. They are methods too close to the rack and the screw to permit of constitutional differentiation.

It has long since ceased to be true that due process of law is heedless of the means by which otherwise relevant and credible evidence is obtained. This was not true even before the series of recent cases enforced the constitutional principle that the States may not base convictions upon confessions, however much verified, obtained by coercion. These decisions are not arbitrary exceptions to the comprehensive right of States to fashion their own rules of evidence for criminal trials. They are not sports in our constitutional law but applications of a general principle. They are only instances of the general requirement that States in their prosecutions respect certain decencies of civilized conduct. Due process of law, as a historic and generative principle, precludes defining, and thereby confining, these standards of conduct more precisely than to say that convictions cannot be brought about by methods that offend "a sense of justice." See Mr. Chief Justice Hughes, speaking for a unanimous Court in Brown v. Mississippi, 297 U.S. 278, 285–286. It would be a stultification of the responsibility which the course of constitutional history has cast upon this Court to hold that in order to convict a man the police cannot extract by force what is in his mind but can extract what is in his stomach.

To attempt in this case to distinguish what lawyers call "real evidence" from verbal evidence is to ignore the reasons for excluding coerced confessions. Use of involuntary verbal confessions in State criminal trials is constitutionally obnoxious not only because of their unreliability. They are inadmissible under the Due Process Clause even though statements contained in them may be independently established as true. Coerced confessions offend the community's sense of fair play and decency. So here, to sanction the brutal conduct which naturally enough was condemned by the court whose judgment is before us, would be to afford brutality the cloak of law. Nothing would be more calculated to discredit law and thereby to brutalize the temper of a society.

In deciding this case we do not heedlessly bring into question decisions in many States dealing with essentially different, even if related, problems. We therefore put to one side cases which have arisen in the State courts through use of modern methods and devices for discovering wrongdoers and bringing them to book. It does not fairly represent these decisions to suggest that they legalize force so brutal and so offensive to human dignity in securing evidence from a suspect as is revealed by this record. Indeed the California Supreme Court has not sanctioned this mode of securing a conviction. It merely exercised its discretion to decline a review of the conviction. All the California judges who have expressed themselves in this case have condemned the conduct in the strongest language.

We are not unmindful that hypothetical situations can be conjured up, shading imperceptibly from the circumstances of this case and by gradations producing practical differences despite seemingly logical extensions. But the Constitution is "intended to preserve practical and substantial rights, not to maintain theories." Davis v. Mills, 194 U.S. 451, 457.

On the facts of this case the conviction of the petitioner has been obtained by methods that offend the Due Process Clause. The judgment below must be

Reversed.

Mapp *v.* Ohio

367 U.S. 643, 81 S.Ct. 1680, 6 L.Ed. 2d. 1081 (1961)

APPEAL FROM THE SUPREME COURT OF OHIO.

Argued March 29, 1961.—Decided June 19, 1961.

. . .

MR. JUSTICE CLARK delivered the opinion of the Court.

Appellant stands convicted of knowingly having had in her possession and under her control certain lewd and lascivious books, pictures, and photographs in violation of § 2905.34 of Ohio's Revised Code. As officially stated in the syllabus to its opinion, the Supreme Court of Ohio found that her conviction was valid though "based primarily upon the introduction in evidence of lewd and lascivious books and pictures unlawfully seized during an unlawful search of defendant's home..." 170 Ohio St. 427–428, 166 N.E. 2d 387. 388.

On May 23, 1957, three Cleveland police officers arrived at appellant's residence in that city pursuant to information that "a person [was] hiding out in the home, who was wanted for questioning in connection with a recent bombing, and that there was a large amount of policy paraphernalia being hidden in the home." Miss Mapp and her daughter by a former marriage lived on the top floor of the two-family dwelling. Upon their arrival at that house, the officers knocked on the door and demanded entrance but appellant, after telephoning her attorney, refused to admit them without a search warrant. They advised their headquarters of the situation and undertook a surveillance of the house.

The officers again sought entrance some three hours later when four or more additional officers arrived on the scene. When Miss Mapp did not come to the door immediately, at least one of the several doors to the house was forcibly opened and the policemen gained admittance. Meanwhile Miss Mapp's attorney arrived, but the officers, having secured their own entry, and continuing in their defiance of the law, would permit him neither to see Miss Mapp nor to enter the house. It appears that Miss Mapp was halfway down the stairs from the upper floor to the front door when the officers, in this highhanded manner, broke into the hall. She demanded to see the search warrant. A paper, claimed to be a warrant, was held up by one of the officers. She grabbed the "warrant" and placed it in her bosom. A struggle ensued in which the officers recovered the piece of paper and as a result of which they handcuffed appellant because she had been "belligerent" in resisting their official rescue of the "warrant" from her person. Running roughshod over appellant, a policeman "grabbed" her, "twisted [her] hand," and she "yelled [and] pleaded with him" because "it was hurting." Appellant, in handcuffs, was then forcibly taken upstairs to her bedroom where the officers searched a dresser, a chest of drawers, a closet and some suitcases. They also looked into a photo album and through personal papers belonging to the appellant. The search spread to the rest of the second floor including the child's bedroom, the living room, the kitchen and a dinette. The basement of the building and a trunk found therein were also searched. The obscene materials for possession of which she was ultimately convicted were discovered in the course of that widespread search.

At the trial no search warrant was produced by the prosecution, nor was the failure to produce one explained or accounted for. At best, "There is, in the record, considerable doubt as to whether there ever was any warrant for the search of defendant's home." 170 Ohio St., at 430, 166 N.E. 2d, at 389. The Ohio Supreme Court believed a "reasonable argument" could be made that the conviction should be reversed "because the 'methods' employed to obtain the [evidence]... were such as to 'offend "a sense of justice,"'" but the court found determinative the fact that the evidence had not been taken "from defendant's person by the use of brutal or offensive physical force against defendant." 170 Ohio St., at 431, 166 N.E. 2d, at 389–390.

The State says that even if the search were made without authority, or otherwise unreasonably, it is not prevented from using the unconstitutionally seized evidence at trial, citing Wolf v. Colorado, 338 U.S. 25 (1949), in which this Court did indeed hold "that in a prosecution in a State court for a State crime the Fourteenth Amendment does not forbid the admission of evidence obtained by an unreasonable search and seizure." At p. 33. On this appeal, of which we have noted probable jurisdiction, 364 U.S. 868, it is urged once again that we review that holding.

I

Seventy-five years ago, in Boyd v. United States, 116 U.S. 616, 630 (1886), considering the Fourth and Fifth Amendments as running "almost into each other" on the facts before it, this Court held that the doctrines of those Amendments

> "apply to all invasions on the part of the government and its employés of the sanctity of a man's home and the privacies of life. It is not the breaking of his doors, and the rummaging of his drawers, that constitutes the essence of the offence; but it is the invasion of his indefeasible right of personal security, personal liberty and private property.... Breaking into a house and opening boxes and drawers are circumstances of aggravation; but any forcible and compulsory extortion of a man's own testimony or of his private papers to be used as evidence to convict him of crime or to forfeit his goods, is within the condemnation ... [of those Amendments]."

The Court noted that

> "constitutional provisions for the security of person and property should be liberally construed.... It is the duty of courts to be watchful for the constitutional rights of the citizen, and against any stealthy encroachments thereon." At p. 635.

In this jealous regard for maintaining the integrity of individual rights, the Court gave life to Madison's prediction that "independent tribunals of justice ... will be naturally led to resist every encroachment upon rights expressly stipulated for in the Constitution by the declaration of rights." I Annals of Cong. 439 (1789). Concluding, the Court specifically referred to the use of the evidence there seized as "unconstitutional." At p. 638.

Less than 30 years after Boyd, this Court, in Weeks v. United States, 232 U.S. 383 (1914), stated that

> "the Fourth Amendment ... put the courts of the United States and Federal officials, in the exercise of their power and authority, under limitations and restraints [and] ... forever secure[d] the people, their persons, houses, papers and effects against all unreasonable searches and seizures under the guise of law ... and the duty of giving to it force and effect is obligatory upon all entrusted under our Federal system with the enforcement of the laws." At pp. 391–392.

Specifically dealing with the use of the evidence unconstitutionally seized, the Court concluded:

> "If letters and private documents can thus be seized and held and used in evidence against a citizen accused of an offense, the protection of the Fourth Amendment declaring his right to be secure against such searches and seizures is of no value, and, so far as those thus placed are concerned, might as well be stricken from the Constitution. The efforts of the courts and their officials to bring the guilty to punishment, praiseworthy as they are, are not to be aided by the sacrifice of those great principles established by years of endeavor and suffering which have resulted in their embodiment in the fundamental law of the land." At p. 393.

Finally, the Court in that case clearly stated that use of the seized evidence involved "a denial of the constitutional rights of the accused." At p. 398. Thus, in the year 1914, in the Weeks case, this Court "for the first time" held that "in a federal prosecution the Fourth Amendment barred the use of evidence secured through an illegal search and seizure." Wolf v. Colorado, supra, at 28. This Court has ever since required of federal law officers a strict adherence to that command which this Court has held to be a clear, specific, and constitutionally required—even if judicially implied—deterrent safeguard without insistence upon which the Fourth Amendment would have been reduced to "a form of words." HOLMES, J., Silverthorne Lumber Co. v. United States, 251 U.S. 385, 392 (1920). It meant, quite simply, that "conviction by means of unlawful seizures and enforced confessions... should find no sanction in the judgments of the courts..." Weeks v. United States, supra, at 392, and that such evidence "shall not be used at all." Silverthorne Lumber Co. v. United States, supra, at 392.

There are in the cases of this Court some passing references to the Weeks rule as being one of evidence. But the plain and unequivocal language of Weeks—and its later paraphrase in Wolf—to the effect that the Weeks rule is of constitutional origin, remains entirely undisturbed. In Byars v. United States, 273 U.S. 28 (1927), a unanimous Court declared that "the doctrine [cannot]... be tolerated *under our constitutional system*, that evidences of crime discovered by a federal officer in making a search without lawful warrant may be used against the victim of the unlawful search where a timely challenge has been interposed." At pp. 29–30 (emphasis added). The Court, in Olmstead v. United States, 277 U.S. 438 (1928), in unmistakable language restated the Weeks rule:

> "The striking outcome of the Weeks case and those which followed it was the sweeping declaration that the Fourth Amendment, although not referring to or limiting the use of evidence in courts, really forbade its introduction if obtained by government officers through a violation of the Amendment." At p. 462.

In McNabb v. United States, 318 U.S. 332 (1943), we note this statement:

> "[A] conviction in the federal courts, the foundation of which is evidence obtained in disregard of liberties deemed fundamental by the Constitution, cannot stand. Boyd v. United States... Weeks v. United States.... And this Court has, on Constitutional grounds, set aside convictions, both in the federal and state courts, which were based upon confessions 'secured by protracted and repeated questioning of ignorant and untutored persons, in whose minds the power of officers was greatly magnified'... or 'who have been unlawfully held incommunicado without advice of friends or counsel'..." At pp. 339–340.

Significantly, in McNabb, the Court did then pass on to formulate a rule of evidence, saying, "[i]n the view we take of the case, however, it becomes unnecessary to reach the Constitutional issue [for]... [t]he principles governing the admissibility of evidence in federal criminal trials have not been restricted... to those derived solely from the Constitution." At pp. 340–341.

II

In 1949, 35 years after *Weeks* was announced, this Court, in Wolf v. Colorado, supra, again for the first time, discussed the effect of the Fourth Amendment upon the States through the operation of the Due Process Clause of the Fourteenth Amendment. It said:

> "[W]e have no hesitation in saying that were a State affirmatively to sanction such police incursion into privacy it would run counter to the guaranty of the Fourteenth Amendment." At p. 28.

Nevertheless, after declaring that the "security of one's privacy against arbitrary intrusion by the police" is "implicit in 'the concept of ordered liberty' and as such enforceable against the States through the Due Process Clause," cf. Palko v. Connecticut, 302 U.S. 319 (1937), and announcing that it "stoutly adhere[d]" to the Weeks decision, the Court decided that the Weeks exclusionary rule would not then be imposed upon the States as "an essential ingredient of the right." 338 U.S., at 27–29. The Court's reasons for not considering essential to the right to privacy, as a curb imposed upon the States by the Due Process Clause, that which decades before had been posited as part and parcel of the Fourth Amendment's limitation upon federal encroachment of individual privacy, were bottomed on factual considerations.

While they are not basically relevant to a decision that the exclusionary rule is an essential ingredient of the Fourth Amendment as the right it embodies is vouchsafed against the States by the Due Process Clause, we will consider the current validity of the factual grounds upon which Wolf was based.

The Court in Wolf first stated that "[t]he contrariety of views of the States" on the adoption of the exclusionary rule of Weeks was "particularly impressive" (at p. 29); and, in this connection, that it could not "brush aside the experience of States which deem the incidence of such conduct by the police too slight to call for a deterrent remedy . . . by overriding the [States'] relevant rules of evidence." At pp. 31–32. While in 1949, prior to the Wolf case, almost two-thirds of the States were opposed to the use of the exclusionary rule, now, despite the Wolf case, more than half of those since passing upon it, by their own legislative or judicial decision, have wholly or partly adopted or adhered to the Weeks rule. See Elkins v. United States, 364 U.S. 206, Appendix, pp. 224–232 (1960). Significantly, among those now following the rule is California, which, according to its highest court, was "compelled to reach that conclusion because other remedies have completely failed to secure compliance with the constitutional provisions . . . ." People v. Cahan, 44 Cal. 2d 434, 445, 282 P. 2d 905, 911 (1955). In connection with this California case, we note that the second basis elaborated in Wolf in support of its failure to enforce the exclusionary doctrine against the States was that "other means of protection" have been afforded "the right to privacy." 338 U.S., at 30. The experience of California that such other remedies have been worthless and futile is buttressed by the experience of other States. The obvious futility of relegating the Fourth Amendment to the protection of other remedies has, moreover, been recognized by this Court since Wolf. See Irvine v. California, 347 U.S. 128, 137 (1954).

Likewise, time has set its face against what Wolf called the "weighty testimony" of People v. Defore, 242 N.Y. 13, 150 N.E. 585 (1926). There JUSTICE (then Judge) CARDOZO, rejecting adoption of the Weeks exclusionary rule in New York, had said that "[t]he Federal rule as it stands is either too strict or too lax." 242 N.Y., at 22, 150 N.E., at 588. However, the force of that reasoning has been largely vitiated by later decisions of this Court. These include the recent discarding of the "silver platter" doctrine which allowed federal judicial use of evidence seized in violation of the Constitution by state agents, Elkins v. United States, supra; the relaxation of the formerly strict requirements as to standing to challenge the use of evidence thus seized, so that now the procedure of exclusion, "ultimately referable to constitutional safeguards," is available to anyone even "legitimately on [the] premises" unlawfully searched, Jones v. United States, 362 U.S. 257, 266–267 (1960); and, finally, the formulation of a method to prevent state use of evidence unconstitutionally seized by federal agents, Rea v. United States, 350 U.S. 214 (1956). Because there can be no fixed formula, we are admittedly met with "recurring questions of the reasonableness of searches," but less is not to be expected when dealing with a Constitution, and, at any rate, "[r]easonableness is in the first instance for the [trial court]... to determine." United States v. Rabinowitz, 339 U.S. 56, 63 (1950).

It, therefore, plainly appears that the factual considerations supporting the failure of the Wolf Court to include the Weeks exclusionary rule when it recognized the enforceability of the right to privacy against the States in 1949, while not basically relevant to the constitutional consideration, could not, in any analysis, now be deemed controlling.

III

Some five years after Wolf, in answer to a plea made here Term after Term that we overturn its doctrine on applicability of the Weeks exclusionary rule, this Court indicated that such should not be done until the States had "adequate opportunity to adopt or reject the [Weeks] rule." Irvine v. California, supra, at 134. There again it was said:

> "Never until June of 1949 did this Court hold the basic search-and-seizure prohibition in any way applicable to the states under the Fourteenth Amendment." Ibid.

And only last Term, after again carefully re-examining the Wolf doctrine in Elkins v. United States, supra, the Court pointed out that "the controlling principles" as to search and seizure and the problem of admissibility "seemed clear" (at p. 212) until the announcement in Wolf "that the Due Process Clause of the Fourteenth Amendment does not itself require state courts to adopt the exclusionary rule" of the Weeks case. At p. 213. At the same time, the Court pointed out, "the underlying constitutional doctrine which Wolf established... that the Federal Constitution... prohibits unreasonable searches and seizures by state officers" had undermined the "foundation upon which the admissibility of state-seized evidence in a federal trial originally rested. . . ." Ibid. The Court concluded that it was therefore obliged to hold, although it chose the narrower ground on which to do so, that all evidence obtained by an unconstitutional search and seizure was inadmissible in a federal court regardless of its source. Today we once again examine Wolf's constitutional documentation of the right to privacy free from unreasonable state intrusion, and, after its dozen years on our books, are led by it to close the only courtroom door remaining open to evidence secured by official lawlessness in flagrant abuse of that basic right, reserved to all persons as a specific guarantee against that very same unlawful conduct. We hold that all evidence obtained by searches and seizures in violation of the Constitution is, by that same authority, inadmissible in a state court.

IV

Since the Fourth Amendment's right of privacy has been declared enforceable against the States through the Due Process Clause of the Fourteenth, it is enforceable against them by the same sanction of exclusion as is used against the Federal Government. Were it otherwise, then just as without the Weeks rule the assurance against unreasonable federal searches and seizures would be "a form of words," valueless and undeserving of mention in a perpetual charter of inestimable human liberties, so too, without that rule the freedom from state invasions of privacy would be so ephemeral and so neatly severed from its conceptual nexus with the freedom from all brutish means of coercing evidence as not to merit this Court's high regard as a freedom "implicit in the concept of ordered liberty." At the time that the Court held in Wolf that the Amendment was applicable to the States through the Due Process Clause, the cases of this Court, as we have seen, had steadfastly held that as to federal officers the Fourth Amendment included the exclusion of the evidence seized in violation of its provisions. Even Wolf "stoutly adhered" to that proposition. The right to privacy, when conceded operatively enforceable against the States, was not susceptible of destruction by avulsion of the sanction upon which its protection and enjoyment had always been deemed dependent under the Boyd, Weeks and Silverthorne cases. Therefore, in extending the substantive protections of due process to all constitutionally unreasonable searches—state or federal—it was logically and constitutionally necessary that the exclusion doctrine—an essential part of the right to privacy—be also insisted upon as an essential ingredient of the right newly recognized by the Wolf case. In short, the admission of the new constitutional right by Wolf could not consistently tolerate denial of its most important constitutional privilege, namely, the exclusion of the evidence which an accused had been forced to give by reason of the unlawful seizure. To hold otherwise is to grant the right but in reality to withhold its privilege and enjoyment. Only last year the Court itself recognized that the purpose of the exclusionary rule "is to deter—to compel respect for the constitutional guaranty in the only effectively available way—by removing the incentive to disregard it." Elkins v. United States, supra, at 217.

Indeed, we are aware of no restraint, similar to that rejected today, conditioning the enforcement of any other basic constitutional right. The right to privacy, no less important than any other right carefully and particularly reserved to the people, would stand in marked contrast to all other rights declared as "basic to a free society." Wolf v. Colorado, supra, at 27. This Court has not hesitated to enforce as strictly against the States as it does against the Federal Government the rights of free speech and of a free press, the rights to notice and to a fair, public trial, including, as it does, the right not to be convicted by use of a coerced confession, however logically relevant it be, and without regard to its reliability. Rogers v. Richmond, 365 U.S. 534 (1961). And nothing could be more certain than that when a coerced confession is involved, "the relevant rules of evidence" are overridden without regard to "the incidence of such conduct by the police," slight or frequent. Why should not the same rule apply to what is tantamount to coerced testimony by way of unconstitutional seizure of goods, papers, effects, documents, etc.? We find that as to the Federal Government, the Fourth and Fifth Amendments and, as to the States, the freedom from unconscionable invasions of privacy and the freedom from convictions based upon coerced confessions do enjoy an "intimate relation" in their perpetuation of "principles of humanity and civil liberty [secured]...only after years of struggle." Bram v. United States, 168 U.S. 532, 543–544 (1897). They express "supplementing phases of the same constitutional purpose—to maintain inviolate large areas of personal privacy." Feldman v. United States, 322 U.S. 487, 489–490 (1944). The philosophy of each Amendment and of each freedom is complementary to, although not dependent upon, that of the other in its sphere of influence—the very least that together they assure in either sphere is that no man is to be convicted on unconstitutional evidence. Cf. Rochin v. California, 342 U.S. 165, 173 (1952).

V

Moreover, our holding that the exclusionary rule is an essential part of both the Fourth and Fourteenth Amendments is not only the logical dictate of prior cases, but it also makes very good sense. There is no war between the Constitution and common sense. Presently, a federal prosecutor may make no use of evidence illegally seized, but a State's attorney across the street may, although he supposedly is operating under the enforceable prohibitions of the same Amendment. Thus the State, by admitting evidence unlawfully seized, serves to encourage disobedience to the Federal Constitution which it is bound to uphold. Moreover, as was said in Elkins, "[t]he very essence of a healthy federalism depends upon the avoidance of needless conflict between state and federal courts." 364 U.S., at 221. Such a conflict, hereafter needless, arose this very Term, in Wilson v. Schnettler, 365 U.S. 381 (1961), in which, and in spite of the promise made by Rea, we gave full recognition to our practice in this regard by refusing to restrain a federal officer from testifying in a state court as to evidence unconstitutionally seized by him in the performance of his duties. Yet the double standard recognized until today hardly put such a thesis into practice. In nonexclusionary States, federal officers, being human, were by it invited to and did, as our cases indicate, step across the street to the State's attorney with their unconstitutionally seized evidence. Prosecution on the basis of that evidence was then had in a state court in utter disregard of the enforceable Fourth Amendment. If the fruits of an unconstitutional search had been inadmissible in both state and federal courts, this inducement to evasion would have been sooner eliminated. There would be no need to reconcile such cases as Rea and Schnettler, each pointing up the hazardous uncertainties of our heretofore ambivalent approach.

Federal-state cooperation in the solution of crime under constitutional standards will be promoted, if only by recognition of their now mutual obligation to respect the same fundamental criteria in their approaches. "However much in a particular case insistence upon such rules may appear as a technicality that inures to the benefit of a guilty person, the history of the criminal law proves that tolerance of shortcut methods in law enforcement impairs its enduring effectiveness." Miller v. United States, 357 U.S. 301, 313 (1958). Denying shortcuts to only one of two cooperating law enforcement agencies tends naturally to breed legitimate suspicion of "working arrangements" whose results are equally tainted. Byars v. United States, 273 U.S. 28 (1927); Lustig v. United States, 338 U.S. 74 (1949).

There are those who say, as did JUSTICE (then Judge) CARDOZO, that under our constitutional exclusionary doctrine "[t]he criminal is to go free because the constable has blundered." People v. Defore, 242 N.Y., at 21, 150 N.E., at 587. In some cases this will undoubtedly be the result. But, as was said in Elkins, "there is another consideration—the imperative of judicial integrity." 364 U.S., at 222. The criminal goes free, if he must, but it is the law that sets him free. Nothing can destroy a government more quickly than its failure to observe its own laws, or worse, its disregard of the charter of its own existence. As MR. JUSTICE BRANDEIS, dissenting, said in Olmstead v. United States, 277 U.S. 438, 485 (1928): "Our Government is the potent, the omnipresent teacher. For good or for ill, it teaches the whole people by its example.... If the Government becomes a lawbreaker, it breeds contempt for law; it invites every man to become a law unto himself; it invites anarchy." Nor can it lightly be assumed that, as a practical matter, adoption of the exclusionary rule fetters law enforcement. Only last year this Court expressly considered that contention and found that "pragmatic evidence of a sort" to the contrary was not wanting. Elkins v. United States, supra, at 218. The Court noted that

> "The federal courts themselves have operated under the exclusionary rule of Weeks for almost half a century; yet it has not been suggested either that the Federal Bureau of Investigation has thereby been rendered ineffective, or that the administration of criminal justice in the federal courts has thereby been disrupted. Moreover, the experience of the states is impressive.... The movement towards the rule of exclusion has been halting but seemingly inexorable." Id., at 218–219.

The ignoble shortcut to conviction left open to the State tends to destroy the entire system of constitutional restraints on which the liberties of the people rest. Having once recognized that the right to privacy embodied in the Fourth Amendment is enforceable against the States, and that the right to be secure against rude invasions of privacy by state officers is, therefore, constitutional in origin, we can no longer permit that right to remain an empty promise. Because it is enforceable in the same manner and to like effect as other basic rights secured by the Due Process Clause, we can no longer permit it to be revocable at the whim of any police officer who, in the name of law enforcement itself, chooses to suspend its enjoyment. Our decision, founded on reason and truth, gives to the individual no more than that which the Constitution guarantees him, to the police officer no less than that to which honest law enforcement is entitled, and, to the courts, that judicial integrity so necessary in the true administration of justice.

The judgment of the Supreme Court of Ohio is reversed and the cause remanded for further proceedings not inconsistent with this opinion.

Reversed and remanded.

Katz *v.* United States

389 U.S. 347, 88 S.Ct. 507, 19 L.Ed. 2d. 576 (1967)

CERTIORARI TO THE UNITED STATES COURT OF APPEALS FOR THE NINTH CIRCUIT.

Argued October 17, 1967.—Decided December 18, 1967.

. . .

MR. JUSTICE STEWART delivered the opinion of the Court.

The petitioner was convicted in the District Court for the Southern District of California under an eight-count indictment charging him with transmitting wagering information by telephone from Los Angeles to Miami and Boston, in violation of a federal statute. At trial the Government was permitted, over the petitioner's objection, to introduce evidence of the petitioner's end of telephone conversations, overheard by FBI agents who had attached an electronic listening and recording device to the outside of the public telephone booth from which he had placed his calls. In affirming his conviction, the Court of Appeals rejected the contention that the recordings had been obtained in violation of the Fourth Amendment, because "[t]here was no physical entrance into the area occupied by [the petitioner]." We granted certiorari in order to consider the constitutional questions thus presented.

The petitioner has phrased those questions as follows:

> "A. Whether a public telephone booth is a constitutionally protected area so that evidence obtained by attaching an electronic listening recording device to the top of such a booth is obtained in violation of the right to privacy of the user of the booth.
>
> "B. Whether physical penetration of a constitutionally protected area is necessary before a search and seizure can be said to be violative of the Fourth Amendment to the United States Constitution."

We decline to adopt this formulation of the issues. In the first place, the correct solution of Fourth Amendment problems is not necessarily promoted by incantation of the phrase "constitutionally protected area." Secondly, the Fourth Amendment cannot be translated into a general constitutional "right to privacy." That Amendment protects individual privacy against certain kinds of governmental intrusion, but its protections go further, and often have nothing to do with privacy at all. Other provisions of the Constitution protect personal privacy from other forms of governmental invasion. But the protection of a person's *general* right to privacy—his right to be let alone by other people—is, like the protection of his property and of his very life, left largely to the law of the individual States.

Because of the misleading way the issues have been formulated, the parties have attached great significance to the characterization of the telephone booth from which the petitioner placed his calls. The petitioner has strenuously argued that the booth was a "constitutionally protected area." The Government has maintained with equal vigor that it was not. But this effort to decide whether or not a given "area," viewed in the abstract, is "constitutionally protected" deflects attention from the problem presented by this case. For the Fourth Amendment protects people, not places. What a person knowingly exposes to the public, even in his own home or office, is not a subject of Fourth Amendment protection. See Lewis v. United States, 385 U.S. 206, 210; United States v. Lee, 274 U.S. 559, 563. But what he seeks to preserve as private, even in an area accessible to the public, may be constitutionally protected. See Rios v. United States, 364 U.S. 253; Ex parte Jackson, 96 U.S. 727, 733.

The Government stresses the fact that the telephone booth from which the petitioner made his calls was constructed partly of glass, so that he was as visible after he entered it as he would have been if he had remained outside. But what he sought to exclude when he entered the booth was not the intruding eye—it was the uninvited ear. He did not shed his right to do so simply because he made his calls from a place where he might be seen. No less than an individual in a business office, in a friend's apartment, or in a taxicab, a person in a telephone booth may rely upon the protection of the Fourth Amendment. One who occupies it, shuts the door behind him, and pays the toll that permits him to place a call is surely entitled to assume that the words he utters into the mouthpiece will not be broadcast to the world. To read the Constitution more narrowly is to ignore the vital role that the public telephone has come to play in private communication.

The Government contends, however, that the activities of its agents in this case should not be tested by Fourth Amendment requirements, for the surveillance technique they employed involved no physical penetration of the telephone booth from which the petitioner placed his calls. It is true that the absence of such penetration was at one time thought to foreclose further Fourth Amendment inquiry, Olmstead v. United States, 277 U.S. 438, 457, 464, 466; Goldman v. United States, 316 U.S. 129, 134–136, for that Amendment was thought to limit only searches and seizures of tangible property. But "[t]he premise that property interests control the right of the Government to search and seize has been discredited." Warden v. Hayden, 387 U.S. 294, 304. Thus, although a closely divided Court supposed in

Olmstead that surveillance without any trespass and without the seizure of any material object fell outside the ambit of the Constitution, we have since departed from the narrow view on which that decision rested. Indeed, we have expressly held that the Fourth Amendment governs not only the seizure of tangible items, but extends as well to the recording of oral statements, overheard without any "technical trespass under... local property law." Silverman v. United States, 365 U.S. 505, 511. Once this much is acknowledged, and once it is recognized that the Fourth Amendment protects people—and not simply "areas"—against unreasonable searches and seizures, it becomes clear that the reach of that Amendment cannot turn upon the presence or absence of a physical intrusion into any given enclosure.

We conclude that the underpinnings of Olmstead and Goldman have been so eroded by our subsequent decisions that the "trespass" doctrine there enunciated can no longer be regarded as controlling. The Government's activities in electronically listening to and recording the petitioner's words violated the privacy upon which he justifiably relied while using the telephone booth and thus constituted a "search and seizure" within the meaning of the Fourth Amendment. The fact that the electronic device employed to achieve that end did not happen to penetrate the wall of the booth can have no constitutional significance.

The question remaining for decision, then, is whether the search and seizure conducted in this case complied with constitutional standards. In that regard, the Government's position is that its agents acted in an entirely defensible manner: They did not begin their electronic surveillance until investigation of the petitioner's activities had established a strong probability that he was using the telephone in question to transmit gambling information to persons in other States, in violation of federal law. Moreover, the surveillance was limited, both in scope and in duration, to the specific purpose of establishing the contents of the petitioner's unlawful telephonic communications. The agents confined their surveillance to the brief periods during which he used the telephone booth, and they took great care to overhear only the conversations of the petitioner himself.

Accepting this account of the Government's actions as accurate, it is clear that this surveillance was so narrowly circumscribed that a duly authorized magistrate, properly notified of the need for such investigation, specifically informed of the basis on which it was to proceed, and clearly apprised of the precise intrusion it would entail, could constitutionally have authorized, with appropriate safeguards, the very limited search and seizure that the Government asserts in fact took place. Only last Term we sustained the validity of such an authorization, holding that, under sufficiently "precise and discriminate circumstances," a federal court may empower government agents to employ a concealed electronic device "for the narrow and particularized purpose of ascertaining the truth of the... allegations" of a "detailed factual affidavit alleging the commission of a specific criminal offense." Osborn v. United States, 385 U.S. 323, 329–330. Discussing that holding, the Court in Berger v. New York, 388 U.S. 41, said that "the order authorizing the use of the electronic device" in Osborn "afforded similar protections to those... of conventional warrants authorizing the seizure of tangible evidence." Through those protections, "no greater invasion of privacy was permitted than was necessary under the circumstances." Id., at 57. Here, too, a similar judicial order could have accommodated "the legitimate needs of law enforcement" by authorizing the carefully limited use of electronic surveillance.

The Government urges that, because its agents relied upon the decisions in Olmstead and Goldman, and because they did no more here than they might properly have done with prior judicial sanction, we should retroactively validate their conduct. That we cannot do. It is apparent that the agents in this case acted with restraint. Yet the inescapable fact is that this restraint was imposed by the agents themselves, not by a judicial officer. They were not required, before commencing the search, to present their estimate of probable cause for detached scrutiny by a neutral magistrate. They were not compelled, during the conduct of the search itself, to observe precise limits established in advance by a specific court order. Nor were they directed, after the search had been completed, to notify the authorizing magistrate in detail of all that had been seized. In the absence of such safeguards, this Court has never sustained a search upon the sole ground that officers reasonably expected to find evidence of a particular crime and voluntarily confined their activities to the least intrusive means consistent with that end. Searches conducted without warrants have been held unlawful "notwithstanding facts unquestionably showing probable cause," Agnello v. United States, 269 U.S. 20, 33, for the Constitution requires "that the deliberate, impartial judgment of a judicial officer . . . be interposed between the citizen and the police . . . ." Wong Sun v. United States, 371 U.S. 471, 481–482. "Over and again this Court has emphasized that the mandate of the [Fourth] Amendment requires adherence to judicial processes," United States v. Jeffers, 342 U.S. 48, 51, and that searches conducted outside the judicial process, without prior approval by judge or magistrate, are per se unreasonable under the Fourth Amendment—subject only to a few specifically established and well-delineated exceptions.

It is difficult to imagine how any of those exceptions could ever apply to the sort of search and seizure involved in this case. Even electronic surveillance substantially contemporaneous with an individual's arrest could hardly be deemed an "incident" of that arrest. Nor could the use of electronic surveillance without prior authorization be justified on grounds of "hot pursuit." And, of course, the very nature of electronic surveillance precludes its use pursuant to the suspect's consent.

The Government does not question these basic principles. Rather, it urges the creation of a new exception to cover this case. It argues that surveillance of a telephone booth should be exempted from the usual requirement of advance authorization by a magistrate upon a showing of probable cause. We cannot agree. Omission of such authorization

> "bypasses the safeguards provided by an objective predetermination of probable cause, and substitutes instead the far less reliable procedure of an after-the-event justification for the . . . search, too likely to be subtly influenced by the familiar shortcomings of hindsight judgment." Beck v. Ohio, 379 U.S. 89, 96.

And bypassing a neutral predetermination of the *scope* of a search leaves individuals secure from Fourth Amendment violations "only in the discretion of the police." Id., at 97.

These considerations do not vanish when the search in question is transferred from the setting of a home, an office, or a hotel room to that of a telephone booth. Wherever a man may be, he is entitled to know that he will remain free from unreasonable searches and seizures. The government agents here ignored "the procedure of antecedent justification... that is central to the Fourth Amendment," a procedure that we hold to be a constitutional precondition of the kind of electronic surveillance involved in this case. Because the surveillance here failed to meet that condition, and because it led to the petitioner's conviction, the judgment must be reversed.

It is so ordered.

Chimel *v.* California

395 U.S. 752, 89 S.Ct. 2034, 23 L.Ed. 2d. 685 (1969)

CERTIORARI TO THE SUPREME COURT OF CALIFORNIA

Argued March 27, 1969.—Decided June 23, 1969.

. . .

MR. JUSTICE STEWART delivered the opinion of the Court.

This case raises basic questions concerning the permissible scope under the Fourth Amendment of a search incident to a lawful arrest.

The relevant facts are essentially undisputed. Late in the afternoon of September 13, 1965, three police officers arrived at the Santa Ana, California, home of the petitioner with a warrant authorizing his arrest for the burglary of a coin shop. The officers knocked on the door, identified themselves to the petitioner's wife, and asked if they might come inside. She ushered them into the house, where they waited 10 or 15 minutes until the petitioner returned home from work. When the petitioner entered the house, one of the officers handed him the arrest warrant and asked for permission to "look around." The petitioner objected, but was advised that "on the basis of the lawful arrest," the officers would nonetheless conduct a search. No search warrant had been issued.

Accompanied by the petitioner's wife, the officers then looked through the entire three-bedroom house, including the attic, the garage, and a small workshop. In some rooms the search was relatively cursory. In the master bedroom and sewing room, however, the officers directed the petitioner's wife to open drawers and "to physically move contents of the drawers from side to side so that [they] might view any items that would have come from [the] burglary." After completing the search, they seized numerous items—primarily coins, but also several medals, tokens, and a few other objects. The entire search took between 45 minutes and an hour.

At the petitioner's subsequent state trial on two charges of burglary, the items taken from his house were admitted into evidence against him, over his objection that they had been unconstitutionally seized. He was convicted, and the judgments of conviction were affirmed by both the California Court of Appeal, 61 Cal. Rptr. 714, and the California Supreme Court, 68 Cal. 2d 436, 439 P. 2d 333. Both courts accepted the petitioner's contention that the arrest warrant was invalid because the supporting affidavit was set out in conclusory terms, but held that since the arresting officers had procured the warrant "in good faith," and since in any event they had had sufficient information to constitute probable cause for the petitioner's arrest, that arrest had been lawful. From this conclusion the appellate courts went on to hold that the search of the petitioner's home had been justified, despite the absence of a search warrant, on the ground that it had been incident to a valid arrest. We granted certiorari in order to consider the petitioner's substantial constitutional claims. 393 U.S. 958.

Without deciding the question, we proceed on the hypothesis that the California courts were correct in holding that the arrest of the petitioner was valid under the Constitution. This brings us directly to the question whether the warrantless search of the petitioner's entire house can be constitutionally justified as incident to that arrest. The decisions of this Court bearing upon that question have been far from consistent, as even the most cursory review makes evident.

Approval of a warrantless search incident to a lawful arrest seems first to have been articulated by the Court in 1914 as dictum in Weeks v. United States, 232 U.S. 383, in which the Court stated:

> "What then is the present case? Before answering that inquiry specifically, it may be well by a process of exclusion to state what it is not. It is not an assertion of the right on the part of the Government, always recognized under English and American law, to search the person of the accused when legally arrested to discover and seize the fruits or evidences of crime." Id., at 392.

That statement made no reference to any right to search the *place* where an arrest occurs, but was limited to a right to search the "person." Eleven years later the case of Carroll v. United States, 267 U.S. 132, brought the following embellishment of the Weeks statement:

> "When a man is legally arrested for an offense, whatever is found upon his person *or in his control* which it is unlawful for him to have and which may be used to prove the offense may be seized and held as evidence in the prosecution." Id., at 158. (Emphasis added.)

Still, that assertion too was far from a claim that the "place" where one is arrested may be searched so long as the arrest is valid. Without explanation, however, the principle emerged in expanded form a few months later in Agnello v. United States, 269 U.S. 20—although still by way of dictum:

> "The right without a search warrant contemporaneously to search persons lawfully arrested while committing crime and to search the place where the arrest is made in order to find and seize things connected with the crime as its fruits or as the means by which it was committed, as well as weapons and other things to effect an

> escape from custody, is not to be doubted. See Carroll v. United States, 267 U.S. 132, 158; Weeks v. United States, 232 U.S. 383, 392." 269 U.S., at 30.

And in Marron v. United States, 275 U.S. 192, two years later, the dictum of Agnello appeared to be the foundation of the Court's decision. In that case federal agents had secured a search warrant authorizing the seizure of liquor and certain articles used in its manufacture. When they arrived at the premises to be searched, they saw "that the place was used for retailing and drinking intoxicating liquors." Id., at 194. They proceeded to arrest the person in charge and to execute the warrant. In searching a closet for the items listed in the warrant they came across an incriminating ledger, concededly not covered by the warrant, which they also seized. The Court upheld the seizure of the ledger by holding that since the agents had made a lawful arrest, "[t]hey had a right without a warrant contemporaneously to search the place in order to find and seize the things used to carry on the criminal enterprise." Id., at 199.

That the Marron opinion did not mean all that it seemed to say became evident, however, a few years later in Go-Bart Importing Co. v. United States, 282 U.S. 344, and United States v. Lefkowitz, 285 U.S. 452. In each of those cases the opinion of the Court was written by MR. JUSTICE BUTLER, the author of the opinion in Marron. In Go-Bart, agents had searched the office of persons whom they had lawfully arrested, and had taken several papers from a desk, a safe, and other parts of the office. The Court noted that no crime had been committed in the agents' presence, and that although the agent in charge "had an abundance of information and time to swear out a valid [search] warrant, he failed to do so." 282 U.S., at 358. In holding the search and seizure unlawful, the Court stated:

> "Plainly the case before us is essentially different from Marron v. United States, 275 U.S. 192. There officers executing a valid search warrant for intoxicating liquors found and arrested one Birdsall who in pursuance of a conspiracy was actually engaged in running a saloon. As an incident to the arrest they seized a ledger in a closet where the liquor or some of it was kept and some bills beside the cash register. These things were visible and accessible and in the offender's immediate custody. There was no threat of force or general search or rummaging of the place." 282 U.S., at 358.

This limited characterization of Marron was reiterated in Lefkowitz, a case in which the Court held unlawful a search of desk drawers and a cabinet despite the fact that the search had accompanied a lawful arrest. 285 U.S., at 465.

The limiting views expressed in Go-Bart and Lefkowitz were thrown to the winds, however, in Harris v. United States, 331 U.S. 145, decided in 1947. In that case, officers had obtained a warrant for Harris' arrest on the basis of his alleged involvement with the cashing and interstate transportation of a forged check. He was arrested in the living room of his four-room apartment, and in an attempt to recover two canceled checks thought to have been used in effecting the forgery, the officers undertook a thorough search of the entire apartment. Inside a desk drawer they found a sealed envelope marked "George Harris, personal papers." The envelope, which was then torn open, was found to contain altered Selective Service documents, and those documents were used to secure Harris' conviction for violating the Selective Training and Service Act of 1940. The Court rejected Harris' Fourth Amendment claim, sustaining the search as "incident to arrest." Id., at 151.

Only a year after Harris, however, the pendulum swung again. In Trupiano v. United States, 334 U.S. 699, agents raided the site of an illicit distillery, saw one of several conspirators operating the still, and arrested him, contemporaneously "seiz[ing] the illicit distillery." Id., at 702. The Court held that the arrest and others made subsequently had been valid, but that the unexplained failure of the agents to procure a search warrant—in spite of the fact that they had had more than enough time before the raid to do so—rendered the search unlawful. The opinion stated:

> "It is a cardinal rule that, in seizing goods and articles, law enforcement agents must secure and use search warrants wherever reasonably practicable.... This rule rests upon the desirability of having magistrates rather than police officers determine when searches and seizures are permissible and what limitations should be placed upon such activities.... To provide the necessary security against unreasonable intrusions upon the private lives of individuals, the framers of the Fourth Amendment required adherence to judicial processes wherever possible. And subsequent history has confirmed the wisdom of that requirement.
>
> . . .
>
> "A search or seizure without a warrant as an incident to a lawful arrest has always been considered to be a strictly limited right. It grows out of the inherent necessities of the situation at the time of the arrest. But there must be something more in the way of necessity than merely a lawful arrest." Id., at 705, 708.

In 1950, two years after Trupiano, came United States v. Rabinowitz, 339 U.S. 56, the decision upon which California primarily relies in the case now before us. In Rabinowitz, federal authorities had been informed that the defendant was dealing in stamps bearing forged overprints. On the basis of that information they secured a warrant for his arrest, which they executed at his one-room business office. At the time of the arrest, the officers "searched the desk, safe, and file cabinets in the office for about an hour and a half," id., at 59, and seized 573 stamps with forged overprints. The stamps were admitted into evidence at the defendant's trial, and this Court affirmed his conviction, rejecting the contention that the warrantless search had been unlawful. The Court held that the search in its entirety fell within the principle giving law enforcement authorities "[t]he right 'to search the place where the arrest is made in order to find and seize things connected with the crime....'" Id., at 61. Harris was regarded as "ample authority" for that conclusion. Id., at 63. The opinion rejected the rule of Trupiano that "in seizing goods and articles, law enforcement agents must secure and use search warrants wherever reasonably practicable." The test, said the Court, "is not whether it is reasonable to procure a search warrant, but whether the search was reasonable." Id., at 66.

Rabinowitz has come to stand for the proposition, inter alia, that a warrantless search "incident to a lawful arrest" may generally extend to the area that is considered to be in the "possession" or under the "control" of the person arrested. And it was on the basis of that proposition that the California courts upheld the search of the petitioner's entire house in this case. That doctrine, however, at least in the broad sense in which it was applied by the California courts in this case, can withstand neither historical nor rational analysis.

Even limited to its own facts, the Rabinowitz decision was, as we have seen, hardly founded on an unimpeachable line of authority. As MR. JUSTICE FRANKFURTER commented in dissent in that case, the "hint" contained in Weeks was, without persuasive justification, "loosely turned into dictum and finally elevated to a decision." 339 U.S., at 75. And the approach taken in cases such as Go-Bart, Lefkowitz, and Trupiano was essentially disregarded by the Rabinowitz Court.

Nor is the rationale by which the State seeks here to sustain the search of the petitioner's house supported by a reasoned view of the background and purpose of the Fourth Amendment. MR. JUSTICE FRANKFURTER wisely pointed out in his Rabinowitz dissent that the Amendment's proscription of "unreasonable searches and seizures" must be read in light of "the history that gave rise to the words"—a history of "abuses so deeply felt by the Colonies as to be one of the potent causes of the Revolution . . . ." 339 U.S., at 69. The Amendment was in large part a reaction to the general warrants and warrantless searches that had so alienated the colonists and had helped speed the movement for independence. In the scheme of the Amendment, therefore, the requirement that "no Warrants shall issue, but upon probable cause," plays a crucial part. As the Court put it in McDonald v. United States, 335 U.S. 451:

> "We are not dealing with formalities. The presence of a search warrant serves a high function. Absent some grave emergency, the Fourth Amendment has interposed a magistrate between the citizen and the police. This was done not to shield criminals nor to make the home a safe haven for illegal activities. It was done so that an objective mind might weigh the need to invade that privacy in order to enforce the law. The right of privacy was deemed too precious to entrust to the discretion of those whose job is the detection of crime and the arrest of criminals. . . . And so the Constitution requires a magistrate to pass on the desires of the police before they violate the privacy of the home. We cannot be true to that constitutional requirement and excuse the absence of a search warrant without a showing by those who seek exemption from the constitutional mandate that the exigencies of the situation made that course imperative." Id., at 455–456.

Even in the Agnello case the Court relied upon the rule that "[b]elief, however well founded, that an article sought is concealed in a dwelling house furnishes no justification for a search of that place without a warrant. And such searches are held unlawful notwithstanding facts unquestionably showing probable cause." 269 U.S., at 33. Clearly, the general requirement that a search warrant be obtained is not lightly to be dispensed with, and "the burden is on those seeking [an] exemption [from the requirement] to show the need for it . . . ." United States v. Jeffers, 342 U.S. 48, 51.

Only last Term in Terry v. Ohio, 392 U.S. 1, we emphasized that "the police must, whenever practicable, obtain advance judicial approval of searches and seizures through the warrant procedure," id., at 20, and that "[t]he scope of [a] search must be 'strictly tied to and justified by' the circumstances which rendered its initiation permissible." Id., at 19. The search undertaken by the officer in that "stop and frisk" case was sustained under that test, because it was no more than a "protective ... search for weapons." Id., at 29. But in a companion case, Sibron v. New York, 392 U.S. 40, we applied the same standard to another set of facts and reached a contrary result, holding that a policeman's action in thrusting his hand into a suspect's pocket had been neither motivated by nor limited to the objective of protection. Rather, the search had been made in order to find narcotics, which were in fact found.

A similar analysis underlies the "search incident to arrest" principle, and marks its proper extent. When an arrest is made, it is reasonable for the arresting officer to search the person arrested in order to remove any weapons that the latter might seek to use in order to resist arrest or effect his escape. Otherwise, the officer's safety might well be endangered, and the arrest itself frustrated. In addition, it is entirely reasonable for the arresting officer to search for and seize any evidence on the arrestee's person in order to prevent its concealment or destruction. And the area into which an arrestee might reach in order to grab a weapon or evidentiary items must, of course, be governed by a like rule. A gun on a table or in a drawer in front of one who is arrested can be as dangerous to the arresting officer as one concealed in the clothing of the person arrested. There is ample justification, therefore, for a search of the arrestee's person and the area "within his immediate control"—construing that phrase to mean the area from within which he might gain possession of a weapon or destructible evidence.

There is no comparable justification, however, for routinely searching any room other than that in which an arrest occurs—or, for that matter, for searching through all the desk drawers or other closed or concealed areas in that room itself. Such searches, in the absence of well-recognized exceptions, may be made only under the authority of a search warrant. The "adherence to judicial processes" mandated by the Fourth Amendment requires no less.

This is the principle that underlay our decision in Preston v. United States, 376 U.S. 364. In that case three men had been arrested in a parked car, which had later been towed to a garage and searched by police. We held the search to have been unlawful under the Fourth Amendment, despite the contention that it had been incidental to a valid arrest. Our reasoning was straightforward:

> "The rule allowing contemporaneous searches is justified, for example, by the need to seize weapons and other things which might be used to assault an officer or effect an escape, as well as by the need to prevent the destruction of evidence of the crime—things which might easily happen where the weapon or evidence is on the accused's person or under his immediate control. But these justifications are absent where a search is remote in time or place from the arrest." Id., at 367.

The same basic principle was reflected in our opinion last Term in Sibron. That opinion dealt with Peters v. New York, No. 74, as well as with Sibron's case, and Peters involved a search that we upheld as incident to a proper arrest. We sustained the search, however, only because its scope had been "reasonably limited" by the "need to seize weapons" and "to prevent the destruction of evidence," to which Preston had referred. We emphasized that the arresting officer "did not engage in an unrestrained and thoroughgoing examination of Peters and his personal effects. He seized him to cut short his flight, and he searched him primarily for weapons." 392 U.S., at 67.

It is argued in the present case that it is "reasonable" to search a man's house when he is arrested in it. But that argument is founded on little more than a subjective view regarding the acceptability of certain sorts of police conduct, and not on considerations relevant to Fourth Amendment interests. Under such an unconfined analysis, Fourth Amendment protection in this area would approach the evaporation point. It is not easy to explain why, for instance, it is less subjectively "reasonable" to search a man's house when he is arrested on his front lawn—or just down the street—than it is when he happens to be in the house at the time of arrest. As MR. JUSTICE FRANKFURTER put it:

> "To say that the search must be reasonable is to require some criterion of reason. It is no guide at all either for a jury or for district judges or the police to say that an 'unreasonable search' is forbidden—that the search must be reasonable. What is the test of reason which makes a search reasonable? The test is the reason underlying and expressed by the Fourth Amendment: the history and the experience which it embodies and the safeguards afforded by it against the evils to which it was a response." United States v. Rabinowitz, 339 U.S., at 83 (dissenting opinion).

Thus, although "[t]he recurring questions of the reasonableness of searches" depend upon "the facts and circumstances—the total atmosphere of the case," id., at 63, 66 (opinion of the Court), those facts and circumstances must be viewed in the light of established Fourth Amendment principles.

It would be possible, of course, to draw a line between Rabinowitz and Harris on the one hand, and this case on the other. For Rabinowitz involved a single room, and Harris a four-room apartment, while in the case before us an entire house was searched. But such a distinction would be highly artificial. The rationale that allowed the searches and seizures in Rabinowitz and Harris would allow the searches and seizures in this case. No consideration relevant to the Fourth Amendment suggests any point of rational limitation, once the search is allowed to go beyond the area from which the person arrested might obtain weapons or evidentiary items. The only reasoned distinction is one between a search of the person arrested and the area within his reach on the one hand, and more extensive searches on the other.

The petitioner correctly points out that one result of decisions such as Rabinowitz and Harris is to give law enforcement officials the opportunity to engage in searches not justified by probable cause, by the simple expedient of arranging to arrest suspects at home rather than elsewhere. We do not suggest that the petitioner is necessarily correct in his assertion that such a strategy was utilized here, but the fact remains that had he been arrested earlier in the day, at his place of employment rather than at home, no search of his house could have been made without a search warrant. In any event, even apart from the possibility of such police tactics, the general point so forcefully made by Judge Learned Hand in United States v. Kirschenblatt, 16 F. 2d 202, remains:

> "After arresting a man in his house, to rummage at will among his papers in search of whatever will convict him, appears to us to be indistinguishable from what might be done under a general warrant; indeed, the warrant would give more protection, for presumably it must be issued by a magistrate. True, by hypothesis the power would not exist, if the supposed offender were not found on the premises; but it is small consolation to know that one's papers are safe only so long as one is not at home." Id., at 203.

Rabinowitz and Harris have been the subject of critical commentary for many years, and have been relied upon less and less in our own decisions. It is time, for the reasons we have stated, to hold that on their own facts, and insofar as the principles they stand for are inconsistent with those that we have endorsed today, they are no longer to be followed.

Application of sound Fourth Amendment principles to the facts of this case produces a clear result. The search here went far beyond the petitioner's person and the area from within which he might have obtained either a weapon or something that could have been used as evidence against him. There was no constitutional justification, in the absence of a search warrant, for extending the search beyond that area. The scope of the search was, therefore, "unreasonable" under the Fourth and Fourteenth Amendments, and the petitioner's conviction cannot stand.

Reversed.

George K. Wyman, Individually and as Commissioner of the State of New York, Department of Social Services, Appellant, *v.* Barbara James, etc.

400 U.S. 309, 91 S.Ct. 381, 21 L.Ed. 2d. 408 (1971)

Argued October 20, 1970.—Decided January 12, 1971.

. . .

Mr. Justice Blackmun delivered the opinion of the Court.

This appeal presents the issue whether a beneficiary of the program for Aid to Families with Dependent Children (AFDC) may refuse a home visit by the caseworker without risking the termination of benefits.

The New York State and City social services commissioners appeal from a judgment and decree of a divided three-judge District Court holding invalid and unconstitutional in application § 134 of the New York Social Services Law, § 175 of the New York Policies Governing the Administration of Public Assistance, and §§ 351.10 and 351.21 of Title 18 of the New York Code of Rules and Regulations, and granting injunctive relief. James v Goldberg, 303 F Supp 935 (SDNY 1969). This Court noted probable jurisdiction but, by a divided vote, denied a requested stay. 397 US 904, 25 L Ed 2d 85, 90 S Ct 921.

The District Court majority held that a mother receiving AFDC relief may refuse, without forfeiting her right to that relief, the periodic home visit which the cited New York statutes and regulations prescribe as a condition for the continuance of assistance under the program. The beneficiary's thesis, and that of the District Court majority is that home visitation is a search and, when not consented to or when not supported by a warrant based on probable cause, violates the beneficiary's Fourth and Fourteenth Amendment rights.

Judge McLean, in dissent, thought it unrealistic to regard the home visit as a search; felt that the requirement of a search warrant to issue only upon a showing of probable cause would make the AFDC program "in effect another criminal statute" and would "introduce a hostile arm's length element into the relationship" between worker and mother, "a relationship which can be effective only when it is based upon mutual confidence and trust"; and concluded that the majority's holding struck "a damaging blow" to an important social welfare program. 303 F Supp, at 946.

I

The case comes to us on the pleadings and supporting affidavits and without the benefit of testimony which an extended hearing would have provided. The pertinent facts, however, are not in dispute.

Plaintiff Barbara James is the mother of a son, Maurice, who was born in May 1967. They reside in New York City. Mrs. James first applied for AFDC assistance shortly before Maurice's birth. A caseworker made a visit to her apartment at that time without objection. The assistance was authorized.

Two years later, on May 8, 1969, a caseworker wrote Mrs. James that she would visit her home on May 14. Upon receipt of this advice, Mrs. James telephoned the worker that, although she was willing to supply information "reasonable and relevant" to her need for public assistance, any discussion was not to take place at her home. The worker told Mrs. James that she was required by law to visit in her home and that refusal to permit the visit would result in the termination of assistance. Permission was still denied.

On May 13 the City Department of Social Services sent Mrs. James a notice of intent to discontinue assistance because of the visitation refusal. The notice advised the beneficiary of her right to a hearing before a review officer. The hearing was requested and was held on May 27. Mrs. James appeared with an attorney at that hearing. They continued to refuse permission for a worker to visit the James home, but again expressed willingness to cooperate and to permit visits elsewhere. The review officer ruled that the refusal was a proper ground for the termination of assistance. His written decision stated:

> "The home visit which Mrs. James refuses to permit is for the purpose of determining if there are any changes in her situation that might affect her eligibility to continue to receive Public Assistance, or that might affect the amount of such assistance, and to see if there are any social services which the Department of Social Services can provide to the family."

A notice of termination issued on June 2.

Thereupon, without seeking a hearing at the state level, Mrs. James, individually and on behalf of Maurice, and purporting to act on behalf of all other persons similarly situated, instituted the present civil rights suit under 42 USC § 1983. She alleged the denial of rights guaranteed to her under the First, Third, Fourth, Fifth, Sixth, Ninth, Tenth, and Fourteenth Amendments, and under Subchapters IV and XVI of the Social Security Act and regulations issued thereunder. She further alleged that she and her son have no income, resources, or support other than the benefits received under the AFDC program. She asked for declaratory and injunctive relief. A temporary restraining order was issued on June 13, James v Goldberg, 302 F Supp 478 (SDNY 1969), and the three-judge District Court was convened.

II

The federal aspects of the AFDC program deserve mention. They are provided for in Subchapter IV, Part A, of the Social Security Act of 1935, 49 Stat 627, as amended, 42 USC §§ 601–610 (1964 ed. and Supp V). Section 401 of the Act, 42 USC § 601 (1964 ed., Supp V), specifies its purpose, namely, "encouraging the care of dependent children in their own homes or in the homes of relatives by enabling each State to furnish financial assistance and rehabilitation and other services . . . to needy dependent children and the parents or relatives with whom they are living to help maintain and strengthen family life . . . ." The same section authorizes the federal appropriation for payments to States that qualify. Section 402, 42 USC §602 (1964 ed., Supp V), provides that a state plan, among other things, must "provide for granting an opportunity for a fair hearing before the State agency to any individual whose claim for aid to families with dependent children is denied or is not acted upon with reasonable promptness"; must "provide that the State agency will make such reports . . . as the Secretary [of Health, Education, and Welfare] may from time to time require"; must "provide that the State agency shall, in determining need, take into consideration any other income and resources of any child or relative claiming aid"; and must "provide that where the State agency has reason to believe that the home in which a relative and child receiving aid reside is unsuitable for the child because of the neglect, abuse, or exploitation of such child it shall bring such condition to the attention of the appropriate court or law enforcement agencies in the State . . . ." Section 405, 42 USC § 605, provides that

> "Whenever the State agency has reason to believe that any payments of aid . . . made with respect to a child are not being or may not be used in the best interests of the child, the State agency may provide for such counseling and guidance services with respect to the use of such payments and the management of other funds by the relative . . . in order to assure use of such payments in the best interests of such child, and may provide for advising such relative that continued failure to so use such payments will result in substitution therefor of protective payments . . . or in seeking the appointment of a guardian . . . or in the imposition of criminal or civil penalties . . . ."

III

When a case involves a home and some type of official intrusion into that home, as this case appears to do, an immediate and natural reaction is one of concern about Fourth Amendment rights and the protection which that Amendment is intended to afford. Its emphasis indeed is upon one of the most precious aspects of personal aspects of personal security in the home: "The right of the people to be secure in their persons, houses, papers, and effects...." This Court has characterized that right as "basic to a free society." Wolf v Colorado, 338 US 25, 27, 93 L Ed 1782, 1785, 69 S Ct 1359 (1949); Camara v Municipal Court, 387 US 523, 528, 18 L Ed 2d 930, 985, 87 S Ct 1727 (1967). And over the years the Court consistently has been most protective of the privacy of the dwelling. See, for example, Boyd v United States, 116 US 616, 626–630, 29 L Ed 746, 749, 751, 6 S Ct 538 (1886); Mapp v Ohio, 367 US 643, 6 L Ed 2d 1081, 81 S Ct 1684, 84 ALR 2d 933 (1961); Chimel v California, 395 US 752, 23 L Ed 2d 685, 89 S Ct 2034 (1969); Vale v Louisiana, 399 US 30, 26 L Ed 2d 409, 90 S Ct 1969 (1970). In Camara MR. JUSTICE WHITE, after noting that the "translation of the abstract prohibition against 'unreasonable searches and seizures' into workable guidelines for the decision of particular cases is a difficult task," went on to observe,

> "Nevertheless, one governing principle, justified by history and by current experience, has consistently been followed: except in certain carefully defined classes of cases, a search of private property without proper consent is 'unreasonable' unless it has been authorized by a valid search warrant." 387 US, at 528–529, 18 L Ed 2d at 935.

He pointed out, too, that one's Fourth Amendment protection subsists apart from his being suspected of criminal behavior. 387 US, at 530, 18 L Ed 2d at 936.

IV

This natural and quite proper protective attitude, however, is not a factor in this case, for the seemingly obvious and simple reasons that we are not concerned here with any search by the New York social service agency in the Fourth Amendment meaning of that term. It is true that the governing statute and regulations appear to make mandatory the initial home visit and the subsequent periodic "contacts" (which may include home visits) for the inception and continuance of aid. It is also true that the caseworker's posture in the home visit is perhaps, in a sense, both rehabilitative and investigative. But this latter aspect, we think, is given too broad a character and far more emphasis than it deserves if it is equated with a search in the traditional criminal law context. We note, too, that the visitation in itself is not forced or compelled, and that the beneficiary's denial of permission is not a criminal act. If consent to the visitation is withheld, no visitation takes place. The aid then never begins or merely ceases, as the case may be. There is no entry of the home and there is no search.

V

If however, we were to assume that a caseworker's home visit, before or subsequent to the beneficiary's initial qualification for benefits, somehow (perhaps because the average beneficiary might feel she is in no position to refuse consent to the visit), and despite its interview nature, does possess some of the characteristics of a search in the traditional sense, we nevertheless conclude that the visit not fall within the Fourth Amendment's proscription. This is because it does not descend to the level of unreasonableness. It is unreasonableness which is the Fourth Amendment's standard. Terry v Ohio, 392 US 1, 9, 20 L Ed 2d 889, 898, 88 S Ct 1868 (1968); Elkins v United States, 364 US 206, 222, 4 L Ed 2d 1669, 1689, 80 S Ct 1437 (1960). And MR. CHIEF JUSTICE WARREN observed in Terry that "the specific content and incidents of this right must be shaped by the context in which it is asserted." 392 US, at 9, 20 L Ed 2d at 898.

There are a number of factors that compel us to conclude that the home visit proposed for Mrs. James is not unreasonable:

1. The public's interest in this particular segment of the area of assistance to the unfortunate is protection and aid for the dependent child whose family requires such aid for that child. The focus is on the *child* and, further, it is on the child who is *dependent*. There is no more worthy object of the public's concern. The dependent child's needs are paramount, and only with hesitancy would we relegate those needs, in the scale of comparative values, to a position secondary to what the mother claims as her rights.

2. The agency, with tax funds provided from federal as well as from state sources, is fulfilling a public trust. The state, working through its qualified welfare agency, has appropriate and paramount interest and concern in seeing and assuring that the intended and proper objects of that tax-produced assistance are the ones who benefit from the aid it dispenses. Surely it is not unreasonable, in the Fourth Amendment sense or in any other sense of that term, that the State have at its command a gentle means, of limited extent and of practical and considerate application, of achieving that assurance.

3. One who dispenses purely private charity naturally has an interest in and expects to know how his charitable funds are utilized and put to work. The public, when it is the provider, rightly expects the same. It might well expect more, because of the trust aspect of public funds, and the recipient, as well as the caseworker, has not only an interest but an obligation.

4. The emphasis of the New York statutes and regulations is upon the home, upon "close contract" with the beneficiary, upon restoring the aid recipient "to a condition of self-support," and upon the relief of his distress. The federal emphasis is no different. It is upon "assistance and rehabilitation," upon maintaining and strengthening family life, and upon "maximum self-support and personal independence consistent with the maintenance of continuing parental care and protec-

tion . . . ." 42 USC § 601 (1964 ed., Supp V); Dandridge v Williams, 397 US 471, 479, 25 L Ed 2d 491, 498, 90 S Ct 1153 (1970), and id., at 510, 25 L Ed 2d at 516 (MARSHALL, J., dissenting). It requires cooperation from the state agency upon specified standards and in specified ways. And it is concerned about any possible exploitation of the child.

5. The home visit it is true, is not required by federal statute or regulation. But it has been noted that the visit is "the heart of welfare administration"; that it affords "a personal, rehabilitative orientation, unlike that of most federal programs"; and that the "more pronounced service orientation" effected by Congress with the 1956 amendments to the Social Security Act "gave redoubled importance to the practice of home visiting." Note, Rehabilitation, Investigation and the Welfare Home Visit, 79 Yale LJ 746, 748 (1970). The home visit is an established routine in States besides New York.

6. The means employed by the New York agency are significant. Mrs. James received written notice several days in advance of the intended home visit. The date was specified. Section 134-a of the New York Social Services Law, effective April 1, 1967 and set forth in n. 2, supra, sets the tone. Privacy is emphasized. The applicant-recipient is made the primary source of information as to eligibility. Outside informational source, other than public records, are to be consulted only with the beneficiary's consent. Forcible entry or entry under false pretenses or visitation outside working hours or snooping in the home are forbidden. HEW Handbook of Public Assistance Administration pt. IV, §§ 2200(a) and 2300; 18 NYCRR §§351.1, 351.6, and 351.7. All this minimizes any "burden" upon the homeowner's right against unreasonable intrusion.

7. Mrs. James, in fact, on this record presents no specific complaint of any unreasonable intrusion of her home and nothing that supports an inference that the desired home visit had as its purpose the obtaining of information as to criminal activity. She complains of no proposed visitation at an awkward or retirement hour. She suggests no forcible entry. She refers to no snooping. She describes no impolite or reprehensible conduct of any kind. She alleges only, in general and nonspecific terms, that on previous visits and, on information and belief, on visitation at the home of other aid recipients, "questions concerning personal relationships, beliefs and behavior are raised and pressed which are unnecessary for a determination of continuing eligibility." Paradoxically, this same complaint could be made of a conference held elsewhere than in the home, and yet this is what is sought by Mrs. James. The same complaint could be made of the census taker's questions. See MR. JUSTICE MARSHALL's opinion, as United States Circuit Judge, in United States v Rickenbacker, 309 F2d 462 (CA2 1962), cert denied, 371 US 962, 9 L Ed 2d 509, 83 S Ct 542. What Mrs. James appears to want from the agency that provides her and her infant son with the necessities for life is the right to receive those necessities upon her own informational terms, to utilize the Fourth Amendment as a wedge for imposing those terms, and to avoid questions of any kind.

8. We are not persuaded, as Mrs. James would have us be, that all information pertinent to the issue of eligibility can be obtained by the agency through an interview at a place other than the home, or, as the District Court majority suggested, by examining a lease or a birth certificate, or by periodic medical examinations, or by interviews with school personnel. 303 F Supp, at 943. Although these secondary sources might be helpful, they would not always assure verification of actual residence or of actual physical presence in the home, which are requisites for AFDC benefits, or of impending medical needs. And, of course, little children, such as Maurice James, are not yet registered in school.

9. The visit is not one by police or uniformed authority. It is made by a caseworker of some training whose primary objective is, or should be, the welfare, not the prosecution, of the aid recipient for whom the worker has profound responsibility. As has already been stressed, the program concerns dependent children and the needy families of those children. It does not deal with crime or with the actual or suspected perpetrators of crime. The caseworker is not a sleuth but rather, we trust, is a friend to one in need.

10. The home visit is not a criminal investigation, does not equate with a criminal investigation, and despite the announced fears of Mrs. James and those who would join her, is not in aid of any criminal proceeding. If the visitation serves to discourage misrepresentation or fraud, such a byproduct of that visit does not impress upon the visit itself a dominant criminal investigative aspect. And if the visit should, by chance, lead to the discovery of fraud and a criminal prosecution should follow, then, even assuming that the evidence discovered upon the home visitation is admissible, an issue upon which we express no opinion, that is a routine and expected fact of life and a consequence no greater than that which necessarily ensues upon any other discovery by a citizen of criminal conduct.

11. The warrant procedure, which the plaintiff appears to claim to be so precious to her, even if civil in nature, is not without its seriously objectionable features in the welfare context. If a warrant could be obtained (the plaintiff affords us little help as to how it would be obtained), it presumably could be applied for ex parte, its execution would require no notice, it would justify entry by force, and its hours for execution would not be so limited as those prescribed for home visitation. The warrant necessarily would imply conduct either criminal or out of compliance with an asserted governing standard. Of course, the force behind the warrant argument, welcome to the one asserting it, is the fact that it would have to rest upon probable cause, and probable cause in the welfare context, as Mrs. James concedes, requires more than the mere need of the caseworker to see the child in the home and to have assurance that the child is there and is receiving the benefit of the aid that has been authorized for it. In this setting the warrant argument is out of place.

It seems to us that the situation is akin to that where an Internal Revenue Service agent, in making a routine civil audit of a taxpayer's income tax return, asks that the taxpayer produce for the agent's review some proof of a deduction the taxpayer has asserted to his benefit in the computation of his tax. If the taxpayer refuses, there is, absent fraud, only a disallowance of the claimed deduction and a consequent additional tax. The taxpayer is fully within his "rights" in refusing to produce the proof, but in maintaining and asserting those rights a tax detriment results and it is a detriment of the taxpayer's own making. So here Mrs. James has the "right" to refuse the home visit, but a consequence in the form of cessation of aid, similar to the taxpayer's resultant additional tax, flows from that refusal. The choice is entirely hers, and nothing of constitutional magnitude is involved.

VI

Camara v Municipal Court, 387 US 523, 18 L Ed 2d 930, 87 S Ct 1727 (1967), and its companion case, See v City of Seattle, 387 US 541, 18 L Ed 2d 943, 87 S Ct 1737 (1967), both by a divided Court, are not inconsistent with our result here. Those cases concerned, respectively, a refusal of entry to city housing inspectors checking for a violation of a building's occupancy permit, and a refusal of entry to a fire department representative interested in compliance with a city's fire code. In each case a majority of this Court held that the Fourth Amendment barred prosecution for refusal to permit the desired warrantless inspection. Frank v Maryland, 359 US 360, 3 L Ed 2d 377, 79 S Ct 804 (1959), a case that reached an opposing result and that concerned a request by a health officer for entry in order to check the source of a rat infestation, was pro tanto overruled. Both Frank and Camara involved dwelling quarters. See had to do with a commercial warehouse.

But the facts of the three cases are significantly different from those before us. Each concerned a true search for violations. Frank was a criminal prosecution for the owner's refusal to permit entry. So, too, was See. Camara had to do with a writ of prohibition sought to prevent an already pending criminal prosecution. The community welfare aspects, of course, were highly important, but each case arose in a criminal context where a genuine search was denied and prosecution followed.

In contrast, Mrs. James is not being prosecuted for her refusal to permit the home visit and is not about to be so prosecuted. Her wishes in that respect are fully honored. We have not been told, and have not found, that her refusal is made a criminal act by any applicable New York or federal statute. The only consequence of her refusal is that the payment of benefits ceases. Important and serious as this is, the situation is no different than if she had exercised a similar negative choice initially and refrained from applying for AFDC benefits. If a statute made her refusal a criminal offense, and if this case were one concerning her prosecution under that statute, Camara and See would have conceivable pertinency.

VII

Our holding today does not mean, of course, that a termination of benefits upon refusal of a home visit is to be upheld against constitutional challenge under all conceivable circumstances. The early morning mass raid upon homes of welfare recipients is not unknown. See Parrish v Civil Service Comm'n, 66 Cal 2d 260, 425

P2d 223 (1967); Reich, Midnight Welfare Searches and the Social Security Act, 72 Yale LJ 1347 (1963). But that is not this case. Facts of that kind present another case for another day.

We therefore conclude that the home visitation as structured by the New York statutes and regulations is a reasonable administrative tool; that it serves a valid and proper administrative purpose for the dispensation of the AFDC program; that it is not an unwarranted invasion of personal privacy; and that it violates no right guaranteed by the Fourth Amendment.

Reversed and remanded with directions to enter a judgment of dismissal.

It is so ordered.

United States *v.* Watson

423 US 411, 46 L Ed 2d 598, 96 S Ct 820 (1976)

. . .

MR. JUSTICE WHITE delivered the opinion of the Court.

This case presents questions under the Fourth Amendment as to the legality of a warrantless arrest and of an ensuing search of the arrestee's automobile carried out with his purported consent.

I

The relevant events began on August 17, 1972, when an informant, one Khoury, telephoned a postal inspector informing him that respondent Watson was in possession of a stolen credit card and had asked Khoury to cooperate in using the card to their mutual advantage. On five to 10 previous occasions Khoury had provided the inspector with reliable information on postal inspection matters, some involving Watson. Later that day Khoury delivered the card to the inspector. On learning that Watson had agreed to furnish additional cards, the inspector asked Khoury to arrange to meet with Watson. Khoury did so, a meeting being scheduled for August 22. Watson canceled that engagement, but at noon on August 23, Khoury met with Watson at a restaurant designated by the latter. Khoury had been instructed that if Watson had additional stolen credit cards, Khoury was to give a designated signal. The signal was given, the officers closed in, and Watson was forthwith arrested. He was removed from the restaurant to the street where he was given the warnings required by Miranda v Arizona, 384 US 436, 16 L Ed 2d 694, 86 S Ct 1602, 10 Ohio Misc 9, 36 Ohio Ops 2d 237, 10 ALR3d 974 (1966). A search having revealed that Watson had no credit cards on his person, the inspector asked if he could look inside Watson's car, which was standing within view. Watson said, "Go ahead," and repeated these words when the inspector cautioned that "[i]f I find anything, it is going to go against you." Using keys furnished by Watson, the inspector entered the car and found under the floor mat an envelope containing two credit cards in the names of other persons. These cards were the basis for two counts of a four-count indictment charging Watson with possessing stolen mail in violation of 18 USC § 1708 [18 USCS § 1708].

Prior to trial, Watson moved to suppress the cards, claiming that his arrest was illegal for want of probable cause and an arrest warrant and that his consent to search the car was involuntary and ineffective because he had not been told that he could withhold consent. The motion was denied, and Watson was convicted of illegally possessing the two cards seized from his car.

A divided panel of the Court of Appeals for the Ninth Circuit reversed, 504 F2d 849 (1974), ruling that the admission in evidence of the two credit cards found in the car was prohibited by the Fourth Amendment. In reaching this judgment, the court decided two issues in Watson's favor. First, notwithstanding its agreement with the District Court that Khoury was reliable and that there was probable cause for arresting Watson, the court held the arrest unconstitutional because the postal inspector had failed to secure an arrest warrant although he concededly had time to do so. Second, based on the totality of the circumstances, one of which was the illegality of the arrest, the court held Watson's consent to search had been coerced and hence was not a valid ground for the warrantless search of the automobile. We granted certiorari. 420 US 924, 43 L Ed 2d 392, 95 S Ct 1117 (1975).

II

A major part of the Court of Appeals' opinion was its holding that Watson's warrantless arrest violated the Fourth Amendment. Although it did not expressly do so, it may have intended to overturn the conviction on the independent ground that the two credit cards were the inadmissible fruits of an unconstitutional arrest. Cf. Brown v Illinois, 422 US 590, 45 L Ed 2d 416, 95 S Ct 2254 (1975). However that may be, the Court of Appeals treated the illegality of Watson's arrest as an important factor in determining the voluntariness of his consent to search his car. We therefore deal first with the arrest issue.

Contrary to the Court of Appeals' view, Watson's arrest was not invalid because executed without a warrant. § 3061(a)(3) Title 18 USC [18 USCS § 3061(a)] expressly empowers the Board of Governors of the Postal Service to authorize Postal Service officers and employees "performing duties related to the inspection of postal matters" to

> "make arrests without warrant for felonies cognizable under the laws of the United States if they have reasonable grounds to believe that the person to be arrested has committed or is committing such a felony."

By regulation, 39 CFR § 232.5(a)(3) (1975), and in identical language, the Board of Governors has exercised that power and authorized warrantless arrests. Because there was probable cause in this case to believe that Watson had violated § 1708, the inspector and his subordinates, in arresting Watson, were acting strictly in accordance with the governing statute and regulations. The effect of the judgment of the Court of Appeals was to invalidate the statute as applied in this case and as applied to all the situations where a court fails to find exigent circumstances justifying a warrantless arrest. We reverse that judgment.

Under the Fourth Amendment, the people are to be "secure in their persons, houses, papers, and effects, against unreasonable searches and seizures, ... and no Warrants shall issue, but upon probable cause ...." Section 3061 represents a judgment by Congress that it is not unreasonable under the Fourth Amendment for postal inspectors to arrest without a warrant provided they have probable cause to do so. This was not an isolated or quixotic judgment of the legislative branch. Other federal law enforcement officers have been expressly authorized by statute for many years to make felony arrests on probable cause but without a warrant. This is true of United States marshals, 18 USC § 3053 [18 USCS §3053], and of agents of the Federal Bureau of Investigation, 18 USC § 3052 [18 USCS § 3052]; the Drug Enforcement Administration, 84 Stat 1273, 21 USC § 878 [21 USCS § 878]; the Secret Service, 18 USC § 3056(a) [18 USCS § 3056(a)]; and the Customs Service, 26 USC § 7607 [26 USCS § 7607].

Because there is a "strong presumption of constitutionality due to an Act of Congress, especially when it turns on what is 'reasonable,'" "[o]bviously the court should be reluctant to decide that a search thus authorized by Congress was unreasonable and that the Act was therefore unconstitutional." United States v Di Re, 332 US 581, 585, 92 L Ed 210, 68 S Ct 222 (1948). Moreover, there is nothing in the Court's prior cases indicating that under the Fourth Amendment a warrant is required to make a valid arrest for a felony. Indeed, the relevant prior decisions are uniformly to the contrary.

"The usual rule is that a police officer may arrest without warrant one believed by the officer upon reasonable cause to have been guilty of a felony ...." Carroll v United States, 267 US 132, 156, 69 L Ed 543, 45 S Ct 280, 39 ALR 790 (1925). In Henry v United States, 361 US 98, 4 L Ed 2d 134, 80 S Ct 168 (1959), the Court dealt with an FBI agent's warrantless arrest under 18 USC § 3052 [18 USCS § 3052], which authorizes a warrantless arrest where there are reasonable grounds to believe that the person to be arrested has committed a felony. The Court declared that "[t]he statute states the constitutional standard ..." 361 US, at 100, 4 L Ed 2d 134, 80 S Ct 168. The necessary inquiry, therefore, was not whether there was a warrant or whether there was time to get one, but whether there was probable cause for the arrest. In Abel v United States, 362 US 217, 232, 4 L Ed 2d 668, 80 S Ct 683 (1960), the Court sustained an administrative arrest made without "a judicial warrant within the scope of the Fourth Amendment." The crucial question in Draper v United States, 358 US 307, 3 L Ed 2d 327, 79 S Ct 329 (1959), was whether there was probable cause for the warrantless arrest. If there was, the Court said, "the arrest, though without a warrant, was lawful ...." Id., at 310, 3 L Ed 2d 327, 79 S Ct 329, Ker v California, 374 US 23, 34–35, 10 L Ed 2d 726, 83 S Ct 1623, 24 Ohio Ops 2d 201 (1963) (opinion of CLARK, J.) reiterated the rule that "[t]he lawfulness of the arrest without warrant, in turn, must be based upon probable cause ..." and went on to sustain the warrantless arrest over other claims going to the mode of entry. Just last Term, while recognizing that maximum protection of individual rights could be assured by requiring a magistrate's review of the factual justification prior to any arrest, we stated that "such a requirement would constitute an intolerable handicap for legitimate law enforcement" and noted that the Court "has never invalidated an arrest supported by probable cause solely because the officers failed to secure a warrant." Gerstein v Pugh, 420 US 103, 113, 43 L Ed 2d 54, 95 S Ct 854 (1975).

The cases construing the Fourth Amendment thus reflect the ancient common-law rule that a peace officer was permitted to arrest without a warrant for a misdemeanor or felony committed in his presence as well as for a felony not committed in his presence if there was reasonable grounds for making the arrest. 10 Halsbury's Laws of England 344–345 (3d ed 1955); 4 W. Blackstone, Commentaries 292; 1 J. Stephen, A History of the Criminal Law of England 193 (1883); 2 M. Hale, Plea of the Crown 72–74; Wilgus, Arrest Without a Warrant, 22 Mich L Rev 541, 547–550, 686–688 (1924); Samuel v Payne, 1 Dougl 359, 99 Eng Rep 230 (KB 1780); Beckwith v Philby, 6 Barn & Cress, 635, 108 Eng Rep 585 (KB 1827). This has also been the prevailing rule under state constitutions and statutes. "The rule of the common law, that a peace officer or a private citizen may arrest a felon without a warrant, has been generally held by the courts of the several States to be in force in cases of felony punishable by the civil tribunals." Kurtz v Moffitt, 115 US 487, 504, 29 L Ed 458, 6 S Ct 148 (1885).

In Rohan v Sawin, 59 Mass 281 (1850), a false-arrest case, the Supreme Judicial Court of Massachusetts held that the common-law rule obtained in that State. Given probable cause to arrest, "[t]he authority of a constable, to arrest without warrant, in cases of felony, is most fully established by the elementary books, and adjudicated cases." Id., at 284. In reaching this judgment the court observed:

> "It has been sometimes contended, that an arrest of this character, without a warrant, was a violation of the great fundamental principles of our national and state constitutions, forbidding unreasonable searches and arrests, except by warrant founded upon a complaint made under oath. Those provisions doubtless had another and different purpose, being in restraint of general warrants to make searches, and requiring warrants to issue only upon a complaint made under oath. They do not conflict with the authority of constables or other peace-officers, or private persons under proper limitations, to arrest without warrant those who have committed felonies. The public safety, and the due apprehension of criminals, charged with heinous offences, imperiously require that such arrests should be made without warrant by officers of the law." Id., at 284–285.

Also rejected, id., at 285–286, was the trial court's view that to justify a warrantless arrest, the State must show "an immediate necessity therefor, arising from the danger, that the plaintiff would otherwise escape, or secrete the stolen property, before a warrant could be procured against him." The Supreme Judicial Court ruled that there was no "authority for thus restricting a constable in the exercise of his authority to arrest for a felony without a warrant." Id., at 286. Other early cases to similar effect were Wakely v Hart, 6 Binn 316 (Pa 1814); Holley v Mix, 3 Wend 350 (NY Sup Ct 1829); State v Brown, 5 Del 505 (Ct Gen Sess 1853); Johnson v State, 30 Ga 426 (1860); Wade v Chaffee, 8 RI 224 (1865). See Reuck v McGregor, 32 NJL 70,

74 (Sup Ct 1866); Baltimore & O.R. Co. v Cain, 81 Md 87, 100, 102, 31 A 801, 803, 804 (1895).

Because the common-law rule authorizing arrests without a warrant generally prevailed in the States, it is important for present purposes to note that in 1792 Congress invested United States marshals and their deputies with "the same powers in executing the laws of the United States, as sheriffs and their deputies in the several states have by law, in executing the laws of their respective states." Act of May 2, 1792, c 28, § 9, 1 Stat 265. The Second Congress thus saw no inconsistency between the Fourth Amendment and legislation giving United States marshals the same power as local peace officers to arrest for a felony without a warrant. This provision equating the power of federal marshals to those of local sheriffs was several times reenacted and is today § 570 of Title 28 of the United States Code. That provision, however, was supplemented in 1935 by § 504a of the Judicial Code, which in its essential elements is now 18 USC § 3053 [18 USCS § 3053] and which expressly empowered marshals to make felony arrests without warrant and on probable cause. It was enacted to furnish a federal standard independent of the vagaries of state laws, the Committee Report remarking that under existing law a "marshal or deputy marshal may make an arrest without a warrant within his district in all cases where the sheriff might do so under the State statutes." HR Rep No. 283, 74th Cong, 1st Sess, 1 (1935). See United States v Riggs, 474 F2d 699, 702–703, n 2 (CA2), cert denied, 414 US 820, 38 L Ed 2d 53, 94 S Ct 115 (1973).

The balance struck by the common law in generally authorizing felony arrests on probable cause, but without a warrant, has survived substantially intact. It appears in almost all of the States in the form of express statutory authorization. In 1963, the American Law Institute undertook the task of formulating a model statute governing police powers and practice in criminal law enforcement and related aspects of pretrial procedure. In 1975, after years of discussion, A Model Code of Pre-arraignment Procedure was proposed. Among its provisions was § 120.1 which authorizes an officer to take a person into custody if the officer has reasonable cause to believe that the person to be arrested has committed a felony, or has committed a misdemeanor or petty misdemeanor in his presence. The commentary to this section said: "The Code thus adopts the traditional and almost universal standard for arrest without a warrant."

This is the rule Congress has long directed its principal law enforcement officers to follow. Congress has plainly decided against conditioning warrantless arrest power on proof of exigent circumstances. Law enforcement officers may find it wise to seek arrest warrants where practicable to do so, and their judgments about probable cause may be more readily accepted where backed by a warrant issued by a magistrate. See United States v Ventresca, 380 US 102, 106, 13 L Ed 2d 684, 85 S Ct 741 (1965); Aguilar v Texas, 378 US 108, 111, 12 L Ed 2d 723, 84 S Ct 1509 (1964); Wong Sun v United States, 371 US 471, 479–480, 9 L Ed 2d 441, 83 S Ct 407 (1963). But we decline to transform this judicial preference into a constitutional rule when the judgment of the Nation and Congress has for so long been to authorize warrantless public arrests on probable cause rather than to encumber criminal prosecutions with endless litigation with respect to the existence of exigent circumstances, whether it was practicable to get a warrant, whether the suspect was about to flee, and the like.

Watson's arrest did not violate the Fourth Amendment, and the Court of Appeals erred in holding to the contrary.

III

Because our judgment is that Watson's arrest comported with the Fourth Amendment, Watson's consent to the search of his car was not the product of an illegal arrest. To the extent that the issue of the voluntariness of Watson's consent was resolved on the premise that his arrest was illegal, the Court of Appeals was also in error.

We are satisfied in addition that the remaining factors relied upon by the Court of Appeals to invalidate Watson's consent are inadequate to demonstrate that, in the totality of the circumstances, Watson's consent was not his own "essentially free and unconstrained choice" because his "will ha[d] been overborne and his capacity for self-determination critically impaired." Schneckloth v Bustamonte, 412 US 218, 225, 36 L Ed 2d 854, 93 S Ct 2041 (1973). There was no overt act or threat of force against Watson proved or claimed. There were no promises made to him and no indication of more subtle forms of coercion that might flaw his judgment. He had been arrested and was in custody, but his consent was given while on a public street, not in the confines of the police station. Moreover, the fact of custody alone has never been enough in itself to demonstrate a coerced confession or consent to search. Similarly, under Schneckloth, the absence of proof that Watson knew he could withhold his consent, though it may be a factor in the overall judgment, is not to be given controlling significance. There is no indication in this record that Watson was a newcomer to the law, mentally deficient, or unable in the face of a custodial arrest to exercise a free choice. He was given Miranda warnings and was further cautioned that the results of the search of his car could be used against him. He persisted in his consent.

In these circumstances, to hold that illegal coercion is made out from the fact of arrest and the failure to inform the arrestee that he could withhold consent would not be consistent with Schneckloth and would distort the voluntariness standard that we reaffirmed in that case.

In consequence, we reverse the judgment of the Court of Appeals.

So ordered.

United States *v.* Santana et al.

427 U.S. 38, 96 S.Ct. 2406, 49 L.Ed. 2d. 300 (1976)

CERTIORARI TO THE UNITED STATES COURT OF APPEALS FOR THE THIRD CIRCUIT

Argued April 27, 1976—Decided June 24, 1976

. . .

MR. JUSTICE REHNQUIST delivered the opinion of the Court.

I

On August 16, 1974, Michael Gilletti, an undercover officer with the Philadelphia Narcotics Squad arranged a heroin "buy" with one Patricia McCafferty (from whom he had purchased narcotics before). McCafferty told him it would cost $115 "and we will go down to Mom Santana's for the dope."

Gilletti notified his superiors of the impending transaction, recorded the serial numbers of $110 [sic] in marked bills, and went to meet McCafferty at a prearranged location. She got in his car and directed him to drive to 2311 North Fifth Street, which, as she had previously informed him, was respondent Santana's residence.

McCafferty took the money and went inside the house, stopping briefly to speak to respondent Alejandro who was sitting on the front steps. She came out shortly afterwards and got into the car. Gilletti asked for the heroin; she thereupon extracted from her bra several glassine envelopes containing a brownish-white powder and gave them to him.

Gilletti then stopped the car, displayed his badge and placed McCafferty under arrest. He told her that the police were going back to 2311 North Fifth Street and that he wanted to know where the money was. She said, "Mom has the money." At this point Sergeant Pruitt and other officers came up to the car. Gilletti showed them the envelope and said "Mom Santana has the money." Gilletti then took McCafferty to the police station.

Pruitt and the others then drove approximately two blocks back to 2311 North Fifth Street. They saw Santana standing in the doorway of the house with a brown paper bag in her hand. They pulled up to within 15 feet of Santana and got out of their van, shouting "police," and displaying their identification. As the officers approached, Santana retreated into the vestibule of her house.

The officers followed through the open door, catching her in the vestibule. As she tried to pull away, the bag tilted and "two bundles of glazed paper packets with a white powder" fell to the floor. Respondent Alejandro tried to make off with the dropped envelopes but was forcibly restrained. When Santana was told to empty her pockets she produced $135, $70 of which could be identified as Gilletti's marked money. The white powder in the bag was later determined to be heroin.

An indictment was filed in the United States District Court for the Eastern District of Pennsylvania charging McCafferty with distribution of heroin, in violation of 21 U.S.C. § 841, and respondents with possession of heroin with intent to distribute in violation of the same section. McCafferty pleaded guilty. Santana and Alejandro moved to suppress the heroin and money found during and after their arrests.

The District Court granted respondents' motion. In an oral opinion the court found that "[t]here was strong probable cause that Defendant Santana had participated in the transaction with Defendant McCafferty." However, the court continued:

> "One of the police officers...testified that the mission was to arrest Defendant Santana. Another police officer testified that the mission was to recover the bait money. Either one would require a warrant, one a warrant of arrest under ordinary circumstances and one a search warrant."

The court further held that Santana's "reentry from the doorway into the house" did not support allowing the police to make a warrantless entry into the house on the grounds of "hot pursuit," because it took "hot pursuit" to mean "a chase in and about public streets." The court did find, however, that the police acted under "extreme emergency" conditions. The Court of Appeals affirmed this decision without opinion.

II

In United States v. Watson, 423 U.S. 411 (1976), we held that the warrantless arrest of an individual in a public place upon probable cause did not violate the Fourth Amendment. Thus the first question we must decide is whether, when the police first sought to arrest Santana, she was in a public place.

While it may be true that under the common law of property the threshold of one's dwelling is "private," as is the yard surrounding the house, it is nonetheless clear that under the cases interpreting the Fourth Amendment Santana was in a "public" place. She was not in an area where she had any expectation of privacy. "What a person knowingly exposes to the public, even in his own house or office, is not a subject of Fourth Amendment protection." Katz v. United States, 389 U.S. 347, 351 (1967). She was not merely visible to the public but was as exposed to public view, speech, hearing, and touch as if she had been standing completely outside her house. Hester v. United States, 265 U.S. 57, 59 (1924). Thus, when the police, who concededly had probable cause to do so, sought to arrest her, they merely intended to perform a function that we have approved in Watson.

The only remaining question is whether her act of retreating into her house could thwart an otherwise proper arrest. We hold that it could not. In Warden v. Hayden, 387 U.S. 294 (1967), we recognized the right of police, who had probable cause to believe that an armed robber had entered a house a few minutes before, to make a warrantless entry to arrest the robber and to search for weapons. This case, involving a true "hot pursuit," is clearly governed by Warden; the need to act quickly here is even greater than in that case while the intrusion is much less. The District Court was correct in concluding that "hot pursuit" means some sort of a chase, but it need not be an extended hue and cry "in and about [the] public streets." The fact that the pursuit here ended almost as soon as it began did not render it any the less a "hot pursuit" sufficient to justify the warrantless entry into Santana's house. Once Santana saw the police, there was likewise a realistic expectation that any delay would result in destruction of evidence. See Vale v. Louisiana, 399 U.S. 30, 35 (1970). Once she had been arrested the search, incident to that arrest, which produced the drugs and money was clearly justified. United States v. Robinson, 414 U.S. 218 (1973); Chimel v. California, 395 U.S. 752, 762–763 (1969).

We thus conclude that a suspect may not defeat an arrest which has been set in motion in a public place, and is therefore proper under Watson, by the expedient of escaping to a private place. The judgment of the Court of Appeals is

Reversed.

United States, Petitioner, *v.* New York Telephone Company

434 U.S. 159, 98 S.Ct. 364, 22 Cr. L. 3001, 54 L.Ed. 2d. 376 (1977)

ON WRIT OF CERTIORARI TO THE UNITED STATES COURT OF APPEALS FOR THE SECOND CIRCUIT.

[December 7, 1977]

. . .

MR. JUSTICE WHITE delivered the opinion of the Court.

This case presents the question of whether a United States District Court may properly direct a telephone company to provide federal law enforcement officials the facilities and technical assistance necessary for the implementation of its order authorizing the use of pen registers* to investigate offenses which there was probable cause to believe were being committed by means of the telephone.

I

On March 19, 1976, the United States District Court for the Southern District of New York issued an order authorizing agents of the Federal Bureau of Investigation (FBI) to install and use pen registers with respect to two telephones and directing the New York Telephone Company (the Company) to furnish the FBI "all information, facilities and technical assistance" necessary to employ the pen registers unobtrusively. The FBI was ordered to compensate the Company at prevailing rates for any assistance which it furnished. App. 6–7. The order was issued on the basis of an affidavit submitted by an FBI agent which stated that certain individuals were conducting an illegal gambling enterprise at 220 East 14th Street in New York City and that, on the basis of facts set forth therein, there was probable cause to believe that two telephones bearing different numbers were being used at that address in furtherance of the illegal activity. App. 1–5. The District Court found that there was probable cause to conclude that an illegal gambling enterprise using the facilities of interstate commerce was being conducted at the East 14th Street address in violation of Title 18, United States Code, §§ 371 and 1952, and that the two telephones had been, were currently being, and would continue to be used in connection with those offenses. Its order authorized the FBI to operate the pen registers with respect

*A pen register is a mechanical device that records the numbers dialed on a telephone by monitoring the electrical impulses caused when the dial on the telephone is released. It does not overhear oral communications and does not indicate whether calls are actually completed.

to the two telephones until knowledge of the numbers dialed led to the identity of the associates and confederates of those believed to be conducting the illegal operation or for 20 days, "whichever is earlier."

The Company declined to comply fully with the court order. It did inform the FBI of the location of the relevant "appearances," that is, the places where specific telephone lines emerge from the sealed telephone cable. In addition, the Company agreed to identify the relevant "pairs," or the specific pairs of wires that constituted the circuits of the two telephone lines. This information is required to install a pen register. The Company, however, refused to lease lines to the FBI which were needed to install the pen registers in an unobtrusive fashion. Such lines were required by the FBI in order to install the pen registers in inconspicuous locations away from the building containing the telephones. A "leased line" is an unused telephone line which makes an "appearance" in the same terminal box as the telephone line in connection with which it is desired to install a pen register. If the leased line is connected to the subject telephone line, the pen register can then be installed on the leased line at a remote location and be monitored from that point. The Company, instead of providing the leased lines, which it conceded that the court's order required it to do, advised the FBI to string cables from the "subject-apartment" to another location where pen registers could be installed. The FBI determined after canvassing the neighborhood of the apartment for four days that there was no location where it could string its own wires and attach the pen registers without alerting the suspects, in which event, of course, the gambling operation would cease to function. App. 15–22.

On March 30, 1976, the Company moved in the District Court to vacate that portion of the pen register order directing it to furnish facilities and technical assistance to the FBI in connection with the use of the pen registers on the ground that such a directive could be issued only in connection with a wiretap order conforming to the requirements of Title III of the Omnibus Crime Control and Safe Streets Act of 1968, 18 U.S.C. §§ 2510–2520 (Title III). It contended that neither Fed. Rule Crim. Proc. 41 nor the All Writs Act, 28 U.S.C. § 1651 (a), provided any basis for such an order. App. 10–14. The District Court ruled that pen registers are not governed by the prescriptions of Title III because they are not devices used to intercept oral communications. It concluded that it had jurisdiction to authorize the installation of the pen registers upon a showing of probable cause and that both the All Writs Act and its inherent powers provided authority for the order directing the Company to assist in the installation of the pen registers.

On April 9, 1976, after the District Court and the Court of Appeals denied the Company's motion to stay the pen register order pending appeal, the Company provided the leased lines.

The Court of Appeals affirmed in part and reversed in part, with one judge dissenting on the ground that the order below should have been affirmed in its entirety. Application of the United States of America in the Matter of an Order Authorizing the Use of a Pen Register or Similar Mechanical Device (Application) 538 F. 2d 956 (CA2 1976). It agreed with the District Court that pen registers do not fall within the scope of Title III and are not otherwise prohibited or regulated by statute. The Court of Appeals also concluded that district courts have the power, either inherently or as a logical derivative of Fed. Rule Crim. Proc. 41, to authorize pen register surveillance upon an adequate showing of probable cause. The majority held, however, that the District Court abused its discretion in ordering the Company to assist in the installation and operation of the pen registers. It assumed, *arguendo,* "that a district court has inherent discretionary authority or discretionary power under the All Writs Act to compel technical assistance by the Telephone Company," but concluded that "in the absence of specific and properly limited Congressional action, it was an abuse of discretion for the District Court to order the Telephone Company to furnish technical assistance." Id., at 961. The majority expressed concern that "such an order could establish a most undesirable, if not dangerous and unwise, precedent for the authority of federal courts to impress unwilling aid on private third parties" and that "there is no assurance that the court will always be able to protect [third parties] from excessive or overzealous Government activity or compulsion." Id., at 962–963.

We granted the United States' petition for certiorari challenging the Court of Appeals' invalidation of the District Court's order against respondent.

II

We first reject respondent's contention, which is renewed here, that the District Court lacked authority to order the Company to provide assistance because the use of pen registers may only be authorized in conformity with the procedures set forth in Title III for securing judicial authority to intercept wire communications. Both the language of the statute and its legislative history establish beyond any doubt that pen registers are not governed by Title III.

Title III is concerned only with orders "authorizing or approving the *interception* of a wire or oral communication. . . ." 18 U.S.C. § 2518 (1) (emphasis added). Congress defined "intercept" to mean "the *aural* acquisition of the *contents* of any wire or oral *communication* through the use of any electronic, mechanical, or other device." 18 U.S.C. § 2510 (4) (emphasis added). Pen registers do not "intercept" because they do not acquire the "contents" of communications, as that term is defined by 18 U.S.C. § 2511 (8). Indeed, a law enforcement official could not even determine from the use of a pen register whether a communication existed. These devices do not hear sound. They disclose only the telephone numbers that have been dialed—a means of establishing communication. Neither the purport of any communication between the caller and the recipient of the call, their identities, nor whether the call was even completed are disclosed by pen registers. Furthermore, pen registers do not accomplish the "aural acquisition" of anything. They decode outgoing telephone numbers by responding to changes in electrical voltage caused by the turning of the telephone dial (or the pressing of buttons on push button telephones) and present the information in a form to be interpreted by sight rather than by hearing.

The legislative history confirms that there was no congressional intent to subject pen registers to the requirements of Title III. The Senate Report explained that the definition of "intercept" was designed to exclude pen registers:

> "Paragraph 4 [of § 2510] defines 'intercept' to include the aural acquisition of the contents of any wire or oral communication by any electronic, mechanical, or other device. Other forms of surveillance are not within the proposed legislation. . . . The proposed legislation is not designed to prevent the tracing of phone calls. The use of a 'pen register,' for example, would be permissible. But see United States v. Dote, 371 F. 2d 176 (7th 1966). The proposed legislation is intended to protect the privacy of the communication itself and not the means of communication." S. Rep. No. 1097, 90th Cong., 2d Sess., p. 90 (1968).

It is clear that Congress did not view pen registers as posing a threat to privacy of the same dimension as the interception of oral communications and did not intend to impose Title III restrictions upon their use.

III

We also agree with the Court of Appeals that the District Court had power to authorize the installation of the pen registers. It is undisputed that the order in this case was predicated upon a proper finding of probable cause, and no claim is made that it was in any way inconsistent with the Fourth Amendment. Fed. Rule Crim. Proc. 41 (b) authorizes the issuance of a warrant to

> "search for and seize any (1) property that constitutes evidence of the commission of a criminal offense; or (2) contraband, the fruits of crime, or things otherwise criminally possessed; or (3) property designed or intended for use or which is or has been used as the means of committing a criminal offense."

This definition is broad enough to encompass a "search" designed to ascertain the use which is being made of a telephone suspected of being employed as a means of facilitating a criminal venture and the "seizure" of evidence which the "search" of the telephone produces. Although Rule 41 (h) defines property "to include documents, books, papers and any other tangible objects," it does not restrict or purport to exhaustively enumerate all the items which may be seized pursuant to Rule 41. Indeed, we recognized in Katz v. United States, 389 U.S. 347 (1967), which held that telephone conversations were protected by the Fourth Amendment, that Rule 41 is not limited to tangible items but is sufficiently flexible to include within its scope electronic intrusions authorized upon a finding of probable cause. 389 U.S., at 354–356, and n. 16. See also Osborn v. United States, 385 U.S. 323, 329–331 (1966).

Our conclusion that Rule 41 authorizes the use of pen registers under appropriate circumstances is supported by Fed. Rule Crim. Proc. 57 (b), which provides: "If no procedure is specifically prescribed by rule, the court may proceed in any lawful manner not inconsistent with these rules or with any applicable statute." Although we need not and do not decide whether Rule 57 (b) by itself would authorize the issuance of pen register orders, it reinforces our conclusion that Rule 41 is sufficiently broad to include seizures of intangible items such as dial impulses recorded by pen registers as well as tangible items.

Finally, we could not hold that the District Court lacked any power to authorize the use of pen registers without defying the congressional judgment that the use of pen registers "be permissible." S. Rep. No. 1097, supra, at 90. Indeed, it would be anomalous to permit the recording of conversations by means of electronic surveillance while prohibiting the far lesser intrusion accomplished by pen registers. Congress intended no such result. We are unwilling to impose it in the absence of some showing that the issuance of such orders would be inconsistent with Rule 41. Cf. Rule 57 (b), supra.

IV

The Court of Appeals held that even though the District Court had ample authority to issue the pen register warrant and even assuming the applicability of the All Writs Act, the order compelling the Company to provide technical assistance constituted an abuse of discretion. Since the Court of Appeals conceded that a compelling case existed for requiring the assistance of the Company and did not point to any fact particular to this case which would warrant a finding of abuse of discretion, we interpret its holding as generally barring district courts from ordering any party to assist in the installation or operation of a pen register. It was apparently concerned that sustaining the District Court's order would authorize courts to compel third parties to render assistance without limitation regardless of the burden involved and pose a severe threat to the autonomy of third parties who for whatever reason prefer not to render such assistance. Consequently the Court of Appeals concluded that courts should not embark upon such a course without specific legislative authorization. We agree that the power of federal courts to impose duties upon third parties is not without limits; unreasonable burdens may not be imposed. We conclude, however, that the order issued here against respondent was clearly authorized by the All Writs Act and was consistent with the intent of Congress.

The All Writs Act provides:

> "The Supreme Court and all courts established by Act of Congress may issue all writs necessary or appropriate in aid of their respective jurisdictions and agreeable to the usages and principles of law." 28 U.S.C. § 1651 (a).

The assistance of the Company was required here to implement a pen register order which we have held the District Court was empowered to issue by Rule 41. This Court has repeatedly recognized the power of a federal court to issue such commands under the All Writs Act as may be necessary or appropriate to effectuate and prevent the frustration of orders it has previously issued in its exercise of jurisdiction otherwise obtained: "This statute has served since its inclusion, in substance, in the original Judiciary Act as a 'legislatively approved source of procedural instruments designed to achieve the rational ends of law.'" Harris v. Nelson, 394 U.S. 286, 299 (1969), quoting Price v. Johnston, 334 U.S. 266, 282 (1948). Indeed, "[u]nless appropriately confined by Congress, a federal court may avail itself of all auxiliary writs as aids in the performance of its duties, when the use of such historic aids is calculated in its sound judgment to achieve the ends of justice entrusted to it." Adams v. United States ex rel. McCann, 317 U.S. 269, 273 (1942).

The Court has consistently applied the Act flexibly in conformity with these principles. Although § 262 of the Judicial Code, the predecessor to § 1651, did not expressly authorize courts, as does § 1651, to issue writs "appropriate" to the proper exercise of their jurisdiction but only "necessary" writs, Adams held that these supplemental powers are not limited to those situations where it is "necessary" to issue the writ or order "in the sense that the court could not otherwise physically discharge its duties." Ibid. In Price v. Johnston, supra, § 262 supplied the authority for a United States Court of Appeals to issue an order commanding that a prisoner be brought before the court for the purpose of arguing his own appeal. Similarly, in order to avoid frustrating the "very purpose" of 28 U.S.C. § 2255, § 1651 furnished the District Court with authority to order that a federal prisoner be produced in court for purposes of a hearing. United States v. Hayman, 342 U.S. 205, 220–222 (1952). The question in Harris v. Nelson, supra, was whether, despite the absence of specific statutory authority, the District Court could issue a discovery order in connection with a habeas corpus proceeding pending before it. Eight Justices agreed that the district courts have power to require discovery when essential to render a habeas corpus proceeding effective. The Court has also held that despite the absence of express statutory authority to do so, the Federal Trade Commission may petition for, and a Court of Appeals may issue, pursuant to § 1651, an order preventing a merger pending hearings before the Commission to avoid impairing or frustrating the Court of Appeals appellate jurisdiction. Federal Trade Comm'n v. Dean Foods Co., 384 U.S. 597 (1966).

The power conferred by the Act extends, under appropriate circumstances, to persons who though not parties to the original action or engaged in wrong doing are in a position to frustrate the implementation of a court order or the proper administration of justice. Mississippi Valley Barge Line Co. v. United States, 273 F. Supp. 1, 6 (FD Mo. 1967), aff'd. 389 U.S. 579 (1968); Board of Education v. York, 429 F. 2d 66 (CA10 1970), cert. denied, 401 U.S. 954 (1971), and encompasses even those who have not taken any affirmative action to hinder justice. United States v. McHie, 196 Fed. 586 (ND Ill. 1912); Field v. United States, 193 F. 2d 92, 95–96 (CA2), cert. denied, 342 U.S. 894 (1951).

Turning to the facts of this case, we do not think that the Company was a third party so far removed from the underlying controversy that its assistance could not be permissibly compelled. A United States District Court found that there was probable cause to believe that the Company's facilities were being employed to facilitate a criminal enterprise on a continuing basis. For the Company, with this knowledge, to refuse to supply the meager assistance required by the FBI in its efforts to put an end to this venture threatened obstruction of an investigation which would determine whether the Company's facilities were being lawfully used. Moreover, it can hardly be contended that the Company, a highly regulated public utility with a duty to serve the public, had a substantial interest in not providing assistance. Certainly the use of pen registers is by no means offensive to it. The Company concedes that it regularly employs such devices without court order for the purposes of checking billing operations, detecting fraud, and preventing violations of law. It also agreed to supply the FBI with all the information required to install its own pen registers. Nor was the District Court's order in any way burdensome. The order provided that the Company be fully reimbursed at prevailing rates, and compliance with it required minimal effort on the part of the Company and no disruption to its operations.

Finally, we note, as the Court of Appeals recognized, that without the Company's assistance there is no conceivable way in which the surveillance authorized by the District Court could have been successfully accomplished. The FBI, after an exhaustive search, was unable to find a location where it could install its own pen registers without tipping off the targets of the investigation. The provision of a leased line by the Company was essential to the fulfillment of the purpose—to learn the identities of those connected with the gambling operation—for which the pen register order had been issued.

The order compelling the Company to provide assistance was not only consistent with the Act but also with more recent congressional actions. As established in Part II, supra, Congress clearly intended to permit the use of pen registers by federal law enforcement officials. Without the assistance of the Company in circumstances such as those presented here, however, these devices simply cannot be effectively employed. Moreover, Congress provided in a 1970 amendment to Title III that "[a]n order authorizing the interception of a wire or oral communication shall, upon request of the applicant, direct that a communication common carrier . . . shall furnish the applicant forthwith all information, facilities, and technical assistance necessary to accomplish the interception unobtrusively. . . ." 18 U.S.C. § 2518 (4). In light of this direct command to federal courts to compel, upon request, any assistance necessary to accomplish an electronic interception, it would be remarkable if Congress thought it beyond the power of the federal courts to exercise, where required, a discretionary authority to order telephone companies to assist in the installation and operation of pen registers, which accomplish a far lesser invasion of privacy. We are convinced that to prohibit the order challenged here would frustrate the clear indication by Congress that the pen register is a permissible law enforcement tool by enabling a public utility to thwart a judicial determination that its use is required to apprehend and prosecute successfully those employing the utility's facilities to conduct a criminal venture. The contrary judgment of the Court of Appeals is accordingly reversed.

So ordered.

W. T. Stone, Warden, Petitioner, *v.* Lloyd Charles Powell; Charles L. Wolff, Jr., Warden, Petitioners, *v.* David L. Rice

428 US 465, 96 S Ct 3037, 49 L Ed 2d 1067 (1976)

Argued February 24, 1976.—Decided July 6, 1976.

. . .

MR. JUSTICE POWELL delivered the opinion of the Court.

Respondents in these cases were convicted of criminal offenses in state courts, and their convictions were affirmed on appeal. The prosecution in each case relied upon evidence obtained by searches and seizures alleged by respondents to have been unlawful. Each respondent subsequently sought relief in a federal district court by filing a petition for a writ of federal habeas corpus under 28 USC § 2254 [28 USCS § 2254]. The question presented is whether a federal court should consider, in ruling on a petition for habeas corpus relief filed by a state prisoner, a claim that evidence obtained by an unconstitutional search or seizure was introduced at his trial, when he has previously been afforded an opportunity for full and fair litigation of his claim in the state courts. The issue is of considerable importance to the administration of criminal justice.

I

We summarize first the relevant facts and procedural history of these cases.

A

Respondent Lloyd Powell was convicted of murder in June 1968 after trial in a California state court. At about midnight on February 17, 1968, he and three companions entered the Bonanza Liquor Store in San Bernardino, Cal., where Powell became involved in an altercation with Gerald Parsons, the store manager, over the theft of a bottle of wine. In the scuffling that followed Powell shot and killed Parsons' wife. Ten hours later an officer of the Henderson, Nev., Police Department arrested Powell for violation of the Henderson vagrancy ordinance, and in the search incident to the arrest discovered a .38 caliber revolver with six expended cartridges in the cylinder.

Powell was extradicted to California and convicted of second-degree murder in the Superior Court of San Bernardino County. Parsons and Powell's accomplices at the liquor store testified against him. A criminologist testified that the revolver found on Powell was the gun that killed Parsons' wife. The trial court rejected Powell's contention that testimony by the Henderson police officer as to the search and the discovery of the revolver should have been excluded because the vagrancy ordinance was unconstitutional. In October 1969, the conviction was affirmed by a California District Court of Appeal. Although the issue was duly presented, that court found it unnecessary to pass upon the legality of the arrest and search because it concluded that the error, if any, in admitting the testimony of the Henderson officer was harmless beyond a reasonable doubt under Chapman v California, 386 US 18, 17 L Ed 2d 705, 87 S Ct 824, 24 ALR3d 1065 (1967). The Supreme Court of California denied Powell's petition for habeas corpus relief.

In August 1971 Powell filed an amended petition for a writ of federal habeas corpus under 28 USC § 2254 [28 USCS § 2254] in the United States District Court for the Northern District of California, contending that the testimony concerning the .38 caliber revolver should have been excluded as the fruit of an illegal search. He argued that his arrest had been unlawful because the Henderson vagrancy ordinance was unconstitutionally vague, and that the arresting officer lacked probable cause to believe that he was violating it. The District Court concluded that the arresting officer had probable cause and held that even if the vagrancy ordinance was unconstitutional, the deterrent purpose of the exclusionary rule does not require that it be applied to bar admission of the fruits of a search incident to an otherwise valid arrest. In the alternative, that court agreed with the California District Court of Appeal that the admission of the evidence concerning Powell's arrest, if error, was harmless beyond a reasonable doubt.

In December 1974, the Court of Appeals for the Ninth Circuit reversed. 507 F2d 93. The Court concluded that the vagrancy ordinance was unconstitutionally vague, that Powell's arrest was therefore illegal, and that although exclusion of the evidence would serve no deterrent purpose with regard to police officers who were enforcing statutes in good faith, exclusion would serve the public interest by deterring legislators from enacting unconstitutional statutes. Id., at 98. After an independent review of the evidence the court concluded that the admission of the evidence was not harmless error since it supported the testimony of Parsons and Powell's accomplices. Id., at 99.

B

Respondent David Rice was convicted of murder in April 1971 after trial in a Nebraska state court. At 2:05 a.m. on August 17, 1970, Omaha police received a telephone call that a woman had been heard screaming at 2867 Ohio Street. As one of the officers sent to that address examined a suitcase lying in the doorway, it exploded, killing him instantly. By August 22 the investigation of the murder centered on Duane Peak, a 15-year-old member of the National Committee to Combat Fascism ("NCCF"), and that afternoon a warrant was issued for Peak's arrest. The investigation also focused on other known members of the NCCF, including Rice, some of whom were believed to be planning to kill Peak before he could incriminate them. In their search for Peak, the police went to Rice's home at 10:30 that night and found lights and a television on, but there was no response to their repeated knocking. While some officers remained to watch the premises, a warrant was obtained to search for explosives and illegal weapons believed to be in Rice's possession. Peak was not in the house, but upon entering the police discovered, in plain view, dynamite, blasting caps, and other materials useful in the construction of explosive devices. Peak subsequently was arrested, and on August 27, Rice voluntarily surrendered. The clothes Rice was wearing at that time were subjected to chemical analysis, disclosing dynamite particles.

Rice was tried for first-degree murder in the District Court of Douglas County. At trial Peak admitted planting the suitcase and making the telephone call, and implicated Rice in the bombing plot. As corroborative evidence the State introduced items seized during the search, as well as the results of the chemical analysis of Rice's clothing. The court denied Rice's motion to suppress this evidence. On appeal the Supreme Court of Nebraska affirmed the conviction, holding that the search of Rice's home had been pursuant to a valid search warrant. State v Rice, 188 Neb 728, 199 NW2d 480 (1972).

In September 1972 Rice filed a petition for a writ of habeas corpus in the United States District Court for Nebraska. Rice's sole contention was that his incarceration was unlawful because the evidence underlying his conviction had been discovered as the result of an illegal search of his home. The District Court concluded that the search warrant was invalid, as the supporting affidavit was defective under Spinelli v United States, 393 US 410, 21 L Ed 2d 637, 89 S Ct 584 (1969), and Aguilar v Texas, 378 US 108, 12 L Ed 2d 723, 84 S Ct 1509 (1964). 388 F Supp 185, 190–194 (1974). The court also rejected the State's contention that even if the warrant was invalid the search was justified because of the valid arrest warrant for Peak and because of the exigent circumstances of the situation—danger to Peak and search for bombs and explosives believed in possession of NCCF. The court reasoned that the arrest warrant did not justify the entry as the police lacked probable cause to believe Peak was in the house, and further concluded that the circumstances were not sufficiently exigent to justify an immediate warrantless search. Id., at 194–202. The Court of Appeals for the Eighth Circuit affirmed, substantially for the reasons stated by the District Court. 513 F2d 1280 (1975).

Petitioners Stone and Wolff, the wardens of the respective state prisons where Powell and Rice are incarcerated, petitioned for review of these decisions, raising questions concerning the scope of federal habeas corpus and the role of the exclusionary rule upon collateral review of cases involving Fourth Amendment claims. We granted their petitions for certiorari. 422 US 1055, 45 L Ed 2d 707, 95 S Ct 2676 (1975). We now reverse.

II

The authority of federal courts to issue the writ of habeas corpus ad subjiciendum was included in the first grant of federal court jurisdiction, made by the Judiciary Act of 1789, c 20 § 14, 1 Stat 81, with the limitation that the writ extend only to prisoners held in custody by the United States. The original statutory authorization did not define the substantive reach of the writ. It merely stated that the courts of the United States "shall have power to issue writs of... habeas corpus...." Ibid. The courts defined the scope of the writ in accordance with the common law and limited it to an inquiry as to the jurisdiction of the sentencing tribunal. See, e.g., Ex parte Watkins, 28 US (3 Pet) 193, 7 L Ed 650 (1830) (MARSHALL, C. J.).

In 1867 the writ was extended to state prisoners. Act of Feb. 5, 1867, c 28, § 1, 14 Stat 385. Under the 1867 Act federal courts were authorized to give relief in "all cases where any person may be restrained of his or her liberty in violation of the constitution, or of any treaty or law of the United States..." But the limitation of federal habeas corpus jurisdiction to consideration of the jurisdiction of the sentencing court persisted. See, e.g., In re Wood, 140 US 278, 35 L Ed 505, 11 S Ct 738 (1891); In re Rahrer, 140 US 545, 35 L Ed 572, 11 S Ct 865 (1891); Andrews v Swartz, 156 US 272, 39 L Ed 422, 15 S Ct 389 (1895); Bergemann v Backer, 157 US 655, 39 L Ed 845, 15 S Ct 727 (1895); Pettibone v Nichols, 203 US 192, 51 L Ed 148, 27 S Ct 111 (1906). And, although the concept of "jurisdiction" was subjected to considerable strain as the substantive scope of the writ was expanded, this expansion was limited to only a few classes of cases until Frank v Mangum, 237 US 309, 59 L Ed 969, 35 S Ct 582, in 1915. In Frank, the prisoner had claimed in the state courts that the proceedings which resulted in his conviction for murder had been dominated by a mob. After the State Supreme Court rejected his contentions, Frank unsuccessfully sought habeas corpus relief in the Federal District Court. This Court affirmed the denial of relief because Frank's federal claims had been considered by a competent and unbiased state tribunal. The Court recognized, however, that if a habeas corpus court found that the State had failed to provide adequate "corrective process" for the full and fair litigation of federal claims, whether or not "jurisdictional," the court could inquire into the merits to determine whether a detention was lawful. Id., at 333–336. 59 L Ed 969, 35 S Ct 582.

In the landmark decision in Brown v Allen, 344 US 443, 482–487, 97 L Ed 469, 73 S Ct 397 (1953), the scope of the writ was expanded still further. In that case and its companion case, Daniels v Allen, state prisoners applied for federal habeas corpus relief claiming that the trial courts had erred in failing to quash their indictments due to alleged discrimination in the selection of grand jurors and in ruling certain confessions admissible. In Brown, the highest court of the State had rejected these claims on direct appeal, State v Brown, 233 NC 202, 63 SE2d 99, and this Court had denied certiorari, 341 US 943, 95 L Ed 1369, 71 S Ct 997 (1951). Despite the apparent adequacy of the state corrective process, the Court reviewed the denial of the writ of habeas corpus and held that Brown was entitled to a full reconsideration of these constitutional claims, including, if appropriate, a hearing in the Federal District Court. In Daniels, however, the state supreme court on direct review had refused to consider the appeal because the papers were filed out of time. This Court held that since the state court judgment rested on a reasonable application of the State's legitimate procedural rules, a ground that would have barred direct review of his federal claims by this Court, the District Court lacked authority to grant habeas corpus relief. See 344 US at 458, 486, 97 L Ed 469, 73 S Ct 397.

This final barrier to broad collateral re-examination of state criminal convictions in federal habeas corpus proceedings was removed in Fay v Noia, 372 US 391, 9 L Ed 2d 837, 83 S Ct 822, 24 Ohio Ops 2d 12 (1963). Noia and two codefendants had been convicted of felony murder. The sole evidence against each defendant was a signed confession. Noia's codefendants, but not Noia himself, appealed their convictions. Although their appeals were unsuccessful, in subsequent state proceedings they were able to establish that their confessions had been coerced and their convictions therefore procured in violation of the Constitution. In a subsequent federal habeas corpus proceeding, it was stipulated that Noia's confession also had been coerced, but the District Court followed Daniels in holding that Noia's failure to appeal barred habeas corpus review. See 183 F Supp 222, 225 (1960). The Court of Appeals reversed, ordering that Noia's conviction be set aside and that he be released from custody or a new trial be granted. This Court affirmed the grant of the writ, narrowly restricting the circumstances in which a federal court may refuse to consider the merits of federal constitutional claims.

During the period in which the substantive scope of the writ was expanded, the Court did not consider whether exceptions to full review might exist with respect to particular categories of constitutional claims. Prior to the Court's decision in Kaufman v United States, 394 US 217, 22 L Ed 2d 227, 89 S Ct 1068 (1969), however, a substantial majority of the federal courts of appeals had concluded that collateral review of search-and-seizure claims was inappropriate on motions filed by federal prisoners under 28 USC § 2255 [28 USCS § 2255], the modern post-conviction procedure available to federal prisoners in lieu of habeas corpus. The primary rationale advanced in support of those decisions was that Fourth Amendment violations are different in kind from denials of Fifth or Sixth Amendment rights in that claims of illegal search and seizure do not "impugn the integrity of the fact-finding process or challenge evidence as inherently unreliable; rather, the exclusion of illegally seized evidence is simply a prophylactic device intended generally to deter Fourth Amendment violations by law enforcement officers." Id., at 224, 22 L Ed 2d 227, 89 S Ct 1068. See Thornton v United States, 125 US App DC 114, 368 F2d 822 (1966).

Kaufman rejected this rationale and held that search-and-seizure claims are cognizable in § 2255 proceedings. The Court noted that "the federal habeas remedy extends to state prisoners alleging that unconstitutionally obtained evidence was admitted against them at trial," 394 US, at 225, 22 L Ed 2d 227, 89 S Ct 1068, citing, e.g., Mancusi v DeForte, 392 US 364, 20 L Ed 2d 1154, 88 S Ct 2120 (1968); Carafas v LaVallee, 391 US 234, 20 L Ed 2d 554, 88 S Ct 1556 (1968), and concluded, as a matter of statutory construction, that there was no basis for restricting "access by federal prisoners with illegal search-and-seizure claims to federal collateral remedies, while placing no similar restriction on access by state prisoners," 394 US, at 226, 22 L Ed 2d 227, 89 S Ct 1068. Although in recent years the view has been expressed that the Court should re-examine the substantive scope of federal habeas jurisdiction and limit collateral review of search-and-seizure claims "solely to the question of whether the petitioner was provided with a fair opportunity to raise and have adjudicated the question in state courts," Schneckloth v Bustamonte, 412 US 218, 250, 36 L Ed 2d 854, 93 S Ct 2041 (1973) (POWELL, J., concurring), the Court, without discussion or consideration of the issue, has continued to accept jurisdiction in cases raising such claims. See Lefkowitz v Newsome, 420 US 283, 43 L Ed 2d 196, 95 S Ct 886 (1975); Cady v Dombrowski, 413 US 433, 37 L Ed 2d 706, 93 S Ct 2523 (1973); Cardwell v Lewis, 417 US 583, 41 L Ed 2d 325, 94 S Ct 2464, 69 Ohio Ops 2d 69 (1974) (plurality opinion).

The discussion in Kaufman of the scope of federal habeas corpus rests on the view that the effectuation of the Fourth Amendment, as applied to the States through the Fourteenth Amendment, requires the granting of habeas corpus relief when a prisoner has been convicted in state court on the basis of evidence obtained in an illegal search or seizure since those Amendments were held in Mapp v Ohio, 367 US 643, 6 L Ed 2d 1081, 81 S Ct 1684, 84 ALR2d 933, 16 Ohio Ops 2d 384, 86 Ohio L Abs 513 (1961), to require exclusion of such evidence at trial and reversal of conviction upon direct review. Until this case we have not had occasion fully to consider the validity of this view. See, e.g., Schneckloth v Bustamonte, supra, at 249 n 38; 36 L Ed 2d 854, 93 S Ct 2041; Cardwell v Lewis, supra, at 596 and n 12, 41 L Ed 2d 325, 94 S Ct 2464, 69 Ohio Ops 2d 69. Upon examination, we conclude, in light of the nature and purpose of the Fourth Amendment exclusionary rule, that this view is unjustified. We hold, therefore, that where the State has provided an opportunity for full and fair litigation of a Fourth Amendment claim, the Constitution does not require that a state prisoner be granted federal habeas corpus relief on the ground that evidence obtained in an unconstitutional search or seizure was introduced at his trial.

III

The Fourth Amendment assures the "right of the people to be secure in their persons, houses, papers, and effects, against unreasonable searches and seizures." The Amendment was primarily a reaction to the evils associated with the use of the general warrant in England and the writs of assistance in the Colonies, Stanford v Texas, 379 US 476, 481–485, 13 L Ed 2d 431, 85 S Ct 506 (1965); Frank v Maryland, 359 US 360, 363–365, 3 L Ed 2d 877, 79 S Ct 804 (1959), and was intended to protect the "sanctity of a man's home and the privacies of life," Boyd v United States, 116 US 616, 630, 29 L Ed 746, 6 S Ct 524 (1886), from searches under unchecked general authority.

The exclusionary rule was a judicially created means of effectuating the rights secured by the Fourth Amendment. Prior to the Court's decisions in Weeks v United States, 232 US 383, 58 L Ed 652, 34 S Ct 341 (1914), and Gouled v United States, 255 US 298, 65 L Ed 647, 41 S Ct 261 (1921), there existed no barrier to the introduction in criminal trials of evidence obtained in violation of the Amendment. See Adams v New York, 192 US 585, 48 L Ed 575, 24 S Ct 372 (1904). In Weeks the Court held that the defendant could petition before trial for the return of property secured through an illegal search or seizure conducted by federal authorities. In Gouled the Court held broadly that such evidence could not be introduced in a federal prosecution. See Warden v Hayden, 387 US 294, 304–305, 18 L Ed 2d 782, 87 S Ct 1642 (1967). See also Silverthorne Lumber Co. v United States, 251 US 385, 64 L Ed 319, 40 S Ct 182, 24 ALR 1426 (1920) (fruits of illegally seized evidence). Thirty-five years after Weeks the Court held in Wolf v Colorado, 338 US 25, 93 L Ed 1782, 69 S Ct 1359 (1949), that the right to be free from arbitrary intrusion by the police that is protected by the Fourth Amendment is "implicit in 'the concept of ordered liberty' and as such enforceable against the States through the [Fourteenth Amendment] Due Process Clause." Id., at 27–28, 93 L Ed 1782, 69 S Ct 1359. The Court concluded, however, that the Weeks exclusionary rule would not be imposed upon the States as "an essential ingredient of that right." Id., at 29, 93 L Ed 1782, 69 S Ct 1359. The full force of Wolf was eroded in subsequent decisions, see Elkins v United States, 364 US 206, 4 L Ed 1669, 80 S Ct 1437 (1960); Rea v United States, 350 US 214, 100 L Ed 233, 76 S Ct 292 (1956), and a little more than a decade later the exclusionary rule was held applicable to the States in Mapp v Ohio, 367 US 643, 6 L Ed 2d 1081, 81 S Ct 1684, 84 ALR2d 933, 16 Ohio Ops 2d 384, 86 Ohio L Abs 513 (1961).

Decisions prior to Mapp advanced two principal reasons for application of the rule in federal trials. The Court in Elkins, for example, in the context of its special supervisory role over the lower federal courts, referred to the "imperative of judicial integrity," suggesting that exclusion of illegally seized evidence prevents contamination of the judicial process. 364 US, at 222, 4 L Ed 2d 1669, 80 S Ct 1437. But even in that context a more pragmatic ground was emphasized:

> "The rule is calculated to prevent, not to repair. Its purpose is to deter—to compel respect for the constitutional guaranty in the only effectively available way—by removing the incentive to disregard it." Id., at 217, 4 L Ed 2d 1669, 80 S Ct 1437.

The Mapp majority justified the application of the rule to the States on several grounds, but relied principally upon the belief that exclusion would deter future unlawful police conduct. 367 US, at 658, 6 L Ed 2d 1081, 81 S Ct 1684, 84 ALR2d 933, 16 Ohio Ops 2d 384, 86 Ohio L Abs 513.

Although our decisions often have alluded to the "imperative of judicial integrity," e.g., United States v Peltier, 422 US 531, 536–539, 45 L Ed 2d 374, 95 S Ct 2313 (1975), they demonstrate the limited role of this justification in the determination whether to apply the rule in a particular context. Logically extended this justification would require that courts exclude unconstitutionally seized evidence despite lack of objection by the defendant, or even over his assent. Cf. Henry v Mississippi, 379 US 443, 13 L Ed 2d 408, 85 S Ct 564 (1965). It also would require abandonment of the standing limitations on who may object to the introduction of unconstitutionally seized evidence, Alderman v United States, 394 US 165, 22 L Ed 2d 176, 89 S Ct 961 (1969), and retreat from the proposition that judicial proceedings need not abate when the defendant's person is unconstitutionally seized, Gerstein v Pugh, 420 US 103, 119, 43 L Ed 2d 54, 95 S Ct 854 (1975); Frisbie v Collins, 342 US 519, 96 L Ed 541, 72 S Ct 509 (1952). Similarly, the interest in promoting judicial integrity does not prevent the use of illegally seized evidence in grand jury proceedings. United States v Calandra, 414 US 338, 38 L Ed 2d 561, 94 S Ct 613, 66 Ohio Ops 2d 320 (1974). Nor does it require that the trial court exclude such evidence from use for impeachment of a defendant, even though its introduction is certain to result in convictions in some cases. Walder v United States, 347 US 62, 98 L Ed 503, 74 S Ct 354 (1954). The teaching of these cases is clear. While courts, of course, must ever be concerned with preserving the integrity of the judicial process, this concern has limited force as a justification for the exclusion of highly probative evidence. The force of this justification becomes minimal where federal habeas corpus relief is sought by a prisoner who previously has been afforded the opportunity for full and fair consideration of his search-and-seizure claim at trial and on direct review.

The primary justification for the exclusionary rule then is the deterrence of police conduct that violates Fourth Amendment rights. Post-Mapp decisions have established that the rule is not a personal constitutional right. It is not calculated to redress the injury to the privacy of the victim of the search or seizure, for any "[r]eparation comes too late." Linkletter v Walker, 381 US 618, 637, 14 L Ed 2d 601, 85 S Ct 1731, 5 Ohio Misc 49, 33 Ohio Ops 2d 118 (1965). Instead,

> "the rule is a judicially created remedy designed to safeguard Fourth Amendment rights generally through its deterrent effect...." United States v Calandra, supra, at 348, 38 L Ed 2d 561, 94 S Ct 613, 66 Ohio Ops 2d 320.

Accord, United States v Peltier, supra, at 538–539, 45 L Ed 2d 374, 95 S Ct 2313; Terry v Ohio, 392 US 1, 28–29, 20 L Ed 2d 889, 88 S Ct 1868 (1968); Linkletter v Walker, 381 US at 636–637, 14 L Ed 2d 601, 85 S Ct 1731, 5 Ohio Misc 49, 33 Ohio Ops 2d 118; Tehan v Shott, 382 US 406, 416, 15 L Ed 2d 453, 86 S Ct 459 (1966).

Mapp involved the enforcement of the exclusionary rule at state trials and on direct review. The decision in Kaufman, as noted above, is premised on the view that implementation of the Fourth Amendment also requires the consideration of search-and-seizure claims upon collateral review of state convictions. But despite the broad deterrent purpose of the exclusionary rule, it has never been interpreted to proscribe the introduction of illegally seized evidence in all proceedings or against all persons. As in the case of any remedial device, "the application of the rule has been restricted to those areas where its remedial objectives are thought most efficaciously served." United States v Calandra, supra, at 348, 38 L Ed 2d 561, 94 S Ct 613, 66 Ohio Ops 2d 320. Thus, our refusal to extend the exclusionary rule to grand jury proceedings was based on a balancing of the potential injury to the historic role and function of the grand jury by such extension against the potential contribution to the effectuation of the Fourth Amendment through deterrence of police misconduct:

> "Any incremental deterrent effect which might be achieved by extending the rule to grand jury proceedings is uncertain at best. Whatever deterrence of police misconduct may result from the exclusion of illegally seized evidence from criminal trials, it is unrealistic to assume that the application of the rule to grand jury proceedings would significantly further that goal. Such an extension would deter only police investigation consciously directed toward the discovery of evidence solely for use in a grand jury investigation. . . .
>
> "We therefore decline to embrace a view that would achieve a speculative and undoubtedly minimal advance in the deterrence of police misconduct at the expense of substantially impeding the role of the grand jury." Id., at 351, 38 L Ed 2d 561, 94 S Ct 613, 66 Ohio Ops 2d 320 (footnote omitted).

The same pragmatic analysis of the exclusionary rule's usefulness in a particular context was evident earlier in Walder v United States, supra, where the Court permitted the Government to use unlawfully seized evidence to impeach the credibility of a defendant who had testified broadly in his own defense. The Court held, in effect, that the interests safeguarded by the exclusionary rule in that context were outweighed by the need to prevent perjury and to assure the integrity of the trial process. The judgment in Walder revealed most clearly that the policies behind the exclusionary rule are not absolute. Rather, they must be evaluated in light of competing policies. In that case, the public interest in determination of truth at trial was deemed to outweigh the incremental contribution that might have been made to the protection of Fourth Amendment values by application of the rule.

The balancing process at work in these cases also finds expression in the standing requirement. Standing to invoke the exclusionary rule has been found to exist only when the Government attempts to use illegally obtained evidence to incriminate the victim of the illegal search. Brown v United States, 411 US 223, 36

L Ed 2d 208, 93 S Ct 1565 (1973); Alderman v United States, 394 US 165, 22 L Ed 2d 176, 89 S Ct 961; Wong Sun v United States, 371 US 471, 491–492, 9 L Ed 2d 441, 83 S Ct 407 (1963). See Jones v United States, 362 US 257, 261, 4 L Ed 2d 697, 80 S Ct 725, 78 ALR2d 233 (1960). The standing requirement is premised on the view that the "additional benefits of extending the rule" to defendants other than the victim of the search or seizure are outweighed by the "further encroachment upon the public interest in prosecuting those accused of crime and having them acquitted or convicted on the basis of all the evidence which exposes the truth." Alderman v United States, supra, at 174–175, 22 L Ed 2d 176, 89 S Ct 961.

IV

We turn now to the specific question presented by these cases. Respondents allege violations of Fourth Amendment rights guaranteed them through the Fourteenth Amendment. The question is whether state prisoners—who have been afforded the opportunity for full and fair consideration of their reliance upon the exclusionary rule with respect to seized evidence by the state courts at trial and on direct review—may invoke their claim again on federal habeas corpus review. The answer is to be found by weighing the utility of the exclusionary rule against the costs of extending it to collateral review of Fourth Amendment claims.

The costs of applying the exclusionary rule even at trial and on direct review are well known: the focus of the trial, and the attention of the participants therein, is diverted from the ultimate question of guilt or innocence that should be the central concern in a criminal proceeding. Moreover, the physical evidence sought to be excluded is typically reliable and often the most probative information bearing on the guilt or innocence of the defendant. As Mr. Justice Black emphasized in his dissent in Kaufman:

> "A claim of illegal search and seizure under the Fourth Amendment is crucially different from many other constitutional rights; ordinarily the evidence seized can in no way have been rendered untrustworthy by the means of its seizure and indeed often this evidence alone establishes beyond virtually any shadow of a doubt that the defendant is guilty." 394 US at 237, 22 L Ed 2d 227, 89 S Ct 1068.

Application of the rule thus deflects the truthfinding process and often frees the guilty. The disparity in particular cases between the error committed by the police officer and the windfall afforded a guilty defendant by application of the rule is contrary to the idea of proportionality that is essential to the concept of justice. Thus, although the rule is thought to deter unlawful police activity in part through the nurturing of respect for Fourth Amendment values, if applied indiscriminately it may well have the opposite effect of generating disrespect for the law and administration of justice. These long-recognized costs of the rule persist when a criminal conviction is sought to be overturned on collateral review on the ground that a search-and-seizure claim was erroneously rejected by two or more tiers of state courts.

Evidence obtained by police officers in violation of the Fourth Amendment is excluded at trial in the hope that the frequency of future violations will decrease. Despite the absence of supportive empirical evidence, we have assumed that the immediate effect of exclusion will be to discourage law enforcement officials from violating the Fourth Amendment by removing the incentive to disregard it. More importantly, over the long term, this demonstration that our society attaches serious consequences to violation of constitutional rights is thought to encourage those who formulate law enforcement policies, and the officers who implement them, to incorporate Fourth Amendment ideals into their value system.

We adhere to the view that these considerations support the implementation of the exclusionary rule at trial and its enforcement on direct appeal of state court convictions. But the additional contribution, if any, of the consideration of search-and-seizure claims of state prisoners on collateral review is small in relation to the costs. To be sure, each case in which such claim is considered may add marginally to an awareness of the values protected by the Fourth Amendment. There is no reason to believe, however, that the overall educative effect of the exclusionary rule would be appreciably diminished if search-and-seizure claims could not be raised in federal habeas corpus review of state convictions. Nor is there reason to assume that any specific disincentive already created by the risk of exclusion of evidence at trial or the reversal of convictions on direct review would be enhanced if there were the further risk that a conviction obtained in state court and affirmed on direct review might be overturned in collateral proceedings often occurring years after the incarceration of the defendant. The view that the deterrence of Fourth Amendment violations would be furthered rests on the dubious assumption that law enforcement authorities would fear that federal habeas review might reveal flaws in a search or seizure that went undetected at trial and on appeal. Even if one rationally could assume that some additional incremental effect would be present in isolated cases, the resulting advance of the legitimate goal of furthering Fourth Amendment rights would be outweighed by the acknowledged costs to other values vital to a rational system of criminal justice.

In sum, we conclude that where the State has provided an opportunity for full and fair litigation of a Fourth Amendment claim, a state prisoner may not be granted federal habeas corpus relief on the ground that evidence obtained in an unconstitutional search or seizure was introduced at his trial. In this context the contribution of the exclusionary rule, if any, to the effectuation of the Fourth Amendment is minimal and the substantial societal costs of application of the rule persist with special force.

Accordingly, the judgments of the Court of Appeals are

Reversed.

UNITED STATES, Petitioner *v.* Rosa Elvira MONTOYA DE HERNANDEZ.

—U.S.—, 105 S.Ct. 3304, —L Ed2—(1985)

Justice REHNQUIST delivered the opinion of the Court.

Respondent Rosa Elvira Montoya de Hernandez was detained by customs officials upon her arrival at the Los Angeles airport on a flight from Bogota, Colombia. She was found to be smuggling 88 cocaine-filled balloons in her alimentary canal, and was convicted after a bench trial of various federal narcotics offenses. A divided panel of the United States Court of Appeals for the Ninth Circuit reversed her convictions, holding that her detention violated the Fourth Amendment to the United States Constitution because the customs inspectors did not have a "clear indication" of alimentary canal smuggling at the time she was detained. 731 F.2d 1369 (1984). Because of a conflict in the decisions of the Courts of Appeals on this question and the importance of its resolution to the enforcement of customs laws, we granted certiorari. 469 U.S.—, 105 S.Ct. 954, 83 L.Ed.2d 961. We now reverse.

Respondent arrived at Los Angeles International Airport shortly after midnight, March 5, 1983, on Avianca Flight 080, a direct 10-hour flight from Bogota, Colombia. Her visa was in order so she was passed through Immigration and proceeded to the customs desk. At the customs desk she encountered Customs Inspector Talamantes, who reviewed her documents and noticed from her passport that she had made at least eight recent trips to either Miami or Los Angeles. Talamantes referred respondent to a secondary customs' desk for further questioning. At this desk Talamantes and another inspector asked respondent general questions concerning herself and the purpose of her trip. Respondent revealed that she spoke no English and had no family or friends in the United States. She explained in Spanish that she had come to the United States to purchase goods for her husband's store in Bogota. The customs inspectors recognized Bogota as a "source city" for narcotics. Respondent possessed $5,000 in cash, mostly $50 bills, but had no billfold. She indicated to the inspectors that she had no appointments with merchandise vendors, but planned to ride around Los Angeles in taxicabs visiting retail stores such as J.C. Penney and K–Mart in order to buy goods for her husband's store with the $5,000.

Respondent admitted that she had no hotel reservations, but stated that she planned to stay at a Holiday Inn. Respondent could not recall how her airline ticket was purchased. When the inspectors opened respondent's one small valise they found about four changes of "cold weather" clothing. Respondent had no shoes other than the high-heeled pair she was wearing. Although respondent possessed no checks, waybills, credit cards, or letters of credit, she did produce a Colombian business card and a number of old receipts, waybills, and fabric swatches displayed in a photo album.

At this point Talamantes and the other inspector suspected that respondent was a "balloon swallower," one who attempts to smuggle narcotics into this country hidden in her alimentary canal. Over the years Inspector Talamantes had apprehended dozens of alimentary canal smugglers arriving on Avianca Flight 080. See App. 42; *United States v. Mendez-Jimenez,* 709 F.2d 1300, 1301 (1983).

The inspectors requested a female customs inspector to take respondent to a private area and conduct a patdown and strip search. During the search the female inspector felt respondent's abdomen area and noticed a firm fullness, as if respondent were wearing a girdle. The search revealed no contraband but the inspector noticed that respondent was wearing two pair of elastic underpants with a paper towel lining the crotch area.

When respondent returned to the customs area and the female inspector reported her discoveries, the inspector in charge told respondent that he suspected she was smuggling drugs in her alimentary canal. Respondent agreed to the inspector's request that she be x rayed at a hospital but in answer to the inspector's query stated that she was pregnant. She agreed to a pregnancy test before the x ray. Respondent withdrew the consent for an x ray when she learned that she would have to be handcuffed en route to the hospital. The inspector then gave respondent the option of returning to Colombia on the next available flight, agreeing to an x ray, or remaining in detention until she produced a monitored bowel movement that would confirm or rebut the inspectors' suspicions. Respondent chose the first option and was placed in a customs' office under observation. She was told that if she went to the toilet she would have to use a wastebasket in the women's restroom, in order that female customs inspectors could inspect her stool for balloons or capsules carrying narcotics. The inspectors refused respondent's request to place a telephone call.

Respondent sat in the customs office, under observation, for the remainder of the night. During the night customs officials attempted to place respondent on a Mexican airline that was flying to Bogota via Mexico City in the morning. The airline refused to transport respondent because she lacked a Mexican visa necessary to land in Mexico City. Respondent was not permitted to leave, and was informed that she would be detained until she agreed to an x ray or her bowels moved. She remained detained in the customs office under observation, for most of the time curled up in a chair leaning to one side. She refused all offers of food and drink, and refused to use the toilet facilities. The Court of Appeals noted that she exhibited symptoms of discomfort consistent with "heroic efforts to resist the usual calls of nature." 731 F.2d, at 1371.

At the shift change at 4:00 p.m. the next afternoon, almost 16 hours after her flight had landed, respondent still had not defecated or urinated or partaken of food or drink. At that time customs officials sought a court order authorizing a pregnancy test, an x ray, and a rectal examination. The Federal Magistrate issued an order just before midnight that evening, which authorized a rectal examination and involuntary x ray, provided that the physician in charge considered respondent's claim of pregnancy. Respondent was taken to a hospital and given a pregnancy test, which later turned out to be negative. Before the results of the pregnancy test were known, a physician conducted a rectal examination and removed from respondent's rectum a balloon containing a foreign substance. Respondent was then placed formally under arrest. By 4:10 a.m. respondent had passed 6 similar balloons; over the next 4 days she passed 88 balloons containing a total of 528 grams of 80% pure cocaine hydrochloride.

After a suppression hearing the District Court admitted the cocaine in evidence against respondent. She was convicted of possession of cocaine with intent to distribute, 21 U.S.C. § 841(a)(1) and unlawful importation of cocaine, 21 U.S.C. §§ 952(a), 960(a).

A divided panel of the United States Court of Appeals for the Ninth Circuit reversed respondent's convictions. The court noted that customs inspectors had a "justifiably high level of official skepticism" about respondent's good motives, but the inspectors decided to let nature take its course rather than seek an immediate magistrate's warrant for an x ray. 731 F.2d, at 1371. Such a magistrate's warrant required a "clear indication" or "plain suggestion" that the traveler was an alimentary canal smuggler under previous decisions of the Court of Appeals. See *United States v. Quintero-Castro,* 705 F.2d 1099 (CA9 1983); *United States v. Mendez-Jimenez,* 709 F.2d 1300, 1302 (CA9 1983); but cf. *South Dakota v. Opperman,* 428 U.S. 367, 370, n. 5, 96 S.Ct. 3092, 3096, 3097, n. 5, 49 L.Ed.2d 1000 (1976). The court applied this required level of suspicion to respondent's case. The court questioned the "humanity" of the inspectors' decision to hold respondent until her bowels moved, knowing that she would suffer "many hours of humiliating discomfort" if she chose not to submit to the x-ray examination. The court concluded that under a "clear indication" standard "the evidence available to the customs officers when they decided to hold [respondent] for continued observation was insufficient to support the 16-hour detention." 731 F.2d, at 1373.

The government contends that the customs inspectors reasonably suspected that respondent was an alimentary canal smuggler, and this suspicion was sufficient to justify the detention. In support of the judgment below respondent argues, *inter alia,* that reasonable suspicion would not support respondent's detention, and in any event the inspectors did not reasonably suspect that respondent was carrying narcotics internally.

[1, 2] The Fourth Amendment commands that searches and seizures be reasonable. What is reasonable depends upon all of the circumstances surrounding the search or seizure and the nature of the search or seizure itself. *New Jersey v. T.L.O.,* 469 U.S.—, — – —, 105 S.Ct. 733, 741–744, 83 L.Ed.2d 720 (1985). The permissibility of a particular law enforcement practice is judged by "balancing its intrusion on the individual's Fourth Amendment interests against its promotion of legitimate governmental interests." *United States v. Villamonte-Marquez,* 462 U.S. 579, ——, 103 S.Ct. 2573, 2579, 77 L.Ed.2d 22 (1983); *Delaware v. Prouse,* 440 U.S. 648, 654, 99 S.Ct. 1391, 1396, 59 L.Ed.2d 660 (1979); *Camara v. Municipal Court,* 387 U.S. 523, 87 S.Ct. 1727, 18 L.Ed.2d 930 (1967).

Here the seizure of respondent took place at the international border. Since the founding of our Republic, Congress has granted the Executive plenary authority to conduct routine searches and seizures at the border, without probable cause or a warrant, in order to regulate the collection of duties and to prevent the introduction of contraband into this country. See *United States v. Ramsey,* 431 U.S. 606, 616–617, 97 S.Ct. 1972, 1978–1979, 52 L.Ed.2d 617 (1977), citing Act of July 31, 1789, ch. 5, 1 Stat. 29. This Court has long recognized Congress' power to police entrants at the border. See *Boyd v. United States,* 116 U.S. 616, 623, 6 S.Ct. 524, 528, 29 L.Ed. 746 (1886). As we stated recently:

> " 'Import restrictions and searches of persons or packages at the national border rest on different considerations and different rules of constitutional law from domestic regulations. The Constitution gives Congress broad comprehensive powers "[t]o regulate Commerce with foreign Nations," Art. I, § 8, cl. 3. Historically such broad powers have been necessary to prevent smuggling and to prevent prohibited articles from entry.' " *Ramsey, supra,* 431 U.S. at 618–619, 97 S.Ct., at 1979–1978, quoting *United States v. 12 200 Ft. Reels of Film,* 413 U.S. 123, 125, 93 S.Ct. 2665, 2667, 37 L.Ed.2d 500 (1973).

[3–4] Consistently, therefore, with Congress' power to protect the Nation by stopping and examining persons entering this country, the Fourth Amendment's balance of reasonableness is qualitatively different at the international border than in the interior. Routine searches of the persons and effects of entrants are not subject to any requirement of reasonable suspicion, probable cause, or warrant, and first-class mail may be opened without a warrant on less than probable cause, *Ramsey, supra.* Automotive travelers may be stopped at fixed check points near the border without individualized suspicion even if the stop is based largely on ethnicity, *United States v. Martinez-Fuerte,* 428 U.S. 543, 562–563, 96 S.Ct. 3074, 3085, 49 L.Ed.2d 1116 (1976), and boats on inland waters with ready access to the sea may be hailed and boarded with no suspicion whatever. *United States v. Villamonte-Marquez, supra,* 462 U.S. at ——, 103 S.Ct., at 2582.

These cases reflect longstanding concern for the protection of the integrity of the border. This concern is, if anything, heightened by the veritable national crisis in law enforcement caused by smuggling of illicit narcotics, see *United States v. Mendenhall,* 446 U.S. 544, 561, 100 S.Ct. 1870, 1880, 64 L.Ed.2d 497 (1980) (POWELL, J., concurring), and in particular by the increasing utilization of alimentary canal smuggling. This desperate practice appears to be a relatively recent addition to the smugglers' repertoire of deceptive practices, and it also appears to be exceedingly difficult to detect. Congress had recognized these difficulties. Title 19 U.S.C. § 1582 provides that "all persons coming into the United States from foreign countries shall be liable to detention and search authorized . . . [by customs regulations]." Customs agents may "stop, search, and examine" any "vehicle, beast or person" upon which an officer suspects there is contraband or "merchandise which is subject to duty." § 482; see also §§ 1467, 1481; 19 CFR §§ 162.6, 162.7 (1984).

[5, 6] Balanced against the sovereign's interests at the border are the Fourth Amendment rights of respondent. Having presented herself at the border for admission, and having subjected herself to the criminal enforcement powers of the Federal Government, 19 U.S.C. § 482, respondent was entitled to be free from unreasonable search and seizure. But not only is the expectation of privacy less at the border than in the interior, see, *e.g., Carroll v. United States,* 267 U.S. 132, 154, 45 S.Ct. 280, 285, 69 L.Ed. 543 (1925); cf. *Florida v. Royer,*

460 U.S. 491, 515, 103 S.Ct. 1319, 1333, 75 L.Ed.2d 229 (1983) (BLACKMUN, J., dissenting), but the Fourth Amendment balance between the interests of the Government and the privacy right of the individual is struck much more favorably to the Government at the border. *Ante,* at 3308–3309.

We have not previously decided what level of suspicion would justify a seizure of an incoming traveler for purposes other than a routine border search. Cf. *Ramsey, supra,* 431 U.S., at 618, n. 13, 97 S.Ct., at 1979, n. 13. The Court of Appeals held that the initial detention of respondent was permissible only if the inspectors possessed a "clear indication" of alimentary canal smuggling. 731 F.2d, at 1372, citing *Quintero-Castro,* 705 F.2d 1099 (1983); cf. *Mendez-Jimenez,* 709 F.2d 1300 (1983). This "clear indication" language comes from our opinion in *Schmerber v. California,* 384 U.S. 757, 86 S.Ct. 1826, 16 L.Ed.2d 908 (1966), but we think that the Court of Appeals misapprehended the significance of that phrase in the context in which it was used in *Schmerber.* The Court of Appeals for the Ninth Circuit viewed "clear indication" as an intermediate standard between "reasonable suspicion" and "probable cause." See *Mendez-Jimenez, supra,* at 1302. But we think that the words in *Schmerber* were used to indicate the necessity for particularized suspicion that the evidence sought might be found within the body of the individual, rather than as enunciating still a third Fourth Amendment threshold between "reasonable suspicion" and "probable cause."

No other court, including this one, has ever adopted *Schmerber*'s "clear indication" language as a Fourth Amendment standard. See, *e.g., Winston v. Lee,* 470 U.S.——, ——, 105 S.Ct. 1611, 1616–1617, 84 L.Ed.2d 662 (1985) (surgical removal of bullet for evidence). Indeed, another Circuit Court of Appeals, faced with facts almost identical to this case, has adopted a less strict standard based upon reasonable suspicion. See *United States v. Mosquera-Ramirez,* 729 F.2d 1352, 1355 (CA11 1984). We do not think that the Fourth Amendment's emphasis upon reasonableness is consistent with the creation of a third verbal standard in addition to "reasonable suspicion" and "probable cause"; we are dealing with a constitutional requirement of reasonableness, not *mens rea,* see *United States v. Bailey,* 444 U.S. 394, 403–406, 100 S.Ct. 624, 631–633, 62 L.Ed.2d 575 (1980), and subtle verbal gradations may obscure rather than elucidate the meaning of the provision in question.

[7] We hold that the detention of a traveler at the border, beyond the scope of a routine customs search and inspection, is justified at its inception if customs agents, considering all the facts surrounding the traveler and her trip, reasonably suspect that the traveler is smuggling contraband in her alimentary canal.

[8] The "reasonable suspicion" standard has been applied in a number of contexts and effects a needed balance between private and public interests when law enforcement officials must make a limited intrusion on less than probable cause. It thus fits well into the situations involving alimentary canal smuggling at the border: this type of smuggling gives no external signs and inspectors will rarely possess probable cause to arrest or search, yet governmental interests in stopping smuggling at the border are high indeed. Under this standard officials at the border must have a "particularized and objective basis for suspecting the particular person" of alimentary canal smuggling. *United States v. Cortez,* 449 U.S. 411, 417, 101 S.Ct. 690, 695, 66 L.Ed.2d 621 (1981), *id.,* at 418, 101 S.Ct., at 695, citing *Terry v. Ohio,* 392 U.S. 1, 21, n. 18, 88 S.Ct. 1868, 1879, n. 18, 20 L.Ed.2d 889 (1968).

[9] The facts, and their rational inferences, known to customs inspectors in this case clearly supported a reasonable suspicion that respondent was an alimentary canal smuggler. We need not belabor the facts, including respondent's implausible story, that supported this suspicion, see *supra,* at 1–4, 88 S.Ct., at 1868–1871. The trained customs inspectors had encountered many alimentary canal smugglers and certainly had more than an "inchoate and unparticularized suspicion or 'hunch,'" *Terry, supra,* at 27, 88 S.Ct., at 1883, that respondent was smuggling narcotics in her alimentary canal. The inspectors' suspicion was a "'common-sense conclusio[n] about human behavior' upon which 'practical people,'—including government officials, are entitled to rely." *T.L.O.,* 469 U.S., at ——, 105 S.Ct., at 746, citing *United States v. Cortez, supra.*

The final issue in this case is whether the detention of respondent was reasonably related in scope to the circumstances which justified it initially. In this regard we have cautioned that courts should not indulge in "unrealistic second-guessing," *United States v. Sharpe,* 470 U.S.——, ——, 105 S.Ct. 1568, 1576, 84 L.Ed.2d 605 (1985), and we have noted that "creative judge[s], engaged in *post hoc* evaluations of police conduct can almost always imagine some alternative means by which the objectives of the police might have been accomplished," *Ibid.* But "[t]he fact that the protection of the public might, in the abstract, have been accomplished by 'less intrusive' means does not, in itself, render the search unreasonable." *Ibid.,* citing *Cady v. Dombrowski,* 413 U.S. 433, 447, 93 S.Ct. 2523, 2531, 37 L.Ed.2d 706 (1983). Authorities must be allowed "to graduate their response to the demands of any particular situation." *United States v. Place,* 462 U.S. 696, 709, n. 10, 103 S.Ct. 2637, 2646, n. 10, 77 L.Ed.2d 110 (1983). Here, respondent was detained *incommunicado* for almost 16 hours before inspectors sought a warrant; the warrant then took a number of hours to procure, through no apparent fault of the inspectors. This length of time undoubtedly exceeds any other detention we have approved under reasonable suspicion. But we have also consistently rejected hard-and-fast time limits, *Sharpe, supra; Place, supra,* at 709, n. 10, 103 S.Ct., at 2646, n. 10. Instead, "common sense and ordinary human experience must govern over rigid criteria." *Sharpe, supra,* 470 U.S., at ——, 105 S.Ct., at 1575.

The rudimentary knowledge of the human body which judges possess in common with the rest of humankind tells us that alimentary canal smuggling cannot be detected in the amount of time in which other illegal activity may be investigated through brief *Terry*-type stops. It presents few, if any external signs; a quick frisk will not do, nor will even a strip search. In the case of respondent the inspectors had available, as an alternative to simply awaiting her bowel movement, an x ray. They offered her the alternative of submitting herself to that procedure. But when she refused that alternative, the customs inspectors were left with only two practical alternatives: detain her for such time as necessary to confirm their suspicions, a detention which would last much longer than the typical "*Terry*" stop, or turn her loose into the interior carrying the reasonably suspected contraband drugs.

The inspectors in this case followed this former procedure. They no doubt expected that respondent, having recently disembarked from a 10-hour direct flight with a full and stiff abdomen, would produce a bowel movement without extended delay. But her visible efforts to resist the call of nature, which the court below labeled "heroic," disappointed this expectation and in turn caused her humiliation and discomfort. Our prior cases have refused to charge police with delays in investigatory detention attributable to the suspect's evasive actions, see *Sharpe,* 470 U.S., at ——, 105 S.Ct., at 1576; *id.,* at ——, 105 S.Ct., at 1584 (MARSHALL, J., concurring in judgment), and that principle applies here as well. Respondent alone was responsible for much of the duration and discomfort of the seizure.

[10] Under these circumstances, we conclude that the detention in this case was not unreasonably long. It occurred at the international border, where the Fourth Amendment balance of interests leans heavily to the Government. At the border, customs officials have more than merely an investigative law enforcement role. They are also charged, along with immigration officials, with protecting this Nation from entrants who may bring anything harmful into this country, whether that be communicable diseases, narcotics, or explosives: See 8 U.S.C. §§ 1182(a)(23), 1182(a)(6), 1222; 19 CFR §§ 162.4–162.7 (1984). See also 19 U.S.C. § 482; 8 U.S.C. § 1103(a). In this regard the detention of a suspected alimentary canal smuggler at the border is analogous to the detention of a suspected tuberculosis carrier at the border: both are detained until their bodily processes dispel the suspicion that they will introduce a harmful agent into this country. Cf. 8 U.S.C. § 1222; 42 CFR pt. 34 (1984); 19 U.S.C. §§ 482, 1582.

Respondent's detention was long, uncomfortable, indeed, humiliating; but both its length and its discomfort resulted solely from the method by which she chose to smuggle illicit drugs into this country. In *Adams v. Williams,* 407 U.S. 143, 92 S.Ct. 1921, 1922, 32 L.Ed.2d 612 (1972), another *Terry*-stop case, we said that "[t]he Fourth Amendment does not require a policeman who lacks the precise level of information necessary for probable cause to arrest to simply shrug his shoulders and allow a crime to occur or a criminal to escape." *Id.,* at 145, 92 S.Ct., at 1923. Here, by analogy, in the presence of articulable suspicion of smuggling in her alimentary canal, the customs officers were not required by the Fourth Amendment to pass respondent and her 88 cocaine-filled balloons into the interior. Her detention for the period of time necessary to either verify or dispel the suspicion was not unreasonable. The judgment of the Court of Appeals is therefore

Reversed.

Justice STEVENS, concurring in the judgment.

If a seizure and a search of the person of the kind disclosed by this record may be made on the basis of reasonable suspicion, we must assume that a significant number of innocent persons will be required to undergo similar procedures. The rule announced in this case cannot, therefore, be supported on the ground that respondent's prolonged and humiliating detention "resulted solely from the method by which she chose to smuggle illicit drugs into this country." *Ante,* at 3312.

The prolonged detention of respondent was, however, justified by a different choice that respondent made; she withdrew her consent to an X-ray examination that would have easily determined whether the reasonable suspicion that she was concealing contraband was justified. I believe that Customs agents may require that a non-pregnant person reasonably suspected of this kind of smuggling submit to an X-ray examination as an incident to a border search. I therefore concur in the judgment. . . .

MASSACHUSETTS, Petitioner *v.* Osborne SHEPPARD.

—U.S,—, 104 S.Ct. 3424, 82 L.Ed.2d 737 (1984)

Justice WHITE delivered the opinion of the Court.

This case involves the application of the rules articulated today in *United States v. Leon, ante,* to a situation in which police officers seize items pursuant to a warrant subsequently invalidated because of a technical error on the part of the issuing judge.

I

The badly burned body of Sandra Boulware was discovered in a vacant lot in the Roxbury section of Boston at approximately 5 a.m., Saturday, May 5, 1979. An autopsy revealed that Boulware had died of multiple compound skull fractures caused by blows to the head. After a brief investigation, the police decided to question one of the victim's boyfriends, Osborne Sheppard. Sheppard told the police that he had last seen the victim on Tuesday night and that he had been at a local gaming house (where cards games were played) from 9 p.m. Friday until 5 a.m. Saturday. He identified several people who would be willing to substantiate the latter claim.

By interviewing the people Sheppard had said were at the gaming house on Friday night, the police learned that although Sheppard was at the gaming house that night, he had borrowed an automobile at about 3 a.m. Saturday morning in order to give two men a ride home. Even though the trip normally took only fifteen minutes, Sheppard did not return with the car until nearly 5 a.m.

On Sunday morning, police officers visited the owner of the car Sheppard had borrowed. He consented to an inspection of the vehicle. Bloodstains and pieces of hair were found on the rear bumper and within the trunk compartment.

In addition, the officers noticed strands of wire in the trunk similar to wire strands found on and near the body of the victim. The owner of the car told the officers that when he last used the car on Friday night, shortly before Sheppard borrowed it, he had placed articles in the trunk and had not noticed any stains on the bumper or in the trunk.

On the basis of the evidence gathered thus far in the investigation, Detective Peter O'Malley drafted an affidavit designed to support an application for an arrest warrant and a search warrant authorizing a search of Sheppard's residence. The affidavit set forth the results of the investigation and stated that the police wished to search for

> "[a] fifth bottle of amaretto liquor, 2 nickel bags of marijuana, a woman's jacket that has been described as black-grey (charcoal), any possessions of Sandra D. Boulware, similar type wire and rope that match those on the body of Sandra D. Boulware, or in the above Thunderbird. A blunt instrument that might have been used on the victim, men's or women's clothing that may have blood, gasoline burns on them. Items that may have fingerprints of the victim."

Detective O'Malley showed the affidavit to the district attorney, the district attorney's first assistant, and a sergeant, who all concluded that it set forth probable cause for the search and the arrest. 387 Mass. 488, 492, 441 N.E.2d 725, 727 (1982).

Because it was Sunday, the local court was closed, and the police had a difficult time finding a warrant application form. Detective O'Malley finally found a warrant form previously in use in the Dorchester District. The form was entitled "Search Warrant—Controlled Substance G.L. c. 276 §§ 1 through 3A." Realizing that some changes had to be made before the form could be used to authorize the search requested in the affidavit, Detective O'Malley deleted the subtitle "controlled substance" with a typewriter. He also substituted "Roxbury" for the printed "Dorchester" and typed Sheppard's name and address into blank spaces provided for that information. However, the reference to "controlled substance" was not deleted in the portion of the form that constituted the warrant application and that, when signed, would constitute the warrant itself.

Detective O'Malley then took the affidavit and the warrant form to the residence of a judge who had consented to consider the warrant application. The judge examined the affidavit and stated that he would authorize the search as requested. Detective O'Malley offered the warrant form and stated that he knew the form as presented dealt with controlled substances. He showed the judge where he had crossed out the subtitles. After unsuccessfully searching for a more suitable form, the judge informed O'Malley that he would make the necessary changes so as to provide a proper search warrant. The judge then took the form, made some changes on it, and dated and signed the warrant. However, he did not change the substantive portion of the warrant, which continued to authorize a search for controlled substances; nor did he alter the form so as to incorporate the affidavit. The judge returned the affidavit and the warrant to O'Malley, informing him that the warrant was sufficient authority in form and content to carry out the search as requested. O'Malley took the two documents and, accompanied by other officers, proceeded to Sheppard's residence. The scope of the ensuing search was limited to the items listed in the affidavit, and several incriminating pieces of evidence were discovered. Sheppard was then charged with first degree murder.

At a pretrial suppression hearing, the trial judge concluded that the warrant failed to conform to the commands of the Fourth Amendment because it did not particularly describe the items to be seized. The judge ruled, however, that the evidence could be admitted notwithstanding the defect in the warrant because the police had acted in good faith in executing what they reasonably thought was a valid warrant. App. 35a. At the subsequent trial, Sheppard was convicted.

On appeal, Sheppard argued that the evidence obtained pursuant to the defective warrant should have been suppressed. The Supreme Judicial Court of Massachusetts agreed. A plurality of the justices concluded that although "the police conducted the search in a good faith belief, reasonably held, that the search was lawful and authorized by the warrant issued by the judge," 387 Mass., at 503, 441 N.E.2d, at 733, the evidence had to be excluded because this Court had not recognized a good-faith exception to the exclusionary rule. Two justices combined in a separate concurrence to stress their rejection of the good-faith exception, and one justice dissented, contending that since exclusion of the evidence in this case would not serve to deter any police misconduct, the evidence should be admitted. We granted certiorari and set the case for argument in conjunction with *United States v. Leon, ante.*

II

[1] Having already decided that the exclusionary rule should not be applied when the officer conducting the search acted in objectively reasonable reliance on a warrant issued by a detached and neutral magistrate that subsequently is determined to be invalid, *id.,* at ——, the sole issue before us in this case is whether the officers reasonably believed that the search they conducted was authorized by a valid warrant. There is no dispute that the officers believed that the warrant authorized the search that they conducted. Thus, the only question is whether there was an objectively reasonable basis for the officers' mistaken belief. Both the trial court, App. 35a, and a majority of the Supreme Judicial Court, 387 Mass., at 503, 441 N.E.2d, at 733; *id.,* at 524–525, 441 N.E.2d, at 745 (Lynch, J., dissenting), concluded that there was. We agree.

The officers in this case took every step that could reasonably be expected of them. Detective O'Malley prepared an affidavit which was reviewed and approved by the District Attorney. He presented that affidavit to a neutral judge. The judge concluded that the affidavit established probable cause to search Sheppard's residence, App. 26a, and informed O'Malley that he would authorize the search as requested. O'Malley then produced the warrant form and informed the judge that it might need to be changed. He was told by the judge that the necessary changes would be made. He then observed the judge make some changes and received the warrant and the affidavit. At this point, a reasonable police officer would have concluded, as O'Malley did, that the warrant authorized a search for the materials outlined in the affidavit.

[2] Sheppard contends that since O'Malley knew the warrant form was defective, he should have examined it to make sure that the necessary changes had been made. However, that argument is based on the premise that O'Malley had a duty to disregard the judge's assurances that the requested search would be authorized and the necessary changes would be made. Whatever an officer may be required to do when he executes a warrant without knowing beforehand what items are to be seized, we refuse to rule that an officer is required to disbelieve a judge who has just advised him, by word and by action, that the warrant he possesses authorizes him to conduct the search he has requested. In Massachusetts, as in most jurisdictions, the determinations of a judge acting within his jurisdiction, even if erroneous, are valid and binding until they are set aside under some recognized procedure. *Streeter v. City of Worcester,* 336 Mass. 469, 472, 146 N.E.2d 514, 517 (1957); *Moll v. Township of Wakefield,* 274 Mass. 505, 507, 175 N.E. 81, 82 (1931). If an officer is required to accept at face value the judge's conclusion that a warrant form is invalid, there is little reason why he should be expected to disregard assurances that everything is all right, especially when he has alerted the judge to the potential problems.

In sum, the police conduct in this case clearly was objectively reasonable and largely error-free. An error of constitutional dimensions may have been committed with respect to the issuance of the warrant, but it was the judge, not the police officers, who made the critical mistake. "[T]he exclusionary rule was adopted to deter unlawful searches by police, not to punish the errors of magistrates and judges." *Illinois v. Gates,* 462 U.S.——, ——, 103 S.Ct. 2317, 2345, 76 L.Ed.2d 527 (1983) (WHITE, J., concurring in the judgment) Suppressing evidence because the judge failed to make all the necessary clerical corrections despite his assurances that such changes would be made will not serve the deterrent function that the exclusionary rule was designed to achieve. Accordingly, federal law does not require the exclusion of the disputed evidence in this case. The judgment of the Supreme Judicial Court is therefore reversed, and the case is remanded for further proceedings not inconsistent with this opinion.

It is so ordered.

UNITED STATES, Petitioner *v.* WILLIAM HARRIS SHARPE and DONALD DAVIS SAVAGE

470 U.S.—, 84 L.Ed.2d 605, 105 S.Ct. 1568 (1985)

Chief Justice **Burger** delivered the opinion of the Court.

[1a] We granted certiorari to decide whether an individual reasonably suspected of engaging in criminal activity may be detained for a period of 20 minutes, when the detention is necessary for law enforcement officers to conduct a limited investigation of the suspected criminal activity.

I

A

On the morning of June 9, 1978, Agent Cooke of the Drug Enforcement Administration (DEA) was on patrol in an unmarked vehicle on a coastal road near Sunset Beach, North Carolina, an area under surveillance for suspected drug trafficking. At approximately 6:30 a. m., Cooke noticed a blue pickup truck with an attached camper shell traveling on the highway in tandem with a blue Pontiac Bonneville. Respondent Savage was driving the pickup, and respondent Sharpe was driving the Pontiac. The Pontiac also carried a passenger, Davis, the charges against whom were later dropped. Observing that the truck was riding low in the rear and that the camper did not bounce or sway appreciably when the truck drove over bumps or around curves, Agent Cooke concluded that it was heavily loaded. A quilted material covered the rear and side windows of the camper.

Cooke's suspicions were sufficiently aroused to follow the two vehicles for approximately 20 miles as they proceeded south into South Carolina. He then decided to make an "investigative stop" and radioed the State Highway Patrol for assistance. Officer Thrasher, driving a marked patrol car, responded to the call. Almost immediately after Thrasher caught up with the procession, the Pontiac and the pickup turned off the highway and onto a campground road. Cooke and Thrasher followed the two vehicles as the latter drove along the road at 55 to 60 miles an hour, exceeding the speed limit of 35 miles an hour. The road eventually looped back to the highway, onto which Savage and Sharpe turned and continued to drive south.

At this point, all four vehicles were in the middle lane of the three right-hand lanes of the highway. Agent Cooke asked Officer Thrasher to signal both vehicles to stop. Thrasher pulled alongside the Pontiac, which was in the lead, turned on his flashing light, and motioned for the driver of the Pontiac to stop. As Sharpe moved the Pontiac into the right lane, the pickup truck cut between the Pontiac and Thrasher's patrol car, nearly hitting the patrol car, and continued down the highway. Thrasher pursued the truck while Cooke pulled up behind the Pontiac.

Cooke approached the Pontiac and identified himself. He requested identification, and Sharpe produced a Georgia driver's license bearing the name of Raymond J. Pavlovich. Cooke then attempted to radio Thrasher to determine whether he had been successful in stopping the pickup truck, but he was unable to make contact for several minutes, apparently because Thrasher was not in his patrol car. Cooke radioed the local police for assistance, and two officers from the Myrtle Beach Police Department arrived about 10 minutes later. Asking the two officers to "maintain the situation," Cooke left to join Thrasher.

In the meantime, Thrasher had stopped the pickup truck about one-half mile down the road. After stopping the truck, Thrasher had approached it with his revolver drawn, ordered the driver, Savage, to get out and assume a "spread eagled" position against the side of the truck, and patted him down. Thrasher then holstered his gun and asked Savage for his driver's license and the truck's vehicle registration. Savage produced his own Florida driver's license and a bill of sale for the truck bearing the name of Pavlovich. In response to questions from Thrasher concerning the ownership of the truck, Savage said that the truck belonged to a friend and that he was taking it to have its shock absorbers repaired. When Thrasher told Savage that he would be held until the arrival of Cooke, whom Thrasher identified as a DEA agent, Savage became nervous, said that he wanted to leave, and requested the return of his driver's license. Thrasher replied that Savage was not free to leave at that time.

Agent Cooke arrived at the scene approximately 15 minutes after the truck had been stopped. Thrasher handed Cooke Savage's license and the bill of sale for the truck; Cooke noted that the bill of sale bore the same name as Sharpe's license. Cooke identified himself to Savage as a DEA agent and said that he thought the truck was loaded with marihuana. Cooke twice sought permission to search the camper, but Savage declined to give it, explaining that he was not the owner of the truck. Cooke then stepped on the rear of the truck and, observing that it did not sink any lower, confirmed his suspicion that it was probably overloaded. He put his nose against the rear window, which was covered from the inside, and reported that he could smell marihuana. Without seeking Savage's permission, Cooke removed the keys from the ignition, opened the rear of the camper, and observed a large number of burlap-wrapped bales resembling bales of marihuana that Cooke had seen in previous investigations. Agent Cooke then placed Savage under arrest and left him with Thrasher.

Cooke returned to the Pontiac and arrested Sharpe and Davis. Approximately 30 to 40 minutes had elapsed between the time Cooke stopped the Pontiac and the time he returned to arrest Sharpe and Davis. Cooke assembled the various parties and vehicles and led them to the Myrtle Beach police station. That evening, DEA agents took the truck to the Federal Building in Charleston, South Carolina. Several days later, Cooke supervised the unloading of the truck, which contained 43 bales weighing a total of 2,629 pounds. Acting without a search warrant, Cooke had eight randomly selected bales opened and sampled. Chemical tests showed that the samples were marihuana.

B

Sharpe and Savage were charged with possession of a controlled substance with intent to distribute it in violation of 21 USC § 841(a)(1) and 18 USC § 2 [21 USCS § 841(a)(1) and 18 USCS § 2]. The United States District Court for the District of South Carolina denied respondents' motion to suppress the contraband, and respondents were convicted.

A divided panel of the Court of Appeals for the Fourth Circuit reversed the convictions. Sharpe v United States, 660 F2d 967 (1981). The majority assumed that Cooke "had an articulable and reasonable suspicion that Sharpe and Savage were engaged in marijuana trafficking when he and Thrasher stopped the Pontiac and the truck." Id., at 970. But the court held the investigative stops unlawful because they "failed to meet the requirement of brevity" thought to govern detentions on less than probable cause. Ibid. Basing its decision solely on the duration of the respondents' detentions, the majority concluded that "the length of the detentions effectively transformed them into de facto arrests without bases in probable cause, unreasonable seizures under the Fourth Amendment." Ibid. The majority then determined that the samples of marihuana should have been suppressed as the fruit of respondents' unlawful seizures. Id., at 971. As an alternative basis for its decision, the majority held that the warrantless search of the bales taken from the pickup violated Robbins v California, 453 US 420, 69 L Ed 2d 744, 101 S Ct 2841 (1981). Judge Russell dissented as to both grounds of the majority's decision.

The Government petitioned for certiorari, asking this Court to review both of the alternative grounds held by the Court of Appeals to justify suppression. We granted the petition, vacated the judgment of the Court of Appeals, and remanded the case for further consideration in the light of the intervening decision in United States v Ross, 456 US 798, 72 L Ed 2d 572, 102 S Ct 2157 (1982). United States v Sharpe, 457 US 1127, 73 L Ed 2d 1345, 102 S Ct 2951 (1982).

On remand, a divided panel of the Court of Appeals again reversed the convictions. 712 F2d 65 (1983). The majority concluded that, in the light of Ross, it was required to "disavow" its alternative holding disapproving the warrantless search of the marihuana bales. But, "[f]inding that Ross does not adversely affect our primary holding" that the detentions of the two defendants constituted illegal seizures, the court readopted the prior opinion as modified. Ibid. The majority declined "to reexamine our principal holding or to reargue the same issues that were addressed in detail in the original majority and dissenting opinions," reasoning that its action complied with this Court's mandate. The panel assumed that "[h]ad [this] Court felt that a reversal was in order, it could and would have said so." Id., at 65, n 1. Judge Russell again dissented.

We granted certiorari, 467 US ——, 82 L Ed 2d 837, 104 S Ct 3531 (1984), and we reverse.

II

A

The Fourth Amendment is not, of course, a guarantee against *all* searches and seizures, but only against *unreasonable* searches and seizures. The authority and limits of the Amendment apply to investigative stops of vehicles such as occurred here. United States v Hensley, 469 US —, —, 83 L Ed 2d 604, 105 S Ct 675 (1985); United States v Cortez, 449 US 411, 417, 66 L Ed 2d 621, 101 S Ct 690 (1981); Delaware v Prouse, 440 US 648, 663, 59 L Ed 2d 660, 99 S Ct 1391 (1979); United States v Brignoni-Ponce, 422 US 873, 878, 880,

45 L Ed 2d 607, 95 S Ct 2574 (1975). In Terry v Ohio, 392 US 1, 20 L Ed 2d 889, 88 S Ct 1868, 44 Ohio Ops 2d 383 (1968), we adopted a dual inquiry for evaluating the reasonableness of an investigative stop. Under this approach, we examine

> "whether the officer's action was justified at its inception, and whether it was reasonably related in scope to the circumstances which justified the interference in the first place." Id., at 20, 20 L Ed 2d 889, 88 S Ct 1868, 44 Ohio Ops 2d 383.

[4a] As to the first part of this inquiry, the Court of Appeals assumed that the police had an articulable and reasonable suspicion that Sharpe and Savage were engaged in marihuana trafficking, given the setting and all the circumstances when the police attempted to stop the Pontiac and the pickup. 660 F2d, at 970. That assumption is abundantly supported by the record. As to the second part of the inquiry, however, the court concluded that the 30- to 40-minute detention of Sharpe and the 20-minute detention of Savage "failed to meet the [Fourth Amendment's] requirement of brevity." Ibid.

[1b] It is not necessary for us to decide whether the length of Sharpe's detention was unreasonable, because that detention bears no causal relation to Agent Cooke's discovery of the marihuana. The marihuana was in Savage's pickup, not in Sharpe's Pontiac; the contraband introduced at respondents' trial cannot logically be considered the "fruit" of Sharpe's detention. The only issue in this case, then, is whether it was reasonable under the circumstances facing Agent Cooke and Officer Thrasher to detain Savage, whose vehicle contained the challenged evidence, for approximately 20 minutes. We conclude that the detention of Savage clearly meets the Fourth Amendment's standard of reasonableness.

The Court of Appeals did not question the reasonableness of Officer Thrasher's or Agent Cooke's conduct during their detention of Savage. Rather, the court concluded that the length of the detention alone transformed it from a Terry stop into a de facto arrest. Counsel for respondents, as amicus curiae, assert that conclusion as their principal argument before this Court, relying particularly upon our decisions in Dunaway v New York, 442 US 200, 60 L Ed 2d 824, 99 S Ct 2248 (1979); Florida v Royer, 460 US 491, 75 L Ed 2d 229, 103 S Ct 1319 (1983); and United States v Place, 462 US 696, 77 L Ed 2d 110, 103 S Ct 2637 (1983). That reliance is misplaced.

In Dunaway, the police picked up a murder suspect from a neighbor's home and brought him to the police station, where, after being interrogated for an hour, he confessed. The state conceded that the police lacked probable cause when they picked up the suspect, but sought to justify the warrantless detention and interrogation as an investigative stop. The Court rejected this argument, concluding that the defendant's detention was "in important respects indistinguishable from a traditional arrest." 442 US, at 212, 60 L Ed 2d 824, 99 S Ct 2248. Dunaway is simply inapposite here: the Court was not concerned with the length of the defendant's detention, but with events occurring during the detention.

In Royer, government agents stopped the defendant in an airport, seized his luggage, and took him to a small room used for questioning, where a search of the luggage revealed narcotics. The Court held that the defendant's detention constituted an arrest. See 460 US, at 503, 75 L Ed 2d 229, 103 S Ct 1319 (plurality opinion); id., at 509, 75 L Ed 2d 229, 103 S Ct 1319 (Powell, J., concurring); ibid. (Brennan, J., concurring in the result). As in Dunaway, though, the focus was primarily on facts other than the duration of the defendant's detention—particularly the fact that the police confined the defendant in a small airport room for questioning.

The plurality in Royer did note that "an investigative detention must be temporary and last no longer than is necessary to effectuate the purpose of the stop." 460 US, at 500, 75 L Ed 2d 229, 103 S Ct 1319. The Court followed a similar approach in Place. In that case, law enforcement agents stopped the defendant after his arrival in an airport and seized his luggage for 90 minutes to take it to a narcotics detection dog for a "sniff test." We decided that an investigative seizure of personal property could be justified under the Terry doctrine, but that "[t]he length of the detention of respondent's luggage alone precludes the conclusion that the seizure was reasonable in the absence of probable cause." 462 US, at 709, 77 L Ed 2d 110, 103 S Ct 2637. However, the rationale underlying that conclusion was premised on the fact that the police knew of respondent's arrival time for several hours beforehand, and the Court assumed that the police could have arranged for a trained narcotics dog in advance and thus avoided the necessity of holding respondent's luggage for 90 minutes. "[I]n assessing the effect of the length of the detention, we take into account whether the police diligently pursue their investigation." Ibid.; see also Royer, supra, at 500, 75 L Ed 2d 229, 103 S Ct 1319.

Here, the Court of Appeals did not conclude that the police acted less than diligently, or that they unnecessarily prolonged Savage's detention. Place and Royer thus provide no support for the Court of Appeals' analysis.

[3b] Admittedly, Terry, Dunaway, Royer, and Place, considered together, may in some instances create difficult line-drawing problems in distinguishing an investigative stop from a de facto arrest. Obviously, if an investigative stop continues indefinitely, at some point it can no longer be justified as an investigative stop. But our cases impose no rigid time limitation on Terry stops. While it is clear that "the brevity of the invasion of the individual's Fourth Amendment interests is an important factor in determining whether the seizure is so minimally intrusive as to be justifiable on reasonable suspicion," United States v Place, supra, at 709, 77 L Ed 2d 110, 103 S Ct 2637, we have emphasized the need to consider the law enforcement purposes to be served by the stop as well as the time reasonably needed to effectuate those purposes. United States v Hensley, 469 US ——, ——, ——, 83 L Ed 2d 604, 105 S Ct 675 (1985); Place, supra, at 703–704, 709, 77 L Ed 2d 110, 103 S Ct 2637; Michigan v Summers, 452 US 692, 700, and n 12, 69 L Ed 2d 340, 101 S Ct 2587 (1981) (quoting 3 W. LaFave, Search and Seizure § 9.2, at 36–37 (1978)). Much as a "bright line" rule would be desirable, in evaluating whether an investigative detention is unreasonable, common sense and ordinary human experience must govern over rigid criteria.

We sought to make this clear in Michigan v Summers, supra:

> "If the purpose underlying a Terry stop—investigating possible criminal activity—is to be served, the police must under certain circumstances be able to detain the individual for longer than the brief time period involved in Terry and Adams [v Williams, 407 US 143 [32 L Ed 2d 612, 92 S Ct 1921] (1972)]." 452 US, at 700, n 12, 69 L Ed 2d 340, 101 S Ct 2587.

Later, in Place, we expressly rejected the suggestion that we adopt a hard-and-fast time limit for a permissible Terry stop:

> "We understand the desirability of providing law enforcement authorities with a clear rule to guide their conduct. Nevertheless, we question the wisdom of a rigid time limitation. Such a limit would undermine the equally important need to allow authorities to graduate their responses to the demands of any particular situation." 462 US, at 709, n 10, 77 L Ed 2d 110, 103 S Ct 2637.

The Court of Appeals' decision would effectively establish a per se rule that a 20-minute detention is too long to be justified under the Terry doctrine. Such a result is clearly and fundamentally at odds with our approach in this area.

B

[5] In assessing whether a detention is too long in duration to be justified as an investigative stop, we consider it appropriate to examine whether the police diligently pursued a means of investigation that was likely to confirm or dispel their suspicions quickly, during which time it was necessary to detain the defendant. See Michigan v Summers, 452 US, at 701, n 14, 69 L Ed 2d 340, 101 S Ct 2587 (quoting 3 W. LaFave, Search and Seizure § 9.2, at 40 (1978)); see also Place, 462 US, at 709, 77 L Ed 2d 110, 103 S Ct 2637; Royer, 460 US, at 500, 75 L Ed 2d 229, 103 S Ct 1319. A court making this assessment should take care to consider whether the police are acting in a swiftly developing situation, and in such cases the court should not indulge in unrealistic second-guessing. See generally post, at —— U.S. ——, 84 L Ed 2d 632–635 (Brennan, J., dissenting). A creative judge engaged in post hoc evaluation of police conduct can almost always imagine some alternative means by which the objectives of the police might have been accomplished. But "[t]he fact that the protection of the public might, in the abstract, have been accomplished by 'less intrusive' means does not, in itself, render the search unreasonable." Cady v Dombrowski, 413 US 433, 447, 37 L Ed 2d 706, 93 S Ct 2523 (1973); see also United States v Martinez-Fuerte, 428 US 543, 557, n 12, 49 L Ed 2d 1116, 96 S Ct 3074 (1976). The question is not simply whether some other alternative was available, but whether the police acted unreasonably in failing to recognize or to pursue it.

[1c] We readily conclude that, given the circumstances facing him, Agent Cooke pursued his investigation in a diligent and reasonable manner. During most of Savage's 20-minute detention, Cooke was attempting to contact Thrasher and enlisting the help of the local police who remained with Sharpe while Cooke left to pursue Officer Thrasher and the pickup. Once Cooke reached Officer Thrasher and Savage, he proceeded expeditiously: within the space of a few minutes, he examined Savage's driver's license and the truck's bill of sale, requested (and was denied) permission to search the truck, stepped on the rear bumper and noted that the truck did not move, confirming his suspicion that it was probably overloaded. He then detected the odor of marihuana.

[1d] Clearly this case does not involve any delay unnecessary to the legitimate investigation of the law enforcement officers. Respondents presented no evidence that the officers were dilatory in their investigation. The delay in this case was attributable almost entirely to the evasive actions of Savage, who sought to elude the police as Sharpe moved his Pontiac to the side of the road. Except for Savage's maneuvers, only a short and certainly permissible pre-arrest detention would likely have taken place. The somewhat longer detention was simply the result of a "graduate[d] . . . respons[e] to the demands of [the] particular situation," Place, supra, at 709, n 10, 77 L Ed 2d 110, 103 S Ct 2637.

We reject the contention that a 20-minute stop is unreasonable when the police have acted diligently and a suspect's actions contribute to the added delay about which he complains. The judgment of the Court of Appeals is reversed, and the case is remanded for further proceedings consistent with this opinion.

Reversed and remanded.

CHAPTER 7

Contents

Fifth Amendment—Prohibitions against Government

§ 7.1 Introduction

The Fifth Amendment provides:

> *No person shall be held to answer for a capital, or otherwise infamous crime, unless on a presentment or indictment of a Grand Jury, except in cases arising in the land or naval forces, or in the Militia, when in actual service in time of War or public danger; nor shall any person be subject for the same offence to be twice put in jeopardy of life or limb; nor shall be compelled in any criminal case to be a witness against himself, nor be deprived of life, liberty, or property, without due process of law; nor shall private property be taken for public use, without just compensation.*

The Fifth Amendment contains rights which relate to criminal law as well as to civil law. The language dealing with the public use of private property for public use (eminent domain) without just compensation is manifestly civil in scope. However, that provision was included as a limitation of the federal government's control over the freedom of the individual along with those limitations relating to the preservation of law and order in order to prevent abuses of sovereign power which had been practiced in England and on the Continent of Europe.

The reader has previously been alerted to the historical reasons for the adoption of the Fifth Amendment in Chapter 4 (supra). To repeat them here would be repetitive and fruitless. However, one should realize that while the wording of the amendment seems very clear on first impression, the courts have been called upon to construe its more finite meaning.

For example, cases have come before the Court to decide the following questions:

1. What is the meaning of the phrase "criminal case"?
2. At what point in the arrest process does the accused enjoy the privilege?
3. What statements are protected?
4. Does the taking of voiceprints, handwriting samples, fingerprints, footprints, lineups, or blood extractions fall within the scope of the self-incrimination prohibition?
5. Does the government or the defendant assume the burden of proof for determining a violation of the constitutional protection?
6. Could psychological compulsion be prohibited as well as physical compulsion?

7. What is the duration of Miranda warnings?
8. Does a judge or prosecutor have the right to comment at the trial that a defendant failed to testify in his own defense?
9. Does this right attach to administrative trials such as police department disciplinary hearings?
10. What is an infamous crime?

§ 7.2 Fifth Amendment Meaning of Criminal Case

If a witness is subpoenaed or appears voluntarily before an investigating commission established by government for the purpose of ferreting out criminal behavior in the community and the persons responsible for the antisocial behavior, the witness may invoke his privilege against self-incrimination. The Court stated in Malloy v. Hogan, 378 U.S. 1, 84 S.Ct. 1489, 12 L.Ed.2d 653 (1964), that it must be considered irrelevant that the petitioner was a witness in a statutory inquiry and not a defendant in a criminal prosecution, for it has been long settled that the privilege protects witnesses in similar federal inquiries. "The privilege afforded not only extends to answers that would in themselves support a conviction . . . but likewise embraces those which furnish a link in the chain of evidence needed to prosecute. . . . To sustain the privilege, it need only be evident from the implications of the question, in the setting in which it is asked, that a responsive answer to the question or an explanation of why it cannot be answered might be dangerous because injurious disclosure could result." Hoffman v. United States, 341 U.S. 479, 71 S.Ct. 814, 95 L.Ed. 1118 (1951).

§ 7.3 Self-Incrimination Privilege

The privilege against self-incrimination is not a blanket protection which attaches in every encounter between law enforcement and a malefactor. A person is not entitled to a Miranda warning during the commission of a crime. Feldstein v. U.S., C.A.Cal. 429 F.2d 1062, cert. den. 400 U.S. 920, 91 S.Ct. 174, 27 L.Ed.2d 159, reh.den. 400 U.S. 1002, 91 S.Ct. 452, 27 L.Ed.2d 454 (1971). If it were otherwise, a murderer could approach a police officer and without warning tell the police officer that he murdered "X." If the privilege were a blanket privilege, the police officer would be precluded from using this statement and any further information which might flow from this statement under the "fruit of the poison tree" doctrine. It can therefore be observed that this would lead to a preposterous situation where every murderer would seek out the first police officer that s/he would see to blurt out the confession to the officer and thereby escape punishment for the crime.

Accordingly, the courts have looked into the history and reason for the self-incrimination privilege in order to establish the point at which the perpetrator is entitled to invoke this privilege. You will remember that it was included in the Bill of Rights to prevent excesses by governmental agents in the prosecution of crime which resulted in the application of torture to obtain confessions. With this in mind, the courts have devised the most practical method that they know to prevent these excesses. This method is the exclusionary rule previously indicated.

If the police force a confession and this is shown to the trial court, the confession is not admitted in evidence and all that flows therefrom is likewise not admitted. Thus, it is not in the interest of law enforcement to force a confession.

For many years, the police contended that police interrogation without advising the prisoner of constitutional rights was indispensible in law enforcement. The fact that the interrogation was conducted away from the eyes of society made it more readily acceptable, notwithstanding the fact that it was general knowledge that "third degree" tactics were in use in practically every police agency in the country.

In Bram v. United States, 168 U.S. 532, 18 S.Ct. 183, 42 L.Ed. 1123 (1897), the Court held that "in criminal trials (i)n the courts of the United States, wherever a question arises whether a confession is incompetent because not voluntary, the issue is controlled by (self-incrimination) portion of the Fifth Amendment...." This was the rule until the Court said in Malloy v. Hogan (supra) that "today the admissibility of a confession in a state criminal prosecution is tested by the same standard applied in federal prosecutions since 1897...."

In Escobedo v. Illinois, 378 U.S. 478, 32 Ohio Op.2d 31, 84 S.Ct. 1758, 12 L.Ed.2d 977 (1964), decided during the same term as Malloy v. Hogan (supra), the Court fixed the point at which the police are no longer able to use statements made to them by a suspect. The Court said, in a 5–4 decision, "... that where, as here, the investigation is no longer a general inquiry into an unsolved crime but has begun to focus on a particular suspect, the suspect has been taken into police custody, the police carry out a process of interrogations that lends itself to eliciting incriminating statements, the suspect has requested and been denied an opportunity to consult with his lawyer, and the police have not effectively warned him of his absolute constitutional right to remain silent, the accused has been denied 'the assistance of counsel' in violation of the Sixth Amendment to the Constitution as 'made obligatory upon the States by the Fourteenth Amendment' and that no statement elicited by the police during the interrogation may be used against him in a criminal trial."

Thus we have what appears to be a marriage of the Fifth Amendment self-incrimination clause and the Sixth Amendment right of counsel clause. We can thus say that when the investigation centers on a particular individual, the police had better advise that person that anything s/he says may be used against him/her in a trial. To do otherwise would invite a dismissal. This rule was further refined in Miranda v. Arizona (infra) and other cases which will be discussed in Chapter 8 (infra).

While the Fifth and Fourteenth Amendments protect a defendant against being convicted on evidence of self-incrimination, and a defendant need not testify at his trial, a problem sometimes arises as to trial strategy when a defendant fails to take the stand in his/her own defense. Some defense attorneys do not want the jury to be reminded in the judge's charge of the defendant's failures to take the stand. Others want it explained to the jury that this fact shall have no inference of guilt or of innocence. In CARTER v. KENTUCKY, 450 U.S. 288, 101 S.Ct. 1112, 67 L.Ed.2d. 241, 28 Cr.L. 3093 (1981) the Court held that if defense counsel requests that the judge charge the jury that "the defendant is not compelled to testify and the fact that he does not cannot be used as an inference of guilt and should not prejudice him in any way," the trial judge is under obligation to so charge inorder to minimize the danger that the jury will give evidentiary weight to the defendant's failure to testify.

A South Dakota statute permits a person suspected of driving while intoxicated to refuse to submit to a blood alcohol test, but authorizes revocation of the driver's license of a person so refusing the test and permits such refusal to be used against him at trial. MASON H. NEVILLE was arrested by police officers in that state for driving while intoxicated. After request, he refused to take the test although he was told that he could lose his license for the refusal. The police did not warn him that the refusal could be used against him at trial. In SOUTH DAKOTA v. MASON HENRY NEVILLE, —U.S.—, 103 S.Ct. 916, L.Ed.2d. 748, 32 Cr.L. 3047 (1983) the Court held that the admission into evidence of a defendant's refusal to submit to a blood alcohol test does not offend his Fifth Amendment right against self incrimination and that it is not fundamentally unfair in violation of due process to use respondent's refusal to take the blood alcohol test as evidence of guilt even though the police failed to warn him that the refusal could be used against him at trial.

§ 7.3(a) Probation Officer—Statements Made to

The Fifth Amendment privilege against self incrimination has been held not to be applicable when a probationer made incriminating statements to his probation officer during a non constodial interview where the officer questioned the client who was required to give truthful answers. He could not have reasonably perceived himself to be threatened with revocation of probation as a punishment for refusing to give answers that would incriminate him. MINNESOTA v. MURPHY, —U.S.—, 104 S.Ct. 1136, 79 L.Ed.2d. 409 (1984).

§ 7.4 Statements Protected by the Self-Incrimination Privilege

Escobedo v. Illinois (supra) and Malloy v. Hogan (supra) are still undergoing refinement in their applicability to the self-incrimination privilege. In Michigan v. Tucker, 417 U.S. 433, 94 S.Ct. 2357, 41 L.Ed.2d 182 (1974), the Court said that the hallmark of all privilege against self-incrimination cases is compulsion, a concern applicable equally to police interrogation. The Miranda warning requirements, however, are only "prophylactic rules developed to protect that right" (self-incrimination) but are not "themselves rights protected by the Constitution; they are only practical reinforcement for the (constitutional) right...." Just as trial procedures must be fair but not perfect, so police are not required to "make no errors whatsoever." Before sanctions are imposed because of police error, they must serve a useful purpose under the deterrent theory. For that to be so, police must have engaged in 'wilful or at the very least, negligent conduct which has deprived the defendant of some right,' so that use of the exclusionary sanction instills in those particular officers, or in their future counterparts, a greater degree of care towards the right of an accused."

In the Tucker case, the arrest had taken place before Miranda v. Arizona (infra) but the Court's decision was post-Miranda. The police warned him of his rights pursuant to Escobedo v. Illinois (supra). In the Tucker case, the Court balanced a technical error against a possible deterrent effect, "the strong interest under any system of justice making available to the trier of the fact all concededly relevant and trustworthy evidence which either party seeks to adduce." The Court distinguished "harmless error" from substantial error. It said "the law does not require that a defendant receive a perfect trial, only a fair one." The statements which are protected are all those which might incriminate the defendant in any way. However, in the Tucker case (supra) the defendant was interrogated about a rape. His statement indicated the existence of an alibi witness who proved to be a prime witness for the prosecution. The confession was never used in evidence. Tucker objected throughout the trial to the testimony of the prosecution witness as the unlawful derivative evidence of a Miranda violation. His claim was rejected by the state courts but the Federal District Court and the Federal Court of Appeals adopted the contention of the defendant on appeal. Notwithstanding this, the Supreme Court, by a divided 5–3–1 court, reversed and adopted the theory of the state courts.

The government frequently employs psychiatrists to interview defendants. In ESTELLE v. SMITH, 451 U.S. 454, 101 S.Ct. 1866, 68 L.Ed.2d. 359, 29 Cr.L. 3031 (1981) Texas employed a psychiatrist to interview a prisoner to determine if he was competent to stand trial in a potential capital case. The determination was that he was competent to stand trial. He went to trial and was convicted. On the sentencing part of a bifurcated trial, the psychiatrist, whose name did not appear on the governments' notice list, testified over objection as to the conversation that the psychiatrist had with the defendant. Held: This was a violation of the Fifth Amendment, self-incrimination clause as well as the denial of his right to counsel. See 8.14 (infra).

§ 7.5 Self-Incrimination Regarding Other Evidence

The rule for the introduction into evidence of voiceprints is not uniform among the states and the federal courts. The law is in a state of flux in this area. The arguments for and against the introduction of this evidence is best left to a course dealing exclusively with the law of evidence. It is interesting to note that in those jurisdictions which admit voiceprints into evidence, they are considered to be no violation of the self-incrimination clause. In Schmerber v. California, 384 U.S. 757, 86 S.Ct. 1826, 16 L.Ed.2d 908 (1966), the Court said "... both federal and state courts have usually held that it (self-incrimination privilege) offers no protection against compulsion to fingerprinting, photographing, or measurements, to write, or speak for identification, to appear in court to stand, to assume a stance, to walk, or to make a particular gesture." In the Schmerber case the trial court admitted evidence to show the alcoholic content of the petitioner's blood which had been extracted under surgically acceptable standards in a hospital by a licensed physician. The Supreme Court held that this, like the other situations indicated above, did not amount to testimonial compulsion which the Fifth Amendment protects.

§ 7.6 Burden to Prove Irregularity Regarding Self-Incrimination

Those readers who have knowledge of the law of evidence are aware of the presence of presumptions. A presumption determines from whom the proof must come. There are conclusive presumptions and rebuttable presumptions. There are presumptions of fact and presumptions of law as well as mixed presumptions of fact and law. A presumption presupposes a circumstance to exist. In the analysis of constitutional law, we presume that government and its agents and servants acted in conformity with law and therefore this presumption must be overcome by the defendant. Many states provide for the defendant to prove that the government violated the defendant's rights by presenting its evidence first. Other states provide by court rule for the state to put in its evidence first, on the assumption that the state has the burden to prove each and every allegation of the crime including the legality of the confession.

It has been held that a statute lifting the burden of proof from the state in a criminal prosecution and casting it on the accused must be kept within the limits of reason and fairness, and these limits are that the state shall have introduced enough evidence having a sinister, criminal, or inculpatory significance to make it just for the accused to be required to repel it with excuse or explanation. Tot v. United States, 319 U.S. 463, 63 S.Ct. 1241, 87 L.Ed. 1519 (1943).

The reader is directed to the rules of the court in his/her jurisdiction to ascertain who has the burden of proof in motions to suppress.

§ 7.7 Psychological Compulsion and Self-Incrimination

The courts have construed psychological compulsion to confess in the same way as if corporeal punishment had been inflicted. When a prisoner is apprehended, s/he should be brought before a magistrate with all reasonable speed. The Federal Rules of Criminal Procedure as of this time, promulgated as rule 52, provides a statutory authority for quick arraignment. All other jurisdictions in the United States known to the author, have similar legislation. The legislation is an outgrowth of McNabb v. United States, 318 U.S. 332, 63 S.Ct. 608, 87 L.Ed. 819 (1957), where the Court said, "... The awful instruments of the criminal law cannot be entrusted to a single functionary. The complicated process of criminal justice is therefore divided into different parts...."

In Mallory v. United States, 354 U.S. 449, 77 S.Ct. 1356, 1 L.Ed.2d 1479 (1957), the Court reversed a conviction of a petitioner who had been arrested as a suspect of a rape and had been held in custody from 2:30 PM of one day to the next morning. During his period of incarceration before arraignment, he was subjected to an almost continuous barrage of questioning by teams of police officers until he said that he could have done this crime, or he might have done it. He finally stated that he was responsible.

The Court held that the police detention of defendants beyond the time when committing magistrate was readily accessible constituted "wilful disobedience of the law." The Court additionally wrote about psychological coercion to confess in Miranda v. Arizona (infra) where they recited the contents of police interrogation manuals which recommended this type of questioning.

§ 7.8 Duration of Miranda Warning

The Court has been reinterpreting Miranda and has placed limitations on the rule. In Michigan v. Mosely, 423 U.S. 96, 96 S.Ct. 321, 46 L.Ed.2d 313 (1975), a defendant was arrested in connection with two robberies and invoked his right to remain silent after a detective gave him Miranda warnings. Two hours later, a second detective repeated the Miranda warnings and questioned the defendant solely with regard to an unrelated homicide. In the second trial, the defendant's inculpatory statements were admitted into evidence over his objection. The Court held that Miranda created no "per se proscription of indefinite duration upon any further questioning by any police officer on any subject." The admissibility of a defendant's statements made after the invocation of silence "depends under Miranda on whether his 'right to cut off questioning' was 'scrupulously honored.'" 384 U.S. 436, 479. The Court concluded that in this case the defendant's right to cut off questioning was in fact honored.

In OREGON v. BRADSHAW, 459 U.S. 966, 103 S.Ct. 292, 74 L.Ed.2d. 276, 51 L.W. 4940 (1983) the Court held that where police officers gave suspect his Miranda rights warning with respect to a possible manslaughter charge and when the suspect was later arrested for furnishing liquor to the victim, a minor, and again advised of his rights, and where the suspect denied his involvement and asked for an attorney. The fact that the respondent subsequently initiated a conversation with a police officer who advised him that he did not have to talk to him and the respondent said that he understood, whereupon the police officer suggested that he take a polygraph examination, which he did, after again being read his Miranda rights, and where the respondent made certain incriminating statements, the incriminating statements were held to be admissible in respondent's trial.

§ 7.9 Judge or Prosecutor's Comments on Defendant's Failure to Testify

The defendant has an absolute right to remain silent so as not to incriminate him/herself. However, if s/he exercises this right, is it permissible for a judge or prosecutor to bring the failure to the attention of the jury? Twining v. New Jersey, 211 U.S. 78, 29 S.Ct. 14, 53 L.Ed. 97 (1908), was the first to treat that issue with respect to the Fifth Amendment right to be effective in state courts. The Court held in that case that the Fifth amendment privilege against self-incrimination is not binding on the states through the Fourteenth Amendment.

The Court continued this line of thinking in Adamson v. California, 332 U.S. 46, 67 S.Ct. 1672, 91 L.Ed. 1093 (1947), where it construed a California statute which authorized the court and counsel to comment upon the "failure of the defendant to explain or to deny by his testimony any evidence or facts in the case against him." However, in Malloy v. Hogan, 378 U.S. 1, 84 S.Ct. 1489, 12 L.Ed.2d 653 (1964), the Court reversed Twining and Adamson by holding in a 5–4 decision that the Fourteenth Amendment guaranteed the petitioner the protection of the Fifth Amendment's privilege against self-incrimination in state criminal prosecutions thereby silencing judicial comment about a defendant's failure to testify. The pendulum swung back a little in Lakeside v. Oregon, 435 U.S. 333, 55 L.Ed.2d 319, 98 S.Ct. 1091 (1978), where the Court held that there is no violation of the Fifth Amendment right to silence if a state judge instructs a jury that the defendant did not testify and that he has a constitutional right not to testify, adding that the jury is not to draw any adverse inference from defendant's decision not to testify.

A further refinement of this concept was found (1983) in U.S. v. HASTINGS, —U.S.—, 104 S.Ct. 3540, 82 L.Ed.2d. 844, where a prosecutor, in summation, commented on defendant's failure to rebut victims' testimony. The Court held that this was harmless error beyond a reasonable doubt. The jury would have convicted the defendant without this error having been made.

A Kentucky law maintained a distinction between an "admonition" and an "instruction" to the jury. In JAMES v. KENTUCKY, —U.S.—, 104 S.Ct. 1803, 80 L.Ed.2d. 346, (1984) a defendant requested that "an admonition be given to the jury that no emphasis be given to defendant's failure to testify." The judge overruled the request. The Kentucky Supreme Court upheld the trial judge saying that there was a vast difference between "admonition" and "instruction" to the jury. The United States Supreme Court held that for federal constitutional purposes, petitioner adequately invoked his substantive right for jury guidance and Kentucky's distinction between admonitions and instructions is not the sort of firmly established and regularly followed state practice that can prevent implementation of a federal constitutional right.

§ 7.10 Separate Sovereignties

For many years the Court held that if one was granted immunity in either the state or federal forum, it would not carry over to the other jurisdictions.

This was overruled in Murphy v. Waterfront Commission, 378 U.S. 52, 84 S.Ct. 1594, 12 L.Ed.2d 678 (1964), where the Court, per Goldberg, J., ruled, "... Most, if not all, of (the) policies and purposes (of the privilege against self-incrimination) are defeated when a witness can be whipsawed into incriminating himself under both state and federal law."

§ 7.11 Self-Incrimination Regarding Administrative Trials

Administrative trials such as police department disciplinary hearings, do not ordinarily require strict adherence to the legal rules of evidence. A defendant in such a trial need not be proven guilty beyond a reasonable doubt as is the rule in the criminal court. The defendant need only be proven guilty by substantial evidence. All relevant evidence is admissible notwithstanding that if it were a criminal trial, it might be excluded because of an exclusionary rule. Under these circumstances it might be natural to assume that a police officer may be required to testify if directed to do so under penalty of loss of job and pension rights. The Court has held to the contrary in Garrity v. New Jersey, 385 U.S. 493, 87 S.Ct. 616, 17 L.Ed.2d 562 (1967).

In a related matter the Court held a New York statute to be unconstitutional which provided for a political party officer to testify before a grand jury or other authorized tribunal concerning the conduct of his office without a waiver of immunity. If there was a refusal to so testify, the officer's political position was to terminate and he was to be disqualified from holding any other party or public office for five years. The Court said that this statute was unconstitutional on the grounds that it infringes on the official's Fifth Amendment rights. Lefkowitz v. Cunningham, 431 U.S. 801, 97 S.Ct. 2132, 52 L.Ed.2d 1, 21 Cr.L. 3109 (1977).

§ 7.12 Infamous Crime Defined

The courts have construed the meaning of the term "infamous crime" as used in the Fifth Amendment as follows: a crime punishable by imprisonment in a state prison or penitentiary with or without hard labor, is an infamous crime within the provision of the Fifth Amendment of the Constitution that "no person shall be held to answer for a capital or other infamous crime unless on presentment and indictment of a grand jury." Brede v. Powers, 263 U.S. 4, 44 S.Ct. 8, 68 L.Ed. 132 (1923).

It would therefore appear that every felony which is punishable by imprisonment in a state prison or penitentiary must be initiated by a presentment and indictment of a grand jury whereas a crime or offense of lesser repugnance to society, such as a violation of a city, county, or village ordinance or a misdemeanor, all of which might be punishable by a fine and/or imprisonment in a city, county, or village jail, need not be initiated by presentment and indictment of a grand jury. Some jurisdictions have statutes which give the defendant the option to move to have the case presented to the grand jury even though the defendant is being charged with a misdemeanor. In this way the defendant has an opportunity to have a group of citizens determine whether charges should be preferred instead of leaving this decision to a prosecutor or a police officer alone.

The right of a defendant to a presentment and indictment by a grand jury has not been made applicable to state prosecutions unless the state itself provides for it by its constitution and by legislation. There is some movement in the direction of disbanding grand juries. Those in favor of its continuance argue that the grand jury acts as a safeguard against power-hungry autocratic prosecutors, while their opponents argue that it delays criminal justice.

§ 7.13 Double Jeopardy

The term "double jeopardy" has been applied to the situation prohibited in the Fifth Amendment which reads:

> *...nor shall any person be subject for the same offence to be twice put in jeopardy of life or limb,...*

The double jeopardy language was incorporated into the Fifth Amendment as a defense against the awesome power of the government to continuously prosecute a defendant until, by sheer exhaustion of purpose or financial resources, the defendant would succumb to plead guilty to a crime that s/he did not commit.

As in all of these rights, the government must protect itself against an abuse of those rights which might lead to a breakdown of law and order. If, for example, a defendant was convicted and s/he was successful in an appellate court which directed a remand for a new trial, the new trial would not be double jeopardy. United States v. Ball, 163 U.S. 662, 16 S.Ct. 1192, 41 L.Ed. 300 (1896). It is quite simple to understand that if it were otherwise, every defendant who would be successful on an appeal from a trial where an unintentional error had occurred might be free to roam the streets.

It has been held that double jeopardy attaches when the jury has been impaneled and sworn, Downom v. United States, 372 U.S. 734, 100 S.Ct. 1033, 10 L.Ed.2d 100 (1963), and in nonjury cases, when the first witness is sworn, but in Florida, it attaches when the court begins to hear evidence,

State v. Berhard, 254 So.2d 38 (1971). However, in Christ v. Bretts, 436 U.S. 908, 98 S.Ct. 2156, 57 L.Ed.2d 124 (1978), the Court held that double jeopardy attaches once a jury is impaneled and sworn, notwithstanding that a Montana statute provided that it did not attach until the first witness is sworn.

For many years the Court held that a citizen's immunity to be twice placed in jeopardy for the same offense was not generally regarded as a fundamental right encompassed within the protection of the Fourteenth Amendment's due process clause. United States ex rel. Martin v. Walker, D.C.Conn., 111 F.Supp. 455, affd. C.A. 203 F.2d 563. However, this concept was changed when the Court said in Benton v. Maryland, 395 U.S. 784, 89 S.Ct. 2056, 23 L.Ed.2d 707 (1969), in remand 260 A.2d 86, 8 Md.App. 388, that the double jeopardy provision of the Fifth Amendment represents a fundamental ideal, and it applies to the states through the Fourteenth Amendment. This case overruled Palko v. Connecticut, 302 U.S. 319, 58 S.Ct. 149, 82 L.Ed. 288 (1937), where an accused was retried for an offense of which he had been acquitted when the state appealed the acquittal.

Some states provide for nonjury trials of minor offenses and if the defendant is found guilty, s/he may move for a trial de novo by a jury in a higher court. In Ludwig v. Massachusetts, 427 U.S. 618, 96 S.Ct. 2781, 49 L.Ed.2d 732, 44 U.S.L.W. 5173 (1976), the Court held that this procedure does not violate the double jeopardy clause. In North v. Russell, 427 U.S. 328, 96 S.Ct. 2709, 49 L.Ed.2d 534 (1976), a Kentucky case, where a defendant who was brought before a police court having jurisdiction over misdemeanors could have a de novo trial in a second-tier circuit court, it was held not to be a violation of the double jeopardy clause because the defendant could merely plead guilty in a police court and the de novo appeal automatically vacated the police court conviction.

Sometimes there is confusion as to the meaning of double jeopardy when it involves being tried for a similar transaction and the court has set up some guidelines:

1. The protection is available to an accused if s/he is being retried for the same offense;
2. It protects an accused from prosecution for any offense where the evidence to be introduced would necessarily include relitigation of a fact or issue which was previously resolved at an earlier trial even though the charges against the accused were different.

In Ashe v. Swenson, 397 U.S. 436, 90 S.Ct. 1189, 25 L.Ed.2d 469 (1970), the accused was tried for robbing a second participant in a card game after he had been previously tried and acquitted of robbing another victim at the same game. The Court majority avoided the issue of double jeopardy and decided that he should not be retried on the theory of collateral estoppel. That is to say that if he had been convicted of robbing one participant, he could still be convicted in a separate trial of robbing another participant, but when he was acquitted of robbing a participant, the government could not relitigate an issue which was resolved in an earlier trial in favor of the accused. In this case it was the issue of whether the defendant was or was not present at the scene.

In order for the theory of collateral estoppel to become operative, the same parties must be adversaries. That is to say that if a defendant is acquitted in a state trial, it does not preclude a second trial by the federal government for a federal crime growing out of the same evidence.

In a 1977 case, a defendant had been convicted of felony murder under a state law which required proof of an underlying robbery with a firearm. He was brought to trial again on the separate robbery arising out of the same incident. The Court held that this second trial constituted double jeopardy, Coker v. Georgia, 433 U.S. 584, 97 S.Ct. 2861, 53 L.Ed.2d 982, 21 Cr.L. 3199 (1977). In another case that came before the same term of the Court, it held that where a defendant was convicted of operating a vehicle without the owner's consent and the defendant was fined for that offense, he could not be brought to another county and be indicted for theft of the car and joyriding. The Court held that the indictments constituted double jeopardy in that it was all part of one transaction and the test as to whether there are two offenses requires proof of a fact which the other does not. Brown v. Ohio, 432 U.S. 161, 97 S.Ct. 187, 53 L.Ed.2d 187, 21 Cr.L. 3137 (1977).

In WHALEN v. U.S., 445 U.S. 684, 100 S.Ct. 1432, 63 L.Ed.2d. 715, 27 Cr.L. 3064 (1980) a defendant was convicted for rape and murder in the perpetration of the rape as two separate violations of the District of Columbia Code. He received separate sentences for each offense to run consecutively. The petitioner contended that his sentence for rape was improper because that offense merged with the felony murder and that the imposition of the two sentences was contrary to the federal statutes and the Double Jeopardy Clause of the Fifth Amendment. The Supreme Court held that multiple punishments for the same offense cannot be imposed for two offenses arising out of the same criminal act unless each offense requires proof of a fact which the other does not.

A conviction for killing in the course of a rape cannot be had without proving all the elements of the offense of rape.

In BUSIC v. UNITED STATES, 446 U.S. 398, 100 S.Ct. 1747, 64 L.Ed.2d. 381, 27 Cr.L. 3109 (1980) the Court held that a federal statute which authorized imposition of increased penalties on a defendant who uses or carries a firearm while committing a federal felony, may not be applied to a defendant charged with violating a statute that increased the punishment for use of a dangerous weapon. In Busic, the defendant and another co-defendant were tried in a joint trial and convicted of, inter alia, armed assault on federal officers. Busic was not the triggerman but was held as an aidor and abbettor and hence as a principal under 18 U.S.C. Sec. 2 and also in violation of 18 U.S.C. 111 which makes it unlawful to assault a federal officer and provides for greater punishment if the perpetrator "uses" a deadly weapon. BUSIC was also convicted of carrying a firearm in the commission of the armed assault in violation of 18 U.S.C. Sect. 924(c).

The court relied on the rule of "lenity" in its holding, i.e. "ambiguity concerning the ambit of criminal statutes should be resolved in favor or lenity." REWIS v. U.S. 401 U.S. 808, 812 (1971) as well as another rule of law that a more specific statute will be given precedence over a more general one regardless of their temporal sequence. PREISER v. RODRIGUES 411 U.S. 475, 489–490 (1973) which authorizes the imposition of enhanced penalties on a defendant who "uses" 924(c)(1) or "carries" 924(c)(2) a firearm while committing a federal felony. As previously indicated, the Court held that Busic can receive the enhanced sentence only under the enhancement provision in the statute defining the felony he committed.

A frequent problem of possible double jeopardy arises when the prosecutor goes to trial but upon a defendant's successful motion to dismiss at the end of the prosecution's case, because of insufficiency of the evidence, as a matter of law, the prosecutor re-indicts and tries the defendant again for the same transaction. The Court addressed itself to the issue of double jeopardy raised by the petitioner in HUDSON v. STATE OF LOUISIANA, 450 U.S. 40, 101 S.Ct. 970, 67 L.Ed.2d. 30, 28 Cr.L. 3081 (1981) and held that a retrial under these circumstances constituted double jeopardy and was constitutionally invalid.

§ 7.14 Nonapplication of Double Jeopardy

There are situations which develop from time to time that present an apparent double jeopardy claim. The courts have held the following not to constitute double jeopardy:

1. *Hung jury:* When a jury fails to get a unanimous verdict (required in some states to convict), the defendant may be tried again. U.S. v. Perez, 9 Wheat. (22 U.S.) 579 (1824);

2. *Mistrial asked for by defendant:* U.S. v. Dinitz, 424 U.S. 600, 96 S.Ct. 1075, 47 L.Ed.2d 267 (1976); Muller v. State, 478 P.2d 822 (Alaska 1971); or directed by the court to protect the defendant's rights, Ill. v. Somerville, 410 U.S. 458, 93 S.Ct. 1066, 35 L.Ed.2d 425 (1973);
3. *Mistrial based on a stipulation* between the prosecution and the defendant: This is a waiver similar to an appeal by defendant;
4. *Mistrial resulting from conduct of defendant or defense counsel:* It is quite apparent that a defendant and/or his/her counsel could be obviously losing the case and decides to do something in the trial which would be prejudicial. If this ploy would result in a bar against a retrial, the ends of public justice would be defeated. See U.S. v. Perez (supra);
5. *Order to suppress evidence:* Where an order to suppress was entered after a general finding of guilt rendered in a bench trial, it was held that an appeal of the order by the government did not pose a double jeopardy problem. United States v. Rose, 429 U.S. 5, 97 S.Ct. 26, 50 L.Ed.2d 5, (1976).
6. *Trial de novo:* Some states provide for bench trials in criminal matters. If the defendant is found guilty at the bench trial, he/she may seek a trial de novo to be conducted before a jury. Massachusetts has such a procedure. In JUSTICES OF BOSTON MUNICIPAL COURT v. LYDON, —U.S.—, 104 S.Ct. 1805, 80 L.Ed.2d. 311 (1984) the defendant was charged with minor crimes and was tried in Boston Municipal Court and found guilty. He requested a de novo trial and was released on personal recognizance. Before the trial commenced, he moved to dismiss on the ground that no evidence of intent (a necessary element of the crime charged) had been presented at the bench trial and thus a retrial should be barred as a violation of the double jeopardy clause under BURKS v. UNITED STATES 437 U.S. 1. The motion was denied and he sought relief from the Massachusetts Supreme Judicial Court that affirmed the lower court. He then sought habeas corpus relief in Federal District Court. The case finally arrived in the United States Supreme Court which held that the District Court had jurisdiction for the habeas corpus petition and, inter alia, held that his retrial de novo without any judicial determination of the sufficiency of the evidence at his prior bench trial does not violate the Double Jeopardy Clause.
7. *No threat of successive prosecutions:* Another case involving the non-application of a double jeopardy defense arose in U.S. v. DIFRANCESCO, 449 U.S. 117, 101 S.Ct. 426, 66 L.Ed.2d. 328, 28 Cr.L. 3009 (1980) where the defendant claimed that the section of the

Organized Crime Control Act, 18 U.S.C. Section 3576 granting the United States the right, under specified conditions to appeal the sentence imposed upon a "dangerous special offender" was unconstitutional in that it violated the Double Jeopardy clause of the Fifth Amendment. The Court held that where the government appeal holds no threat of successive prosecutions, the Double Jeopardy Clause is not offended.

8. *Mistrial on motion of defendant:* Where a defendant in a criminal trial successfully moves for a mistrial, he may invoke the bar of double jeopardy in a second effort to try him only if the conduct giving rise to the successful motion for a mistrial was prosecutorial or judicial conduct INTENDED to provoke the defendant into moving for a mistrial. OREGON, PETITIONER vs. BRUCE ALAN KENNEDY, —U.S.—, 102 S.Ct. 2083, L.Ed.2d. 416, 31 Cr.L. 3044 (1982).

9. *Insufficient weight of evidence:* In TIBBS v. FLORIDA, —U.S.—, 102 S.Ct. 2211, 72 L.Ed.2d. 652, 31 Cr.L. 3065 (1982) it was held in a 5–4 decision that the Double Jeopardy Clause does not bar the retrial of a defendant whose conviction was reversed on appeal due to the weight of the evidence, rather than its sufficiency. The difference between the weight and sufficiency of evidence was stated in the intermediate decision in this case in the Florida Supreme Court and adopted by the United States Supreme Court by implication. The Florida Supreme Court held that a conviction rests upon insufficient evidence when, even after viewing the evidence in the light most favorable to the prosecution, no rational factfinder could have found the defendant guilty beyond a reasonable doubt. A reversal based on the weight of the evidence, on the other hand, draws the appellate court into questions of credibility. In this case there was a serious question of the veracity of a drug using "naer do well" female in her accusations against the defendant, a college educated male of good reputation who stood charged with murder and rape. The Florida Supreme Court reversed his capital punishment conviction saying that the "interests of justice" required a new trial.

10. *Cumulative punishment:* Missouri has a statute that provides that any person who commits a felony under the laws of the state through the use of a dangerous or deadly weapon is also guilty of the crime of armed criminal action punishable by imprisonment for not less than three years which punishment shall be in addition to any punishment provided by law for the felony. Danny Hunter was convicted in a Missouri state court of both first degree robbery and armed criminal action, and pursuant to statutes was sentenced to concurrent prison terms of 10 years for robbery and 15 years for armed criminal action. The Missouri Court of Appeals reversed the conviction and sentence for armed criminal action on the ground that his sentence for both crimes violated his protection against double jeopardy. The United States Supreme Court in MISSOURI v. HUNTER, —U.S.—, 103 S.Ct. 673, L.Ed.2d. 535, 32 Cr.L. 3021 (1983) held that this was not a violation of the respondent's double jeopardy protection because, inter alia, that if two criminal statutes proscribe the same conduct, the double jeopardy clause does not preclude the imposition, in a single trial of cumulative punishments pursuant to those statutes, citing WHALEN v. U.S. 445 U.S. 684 . . . Where, as here, a legislature specifically authorizes cumulative punishment under two statutes, regardless of whether those statutes proscribe the "same" conduct . . . a court's task of statutory construction is at an end.

§ 7.15 Sentence on Second Trial

A defendant who appeals and gets a retrial has no assurance that upon conviction in the subsequent trial his/her sentence may be longer or shorter than what s/he had received in the earlier trial. North Carolina v. Pearce, 395 U.S. 711, 89 S.Ct. 2072, 23 L.Ed.2d 658 (1969). The judge who imposes a more severe sentence, however, must place objective reasons on the record.

Where a state statute provides in possible capital punishment cases for the jury to determine whether the prosecution has "proved its case" in the sentencing procedure of a bifurcated trial held before the same jury that had convicted the defendant, the Court has held that on the second trial, the matter of sentencing is res adjudicata in that the jury had already acquitted him of whatever was necessary to impose the death sentence. BULLINGTON v. STATE OF MISSOURI, 431 U.S. 430, S.Ct. 1852, 68 L.Ed.2d. 270, 29 Cr.L. 3023 (1981).

§ 7.16 Double Sovereignties and Double Jeopardy

A problem arises when the federal government prosecutes a defendant for a violation of a federal law which is also a violation of a state law, or conversely. Another similar situation might occur when more than one state claims that a defendant has violated its laws although the act was all part of one transaction. This theory can be further extended to violations of laws of different jurisdictions within a state, e.g., village, municipal, county, state law, all arising out of the same transaction.

A. Federal and state sovereignties: United States v. Lanza, 260 U.S. 377, 43 S.Ct. 141, 67 L.Ed. 314 (1922), was the bellwether case for this problem. The Court held there that each citizen of the United States is also a citizen of a state and owes allegiance to both sovereigns. An act denounced as a crime by both the state and the federal government is an offense against the peace and dignity of each and may be separately punished by each.

This was followed, among others, by Bartkus v. Illinois, 359 U.S. 121, 79 S.Ct. 676, 3 L.Ed.2d 684 (1959), where a divided court permitted a state conviction for robbery of a federally insured bank after the defendant had been acquitted on federal charges arising out of the same transaction and Abbate v. United States, 359 U.S. 187, 798 S.Ct. 666, 3 L.Ed.2d 729 (1959), where the defendants pleaded guilty in an Illinois state court for conspiring to injure or destroy the property of another in violation of state law. However, the act was also conspiring to dynamite telephone company facilities and this was a federal crime. They were again tried in a federal court and convicted. The Court sustained the second conviction.

The overriding reasoning of the Court appears to be that a state may make a "deal" with a defendant who is well placed politically, mete out little or no punishment for a violation that may also be a violation of federal law, and law enforcement would be hindered. However, pursuant to Murphy v. Waterfront Commission, 378 U.S. 52, 84 S.Ct. 1594, 12 L.Ed.2d 678 (1964), it was held that a constitutional privilege against self-incrimination protects a state witness against incrimination in a federal prosecution. Therefore where a witness testifies under amnesty granted by a state, neither the testimony nor its fruits may be used in a subsequent prosecution by the federal government.

The student is left to his/her own imagination as to how this procedure can be used in a corrupt jurisdiction.

Illinois later adopted legislation forbidding state prosecution of any person acquitted or convicted by the federal government for the same criminal act. Ill. Re. Stat. Ch. 38 Section 3-4 (1968 supp). Many other states have similar statutes.

B. More than one state sovereignty: Following the thinking of United States v. Lanza (supra) each state may prosecute for an offense against the peace and dignity of each where the act was committed within its borders, and hence no double jeopardy attaches.

C. Municipal and state sovereignties: The problem of municipal and state sovereignty regarding double jeopardy prosecution was met in Waller v. Florida, 397 U.S. 387, 90 S.Ct. 1184, 25 L.Ed.2d 435 (1970), where a unanimous Court rejected the extension of the Bartkus rule (supra) when petitioner had removed a canvas mural which was affixed inside the City Hall and carried it through the streets until, after a scuffle with the police, it was recovered in a damaged condition. He was convicted of two city ordinances (destruction of city property; disorderly breach of the peace) and also convicted of a felony of grand larceny. The court held that the second trial on the state charge was double jeopardy in that the city and state are not separate sovereigns.

The courts have made some other fine distinctions which are not, in the author's opinion, proper to be included in a text of this scope. For an extensive treatment of this topic the reader is referred to Comment, Twice in Jeopardy, 75 Yale Law Journal 262 (1966).

§ 7.17 Second Trial for More Serious Offense

Sometimes facts change during the course of a trial or after a trial is completed, which may justify a second trial for a more serious offense. Such a situation might occur where the victim of an assault dies as a result of injuries received in the assault. The trial for the assault may have been concluded and the defendant convicted before the victim has died. If it can be determined that the victim died as a result of the assault, the second trial for homicide, whether it be for manslaughter or murder, depending on the facts, will not be barred because of the assault trial. Where the same act or transaction constitutes a violation of the distinct statutory provisions, the test to be applied to determine whether there are two offenses or only one, is whether each provision requires proof of an additional fact which the other does not, Blockbuster v. U.S., 284 U.S. 299 (1932).

§ 7.18 Effect of Double Jeopardy

If the defendant is successful in invoking a claim that s/he is being tried in violation of the double jeopardy privilege, the defendant is entitled to a dismissal of the charges presently before the court.

The defendant can also not be found guilty of a lesser included offense. For example: if a defendant is found not guilty of robbery, s/he cannot be retried and found guilty of larceny arising out of the same transaction which relitigates the issue of whether property was taken unlawfully by the defendant from the person of the same victim. This is so because larceny is a lesser included offense of the robbery, thereby making it part of the same offense. The defendant who was tried for robbery could have been found guilty of the larceny or assault but was not so found. Reading the definitions below may make this more understandable:

Larceny: The taking of another's property unlawfully, with the intention of depriving the owner of its use;

Assault: An attempt, with unlawful force, to inflict bodily injury upon another, accompanied by the apparent present ability to give effect to the attempt if not prevented;

Robbery: A person commits robbery when in the course of committing a larceny, s/he uses or threatens the immediate use of physical force upon another person for the purpose of:

(1) preventing or overcoming resistance to the taking of the property or to the retention thereof immediately after the taking, or

(2) compelling the owner of such property or another person to deliver up the property or to engage in other conduct which aids in the commission of the larceny.

§ 7.19 Doctrine of Res Adjudicata

Res adjudicata is sometimes shortened to read "res judicata." Both terms have the same meaning. This phrase has Latin origin. The term "res" meaning "the thing," and the term "adjudicata" meaning "decided." Taken together the phrase means literally "the thing decided." It is a doctrine in law by which a final judgment of a court of competent jurisdiction is conclusive upon the parties to the litigation and therefore may not be relitigated by the same parties in any subsequent litigation. Therefore the issue, having been once decided, is put to "sleep" never to be brought up again.

The idea of double jeopardy is directly related to res judicata except that double jeopardy is directed against government alone whereas res judicata may apply to both criminal and civil trials.

A case involving res adjudicata arose in 1980 in UNITED STATES v. DIFRANCESCO. (supra in Section 7.14) The reader is referred to the preceding section for a discussion of this case.

§ 7.20 Confessions and Admissions

The privilege against self-incrimination naturally includes the right of a suspect not to be compelled to confess the crime or make admissions with respect to it. There is a different meaning given to confessions when compared to admissions, but both confessions and/or admissions may not be forced involuntarily from a suspect.

A confession is a direct acknowledgment of guilt whereas an admission is a statement or an act done which is inconsistent with the party's present position on trial. An example of a confession occurs where the suspect makes a statement as follows: "I killed Jane Doe." On the other hand, an example of an admission might be where the defendant testifies on the trial "I did not see Jane Doe that night"; however, he had previously stated to someone else that he had taken Jane Doe to a movie on the night in question.

§ 7.21 Prohibition against Involuntary Confessions or Admissions

We have previously discussed the reasons for the prohibition against self-incrimination as contained in the Fifth Amendment. We have also discussed the experience of the author while he and his wife were in the Lisbon, Portugal, airport where the young Portuguese man indicated that there was freedom of speech written in the nation's constitution but if anything was said against the government, the speaker was placed in jail. The United States Supreme Court has been particularly active in protecting persons from the excesses of law enforcement by excluding evidence induced by involuntary statements made by the accused.

Police departments and officers, in the interest of effective law enforcement, had for many years adopted a procedure which came to be known as "Third Degree Method" of interrogation. A suspect would be subjected to many forms of physical and/or psychological torture to confess to a crime. The answer that the police were looking for under these conditions was the expected answer involving the suspect in the commission of the crime. This was brought out in the Wickersham Report to Congress by a Presidential Commission from factual studies conducted in the early 1930s.

The initial theory preventing the admissibility of coerced incriminating evidence was the probability of its unreliability. This was later joined by an abhorrence of police practices which were in violation of the law, that is, in the end life and liberty could be as much endangered from illegal methods used to convict those thought to be criminals as from the actual criminals themselves. This was therefore a violation of the Due Process of Law Clause of the Fourteenth Amendment, when applied to actions of state law enforcement officers. Theoretically the two standards, i.e., lack of trustworthiness, lack of due process of law, are applied independently of each other; in practice they often overlap.

The Court treated this problem in Brown v. Mississippi, 297 U.S. 278, 56 S.Ct. 461, 80 L.Ed. 682 (1936). This was the first Fourteenth Amendment due process case. In that case a black defendant had been beaten unmercifully into a confession. The Court excluded this confession based on the lack of veracity of the confession under the circumstances of that case. Similar cases followed Brown (supra) but Ashcraft v. Tennessee, 322 U.S. 143, 64 S.Ct. 921, 88 L.Ed. 1194 (1944), extended the concept to include psychological coercion where the defendant had been subjected to some thirty-six hours of continuous interrogation by the police. The Court ruled that this type of questioning raised a conclusive presumption of coercion. Spano v. New York, 360 U.S. 315, 79 S.Ct. 1202, 3 L.Ed.2d 1265 (1959), combined the two constitutional standards, i.e., police methods test and the trustworthiness test.

The Court in McNabb v. United States, 318 U.S. 332, 63 S.Ct. 608, 87 L.Ed.2d 1479 (1957), held for the general principle that police detention of defendants beyond the time when a committing magistrate was readily accessible constituted "wilful disobedience of law." This became known as the McNabb-Mallory rule and, of course, as the case titles indicated, it was applicable at that time to federal prosecutions. The Court went much further in state prosecution in this doctrine but covered it under the right to counsel as well as self-incrimination considerations.

A question was raised as to whether a federal court can review the voluntariness of a confession. In MILLER v. FENTON, 38 Cr.L. 3025 (1985) the Court of Appeals of New Jersey had concluded that the voluntariness of a confession is a "factual issue," which 28 USC 2254(d) provided was a state-court finding of fact, with certain exceptions, shall be presumed to be correct in a federal habeas corpus proceeding. . . . The United States Supreme Court held to the contrary. It held that the voluntariness of a confession is not an issue of fact entitled to 2254(d) presumption but is a legal question meriting independent consideration in a habeas corpus proceeding.

§ 7.22 Custodial Interrogation

The Court has construed custodial interrogation to be a questioning initiated by law enforcement officers after a person has been taken into custody or otherwise deprived of his freedom of action in any significant way. Miranda v. Arizona, 384 U.S. 436, 86 S.Ct. 1602, 16 L.Ed.2d 694 (1966). You will note that the Court emphasized that law enforcement officers must be involved. It would appear that private security guards such as those found in department stores or commercial establishments need not be affected by the privilege against self-incrimination or other personal rights. The rights of the individual as contained in the Bill of Rights are directed only against government and its propensity for abuse.

Miranda (supra) held for the principle that the prosecution may not use statements made by the accused, whether inculpatory or exculpatory, stemming from custodial interrogations of the defendant unless it demonstrates the use of procedural safeguards effective to secure the privilege against self-incrimination.

We now come to a joining of the legal history in state criminal procedure of the right against self-incrimination and the right of counsel as is guaranteed in the Sixth Amendment. This will be treated more fully in Chapter 8 infra. Likewise, the issue of cruel and unusual punishment as it relates to capital punishment is discussed in Chapter 9 infra.

§ 7.23 Probation—Automatic Revocation

BEARDEN v. GEORGIA, 461 U.S. 660, 103 S.Ct. 2064, 76 L.Ed.2d. 221, 33 Cr.L. 3103 (1983) involved a petitioner who plead guilty in a Georgia trial court to burglary and theft by receiving stolen property. The Court sentenced him to probation on condition that he pay a $500 fine and $250 in restitution. $100 was to be paid on the sentence date, $100 the following day and $550 within four months. He paid the $200 but was terminated from his job and was unable to find work. Shortly before the $550 payment date, he notified his probation officer that the payment would be late. A petition for revocation of probation was filed because of no payment of the balance of $500. After a hearing, probation was revoked, a conviction was entered and he was sentenced to prison. The record indicated that he was unable to find employment, had no assets nor any income. The Court held that a sentencing court may not revoke a defendant's probation for failure to pay a fine and make restitution absence evidence and findings that he was somehow responsible for the failure. . . .

Judicial Decisions Relating to Chapter 7

Miranda *v.* Arizona

384 U.S. 436, 86 S.Ct. 1602, 16 L.Ed.2d 694 (1966)

CERTIORARI TO THE SUPREME COURT OF ARIZONA

. . .

MR. CHIEF JUSTICE WARREN delivered the opinion of the Court.

The cases before us raise questions which go to the roots of our concepts of American criminal jurisprudence: the restraints society must observe consistent with the Federal Constitution in prosecuting individuals for crime. More specifically, we deal with the admissibility of statements obtained from an individual who is subjected to custodial police interrogation and the necessity for procedures which assure that the individual is accorded his privilege under the Fifth Amendment to the Constitution not to be compelled to incriminate himself.

We dealt with certain phases of this problem recently in Escobedo v. Illinois, 378 U.S. 478 (1964). There, as in the four cases before us, law enforcement officials took the defendant into custody and interrogated him in a police station for the purpose of obtaining a confession. The police did not effectively advise him of his right to remain silent or of his right to consult with his attorney. Rather, they confronted him with an alleged accomplice who accused him of having perpetrated a murder. When the defendant denied the accusation and said "I didn't shoot Manuel, you did it," they handcuffed him and took him to an interrogation room. There, while handcuffed and standing, he was questioned for four hours until he confessed. During this interrogation, the police denied his request to speak to his attorney, and they prevented his retained attorney, who had come to the police station, from consulting with him. At his trial, the State, over his objection, introduced the confession against him. We held that the statements thus made were constitutionally inadmissible.

This case has been the subject of judicial interpretation and spirited legal debate since it was decided two years ago. Both state and federal courts, in assessing its implications, have arrived at varying conclusions. A wealth of scholarly material has been written tracing its ramifications and underpinnings. Police and prosecutor have speculated on its range and desirability. We granted certiorari in these cases, 382 U.S. 924, 925, 937, in order further to explore some facets of the problems, thus exposed, of applying the privilege against self-incrimination to in-custody interrogation, and to give concrete constitutional guidelines for law enforcement agencies and courts to follow.

We start here, as we did in Escobedo, with the premise that our holding is not an innovation in our jurisprudence, but is an application of principles long recognized and applied in other settings. We have undertaken a thorough re-examination of the Escobedo decision and the principles it announced, and we reaffirm it. That case was but an explication of basic rights that are enshrined in our Constitution—that "No person . . . shall be compelled in any criminal case to be a witness against himself," and that "the accused shall . . . have the Assistance of Counsel"—rights which were put in jeopardy in that case through official overbearing. These precious rights were fixed in our Constitution only after centuries of persecution and struggle. And in the words of CHIEF JUSTICE MARSHALL, they were secured "for ages to come, and . . . designed to approach immortality as nearly as human institutions can approach it," Cohens v. Virginia, 6 Wheat. 264, 387 (1821).

Over 70 years ago, our predecessors on this Court eloquently stated:

> "The maxim *nemo tenetur seipsum accusare* had its origin in a protest against the inquisitorial and manifestly unjust methods of interrogating accused persons, which [have] long obtained in the continental system, and, until the expulsion of the Stuarts from the British throne in 1688, and the erection of additional barriers for the protection of the people against the exercise of arbitrary power, [were] not uncommon even in England. While the admissions or confessions of the prisoner, when voluntarily and freely made, have always ranked high in the scale of incriminating evidence, if an accused person be asked to explain his apparent connection with a crime under investigation, the ease with which the questions put to him may assume an inquisitorial character, the temptation to press the witness unduly, to browbeat him if he be timid or reluctant, to push him into a corner, and to entrap him into fatal contradictions, which is so painfully evident in many of the earlier state trials, notably in those of Sir Nicholas Throckmorton, and Udal, the Puritan minister, made the system so odious as to give rise to a demand for its total abolition. The change in the English criminal procedure in that particular seems to be founded upon no statute and no judicial opinion, but upon a general and silent acquiescence of the courts in a popular demand. But, however adopted, it has become firmly embedded in English, as well as in American jurisprudence. So deeply, did the iniquities of the ancient system impress themselves upon the minds of the American colonists that the States, with one accord, made a denial of the right to question an accused person a part of their fundamental law, so that a maxim, which in England was a mere rule of evidence, became clothed in this country with the impregnability of a constitutional enactment." Brown v. Walker, 161 U.S. 591, 596–597 (1896).

In stating the obligation of the judiciary to apply these constitutional rights, this Court declared in Weems v. United States, 217 U.S. 349, 373 (1910):

> ". . . our contemplation cannot be only of what has been but of what may be. Under any other rule a constitution would indeed be as easy of application as it would be deficient in efficacy and power. Its general principles would have little value and be converted by precedent into impotent and lifeless formulas. Rights declared in words might be lost in reality. And this has been recognized. The meaning and vitality of the Constitution have developed against narrow and restrictive construction."

This was the spirit in which we delineated, in meaningful language, the manner in which the constitutional rights of the individual could be enforced against overzealous police practices. It was necessary in Escobedo, as here, to insure that what was proclaimed in the Constitution had not become but a "form of words," Silverthorne Lumber Co. v. United States, 251 U.S. 385, 392 (1920), in the hands of government officials. And it is in this spirit, consistent with our role as judges, that we adhere to the principles of Escobedo today.

Our holding will be spelled out with some specificity in the pages which follow but briefly stated it is this: the prosecution may not use statements, whether exculpatory or inculpatory, stemming from custodial interrogation of the defendant unless it demonstrates the use of procedural safeguards effective to secure the privilege against self-incrimination. By custodial interrogation, we mean questioning initiated by law enforcement officers after a person has been taken into custody or otherwise deprived of his freedom of action in any significant way. As for the procedural safeguards to be employed, unless other fully effective means are devised to inform accused persons of their right of silence and to assure a continuous opportunity to exercise it, the following measures are required. Prior to any questioning, the person must be warned that he has a right to remain silent, that any statement he does make may be used as evidence against him, and that he has a right to the presence of an attorney, either retained or appointed. The defendant may waive effectuation of these rights, provided the waiver is made voluntarily, knowingly and intelligently. If, however, he indicates in any manner and at any stage of the process that he wishes to consult with an attorney before speaking there can be no questioning. Likewise, if the individual is alone and indicates in any manner that he does not wish to be interrogated, the police may not question him. The mere fact that he may have answered some questions or volunteered some statements on his own does not deprive him of the right to refrain from answering any further inquiries until he has consulted with an attorney and thereafter consents to be questioned.

I

The constitutional issue we decide in each of these cases is the admissibility of statements obtained from a defendant questioned while in custody or otherwise deprived of his freedom of action in any significant way. In each, the defendant was questioned by police officers, detectives, or a prosecuting attorney in a room in which he was cut off from the outside world. In none of these cases was the defendant given a full and effective warning of his rights at the outset of the interrogation process. In all the cases, the questioning elicited oral admissions, and in three of them, signed statements as well which were admitted at their trials. They all thus share salient features—incommunicado interrogation of individuals in a police-dominated atmosphere, resulting in self-incriminating statements without full warnings of constitutional rights.

An understanding of the nature and setting of this in-custody interrogation is essential to our decisions today. The difficulty in depicting what transpires at such interrogations stems from the fact that in this country they have largely taken place incommunicado. From extensive factual studies undertaken in the early 1930's, including the famous Wickersham Report to Congress by a Presidential

Commission, it is clear that police violence and the "third degree" flourished at that time. In a series of cases decided by this Court long after these studies, the police resorted to physical brutality—beating, hanging, whipping—and to sustained and protracted questioning incommunicado in order to extort confessions. The Commission on Civil Rights in 1961 found much evidence to indicate that "some policemen still resort to physical force to obtain confessions," 1961 Comm'n on Civil Rights Rep., Justice, pt. 5, 17. The use of physical brutality and violence is not, unfortunately, relegated to the past or to any part of the country. Only recently in Kings County, New York, the police brutally beat, kicked and placed lighted cigarette butts on the back of a potential witness under interrogation for the purpose of securing a statement incriminating a third party. People v. Portelli, 15 N.Y.2d 235, 205 N.E.2d 857, 257 N.Y.S.2d 931 (1965).

The examples given above are undoubtedly the exception now, but they are sufficiently widespread to be the object of concern. Unless a proper limitation upon custodial interrogation is achieved—such as these decisions will advance—there can be no assurance that practices of this nature will be eradicated in the foreseeable future. The conclusion of the Wickersham Commission Report, made over 30 years ago, is still pertinent:

> "To the contention that the third degree is necessary to get the facts, the reporters aptly reply in the language of the present Lord Chancellor of England (Lord Sankey): 'It is not admissible to do a great right by doing a little wrong. . . . It is not sufficient to do justice by obtaining a proper result by irregular or improper means.' Not only does the use of the third degree involve a flagrant violation of law by the officers of the law, but it involves also the dangers of false confessions, and it tends to make police and prosecutors less zealous in the search for objective evidence. As the New York prosecutor quoted in the report said, 'It is a short cut and makes the police lazy and unenterprising.' Or, as another official quoted remarked: 'If you use your fists, you are not so likely to use your wits.' We agree with the conclusion expressed in the report, that 'The third degree brutalizes the police, hardens the prisoner against society, and lowers the esteem in which the administration of justice is held by the public.'" IV National Commission on Law Observance and Enforcement, Report on Lawlessness in Law Enforcement 5 (1931).

Again we stress that the modern practice of in-custody interrogation is psychologically rather than physically oriented. As we have stated before, "Since Chambers v. Florida, 309 U.S. 227, this Court has recognized that coercion can be mental as well as physical, and that the blood of the accused is not the only hallmark of an unconstitutional inquisition." Blackburn v. Alabama, 361 U.S. 199, 206 (1960). Interrogation still takes place in privacy. Privacy results in secrecy and this in turn results in a gap in our knowledge as to what in fact goes on in the interrogation rooms. A valuable source of information about present police practices, however, may be found in various police manuals and texts which document procedures employed with success in the past, and which recommend various other effective tactics. These texts are used by law enforcement agencies themselves as guides. It should be noted that these texts professedly present the most enlightened and effective means presently used to obtain statements through custodial interrogation. By considering these texts and other data, it is possible to describe procedures observed and noted around the country.

The officers are told by the manuals that the "principal psychological factor contributing to a successful interrogation is *privacy*—being alone with the person under interrogation." The efficacy of this tactic has been explained as follows:

> "If at all practicable, the interrogation should take place in the investigator's office or at least in a room of his own choice. The subject should be deprived of every psychological advantage. In his own home he may be confident, indignant, or recalcitrant. He is more keenly aware of his rights and more reluctant to tell of his indiscretions or criminal behavior within the walls of his home. Moreover his family and other friends are nearby, their presence lending moral support. In his own office, the investigator possesses all the advantages. The atmosphere suggests the invincibility of the forces of the law."

To highlight the isolation and unfamiliar surroundings, the manuals instruct the police to display an air of confidence in the suspect's guilt and from outward appearance to maintain only an interest in confirming certain details. The guilt of the subject is to be posited as a fact. The interrogator should direct his comments toward the reasons why the subject committed the act, rather than court failure by asking the subject whether he did it. Like other men, perhaps the subject has had a bad family life, had an unhappy childhood, had too much to drink, had an unrequited desire for women. The officers are instructed to minimize the moral seriousness of the offense, to cast blame on the victim or on society. These tactics are designed to put the subject in a psychological state where his story is but an elaboration of what the police purport to know already—that he is guilty. Explanations to the contrary are dismissed and discouraged.

The texts thus stress that the major qualities an interrogator should possess are patience and perseverance. One writer describes the efficacy of these characteristics in this manner:

> "In the preceding paragraphs emphasis has been placed on kindness and strategems. The investigator will, however, encounter many situations where the sheer weight of his personality will be the deciding factor. Where emotional appeals and tricks are employed to no avail, he must rely on an oppressive atmosphere of dogged persistence. He must interrogate steadily and without relent, leaving the subject no prospect of surcease. He must dominate his subject and overwhelm him with his inexorable will to obtain the truth. He should interrogate for a spell of several hours pausing only for the subject's necessities in acknowledgment of the need to avoid a charge of duress that can be technically substantiated. In a serious case, the interrogation may continue for days, with the required intervals for food and sleep, but with no respite from the atmosphere of domination. It is possible in this way to induce the subject to talk without resorting to duress or coercion. The method should be used only when the guilt of the subject appears highly probable."

The manuals suggest that the suspect be offered legal excuses for his actions in order to obtain an initial admission of guilt. Where there is a suspected revenge-killing, for example, the interrogator may say:

> "Joe, you probably didn't go out looking for this fellow with the purpose of shooting him. My guess is, however, that you expected something from him and that's why you carried a gun—for your own protection. You knew him for what he was, no good. Then when you met him he probably started using foul, abusive language and he gave some indication that he was about to pull a gun on you, and that's when you had to act to save your own life. That's about it, isn't it, Joe?"

Having then obtained the admission of shooting, the interrogator is advised to refer to circumstantial evidence which negates the self-defense explanation. This should enable him to secure the entire story. One text notes that "Even if he fails to do so, the inconsistency between the subject's original denial of the shooting and his present admission of at least doing the shooting will serve to deprive him of a self-defense 'out' at the time of trial."

When the techniques described above prove unavailing, the texts recommend they be alternated with a show of some hostility. One ploy often used has been termed the "friendly-unfriendly" or the "Mutt and Jeff" act:

> "...In this technique, two agents are employed. Mutt, the relentless investigator, who knows the subject is guilty and is not going to waste any time. He's sent a dozen men away for this crime and he's going to send the subject away for the full term. Jeff, on the other hand, is obviously a kindhearted man. He has a family himself. He has a brother who was involved in a little scrape like this. He disapproves of Mutt and his tactics and will arrange to get him off the case if the subject will cooperate. He can't hold Mutt off for very long. The subject would be wise to make a quick decision. The technique is applied by having both investigators present while Mutt acts out his role. Jeff may stand by quietly and demur at some of Mutt's tactics. When Jeff makes his plea for cooperation, Mutt is not present in the room."

The interrogators sometimes are instructed to induce a confession out of trickery. The technique here is quite effective in crimes which require identification or which run in series. In the identification situation, the interrogator may take a break in his questioning to place the subject among a group of men in a line-up. "The witness or complainant (previously coached, if necessary) studies the line-up and confidently points out the subject as the guilty party." Then the questioning resumes "as though there were now no doubt about the guilt of the subject." A variation on this technique is called the "reverse line-up":

> "The accused is placed in a line-up, but this time he is identified by several fictitious witnesses or victims who associated him with different offenses. It is expected that the subject will become desperate and confess to the offense under investigation in order to escape from the false accusations."

The manuals also contain instructions for police on how to handle the individual who refuses to discuss the matter entirely, or who asks for an attorney or relatives. The examiner is to concede him the right to remain silent. "This usually has a very undermining effect. First of all, he is disappointed in his expectation of an unfavorable reaction on the part of the interrogator. Secondly, a concession of this right to remain silent impresses the subject with the apparent fairness of his interrogator." After this psychological conditioning, however, the officer is told to point out the incriminating significance of the suspect's refusal to talk:

> "Joe, you have a right to remain silent. That's your privilege and I'm the last person in the world who'll try to take it away from you. If that's the way you want to leave this, O.K. But let me ask you this. Suppose you were in my shoes and I were in yours and you called me in to ask me about this and I told you, 'I don't want to answer any of your questions.' You'd think I had something to hide, and you'd probably be right in thinking that. That's exactly what I'll have to think about you, and so will everybody else. So let's sit here and talk this whole thing over."

Few will persist in their initial refusal to talk, it is said, if this monologue is employed correctly.

In the event that the subject wishes to speak to a relative or an attorney, the following advice is tendered:

> "[T]he interrogator should respond by suggesting that the subject first tell the truth to the interrogator himself rather than get anyone else involved in the matter. If the request is for an attorney the interrogator may suggest that the subject save himself or his family the expense of any such professional service, particularly if he is innocent of the offense under investigation. The interrogator may also add, 'Joe, I'm only looking for the truth, and if you're telling the truth, that's it. You can handle this by yourself.'"

From these representative samples of interrogation techniques, the setting prescribed by the manuals and observed in practice becomes clear. In essence, it is this: To be alone with the subject is essential to prevent distraction and to deprive him of any outside support. The aura of confidence in his guilt undermines his will to resist. He merely confirms the preconceived story the police seek to have him describe. Patience and persistence, at times relentless questioning, are employed. To obtain a confession, the interrogator must "patiently maneuver himself or his quarry into a position from which the desired objective may be attained." When normal procedures fail to produce the needed result, the police may resort to deceptive strategems such as giving false legal advice. It is important to keep the subject off balance, for example, by trading on his insecurity about himself or his surroundings. The police then persuade, trick, or cajole him out of exercising his constitutional rights.

Even without employing brutality, the "third degree" or the specific stratagems described above, the very fact of custodial interrogation exacts a heavy toll on individual liberty and trades on the weakness of individuals. This fact may be illustrated simply by referring to three confession cases decided by this Court in the Term immediately preceding our Escobedo decision. In Townsend v. Sain, 372 U.S. 293 (1963), the defendant was a 19-year-old heroin addict, described as a "near mental defective," id., at 307–310. The defendant in Lynumn v. Illinois, 372 U.S. 528 (1963), was a woman who confessed to the arresting officer after being importuned to "cooperate" in order to prevent her children from being taken by relief authorities. This Court as in those cases reversed the conviction of a defendant in Haynes v. Washington, 373 U.S. 503 (1963), whose persistent request during his interrogation was to phone his wife or attorney. In other settings, these individuals might have exercised their constitutional rights. In the incommunicado police-dominated atmosphere, they succumbed.

In the cases before us today, given this background, we concern ourselves primarily with this interrogation atmosphere and the evils it can bring. In No. 759, Miranda v. Arizona, the police arrested the defendant and took him to a special interrogation room where they secured a confession. In No. 760, Vignera v. New York, the defendant made oral admissions to the police after interrogation in the afternoon, and then signed an inculpatory statement upon being questioned by an assistant district attorney later the same evening. In No. 761, Westover v. United States, the defendant was handed over to the Federal Bureau of Investigation by local authorities after they had detained and interrogated him for a lengthy period, both at night and the following morning. After some two hours of questioning, the federal officers had obtained signed statements from the defendant. Lastly, in No. 584, California v. Stewart, the local police held the defendant five days in the station and interrogated him on nine separate occasions before they secured his inculpatory statement.

In these cases, we might not find the defendants' statements to have been involuntary in traditional terms. Our concern for adequate safeguards to protect precious Fifth Amendment rights is, of course, not lessened in the slightest. In each of the cases, the defendant was thrust into an unfamiliar atmosphere and run through menacing police interrogation procedures. The potentiality for compulsion is forcefully apparent, for example, in Miranda, where the indigent Mexican defendant was a seriously disturbed individual with pronounced sexual fantasies, and in Stewart, in which the defendant was an indigent Los Angeles Negro who had dropped out of school in the sixth grade. To be sure, the records do not evince overt physical coercion or patent psychological ploys. The fact remains that in none of these cases did the officers undertake to afford appropriate safeguards at the outset of the interrogation to insure that the statements were truly the product of free choice.

It is obvious that such an interrogation environment is created for no purpose other than to subjugate the individual to the will of his examiner. This atmosphere carries its own badge of intimidation. To be sure, this is not physical intimidation, but it is equally destructive of human dignity. The current practice of incommunicado interrogation is at odds with one of our Nation's most cherished principles—that the individual may not be compelled to incriminate himself. Unless adequate protective devices are employed to dispel the compulsion inherent in custodial surroundings, no statement obtained from the defendant can truly be the product of his free choice.

From the foregoing, we can readily perceive an intimate connection between the privilege against self-incrimination and police custodial questioning. It is fitting to turn to history and precedent underlying the Self-Incrimination Clause to determine its applicability in this situation.

II

We sometimes forget how long it has taken to establish the privilege against self-incrimination, the sources from which it came and the fervor with which it was defended. Its roots go back into ancient times. Perhaps the critical historical event shedding light on its origins and evolution was the trial of one John Lilburn, a vocal anti-Stuart Leveller, who was made to take the Star Chamber Oath in 1637. The oath would have bound him to answer to all questions posed to him on any subject. The Trial of John Lilburn and John Wharton, 3 How.St.Tr. 1315 (1637). He resisted the oath and declaimed the proceedings, stating:

> "Another fundamental right I then contended for, was, that no man's conscience ought to be racked by oaths imposed, to answer to questions concerning himself in matters criminal, or pretended to be so." Haller & Davies, The Leveller Tracts 1647–1653, p. 454 (1944).

On account of the Lilburn Trial, Parliament abolished the inquisitorial Court of Star Chamber and went further in giving him generous reparation. The lofty principles to which Lilburn had appealed during his trial gained popular acceptance in England. These sentiments worked their way over to the Colonies and were implanted after great struggle into the Bill of Rights. Those who framed our Constitution and the Bill of Rights were ever aware of subtle encroachments on individual liberty. They knew that "illegitimate and unconstitutional practices get their first footing . . . by silent approaches and slight deviations from legal modes of procedure." Boyd v. United States, 116 U.S. 616, 635 (1886). The privilege was elevated to constitutional status and has always been "as broad as the mischief against which it seeks to guard." Counselman v. Hitchcock, 142 U.S. 547, 562 (1892). We cannot depart from this noble heritage.

Thus we may view the historical development of the privilege as one which groped for the proper scope of governmental power over the citizen. As a "noble principle often transcends its origins," the privilege has come rightfully to be recognized in part as an individual's substantive right, a "right to a private enclave where he may lead a private life. That right is the hallmark of our democracy." United States v. Grunewald, 233 F.2d 556, 579, 581–582 (FRANK, J., dissenting), rev'd, 353 U.S. 391 (1957). We have recently noted that the privilege against self-incrimination—the essential mainstay of our adversary system—is founded on a complex of values. Murphy v. Waterfront Comm'n, 378 U.S. 52, 55–57, n. 5 (1964); Tehan v. Shott, 382 U.S. 406, 414–415, n. 12 (1966). All these policies point to one overriding thought: the constitutional foundation underlying the privilege is the respect a government—state or federal—must accord to the dignity and integrity of its citizens. To maintain a "fair state-individual balance," to require the government "to shoulder the entire load," 8 Wigmore, Evidence 317 (McNaughton rev. 1961), to respect the inviolability of the human personality, our accusatory system of criminal justice demands that the government seeking to punish an individual produce the evidence against him by its own independent labors, rather than by the cruel, simple expedient of compelling it from his own mouth. Chambers v. Florida, 309 U.S. 227, 235–238 (1940). In sum, the privilege is fulfilled only when the person is guaranteed the right "to remain silent unless he chooses to speak in the unfettered exercise of his own will." Malloy v. Hogan, 378 U.S. 1, 8 (1964).

The question in these cases is whether the privilege is fully applicable during a period of custodial interrogation. In this Court, the privilege has consistently been accorded a liberal construction. Albertson v. SACB, 382 U.S. 70, 81 (1965); Hoffman v. United States, 341 U.S. 479, 486 (1951); Arndstein v. McCarthy, 254 U.S. 71, 72–73 (1920); Counselman v. Hitchock, 142 U.S. 547, 562 (1892). We are satisfied that all the principles embodied in the privilege apply to informal compulsion exerted by law-enforcement officers during in-custody questioning. An individual swept from familiar surroundings into police custody, surrounded by antagonistic forces, and subjected to the techniques of persuasion described above cannot be otherwise than under compulsion to speak. As a practical matter, the compulsion to speak in the isolated setting of the police station may well be greater than in courts or other official investigations, where there are often impartial observers to guard against intimidation or trickery.

This question, in fact, could have been taken as settled in federal courts almost 70 years ago, when, in Bram v. United States, 168 U.S. 532, 542 (1897), this Court held:

> "In criminal trials, in the courts of the United States, wherever a question arises whether a confession is incompetent because not voluntary, the issue is controlled by that portion of the Fifth Amendment . . . commanding that no person 'shall be compelled in any criminal case to be a witness against himself.'"

In Bram, the Court reviewed the British and American history and case law and set down the Fifth Amendment standard for compulsion which we implement today:

> "Much of the confusion which has resulted from the effort to deduce from the adjudged cases what would be a sufficient quantum of proof to show that a confession was or was not voluntary, has arisen from a misconception of the subject to which the proof must address itself. The rule is not that in order to render a statement admissible the proof must be adequate to establish that the particular communications contained in a statement were voluntarily made, but it must be sufficient to establish that the making of the statement was voluntary; that is to say, that from the causes, which the law treats as legally sufficient to engender in the mind of the accused hope or fear in respect to the crime charged, the accused was not involuntarily impelled to make a statement, when but for the improper influences he would have remained silent. . . ." 168 U.S., at 549. And see, id., at 542.

The Court has adhered to this reasoning. In 1924, MR. JUSTICE BRANDEIS wrote for a unanimous Court in reversing a conviction resting on a compelled confession, Wan v. United States, 266 U.S. 1. He stated:

> "In the federal courts, the requisite of voluntariness is not satisfied by establishing merely that the confession was not induced by a promise or a threat. A confession is voluntary in law if, and only if, it was, in fact, voluntarily made. A confession may have been given voluntarily, although it was made to police officers, while in custody, and in answer to an examination conducted by them. But a confession obtained by compulsion must be excluded whatever may have been the character of the compulsion, and whether the compulsion was applied in a judicial proceeding or otherwise. Bram v. United States, 168 U.S. 532." 266 U.S., at 14–15.

In addition to the expansive historical development of the privilege and the sound policies which have nurtured its evolution, judicial precedent thus clearly establishes its application to incommunicado interrogation. In fact, the Government concedes this point as well established in No. 761, Westover v. United States, stating: "We have no doubt... that it is possible for a suspect's Fifth Amendment right to be violated during in-custody questioning by a law-enforcement officer."

Because of the adoption by Congress of Rule 5(a) of the Federal Rules of Criminal Procedure, and this Court's effectuation of that Rule in McNabb v. United States, 318 U.S. 332 (1943), and Mallory v. United States, 354 U.S. 449 (1957), we have had little occasion in the past quarter century to reach the constitutional issues in dealing with federal interrogations. These supervisory rules, requiring production of an arrested person before a commissioner "without unnecessary delay" and excluding evidence obtained in default of that statutory obligation, were nonetheless responsive to the same considerations of Fifth Amendment policy that unavoidably face us now as to the States. In McNabb, 318 U.S., at 343–344, and in Mallory, 354 U.S., at 455–456, we recognized both the dangers of interrogation and the appropriateness of prophylaxis stemming from the very fact of interrogation itself.

Our decision in Malloy v. Hogan, 378 U.S. 1 (1964), necessitates an examination of the scope of the privilege in state cases as well. In Malloy, we squarely held the privilege applicable to the States, and held that the substantive standards underlying the privilege applied with full force to state court proceedings. There, as in Murphy v. Waterfront Comm'n, 378 U.S. 52 (1964), and Griffin v. California, 380 U.S. 609 (1965), we applied the existing Fifth Amendment standards to the case before us. Aside from the holding itself, the reasoning in Malloy made clear what had already become apparent—that the substantive and procedural safeguards surrounding admissibility of confessions in state cases had become exceedingly exacting, reflecting all the policies embedded in the privilege, 378 U.S., at 7–8. The voluntariness doctrine in the state cases, as Malloy indicates, encompasses all interrogation practices which are likely to exert such pressure upon an individual as to disable him from making a free and rational choice. The implications of this proposition were elaborated in our decision in Escobedo v. Illinois, 378 U.S. 478, decided one week after Malloy applied the privilege to the States.

Our holding there stressed the fact that the police had not advised the defendant of his constitutional privilege to remain silent at the outset of the interrogation, and we drew attention to that fact at several points in the decision, 378 U.S., at 483, 485, 491. This was no isolated factor, but an essential ingredient in our decision. The entire thrust of police interrogation there, as in all the cases today, was to put the defendant in such an emotional state as to impair his capacity for rational judgment. The abdication of the constitutional privilege—the choice on his part to speak to the police—was not made knowingly or competently because of the failure to apprise him of his rights; the compelling atmosphere of the in-custody interrogation, and not an independent decision on his part, caused the defendant to speak.

A different phase of the Escobedo decision was significant in its attention to the absence of counsel during the questioning. There, as in the cases today, we sought a protective device to dispel the compelling atmosphere of the interrogation. In Escobedo, however, the police did not relieve the defendant of the anxieties which they had created in the interrogation rooms. Rather, they denied his request for the assistance of counsel, 378 U.S., at 481, 488, 491. This heightened his dilemma, and made his later statements the product of this compulsion. Cf. Haynes v. Washington, 373 U.S. 503, 514 (1963). The denial of the defendant's request for his attorney thus undermined his ability to exercise the privilege—to remain silent if he chose or to speak without any intimidation, blatant or subtle. The presence of counsel, in all the cases before us today, would be the adequate protective device necessary to make the process of police interrogation conform to the dictates of the privilege. His presence would insure that statements made in the government-established atmosphere are not the product of compulsion.

It was in this manner that Escobedo explicated another facet of the pretrial privilege, noted in many of the Court's prior decisions: the protection of rights at trial. That counsel is present when statements are taken from an individual during interrogation obviously enhances the integrity of the fact-finding processes in court. The presence of an attorney, and the warnings delivered to the individual, enable the defendant under otherwise compelling circumstances to tell his story without fear, effectively, and in a way that eliminates the evils in the interrogation process. Without the protections flowing from adequate warnings and the rights of counsel, "all the careful safeguards erected around the giving of testimony, whether by an accused or any other witness, would become empty formalities in a procedure where the most compelling possible evidence of guilt, a confession, would have already been obtained at the unsupervised pleasure of the police." Mapp v. Ohio, 367 U.S. 643, 685 (1961) (Harlan, J., dissenting). Cf. Pointer v. Texas, 380 U.S. 400 (1965).

III

Today, then, there can be no doubt that the Fifth Amendment privilege is available outside of criminal court proceedings and serves to protect persons in all settings in which their freedom of action is curtailed in any significant way from being compelled to incriminate themselves. We have concluded that without proper safeguards the process of in-custody interrogation of persons suspected or accused of crime contains inherently compelling pressures which work to undermine the individual's will to resist and to compel him to speak where he would not otherwise do so freely. In order to combat these pressures and to permit a full opportunity to exercise the privilege against self-incrimination, the accused must be adequately and effectively apprised of his rights and the exercise of those rights must be fully honored.

It is impossible for us to foresee the potential alternatives for protecting the privilege which might be devised by Congress or the States in the exercise of their creative rule-making capacities. Therefore we cannot say that the Constitution necessarily requires adherence to any particular solution for the inherent compulsions of the interrogation process as it is presently conducted. Our decision in no way creates a constitutional straitjacket which will handicap sound efforts at reform, nor is it intended to have this effect. We encourage Congress and the States to continue their laudable search for increasingly effective ways of protecting the rights of the individual while promoting efficient enforcement of our criminal laws. However, unless we are shown other procedures which are at least as effective in apprising accused persons of their right of silence and in assuring a continuous opportunity to exercise it, the following safeguards must be observed.

At the outset, if a person in custody is to be subjected to interrogation, he must first be informed in clear and unequivocal terms that he has the right to remain silent. For those unaware of the privilege, the warning is needed simply to make them aware of it—the threshold requirement for an intelligent decision as to its exercise. More important, such a warning is an absolute prerequisite in overcoming the inherent pressures of the interrogation atmosphere. It is not just the subnormal or woefully ignorant who succumb to an interrogator's imprecations, whether implied or expressly stated, that the interrogation will continue until a confession is obtained or that silence in the face of accusation is itself damning and will bode ill when presented to a jury. Further, the warning will show the individual that is interrogators are prepared to recognize his privilege should he choose to exercise it.

The Fifth Amendment privilege is so fundamental to our system of constitutional rule and the expedient of giving an adequate warning as to the availability of the privilege so simple, we will not pause to inquire in individual cases whether the defendant was aware of his rights without a warning being given. Assessments of the knowledge the defendant possessed, based on information as to his age, education, intelligence, or prior contact with authorities, can never be more than speculation; a warning is a clearcut fact. More important, whatever the background of the person interrogated, a warning at the time of the interrogation is indispensable to overcome its pressures and to insure that the individual knows he is free to exercise the privilege at that point in time.

The warning of the right to remain silent must be accompanied by the explanation that anything said can and will be used against the individual in court. This warning is needed in order to make him aware not only of the privilege, but also of the consequences of forgoing it. It is only through an awareness of these consequences that there can be any assurance of real understanding and intelligent exercise of the privilege. Moreover, this warning may serve to make the individual more acutely aware that he is faced with a phase of the adversary system—that he is not in the presence of persons acting solely in his interest.

The circumstances surrounding in-custody interrogation can operate very quickly to overbear the will of one merely made aware of his privilege by his interrogators. Therefore, the right to have counsel present at the interrogation is indispensable to the protection of the Fifth Amendment privilege under the system we delineate today. Our aim is to assure that the individual's right to choose between silence and speech remains unfettered throughout the interrogation process. A once-stated warning, delivered by those who will conduct the interrogation, cannot itself suffice to that end among those who most require knowledge of their rights. A mere warning given by the interrogators is not alone sufficient to accomplish that end. Prosecutors themselves claim that the admonishment of the right to remain silent without more "will benefit only the recidivist and the professional." Brief for the National District Attorneys Association as amicus curiae, p. 14. Even preliminary advice given to the accused by his own attorney can be swiftly overcome by the secret interrogation process. Cf. Escobedo v. Illinois, 378 U.S. 478, 485, n. 5. Thus, the need for counsel to protect the Fifth Amendment privilege comprehends not merely a right to consult with counsel prior to questioning, but also to have counsel present during any questioning if the defendant so desires.

The presence of counsel at the interrogation may serve several significant subsidiary functions as well. If the accused decides to talk to his interrogators, the assistance of counsel can mitigate the dangers of untrustworthiness. With a lawyer present the likelihood that the police will practice coercion is reduced, and if coercion is nevertheless exercised the lawyer can testify to it in court. The presence of a lawyer can also help to guarantee that the accused gives a fully accurate statement to the police and that the statement is rightly reported by the prosecution at trial. See Crooker v. California, 357 U.S. 433, 443–448 (1958) (Douglas, J., dissenting).

An individual need not make a pre-interrogation request for a lawyer. While such request affirmatively secures his right to have one, his failure to ask for a lawyer does not constitute a waiver. No effective waiver of the right to counsel during interrogation can be recognized unless specifically made after the warnings we here delineate have been given. The accused who does not know his rights and therefore does not make a request may be the person who most needs counsel. As the California Supreme Court has aptly put it:

> "Finally, we must recognize that the imposition of the requirement for the request would discriminate against the defendant who does not know his rights. The defendant who does not ask for counsel is the very defendant who most needs counsel. We cannot penalize a defendant who, not understanding his constitutional rights, does not make the formal request and by such failure demonstrates his helplessness. To require the request would be to favor the defendant whose sophistication or status had fortuitously prompted him to make it." People v. Dorado, 62 Cal.2d 338, 351, 398 P. 2d 361, 369–370, 42 Cal.Rptr. 169, 177–178 (1965) (Tobriner, J.).

In Carnley v. Cochran, 369 U.S. 506, 513 (1962), we stated: "[I]t is settled that where the assistance of counsel is a constitutional requisite, the right to be furnished counsel does not depend on a request." This proposition applies with equal force in the context of providing counsel to protect an accused's Fifth Amendment privilege in the face of interrogation. Although the role of counsel at trial differs from the role during interrogation, the differences are not relevant to the question whether a request is a prerequisite.

Accordingly we hold that an individual held for interrogation must be clearly informed that he has the right to consult with a lawyer and to have the lawyer with him during interrogation under the system for protecting the privilege we delineate today. As with the warnings of the right to remain silent and that anything stated can be used in evidence against him, this warning is an absolute prerequisite to interrogation. No amount of circumstantial evidence that the person may have been aware of this right will suffice to stand in its stead. Only through such a warning is there ascertainable assurance that the accused was aware of this right.

If an individual indicates that he wishes the assistance of counsel before any interrogation occurs, the authorities cannot rationally ignore or deny his request on the basis that the individual does not have or cannot afford a retained attorney. The financial ability of the individual has no relationship to the scope of the rights involved here. The privilege against self-incrimination secured by the Constitution applies to all individuals. The need for counsel in order to protect the privilege exists for the indigent as well as the affluent. In fact, were we to limit these constitutional rights to those who can retain an attorney, our decisions today would be of little significance. The cases before us as well as the vast majority of confession cases with which we have dealt in the past involve those unable to retain counsel. While authorities are not required to relieve the accused of his poverty, they have the obligation not to take advantage of indigence in the administration of justice. Denial of counsel to the indigent at the time of interrogation while allowing an attorney to those who can afford one would be no more supportable by reason or logic than the similar situation at trial and on appeal struck down in Gideon v. Wainwright, 372 U.S. 335 (1963), and Douglas v. California, 372 U.S. 353 (1963).

In order fully to apprise a person interrogated of the extent of his rights under this system then, it is necessary to warn him not only that he has the right to consult with an attorney, but also that if he is indigent a lawyer will be appointed to represent him. Without this additional warning, the admonition of the right to consult with counsel would often be understood as meaning only that he can consult with a lawyer if he has one or has the funds to obtain one. The warning of a right to counsel would be hollow if not couched in terms that would convey to the indigent—the person most often subjected to interrogation—the knowledge that he too has a right to have counsel present. As with the warnings of the right to remain silent and of the general right to counsel, only by effective and express explanation to the indigent of this right can there be assurance that he was truly in a position to exercise it.

Once warnings have been given, the subsequent procedure is clear. If the individual indicates in any manner, at any time prior to or during questioning, that he wishes to remain silent, the interrogation must cease. At this point he has shown that he intends to exercise his Fifth Amendment privilege; any statement taken after the person invokes his privilege cannot be other than the product of compulsion, subtle or otherwise. Without the right to cut off questioning, the setting of in-custody interrogation operates on the individual to overcome free choice in producing a statement after the privilege has been once invoked. If the individual states that he wants an attorney, the interrogation must cease until an attorney is present. At that time, the individual must have an opportunity to confer with the attorney and to have him present during any subsequent questioning. If the individual cannot obtain an attorney and he indicates that he wants one before speaking to police, they must respect his decision to remain silent.

This does not mean, as some have suggested, that each police station must have a "station house lawyer" present at all times to advise prisoners. It does mean, however, that if police propose to interrogate a person they must make known to him that he is entitled to a lawyer and that if he cannot afford one, a lawyer will be provided for him prior to any interrogation. If authorities conclude that they will not provide counsel during a reasonable period of time in which investigation in the field is carried out, they may refrain from doing so without violating the person's Fifth Amendment privilege so long as they do not question him during that time.

If the interrogation continues without the presence of an attorney and a statement is taken, a heavy burden rests on the government to demonstrate that the defendant knowingly and intelligently waived his privilege against self-incrimination and his right to retained or appointed counsel. Escobedo v. Illinois, 378 U.S. 478, 490, n. 14. This Court has always set high standards of proof for the waiver of constitutional rights, Johnson v. Zerbst, 304 U.S. 458 (1938), and we re-assert these standards as applied to in-custody interrogation. Since the State is responsible for establishing the isolated circumstances under which the interrogation takes place and has the only means of making available corroborated evidence of warnings given during incommunicado interrogation, the burden is rightly on its shoulders.

An express statement that the individual is willing to make a statement and does not want an attorney followed closely by a statement could constitute a waiver. But a valid waiver will not be presumed simply from the silence of the accused after warnings are given or simply from the fact that a confession was in fact eventually obtained. A statement we made in Carnley v. Cochran, 369 U.S. 506, 516 (1962), is applicable here:

> "Presuming waiver from a silent record is impermissible. The record must show, or there must be an allegation and evidence which show, that an accused was offered counsel but intelligently and understandingly rejected the offer. Anything less is not waiver."

See also Glasser v. United States, 315 U.S. 60 (1942). Moreover, where in-custody interrogation is involved, there is no room for the contention that the privilege is waived if the individual answers some questions or gives some information on his own prior to invoking his right to remain silent when interrogated.

Whatever the testimony of the authorities as to waiver of rights by an accused, the fact of lengthy interrogation or incommunicado incarceration before a statement is made is strong evidence that the accused did not validly waive his rights. In these circumstances the fact that the individual eventually made a statement is consistent with the conclusion that the compelling influence of the interrogation finally forced him to do so. It is inconsistent with any notion of a voluntary relinquishment of the privilege. Moreover, any evidence that the accused was threatened, tricked, or cajoled into a waiver will, of course, show that the defendant did not voluntarily waive his privilege. The requirement of warnings and waiver of rights is a fundamental with respect to the Fifth Amendment privilege and not simply a preliminary ritual to existing methods of interrogation.

The warnings required and the waiver necessary in accordance with our opinion today are, in the absence of a fully effective equivalent, prerequisites to the admissibility of any statement made by a defendant. No distinction can be drawn between statements which are direct confessions and statements which amount to "admissions" of part or all of an offense. The privilege against self-incrimination protects the individual from being compelled to incriminate himself in any manner; it does not distinguish degrees of incrimination. Similarly, for precisely the same reason, no distinction may be drawn between inculpatory statements and statements alleged to be merely "exculpatory." If a statement made were in fact truly exculpatory it would, of course, never be used by the prosecution. In fact, statements merely intended to be exculpatory by the defendant are often used to impeach his testimony at trial or to demonstrate untruths in the statement given under interrogation and thus to prove guilt by implication. These statements are incriminating in any meaningful sense of the word and may not be used without the full warnings and effective waiver required for any other statement. In Escobedo itself, the defendant fully intended his accusation of another as the slayer to be exculpatory as to himself.

The principles announced today deal with the protection which must be given to the privilege against self-incrimination when the individual is first subjected to police interrogation while in custody at the station or otherwise deprived of his freedom of action in any significant way. It is at this point that our adversary system of criminal proceedings commences, distinguishing itself at the outset from the inquisitorial system recognized in some countries. Under the system of warnings we delineate today or under any other system which may be devised and found effective, the safeguards to be erected about the privilege must come into play at this point.

Our decision is not intended to hamper the traditional function of police officers in investigating crime. See Escobedo v. Illinois, 378 U.S. 478, 492. When an individual is in custody on probable cause, the police may, of course, seek out evidence in the field to be used at trial against him. Such investigation may include inquiry of persons not under restraint. General on-the-scene questioning as to facts surrounding a crime or other general questioning of citizens in the fact-finding process is not affected by our holding. It is an act of responsible citizenship for individuals to give whatever information they may have to aid in law enforcement. In such situations the compelling atmosphere inherent in the process of in-custody interrogation is not necessarily present.

In dealing with statements obtained through interrogation, we do not purport to find all confessions inadmissible. Confessions remain a proper element in law enforcement. Any statement given freely and voluntarily without any compelling influences is, of course, admissible in evidence. The fundamental import of the privilege while an individual is in custody is not whether he is allowed to talk to the police without the benefit of warnings and counsel, but whether he can be interrogated. There is no requirement that police stop a person who enters a police station and states that he wishes to confess to a crime, or a person who calls the police to offer a confession or any other statement he desires to make. Volunteered statements of any kind are not barred by the Fifth Amendment and their admissibility is not affected by our holding today.

To summarize, we hold that when an individual is taken into custody or otherwise deprived of his freedom by the authorities in any significant way and is subjected to questioning, the privilege against self-incrimination is jeopardized. Procedural safeguards must be employed to protect the privilege, and unless other fully effective means are adopted to notify the person of his right of silence and to assure that the exercise of the right will be scrupulously honored, the following measures are required. He must be warned prior to any questioning that he has the right to remain silent, that anything he says can be used against him in a court of law, that he has the right to the presence of an attorney, and that if he cannot afford an attorney one will be appointed for him prior to any questioning if he so desires. Opportunity to exercise these rights must be afforded to him throughout the interrogation. After such warnings have been given, and such opportunity afforded him, the individual may knowingly and intelligently waive these rights and agree to answer questions or make a statement. But unless and until such warnings and waiver are demonstrated by the prosecution at trial, no evidence obtained as a result of interrogation can be used against him.

IV

A recurrent argument made in these cases is that society's need for interrogation outweighs the privilege. This argument is not unfamiliar to this Court. See, e.g., Chambers v. Florida, 309 U.S. 227, 240–241 (1940). The whole thrust of our foregoing discussion demonstrates that the Constitution has prescribed the rights of the individual when confronted with the power of government when it provided in the Fifth Amendment that an individual cannot be compelled to be a witness against himself. That right cannot be abridged. As Mr. Justice Brandeis once observed:

> "Decency, security and liberty alike demand that government officials shall be subjected to the same rules of conduct that are commands to the citizen. In a government of laws, existence of the government will be imperilled if it fails to observe the law scrupulously. Our Government is the potent, the omnipresent teacher. For

> good or for ill, it teaches the whole people by its example. Crime is contagious. If the Government becomes a lawbreaker, it breeds contempt for law; it invites every man to become a law unto himself; it invites anarchy. To declare that in the administration of the criminal law the end justifies the means . . . would bring terrible retribution. Against that pernicious doctrine this Court should resolutely set its face." Olmstead v. United States, 277 U.S. 438, 485 (1928) (dissenting opinion).

In this connection, one of our country's distinguished jurists has pointed out: "The quality of a nation's civilization can be largely measured by the methods it uses in the enforcement of its criminal law."

If the individual desires to exercise his privilege, he has the right to do so. This is not for the authorities to decide. An attorney may advise his client not to talk to police until he has had an opportunity to investigate the case, or he may wish to be present with his client during any police questioning. In doing so an attorney is merely exercising the good professional judgment he has been taught. This is not cause for considering the attorney a menace to law enforcement. He is merely carrying out what he is sworn to do under his oath—to protect to the extent of his ability the rights of his client. In fulfilling this responsibility the attorney plays a vital role in the administration of criminal justice under our Constitution.

In announcing these principles, we are not unmindful of the burdens that law enforcement officials must bear, often under trying circumstances. We also fully recognize the obligation of all citizens to aid in enforcing the criminal laws. This Court, while protecting individual rights, has always given ample latitude to law enforcement agencies in the legitimate exercise of their duties. The limits we have placed on the interrogation process should not constitute an undue interference with a proper system of law enforcement. As we have noted, our decision does not in any way preclude police from carrying out their traditional investigatory functions. Although confessions may play an important role in some convictions, the cases before us present graphic examples of the overstatement of the "need" for confessions. In each case authorities conducted interrogations ranging up to five days in duration despite the presence, through standard investigating practices, of considerable evidence against each defendant. Further examples are chronicled in our prior cases. See, e.g., Haynes v. Washington, 373 U.S. 503, 518–519 (1963); Rogers v. Richmond, 365 U.S. 534, 541 (1961); Malinski v. New York, 324 U.S. 401, 402 (1945).

It is also urged that an unfettered right to detention for interrogation should be allowed because it will often redound to the benefit of the person questioned. When police inquiry determines that there is no reason to believe that the person has committed any crime, it is said, he will be released without need for further formal procedures. The person who has committed no offense, however, will be better able to clear himself after warnings with counsel present than without. It can be assumed that in such circumstances a lawyer would advise his client to talk freely to police in order to clear himself.

Custodial interrogation, by contrast, does not necessarily afford the innocent an opportunity to clear themselves. A serious consequence of the present practice of the interrogation alleged to be beneficial for the innocent is that many arrests "for investigation" subject large numbers of innocent persons to detention and interrogation. In one of the cases before us, No. 584, California v. Stewart, police held four persons, who were in the defendant's house at the time of the arrest, in jail for five days until defendant confessed. At that time they were finally released. Police stated that there was "no evidence to connect them with any crime." Available statistics on the extent of this practice where it is condoned indicate that these four are far from alone in being subjected to arrest, prolonged detention, and interrogation without the requisite probable cause.

Over the years the Federal Bureau of Investigation has compiled an exemplary record of effective law enforcement while advising any suspect or arrested person, at the outset of an interview, that he is not required to make a statement, that any statement may be used against him in court, that the individual may obtain the services of an attorney of his own choice and, more recently, that he has a right to free counsel if he is unable to pay. A letter received from the Solicitor General in response to a question from the Bench makes it clear that the present pattern of warnings and respect for the rights of the individual followed as a practice by the FBI is consistent with the procedure which we delineate today. It states:

> At the oral argument of the above cause, MR. JUSTICE FORTAS asked whether I could provide certain information as to the practices followed by the Federal Bureau of Investigation. I have directed these questions to the attention of the Director of the Federal Bureau of Investigation and am submitting herewith a statement of the questions and of the answers which we have received.
>
> "(1) When an individual is interviewed by agents of the Bureau, what warning is given to him?
>
> "The standard warning long given by Special Agents of the FBI to both suspects and persons under arrest is that the person has a right to say nothing and a right to counsel, and that any statement he does make may be used against him in court. Examples of this warning are to be found in the Westover case at 342 F.2d 684 (1965), and Jackson v. U.S., 337 F.2d 136 (1964), cert. den. 380 U.S. 935.
>
> "After passage of the Criminal Justice Act of 1964, which provides free counsel for Federal defendants unable to pay, we added to our instructions to Special Agents the requirement that any person who is under arrest for an offense under FBI jurisdiction, or whose arrest is contemplated following the interview, must also be advised of his right to free counsel if he is unable to pay, and the fact that such counsel will be assigned by the Judge. At the same time, we broadened the right to counsel warning to read counsel of his own choice, or anyone else with whom he might wish to speak.
>
> "(2) When is the warning given?
>
> "The FBI warning is given to a suspect at the very outset of the interview, as shown in the Westover case, cited above. The warning may be given to a person arrested as soon as practicable after the arrest, as shown in the Jackson case, also cited above, and in U.S. v. Konigsberg, 336 F.2d 844 (1964), cert. den. 379 U.S. 933, but in any event it must precede the interview with the person for a confession or admission of his own guilt.
>
> "(3) What is the Bureau's practice in the event that (a) the individual requests counsel and (b) counsel appears?
>
> "When the person who has been warned of his right to counsel decides that he

wishes to consult with counsel before making a statement, the interview is terminated at that point, Shultz v. U.S., 351 F.2d 287 (1965). It may be continued, however, as to all matters *other* than the person's own guilt or innocence. If he is indecisive in his request for counsel, there may be some question on whether he did or did not waive counsel. Situations of this kind must necessarily be left to the judgment of the interviewing Agent. For example, in Hiram v. U.S., 354 F.2d 4 (1965), the Agent's conclusion that the person arrested had waived his right to counsel was upheld by the courts.

"A person being interviewed and desiring to consult counsel by telephone must be permitted to do so, as shown in Caldwell v. U.S., 351 F.2d 459 (1965). When counsel appears in person, he is permitted to confer with his client in private.

"(4) What is the Bureau's practice if the individual requests counsel, but cannot afford to retain an attorney?

"If any person being interviewed after warning of counsel decides that he wishes to consult with counsel before proceeding further the interview is terminated, as shown above. FBI Agents do not pass judgment on the ability of the person to pay for counsel. They do, however, advise those who have been arrested for an offense under FBI jurisdiction, or whose arrest is contemplated following the interview, of a right to free counsel *if* they are unable to pay, and the availability of such counsel from the Judge."

The practice of the FBI can readily be emulated by state and local enforcement agencies. The argument that the FBI deals with different crimes than are dealt with by state authorities does not mitigate the significance of the FBI experience.

The experience in some other countries also suggests that the danger to law enforcement in curbs on interrogation is overplayed. The English procedure since 1912 under the Judges' Rules is significant. As recently strengthened, the Rules require that a cautionary warning be given an accused by a police officer as soon as he has evidence that affords reasonable grounds for suspicion; they also require that any statement made be given by the accused without questioning by police. The right of the individual to consult with an attorney during this period is expressly recognized.

The safeguards present under Scottish law may be even greater than in England. Scottish judicial decisions bar use in evidence of most confessions obtained through police interrogation. In India, confessions made to police not in the presence of a magistrate have been excluded by rule of evidence since 1872, at a time when it operated under British law. Identical provisions appear in the Evidence Ordinance of Ceylon, enacted in 1895. Similarly, in our country the Uniform Code of Military Justice has long provided that no suspect may be interrogated without first being warned of his right not to make a statement and that any statement he makes may be used against him. Denial of the right to consult counsel during interrogation has also been proscribed by military tribunals. There appears to have been no marked detrimental effect on criminal law enforcement in these jurisdictions as a result of these rules. Conditions of law enforcement in our country are sufficiently similar to permit reference to this experience as assurance that lawlessness will not result from warning an individual of his rights or allowing him to exercise them. Moreover, it is consistent with our legal system that we give at least as much protection to these rights as is given in the jurisdictions described. We deal in our country with rights grounded in a specific requirement of the Fifth Amendment of the Constitution, whereas other jurisdictions arrived at their conclusions on the basis of principles of justice not so specifically defined.

It is also urged upon us that we withhold decision on this issue until state legislative bodies and advisory groups have had an opportunity to deal with these problems by rule making. We have already pointed out that the Constitution does not require any specific code of procedures for protecting the privilege against self-incrimination during custodial interrogation. Congress and the States are free to develop their own safeguards for the privilege, so long as they are fully as effective as those described above in informing accused persons of their right of silence and in affording a continuous opportunity to exercise it. In any event, however, the issues presented are of constitutional dimensions and must be determined by the courts. The admissibility of a statement in the face of a claim that it was obtained in violation of the defendant's constitutional rights is an issue the resolution of which has long since been undertaken by this Court. See Hopt v. Utah, 110 U.S. 574 (1884). Judicial solutions to problems of constitutional dimension have evolved decade by decade. As courts have been presented with the need to enforce constitutional rights, they have found means of doing so. That was our responsibility when Escobedo was before us and it is our responsibility today. Where rights secured by the Constitution are involved, there can be no rule making or legislation which would abrogate them.

V

Because of the nature of the problem and because of its recurrent significance in numerous cases, we have to this point discussed the relationship of the Fifth Amendment privilege to police interrogation without specific concentration on the facts of the cases before us. We turn now to these facts to consider the application to these cases of the constitutional principles discussed above. In each instance, we have concluded that statements were obtained from the defendant under circumstances that did not meet constitutional standards for protection of the privilege.

No. 759. Miranda v. Arizona.

On March 13, 1963, petitioner, Ernesto Miranda, was arrested at his home and taken in custody to a Phoenix police station. He was there identified by the complaining witness. The police then took him to "Interrogation Room No. 2" of the detective bureau. There he was questioned by two police officers. The officers admitted at trial that Miranda was not advised that he had a right to have an attorney present. Two hours later, the officers emerged from the interrogation room with a written confession signed by Miranda. At the top of the statement was a typed paragraph stating that the confession was made voluntarily, without threats or promises of immunity and "with full knowledge of my legal rights, understanding any statement I make may be used against me."

At his trial before a jury, the written confession was admitted into evidence over the objection of defense counsel, and the officers testified to the prior oral confession made by Miranda during the interrogation. Miranda was found guilty of kidnapping and rape. He was sentenced to 20 to 30 years' imprisonment on each count, the sentences to run concurrently. On appeal, the Supreme Court of Arizona held that Miranda's constitutional rights were not violated in obtaining the confession and affirmed the conviction. 98 Ariz. 18, 401 P.2d 721. In reaching its decision, the court emphasized heavily the fact that Miranda did not specifically request counsel.

We reverse. From the testimony of the officers and by the admission of respondent, it is clear that Miranda was not in any way apprised of his right to consult with an attorney and to have one present during the interrogation, nor was his right not to be compelled to incriminate himself effectively protected in any other manner. Without these warnings the statements were inadmissible. The mere fact that he signed a statement which contained a typed-in clause stating that he had "full knowledge" of his "legal rights" does not approach the knowing and intelligent waiver required to relinquish constitutional rights. Cf. Haynes v. Washington, 373 U.S. 503, 512–513 (1963); Haley v. Ohio, 332 U.S. 596, 601 (1948) (opinion of Mr. Justice Douglas).

No. 760. Vignera v. New York.

Petitioner, Michael Vignera, was picked up by New York police on October 14, 1960, in connection with the robbery three days earlier of a Brooklyn dress shop. They took him to the 17th Detective Squad headquarters in Manhattan. Sometime thereafter he was taken to the 66th Detective Squad. There a detective questioned Vignera with respect to the robbery. Vignera orally admitted the robbery to the detective. The detective was asked on cross-examination at trial by defense counsel whether Vignera was warned of his right to counsel before being interrogated. The prosecution objected to the question and the trial judge sustained the objection. Thus, the defense was precluded from making any showing that warnings had not been given. While at the 66th Detective Squad, Vignera was identified by the store owner and a saleslady as the man who robbed the dress shop. At about 3 p.m. he was formally arrested. The police then transported him to still another station, the 70th Precinct in Brooklyn, "for detention." At 11 p.m. Vignera was questioned by an assistant district attorney in the presence of a hearing reporter who transcribed the questions and Vignera's answers. This verbatim account of these proceedings contains no statement of any warnings given by the assistant district attorney. At Vignera's trial on a charge of first degree robbery, the detective testified as to the oral confession. The transcription of the statement taken was also introduced in evidence. At the conclusion of the testimony, the trial judge charged the jury in part as follows:

> "The law doesn't say that the confession is void or invalidated because the police officer didn't advise the defendant as to his rights. Did you hear what I said? I am telling you what the law of the State of New York is."

Vignera was found guilty of first degree robbery. He was subsequently adjudged a third-felony offender and sentenced to 30 to 60 years' imprisonment. The conviction was affirmed without opinion by the Appellate Division, Second Department, 21 App.Div.2d 752, 252 N.Y.S.2d 19, and by the Court of Appeals, also without opinion, 15 N.Y.2d 970, 207 N.E.2d 527, 259 N.Y.S.2d 857, remittitur amended, 16 N.Y.2d 614, 209 N.E.2d 110, 261 N.Y.S.2d 65. In argument to the Court of Appeals, the State contended that Vignera had no constitutional right to be advised of his right to counsel or his privilege against self-incrimination.

We reverse. The foregoing indicates that Vignera was not warned of any of his rights before the questioning by the detective and by the assistant district attorney. No other steps were taken to protect these rights. Thus he was not effectively apprised of his Fifth Amendment privilege or of his right to have counsel present and his statements are inadmissible.

No. 761. Westover v. United States.

At approximately 9:45 p.m. on March 20, 1963, petitioner, Carl Calvin Westover, was arrested by local police in Kansas City as a suspect in two Kansas City robberies. A report was also received from the FBI that he was wanted on a felony charge in California. The local authorities took him to a police station and placed him in a line-up on the local charges, and at about 11:45 p.m. he was booked. Kansas City police interrogated Westover on the night of his arrest. He denied any knowledge of criminal activities. The next day local officers interrogated him again throughout the morning. Shortly before noon they informed the FBI that they were through interrogating Westover and that the FBI could proceed to interrogate him. There is nothing in the record to indicate that Westover was ever given any warning as to his rights by local police. At noon, three special agents of the FBI continued the interrogation in a private interview room of the Kansas City Police Department, this time with respect to the robbery of a savings and loan association and a bank in Sacramento, California. After two or two and one-half hours, Westover signed separate confessions to each of these two robberies which had been prepared by one of the agents during the interrogation. At trial one of the agents testified, and a paragraph on each of the statements states, that the agents advised Westover that he did not have to make a statement, that any statement he made could be used against him, and that he had the right to see an attorney.

Westover was tried by a jury in federal court and convicted of the California robberies. His statements were introduced at trial. He was sentenced to 15 years' imprisonment on each count, the sentences to run consecutively. On appeal, the conviction was affirmed by the Court of Appeals for the Ninth Circuit. 342 F.2d 684.

We reverse. On the facts of this case we cannot find that Westover knowingly and intelligently waived his right to remain silent and his right to consult with counsel prior to the time he made the statement. At the time the FBI agents began questioning Westover, he had been in custody for over 14 hours and had been interrogated at length during that period. The FBI interrogation began immediately upon the conclusion of the interrogation by Kansas City police and was conducted in local police headquarters. Although the two law enforcement authorities are legally distinct and the crimes for which they interrogated Westover were different, the impact on him was that of a continuous period of questioning. There is no evidence of any warning given prior to the FBI interrogation nor is there any evidence of an articulated waiver of rights after the FBI commenced its interrogation. The record simply shows that the defendant did in fact confess a short time after being turned over to the FBI following interrogation by local police. Despite the fact that the FBI agents gave warnings at the outset of their interview, from Westover's point of view the warnings came at the end of the interrogation process. In these circumstances an intelligent waiver of constitutional rights cannot be assumed.

We do not suggest that law enforcement authorities are precluded from questioning any individual who has been held for a period of time by other authorities and interrogated by them without appropriate warnings. A different case would be presented if an accused were taken into custody by the second authority, removed both in time and place from his original surroundings, and then adequately advised of his rights and given an opportunity to exercise them. But here the FBI interrogation was conducted immediately following the state interrogation in the same police station—in the same compelling surroundings. Thus, in obtaining a confession from Westover the federal authorities were the beneficiaries of the pressure applied by the local in-custody interrogation. In these circumstances the giving of warnings alone was not sufficient to protect the privilege.

No. 584. California v. Stewart.

In the course of investigating a series of purse-snatch robberies in which one of the victims had died of injuries inflicted by her assailant, respondent, Roy Allen Stewart, was pointed out to Los Angeles police as the endorser of dividend checks taken in one of the robberies. At about 7:15 p.m., January 31, 1963, police officers went to Stewart's house and arrested him. One of the officers asked Stewart if they could search the house, to which he replied, "Go ahead." The search turned up various items taken from the five robbery victims. At the time of Stewart's arrest, police also arrested Stewart's wife and three other persons who were visiting him. These four were jailed along with Stewart and were interrogated. Stewart was taken to the University Station of the Los Angeles Police Department where he was placed in a cell. During the next five days, police interrogated Stewart on nine different occasions. Except during the first interrogation session, when he was confronted with an accusing witness, Stewart was isolated with his interrogators.

During the ninth interrogation session, Stewart admitted that he had robbed the deceased and stated that he had not meant to hurt her. Police then brought Stewart before a magistrate for the first time. Since there was no evidence to connect them with any crime, the police then released the other four persons arrested with him.

Nothing in the record specifically indicates whether Stewart was or was not advised of his right to remain silent or his right to counsel. In a number of instances, however, the interrogating officers were asked to recount everything that was said during the interrogations. None indicated that Stewart was ever advised of his rights.

Stewart was charged with kidnapping to commit robbery, rape, and murder. At his trial, transcripts of the first interrogation and the confession at the last interrogation were introduced in evidence. The jury found Stewart guilty of robbery and first degree murder and fixed the penalty as death. On appeal, the Supreme Court of California reversed. 62 Cal.2d 571, 400 P.2d 97, 43 Cal.Rptr. 201. It held that under this Court's decision in Escobedo, Stewart should have been advised of his right to remain silent and of his right to counsel and that it would not presume in the face of a silent record that the police advised Stewart of his rights.

We affirm. In dealing with custodial interrogation, we will not presume that a defendant has been effectively apprised of his rights and that his privilege against self-incrimination has been adequately safeguarded on a record that does not show that any warnings have been given or that any effective alternative has been employed. Nor can a knowing and intelligent waiver of these rights be assumed on a silent record. Furthermore, Stewart's steadfast denial of the alleged offenses through eight of the nine interrogations over a period of five days is subject to no other construction than that he was compelled by persistent interrogation to forgo his Fifth Amendment privilege.

Therefore, in accordance with the foregoing, the judgments of the Supreme Court of Arizona in No. 759, of the New York Court of Appeals in No. 760, and of the Court of Appeals for the Ninth Circuit in No. 761 are reversed. The judgment of the Supreme Court of California in No. 584 is affirmed.

It is so ordered.

Schmerber *v.* California

384 U.S. 757, 86 S.Ct. 1826, 16 L.Ed.2d 908 (1966)

CERTIORARI TO THE APPELLATE DEPARTMENT OF THE SUPERIOR COURT OF CALIFORNIA, COUNTY OF LOS ANGELES.

Argued April 25, 1966.—Decided June 20, 1966.

. . .

Mr. Justice Brennan delivered the opinion of the Court.

Petitioner was convicted in Los Angeles Municipal Court of the criminal offense of driving an automobile while under the influence of intoxicating liquor. He had been arrested at a hospital while receiving treatment for injuries suffered in an accident involving the automobile that he had apparently been driving. At the direction of a police officer, a blood sample was then withdrawn from petitioner's body by a physician at the hospital. The chemical analysis of this sample revealed a percent by weight of alcohol in his blood at the time of the offense which indicated intoxication, and the report of this analysis was admitted in evidence at the trial. Petitioner objected to receipt of this evidence of the analysis on the ground that the blood had been withdrawn despite his refusal, on the advice of his counsel, to consent to the test. He contended that in that circumstance the withdrawal of the blood and the admission of the analysis in evidence denied him due process of law under the Fourteenth Amendment, as well as specific guarantees of the Bill of Rights secured against the States by that Amendment: his privilege against self-incrimination under the Fifth Amendment; his right to counsel under the Sixth Amendment; and his right not to be subjected to unreasonable searches and seizures in violation of the Fourth Amendment. The Appellate Department of the California Superior Court rejected these contentions and affirmed the conviction. In view of constitutional decisions since we last considered these issues in Breithaupt v. Abram, 352 U.S. 432—see Escobedo v. Illinois, 378 U.S. 478; Malloy v. Hogan, 378 U.S. 1, and Mapp v. Ohio, 367 U.S. 643—we granted certiorari. 382 U.S. 971. We affirm.

I. The Due Process Clause Claim

Breithaupt was also a case in which police officers caused blood to be withdrawn from the driver of an automobile involved in an accident, and in which there was ample justification for the officer's conclusion that the driver was under the influence of alcohol. There, as here, the extraction was made by a physician in a simple, medically acceptable manner in a hospital environment. There, however, the driver was unconscious at the time the blood was withdrawn and hence had no opportunity to object to the procedure. We affirmed the conviction there resulting from the use of the test in evidence, holding that under such circumstances the withdrawal did not offend "that 'sense of justice' of which we spoke in Rochin v. California, 342 U.S. 165." 352 U.S., at 435. Breithaupt thus requires the rejection of petitioner's due process argument, and nothing in the circumstances of this case or in supervening events persuades us that this aspect of Breithaupt should be overruled.

II. The Privilege Against Self-Incrimination Claim

Breithaupt summarily rejected an argument that the withdrawal of blood and the admission of the analysis report involved in that state case violated the Fifth Amendment privilege of any person not to "be compelled in any criminal case to be a witness against himself," citing Twining v. New Jersey, 211 U.S. 78. But that case, holding that the protections of the Fourteenth Amendment do not embrace this Fifth Amendment privilege, has been succeeded by Malloy v. Hogan, 378 U.S. 1, 8. We there held that "[t]he Fourteenth Amendment secures against state invasion the same privilege that the Fifth Amendment guarantees against federal infringement—the right of a person to remain silent unless he chooses to speak in the unfettered exercise of his own will, and to suffer no penalty . . . for such silence." We therefore must now decide whether the withdrawal of the blood and admission in evidence of the analysis involved in this case violated petitioner's privilege. We hold that the privilege protects an accused only from being compelled to testify against himself, or otherwise provide the State with evidence of a testimonial or communicative nature, and that the withdrawal of blood and use of the analysis in question in this case did not involve compulsion to these ends.

It could not be denied that in requiring petitioner to submit to the withdrawal and chemical analysis of his blood the State compelled him to submit to an attempt to discover evidence that might be used to prosecute him for a criminal offense. He submitted only after the police officer rejected his objection and directed the physician to proceed. The officer's direction to the physician to administer the test over petitioner's objection constituted compulsion for the purposes of the privilege. The critical question, then, is whether petitioner was thus compelled "to be a witness against himself."

If the scope of the privilege coincided with the complex of values it helps to protect, we might be obliged to conclude that the privilege was violated. In Miranda v. Arizona, ante, at 460, the Court said of the interests protected by the privilege: "All these policies point to one overriding thought: the constitutional foundation underlying the privilege is the respect a government—state or federal—must accord to the dignity and integrity of its citizens. To maintain a 'fair state-individual balance,' to require the government 'to shoulder the entire load'... to respect the inviolability of the human personality, our accusatory system of criminal justice demands that the government seeking to punish an individual produce the evidence against him by its own independent labors, rather than by the cruel, simple expedient of compelling it from his own mouth." The withdrawal of blood necessarily involves puncturing the skin for extraction, and the percent by weight of alcohol in that blood, as established by chemical analysis, is evidence of criminal guilt. Compelled submission fails on one view to respect the "inviolability of the human personality." Moreover, since it enables the State to rely on evidence forced from the accused, the compulsion violates at least one meaning of the requirement that the State procure the evidence against an accused "by its own independent labors."

As the passage in Miranda implicitly recognizes, however, the privilege has never been given the full scope which the values it helps to protect suggest. History and a long line of authorities in lower courts have consistently limited its protection to situations in which the State seeks to submerge those values by obtaining the evidence against an accused through "the cruel, simple expedient of compelling it from his own mouth.... In sum, the privilege is fulfilled only when the person is guaranteed the right 'to remain silent unless he chooses to speak in the unfettered exercise of his own will.'" Ibid. The leading case in this Court is Holt v. United States, 218 U.S. 245. There the question was whether evidence was admissible that the accused, prior to trial and over his protest, put on a blouse that fitted him. It was contended that compelling the accused to submit to the demand that he model the blouse violated the privilege. MR. JUSTICE HOLMES, speaking for the Court, rejected the argument as "based upon an extravagant extension of the Fifth Amendment," and went on to say: "[T]he prohibition of compelling a man in a criminal court to be witness against himself is a prohibition of the use of physical or moral compulsion to extort communications from him, not an exclusion of his body as evidence when it may be material. The objection in principle would forbid a jury to look at a prisoner and compare his features with a photograph in proof." 218 U.S., at 252–253.

It is clear that the protection of the privilege reaches an accused's communications, whatever form they might take, and the compulsion of responses which are also communications, for example, compliance with a subpoena to produce one's papers. Boyd v. United States, 116 U.S. 616. On the other hand, both federal and state courts have usually held that it offers no protection against compulsion to submit to fingerprinting, photographing, or measurements, to write or speak for identification, to appear in court, to stand, to assume a stance, to walk, or to make a particular gesture. The distinction which has emerged, often expressed in different ways, is that the privilege is a bar against compelling "communications" or "testimony," but that compulsion which makes a suspect or accused the source of "real or physical evidence" does not violate it.

Although we agree that this distinction is a helpful framework for analysis, we are not to be understood to agree with past applications in all instances. There will be many cases in which such a distinction is not readily drawn. Some tests seemingly directed to obtain "physical evidence," for example, lie detector tests measuring changes in body function during interrogation, may actually be directed to eliciting responses which are essentially testimonial. To compel a person to submit to testing in which an effort will be made to determine his guilt or innocence on the basis of physiological responses, whether willed or not, is to evoke the spirit and history of the Fifth Amendment. Such situations call to mind the principle that the protection of the privilege "is as broad as the mischief against which it seeks to guard," Counselman v. Hitchcock, 142 U.S. 547, 562.

In the present case, however, no such problem of application is presented. Not even a shadow of testimonial compulsion upon or enforced communication by the accused was involved either in the extraction or in the chemical analysis. Petitioner's testimonial capacities were in no way implicated; indeed, his participation, except as a donor, was irrelevant to the results of the test, which depend on chemical analysis and on that alone. Since the blood test evidence, although an incriminating product of compulsion, was neither petitioner's testimony nor evidence relating to some communicative act or writing by the petitioner, it was not inadmissible on privilege grounds.

III. The Right to Counsel Claim

This conclusion also answers petitioner's claim that, in compelling him to submit to the test in face of the fact that his objection was made on the advice of counsel, he was denied his Sixth Amendment right to the assistance of counsel. Since petitioner was not entitled to assert the privilege, he has no greater right because counsel erroneously advised him that he could assert it. His claim is strictly limited to the failure of the police to respect his wish, reinforced by counsel's advice, to be left inviolate. No issue of counsel's ability to assist petitioner in respect of any rights he did possess is presented. The limited claim thus made must be rejected.

IV. The Search and Seizure Claim

In Breithaupt, as here, it was also contended that the chemical analysis should be excluded from evidence as the product of an unlawful search and seizure in violation of the Fourth and Fourteenth Amendments. The Court did not decide whether the extraction of blood in that case was unlawful, but rejected the claim on the basis of Wolf v. Colorado, 338 U.S. 25. That case had held that the Constitution did not require, in state prosecutions for state crimes, the exclusion of evidence obtained in violation of the Fourth Amendment's provisions. We have since overruled Wolf in that respect, holding in Mapp v. Ohio, 367 U.S. 643, that the exclusionary rule adopted for federal prosecutions in Weeks v. United States, 232 U.S. 383, must also be applied in criminal prosecutions in state courts. The question is squarely presented therefore, whether the chemical analysis introduced in evidence in this case should have been excluded as the product of an unconstitutional search and seizure.

The overriding function of the Fourth Amendment is to protect personal privacy and dignity against unwarranted intrusion by the State. In Wolf we recognized "[t]he security of one's privacy against arbitrary intrusion by the police" as being "at the core of the Fourth Amendment" and "basic to a free society." 338 U.S., at 27. We reaffirmed that broad view of the Amendment's purpose in applying the federal exclusionary rule to the States in Mapp.

The values protected by the Fourth Amendment thus substantially overlap those the Fifth Amendment helps to protect. History and precedent have required that we today reject the claim that the Self-Incrimination Clause of the Fifth Amendment requires the human body in all circumstances to be held inviolate against state expeditions seeking evidence of crime. But if compulsory administration of a blood test does not implicate the Fifth Amendment, it plainly involves the broadly conceived reach of a search and seizure under the Fourth Amendment. That Amendment expressly provides that "[t]he right of the people to be secure in their *persons,* houses, papers, and effects, against unreasonable searches and seizures, shall not be violated. . . ." (Emphasis added.) It could not reasonably be argued, and indeed respondent does not argue, that the administration of the blood test in this case was free of the constraints of the Fourth Amendment. Such testing procedures plainly constitute searches of "persons," and depend antecedently upon seizures of "persons," within the meaning of that Amendment.

Because we are dealing with intrusions into the human body rather than with state interferences with property relationships or private papers—"houses, papers, and effects"—we write on a clean slate. Limitations on the kinds of property which may be seized under warrant, as distinct from the procedures for search and the permissible scope of search, are not instructive in this context. We begin with the assumption that once the privilege against self-incrimination has been found not to bar compelled intrusions into the body for blood to be analyzed for alcohol content, the Fourth Amendment's proper function is to constrain, not against all intrusions as such, but against intrusions which are not justified in the circumstances, or which are made in an improper manner. In other words, the questions we must decide in this case are whether the police were justified in requiring petitioner to submit to the blood test, and whether the means and procedures employed in taking his blood respected relevant Fourth Amendment standards of reasonableness.

In this case, as will often be true when charges of driving under the influence of alcohol are pressed, these questions arise in the context of an arrest made by an officer without a warrant. Here, there was plainly probable cause for the officer to arrest petitioner and charge him with driving an automobile while under the influence of intoxicating liquor. The police officer who arrived at the scene shortly after the accident smelled liquor on petitioner's breath, and testified that petitioner's eyes were "bloodshot, watery, sort of a glassy appearance." The officer saw petitioner again at the hospital, within two hours of the accident. There he noticed similar symptoms of drunkenness. He thereupon informed petitioner "that he was under arrest and that he was entitled to the services of an attorney, and that he could remain silent, and that anything that he told me would be used against him in evidence."

While early cases suggest that there is an unrestricted "right on the part of the Government, always recognized under English and American law, to search the person of the accused when legally arrested to discover and seize the fruits or evidences of crime," Weeks v. United States, 232 U.S. 383, 392; People v. Chiagles, 237 N.Y. 193, 142 N.E. 583 (1923) (CARDOZO, J.), the mere fact of a lawful arrest does not end our inquiry. The suggestion of these cases apparently rests on two factors—first, there may be more immediate danger of concealed weapons or of destruction of evidence under the direct control of the accused, United States v. Rabinowitz, 339 U.S. 56, 72–73 (FRANKFURTER, J., dissenting); second, once a search of the arrested person for weapons is permitted, it would be both impractical and unnecessary to enforcement of the Fourth Amendment's purpose to attempt to confine the search to those objects alone. People v. Chiagles, 237 N.Y., at 197–198, 142 N.E., at 584. Whatever the validity of these considerations in general, they have little applicability with respect to searches involving intrusions beyond the body's surface. The interests in human dignity and privacy which the Fourth Amendment protects forbid any such intrusions on the mere chance that desired evidence might be obtained. In the absence of a clear indication that in fact such evidence will be found, these fundamental human interests require law officers to suffer the risk that such evidence may disappear unless there is an immediate search.

Although the facts which established probable cause to arrest in this case also suggested the required relevance and likely success of a test of petitioner's blood for alcohol, the question remains whether the arresting officer was permitted to draw these inferences himself, or was required instead to procure a warrant before proceeding with the test. Search warrants are ordinarily required for searches of dwellings, and, absent an emergency, no less could be required where intrusions into the human body are concerned. The requirement that a warrant be obtained is a requirement that the inferences to support the search "be drawn by a neutral and detached magistrate instead of being judged by the officer engaged in the often competitive enterprise of ferreting out crime." Johnson v. United States, 333 U.S. 10, 13–14; see also Aguilar v. Texas, 378 U.S. 108, 110–111. The importance of informed, detached and deliberate determinations of the issue whether or not to invade another's body in search of evidence of guilt is indisputable and great.

The officer in the present case, however, might reasonably have believed that he was confronted with an emergency, in which the delay necessary to obtain a warrant, under the circumstances, threatened "the destruction of evidence," Preston v.

United States, 376 U.S. 364, 367. We are told that the percentage of alcohol in the blood begins to diminish shortly after drinking stops, as the body functions to eliminate it from the system. Particularly in a case such as this, where time had to be taken to bring the accused to a hospital and to investigate the scene of the accident, there was no time to seek out a magistrate and secure a warrant. Given these special facts, we conclude that the attempt to secure evidence of blood-alcohol content in this case was an appropriate incident to petitioner's arrest.

Similarly, we are satisfied that the test chosen to measure petitioner's blood-alcohol level was a reasonable one. Extraction of blood samples for testing is a highly effective means of determining the degree to which a person is under the influence of alcohol. See Breithaupt v. Abram, 352 U.S., at 436, n. 3. Such tests are a commonplace in these days of periodic physical examinations and experience with them teaches that the quantity of blood extracted is minimal, and that for most people the procedure involves virtually no risk, trauma, or pain. Petitioner is not one of the few who on grounds of fear, concern for health, or religious scruple might prefer some other means of testing, such as the "breathalyzer" test petitioner refused, see n. 9, supra. We need not decide whether such wishes would have to be respected.

Finally, the record shows that the test was performed in a reasonable manner. Petitioner's blood was taken by a physician in a hospital environment according to accepted medical practices. We are thus not presented with the serious questions which would arise if a search involving use of a medical technique, even of the most rudimentary sort, were made by other than medical personnel or in other than a medical environment—for example, if it were administered by police in the privacy of the stationhouse. To tolerate searches under these conditions might be to invite an unjustified element of personal risk of infection and pain.

We thus conclude that the present record shows no violation of petitioner's right under the Fourth and Fourteenth Amendments to be free of unreasonable searches and seizures. It bears repeating, however, that we reach this judgment only on the facts of the present record. The integrity of an individual's person is a cherished value of our society. That we today hold that the Constitution does not forbid the States minor intrusions into an individual's body under stringently limited conditions in no way indicates that it permits more substantial intrusions, or intrusions under other conditions.

Affirmed.

CHAPTER 8

Contents

Sixth Amendment Trial Guarantees

§ 8.1 Speedy Trial

The Sixth Amendment provides:

> *In all criminal prosecutions, the accused shall enjoy the right to a speedy and public trial, by an impartial jury of the State and district wherein the crime shall have been committed, which district shall have been previously ascertained by law, and to be informed of the nature and cause of the accusation; to be confronted with the witnesses against him; to have compulsory process for obtaining witnesses in his favor, and to have the Assistance of Counsel for his defence.*

Where provisions are contained in the Constitution which direct criminal justice procedure, they are self-executing and require no other legislation. Iowa—Jones v. McClaughry, 169 Iowa 281, 151 N.W. 210.

Most persons reading this text who occasionally watch an old western motion picture on television or have seen such films in a theater will have little difficulty in conjuring in their mind the hastily convened court beneath an old elm tree where the hangmen are waiting on the sidelines until the defendant has been found guilty, whereupon they will immediately go into their act to hang the "culprit" who is usually (according to the script) an innocent person. Make no mistake about it, these hangings did occur and would probably still occur were it not for the influence of the Court and public opinion throughout the nation.

The contrary condition wherein a person is arrested only to languish in jail for a protracted period of time, awaiting trial, also has occurred and in some jurisdictions is still occurring. As late as 1975, the Court in Dillingham v. United States, 423 U.S. 64, 95 S.Ct. 303, 46 L.Ed.2d 205, held that a twenty-two month delay between the defendant's arrest and his indictment was a violation of his right to a speedy trial. The Court held that formal arrest engages the speedy trial protection of the Sixth Amendment citing Barker v. Wingo, 407 U.S. 514, 92 S.Ct. 2182, 33 L.Ed.2d 101 (1972).

An extension of the speedy trial idea was attempted in Moody v. Daggett, 429 U.S. 78, 97 S.Ct. 274, 50 L.Ed.2d 236 (1976), where a parolee who was imprisoned for a crime that was committed while he was on parole was held not to be constitutionally entitled to a prompt parole revocation hearing when a parole violator warrant was issued and lodged with the confinement institution as a detainer.

§ 8.2 The Balancing Test

In Barker (supra), the Court adopted a balancing test to determine whether a defendant was denied a speedy trial. It identified four factors:

1. Length of the delay;
2. The reason for the delay;
3. The defendant's assertion of his right;
4. Prejudice to the defendant.

The length of the delay is to some extent a triggering mechanism. Until there is some delay which is presumptively prejudicial, there is no necessity for inquiry into the other factors that go into the balance.

A defendant may lose the ability to have witnesses in his own defense if the trial is delayed. Some jurisdictions have statutory procedural devices to have pretrial examinations of witnesses for the defense. These procedural devices are not often used and many attorneys who represent a defendant who has a good defense are not aware of the existence of these pretrial examinations of witnesses.

§ 8.3 Delays Caused by Defendant

Many delays in the prosecution are caused by the defendant or his attorney. The reason for the request for the adjournment might be that the defendant is attempting to delay his/her day of reckoning, or that, in some jurisdictions, the judge who is sitting is not to the defendant's liking and "judge shopping" occurs, or the defendant is waiting for a new prosecutor to take office, or the attorney has not been paid his fee, or the witnesses against the defendant will lose their zeal to testify or will disappear or die. These and other reasons are tools used in the defense of a criminal action. The courts have held that the defendant who brings about the delay cannot be heard to complain that s/he has been denied a speedy trial. In effect, the defendant by his/her actions thereby waives the right to a speedy trial.

§ 8.4 Delays Caused by Prosecution

On the other side of the coin, the prosecution may intentionally delay the trial to wear out the defendant monetarily and emotionally, or to cause the defendant to lose witnesses in his/her defense. Many times the prosecutor will delay a trial also where s/he has a weak case and does not want to have the evidence closely scrutinized or have the prosecution witness exposed if the witness is an informer or undercover police officer. In these cases the prosecutor hopes for and is many times successful in getting the defendant to plead guilty to a lesser included offense in some jurisdictions or to one or more counts to a multicount indictment in the federal jurisdiction and some state courts where pleas to lesser included offenses are not permitted.

§ 8.5 Role of Court in Deciding the Speedy Trial Issue

To lay aside any contention that it was not a judicial power to determine whether a speedy trial existed, it has been held that it is a judicial power to determine whether an accused in a criminal prosecution has had a speedy trial. Minn.—State v. Artz, 154 Minn. 290, 191 N.W. 605 (1923).

The Court has assigned different weights to the prosecution's delay. If it was caused by negligence or overcrowded courts, it is weighed less heavily but, nevertheless, is considered since the ultimate responsibility for such circumstances must rest with the government rather than with the defendant. A valid reason, such as a missing witness, also serves to justify an appropriate delay. See Barker v. Wingo (supra).

The speedy trial issue has been a troublesome one which has to be construed by the court almost on an ad hoc basis. In construing this right, U.S. v. MACDONALD, 456 U.S. 1, 102 S.Ct. 1497, 71 L.Ed.2d. 696, 30 Cr.L. 3111 (1982) was an unusual case. There a captain in the Army Medical Corps was formally charged by the Army with the murders of his pregnant wife and two children on a military reservation. The Army dropped the charges in 1970 but reopened the investigation at the request of the Justice Department and in 1972 handed over a comprehensive report. The Justice Department did not convene a Grand Jury until 1974. Meanwhile the Captain had been discharged from the service on hardship grounds. On January 1975, McDonald was indicted by a civilian grand jury on three counts of murder, the same charges that the military authorities had dropped. The majority of the Court held that the speedy trial right is not implicated at all when the same sovereign initiates, drops and then reinstates criminal charges. Furthermore, the Speedy Trial Clause of the Sixth Amendment does not apply to the period before a defendant is indicted, arrested, or otherwise officially accused.

§ 8.6 Waiver of Right of Speedy Trial

A defendant may stipulate with the prosecution that s/he will waive the right to a speedy trial. This is sometimes done in order to get some concession from the prosecution. An attorney representing a defendant may be engaged in another matter in a court of equal jurisdiction. If the other engagement is for a lengthy period of time, the judge in which the instant matter is pending may force the attorney to retain other counsel to represent the defendant in the instant case. The defendant may not want other counsel or the attorney may not like to give up the retainer. A problem may arise as to the defendant's right of counsel if s/he is compelled to retain an attorney other than the one s/he initially retained. In this situation, with the judge's permission, counsel may stipulate either in open court or in writing that the defendant waives her/his right to a speedy trial. The prosecution thereby is avoiding a later appellate challenge to the defendant's right to counsel if the defendant was compelled to go to trial with other than the counsel of his/her choice and the defendant and the defense attorney are satisfied because the trial will occur later under conditions more acceptable to the defense.

A defendant may also bring about a waiver of the speedy trial right by his/her actions in delaying the trial (see § 8.3 supra).

§ 8.7 Public Trial

The idea that a defendant in a criminal case be afforded a public trial was advanced to prohibit secret trials where defendants were convicted without due process of law or, in the alternative, where defendants might be able to subvert justice by bribery or threats to be found innocent. The presence of an audience in the courtroom also inhibits false testimony. The right to a public trial in a criminal case has been regarded as a fundamental right of due process of law.

Problems sometimes arise when the subject of the trial is such that it becomes one of extreme public interest. Where a famous person is the defendant or a witness is one such example; another may be a horrendous murder or one based on a sex crime. The presiding judge is given some discretion in these cases as to how many people may be permitted into the courtroom and what their behavior pattern will be. The discretion, however, must meet certain limitations so as not to deprive the defendant of a fair trial. One such abuse of this discretion occurred in the trial of Dr. Sam Sheppard, where the presiding judge permitted television crews and newspaperpeople to take over the courtroom. Sheppard v. Maxwell, 384 U.S. 332, 86 S.Ct. 1507, 16 L.Ed.2d 600 (1966). Television reporting of a trial was also not permitted in Estes v. Texas, 381 U.S. 532, 85 S.Ct. 1628, 14 L.Ed.2d 543 (1965).

However, the public has the right to be informed as to what occurs in its courts; but reporters of all media, including television, are always present if they wish to be and are plainly free to report whatever occurs in open court through their respective media. Bridges v. California, 314 U.S. 2521, 62 S.Ct. 190, 85 L.Ed. 192 (1941); Pennekamp v. Florida, 328 U.S. 331, 66 S.Ct. 1029, 90 L.Ed. 1295 (1946); Estes v. Texas (supra).

Courts are also limited by their size. If a case is one that is well known, it would appear that the court administration should assign the trial to the largest courtroom available. This does not mean that loudspeakers have to be set up in other areas to disseminate the court proceedings to the multitudes. The right of a public trial does not require that spectators not directly concerned with the case be admitted in such numbers as to overcrowd the courtroom and take up space required for jurors, witnesses, court officers, and friends and relatives of the defendant. Cal.—People v. Byrnes, 84 Cal.App.2d 72, 190 P.2d 290 (1948).

Those readers who have experience with juvenile court proceedings may question how and why the case of a juvenile offender is tried in a semi-secret atmosphere where the general public is excluded. This is possible only because juvenile court proceedings are not denominated as criminal trials. The intent is to protect the juveniles' reputations so that they are not branded as criminals in later life.

The court may also exercise sound discretion when a young person is required to testify about facts which might be embarrassing to the witness because of their sexual nature. In such a case, a judge may take testimony in his/her robing room or chambers. N.Y.—Peo. v. Jelke, 308 N.Y. 56, 123 N.E.2d 769 (1954).

RICHMOND NEWSPAPER INC. v. VIRGINIA, 488 U.S. 555, 100 S.Ct. 2814, 65 L.Ed.2d. 973, 27 Cr.L. 324 (1980) held that even though both prosecution and defense in a state criminal trial agree that the trial be closed to the public, the granting of a motion to that effect is violative of the FIRST and FOURTEENTH Amendments of the United States Constitution unless there is an overriding interest articulated in findings. This case expands on GAMMET CO. v. DEPASQUALE, 443 U.S. 368 where the Court held that the Sixth Amendment right to public trial was personal to the accused conferring no right of access to pretrial proceedings that is separately enforceable by the public or the press.

Public knowledge of the contents of pre-trial suppression hearings present a particular problem. The purpose of the suppression hearing requested by the defendant is to keep from the trial jury certain types of inadmissible evidence. If the jury knows about the existence of facts that are not admissible, it may influence the verdict of the jury and a fair trial cannot be conducted. On the other hand, the constitution requires a public trial and all proceedings should be public. This problem arose in WALLER v. GEORGIA, —U.S.—, 104 S.Ct. 2210, 81 L.Ed.2d. 31 (1984). In that case, the defendant moved to suppress evidence but also objected that it be closed to the public citing the Sixth and Fourteenth Amendments right to a public trial. The Court held that under the Sixth Amendment, any closure of a suppression hearing over the objections of the accused must meet the following tests:

The party seeking to close the hearing must advance an overriding interest that is likely to be prejudiced;

The closure must be no broader than necessary to protect that interest;

The trial court must consider reasonable alternatives to closing the hearing; and it must make findings adequate to support the closure, citing PRESS ENTERPRISE CO. v. SUPERIOR COURT OF CALIFORNIA, 464 U.S.—, 103 S.Ct. 2081, 77 L.Ed.2d. 294 (1983).

The Court in the instant case remanded the case to the state courts to decide what portions, if any, of a new suppression hearing may be closed to the public in light of conditions at the time of that hearing.

§ 8.8 Pretrial Publicity

A fair trial is sometimes almost impossible if there is a great deal of pretrial publicity to the facts of the case. The news media characteristically do not report the news as accurately as they should and many mistakes of fact occur. Almost everyone who has been the subject of a newspaper article can attest to the veracity of this statement. In assembling a jury to try the facts of a case, a lawyer representing the client and, in the final analysis, the presiding judge are charged with the impaneling of a fair jury, whose members will decide the issues of the case solely on the facts brought out in testimony in the courtroom. The federal courts and some state courts give the responsibility of the voire dire (questioning of prospective jury persons) to the presiding judge who may be asked by the trial lawyers to pose certain questions to the prospective jurors. Other states give this responsibility to the respective trial attorneys.

When there is a lot of pretrial publicity, the prospective juror should be asked whether s/he has heard of or read about the case. If the prospective juror answers negatively, one wonders if s/he is telling the truth and if so, whether that person is aware of what is happening in the world. If the prospective juror admits the prior knowledge of the case, the question is usually asked as to whether they would decide the case on the facts presented at the trial or on what they had previously heard or read. Some jurors who are anxious to serve on the case will say that they will decide the case solely on what they hear from testimony in the courtroom. The lawyers are then in a dilemma as to whether these persons should be believed.

In Marshall v. United States, 360 U.S. 310, 79 S.Ct. 1171, 3 L.Ed.2d 1250 (1959), the Court set aside a federal conviction where the jurors were exposed "through news accounts" to information that was not admitted at the trial. In order to prevent a reversal on appeal, it is sometimes good judgment for a prosecutor to acquiesce to requests for adjournment or a change of venue in order to relieve the trial of any kind of reversible prejudicial error.

§ 8.9 Compulsory Process for Obtaining Witnesses

A witness may come to court voluntarily or s/he might come in response to a subpoena which has been served upon the witness. Failure of the witness to appear in court when the witness was served with a subpoena might result in the witness's being fined and/or imprisoned after being found in contempt of court. Some states provide that an attorney has the power to subpoena a witness by preparing a piece of paper known as a subpoena and having himself, a person in his office, any adult person, a sheriff, or city marshal present the paper to the witness. The federal government and some state governments provide that the Clerk of the Court prepare and issue the subpoena and the United States Marshal or the Sheriff of the County in state cases serve the witness.

In United States Courts, the jurisdiction of the court is nationwide and hence a United States Marshal can serve anyone anywhere in the United States. State courts have limited jurisdiction within that state's borders but there are statutes known as "long arm statutes" where state courts have assumed extraterritorial jurisdiction. The "long arm" statutes are only valid in civil actions where the "res" of the court action is situated within the borders of the state court where the matter is pending. An example of this is a marital action where one of the parties is within the state court's jurisdiction. A state, however, cannot assume jurisdiction of a person in a criminal action if that person is outside the state except for extradition or intrastate rendition proceedings where both states cooperate with each other.

United States marshals, sheriffs, or other process servers charge a fee for these services. The nonindigent defendant is expected to pay for this service, but the process is made available to him/her. The indigent defendant gets this service provided free of any charge. This is given as a necessary tool of defense counsel and is provided for by statute both in federal and state procedural laws.

§ 8.10 Defendant's Right of Counsel

It has often been said that a lawyer who represents himself has a fool for a client. This is usually a truism because when one is involved in litigation, s/he becomes so emotionally involved in the dispute that clarity of thought is lost. If one trained in the law, in court procedure, and in the rules of evidence should not represent him/herself, then a layman without such training certainly requires the guiding hand of counsel throughout the proceedings from beginning to end. The courts have not been quick to recognize this.

For many years, counsel was only required in federal courts; later, in state courts for capital offenses; still later, in state courts for felonies; then, for misdemeanors where there was a possibility of incarceration for an extended period of time; then, to juvenile proceedings; and finally, to parole revocation hearings and appeals. We will now treat each of these situations and a few additional problems where the court has ruled on the right of counsel to a defendant in a criminal action.

In BALDASAR v. ILLINOIS, 446 U.S. 222, 100 S.Ct. 1585, 64 L.Ed.2d 169, 27 Cr.L. 3084 (1980) the Court held that a defendant who did not have counsel at a misdemeanor trial because there was no thought of incarcerating the defendant for that charge could not have his punishment for a second misdemeanor increased to that of a felony where the state provided that if the defendant had a previous conviction for the same offense it may be treated as a felony with a one to three year prison term. In this case, the second conviction was for stealing a shower head worth $29.00 and he was sentenced to prison for one to three years.

U.S. v. HENRY, 447 U.S. 264, 100 S.Ct. 2183, 65 L.Ed.2d. 115, 27 Cr.L. 3155 (1980) held that admission of incriminating statements at trial of defendant who made these statements to his cellmate who was a paid government informer violated the defendant's right to the assistance of counsel.

§ 8.11 Custodial Interrogation

When a person suspected of criminal activity is taken into custody by law enforcement officers, s/he is usually in a state of shock when s/he is a neophyte to this experience. It once was said by a person of middle age, who had no prior police record, that when he was arrested for intoxicated driving and placed in a police detention cell, he saw his whole life go down in shambles when the iron gate of the cell slammed shut. For the average American law-abiding person who has had no criminal contact with the police, it is a harrowing experience to have his/her liberty curtailed in this way. The Court has decided that when a person is in the custody of the police for interrogation purposes, if the police deny that person the aid of counsel after a request for counsel's assistance, the police are denying that person a fundamental right to the assistance of counsel as provided for in the Sixth Amendment as it was made applicable to the states by the due process clause of the Fourteenth Amendment. Escobedo v. Illinois, 378 U.S. 478, 84 S.Ct. 1758, 12 L.Ed.2d 977 (1964). Any evidence obtained as a result of this interrogation was to be excluded from the trial. The Court held that when the process shifts from investigatory to accusatory—when its focus is on the accused and its purpose is to elicit a confession—our adversary system begins to operate, and, under the circumstances here, the accused must be permitted to consult with his/her lawyer.

The Escobedo case was followed by Miranda v. Arizona, 384 U.S. 436, 86 S.Ct. 1602, 16 L.Ed.2d 694 (1966). The Court extended the Escobedo rule and defined what custodial interrogation is. They further extended the right to counsel during custodial interrogation beyond the circumstances when the accused asks for counsel to be present. The Court said that it is the duty of the police to inform the suspect of his right to counsel even if he does not specifically ask for it. The language of the Court follows:

> Our holding will be spelled out with some specificity in the pages which follow but briefly stated it is this: the prosecution may not use statements, whether exculpatory or inculpatory stemming from custodial interrogation of the defendant unless it demonstrates the use of procedural safeguards effective to secure the privilege against self-incrimination. By custodial interrogation, we mean questioning initiated by law enforcement officers after a person has been taken into custody or otherwise deprived of his freedom of action in any significant way. As for the procedural safeguards to be employed, unless other fully effective means are devised to inform accused persons of their right of silence and to assure a continuous opportunity to exercise it, the following measures are required. Prior to any questioning, the person must be warned that he has a right to remain silent, that any statement he does make may be used as evidence against him, and that he has a right to the presence of an attorney, either retained or appointed. The defendant may waive effectuation of these rights, provided the waiver is made voluntarily, knowingly, and intelligently. If however, he indicates in any manner and at any stage of the process that he wishes to consult with an attorney before speaking there can be no questioning. Likewise, if the individual is alone and indicates in any manner that he does not wish to be interrogated, the police may not question him. The mere fact that he may have answered some questions or volunteered

some statements on his own does not deprive him of the right to refrain from answering any further inquiries until he has consulted with an attorney and thereafter consents to be questioned.

The Miranda case was decided simultaneously with Vignera v. New York, Westover v. United States, and California v. Stewart. These cases raised a furor within the police agencies of the United States. However, acting true to form, the police of the nation learned to live with the decision. They prepared printed cards which were distributed to members of the force, the contents of which were to be read to prisoners at the first available and reasonable opportunity. Signs were posted in station houses in conspicuous places to give the prisoner adequate warnings. Where English and another language were frequently used, the signs might be in two or several languages. They became known in the police profession as the "Miranda Warnings."

Miranda was not the final word of the court with respect to custodial interrogation and right of counsel. In Michigan v. Mosely, 423 U.S. 96, 96 S.Ct. 321, 46 L.Ed.2d 313 (1975), a defendant asserted his Miranda rights and the interrogation ceased. About two hours later another interrogation was commenced for another crime (homicide). The Court said that the fact that one in custody initially asserts Miranda rights does not rule out absolutely the possibility of a subsequent valid waiver. Counsel need not be present before a later waiver is possible. The Court, in effect, said that the right to cut off questioning was in fact honored in this case. The first detective immediately ceased his interrogation. The second detective fully advised the defendant of his Miranda rights. The second questioning was a "reasonable interpretation" of defendant's earlier refusal to answer questions about the first crime (robbery). However, in a Ninth Circuit Court of Appeals case, it was held that officers cannot ignore a clear indication of desire to remain silent. United States v. Kinsman, 540 F.2d 1017 (1976). Other cases have held that officers must allow defendant to contact an attorney even though retained counsel is unavailable.

The waiver must be an intelligent waiver. See effect of influence of drugs. United States v. Cox, 487 F.2d 634 (5th Cir. 1973); intoxication, Kennedy v. State, 499 S.W. 842 (Ark. 1973), Hart v. State, 224 S.E. 2d 755 (Ga. App. 1976). Even an attorney is fully entitled to Miranda warnings. State v. Stein, 360 A. 2d 347 (N.J. 1976).

In Beckwith v. United States, 425 U.S. 341, 96 S.Ct. 1612, 48 L.Ed.2d 1 (1976), the Court rejected the "focus" test of Escobedo and Miranda. In that case agents of the Intelligence Division of the Internal Revenue Service did not arrest petitioner but met with him in his home. The Court said, "An interview with government agents such as (this one) simply does not present the elements which the Miranda court found so inherently coercive as to require its holding." The Court did not find Beckwith in a custodial situation.

In Brewer v. Williams, 430 U.S. 387, 97 S.Ct. 1232, 51 L.Ed. 424, 45 L.W. 4287 (1977), the Court reversed a conviction of a defendant who was found guilty of murder when he gave information as to the location of the victim while he was in custody of the police on a long automobile ride to a place of detention. The defendant had been represented by counsel and the police had promised that they would not interrogate the prisoner while enroute. Notwithstanding this, the police, knowing that the prisoner was a deeply religious Christian, worked on his emotions by intimating that it was a shame that the victim was not able to get a Christian burial because no one knew where she was. The prisoner then led the police to the location where she was buried in a shallow grave. It appears that the Court wanted to punish the police for not keeping their word and this case acts as a warning to any law enforcement officer that an agreement made is not to be broken or the defendant's case will be dismissed.

In Geders v. United States, 425 U.S. 80, 96 S.Ct. 1330, 47 L.Ed.2d 592 (1976), it was held that a trial court's order directing the defendant not to consult with his attorney during a regular overnight recess was held to be a violation of defendant's right to counsel.

The claim that the Miranda warnings were not understood by the prisoner reached the Court in Wainright v. Sypes, 432 U.S. 72, 97 S.Ct. 2497, 53 L.Ed.2d 594, 21 Cr.L. 3177 (1977). In that case the petitioner claimed that he did not understand the Miranda warnings and made a statement to the police which inculpated himself in a murder. Prior to and during the trial, there was no motion to suppress these statements and he was convicted. The issue was first raised on appeal and the Court was of the opinion that the fact that it was first raised on appeal precluded habeas corpus relief absent a showing of actual prejudice and cause for his failure to make a timely objection.

In Massachusetts v. White, #77-1388 (1978), the Court affirmed by a 4–4 decision that a defendant legally intoxicated could not waive his right to remain silent and consult a lawyer.

Once an accused has invoked his right to counsel under MIRANDA v. ARIZONA, 384 U.S. 466 (1966), he may not be subjected to further interrogation until counsel has been made available to him, unless the accused initiates further communications, exchanges or conversations with the police. In EDWARDS v. ARIZONA 451 U.S. 477, 101 S.Ct. 1880, 68 L.Ed.2d. 378, reh den (US) 101 S.Ct. 3128, 69 L.Ed.2d. 984, 29 Cr.L. 3037 (1981) the petitioner was in custody and was given Miranda warnings. He asked for counsel and questioning ceased. The following day the police returned, gave him Miranda warnings again, and for an unknown reason, the petitioner implicated himself in the crime of robbery, burglary and 1st degree murder. Counsel had not been supplied to him after his first request the previous day. The Court held that his conviction was reversed. There was no direction for a remand for a new trial in this case.

In RHODE ISLAND v. INNES, —U.S.—, —S.Ct.—, 64 L.Ed.2d. 297 (1980), an off-hand remark was made to defendant by police officer, that a handicapped child at a nearby school might find the gun. This lead defendant to tell where the gun was. The Court held that this did not constitute interrogation. It held further that in cases like this, interrogation might occur when the suspect could reasonably be expected to be particularly vulnerable, i.e., an express question is asked by the police.

In NEW YORK v. QUARLES, —U.S.—, 104 S.Ct. 2626, 81 L.Ed.2d. 550 (1984), the majority held in a 5–1–3 decision that a police officer need not recite Miranda warnings before asking a custodial suspect immediately at the time of arrest, "where is the gun," when the officer had knowledge that the suspect was reported to have recently possessed a gun and the gun was not in the possession of the suspect at the time of the arrest. The question could reasonably be said to have been prompted by the officer's concern for public safety. In that case the apprehension was made in a supermarket and other persons were present. The Court thus enunciated a "public safety" exception to the Miranda warnings.

In BERKEMER v. MCCARTY, —U.S.—, 104 S.Ct. 3138, 82 L.Ed.2d 317 (1984) it was held that an officer need not give Miranda warnings to a driver of a motor vehicle in a routine traffic stop before the officer asks the driver questions. However, once the motorist has been detained pursuant to a traffic stop, and thereafter is subjected to treatment that renders him "in custody" for practical purposes, he is entitled to the full panoply of protections prescribed by Miranda.

The Court modified BREWER v. WILLIAMS, supra, in NIX v. WILLIAMS, —U.S.—, —S.Ct.—, —L.Ed.2d.—, 35 Cr.L. 3119 (1984) where volunteers were searching for the body of a 10 year old girl. The respondent had been arrested and was being transported to a place of incarceration. The police informed his counsel that during the drive they would not question the respondent. However, one of the officers began a conversation with the respondent that resulted in him making incriminating statements and directed the officers to the child's body. A systematic search of the area by 200 volunteers was then terminated. The Court held that these were different facts from Brewer (supra) because in the instant case, the volunteers would have discovered the body without the aid of the respondent. The Court held further that the evidence pertaining to the discovery and the condition of the body was properly admitted in the second trial (no evidence was introduced as to how police found the body in the second trial) on the ground that the body ultimately or inevitably would have been discovered even if no violation of any constitutional provision had taken place. . . . If the prosecution can establish by a preponderance of the evidence that the information ultimately or inevitably would have been discovered by lawful means, then the deterrence rational has little basis, and the evidence should be received.

Another decision of importance to police and prosecutorial personnel is found in OREGON v. ELSTAD, 468 U.S.—, 105 S.Ct. 1285, 84 L.Ed.2d. 222, 36 Cr.L. 3167 (1985). There the respondent was picked up at his home as a burglary suspect. At his home he made an incriminating statement without having been given Miranda warnings. Later at the station house, he was given Miranda warnings and he then decided to give a written confession without the assistance of counsel. The Court held that the Fifth Amendment guarantee against self incrimination does not require suppression of a confession, made after proper Miranda warnings and a valid waiver of rights, solely because the police had obtained an earlier voluntary statement without the prior Miranda warnings having been given.

To this date, it appears that we have not heard the last word from the Court on Miranda warning requirements. The trend seems to be towards an erosion of defendant's rights in this area of the law.

§ 8.12 Lineup and Show-Up Identification

There have been many problems associated with lineup identification. When a suspect is placed in a lineup with other persons to be shown to the victim for the purpose of identifying the perpetrator of a crime, there is a great possibility of suggestiveness. If a white man is the suspect, surely it would not be due process of law if the white suspect was placed in a lineup with five others who were black. If the white man is alleged to have had blond hair, it would not be credible identification if he was placed in a lineup with those having dark brown or black hair. Other prejudicial procedures might occur where several persons, all in each other's presence, identified the suspect, thereby creating a stampede effect, or where an officer might suggest to the victim that he look over a particular person with great care. Each of these examples manifests prejudicial conduct on the part of the police. If this is demonstrated to the court on motion, there is great likelihood that all evidence which flowed from that identification will be excluded from the trial and the prosecutor will have no further evidence to present, thus allowing a guilty person to go unpunished.

There are innumerable cases where a police officer resembling the suspect was picked out of the lineup as the guilty person. Usually in these cases, the police officer can prove where s/he was at the time of the commission of the crime or s/he is in great trouble. In order to prevent the slightest stigma of suggestiveness, it is recommended that the police insist that a retained or appointed counsel be present during the lineup identification proceedings.

Experience has demonstrated that if an eyewitness makes a mistaken identification at a lineup, the witness will usually continue in his/her assertion because of the possibility of a recovery against him/her in a civil action for false imprisonment. This problem always exists, even in a very fairly conducted lineup procedure where the victim is a person who has much to lose if the identified person is not found guilty or does not plead guilty. Accordingly, where money or property which has been insured has been taken by the perpetrator, the attorney for the victim may point out the risks to the victim, so as to allow the victim to make up his/her mind as to whether the identification should be made.

There is a difference between a show-up (confrontation) and a lineup. A show-up occurs when shortly after the commission of a crime the suspect is brought before the victim for identification purposes. The lineup will occur after a significant interval of time has passed and the suspect will be placed among a group of similarly appearing persons for the purpose of having the suspect identified.

Effective law enforcement requires that suspects be identified prior to courtroom identification. The Court recognizes this but because the identification procedure has been held to be a critical stage of the adversary process, the Court has required that great efforts at fairness be made by the police in conducting both lineups and show-ups. There is an adage which reads as follows:

> First, one has privilege,
> Then there is abuse of that privilege,
> Then there is reform.

This proverb can be applied to police conduct in many areas where the pendulum has been swung in favor of the defendant's rights. The lineup process has been such an example. The Court initially treated the lineup identification problem in two landmark cases. They are United States v. Wade, 388 U.S. 219, 87 S.Ct. 1926, 18 L.Ed.2d 1149 (1967), and Gilbert v. California, 388 U.S. 293, 87 S.Ct. 1967, 18 L.Ed.2d 1199 (1967). Both cases held that a lineup, voice identification, and direct confrontation between a victim and a suspected perpetrator do not constitute a violation of the Fifth Amendment self-incrimination clause but that there may be a violation of the Sixth Amendment right of counsel clause, unless the suspect has had a reasonable opportunity to have a counsel present to represent him.

The Court indicated that prior to the necessity of having counsel present, it should be determined whether the procedure is critical to the defense of the case and, secondly, whether the presence of counsel might have made a difference to the defendant. The Court felt that both of the aforementioned requirements are present in a lineup identification procedure. The Court did not mandate that counsel be present at lineups but it held that an accused could waive the constitutional guarantee of right of counsel at any critical state including this one. It further held that absent a knowing and intelligent waiver, the witness's in-court identification will be excluded unless the prosecution can show an independent source for the in-court identification. There were other points that were made which will be best remembered by reading the case at the end of this chapter.

In Kirby v. Ill., 406 U.S. 682, 92 S.Ct. 1877, 32 L.Ed.2d 411 (1972), the Court limited the right to counsel in lineups until after the initiation of judicial criminal proceedings by way of formal charge, preliminary hearing, indictment, information, or arraignment.

The courts have generally denied a right of counsel at field confrontations. Arizona—State v. Armyo, 26 Ariz.App. 52, 549 P.2d 616 (1976). There is a conflict of authority with respect to whether counsel is required after the filing of the complaint and the issuance of an arrest warrant. United States ex rel. Robinson v. Zelker, 468 F.2d 159 (2nd Cir. 1972); Mo.—Arnold v. State, 284 S.W.2d 248 (1972); S.D.—State v. Johnson, 202 N.W.2d 132 (1972). The prevailing view is that a post arrest confrontation does not require counsel to be present in that the arrest is not the beginning of judicial criminal proceedings, 1975 Washington University Law Quarterly 423. Most states interpreting the Kirby (supra) rule consider the following as triggers so as to require the presence of counsel: confrontation after (1) indictment, (2) information, (3) preliminary arraignment or (4) preliminary examination.

It is therefore suggested that if a lineup is to be conducted, every reasonable effort be made to have a counsel present who would represent the defendant's interests. He need not be the counsel who will conduct the defense at the trial of the defendant. In many ways, it might be to the defendant's best interest to have other than trial counsel present at the lineup should it become necessary for the counsel to testify at a subsequent hearing or trial with respect to the unfairness of the lineup identification procedure. The Code of Professional Responsibility of the American Bar Association and the Codes of Ethics of State and Local Bar Associations frown on the practice of a trial attorney acting as a witness except when it is essential to the ends of justice.

The presence of counsel requirement in the show-up situation was treated differently in Stoval v. Denno, 388 U.S. 293, 87 S.Ct. 1967, 18 L.Ed.2d 1199 (1967). In that case the Court said, "... The practice of showing suspects singly to persons for purpose of identification, and not a part of a line-up, has been unduly condemned... However, a claimed violation of due process of law in the conduct of a confrontation depends on the totality of the circumstances surrounding it and the record in the present case reveals that the showing of Stoval to Mrs. Behrendt in an immediate hospital confrontation was imperative." In that case there was a question as to how long the victim would live.

Thompson v. State, 438 P.2d 287, Okla.Crim.App. (1968), in a state decision prepared a rule of procedure which could be followed by police officers in order to prevent suppression of evidence following the Wade and Gilbert decisions. It recommended the following at 438 P.2d at 289:

1. The suspect should be advised of his right to be represented by counsel and to have counsel present if he so desires. He should be further advised that he does not have a right to refuse to participate in the line-up.
2. The witness or victim attending such line-up should be advised of the purpose for which it is being conducted but the officers should not, directly or indirectly, single out one suspect and suggest that he is the person sought.
3. Other people participating in the line-up should be of the same general weight, height, age, color and race, whenever possible and the suspect should not be clothed in such a manner as to attract special attention or make him stand out from the other persons in the line-up.
4. The names of all persons participating in the line-up should be recorded and preserved together with the names of the officers conducting said line-up.
5. The suspect's waiver of his right to counsel and voluntary participation in said line-up should be recorded and it should also be recorded if he has counsel present during the line-up.
6. Not more than one victim should be presented at the line-up at the same time. Victims previously having attended a line-up should not be allowed to converse with other victims prior to their viewing the line-up.
7. Pictures of the persons participating in the line-up, taken at the line-

up, could be of invaluable aid to the trial judge before whom the identification question is raised.

8. Line-ups should be conducted whenever possible during the daylight hours and witnesses not connected with the police should be encouraged to attend in order that they might later testify as to the method in which the line-up was conducted.
9. Lastly, we emphasize that typewritten records of the manner and mode of conducting the line-up should be prepared and preserved for their later use.

A case setting forth guidelines for police to conduct a show-up in the absence of counsel, occurred in United States v. O'Connor, 282 F.Supp. 963 (D.D.C. 1968). The Court set these guidelines in the form of questions which must be answered to satisfy the due process of law requirement of Stoval v. Denno (supra). They were:

1. Was the defendant the only individual that could possibly be identified as the guilty party by the complaining witness, or were there others near him at the time of the confrontation so as to negate the assertion that he was shown alone to the witness?
2. Where did the confrontation take place?
3. Were there any compelling reasons for a prompt confrontation so as to deprive the police of the opportunity of securing other similar individuals for the purpose of holding a line-up?
4. Was the witness aware of any observation by another or other evidence indicating the guilt of the suspect at the time of the confrontation?
5. Were any tangible objects related to the offense placed before the witness that would encourage identification?
6. Was the witness identification based on only part of the suspect's total personality?
7. Was the identification a product of mutual reinforcement of opinion among witnesses simultaneously viewing the defendant?
8. Was the emotional state of the witness such as to preclude identification?

There were other criteria indicated in the decision as representative of a violation of due process of law. By reading the above, the student should be able to get a feel of the situation if a violation of due process will occur in a particular case. In essence, it appears that when, in the interest of justice, speed of the identification is necessary because of a compelling factor, the identification may be made on a show-up basis without a counsel being present to represent the suspect. See Va.—Martin v. Commonwealth, 173 S.E.2d 794 (1970). The Kirby case (supra) extended the area where counsel need not be present, but it is recommended that the guidelines of United States v. O'Connor be practiced in order to be reasonably certain that evidence is not suppressed.

The United States Congress has attempted to vitiate the Court's holding in Wade and Gilbert (supra) by the enactment of Section 3502 of the Omnibus Crime Control Act of 1968:

> *Section 3502—Admissibility in evidence of eyewitness testimony*
> The testimony of a witness that he saw the accused commit or participate in the commission of the crime for which the accused is being tried shall be admissible in evidence in a criminal prosecution in any trial court ordained and established under Article III of the Constitution of the United States.

The natural intent is that counsel need not be present at lineup identification. There is a great question as to the constitutionality of this section, because the statute overlooks a possible due process violation.

However, in 1977, the Court appears to have moved away from the per se exclusionary rule against overzealous police identification practices. It now seems to favor a flexible test for admissibility of evidence for identification which considers the totality of the circumstances. In Manson v. Brathwaite, 432 U.S. 98, 97 S.Ct. 2243, 53 L.Ed.2d 140, 21 Cr.L. 3120 (1977), the Court held that even an unnecessarily suggestive identification procedure may produce admissible evidence so long as that evidence passes the Biggers test (Neil v. Biggers, 409 U.S. 188 [1972]) for reliability, i.e., undercover state narcotics officer identified the defendant from a single photograph shown to him by a fellow officer who suspected the defendant.

Following Manson v. Brathwaite (supra) the Court decided Moore v. Illinois, 434 U.S. 220, 98 S.Ct. 458, 54 L.Ed.2d 424 (1977). In this case the victim was told that she was going to view the suspect in court. His name was called and he was led before the bench whereupon the prosecutor recited the evidence against the defendant. Defendant had no counsel present. The Court held that the factors to be considered if the in-court identification is to have an independent basis away from tainted pretrial corporeal identification are:

1. Prior opportunity to observe the alleged criminal act.
2. Existence of any discrepancy between pre-lineup description and defendant's actual description.
3. Any identification of any other person before lineup.
4. Identification by picture prior to lineup.
5. Failure on prior occasion to identify defendant.
6. Lapse of time between alleged act and witness identification.

In WATKINS v. SOWDERS, 449 U.S. 341, 101 S.Ct. 654, 66 L.Ed.2d. 549, 28 Cr.L. 3037 (1981) the Court held that a trial court was not required in every case to conduct an identification hearing outside the presence of the jury. A divided Court held that, in some circumstances, not presented here, such determination may be constitutionally necessary. But it does not follow that the Constitution requires a per se rule compelling such a procedure in every case.

§ 8.13 Counsel at Arraignment or Preliminary Hearing

The term "arraignment," like many other terms in the English language, may have several meanings, depending on the circumstances in which it is used. Most often it applies to the first step in the judicial process that a defendant in a criminal matter experiences. It is her/his first appearance before a judicial officer at which time the defendant is advised as to the nature of the charges; the constitutional rights with respect to the right of counsel, either retained or assigned, if the defendant is unable to retain counsel privately; and the right to a jury trial (in some cases). The defendant is also asked as to how s/he pleads to the charge, i.e., guilty, not guilty. In most state and federal courts the defendant is also given the option to plead nolo contendere. At this arraignment, bail conditions are set by the judge. This means that the judge determines the seriousness of the charge, the roots of the defendant in the community, the ability of the defendant to raise bail and the likelihood that the amount of money or other bail conditions determined by the judge will insure the presence of the defendant at all subsequent required appearances and at trial.

Some jurisdictions use the term "arraignment" for a procedure which is really a "presentment." In a presentment, notwithstanding the fact that it is an initial appearance before a judicial officer, no plea is taken, and the defendant is held over for a grand jury until a formal indictment is presented or, in the alternative, no true bill is found.

We run into a little difficulty in using the term "presentment" because here too, there is more than one legal meaning for this word. It may also refer to a presentment of a grand jury where, after investigating an allegation of a commission of a crime on its own initiative without the participation of a prosecutor, the grand jury fails to indict the defendant. In such a presentment, the grand jury criticizes the conduct of a person or persons.

A preliminary hearing is the taking of testimony before a judge who will determine whether a prima facie case exists. This is prior to a trial. If it is a felony, the judge may hold the case for the grand jury, fix bail conditions, and accept a plea.

With this limited background, we now attack the problem of legal representation of a defendant at an arraignment. We must first determine whether this initial appearance before a judicial officer is a critical stage of the judicial proceedings. If, for example, the defendant is given the opportunity to plead guilty or to make incriminating statements at this appearance, surely it must be considered to be a critical stage in the judicial process and fundamental fairness requires the presence of counsel for the defendant. If, on the other hand, no statements are made by the defendant and s/he is not asked any questions which might incriminate the defendant, a counsel need not be present, although one might be present if the defendant wanted it that way. This is in essence the present ruling of the United States Supreme Court as it has developed after a series of cases had been decided dealing with this subject.

Chandler v. Fretag, 348 U.S. 3, 75 S.Ct. 1, 99 L.Ed. 4, decided in 1954, held that in state court criminal proceedings, fundamental fairness required that the accused receive legal assistance by his own retained counsel at every stage in the proceedings. The Court did not indicate in this case that appointed counsel was required for an indigent at this state of the criminal proceedings but instead relied on Betts v. Brady, 316 U.S. 455, 62 S.Ct. 1252, 86 L.Ed. 1595 (1942), where the Court held that appointed counsel is required in capital cases. Hamilton v. Alabama, 368 U.S. 52, 82 S.Ct. 157, 7 L.Ed.2d 114 (1961), held that when a plea is received in a capital case, retained or appointed counsel should be present.

The Hamilton case was followed by White v. Maryland, 373 U.S. 59, 83 S.Ct. 1050, 10 L.Ed.2d 193 (1963), where in another capital case, a preliminary hearing was conducted in the absence of counsel. The Court reversed the conviction in this case on the grounds that the preliminary hearing under Maryland law was as critical a stage in the judicial proceedings as arraignment was under the Alabama law in Hamilton v. Alabama (supra).

The preliminary hearing requirement of the assistance of counsel was extended to noncapital cases in Coleman v. Alabama, 399 U.S. 1, 90 S.Ct. 1999, 26 L.Ed.2d 387 (1970). However in Gerstein v. Pugh, 420 U.S. 103, 95 S.Ct. 854, 43 L.Ed.2d 54 (1975), a Florida case, it was held that a hearing to determine probable cause to arrest (a prima facie case) was not a critical stage which requires the presence of counsel.

In a 1977 case, a rape victim's identification of an indicted defendant at a preliminary hearing without the presence of defendant's counsel was held to violate his Sixth Amendment rights. Moore v. Illinois, 434 U.S. 220, 98 S.Ct. 458, 54 L.Ed.2d 424, 22 Cr.L. 3011 (1977).

Most states and the Federal Rules of Criminal Procedure require the presence of counsel at probable cause hearings. This is not due to federal constitutional requirements but due to a great extension of personal rights afforded to criminal defendants by state constitutions or state and federal legislation. In Ill.—Hessenauer v. People, 256 N.E.2d 791 (1970), the Court said that it is now well established that arraignment is a critical stage in a felony case and the right to counsel attaches automatically before any plea is made and accepted.

§ 8.14 Counsel at Trial

Although the Sixth Amendment clearly provided that the accused shall have the right to the assistance of counsel "in all criminal prosecutions," there was little case law on the subject for many years. Barron v. Baltimore, 32 U.S. 243, 8 L.Ed. 672 (1833), held that none of the Bill of Rights applied to the states. Hurtado v. California, 110 U.S. 516, 4 S.Ct. 111, 28 L.Ed. 232 (1884), continued this thinking even after the passage of the Fourteenth Amendment.

In Johnson v. Zerbst, 304 U.S. 458, 58 S.Ct. 1019, 82 L.Ed. 1461 (1938), the Court held that the assistance of counsel for a criminal defendant was one of the safeguards of the Sixth Amendment which was deemed necessary to insure fundamental human rights of life and liberty. Johnson v. Zerbst was a federal case involving two United States Marines who were charged with feloniously uttering and passing four counterfeit twenty-dollar Federal Reserve Notes and possessing twenty-one such notes. They had counsel at a preliminary hearing but not at the trial. This conviction was overturned by the Court. This case, however, was only applicable to federal courts.

Congress passed the Federal Rules of Criminal Procedure in 1945 where in Rule 44 it provided for a defendant to have counsel either retained or appointed at every stage of the proceedings from the initial appearance through appeal. There was difficulty in implementing this rule and in 1964, Congress passed and the President signed the Criminal Justice Act of 1964 which was a national system for providing counsel to indigent defendants in federal courts.

Each state, having its own constitution and its own laws, may afford more individual rights to those accused of crime than those provided for in the Federal Constitution and Supreme Court decisions. The federal guarantee of the right of counsel as proclaimed in the Sixth Amendment did not reach into state court procedures until the court decided Powell v. Alabama, 287 U.S. 45, 53 S.Ct. 55, 77 L.Ed. 158 (1932). In that case, seven black youths were identified as having perpetrated a gang rape upon two white girls. All of the participants were hitching a ride through Alabama on a freight train. No specific counsel was supplied to them during the trial except that the judge appointed the entire local bar to represent the defendants. The trial was conducted in a hostile environment in Scottsboro, Alabama. The defendants later became known as the "Scottsboro Boys." They did have one attorney, a Mr. Roddy, who was not a member of the local bar but was apparently admitted to practice law in Tennessee. He said that he was not employed to represent the defendants but would like to appear for them if he was assisted by the local bar. The defendants were tried in three separate groups, all on one day, and were convicted of rape. They were sentenced to death, by the jury, under Alabama law. The Supreme Court of Alabama affirmed and the United States Supreme Court reviewed it on certiorari.

The Court held that the defendants in this case, because they were ignorant, illiterate, etc., had been denied their right to counsel to an extent sufficient to violate the notion of fundamental fairness conveyed by the Due Process Clause of the Fourteenth Amendment. Thus the Court had extended the right of counsel at trial to state trials in capital cases where the defendant's intelligence was minimal. This was characterized as "special circumstances." This was the hole in the dike which would make the entire dike cave in to require the right of counsel in state criminal prosecutions in other situations.

The next landmark case in this area was Betts v. Brady, 316 U.S. 455, 62 S.Ct. 1252, 86 L.Ed. 1595 (1942). Betts had insufficient funds to hire counsel to represent him in a robbery charge in Maryland. He asked for assigned counsel and was refused on the ground that Maryland only provided counsel to indigents in capital offenses. The Court affirmed the right of Maryland to continue this practice in that case but when Gideon v. Wainright, 372 U.S. 335, 83 S.Ct. 792, 9 L.Ed.2d 799 (1963), was decided, the Court had almost come around full circle. By a unanimous decision, it reversed the Betts v. Brady (supra) rule by holding that the Sixth Amendment right of counsel was a fundamental right made applicable to the states through the Due Process Clause of the Fourteenth Amendment. Gideon was retried in the same court, with the aid of counsel. In deciding this case, the Court did not yet concern itself with misdemeanor charges. This was left to later judges to determine and this they did.

A felony in one state might be a misdemeanor in another, or conversely. Therefore, different rights of counsel obtained for the same crime in different states. This was resolved in Argersinger v. Hamlin, 407 U.S. 25, 92 S.Ct. 2006, 32 L.Ed.2d 530 (1972), where the Court put the judiciary on notice that if imprisonment is to be imposed if the defendant is found guilty, a counsel should represent the defendant. It did not require counsel to be appointed in every case where the statute provided for imprisonment upon conviction but only in those cases where the judge may decide to impose a sentence of imprisonment upon conviction. Therefore, the judge can preserve the option to send the defendant to jail upon conviction only if the defendant is represented by counsel at the trial.

In Halloway v. Arkansas, 435 U.S. 475, 55 L.Ed.2d 426, 98 S.Ct. 1173 (1978), a defense counsel representing two defendants asked the trial court to be relieved of the representation of one defendant on the grounds that there might be a conflict of interest between the defendants' positions. The trial judge refused to relieve the attorney. The Court held that the trial court's failure, in the absence of dilatory tactics, to appoint separate counsel or inquire whether the conflict was too remote to warrant separate counsel, was a deprivation of the right of counsel under the Sixth Amendment, provided timely objection was made.

In MORRIS v. SLAPPY, 461 U.S. 103, 103 S.Ct. 1610, 75 L.Ed.2d. 610 (1983), the Court held that the right to appointed counsel does not guarantee the right to a "meaningful attorney-client relationship." In the Morris case, the defendant made a request for a continuance on the first day of trial to permit further investigation by a substitute public defender. The public defender however told the court that he was prepared to go to trial even though he was substituting for the assigned public offender who shortly before the trial underwent surgery. The Court denied the continuance. Because of a mistrial, a second trial followed, but respondent refused to cooperate with his appointed lawyer and was convicted.

§ 8.15 Counsel at Post Trial Proceedings

When a trial has been completed and the defendant is found guilty, the defendant is usually remanded to custody and bail conditions, if any, are revoked. The attorney representing the defendant has the legal obligation to make post trial motions to preserve the defendant's rights. The Sixth Amendment mandate of the assistance of counsel does not cease when the finder of the facts pronounces the defendant guilty. A probation report calling for an investigation by a probation agency is usually requested by the judge to assist the judge in the sentencing procedure. The assistance of counsel during this period is essential to insure fundamental fairness. Counsel is provided for the indigent during this period and through the appellate process pursuant to Douglas v. California, 372 U.S. 353, 83 S.Ct. 814, 9 L.Ed.2d 811 (1963). However, after the appeal has been dismissed, the indigent defendant is on his own in most jurisdictions. There are common law writs of habeas corpus or coram nobis available to the prisoner but there has been no decision mandating the appointment of counsel at this juncture. The Tennessee State Penitentiary went one step further. Instead of providing counsel for these writs, in February 1965, a petitioner serving a life sentence was transferred to a maximum security building in the prison for violating a prison regulation which prohibited an inmate to advise, assess, or otherwise contract to aid another either with or without a fee, to prepare writs or other legal matters. The Court held that the regulation was void because it, in effect, barred illiterate prisoners from access to federal habeas corpus and conflicted with 28 U.S.C. 2242 which expressly gave the right to have assistance in writs of habeas corpus. Johnson v. Avery, 393 U.S. 483, 89 S.Ct. 747, 21 L.Ed.2d 718 (1969).

§ 8.16 Counsel at Probation and Parole Revocation Hearings

The underlying theory of probation and parole is to aid those convicted of crime to reenter the community to be useful persons, to themselves, their families, and to the community. To facilitate this goal, the probation officer and the parole officer are social workers who are expected to exercise control over their clients in a beneficent way. In an ideal setting, they become the confidant of the client, someone to whom the client can speak his/her mind and look for guidance. Frequently, the officer does the job so well that even after the client leaves the supervision of the officer, the client expresses a desire to visit and talk with the probation or parole officer.

Many instances of rehabilitation have been brought about in this manner. Not every case is a successful one however. There are clients who, while on probation or parole, commit other crimes or violate the restrictive terms of their release. It then becomes necessary for the officer to advise the court, if it be a probation case, or the parole board, if it be a parole case, to hold a hearing to determine the sanction, if any, that the client shall receive if the charges contained in the violation of probation or parole are proved. This procedure changes the status of the officer from being a beneficent friend and adviser to that of being a law enforcement officer or accuser.

The question then arises as to whether at this point, the client should have the assistance of counsel. While the Sixth Amendment, as interpreted by the Court, has provided for counsel from the beginning of the adversary judicial process up to and including appeal, as has been noted in the previous section, the Court is reluctant to extend this right to post appeal writs. Here too, the Court has been very sparing in granting the right to counsel to those who have been accused of violating a condition of probation or parole.

In a revocation hearing, the legal rules of evidence and formal procedure are not adhered to. The state would argue in probation revocation hearings that the probationers were sentenced at the time that they were originally placed on probation and that the imposition of sentence following probation revocation is, in effect, a mere formality comprising part of the probation revocation proceeding and should not require counsel to be present. The Court treated this problem in Mempa v. Rhay, 389 U.S. 128, 88 S.Ct. 254, 19 L.Ed.2d 336 (1967), where the petitioner was placed on probation for two years after pleading guilty to "joyriding" but the first thirty days were to be spent in the county jail. The imposition of sentence was deferred. About four months later, the prosecutor moved to have petitioner's probation revoked on the ground that he had been involved in a burglary. The petitioner, who was seventeen years old at the time, was not represented by counsel at the hearing and he confessed at the hearing that he had been involved in the burglary.

The Court reasoned that in a deferred sentencing hearing involving a revocation of probation, counsel should be provided. It reasoned that there might be a case where an accused agreed to plead guilty, although he had a valid defense, because he was offered probation; absence of counsel at the imposition of sentence might well result in loss of the right to appeal. Washington (the situs of the hearing) statutes provided that a plea of guilty can be withdrawn at any time prior to the imposition of sentence. This withdrawal privilege is customary throughout the United States but the acceptance of the withdrawal of a plea is up to the discretion of the judge in most jurisdictions.

Following Mempa v. Rhay (supra), the Court again treated a similar but slightly different issue in Gagnon v. Scarpelli, 411 U.S. 778, 93 S.Ct. 1756, 36 L.Ed.2d 656 (1973). This case involved a revocation of probation based upon a confession made by the petitioner that he had committed burglary while he was on probation. He had been previously sentenced to fifteen years imprisonment on an armed robbery charge but the judge suspended the sentence and placed him on probation for seven years. The Court said that in this case, where there was no preliminary hearing or final hearing, the revocation of the probation did not meet the standards of due process as prescribed in Morrisey v. Brewer, 408 U.S. 471, 92 S.Ct. 2593, 33 L.Ed.2d 484 (1972); therefore, petitioner was entitled to a writ of habeas corpus, but the Court also said: "We find no justification for a new inflexible constitutional rule with respect to the requirement of counsel. We think, rather, that the decision as to the need for counsel must be made on a case-by-case basis in the exercise of a sound discretion by the state authority charged with responsibility for administrating the probation and parole system... Presumptively, it may be said that counsel should be provided in cases where, after being informed of his right to request counsel, the probationer or parolee makes such a request, based on a timely and colorable claim (i) that he has not committed the alleged violation of conditions upon which he is at liberty; or (ii) that, even if the violation is a matter of public record or is uncontested, there are substantial reasons which justified or mitigated the violation and make revocation inappropriate and that the reasons are complex or otherwise difficult to present. In passing on a request for the appointment of counsel, the responsible agency should also consider, especially in doubtful cases, whether probationer appears to be capable of speaking effectively for himself. In every case in which a request for counsel at a preliminary or final hearing is refused, the grounds for refusal should be stated succinctly in the record."

§ 8.17 Counsel for Appeals

The appellate process is a very expensive one. The court stenographer is required to translate stenotype machine notes or shorthand notes and have them typed and a record of the trial is thus made. Every word in this transcript is important and a mistake here might make a difference in the outcome of an appeal. The attorney must spend many hours in reading the transcript, make notes of critical points of possible reversible error, spend many hours in a library researching previous decisions of applicable law, write a brief, and have it typed according to very precise rules of the appellate court. S/He must settle the record of the trial, serve a notice of appeal, and provide for either duplication of the record and brief as required by the respective courts or arrange for printing of the record on appeal and brief, depending on the rules of the court. A note of issue must also be prepared and served. The attorney must prepare for oral argument before the appellate judges where s/he may be asked questions by the jurists.

The preceding are the general requirements of the appellate process. They may vary slightly in different jurisdictions but it is easy to understand that many hours and the services of many people are required.

The indigents are certainly not in a position to pay for these services. However, up to 1956, a state did not have to provide a transcript for an indigent who wished to appeal a conviction. In that year the Court decided Griffin v. Illinois, 351 U.S. 12, 76 S.Ct. 585, 100 L.Ed. 891, where, in a 5–4 decision, the Court upheld the contention that the due process and equal protection clauses of the Fourteenth Amendment require that all indigent defendants be furnished a transcript, at least where allegations that manifest error occurred at the trial are not denied. Justice Black observed, "... In criminal trials a State can no more discriminate on account of poverty than on account of religion, race or color... It is true that a State is not required by the federal constitution to provide appellate review at all... But this is not to say that a State that does grant appellate review can do so in a way that discriminates against some convicted defendant on account of their poverty."

This theory was carried to its natural conclusion when in Douglas v. California, 372 U.S. 353, 83 S.Ct. 814, 9 L.Ed.2d 811 (1963), the Court provided that the assistance of counsel for first appeals should be granted as a matter of right to all indigents who have been convicted of crime.

§ 8.18 Right to Effective Counsel

There is a legend that a famous trial prosecutor was prosecuting twelve defendants in a consolidated trial in which each defendant had his own lawyer representing him. When the prosecutor was asked how he felt having twelve lawyers opposing him, his answer was, "Great—the lawyers disagreed among themselves."

This is an example of the varied tactics that are employed by the trial bar in the defense of an action. For this reason, it is extremely difficult for an appeals court to flatly decide from the position of hindsight that a defendant had ineffective counsel. Notwithstanding this, if a court would find that the trial was a "mockery of justice," see People v. Washington, 41 Ill.2d 16, 241 N.E.2d 425 (1968), the Court will reverse a conviction. In Powell v. Alabama (supra), the Court pointed out that the duty to appoint counsel "is not discharged by an assignment at such time or under such circumstances as to preclude the giving of effective aid in the preparation and trial of the case."

One could fairly say that the appellate courts will not reverse where counsel's behavior was such that reasonably competent and fairly experienced criminal defense lawyers might find room for debate about its propriety. If there is room for debate about the propriety of counsel's representation, then the appellate court should find that the defendant had effective counsel and the conviction should stand on these grounds.

Many states are permitting lawyers to designate certain areas of law in which they hold themselves out to be expert. To qualify for this designation, some states will merely require a showing that the attorney has engaged in "X" number of cases in that specialty within "Y" years prior to the application. This is not a panacea but it is a starting point for some sort of gradation of competence. Other states are permitting senior law students, under the supervision of a licensed attorney, to represent indigents. This has not been tested to date in the United States Supreme Court, but it is expected that it may reach the Court someday in the not too distant future. Most courts seem to assume that an ineffective representation claim is a valid basis for review to cause a reversal but few courts seem to have sustained this claim.

In JONES v. BARNES, 463 U.S. 745, 103 S.Ct. 3308, 77 L.Ed.2d. 987, (1983), an indigent defendant complained and sought Federal habeas corpus relief because his appointed appellate counsel refused to include in the brief points of argument proposed by appellant. The appellant filed a pro se supplemental brief. Furthermore, the attorney did not present oral argument of the points set forth by the appellant. The Court held that a criminal defendant has no constitutional right to compel his appointed lawyer to argue non-frivolous issues that the defendant wishes to press, but that counsel may decide, exercising his professional judgment, not to present these arguments to the appellate court. Experienced lawyers know that weak arguments should be deleted and focus should be on one or at most a few central issues.

A 1984 case on this point arose in UNITED STATES v. CRONIC, —U.S.—, 104 S.Ct. 2039, 80 L.Ed.2d. 657 where the defendant in a mail fraud case represented that his appointed counsel was a real estate specialist who had never participated in a criminal trial and had less time to prepare than did the government. The Court held that these facts did not justify a presumption that he was denied constitutionally effective counsel, and therefore he can make out such a claim only by pointing to specific errors made by trial counsel.

However in EVITTS v. LUCEY, —U.S.—, 105 S.Ct. 830, 83 L.Ed.2d. 821 (1985) the Court did sustain such a claim. In that case, a respondent had retained counsel at his trial and was convicted of a drug offense. Counsel filed timely notice of appeal to the Kentucky Court of Appeals. However he failed to file the statement of appeal required by a Kentucky Rule of Appellate Procedure when he filed his brief and record on Appeals. The Court of Appeals dismissed the appeal and later denied a motion for reconsideration. The Kentucky Supreme Court affirmed. The United States Supreme Court considered the case and reversed. The Court held substantially that Kentucky gives a defendant a right for a first appeal. This right cannot be taken away because of a counsel's procedural error. The respondent is entitled to effective counsel and the lower court's action denied him that right.

§ 8.19 Indigents' Right to Counsel Defined

The question of who is indigent and who is not has been plaguing the courts in recent years. The cost to the public treasury in representing indigent defendants has been enormous and continues to rise. Defendants who are earning a reasonable livelihood to support themselves are unable to raise the funds required for the services of a good defense attorney. Other defendants who may be riding around in expensive automobiles and are able to enjoy many other luxuries of life never have enough money (so they tell the court) to pay for an attorney to represent them. This leads to abuse of the free legal assistance program with its consequent drain on the taxpayers. Attorneys who represent the indigent may do it on a pro-bono basis even though they are remunerated in a small way from the government coffers. Some attorneys cannot afford to support themselves and/or their families in this area of law practice and many competent and dedicated persons leave for other pursuits.

The problem of abuse is being attacked in various states by having the judge fix the value of the attorney's services at the end of the representation and entering a judgment for that amount against the name of the defendant. The defendant thus has the obligation to pay and if s/he acquires some wealth, the judgment can be executed against this property. See Florida Statutes, Chapter 27, Section 27.50 et seq. There is no question now but that the indigent defendant is entitled to representation from the time that the investigation centers on the suspect through appeal and it is the obligation of the government to supply the defendant with an attorney for this purpose unless a private attorney is retained.

§ 8.20 Counsel at Juvenile Courts

Juvenile courts are conducted differently from the public trial that takes place in other tribunals dealing with persons who have broken the law. The theory for this is that the juvenile, in his/her tender formative years should not be held accountable for the rest of his/her life for some young child's misdeed.

The juvenile court is a quasi-criminal forum. The complainant is usually referred to as a "petitioner" and the malefactor is usually referred to as a "respondent." The trial is normally conducted behind a closed door, not open to the public. For many years, these trials were conducted without an attorney representing the child, in a court where the judge had virtually unlimited discretion. The following basic rights were denied:

1. Notice of charges;
2. Right to counsel;
3. Right to confrontation and cross-examination;
4. Privilege against self-incrimination;

5. Right to a transcript of the proceedings;
6. Right to appellate review.

The theory was that a fatherly judge would affect the emotions of the child by talking over the problems with the juvenile. This would provide guidance and prevent the child from getting into further difficulties. In re Gault, 387 U.S. 1, 87 S.Ct. 1428, 18 L.Ed.2d 527 (1967), brought this era to an end.

In the Gault case, the Court held that neither the Fourteenth Amendment nor the Bill of Rights is for adults alone. It concluded that a juvenile offender was entitled to reasonable notice of charges, the right to counsel, the right to confrontation and cross-examination, and the privilege against self-incrimination, by reason of the due process clause of the Fourteenth Amendment. The Court did not rule on the failure to provide a transcript of the hearings or the failure of the juvenile court judge to state the grounds for his conclusion, but did explain that "as the present case illustrates, the consequences of failure to provide an appeal, to record the proceedings, or to make findings or state the grounds for the juvenile court's conclusion may be to throw a burden upon the machinery for habeas corpus, to saddle the reviewing process with the burden of attempting to reconstruct a record, and to impose upon the juvenile judge the unseemly duty of testifying under cross-examination as to the events that transpired in the hearings before him."

In re Gault specifically ruled that these rights were to be granted to juveniles brought before the court who were in jeopardy of being sent to an institution. The Court did not rule upon the question whether ordinary due process requirements must be observed with respect to hearings to determine the disposition of the delinquent child.

A sequel to Gault was In Re Winship, 397 U.S. 358, 90 S.Ct. 1068, 25 L.Ed.2d 368 (1970). This case held for the principle that proof beyond a reasonable doubt was an essential ingredient of due process for adult criminal trials as well as for juvenile delinquency proceedings.

§ 8.21 Counsel during Overnight Recess

In Geders v. U.S., 425 U.S. 80, 96 S.Ct. 1330, 47 L.Ed.2d 592 (1976), the trial court ordered the defendant not to consult with his attorney during a regular overnight recess. The defendant had been testifying as a witness on direct examination when an overnight recess was called. Cross-examination was to be pursued shortly thereafter. The Court reasoned that any conflict between a testifying defendant's right to consult with counsel during a recess and the prosecution's desire to cross-examine without intervention of counsel must be resolved in favor of defendant's right to the assistance of counsel, citing Brooks v. Tennessee, 406 U.S. 605 (1972).

§ 8.22 Government's Obligation to Supply Counsel

The reader will remember that in Betts v. Brady, 316 U.S. 455, 62 S.Ct. 1252, 86 L.Ed. 1595 (1942), the Court sustained a Maryland statute which supplied counsel to indigents who were charged with a capital offense and did not require counsel to be supplied in other cases.

The reader will also remember Powell v. Alabama, 287 U.S. 45, 53 S.Ct. 55, 77 L.Ed. 158 (1932), where a conviction was reversed of ignorant, friendless youths traveling through Scottsboro, Alabama, who were tried for rape, etc. and were sentenced for execution, all without the benefit of counsel, and finally the case of Gideon v. Wainright, 372 U.S. 335, 83 S.Ct. 792, 9 L.Ed.2d 799 (1963), which reversed Betts v. Brady (supra) to hold that a defendant in a state prosecution is entitled to have counsel supplied to him at trial if he cannot afford to retain one privately, where the charges are capital or noncapital, felony, misdemeanor, or petty, state or local, where upon conviction he may be sentenced to confinement (see Argersinger v. Hamlin, 407 U.S. 25, 25 S.Ct. 2006, 32 L.Ed.2d 530 [1972]). In all felony cases, counsel is required at trial regardless of the ultimate adjudication or sentence. The trial court must appoint, or otherwise provide, effective counsel for indigent defendants in all such cases. In Halloway v. Arkansas, 435 U.S. 475, 98 S.Ct. 1173, 55 L.Ed.2d 426, 46 L.W. 4289 (1978), the Court held that the trial judge's failure to appoint separate counsel for three jointly tried defendants, or to take adequate steps to determine whether the risk of conflict of interest was too remote to require separate counsel, deprived defendant of right to effective assistance of counsel regardless of whether prejudice has been independently established and is reversible error.

In Scott v. Illinois, U.S. 99 S.Ct. 1158, 59 L.Ed.2d 383, 24 Cr.L. 3053 (1979), the Court held "that the Sixth and Fourteenth Amendments to the United States Constitution require only that no indigent criminal defendant be sentenced to a term of imprisonment unless the State has afforded him the right to assistance of appointed counsel in his defense." Thus, where a statute calls for a fine and/or imprisonment or both, the imprisonment part of the sanction cannot be imposed on an indigent defendant unless the State has afforded the defendant an opportunity to have the assistance of assigned counsel in his/her defense.

§ 8.23 No Counsel Regarding Blood Sample

There are various methods to ascertain the percentage of alcohol in a person's blood. The legislatures of the states have provided several percentages of alcohol in a person's blood to spell out different degrees of intoxication. The finding of a larger percentage would constitute the elements for a more serious offense if the tested person were driving a vehicle. Some jurisdictions use a breath test while others resort to an extraction of a small quantity of blood from the suspect. The blood is then put through prescribed tests and a reading results.

The blood extraction method was used in the case of Schmerber v. California, 384 U.S. 757, 86 S.Ct. 1826, 16 L.Ed.2d 908 (1966). In that case the petitioner raised the argument, inter alia, that he was deprived of his right to object to the test upon the advice of counsel and was accordingly denied his Sixth Amendment right to the assistance of counsel. The Court said, "... Since petitioner was not entitled to assert the privilege, he has no greater right because counsel erroneously advised him that he could assert it. His claim is strictly limited to the failure of the police to respect his wish, reinforced by counsel's advice, to be left inviolate. No issue of counsel's ability to assist petitioner in respect of any rights he did possess is presented. The limited claim made must be rejected."

It should be noted that Schmerber v. California (supra) holds that the test must be conducted under medically approved conditions. If a counsel's advice is not constitutionally required or permitted in blood extraction cases to determine alcoholic content of a person's blood, certainly it will not be required or permitted in a chemical breath test.

§ 8.24 No Counsel Regarding Handwriting Exemplar

It sometimes becomes necessary in a trial to compare the handwriting of a witness or suspect with the handwriting of a document which has been placed in evidence. The question of the right to counsel in handwriting exemplar situations was answered by the Court in Gilbert v. California, 388 U.S. 263, 87 S.Ct. 1951, 18 L.Ed.2d 1178 (1967), where it was held that to require a handwriting exemplar did not impair the defendant's privilege against self-incrimination. It held further that this form of investigation was not a part of a witness identification procedure; there was no application of the right to counsel concept, since the taking of the exemplar was not a "critical" stage and the absence of counsel did not promote unfairness.

§ 8.25 Other Instances of No Right to Counsel

Schmerber v. California (supra), while not directly deciding the issue of the right of counsel to object to the taking of fingerprints, etc., did give these principles negative glancing blows when the Court said, "On the other hand, both federal and state courts have usually held that it (meaning right of counsel) offers no protection against compulsion to submit to fingerprinting, photographing, or measurements, to write or speak for identification, to appear in court, to stand, to assume a stance, to walk, or to make a particular gesture. The distinction which has emerged, often expressed in different ways, is that the privilege is a bar against compelling 'communications' or 'testimony' but that compulsion which makes a suspect or accused the source of 'real or physical evidence' does not violate it."

Wade v. United States, 388 U.S. 219, 87 S.Ct. 1926, 18 L.Ed.2d 1149 (1967), reinforced the concept that speaking for identification is not a constitutional privilege. In that case the suspect was required to stand in a lineup and say something like "put the money in the bag," the words allegedly uttered by the robber. The Court held that "Neither the lineup itself nor anything shown by this record that Wade was required to do in the lineup violated his privilege against self incrimination...."

§ 8.26 Constitutional Guarantee of Jury Trial

It has been previously indicated that each right of the Bill of Rights of the United States Constitution was not applicable to state criminal justice procedure. One by one, each of them was incorporated or absorbed into the state criminal justice procedure. The federal right of a jury trial of the Sixth Amendment was absorbed into state action by the Court's decision in Duncan v. Louisiana, 391 U.S. 145, 88 S.Ct. 1444, 20 L.Ed.2d 491 (1968), wherein the Court held that the Sixth Amendment right to a jury trial was applicable to the states via the Fourteenth Amendment.

The Duncan decision was further extended in Baldwin v. New York, 399 U.S. 66, 90 S.Ct. 1914, 26 L.Ed.2d 437 (1970), by a 5–3 decision. The Baldwin case originated in New York City where the calendar of misdemeanor cases was so great that a statute provided that a person charged with a misdemeanor could select to be tried by one judge or, in the alternative, a three judge bench. There was no provision for a jury trial. The case found its way to the United States Supreme Court and the Justices, in a 5–3 decision, held that "no offense can be deemed 'petty' for purposes of the right to trial by jury where imprisonment for more than six months is authorized." There was no opinion of the Court.

However, in Ludwig v. Massachusetts, 427 U.S. 618, 96 S.Ct. 2781, 49 L.Ed.2d 534 (1976), where a two-tier trial court system provided a de novo trial in a higher court, if the first trial results were appealed, the Court said that this procedure was constitutional. Where no imprisonment is involved the Court held that no jury is required. Muniz v. Hoffman, 422 U.S. 454, 95 S.Ct. 2178, 45 L.Ed.2d 319 (1975).

§ 8.27 Discrimination in Jury Selection

The Sixth Amendment mandates that "In all criminal prosecutions, the accused shall enjoy . . . public trial, by an impartial jury of the State and district wherein the crime shall have been committed, which district shall have been previously ascertained by law . . . ."

Some defendants complained that they could not get an impartial jury because members of their race were systematically excluded from jury service and those who were eligible were prejudiced against the defendant.

The Court has rendered some opinions with respect to this problem but a reading of them gives one the impression that the Court will not interfere unless the defendant proves arbitrary discrimination. This is not an easy burden. In Swain v. Alabama, 380 U.S. 202, 85 S.Ct. 824, 13 L.Ed.2d 759 (1965), the Court held that the Fourteenth Amendment does not require mathematical precision in the composition of state juries.

Each state's criminal procedure allows peremptory challenge in the selection of a jury. The number of peremptory challenges permitted varies with the number of the persons on the jury and with each jurisdiction. A lawyer selecting a jury on a voir dire may exercise peremptory challenges. The lawyer usually does this after hearing the prospective juror respond to questions asked either by the judge or the lawyer, depending upon the rules of the court. The lawyer excuses a juror if s/he has any doubts about the good rapport that the juror has with the lawyer, the case, or the client. Usually it is a hunch or a feeling that the lawyer gets that this particular juror is not a good one for the side of the controversy that the lawyer represents.

To successfully attack a prosecutor in the prosecutor's method of exercising his peremptory challenges, the defendant must demonstrate not only that the prosecutor excluded all members of his race from the jury that tried him, but that the prosecutor has consistently exercised his challenges in a racially similar manner over a period of years, thus establishing a pattern or practice of improper exercise. Swain v Alabama (supra).

However, in Taylor v. Louisiana, 419 U.S. 522, 95 S.Ct. 692, 42 L.Ed.2d 690 (1975), the Court held that systematic exclusion of women from a jury panel was a violation of the Fourteenth Amendment in that the resulting jury was not a fair cross section of the community.

§ 8.28 Jury Trial and Due Process

It is possible for a criminal justice system to operate fairly and equitably without a jury requirement. The system could make use of alternative guarantees and protections that would serve the same purpose as a jury. However, no American state, including Louisiana, has adopted such a system for serious crimes. The right to a jury trial in federal criminal prosecutions was provided for in Article III, Section 2, and the Sixth Amendment. Jury trials were omitted, however, in some states for misdemeanors, as has been explained in Section 8.26 (supra). Maxwell v. Dow, 176 U.S. 581, 20 S.Ct. 448, 44 L.Ed. 597 (1900), held for the principle that no provision of the Bill of Rights applied to the states. This principle, of course, was repudiated in later decisions. The case also held that the Due Process Clause of the Fourteenth Amendment did not prevent a state from trying a defendant for a noncapital offense with fewer than twelve persons on a jury.

Duncan v. Louisiana, 391 U.S. 145, 88 S.Ct. 1444, 20 L.Ed.2d 491 (1968), referred to in Section 8.26 (supra) decided as to whether the Sixth Amendment jury trial right should be incorporated into state criminal trials via the Due Process Clause of the Fourteenth Amendment. Mr. Justice White, delivering the opinion of the court said, "... Those who wrote our constitutions knew from history and experience that it was necessary to protect against unfounded criminal charges brought to eliminate enemies and against judges too responsible to the voice of higher authority ... We need not, however settle in this case the exact location of the line between petty offenses and serious crimes. It is sufficient for our purpose to hold that a crime punishable by two years in prison is, based on past and contemporary standards in this country, a serious crime and not a petty offense. Consequently, appellant was entitled to a jury trial and it was error to deny it."

As you know from reading Section 8.26, Baldwin v. New York, 399 U.S. 66, 90 S.Ct. 1914, 26 L.Ed.2d 437 (1970), required a jury trial where the punishment or conviction might be more than six months' incarceration. Duncan v. Louisiana (supra) was the first case of the court that made the Due Process Clause of the Fourteenth Amendment require the states to adhere to the Sixth Amendment right to a jury trial. The Court therefore was including the right to a jury trial as one of those fundamental rights guaranteed and necessary to an Anglo-American system of ordered liberty, using the Fourteenth Amendment Due Process Clause for its reasoning.

Florida has been one of the States that has given us many landmark cases. It is a state that appears to the author, to be innovative in its justice system. Acting true to its reputation, it introduced, on a pilot program under Canon 3A (7) of the Florida Code of Judicial Conduct wherein the presiding judge is permitted to allow electronic media and still photography coverage of judicial proceedings, subject to the control of the presiding judge and to implementing guidelines placing on trial judges, obligations to protect the fundamental right of the accused in a criminal case, to a fair trial.

It wasn't long before a case challenging the constitutionality of this procedure came on to be heard before the United States Supreme Court. The case was CHANDLER v. STATE OF FLORIDA, 449 U.S. 560, 101 S.Ct. 802, 66 L.Ed.2d. 740, 28 Cr.L. 3067 (1981). In that case, the two petitioners claimed that after they objected to the presence of television and broadcasts of parts of their trial, and the court overruled their objections and conducted the trial with the media coverage, they were denied a fair and impartial jury in violation of the process clauses of the 14th and 5th Amendments. The Court held otherwise. It said a defendant must show that the media coverage of the trial compromises the jury's ability to judge fairly or that the broadcast coverage of the case had an adverse impact on the trial participants. The petitioner was unable to do this in the instant case.

§ 8.29 Function of Jury

Ordinarily the function of the petty jury is to determine the issues of fact in a trial, whereas the function of the judge is to determine the issue of law. An illustration might serve to make this distinction more understandable.

If a defendant in a criminal trial is charged with homicide, there may be a question of what crime of homicide s/he committed. It might be murder (intentional homicide) (some states have Murder 1st Degree and Murder 2nd Degree) or Manslaughter (killing a human being without deliberate intent). The judge would explain to the jury the elements required for the commission of each crime and the jury would decide the issue of fact as to whether it was an intentional killing or committed without intent. There are further refinements present in the statutes of all jurisdictions which the judge will explain to the jury to assist it to decide as to what category of crime the defendant's actions should fit into. The jury also decides whose conflicting testimony it will accept as a true account of what actually occurred.

Some states place an additional responsibility on the jury to decide the punishment that should be meted out to the defendant after the defendant has been found guilty.

§ 8.30 Size of Jury

Article III, Section 2, and the Sixth Amendment, read together, provided initially for jury trials in federal criminal prosecutions.

Pursuant to the decision in Patton v. United States, 281 U.S. 276, 50 S.Ct. 253, 74 L.Ed. 8544 (1930), these provisions referred to the petit jury as it was developed at common law at the times of the adoption of the Constitution and the Sixth Amendment, i.e., that the jury should be composed of twelve persons, no more or less; that the trial should take place in the presence and under the supervision of a judge having power to instruct them as to the law and advise them as to the facts; and that the verdict should be unanimous. The issue of a twelve person jury in state criminal procedure was treated in Mr. Justice Fortas' concurring decision in Duncan v. Louisiana (supra), where he said, "... I see no reason whatever, for example, to assume that our decision today should require us to impose federal requirements such as unanimous verdicts or a jury of twelve upon the states. We may well conclude that these and other features of federal jury practice are by no means fundamental—that they are not essential to due process—and that they are not obligatory on the states...."

A subsequent court did just as Mr. Justice Fortas had predicted when it decided Williams v. Florida, 399 U.S. 78, 90 S.Ct. 1893, 26 L.Ed.2d 446 (1970), wherein the petitioner was objecting to Florida procedure of using a six member jury in a robbery case resulting in his conviction. The defendant's pretrial motion asking for a twelve member jury had been denied. The court reasoned that although common law at the time of the adoption of the Constitution and the Sixth Amendment required a twelve person jury, if a state provided for a jury of less than twelve, it was not a deprivation of a fundamental privilege because the purpose of the trial jury as an interposition between the accused and his accuser of the commonsense judgment of a group of laymen, and the community participation and shared responsibility that results from the group's determination of guilt or innocence would still be present whether it was a jury of twelve or a jury of six.

However, it appears that Georgia went too far when it provided for a five person jury for nonpetty offenses. The Court held that such a statute is unconstitutional, holding that a six person jury is the minimum requirement for due process. Ballew v. Georgia, 435 U.S. 223, 98 S.Ct. 1029, 55 L.Ed.2d 234 (1978).

§ 8.31 Impartiality of Jurors

Even a jury of twelve persons may not be a fair and impartial jury. This requirement, called for in the Sixth Amendment and made applicable to the states by the Fourteenth Amendment Due Process Clause, is not easily attained in certain situations. For example, a community may be so incensed over the factual situation of the commission of the crime, that they would rather lynch the defendant than give him/her a fair trial. It becomes necessary in such a case to be extra careful in the impaneling of the jury to obtain jurors who will reach their verdict solely on the testimony presented in the courtroom.

Defendants often are of the opinion that they will not get a fair trial from jurors who are different from the defendant's racial or ethnic group. As indicated previously, the court does not usually interfere in these matters where there is economic- and social-class underrepresentation on state juries, but the court has interfered where members of the defendant's racial or ethnic group have been systematically excluded from jury service. The court has done this in reliance on the Equal Protection Clause of the Fourteenth Amendment. Hernandez v. Texas, 347 U.S. 475, 74 S.Ct. 667, 98 L.Ed. 866 (1954).

In SMITH v. PHILIPS, —U.S.—, 102 S.Ct. 940, 71 L.Ed.2d. 78, 30 Cr.L. 3055 (1982) a defendant was tried and convicted of murder. During the trial, one of the jurors submitted an application to the District Attorney's office for a position as an investigator. The trial assistants learned of this application before the end of the trial but did not advise defense counsel or the presiding justice of the application. Approximately fifteen days after the jury rendered a verdict of conviction, the District Attorney learned of the application. Five days later, after an investigation to verify the information, the District Attorney informed the trial court and defense counsel. The trial court ordered a hearing to take place and found that the application was an indiscretion but in "in no way reflected a premature conclusion as to the [respondent's] guilt or prejudice against the [respondent] or an inability to consider the guilt or innocence of the respondent solely on the evidence." 384 NYS 2d. 915. The United States Supreme Court affirmed the trial judges reasoning by saying, inter alia, respondent was not denied due process of law either by the juror's or by the prosecutor's failure to disclose the juror's job application.

§ 8.32 Unanimity of Jury Verdict

A criminal defendant is proven guilty when in the minds of the trier of the facts that defendant is guilty of the crime charged beyond a reasonable doubt. Over the years, this has come to mean, in the case of jury trials, a verdict of conviction by a unanimous vote of all jury members. Thus, as little as one juror could prevent the conviction of a defendant with the result that instead of getting the viewpoint of representatives of the community, the community many times got the viewpoint of one person, to its detriment. To counter this, many state legislatures have provided that in criminal trials, juries need not have a unanimous vote in order to convict. Instead, various proportions have been provided such as 10 to 2, or 6 to 1, etc. In Apodaca v. Oregon, 406 U.S. 404, 92 S.Ct. 1628, 32 L.Ed.2d 184 (1972), petitioners were convicted of felonies by jury votes of 11–1 and 10–2. The petitioners were unsuccessful in their challenge of a state constitutional provision which permitted ten members of the jury to render guilty verdicts in noncapital cases. The Court, by Mr. Justice White, stated, "As we said in DUNCAN, the purpose of trial by jury is to prevent oppression by the government by providing a 'safeguard against the corrupt or overzealous prosecutor and against the compliant, biased or eccentric judge'. Given this purpose, the essential feature of a jury obviously lies in the interposition between the accused and his accusor of the common-sense judgment of a group of lavmen . . . A requirement of unanimity, however, does not materially contribute to the exercise of this common-sense judgment . . . In terms of this function we perceive no difference between juries required to act unanimously and those permitted to convict or acquit by votes of ten to two or eleven to one . . . ."

BROWN v. LOUISIANA, 447 U.S. 323, 100 S.Ct. 2214, 65 L.Ed.2d. 159, 27 Cr.L. 3166 (1980) held that a conviction of a defendant who had been found guilty of a nonpetty criminal offense by a non unanimous six person jury violated his right to a trial by jury citing BURCH v. LOUISIANA, 441 U.S. 130 and that this rule is retroactive to all cases still pending on direct review.

§ 8.33 Waiver by Defendant of Jury

It may seem that if a defendant does not want a jury he need not have one imposed upon him. A little further thought might reveal that if it is easy to waive a jury, the defendant placing his fate in the hands of a judge might be in a better position, particularly if the judge was known to be lenient, or corrupt.

There is also an additional problem that the defendant may not have been made aware of the right to trial by jury. The most experienced defendants are nervous when they appear before the bench. Things are said and done which require great reliance on the coaching of the defendant's attorney. The judge must be particularly careful that if the defendant wishes to waive a jury trial that the waiver is an intelligent willful waiver. There was great doubt as to the ability of a federal defendant to waive a jury trial until it was decided in Patton v. United States, 281 U.S. 276, 50 S.Ct. 253, 74 L.Ed. 854 (1930), that it was permissible to waive a jury trial. The state courts did not necessarily go along with Patton (supra) but in 1957, New York permitted waiver in People v. Carrol, 7 Misc.2d 581, 161 N.Y.S.2d 339, affd. 3 N.Y.2d 686, 148 N.E.2d 875.

§ 8.34 Jury Trial and Juvenile Proceedings

The reader may recall that the juvenile proceedings were first thought to be similar to a family disciplinary session where the judge would assume the role of the father who would talk out the problems with the juvenile and have almost unfettered discretion with respect to the fact-finding process and the dispositional process. The reader will also recall that In Re Gault (supra) provided that a counsel should be present, either retained or assigned, to represent the best interests of the defendant in all juvenile proceedings resulting in institutionalization. Later In Re Winship (supra) provided that in a delinquency proceeding the respondent (juvenile) must be found guilty beyond a reasonable doubt in order to sustain an adjudication of delinquency.

The Court has not been willing to go any further to extend the right of a jury trial to juvenile proceedings. The decisions of McKeiver v. Pennsylvania and In Re Burruss, 403 U.S. 528, 91 S.Ct. 1976, 29 L.Ed.2d 647 (1971), as written by Mr. Justice Blackman, indicated that if a jury were provided as fact finders in juvenile proceedings, it would make it into a more extensive adversary hearing than was desirable in light of the purposes of juvenile courts. It should be noted that there were three dissents to the majority decision in this case. It might foretell change if another case reaches the Court.

§ 8.35 Defendant's Right to Cross Examine Witnesses

The defendant has a constitutional right to be confronted by witnesses against him and to cross-examine these witnesses. The trial court may limit the amount of cross examination but the court may not do this in an arbitrary and capricious manner.

The rules of evidence of the several states may govern this procedure but no state shall, in so doing, deprive a defendant of a fundamental right guaranteed to all by the United States Constitution. The right of cross examination is a broad right and counsel often does not know in advance where the cross examination may lead.

Therefore the trial court should give great latitude to the cross-examining counsel in the conduct of the cross-examination.

In POINTER v. TEXAS, 380 U.S. 400; 403–405 (1965) the Sixth Amendment confrontation clause was made applicable to the states through the Fourteenth Amendment. It very often occurs that a prosecution witness appears at a preliminary hearing and is not to be found at the time of trial. If the defendant has had opportunity to cross-examine the witness, whether or not the actual cross examination took place, some courts have held that the testimony taken at the preliminary hearing may be read into evidence CALIFORNIA v. GREEN, 309 U.S. 649 (1970) if the witness cannot be located at the time of trial.

A slightly different factual situation was found in OHIO v. ROBERTS, 448 U.S. 56, 100 S.Ct. 2531, 65 L.Ed.2d. 597, 27 Cr.L. 3234 (1980). In that case the defendant had access to a young lady's apartment, while there, he made use of checks and credit cards belonging to the parents of the young lady. At the preliminary hearing, the defendant subpoenaed the young woman and she refused to testify that she had given respondent checks and credit cards without informing him that she did not have permission to use them. Respondent's counsel did not request that she be considered hostile or place her on cross examination. At the subsequent trial, defendant testified that the daughter had given him her parents checks and credit cards with the understanding that he could use them. The trial court admitted the reading of the transcript of the daughter's preliminary hearing testimony and objection because she was not able to be located at the time of trial. The Ohio Court of Appeals reversed the conviction holding the transcript inadmissible on Sixth Amendment grounds and the Ohio Supreme Court affirmed. The United States Supreme Court reversed the Ohio Supreme Court saying ". . . defense counsel tested the daughter's testimony with the equivalent of significant cross-examination . . . The introduction in evidence at respondent's trial of the daughter's preliminary hearing was constitutionally permissible in that the prosecutor had carried its burden of demonstrating that the daughter (witness) was constitutionally unavailable for purposes of respondent's trial.

Judicial Decisions Relating to Chapter 8

Gideon *v.* Wainwright, Corrections Director

372 U.S. 335, 83 S.Ct. 792, 9 L.Ed.2d 799 (1963)

CERTIORARI TO THE SUPREME COURT OF FLORIDA.

Argued January 15, 1963.—Decided March 18, 1963.

. . .

MR. JUSTICE BLACK delivered the opinion of the Court.

Petitioner was charged in a Florida state court with having broken and entered a poolroom with intent to commit a misdemeanor. This offense is a felony under Florida law. Appearing in court without funds and without a lawyer, petitioner asked the court to appoint counsel for him, whereupon the following colloquy took place:

"*The Court:* Mr. Gideon, I am sorry, but I cannot appoint Counsel to represent you in this case. Under the laws of the State of Florida, the only time the Court can appoint Counsel to represent a Defendant is when that person is charged with a capital offense. I am sorry, but I will have to deny your request to appoint Counsel to defend you in this case.

"*The Defendant:* The United States Supreme Court says I am entitled to be represented by Counsel."

Put to trial before a jury, Gideon conducted his defense about as well as could be expected from a layman. He made an opening statement to the jury, cross-examined the State's witnesses, presented witnesses in his own defense, declined to testify himself, and made a short argument "emphasizing his innocence to the charge contained in the Information filed in this case." The jury returned a verdict of guilty, and petitioner was sentenced to serve five years in the state prison. Later, petitioner filed in the Florida Supreme Court this habeas corpus petition attacking his conviction and sentence on the ground that the trial court's refusal to appoint counsel for him denied him rights "guaranteed by the Constitution and the Bill of Rights by the United States Government." Treating the petition for habeas corpus as properly before it, the State Supreme Court, "upon consideration thereof" but without an opinion, denied all relief. Since 1942, when Betts v. Brady, 316 U.S. 455, was decided by a divided Court, the problem of a defendant's federal constitutional right to counsel in a state court has been a continuing source of controversy and litigation in both state and federal courts. To give this problem another review here, we granted certiorari. 370 U.S. 908. Since Gideon was proceeding in forma pauperis, we appointed counsel to represent him and requested both sides to discuss in their briefs and oral arguments the following: "Should this Court's holding in Betts v. Brady, 316 U.S. 455, be reconsidered?"

I

The facts upon which Betts claimed that he had been unconstitutionally denied the right to have counsel appointed to assist him are strikingly like the facts upon which Gideon here bases his federal constitutional claim. Betts was indicted for robbery in a Maryland state court. On arraignment, he told the trial judge of his lack of funds to hire a lawyer and asked the court to appoint one for him. Betts was advised that it was not the practice in that county to appoint counsel for indigent defendants except in murder and rape cases. He then pleaded not guilty, had witnesses summoned, cross-examined the State's witnesses, examined his own, and chose not to testify himself. He was found guilty by the judge, sitting without a jury, and sentenced to eight years in prison. Like Gideon, Betts sought release by habeas corpus, alleging that he had been denied the right to assistance of counsel in violation of the Fourteenth Amendment. Betts was denied any relief, and on review this Court affirmed. It was held that a refusal to appoint counsel for an indigent defendant charged with a felony did not necessarily violate the Due Process Clause of the Fourteenth Amendment, which for reasons given the Court deemed to be the only applicable federal constitutional provision. The Court said:

> "Asserted denial [of due process] is to be tested by an appraisal of the totality of facts in a given case. That which may, in one setting, constitute a denial of fundamental fairness, shocking to the universal sense of justice, may, in other circumstances, and in the light of other considerations, fall short of such denial." 316 U.S., at 462.

Treating due process as "a concept less rigid and more fluid than those envisaged in other specific and particular provisions of the Bill of Rights," the Court held that refusal to appoint counsel under the particular facts and circumstances in the Betts case was not so "offensive to the common and fundamental ideas of fairness" as to amount to a denial of due process. Since the facts and circumstances of the two cases are so nearly indistinguishable, we think the Betts v. Brady holding if left standing would require us to reject Gideon's claim that the Constitution guarantees him the assistance of counsel. Upon full reconsideration we conclude that Betts v. Brady should be overruled.

II

The Sixth Amendment provides, "In all criminal prosecutions, the accused shall enjoy the right . . . to have the Assistance of Counsel for his defence." We have construed this to mean that in federal courts counsel must be provided for defendants unable to employ counsel unless the right is competently and intelligently waived. Betts argued that this right is extended to indigent defendants in state courts by the Fourteenth Amendment. In response the Court stated that, while the Sixth Amendment laid down "no rule for the conduct of the States, the question recurs whether the constraint laid by the Amendment upon the national courts expresses a rule so fundamental and essential to a fair trial, and so, to due process of law, that it is made obligatory upon the States by the Fourteenth Amendment." 316 U.S., at 465. In order to decide whether the Sixth Amendment's guarantee of counsel is of this fundamental nature, the Court in Betts set out and considered "[r]elevant data on the subject . . . afforded by constitutional and statutory provisions subsisting in the colonies and the States prior to the inclusion of the Bill of Rights in the national Constitution, and in the constitutional, legislative, and judicial history of the States to the present date." 316 U.S., at 465. On the basis of this historical data the Court concluded that "appointment of counsel is not a fundamental right, essential to a fair trial." 316 U.S., at 471. It was for this reason the Betts Court refused to accept the contention that the Sixth Amendment's guarantee of counsel for indigent federal defendants was extended to or, in the words of that Court, "made obligatory upon the States by the Fourteenth Amendment." Plainly, had the Court concluded that appointment of counsel for an indigent criminal defendant was "a fundamental right, essential to a fair trial," it would have held that the Fourteenth Amendment requires appointment of counsel in a state court, just as the Sixth Amendment requires in a federal court.

We think the Court in Betts had ample precedent for acknowledging that those guarantees of the Bill of Rights which are fundamental safeguards of liberty immune from federal abridgment are equally protected against state invasion by the Due Process Clause of the Fourteenth Amendment. This same principle was recognized, explained, and applied in Powell v. Alabama, 287 U.S. 45 (1932), a case upholding the right of counsel, where the Court held that despite sweeping language to the contrary in Hurtado v. California, 110 U.S. 516 (1884), the Fourteenth Amendment "embraced" those "'fundamental principles of liberty and justice which lie at the base of all our civil and political institutions,'" even though they had been "specifically dealt with in another part of the federal Constitution." 287 U.S., at 67. In many cases other than Powell and Betts, this Court has looked to the fundamental nature of original Bill of Rights guarantees to decide whether the Fourteenth Amendment makes them obligatory on the States. Explicitly recognized to be of this "fundamental nature" and therefore made immune from state invasion by the Fourteenth, or some part of it, are the First Amendment's freedoms of speech, press, religion, assembly, association, and petition for redress of grievances. For the same reason, though not always in precisely the same terminology, the Court has made obligatory on the States the Fifth Amendment's command that private property shall not be taken for public use without just compensation, the Fourth Amendment's prohibition of unreasonable searches and seizures, and the Eighth's ban on cruel and unusual punishment. On the other hand, this Court in Palko v. Connecticut, 302 U.S. 319 (1937), refused to hold that the Fourteenth Amendment made the double jeopardy provision of the Fifth Amendment obligatory on the States. In so refusing, however, the Court, speaking through MR. JUSTICE CARDOZO, was careful to emphasize that "immunities that are valid as against the federal government by force of the specific pledges of particular amendments have been found to be implicit in the concept of ordered liberty, and thus, through the Fourteenth Amendment, become valid as against the states" and that guarantees "in their origin . . . effective against the federal government alone" had by prior cases "been taken over from the earlier articles of the federal bill of rights and brought within the Fourteenth Amendment by a process of absorption." 302 U.S., at 324–325, 326.

We accept Betts v. Brady's assumption, based as it was on our prior cases, that a provision of the Bill of Rights which is "fundamental and essential to a fair trial" is made obligatory upon the States by the Fourteenth Amendment. We think the Court in Betts was wrong, however, in concluding that the Sixth Amendment's guarantee of counsel is not one of these fundamental rights. Ten years before Betts v. Brady, this Court, after full consideration of all the historical data examined in Betts, had unequivocally declared that "the right to the aid of counsel is of this fundamental character." Powell v. Alabama, 287 U.S. 45, 68 (1932). While the Court at the close of its Powell opinion did by its language, as this Court frequently does, limit its holding to the particular facts and circumstances of that case, its conclusions about the fundamental nature of the right to counsel are unmistakable. Several years later, in 1936, the Court reemphasized what it had said about the fundamental nature of the right to counsel in this language:

> "We concluded that certain fundamental rights, safeguarded by the first eight amendments against federal action, were also safeguarded against state action by the due process of law clause of the Fourteenth Amendment, and among them the fundamental right of the accused to the aid of counsel in a criminal prosecution." Grosjean v. American Press Co., 297 U.S. 233, 243–244 (1936).

And again in 1938 this Court said:

> "[The assistance of counsel] is one of the safeguards of the Sixth Amendment deemed necessary to insure fundamental human rights of life and liberty.... The Sixth Amendment stands as a constant admonition that if the constitutional safeguards it provides be lost, justice will not 'still be done.'" Johnson v. Zerbst, 304 U.S. 458, 462 (1938). To the same effect, see Avery v. Alabama, 308 U.S. 444 (1940), and Smith v. O'Grady, 312 U.S. 329 (1941).

In light of these and many other prior decisions of this Court, it is not surprising that the Betts Court, when faced with the contention that "one charged with crime, who is unable to obtain counsel, must be furnished counsel by the State," conceded that "[e]xpressions in the opinions of this court lend color to the argument...." 316 U.S., at 462–463. The fact is that in deciding as it did—that "appointment of counsel is not a fundamental right, essential to a fair trial"—the Court in Betts v. Brady made an abrupt break with its own well-considered precedents. In returning to these old precedents, sounder we believe than the new, we but restore constitutional principles established to achieve a fair system of justice. Not only these precedents but also reason and reflection require us to recognize that in our adversary system of criminal justice, any person haled into court, who is too poor to hire a lawyer, cannot be assured a fair trial unless counsel is provided for him. This seems to us to be an obvious truth. Governments, both state and federal, quite properly spend vast sums of money to establish machinery to try defendants accused of crime. Lawyers to prosecute are everywhere deemed essential to protect the public's interest in an orderly society. Similarly, there are few defendants charged with crime, few indeed, who fail to hire the best lawyers they can get to prepare and present their defenses. That government hires lawyers to prosecute and defendants who have the money hire lawyers to defend are the strongest indications of the widespread belief that lawyers in criminal courts are necessities, not luxuries. The right of one charged with crime to counsel may not be deemed fundamental and essential to fair trials in some countries, but it is in ours. From the very beginning, our state and national constitutions and laws have laid great emphasis on procedural and substantive safeguards designed to assure fair trials before impartial tribunals in which every defendant stands equal before the law. This noble ideal cannot be realized if the poor man charged with crime has to face his accusers without a lawyer to assist him. A defendant's need for a lawyer is nowhere better stated than in the moving words of MR. JUSTICE SUTHERLAND in Powell v. Alabama:

> "The right to be heard would be, in many cases, of little avail if it did not comprehend the right to be heard by counsel. Even the intelligent and educated layman has small and sometimes no skill in the science of law. If charged with crime, he is incapable, generally, of determining for himself whether the indictment is good or bad. He is unfamiliar with the rules of evidence. Left without the aid of counsel he may be put on trial without a proper charge, and convicted upon incompetent evidence, or evidence irrelevant to the issue or otherwise inadmissible. He lacks both the skill and knowledge adequately to prepare his defense, even though he have a perfect one. He requires the guiding hand of counsel at every step in the proceedings against him. Without it, though he be not guilty, he faces the danger of conviction because he does not know how to establish his innocence." 287 U.S., at 68–69.

The Court in Betts v. Brady departed from the sound wisdom upon which the Court's holding in Powell v. Alabama rested. Florida, supported by two other States, has asked that Betts v. Brady be left intact. Twenty-two States, as friends of the Court, argue that Betts was "an anachronism when handed down" and that it should now be overruled. We agree.

The judgment is reversed and the cause is remanded to the Supreme Court of Florida for further action not inconsistent with this opinion.

Reversed.

United States *v.* Wade

388 U.S. 218, 87 S.Ct. 1926, 18 L.Ed. 2d. 1149 (1967)

CERTIORARI TO THE UNITED STATES COURT OF APPEALS FOR THE FIFTH CIRCUIT.

Argued February 16, 1967.—Decided June 12, 1967.

. . .

MR. JUSTICE BRENNAN delivered the opinion of the Court.

The question here is whether courtroom identifications of an accused at trial are to be excluded from evidence because the accused was exhibited to the witnesses before trial at a post-indictment lineup conducted for identification purposes without notice to and in the absence of the accused's appointed counsel.

The federally insured bank in Eustace, Texas, was robbed on September 21, 1964. A man with a small strip of tape on each side of his face entered the bank, pointed a pistol at the female cashier and the vice president, the only persons in the bank at the time, and forced them to fill a pillowcase with the bank's money. The man then drove away with an accomplice who had been waiting in a stolen car outside the bank. On March 23, 1965, an indictment was returned against respondent, Wade, and two others for conspiring to rob the bank, and against Wade and the accomplice for the robbery itself. Wade was arrested on April 2, and counsel was appointed to represent him on April 26. Fifteen days later an FBI agent, without notice to Wade's lawyer, arranged to have the two bank employees observe a lineup made up of Wade and five or six other prisoners and conducted in a courtroom of the local county courthouse. Each person in the line wore strips of tape such as allegedly worn by the robber and upon direction each said something like "put the money in the bag," the words allegedly uttered by the robber. Both bank employees identified Wade in the lineup as the bank robber.

At trial, the two employees, when asked on direct examination if the robber was in the courtroom, pointed to Wade. The prior lineup identification was then elicited from both employees on cross-examination. At the close of testimony, Wade's counsel moved for a judgment of acquittal or, alternatively, to strike the bank officials' courtroom identifications on the ground that conduct of the lineup, without notice to and in the absence of his appointed counsel, violated his Fifth Amendment privilege against self-incrimination and his Sixth Amendment right to the assistance of counsel. The motion was denied, and Wade was convicted. The Court of Appeals for the Fifth Circuit reversed the conviction and ordered a new trial at which the in-court identification evidence was to be excluded, holding that, though the lineup did not violate Wade's Fifth Amendment rights, "the lineup, held as it was, in the absence of counsel, already chosen to represent appellant, was a violation of his Sixth Amendment rights . . . ." 358 F. 2d 557, 560. We granted certiorari, 385 U.S. 811, and set the case for oral argument with No. 223, Gilbert v. California, post, p. 263, and No. 254, Stovall v. Denno, post, p. 293, which represent similar questions. We reverse the judgment of the Court of Appeals and remand to that court with direction to enter a new judgment vacating the conviction and remanding the case to the District Court for further proceedings consistent with this opinion.

I

Neither the lineup itself nor anything shown by this record that Wade was required to do in the lineup violated his privilege against self-incrimination. We have only recently reaffirmed that the privilege "protects an accused only from being compelled to testify against himself, or otherwise provide the State with evidence of a testimonial or communicative nature . . . ." Schmerber v. California, 384 U.S. 757, 761. We there held that compelling a suspect to submit to a withdrawal of a sample of his blood for analysis for alcohol content and the admission in evidence of the analysis report were not compulsion to those ends. That holding was supported by the opinion in Holt v. United States, 218 U.S. 245, in which case a question arose as to whether a blouse belonged to the defendant. A witness testified at trial that the defendant put on the blouse and it had fit him. The defendant argued that the admission of the testimony was error because compelling him to put on the blouse was a violation of his privilege. The Court rejected the claim as "an extravagant extension of the Fifth Amendment," MR. JUSTICE HOLMES saying for the Court:

> "[T]he prohibition of compelling a man in a criminal court to be a witness against himself is a prohibition of the use of physical or moral compulsion to extort communications from him, not an exclusion of his body as evidence when it may be material." 218 U.S., at 252–253.

The Court in Holt, however, put aside any constitutional questions which might be involved in compelling an accused, as here, to exhibit himself before victims of or witnesses to an alleged crime; the Court stated, "we need not consider how far a court would go in compelling a man to exhibit himself." Id., at 253.

We have no doubt that compelling the accused merely to exhibit his person for observation by a prosecution witness prior to trial involves no compulsion of the accused to give evidence having testimonial significance. It is compulsion of the accused to exhibit his physical characteristics, not compulsion to disclose any knowledge he might have. It is no different from compelling Schmerber to provide a blood sample or Holt to wear the blouse, and, as in those instances, is not within the cover of the privilege. Similarly, compelling Wade to speak within hearing distance of the witnesses, even to utter words purportedly uttered by the robber, was not compulsion to utter statements of a "testimonial" nature; he was required to use his voice as an identifying physical characteristic, not to speak his guilt. We held in Schmerber, supra, at 761, that the distinction to be drawn under the Fifth Amendment privilege against self-incrimination is one between an accused's "communications" in whatever form, vocal or physical, and "compulsion which makes a suspect or accused the source of 'real or physical evidence,'" Schmerber, supra, at 764. We recognized that "both federal and state courts have usually held that... [the privilege] offers no protection against compulsion to submit to fingerprinting, photography, or measurements, to write or speak for identification, to appear in court, to stand, to assume a stance, to walk, or to make a particular gesture." Id., at 764. None of these activities becomes testimonial within the scope of the privilege because required of the accused in a pretrial lineup.

Moreover, it deserves emphasis that this case presents no question of the admissibility in evidence of anything Wade said or did at the lineup which implicates his privilege. The Government offered no such evidence as part of its case, and what came out about the lineup proceedings on Wade's cross-examination of the bank employees involved no violation of Wade's privilege.

II

The fact that the lineup involved no violation of Wade's privilege against self-incrimination does not, however, dispose of his contention that the courtroom identifications should have been excluded because the lineup was conducted without notice to and in the absence of his counsel. Our rejection of the right to counsel claim in Schmerber rested on our conclusion in that case that "[n]o issue of counsel's ability to assist petitioner in respect to any rights he did possess is presented." 384 U.S., at 766. In contrast, in this case it is urged that the assistance of counsel at the lineup was indispensable to protect Wade's most basic right as a criminal defendant—his right to a fair trial at which the witnesses against him might be meaningfully cross-examined.

The Framers of the Bill of Rights envisaged a broader role for counsel than under the practice then prevailing in England of merely advising his client in "matters of law," and eschewing any responsibility for "matters of fact." The constitutions in at least 11 of the 13 States expressly or impliedly abolished this distinction. Powell v. Alabama, 287 U.S. 45, 60–65; Note, 73 Yale L.J. 1000, 1030–1033 (1964). "Though the colonial provisions about counsel were in accord on few things, they agreed on the necessity of abolishing the facts-law distinction; the colonists appreciated that if a defendant were forced to stand alone against the state, his case was foredoomed." 73 Yale L.J., supra, at 1033–1034. This background is reflected in the scope given by our decisions to the Sixth Amendment's guarantee to an accused of the assistance of counsel for his defense. When the Bill of Rights was adopted, there were no organized police forces as we know them today. The accused confronted the prosecutor and the witnesses against him, and the evidence was marshalled, largely at the trial itself. In contrast, today's law enforcement machinery involves critical confrontations of the accused by the prosecution at pretrial proceedings where the results might well settle the accused's fate and reduce the trial itself to a mere formality. In recognition of these realities of modern criminal prosecution, our cases have construed the Sixth Amendment guarantee to apply to "critical" stages of the proceedings. The guarantee reads: "In all criminal prosecutions, the accused shall enjoy the right . . . to have the Assistance of Counsel *for his defence*." (Emphasis supplied.) The plain wording of this guarantee thus encompasses counsel's assistance whenever necessary to assure a meaningful "defence."

As early as Powell v. Alabama, supra, we recognized that the period from arraignment to trial was "perhaps the most critical period of the proceedings . . . ," id., at 57, during which the accused "requires the guiding hand of counsel . . . ," id., at 69, if the guarantee is not to prove an empty right. That principle has since been applied to require the assistance of counsel at the type of arraignment—for example, that provided by Alabama—where certain rights might be sacrificed or lost: "What happens there may affect the whole trial. Available defenses may be irretrievably lost, if not then and there asserted . . . ." Hamilton v. Alabama, 368 U.S. 52, 54. See White v. Maryland, 373 U.S. 59. The principle was also applied in Massiah v. United States, 377 U.S. 201, where we held that incriminating statements of the defendant should have been excluded from evidence when it appeared that they were overheard by federal agents who, without notice to the defendant's lawyer, arranged a meeting between the defendant and an accomplice turned informant. We said, quoting a concurring opinion in Spano v. New York, 360 U.S. 315, 326, that "[a]nything less . . . might deny a defendant 'effective representation by counsel at the only stage when legal aid and advice would help him.'" 377 U.S., at 204.

In Escobedo v. Illinois, 378 U.S. 478, we drew upon the rationale of Hamilton and Massiah in holding that the right to counsel was guaranteed at the point where the accused, prior to arraignment, was subjected to secret interrogation despite repeated requests to see his lawyer. We again noted the necessity of counsel's presence if the accused was to have a fair opportunity to present a defense at the trial itself:

> "The rule sought by the State here, however, would make the trial no more than an appeal from the interrogation; and the 'right to use counsel at the formal trial [would be] a very hollow thing [if], for all practical purposes, the conviction is already assured by pretrial examination' . . . . 'One can imagine a cynical prosecutor saying: "Let them have the most illustrious counsel, now. They can't escape the noose. There is nothing that counsel can do for them at the trial."'" 378 U.S., at 487–488.

Finally in Miranda v. Arizona, 384 U.S. 436, the rules established for custodial interrogation included the right to the presence of counsel. The result was rested on our finding that this and the other rules were necessary to safeguard the privilege against self-incrimination from being jeopardized by such interrogation.

Of course, nothing decided or said in the opinions in the cited cases links the right to counsel only to protection of Fifth Amendment rights. Rather those decisions "no more than reflect a constitutional principle established as long ago as Powell v. Alabama . . . ." Massiah v. United States, supra, at 205. It is central to that principle that in addition to counsel's presence at trial, the accused is guaranteed that he need not stand alone against the State at any stage of the prosecution, formal or informal, in court or out, where counsel's absence might derogate from the accused's right to a fair trial. The security of that right is as much the aim of the right to counsel as it is of the other guarantees of the Sixth Amendment—the right of the accused to a speedy and public trial by an impartial jury, his right to be informed of the nature and cause of the accusation, and his right to be confronted with the witnesses against him and to have compulsory process for obtaining witnesses in his favor. The presence of counsel at such critical confrontations, as at the trial itself, operates to assure that the accused's interests will be protected consistently with our adversary theory of criminal prosecution. Cf. Pointer v. Texas, 380 U.S. 400.

In sum, the principle of Powell v. Alabama and succeeding cases requires that we scrutinize *any* pretrial confrontation of the accused to determine whether the presence of his counsel is necessary to preserve the defendant's basic right to a fair trial as affected by his right meaningfully to cross-examine the witnesses against him and to have effective assistance of counsel at the trial itself. It calls upon us to analyze whether potential substantial prejudice to defendant's rights inheres in the particular confrontation and the ability of counsel to help avoid that prejudice.

III

The Government characterizes the lineup as a mere preparatory step in the gathering of the prosecution's evidence, not different—for Sixth Amendment purposes—from various other preparatory steps, such as systematized or scientific analyzing of the accused's fingerprints, blood sample, clothing, hair, and the like. We think there are differences which preclude such stages being characterized as critical stages at which the accused has the right to the presence of his counsel. Knowledge of the techniques of science and technology is sufficiently available, and the variables in techniques few enough, that the accused has the opportunity for a meaningful confrontation of the Government's case at trial through the ordinary processes of cross-examination of the Government's expert witnesses and the presentation of the evidence of his own experts. The denial of a right to have his counsel present at such analyses does not therefore violate the Sixth Amendment; they are not critical stages since there is minimal risk that his counsel's absence at such stages might derogate from his right to a fair trial.

IV

But the confrontation compelled by the State between the accused and the victim or witnesses to a crime to elicit identification evidence is peculiarly riddled with innumerable dangers and variable factors which might seriously, even crucially, derogate from a fair trial. The vagaries of eyewitness identification are well-known; the annals of criminal law are rife with instances of mistaken identification. Mr. Justice Frankfurter once said: "What is the worth of identification testimony even when uncontradicted? The identification of strangers is proverbially untrustworthy. The hazards of such testimony are established by a formidable number of instances in the records of English and American trials. These instances are recent—not due to the brutalities of ancient criminal procedure." The Case of Sacco and Vanzetti 30 (1927). A major factor contributing to the high incidence of miscarriage of justice from mistaken identification has been the degree of suggestion inherent in the manner in which the prosecution presents the suspect to witnesses for pretrial identification. A commentator has observed that "[t]he influence of improper suggestion upon identifying witnesses probably accounts for more miscarriages of justice than any other single factor—perhaps it is responsible for more such errors than all other factors combined." Wall, Eye-Witness Identification in Criminal Cases 26. Suggestion can be created intentionally or unintentionally in many subtle ways. And the dangers for the suspect are particularly grave when the witness' opportunity for observation was insubstantial, and thus his susceptibility to suggestion the greatest.

Moreover, "[i]t is a matter of common experience that, once a witness has picked out the accused at the line-up, he is not likely to go back on his word later on, so that in practice the issue of identity may (in the absence of other relevant evidence) for all practical purposes be determined there and then, before the trial."

The pretrial confrontation for purpose of identification may take the form of a lineup, also known as an "identification parade" or "showup," as in the present case, or presentation of the suspect alone to the witness, as in Stovall v. Denno, supra. It is obvious that risks of suggestion attend either form of confrontation and increase the dangers inhering in eyewitness identification. But as is the case with secret interrogations, there is serious difficulty in depicting what transpires at lineups and other forms of identification confrontations. "Privacy results in secrecy and this in turn results in a gap in our knowledge as to what in fact goes on. . . ." Miranda v. Arizona, supra, at 448. For the same reasons, the defense can seldom reconstruct the manner and mode of lineup identification for judge or jury at trial. Those participating in a lineup with the accused may often be police officers; in any event, the participants' names are rarely recorded or divulged at trial. The impediments to an objective observation are increased when the victim is the witness. Lineups are prevalent in rape and robbery prosecutions and present a particular hazard that a victim's understandable outrage may excite vengeful or spiteful motives. In any event, neither witnesses nor lineup participants are apt to be alert for conditions prejudicial to the suspect. And if they were, it would likely be of scant benefit to the suspect since neither witnesses nor lineup participants are likely to be schooled in the detection of suggestive influences. Improper influences may go undetected by a suspect, guilty or not, who experiences the emotional tension that we might expect in one being confronted with potential accusers. Even when he does observe abuse, if he has a criminal record he may be reluctant to take the stand and open up the admission of prior convictions. Moreover, any protestations by the suspect of the fairness of the lineup made at trial are likely to be in vain; the jury's choice is between the accused's unsupported version and that of the police officers present. In short, the accused's inability effectively to reconstruct at trial any unfairness that occurred at the lineup may deprive him of his only opportunity meaningfully to attack the credibility of the witness' courtroom identification.

What facts have been disclosed in specific cases about the conduct of pretrial confrontations for identification illustrate both the potential for substantial prejudice to the accused at that stage and the need for its revelation at trial. A commentator provides some striking examples:

> "In a Canadian case . . . the defendant had been picked out of a line-up of six men, of which he was the only Oriental. In other cases, a black-haired suspect was placed among a group of light-haired persons, tall suspects have been made to stand with short non-suspects, and, in a case where the perpetrator of the crime was known to be a youth, a suspect under twenty was placed in a line-up with five other persons, all of whom were forty or over."

Similarly state reports, in the course of describing prior identifications admitted as evidence of guilt, reveal numerous instances of suggestive procedures, for example, that all in the lineup but the suspect were known to the identifying witness, that the other participants in a lineup were grossly dissimilar in appearance to the suspect, that only the suspect was required to wear distinctive clothing which the culprit allegedly wore, that the witness is told by the police that they have caught the culprit after which the defendant is brought before the witness alone or is viewed in jail, that the suspect is pointed out before or during a lineup, and that the participants in the lineup are asked to try on an article of clothing which fits only the suspect.

The potential for improper influence is illustrated by the circumstances, insofar as they appear, surrounding the prior identifications in the three cases we decide today. In the present case, the testimony of the identifying witnesses elicited on cross-examination revealed that those witnesses were taken to the courthouse and seated in the courtroom to await assembly of the lineup. The courtroom faced on a hallway observable to the witnesses through an open door. The cashier testified that she saw Wade "standing in the hall" within sight of an FBI agent. Five or six other prisoners later appeared in the hall. The vice president testified that he saw a person in the hall in the custody of the agent who "resembled the person that we identified as the one that had entered the bank."

The lineup in Gilbert, supra, was conducted in an auditorium in which some 100 witnesses to several alleged state and federal robberies charged to Gilbert made wholesale identifications of Gilbert as the robber in each other's presence, a procedure said to be fraught with dangers of suggestion. And the vice of suggestion created by the identification in Stovall, supra, was the presentation to the witness of the suspect alone handcuffed to police officers. It is hard to imagine a situation more clearly conveying the suggestion to the witness that the one presented is believed guilty by the police. See Frankfurter, The Case of Sacco and Vanzetti 31–32.

The few cases that have surfaced therefore reveal the existence of a process attended with hazards of serious unfairness to the criminal accused and strongly suggest the plight of the more numerous defendants who are unable to ferret out suggestive influences in the secrecy of the confrontation. We do not assume that these risks are the result of police procedures intentionally designed to prejudice an accused. Rather we assume they derive from the dangers inherent in eyewitness identification and the suggestibility inherent in the context of the pretrial identification. Williams & Hammelmann, in one of the most comprehensive studies of such forms of identification, said, "[T]he fact that the police themselves have, in a given case, little or no doubt that the man put up for identification has committed the offense, and that their chief pre-occupation is with the problem of getting sufficient proof, because he has not 'come clean,' involves a danger that his persuasion may communicate itself even in a doubtful case to the witness in some way. . . ." Identification Parades, Part I, [1963] Crim. L. Rev. 479, 483.

Insofar as the accused's conviction may rest on a courtroom identification in fact the fruit of a suspect pretrial identification which the accused is helpless to subject to effective scrutiny at trial, the accused is deprived of that right of cross-examination which is an essential safeguard to his right to confront the witnesses against him. Pointer v. Texas, 380 U.S. 400. And even though cross-examination is a precious safeguard to a fair trial, it cannot be viewed as an absolute assurance of accuracy and reliability. Thus in the present context, where so many variables and pitfalls exist, the first line of defense must be the prevention of unfairness and the lessening of the hazards of eyewitness identification at the lineup itself. The trial which might determine the accused's fate may well not be that in the courtroom but that at the pretrial confrontation, with the State aligned against the accused, the witness the sole jury, and the accused unprotected against the overreaching, intentional or unintentional, and with little or no effective appeal from the judgment there rendered by the witness—"that's the man."

Since it appears that there is grave potential for prejudice, intentional or not, in the pretrial lineup, which may not be capable of reconstruction at trial, and since presence of counsel itself can often avert prejudice and assure a meaningful confrontation at trial, there can be little doubt that for Wade the post-indictment lineup was a critical stage of the prosecution at which he was "as much entitled to such aid [of counsel]... as at the trial itself." Powell v. Alabama, 287 U.S. 45, 57. Thus both Wade and his counsel should have been notified of the impending lineup, and counsel's presence should have been a requisite to conduct of the lineup, absent an "intelligent waiver." See Carnley v. Cochran, 369 U.S. 506. No substantial countervailing policy considerations have been advanced against the requirement of the presence of counsel. Concern is expressed that the requirement will forestall prompt identifications and result in obstruction of the confrontations. As for the first, we note that in the two cases in which the right to counsel is today held to apply, counsel had already been appointed and no argument is made in either case that notice to counsel would have prejudicially delayed the confrontations. Moreover, we leave open the question whether the presence of substitute counsel might not suffice where notification and presence of the suspect's own counsel would result in prejudicial delay. And to refuse to recognize the right to counsel for fear that counsel will obstruct the course of justice is contrary to the basic assumptions upon which this Court has operated in Sixth Amendment cases. We rejected similar logic in Miranda v. Arizona concerning presence of counsel during custodial interrogation, 384 U.S., at 480–481:

> "[A]n attorney is merely exercising the good professional judgment he has been taught. This is not cause for considering the attorney a menace to law enforcement. He is merely carrying out what he is sworn to do under his oath—to protect to the extent of his ability the rights of his client. In fulfilling this responsibility the attorney plays a vital role in the administration of criminal justice under our Constitution."

In our view counsel can hardly impede legitimate law enforcement; on the contrary, for the reasons expressed, law enforcement may be assisted by preventing the infiltration of taint in the prosecution's identification evidence. That result cannot help the guilty avoid conviction but can only help assure that the right man has been brought to justice.

Legislative or other regulations, such as those of local police departments, which eliminate the risks of abuse and unintentional suggestion at lineup proceedings and the impediments to meaningful confrontation at trial may also remove the basis for regarding the stage as "critical." But neither Congress nor the federal authorities have seen fit to provide a solution. What we hold today "in no way creates a constitutional straitjacket which will handicap sound efforts at reform, nor is it intended to have this effect." Miranda v. Arizona, supra, at 467.

V

We come now to the question whether the denial of Wade's motion to strike the courtroom identification by the bank witnesses at trial because of the absence of his counsel at the lineup required, as the Court of Appeals held, the grant of a new trial at which such evidence is to be excluded. We do not think this disposition can be justified without first giving the Government the opportunity to establish by clear and convincing evidence that the in-court identifications were based upon observations of the suspect other than the lineup identification. See Murphy v. Waterfront Commission, 378 U.S. 52, 79, n. 18. Where, as here, the admissibility of evidence of the lineup identification itself is not involved, a per se rule of exclusion of courtroom identification would be unjustified. See Nardone v. United States, 308 U.S. 338, 341. A rule limited solely to the exclusion of testimony concerning identification at the lineup itself, without regard to admissibility of the courtroom identification, would render the right to counsel an empty one. The lineup is most often used, as in the present case, to crystallize the witnesses' identification of the defendant for future reference. We have already noted that the lineup identification will have that effect. The State may then rest upon the witnesses' unequivocal courtroom identification, and not mention the pretrial identification as part of the State's case at trial. Counsel is then in the predicament in which Wade's counsel found himself—realizing that possible unfairness at the lineup may be the sole means of attack upon the unequivocal courtroom identification, and having to probe in the dark in an attempt to discover and reveal unfairness, while bolstering the government witness' courtroom identification by bringing out and dwelling upon his prior identification. Since counsel's presence at the lineup would equip him to attack not only the lineup identification but the courtroom identification as well, limiting the impact of violation of the right to counsel to exclusion of evidence only of identification at the lineup itself disregards a critical element of that right.

We think it follows that the proper test to be applied in these situations is that quoted in Wong Sun v. United States, 371 U.S. 471, 488, "'[W]hether, granting establishment of the primary illegality, the evidence to which instant objection is made has been come at by exploitation of that illegality or instead by means sufficiently distinguishable to be purged of the primary taint.' Maguire, Evidence of Guilt 221 (1959)." See also Hoffa v. United States, 385 U.S. 293, 309. Application of this test in the present context requires consideration of various factors; for example, the prior opportunity to observe the alleged criminal act, the existence of any discrepancy between any pre-lineup description and the defendant's actual description, any identification prior to lineup of another person, the identification by picture of the defendant prior to the lineup, failure to identify the defendant on a prior occasion, and the lapse of time between the alleged act and the lineup identification. It is also relevant to consider those facts which, despite the absence of counsel, are disclosed concerning the conduct of the lineup.

We doubt that the Court of Appeals applied the proper test for exclusion of the in-court identification of the two witnesses. The court stated that "it cannot be said with any certainty that they would have recognized appellant at the time of trial if this intervening lineup had not occurred," and that the testimony of the two witnesses "may well have been colored by the illegal procedure [and] was prejudicial." 358 F. 2d, at 560. Moreover, the court was persuaded, in part, by the "compulsory verbal responses made by Wade at the instance of the Special Agent." Ibid. This implies the erroneous holding that Wade's privilege against self-incrimination was violated so that the denial of counsel required exclusion.

On the record now before us we cannot make the determination whether the in-court identifications had an independent origin. This was not an issue at trial, although there is some evidence relevant to a determination. That inquiry is most properly made in the District Court. We therefore think the appropriate procedure to be followed is to vacate the conviction pending a hearing to determine whether the in-court identifications had an independent source, or whether, in any event, the introduction of the evidence was harmless error, Chapman v. California, 386 U.S. 18, and for the District Court to reinstate the conviction or order a new trial, as may be proper. See United States v. Shotwell Mfg. Co., 355 U.S. 233, 245–246.

The judgment of the Court of Appeals is vacated and the case is remanded to that court with direction to enter a new judgment vacating the conviction and remanding the case to the District Court for further proceedings consistent with this opinion.

It is so ordered.

John R. Manson, Commissioner of Correction of Connecticut, Petitioner, *v.* Nowell A. Brathwaite

432 U.S. 98, 97 S.Ct. 2243, 53 L.Ed. 2d. 140 (1977)

Argued November 29, 1976.—Decided June 16, 1977.

. . .

MR. JUSTICE BLACKMUN delivered the opinion of the Court.

This case presents the issue as to whether the Due Process Clause of the Fourteenth Amendment compels the exclusion, in a state criminal trial, apart from any consideration of reliability, of pretrial identification evidence obtained by a police procedure that was both suggestive and unnecessary. This Court's decisions in Stovall v Denno, 388 US 293, 18 L Ed 2d 1199, 87 S Ct 1967 (1967), and Neil v Biggers, 409 US 188, 34 L Ed 2d 401, 93 S Ct 375 (1972), are particularly implicated.

I

Jimmy D. Glover, a full-time trooper of the Connecticut State Police, in 1970 was assigned to the Narcotics Division in an undercover capacity. On May 5 of that year, about 7:45 p.m. E.D.T. and while there was still daylight, Glover and Henry Alton Brown, an informant, went to an apartment building at 201 Westland, in Hartford, for the purpose of purchasing narcotics from "Dickie Boy" Cicero, a known narcotics dealer. Cicero, it was thought, lived on the third floor of that apartment building. Tr 45, 68. Glover and Brown entered the building, observed by back-up Officers D'Onofrio and Gaffey, and proceeded by stairs to the third floor. Glover knocked at the door of one of the two apartments served by the stairway. The area was illuminated by natural light from a window in the third floor hallway. Id., at 27–28. The door was opened 12 to 18 inches in response to the knock. Glover observed a man standing at the door and, behind him, a woman. Brown identified himself. Glover then asked for "two things" of narcotics. Id., at 29. The man at the door held out his hand, and Glover gave him two $10 bills. The door closed. Soon the man returned and handed Glover two glassine bags. While the door was open, Glover stood within two feet of the person from whom he made the purchase and observed his face. Five to seven minutes elapsed from the time the door first opened until it closed the second time. Id., at 30–33.

Glover and Brown then left the building. This was about eight minutes after their arrival. Glover drove to headquarters where he described the seller to D'Onofrio and Gaffey. Glover at that time did not know the identity of the seller. Id., at 36. He described him as being "a colored man, approximately five feet eleven inches tall, dark complexion, black hair, short Afro style, and having high cheekbones, and of heavy build. He was wearing at the time blue pants and a plaid shirt." Id., at 37. D'Onofrio, suspecting from this description that respondent might be the seller, obtained a photograph of respondent for the Records Division of the Hartford Police Department. He left it at Glover's office. D'Onofrio was not acquainted with respondent personally, but did know him by sight and had seen him "[s]everal times" prior to May 5. Id., at 63–65. Glover, when alone, viewed the photograph for the first time upon his return to headquarters on May 7; he identified the person shown as the one from whom he had purchased the narcotics. Id., at 36–38.

The toxicological report on the contents of the glassine bags revealed the presence of heroin. The report was dated July 16, 1970. Id., at 75–76.

Respondent was arrested on July 27 while visiting at the apartment of a Mrs. Ramsey on the third floor of 201 Westland. This was the apartment at which the narcotics sale had taken place on May 5.

Respondent was charged, in a two-count information, with possession and sale of heroin, in violation of Conn Gen Stat (Rev of 1958, as amended in 1969), §§ 19-481(a) and 19-480(a). At his trial in January 1971, the photograph from which Glover had identified respondent was received in evidence without objection on the part of the defense. Tr 38. Glover also testified that, although he had not seen respondent in the eight months that had elapsed since the sale, "there [was] no doubt whatsoever" in his mind that the person shown on the photograph was respondent. Id., at 41–42. Glover also made a positive in-court identification without objection. Id., at 37–38.

No explanation was offered by the prosecution for the failure to utilize a photographic array or to conduct a lineup.

Respondent, who took the stand in his own defense, testified that on May 5, the day in question, he had been ill at his Albany Avenue apartment ("a lot of back pains, muscle spasms . . . a bad heart . . . high blood pressure . . . neuralgia in my face, and sinus," id., at 106), and that at no time on that particular day had he been at

201 Westland. Id., at 106, 113–114. His wife testified that she recalled, after her husband had refreshed her memory, that he was home all day on May 5. Id., at 164–165. Doctor Wesley M. Vietzke, an internist and assistant professor of medicine at the University of Connecticut, testified that respondent had consulted him on April 15, 1970, and that he took a medical history from him, heard his complaints about his back and facial pain, and discovered that he had high blood pressure. Id., at 129–131. The physician found respondent, subjectively, "in great discomfort." Id., at 135. Respondent in fact underwent surgery for a herniated disc at L5 and S1 on August 17. Id., at 157.

The jury found respondent guilty on both counts of the information. He received a sentence of not less than six nor more than nine years. His conviction was affirmed per curiam by the Supreme Court of Connecticut. State v Brathwaite, 164 Conn 617, 325 A2d 284 (1973). That court noted the absence of an objection to Glover's in-court identification and concluded that respondent "has not shown that substantial injustice resulted from the admission of this evidence." Id., at 619, 325 A2d, at 285. Under Connecticut law, substantial injustice must be shown before a claim of error not made or passed on by the trial court will be considered on appeal. Ibid.

Fourteen months later, respondent filed a petition for habeas corpus in the United States District Court for the District of Connecticut. He alleged that the admission of the identification testimony at his state trial deprived him of due process of law to which he was entitled under the Fourteenth Amendment. The District Court, by an unreported written opinion based on the court's review of the state trial transcript, dismissed respondent's petition. On appeal, the United States Court of Appeals for the Second Circuit reversed, with instructions to issue the writ unless the State gave notice of a desire to retry respondent and the new trial occurred within a reasonable time to be fixed by the District Judge. 527 F2d 363 (1975).

In brief summary, the court felt that evidence as to the photograph should have been excluded, regardless of reliability, because the examination of the single photograph was unnecessary and suggestive. And, in the court's view, the evidence was unreliable in any event. We granted certiorari. 425 US 957, 48 L Ed 2d 202, 96 S Ct 1737 (1976).

II

Stovall v United States, supra, decided in 1967, concerned a petitioner who had been convicted in a New York court of murder. He was arrested the day following the crime and was taken by the police to a hospital where the victim's wife, also wounded in the assault, was a patient. After observing Stovall and hearing him speak, she identified him as the murderer. She later made an in-court identification. On federal habeas, Stovall claimed the identification testimony violated his Fifth, Sixth, and Fourteenth Amendment rights. The District Court dismissed the petition, and the Court of Appeals, en banc, affirmed. This Court also affirmed. On the identification issue, the Court reviewed the practice of showing a suspect singly for purposes of identification, and the claim that this was so unnecessarily suggestive and conducive to irreparable mistaken identification that it constituted a denial of due process of law. The Court noted that the practice "has been widely condemned," 388 US, at 302, 18 L Ed 2d 1199, 87 S Ct 1967, but it concluded that "a claimed violation of due process of law in the conduct of a confrontation depends on the totality of the circumstances surrounding it." Ibid. In that case, showing Stovall to the victim's spouse "was imperative." The Court then quoted the observations of the Court of Appeals, 355 F2d 731, 735, to the effect that the spouse was the only person who could possibly exonerate the accused; that the hospital was not far from the courthouse and jail; that no one knew how long she might live; that she was not able to visit the jail; and that taking Stovall to the hospital room was the only feasible procedure, and, under the circumstances, "'the usual police station line-up... was out of the question.'" 388 US, at 302, 18 L Ed 2d 1199, 87 S Ct 1967.

Neil v Biggers, supra, decided in 1972, concerned a respondent who had been convicted in a Tennessee court of rape, on evidence consisting in part of the victim's visual and voice identification of Biggers at a station-house showup seven months after the crime. The victim had been in her assailant's presence for some time and had directly observed him indoors and under a full moon outdoors. She testified that she had "no doubt" that Biggers was her assailant. She previously had given the police a description of the assailant. She had made no identification of others presented at previous showups, lineups, or through photographs. On federal habeas, the District Court held that the confrontation was so suggestive as to violate due process. The Court of Appeals affirmed. This Court reversed on that issue, and held that the evidence properly had been allowed to go to the jury. The Court reviewed Stovall and certain later cases where it had considered the scope of due process protection against the admission of evidence derived from suggestive identification procedures, namely, Simmons v United States, 390 US 377, 19 L Ed 2d 1247, 88 S Ct 967 (1968); Foster v California, 394 US 440, 22 L Ed 2d 402, 89 S Ct 1127 (1969); and Coleman v Alabama, 399 US 1, 26 L Ed 2d 387, 90 S Ct 1999 (1970). The Court concluded that general guidelines emerged from these cases "as to the relationship between suggestiveness and misidentification." The "admission of evidence of a showup without more does not violate due process." 409 US, at 198, 34 L Ed 2d 401, 93 S Ct 375. The Court expressed concern about the lapse of seven months between the crime and the confrontation and observed that this "would be a seriously negative factor in most cases." Id., at 201, 34 L Ed 2d 401, 93 S Ct 375. The "central question," however, was "whether under the 'totality of the circumstances' the identification was reliable even though the confrontation procedure was suggestive." Applying that test, the Court found "no substantial likelihood of misidentification. The evidence was properly allowed to go to the jury." Ibid.

Biggers well might be seen to provide an unambiguous answer to the question before us: the admission of testimony concerning a suggestive and unnecessary identification procedure does not violate due process so long as the identification possesses sufficient aspects of reliability. In one passage, however, the Court observed that the challenged procedure occurred pre-Stovall and that a strict rule would make little sense with regard to a confrontation that preceded the Court's first indication that a suggestive procedure might lead to the exclusion of evidence. Id., at 199, 34 L Ed 2d 401, 93 S Ct 375. One perhaps might argue that, by implication, the Court suggested that a different rule could apply post-Stovall. The question before us, then, is simply whether the Biggers analysis applies to post-Stovall confrontations as well to those pre-Stovall.

III

In the present case the District Court observed that the "sole evidence tying Brathwaite to the possession and sale of the heroin consisted in his identifications by the police undercover agent, Jimmy Glover." Petition for Certiorari, App 6a. On the constitutional issue, the court stated that the first inquiry was whether the police used an impermissibly suggestive procedure in obtaining the out-of-court identification. If so, the second inquiry is whether, under all the circumstances, that suggestive procedure gave rise to a substantial likelihood of irreparable misidentification. Id., at 9a. Biggers and Simmons were cited. The court noted that in the Second Circuit, its controlling court, it was clear that "this type of identification procedure [display of a single photograph] is impermissibly suggestive," and turned to the second inquiry. Petition for Certiorari, App 9a. The factors Biggers specified for consideration were recited and applied. The court concluded that there was no substantial likelihood of irreparable misidentification. It referred to the facts: Glover was within two feet of the seller. The duration of the confrontation was at least a "couple of minutes." There was natural light from a window or skylight and there was adequate light to see clearly in the hall. Glover "certainly was paying attention to identify the seller." Id., at 10a. He was a trained police office who realized that later he would have to find and arrest the person with whom he was dealing. He gave a detailed description to D'Onofrio. The reliability of this description was supported by the fact that it enabled D'Onofrio to pick out a single photograph that was thereafter positively identified by Glover. Only two days elapsed between the crime and the photographic identification. Despite the fact that another eight months passed before the in-court identification, Glover had "no doubt" that Brathwaite was the person who had sold him heroin.

The Court of Appeals confirmed that the exhibition of the single photograph to Glover was "impermissibly suggestive," 527 F2d, at 366, and felt that, in addition, "it was unnecessarily so." Id., at 367. There was no emergency and little urgency. The court said that prior to the decision in Biggers, except in cases of harmless error, "a conviction secured as the result of admitting an identification obtained by impermissibly suggestive and unnecessary measures could not stand." Ibid. It noted what it felt might be opposing inferences to be drawn from passages in Biggers, but concluded that the case preserved the principle "requiring the exclusion of identifications resulting from 'unnecessarily suggestive confrontation'" in post-Stovall situations. Id., at 368. The court also concluded that for post-Stovall identifications, Biggers had not changed the existing rule. Thus: "Evidence of an identification unnecessarily obtained by impermissibly suggestive means must be excluded under Stovall.... No rules less stringent than these can force police administrators and prosecutors to adopt procedures that will give fair assurance against the awful risks of misidentification." Id., at 371. Finally, the court said, even if this conclusion were wrong, the writ, nevertheless, should issue. It took judicial notice that on May 5, 1970, sunset at Hartford was at 7:53 p.m. It characterized Glover's duty as an undercover agent as one "to cause arrests to be made," and his description of the suspect as one that "could have applied to hundreds of Hartford black males." Ibid. The in-court identification had "little meaning," for Brathwaite was at the counsel table. The fact that respondent was arrested in the very apartment where the sale was made was subject to a "not implausible" explanation from the respondent, "although evidently not credited by the jury." And the court was troubled by "the long and unexplained delay" in the arrest. It was too great a danger that the respondent was convicted because he was a man D'Onofrio had previously observed near the scene, was thought to be a likely offender, and was arrested when he was known to be in Mrs. Ramsey's apartment, rather than because Glover "really remembered him as the seller." Id., at 371–372.

IV

The State at the outset acknowledges that "the procedure in the instant case was suggestive [because only one photograph was used] and unnecessary" [because there was no emergency or exigent circumstance]. Brief for Petitioner 10; Tr of Oral Arg 7. The respondent, in agreement with the Court of Appeals, proposes a per se rule of exclusion that he claims is dictated by the demands of the Fourteenth Amendment's guarantee of due process. He rightly observes that this is the first case in which this Court has had occasion to rule upon strictly post-Stovall out-of-court identification evidence of the challenged kind.

Since the decision in Biggers, the courts of appeals appear to have developed at least two approaches to such evidence. See Pulaski, Neil v Biggers: The Supreme Court Dismantles the Wade Trilogy's Due Process Protection, 26 Stan L Rev 1097, 1111–1114 (1974). The first, or per se approach, employed by the Second Circuit in the present case, focuses on the procedures employed and requires exclusion of the out-of-court identification evidence, without regard to reliability, whenever it has been obtained through unnecessarily suggested confrontation procedures. The justifications advanced are the elimination of evidence of uncertain reliability, deterrence of the police and prosecutors, and the stated "fair assurance against the awful risks of misidentification." 527 F2d, at 371. See Smith v Coiner, 473 F2d 877, 882 (CA4), cert denied sub nom Wallace v Smith, 414 US 1115, 38 L Ed 2d 743, 94 S Ct 848 (1973).

The second, or more lenient, approach is one that continues to rely on the totality of the circumstances. It permits the admission of the confrontation evidence if, despite the suggestive aspect, the out-of-court identification possesses certain features of reliability. Its adherents feel that the per se approach is not mandated by the Due Process Clause of the Fourteenth Amendment. This second approach, in contrast to the other, is ad hoc and serves to limit the societal costs imposed by a sanction that excludes relevant evidence from consideration and evaluation by the trier of fact. See United States ex rel. Kirby v Sturges, 510 F2d 397, 407–408 (CA7; opinion by Judge, now MR. JUSTICE STEVENS), cert denied, 421 US 1016, 44 L Ed 2d 685, 95 S Ct 2424 (1975); Stanley v Cox, 486 F2d 48 (CA4), cert denied sub nom Stanley v Slayton, 416 US 958, 40 L Ed 2d 309, 94 S Ct 1975 (1973).

MR. JUSTICE STEVENS, in writing for the Seventh Circuit in Kirby, supra, observed: "There is surprising unanimity among scholars in regarding such a rule [the per se approach] as essential to avoid serious risk of miscarriage of justice." 510 F2d, at 405. He pointed out that well-known federal judges have taken the position that "evidence of, or derived from, a showup identification should be inadmissible unless the prosecutor can justify his failure to use a more reliable identification procedure." Id., at 406. Indeed, the American Law Institute's Model Code of Pre-Arraignment Procedure, §§ 160.1 and 160.2 (1975), frowns upon the use of a showup or the display of only a single photograph.

The respondent here stresses the same theme and the need for deterrence of improper identification practice, a factor he regards as preeminent. Photographic identification, it is said, continues to be needlessly employed. He notes that the legislative regulation "the Court hoped Wade [388 US 218, 239, 18 L Ed 2d 1149, 87 S Ct 1926 (1967)] would engender," Brief for Respondent 15, has not been forthcoming. He argues that a totality rule cannot be expected to have a significant deterrent impact; only a strict rule of exclusion will have direct and immediate impact on law enforcement agents. Identification evidence is so convincing to the jury that sweeping exclusionary rules are required. Fairness of the trial is threatened by suggestive confrontation evidence, and thus, it is said, an exclusionary rule has an established constitutional predicate.

There are, of course, several interests to be considered and taken into account. The driving force behind United States v Wade, 388 US 218, 18 L Ed 2d 1149, 87 S Ct 1926 (1967), and Gilbert v California, 388 US 263, 18 L Ed 2d 1178, 87 S Ct 1951 (1967) [right to counsel at a post-indictment line-up], and Stovall, all decided on the same day, was the Court's concern with the problems of eyewitness identification. Usually the witness must testify about an encounter with a total stranger under circumstances of emergency or emotional stress. The witness' recollection of the stranger can be distorted easily by the circumstances or by later actions of the police. Thus, Wade and its companion cases reflect the concern that the jury not hear eyewitness testimony unless that evidence has aspects of reliability. It must be observed that both approaches before us are responsive to this concern. The per se rule, however, goes too far since its application automatically and peremptorily, and without consideration of alleviating factors, keeps evidence from the jury that is reliable and relevant.

The second factor is deterrence. Although the per se approach has the more significant deterrent effect, the totality approach also has an influence on police behavior. The police will guard against unnecessarily suggestive procedures under the totality rule, as well as the per se one, for fear that their actions will lead to the exclusion of identifications as unreliable.

The third factor is the effect on the administration of justice. Here the per se approach suffers serious drawbacks. Since it denies the trier reliable evidence, it may result, on occasion, in the guilty going free. Also, because of its rigidity, the per se approach may make error by the trial judge more likely than the totality approach. And in those cases in which the admission of identification evidence is error under the per se approach but not under the totality approach—cases in which the identification is reliable despite an unnecessarily suggestive identification procedure—reversal is a draconian sanction. Certainly, inflexible rules of exclusion, that may frustrate rather than promote justice, have not been viewed recently by this Court with unlimited enthusiasm. See, for example, the several opinions in Brewer v Williams, ___ US ___, 51 L Ed 2d 424, 97 S Ct 1232 (1977). See also United States v Janis, 428 US 433, 49 L Ed 2d 1046, 96 S Ct 3021 (1976).

It is true, as has been noted, that the Court in Biggers referred to the pre-Stovall character of the confrontation in that case. 409 US, at 199, 34 L Ed 2d 401, 93 S Ct 375. But that observation was only one factor in the judgmental process. It does not translate into a holding that post-Stovall confrontation evidence automatically is to be excluded.

The standard, after all, is that of fairness as required by the Due Process Clause of the Fourteenth Amendment. See United States v Lovasco, ___ US ___, ___, 52 L Ed 2d 752, 97 S Ct ___ (1977); Rochin v California, 342 US 165, 170–172 96 L Ed 183, 72 S Ct 205, 25 ALR2d 1396 (1952). Stovall, with its reference to "the totality of the circumstances," 388 US, at 302, 18 L Ed 2d 1199, 87 S Ct 1967, and Biggers, with its continuing stress on the same totality, 409 US, at 199, 34 L Ed 2d 401, 93 S Ct 375, did not, singly or together, establish a strict exclusionary rule or new standard of due process. Judge Leventhal, although speaking pre-Biggers and of a pre-Wade situation, correctly has described Stovall as protecting an *evidentiary* interest and, at the same time, as recognizing the limited extent of that interest in our adversary system.

We therefore conclude that reliability is the linchpin in determining the admissibility of identification testimony for both pre- and post-Stovall confrontations. The factors to be considered are set out in Biggers. 409 US, at 199–200, 34 L Ed 2d 401, 93 S Ct 375. These include the opportunity of the witness to view the criminal at the time of the crime, the witness' degree of attention, the accuracy of his prior description of the criminal, the level of certainty demonstrated at the confrontation, and the time between the crime and the confrontation. Against these factors is to be weighed the corrupting effect of the suggestive identification itself.

V

We turn, then, to the facts of this case and apply the analysis:

1. *The opportunity to view.* Glover testified that for two to three minutes he stood at the apartment door, within two feet of the respondent. The door opened twice, and each time the man stood at the door. The moments passed, the conversation took place, and payment was made. Glover looked directly at his vendor. It was near sunset, to be sure, but the sun had not yet set, so it was not dark or even dusk or twilight. Natural light from outside entered the hallway through a window. There was natural light, as well, from inside the apartment.

2. *The degree of attention.* Glover was not a casual or passing observer, as is so often the case with eyewitness identification. Trooper Glover was a trained police officer on duty—and specialized and dangerous duty—when he called at the

third floor of 201 Westland in Hartford on May 5, 1970. Glover himself was a Negro and unlikely to perceive only general features of "hundreds of Hartford black males," as the Court of Appeals stated. 527 F2d, at 371. It is true that Glover's duty was that of ferreting out narcotics offenders and that he would be expected in his work to produce results. But it is also true that, as a specially trained, assigned, and experienced officer, he could be expected to pay scrupulous attention to detail, for he knew that subsequently he would have to find and arrest his vendor. In addition, he knew that his claimed observations would be subject later to close scrutiny and examination at any trial.

3. *The accuracy of the description.* Glover's description was given to D'Onofrio within minutes after the transaction. It included the vendor's race, his height, his build, the color and style of his hair, and the high cheekbone facial feature. It also included clothing the vendor wore. No claim has been made that respondent did not possess the physical characteristics so described. D'Onofrio reacted positively at once. Two days later, when Glover was alone, he viewed the photograph D'Onofrio produced and identified its subject as the narcotics seller.

4. *The witness' level of certainty.* There is no dispute that the photograph in question was that of respondent. Glover, in response to a question whether the photograph was that of the person from whom he made the purchase, testified: "There is no question whatsoever." Tr 38. This positive assurance was repeated. Id., at 41–42.

5. *The time between the crime and the confrontation.* Glover's description of his vendor was given to D'Onofrio within minutes of the crime. The photographic identification took place only two days later. We do not have here the passage of weeks or months between the crime and the viewing of the photograph.

These indicators of Glover's ability to make an accurate identification are hardly outweighed by the corrupting effect of the challenged identification itself. Although identifications arising from single-photograph displays may be viewed in general with suspicion, see Simmons v United States, 390 US, at 383, 19 L Ed 2d 1247, 88 S Ct 967, we find in the instant case little pressure on the witness to acquiesce in the suggestion that such a display entails. D'Onofrio had left the photograph at Glover's office and was not present when Glover first viewed it two days after the event. There thus was little urgency and Glover could view the photograph at his leisure. And since Glover examined the photograph alone, there was no coercive pressure to make an identification arising from the presence of another. The identification was made in circumstances allowing care and reflection.

Although it plays no part in our analysis, all this assurance as to the reliability of the identification is hardly undermined by the facts that respondent was arrested in the very apartment where the sale had taken place, and that he acknowledged his frequent visits to that apartment.

Surely, we cannot say that under all the circumstances of this case there is "a very substantial likelihood of irreparable misidentification." Simmons v United States, 390 US, at 384, 19 L Ed 2d 1247, 88 S Ct 967. Short of that point, such evidence is for the jury to weigh. We are content to rely upon the good sense and judgment of American juries, for evidence with some element of untrustworthiness is customary grist for the jury mill. Juries are not so susceptible that they cannot measure intelligently the weight of identification testimony that has some questionable feature.

Of course, it would have been better had D'Onofrio presented Glover with a photographic array including "so far as practicable . . . a reasonable number of persons similar to any person then suspected whose likeness is included in the array." Model Code, supra, § 160.2(2). The use of that procedure would have enhanced the force of the identification at trial and would have avoided the risk that the evidence would be excluded as unreliable. But we are not disposed to view D'Onofrio's failure as one of constitutional dimension to be enforced by a rigorous and unbending exclusionary rule. The defect, if there be one, goes to weight and not to substance.

We conclude that the criteria laid down in Biggers are to be applied in determining the admissibility of evidence offered by the prosecution concerning a post-Stovall identification, and that those criteria are satisfactorily met and complied with here.

The judgment of the Court of Appeals is reversed.

It is so ordered.

James Raymond Moore, Petitioner, *v.* State of Illinois

434 U.S. 220, 98 S.Ct. 458, 54 L.Ed. 2d. 424 (1977)

Argued October 3, 1977.—Decided December 12, 1977.

. . .

MR. JUSTICE POWELL delivered the opinion of the Court.

Petitioner was convicted of rape and related offenses. At trial the complaining witness testified on direct examination by the prosecution that she had identified petitioner at a preliminary hearing at which he was not represented by counsel. The state supreme court affirmed petitioner's convictions, and the Federal District Court and Court of Appeals denied habeas corpus relief. We granted certiorari because of an apparent conflict between the decisions below and our holdings with respect to the right to counsel at corporeal identifications in Wade v United States, 388 US 218, 18 L Ed 2d 1149, 87 S Ct 1926 (1967), Gilbert v California, 388 US 263, 18 L Ed 2d 1178, 87 S Ct 1951 (1967), and Kirby v Illinois, 406 US 682, 32 L Ed 2d 411, 92 S Ct 1877 (1972). We reverse.

I

The victim of the offenses in question lived in an apartment on the south side of Chicago. Shortly after noon on December 14, 1967, she awakened from a nap to find a man standing in the doorway to her bedroom holding a knife. The man entered the bedroom, threw her face down on the bed, and choked her until she was quiet. After covering his face with a bandana, the intruder partially undressed the victim, forced her to commit oral sodomy, and raped her. Then he left, taking a guitar and a flute from the apartment.

When police arrived, the victim gave them a description of her assailant. Although she did not know who he was and had seen his face for only 10 to 15 seconds during the attack, she thought he was the same man who had made offensive remarks to her in a neighborhood bar the night before. She also gave police a notebook she had found next to her bed after the attack.

In the week that followed, police showed the victim two groups of photographs of men. From the first group of 200 she picked about 30 who resembled her assailant in height, weight, and build. From the second group of about 10, she picked two or three. One of these was of petitioner. Police also found a letter in the notebook that the victim had given them. Investigation revealed that it was written by a woman with whom petitioner had been staying. The letter had been taken from the woman's home in her absence, and petitioner appeared to be the only other person who had access to the home.

On the evening of December 20, 1967, police arrested petitioner at his apartment and held him overnight pending a preliminary hearing to determine whether he should be bound over to the grand jury and to set bail. The next morning, a policeman accompanied the victim to Cook County Municipal Court for the hearing. The policeman told her she was going to view a suspect and should identify him if she could. He also had her sign a complaint that named petitioner as her assailant. At the hearing, petitioner's name was called and he was led before the bench. The judge told petitioner that he was charged with rape and deviate sexual behavior. The judge then called the victim, who had been in the courtroom waiting for the case to be called, to come before the bench. The State's attorney stated that police had found evidence linking petitioner with the offenses charged. He asked the victim whether she saw her assailant in the courtroom, and she pointed at petitioner. The State's attorney then requested a continuance of the hearing because more time was needed to check fingerprints. The judge granted the continuance and fixed bail. Petitioner was not represented by counsel at this hearing, and the court did not offer to appoint counsel.

At a subsequent hearing, petitioner was bound over to the grand jury, which indicted him for rape, deviate sexual behavior, burglary, and robbery. Counsel was appointed, and he moved to suppress the victim's identification of petitioner because it had been elicited at the preliminary hearing through an unnecessarily suggestive procedure at which petitioner was not represented by counsel. After an evidentiary hearing the trial court denied the motion on the ground that the prosecution had shown an independent basis for the victim's identification.

At trial, the victim testified on direct examination by the prosecution that she had identified petitioner as her assailant at the preliminary hearing. She also testified that the defendant on trial was the man who had raped her. The prosecution's other evidence linking petitioner with the crimes was the letter found in the victim's apartment. Defense counsel stipulated that petitioner had taken the letter from his woman friend's home, but he presented evidence that petitioner might have lost the notebook containing the letter at the neighborhood bar the night before the attack. The defense theory was that the victim, who also was in the bar that night, could have picked up the notebook by mistake and taken it home. The defense also called witnesses who testified that petitioner was with them in a college lunchroom in another part of Chicago at the time the attack was committed.

The jury found petitioner guilty on all four counts, thus rejecting his theory and alibi. The trial court sentenced him to 30 to 50 years in prison. The Illinois Supreme Court affirmed. People v Moore, 51 Ill 2d 79, 281 NE2d 294 (1972). It rejected petitioner's argument that the victim's identification testimony should have been excluded, on the ground that the prosecution had shown an "independent basis" for the identification. Id., at 86–87, 281 NE2d, at 298. After this Court denied certiorari, 409 US 979, 34 L Ed 2d 242, 93 S Ct 331 (1972), petitioner sought a writ of habeas corpus from the Federal District Court. He contended that admission of the identification testimony at trial violated his Sixth and Fourteenth Amendment rights. Relying on the transcript from the state proceedings, the District Court denied the writ in an unpublished opinion, again on the ground that the prosecution had shown an independent basis for the identification. App 31–35. The Court of Appeals for the Seventh Circuit affirmed in an unpublished opinion, App 38–46, and we granted certiorari. 429 US 1061, 50 L Ed 2d 776, 97 S Ct 783 (1977).

II

United States v Wade, 388 US 218, 18 L Ed 2d 1149, 87 S Ct 1926 (1967), held that a pretrial corporeal identification conducted after a suspect has been indicted is a critical stage in a criminal prosecution at which the Sixth Amendment entitles the accused to the presence of counsel. The Court emphasized the dangers inherent in a pretrial identification conducted in the absence of counsel. Persons who conduct the identification procedure may suggest, intentionally or unintentionally, that they expect the witness to identify the accused. Such a suggestion, coming from a police officer or prosecutor, can lead a witness to make a mistaken identification. The witness then will be predisposed to adhere to this identification in subsequent testimony at trial. 388 US, at 229, 235–236, 18 L Ed 2d 1149, 87 S Ct 1926. If an accused's counsel is present at the pretrial identification, he can serve both his client's and the prosecution's interests by objecting to suggestive features of a procedure before they influence a witness' identification. Id., at 236, 238, 18 L Ed 2d 1149, 87 S Ct 1926. In view of the "variables and pitfalls" that exist at an uncounseled pretrial identification, id., at 235, 18 L Ed 2d 1149, 87 S Ct 1926, the Wade Court reasoned that

> "the first line of defense must be the prevention of unfairness and the lessening of the hazards of eyewitness identification at the lineup itself. The trial which might determine the accused's fate may well not be that in the courtroom but that at the

pretrial confrontation, with the State aligned against the accused, the witness the sole jury, and the accused unprotected against the overreaching, intentional or unintentional, and with little or no effective appeal from the judgment there rendered by the witness—'that's the man.'" Id., at 235–236, 18 L Ed 2d 1149, 87 S Ct 1926.

Wade and its companion case, Gilbert v California, 388 US 263, 18 L Ed 2d 1178, 87 S Ct 1951 (1967), also considered the admissibility of evidence derived from a corporeal identification conducted in violation of the accused's right to counsel. In Wade, witnesses to a robbery who had identified the defendant at the uncounseled pretrial lineup testified at trial on direct examination by the prosecution that he was the man who had committed the robbery. The prosecution did not elicit from the witnesses the fact that they had identified the defendant at the pretrial lineup. Nevertheless, because of the likelihood that the witnesses' in-court identifications were based on their observations of the defendant at the uncounseled lineup rather than at the scene of the crime, the Court held that this testimony should have been excluded unless the prosecution could "establish by clear and convincing evidence that the in-court identifications were based upon observations of the suspect other than the lineup identification." 388 US, at 240, 18 L Ed 2d 1149, 87 S Ct 1926.

Gilbert differed from Wade in one critical respect. In Gilbert the prosecution did elicit testimony in its case-in-chief that witnesses had identified the accused at an uncounseled pretrial lineup. The Court recognized that such testimony would "enhance the impact of [a witness'] in-court identification on the jury and seriously aggravate whatever derogation exists of the accused's right to a fair trial." 388 US, at 273–274, 18 L Ed 2d 1178, 87 S Ct 1951. Because "[t]hat testimony [was] the direct result of the illegal lineup 'come at by exploitation of [the primary] illegality[,]' Wong Sun v United States, 371 US 471, 478, [9 L Ed 2d 441, 83 S Ct 407]," the prosecution was "not entitled to show that the testimony had an independent source." Id., at 272–273, 18 L Ed 2d 1178, 87 S Ct 1951; see also Wade, supra, at 240 n 32, 18 L Ed 2d 1149, 87 S Ct 1926. The Court announced this exclusionary rule in the belief that such a sanction is necessary "to assure that law enforcement officers will respect the accused's constitutional right to the presence of his counsel at the critical lineup." Id., at 273, 18 L Ed 2d 1178, 87 S Ct 1951. The Court therefore reversed the conviction and remanded to the state court for a determination of whether admission of this evidence was harmless constitutional error under Chapman v California, 386 US 18, 17 L Ed 2d 705, 87 S Ct 824, 24 ALR3d 1065 (1967), 388 US, at 274, 18 L Ed 2d 1178, 87 S Ct 1951.

In Kirby v Illinois, 406 US 682, 32 L Ed 2d 411, 92 S Ct 1877 (1972), the Court made clear that the right to counsel announced in Wade and Gilbert attaches only to corporeal identifications conducted "at or after the initiation of adversary judicial criminal proceedings—whether by way of formal charge, preliminary hearing, indictment, information, or arraignment." Id., at 689, 32 L Ed 2d 411, 92 S Ct 1877 (plurality opinion). This is so because the initiation of such proceedings "marks the commencement of the 'criminal prosecutions' to which alone the explicit guarantees of the Sixth Amendment are applicable." Id., at 690, 32 L Ed 2d 411, 92 S Ct

1877. Thus, in Kirby the Court held that the prosecution's evidence of a robbery victim's one-on-one stationhouse identification of an uncounseled suspect shortly after the suspect's arrest was admissible because adversary judicial criminal proceedings had not yet been initiated. In such cases, however, due process protects the accused against the introduction of evidence of, or tainted by, unreliable pretrial identifications obtained through unnecessarily suggestive procedures. Id., at 690–691, 32 L Ed 2d 411, 92 S Ct 1877; Neil v Biggers, 409 US 188, 34 L Ed 2d 401, 93 S Ct 375 (1972); Stovall v Denno, 388 US 293, 18 L Ed 2d 1199, 87 S Ct 1967 (1967); see generally Manson v Brathwaite, ___ US ___, 53 L Ed 2d 140, 97 S Ct 2243 (1977).

III

In the instant case, petitioner argues that the preliminary hearing at which the victim identified him marked the initiation of adversary judicial criminal proceedings against him. Hence, under Wade, Gilbert, and Kirby, he was entitled to the presence of counsel at that confrontation. Moreover, the prosecution introduced evidence of this uncounseled corporeal identification at trial in its case-in-chief. Petitioner contends that under Gilbert, this evidence should have been excluded, without regard to whether there was an "independent source" for it.

The Court of Appeals took a different view of the case. It read Kirby as holding that evidence of a corporeal identification conducted in the absence of defense counsel must be excluded only if the identification is made after the defendant is indicted. App 45–46. Such a reading cannot be squared with Kirby itself, which held that an accused's rights under Wade and Gilbert attach to identifications conducted "at or after the initiation of adversary judicial criminal proceedings," including proceedings instituted "by way of formal charge [or] preliminary hearing." 406 US, at 689, 32 L Ed 2d 411, 92 S Ct 1877. The prosecution in this case was commenced under Illinois law when the victim's complaint was filed in court. See Ill Rev Stat Ch 38, § 111 (1970). The purpose of the preliminary hearing was to determine whether there was probable cause to bind petitioner over to the grand jury and to set bail. Id., §§ 109–1, 109–3. Petitioner had the right to oppose the prosecution at that hearing by moving to dismiss the charges and to suppress the evidence against him. Id., § 109-3(e). He faced counsel for the State, who elicited the victim's identification, summarized the State's other evidence against petitioner, and urged that the State be given more time to marshal its evidence. It is plain that "[t]he government ha[d] committed itself to prosecute," and that petitioner found "himself faced with the prosecutorial forces of organized society, and immersed in the intricacies of substantive and procedural criminal law." Kirby, supra, at 689, 32 L Ed 2d 411, 92 S Ct 1877. The State candidly concedes that this preliminary hearing marked the "initiation of adversary judicial criminal proceedings" against petitioner. Brief for Respondent, at 8, and n 1; Tr of Oral Arg, at 32, 34, and it hardly could contend otherwise. The Court of Appeals therefore erred in holding that petitioner's rights under Wade and Gilbert had not yet attached at the time of the preliminary hearing.

The Court of Appeals also suggested that Wade and Gilbert did not apply here because the "in-court identification could hardly be considered a lineup." App 45. The meaning of this statement is not entirely clear. If the court meant that a one-on-one identification procedure, as distinguished from a lineup, is not subject to the counsel requirement, it was mistaken. Although Wade and Gilbert both involved lineups, Wade clearly contemplated that counsel would be required in both situations: "The pretrial confrontation for purpose of identification may take the form of a lineup . . . or presentation of the suspect alone to the witness. . . . It is obvious that risks of suggestion attend either form of confrontation. . . ." 388 US at 229, 18 L Ed 2d 1149, 87 S Ct 1926; see also id., at 251, 18 L Ed 2d 1149, 87 S Ct 1926 (WHITE, J., dissenting in part and concurring in part); cf. Stovall v Denno, supra; Kirby v Illinois, supra. Indeed, a one-on-one confrontation generally is thought to present greater risks of mistaken identification than a lineup. E.g., P. Wall, Eye-Witness Identification in Criminal Cases 27–40 (1965); Williams & Hammelmann, Identification Parades, Part I, [1963] Crim L Rev 480–481. There is no reason, then, to hold that a one-on-one identification procedure is not subject to the same requirements as a lineup.

If the court believed that petitioner did not have a right to counsel at this identification procedure because it was conducted in the course of a judicial proceeding, we do not agree. The reasons supporting Wade's holding that a corporeal identification is a critical stage of a criminal prosecution for Sixth Amendment purposes apply with equal force to this identification. It is difficult to imagine a more suggestive manner in which to present a suspect to a witness for their critical first confrontation than was employed in this case. The victim, who had seen her assailant for only 10 to 15 seconds, was asked to make her identification after she was told that she was going to view a suspect, after she was told his name and heard it called as he was led before the bench, and after she heard the prosecutor recite the evidence believed to implicate petitioner. Had petitioner been represented by counsel, some or all of this suggestiveness could have been avoided.

In sum, we are unpersuaded by the reasons advanced by the Court of Appeals for distinguishing the identification procedure in this case from those considered in Wade and Gilbert. Here, as in those cases, petitioner's Sixth Amendment rights were violated by a corporeal identification conducted after the initiation of adversary judicial criminal proceedings and in the absence of counsel. The courts below thought that the victim's testimony at trial that she had identified petitioner at an uncounseled pretrial confrontation was admissible even if petitioner's rights had been violated, because there was an "independent source" for the victim's identification at the uncounseled confrontation. 51 Ill 2d, at 86–87, 281 NE2d, at 298; App 35 (District Court), 45–46 (Court of Appeals). But Gilbert held that the prosecution cannot buttress its case-in-chief by introducing evidence of a pretrial identification made in violation of the accused's Sixth Amendment rights, even if it can prove that the pretrial identification had an independent source. "That testimony is the direct result of the illegal lineup 'come at by exploitation of [the primary] illegality.'" Gilbert, supra, at 272–273, 18 L Ed 2d 1178, 87 S Ct 1951, and the prosecution is "therefore not entitled to show that the testimony had an independent source." Id., at 273, 18 L Ed 2d 1178, 87 S Ct 1951. Because the prosecution made use of such testimony in this case, petitioner is entitled to the benefit of the strict rule of Gilbert.

IV

In view of the violation of petitioner's Sixth and Fourteenth Amendment right to counsel at the pretrial corporeal identification, and of the prosecution's exploitation at trial of evidence derived directly from that violation, we reverse the judgment of the Court of Appeals and remand for a determination of whether the failure to exclude that evidence was harmless constitutional error under Chapman v California, 386 US 18, 17 L Ed 2d 705, 87 S Ct 824, 24 ALR3d 1065 (1967). See Gilbert, supra, at 274, 18 L Ed 2d 1178, 87 S Ct 1951. That court also will be free on remand to re-examine the other issues presented by the petition, upon which we do not pass.

Reversed and remanded.

MINNESOTA, Petitioner *v.* MARSHALL DONALD MURPHY

—US —, 104 S.C. 1136 79 L Ed 2d 409, (1984)

Justice White delivered the opinion of the Court.

[1a] In this case, respondent Murphy, who was on probation, made incriminating admissions during a meeting with his probation officer. The issue before us is whether the Fifth and Fourteenth Amendments prohibit the introduction into evidence of the admissions in Murphy's subsequent criminal prosecution.

I

In 1974, Marshall Murphy was twice questioned by Minneapolis Police concerning the rape and murder of a teenage girl. No charges were then brought. In 1980, in connection with a prosecution for criminal sexual conduct arising out of an unrelated incident, Murphy pleaded guilty to a reduced charge of false imprisonment. He was sentenced to a prison term of 16 months, which was suspended, and three years' probation. The terms of Murphy's probation required, among other things, that he participate in a treatment program for sexual offenders at Alpha House, report to his probation officer as directed, and be truthful with the probation officer "in all matters." Failure to comply with these conditions, Murphy was informed, could result in his return to the sentencing court for a probation revocation hearing. App to Pet for Cert C33–C35.

Murphy met with his probation officer at her office approximately once a month, and his probation continued without incident until July 1981, when the officer learned that he had abandoned the treatment program. The probation officer then wrote to Murphy and informed him that failure to set up a meeting would "result in an immediate request for a warrant." Id., at C35. At a meeting in late July, the officer agreed not to seek revocation of probation for nonparticipation in the treatment program since Murphy was employed and doing well in other areas.

[2a] In September 1981, an Alpha House counselor informed the probation officer that, during the course of treatment, Murphy had admitted to a rape and murder in 1974. After discussions with her superior, the officer determined that the police should have this information. She then wrote to Murphy and asked him to contact her to discuss a treatment plan for the remainder of his probationary period. Although she did not contact the police before the meeting, the probation officer knew in advance that she would report any incriminating statements.

[3a] Upon receipt of the letter, Murphy arranged to meet with his probation officer in her office on September 28, 1981. The officer opened the meeting by telling Murphy about the information she had received from the Alpha House counselor and expressing her belief that this information evinced his continued need for treatment. Murphy became angry about what he considered to be a breach of his confidences and stated that he "felt like calling a lawyer." The probation officer replied that Murphy would have to deal with that problem outside the office; for the moment, their primary concern was the relationship between the crimes that Murphy had admitted to the Alpha House counselor and the incident that led to his conviction for false imprisonment.

During the course of the meeting, Murphy denied the false imprisonment charge, admitted that he had committed the rape and murder, and attempted to persuade the probation officer that further treatment was unnecessary because several extenuating circumstances explained the prior crimes. At the conclusion of the meeting, the officer told Murphy that she had a duty to relay the information to the authorities and encouraged him to turn himself in. Murphy then left the office. Two days later, Murphy called his probation officer and told her that he had been advised by counsel not to surrender himself to the police. The officer then procured the issuance of an arrest and detention order from the judge who had sentenced Murphy on the false imprisonment charge. On October 29, 1981, a State grand jury returned an indictment charging Murphy with first-degree murder.

Murphy sought to suppress testimony concerning his confession on the ground that it was obtained in violation of the Fifth and Fourteenth Amendments. The trial court found that he was not "in custody" at the time of the statement and that the confession was neither compelled nor involuntary despite the absence of warnings similar to those required by Miranda v Arizona, 384 US 436, 16 L Ed 2d 694, 86 S Ct 1602, 10 Ohio Misc 9, 36 Ohio Ops 2d 237, 10 ALR3d 974 (1966). The Minnesota Supreme Court reversed on federal constitutional grounds. Although recognizing that the Fifth Amendment privilege generally is not self-executing, it concluded that, notwithstanding the lack of custody in the usual sense, Murphy's failure to claim the privilege when he was questioned was not fatal to his claim "[b]ecause of the compulsory nature of the meeting, because [Murphy] was under court order to respond truthfully to his agent's questions, and because the agent had substantial reason to believe that [Murphy's] answers were likely to be incriminating." 324 NW2d 340, 344 (1982). In the court's view, "the agent should have warned [Murphy] of his privilege against self-incrimination before she questioned him and . . . her failure to do so, when she had already decided to report his answers to the police, bars use of [Murphy's] confession at this trial." Ibid.

[1b] We granted certiorari to resolve a conflict among state and federal courts concerning whether a statement made by a probationer to his probation officer without prior warnings is admissible in a subsequent criminal proceeding. 459 US ——, 74 L Ed 2d 992, 103 S Ct 784 (1983). We now reverse.

II

[4, 5, 6] The Fifth Amendment, in relevant part, provides that no person "shall be compelled in any criminal case to be a witness against himself." It has long been held that this prohibition not only permits a person to refuse to testify against himself at a criminal trial in which he is a defendant, but also "privileges him not to answer official questions put to him in any other proceeding, civil or criminal, formal or informal, where the answers might incriminate him in future criminal proceedings." Lefkowitz v Turley, 414 US 70, 77, 38 L Ed 2d 274, 94 S Ct 316 (1973). In all such proceedings,

> "a witness protected by the privilege may rightfully refuse to answer unless and until he is protected at least against the use of his compelled answers and evidence derived therefrom in any subsequent criminal case in which he is a defendant. . . . Absent such protection, if he is nevertheless compelled to answer, his answers are inadmissible against him in a later criminal prosecution." Id., at 78, 38 L Ed 2d 274, 94 S Ct 316.

A defendant does not lose this protection by reason of his conviction of a crime; notwithstanding that a defendant is imprisoned or on probation at the time he makes incriminating statements, if those statements are compelled they are inadmissible in a subsequent trial for a crime other than that for which he has been convicted. See Baxter v Palmigiano, 425 U S 308, 316, 47 L Ed 2d 810, 96 S Ct 1551 (1976). The issue in this case is whether the Fifth Amendment right that Murphy enjoyed was violated by the admission into evidence at his trial for another crime of the prior statements made by him to his probation officer.

A

[7, 8, 9] We note first that the general obligation to appear and answer questions truthfully did not in itself convert Murphy's otherwise voluntary statements into compelled ones. In that respect, Murphy was in no better position than the ordinary witness at a trial or before a grand jury who is subpoenaed, sworn to tell the truth, and obligated to answer on the pain of contempt, unless he invokes the privilege and shows that he faces a realistic threat of self-incrimination. The answers of such a witness to questions put to him are not compelled within the meaning of the Fifth Amendment unless the witness is required to answer over his valid claim of the privilege. This much is reasonably clear from our cases.

As this Court has long acknowledged,

> "[t]he [Fifth] Amendment speaks of compulsion. It does not preclude a witness from testifying voluntarily in matters which may incriminate him. If, therefore, he desires the protection of the privilege, he must claim it or he will not be considered to have been 'compelled' within the meaning of the Amendment." United States v Monia, 317 US 424, 427, 87 L Ed 376, 63 S Ct 409 (1943) (footnote omitted).

This principle has been applied in cases involving a variety of criminal and noncriminal investigations. See, e.g., United States v Kordel, 397 US 1, 7–10, 25 L Ed 2d 1, 90 S Ct 763 (1970); Rogers v United States, 340 US 367, 370–371, 95 L Ed 344, 71 S Ct 438, 19 ALR2d 378 (1951); Vajtauer v Commissioner of Immigration, 273 US 103, 112–113, 71 L Ed 560, 47 S Ct 302 (1927). These cases, taken together, "stand for the proposition that, in the ordinary case, if a witness under compulsion to testify makes disclosures instead of claiming the privilege, the government has not 'compelled' him to incriminate himself." Garner v United States, 424 US 648, 654, 47 L Ed 2d 370, 96 S Ct 1178 (1976) (footnote omitted). Witnesses who failed to claim the privilege were once said to have "waived" it, but we have recently abandoned this "vague term," Green v United States, 355 US 184, 191, 2 L Ed 2d 199, 78 S Ct 221, 7 Ohio L Abs 202, 61 ALR2d 1119 (1957), and "made clear that an individual may lose the benefit of the privilege without making a knowing and intelligent waiver." Garner v United States, supra, at 654, n 9, 47 L Ed 2d 370, 96 S Ct 1178.

[10] Although we have sometimes suggested in dicta that the usual rule might give way in situations where the government has "substantial reason to believe that the requested disclosures are likely to be incriminating," Roberts v United States, 445 US 552, 559, 63 L Ed 2d 622, 100 S Ct 1358 (1980), we have never adopted the view that a witness must "put the Government on notice by formally availing himself of the privilege" only when he alone "is reasonably aware of the incriminating tendency of the questions." Id., at 562, n *, 63 L Ed 2d 622, 100 S Ct 1358 (Brennan, J., concurring). It has long been recognized that "[t]he Constitution does not forbid the asking of criminative questions," United States v Monia, supra, at 433, 87 L Ed 376, 63 S Ct 409 (Frankfurter, J., dissenting), and nothing in our prior cases suggests that the incriminating nature of a question, by itself, excuses a timely assertion of the privilege. See, e.g., United States v Mandujano, 425 US 564, 574–575, 48 L Ed 2d 212, 96 S Ct 1768 (1976) (plurality opinion). If a witness—even one under a general compulsion to testify—answers a question that both he and the government should reasonably expect to incriminate him, the Court need ask only whether the particular disclosure was "compelled" within the meaning of the Fifth Amendment.

United States v Kordel, supra, perhaps the first case squarely to hold that a witness under compulsion to make disclosures must assert the privilege in a timely manner, is illustrative. In answering interrogatories submitted by the Government in a civil case against a corporation, a corporate officer who had been notified of contemplated criminal action against him supplied evidence and leads helpful in securing his indictment and conviction. Although the relationship between the civil and criminal actions was clear and "[w]ithout question [the officer] could have invoked his Fifth Amendment privilege," 397 US, at 7, 25 L Ed 2d 1, 90 S Ct 763, he did not do so. The Court concluded without hesitation that "[h]is failure at any time to assert the constitutional privilege leaves him in no position to complain now that he was compelled to give testimony against himself." Id., at 10, 25 L Ed 2d 1, 90 S Ct 763 (footnote omitted).

B

[11] Thus it is that a witness confronted with questions that the government should reasonably expect to elicit incriminating evidence ordinarily must assert the privilege rather than answer if he desires not to incriminate himself. If he asserts the privilege, he "may not be required to answer a question if there is some rational basis for believing that it will incriminate him, at least without *at that time* being assured that neither it nor its fruits may be used against him" in a subsequent criminal proceeding. Maness v Meyers, 419 US 449, 473, 42 L Ed 2d 574, 95 S Ct 584 (1975) (1976) (White, J., concurring in the result) (emphasis in original). But if he chooses to answer, his choice is considered to be voluntary since he was free to claim the privilege and would suffer no penalty as the result of his decision to do so. As the Minnesota Supreme Court recognized, application of this general rule is inappropriate in certain well-defined situations. In each of those situations, however, some identifiable factor "was held to deny the individual a 'free choice to admit, to deny, or to refuse to answer.' " Garner v United States, supra, at 657, 47 L Ed 2d 370, 96 S Ct 1178 (quoting Lisenba v California, 314 US 219, 241, 86 L Ed 166, 62 S Ct 280 (1941)). Because we conclude that no such factor was present here, we hold that the Minnesota Supreme Court erred in excluding the probation officer's testimony.

I

[12] A well-known exception to the general rule addresses the problem of confessions obtained from suspects in police custody. Not only is custodial interrogation ordinarily conducted by officers who are "acutely aware of the potentially incriminatory nature of the disclosures sought," Garner v United

States, supra, at 657, 47 L Ed 2d 370, 96 S Ct 1178, but also the custodial setting is thought to contain "inherently compelling pressures which work to undermine the individual's will to resist and to compel him to speak where he would not otherwise do so freely." Miranda v Arizona, 384 US, at 467, 16 L Ed 2d 694, 86 S Ct 1602, 10 Ohio Misc 9, 36 Ohio Ops 2d 237, 10 ALR3d 974. See Schneckloth v Bustamonte, 412 US 218, 246–247, 36 L Ed 2d 854, 93 S Ct 2041 (1973). [To dissipate "the overbearing compulsion . . . caused by isolation of a suspect in police custody," United States v Washington, 431 US 181, 187, n 5, 52 L Ed 2d 238, 97 S Ct 1814 (1977), the Miranda Court required the exclusion of incriminating statements obtained during custodial interrogation unless the suspect fails to claim the Fifth Amendment privilege after being suitably warned of his right to remain silent and of the consequences of his failure to assert it. 384 US, at 467–469, 475–477, 16 L Ed 2d 694, 86 S Ct 1602, 10 Ohio Misc 9, 36 Ohio Ops 2d 237, 10 ALR3d 974. We have consistently held, however, that this extraordinary safeguard "does not apply outside the context of the inherently coercive custodial interrogations for which it was designed." Roberts v United States, 445 U S, at 560, 63 L Ed 2d 622, 100 S Ct 1358.

[13] The Minnesota Supreme Court recognized that Murphy was not "in custody" when he made his incriminating admissions. He was, to be sure, subject to a number of restrictive conditions governing various aspects of his life, and he would be regarded as "in custody" for purposes of federal habeas corpus. See Jones v Cunningham, 371 US 236, 241–243, 9 L Ed 2d 285, 83 S Ct 373, 92 ALR3d 675 (1963). But custody in that context has been defined broadly to effectuate the purposes of the writ, id., at 243, 9 L Ed 2d 285, 83 S Ct 373, 92 ALR2d 675; Hensley v Municipal Court, 411 US 345, 349–351, 36 L Ed 2d 294, 93 S Ct 1571 (1973), and custody for Miranda purposes has been more narrowly circumscribed. See Oregon v Mathiason, 429 US 492, 50 L Ed 2d 714, 97 S Ct 711 (1977) (per curiam). Under the narrower standard appropriate in the Miranda context, it is clear that Murphy was not "in custody" for purposes of receiving Miranda protection since there was no " 'formal arrest or restraint on freedom of movement' of the degree associated with a formal arrest." California v Beheler, 463 US ——, 77 L Ed 2d 1275, 103 S Ct 3517 (1983) (per curiam) (quoting Oregon v Mathiason, supra, at 495, 50 L Ed 2d 714, 97 S Ct 711).]

[14a] Notwithstanding the inapplicability of Miranda, the Minnesota Supreme Court held that the probation officer's failure to inform Murphy of the Fifth Amendment privilege barred use of his confession at trial. Four factors have been advanced in support of this conclusion, but we find them, alone or in combination, insufficient to excuse Murphy's failure to claim the privilege in a timely manner.

[14b] First, the probation officer could compel Murphy's attendance and truthful answers. The Minnesota Supreme Court failed to explain how this transformed a routine interview into an inherently coercive setting. In our view, this factor subjected Murphy to less intimidating pressure than is imposed on grand jury witnesses, who are sworn to tell the truth and placed in a setting conducive to truthtelling. Although warnings in both contexts might serve to dissipate "any possible coercion or unfairness resulting from a witness' misimpression that he must answer truthfully even questions with incriminating aspects," United States v Washington, supra, at 188, 52 L Ed 2d 238, 97 S Ct 1814, we have never held that they must be given to grand jury witnesses, id., at 186, 52 L Ed 2d 238, 97 S Ct 1814, and we decline to require them here since the totality of the circumstances is not such as to overbear a probationer's free will. See Rogers v Richmond, 365 US 534, 544, 5 L Ed 2d 760, 81 S Ct 735 (1961).

[14c, 15] Second, the probation officer consciously sought incriminating evidence. We have already explained that this factor does not give rise to a self-executing privilege, ante, at ——, 79 L Ed 2d ——, and we pause here only to emphasize that police officers questioning persons suspected of crimes often consciously seek incriminating statements. The mere fact that an investigation has focused on a suspect does not trigger the need for Miranda warnings in noncustodial settings, Beckwith v United States, 425 US 341, 48 L Ed 2d 1, 96 S Ct 1612 (1976), and the probation officer's knowledge and intent have no bearing on the outcome of this case.

[14d] Third, Murphy did not expect questions about prior criminal conduct and could not seek counsel before attending the meeting. But the nature of probation is such that probationers should expect to be questioned on a wide range of topics relating to their past criminality. Moreover, the probation officer's letter, which suggested a need to discuss treatment from which Murphy had already been excused, would have led a reasonable probationer to conclude that new information had come to her attention. In any event, Murphy's situation was in this regard indistinguishable from that facing suspects who are questioned in noncustodial settings and grand jury witnesses who are unaware of the scope of an investigation or that they are considered potential defendants. See United States v Washington, supra, at 188–189, 52 L Ed 2d 238, 97 S Ct 1814; Beckwith v United States, supra, at 346–348, 48 L Ed 2d 1, 96 S Ct 1612.

[14e] Fourth, there were no observers to guard against abuse or trickery. Again, this often will be true when a suspect is subjected to noncustodial interrogation, where no warnings are required. Murphy does not allege that the probation officer was not legitimately concerned with the need for further treatment, and we cannot conclude that her actions would have led a reasonable probationer to believe that his statements to her would remain confidential. A probationer cannot pretend ignorance of the fact that his probation officer "is a peace officer, and as such is allied, to a greater or lesser extent, with his fellow peace officers." Fare v Michael C., 442 US 707, 720, 61 L Ed 2d 197, 99 S Ct 2560 (1979). See Cabell v Chavez-Salido, 454 US 432, 447, 70 L Ed 2d 677, 102 S Ct 735 (1982). Absent some express or implied promise to the contrary, he may also be charged with knowledge that "the probation officer is duty bound to report wrongdoing by the [probationer] when it comes to his attention, even if by communication from the [probationer] himself." Fare v Michael C., supra, at

720, 61 L Ed 2d 197, 99 S Ct 2560. The fact that Murphy apparently expressed no surprise on being informed that his statements would be made available to the police, moreover, strongly suggests that he was not misled by any expectation that his statements would remain confidential. See App to Pet for Cert C21 (testimony of Mara Widseth); id., at C28 (testimony of Marshall Murphy).

Even a cursory comparison of custodial interrogation and probation interviews reveals the inaptness of the Minnesota Supreme Court's analogy to Miranda. Custodial arrest is said to convey to the suspect a message that he has no choice but to submit to the officers' will and to confess. Miranda v Arizona, 384 US, at 456–457, 16 L Ed 2d 694, 86 S Ct 1602, 10 Ohio Misc 9, 36 Ohio Ops 2d 237, 10 ALR3d 974. It is unlikely that a probation interview, arranged by appointment at a mutually convenient time, would give rise to a similar impression. Moreover, custodial arrest thrusts an individual into "an unfamiliar atmosphere" or "an interrogation environment . . . created for no purpose other than to subjugate the individual to the will of his examiner." Id., at 457, 16 L Ed 2d 694, 86 S Ct 1602, 10 Ohio Misc 9, 36 Ohio Ops 2d 237, 10 ALR3d 974. Many of the psychological ploys discussed in Miranda capitalize on the suspect's unfamiliarity with the officers and the environment. Murphy's regular meetings with his probation officer should have served to familiarize him with her and her office and to insulate him from psychological intimidation that might overbear his desire to claim the privilege. Finally, the coercion inherent in custodial interrogation derives in large measure from an interrogator's insinuations that the interrogation will continue until a confession is obtained. Id., at 468, 16 L Ed 2d 694, 86 S Ct 1602, 10 Ohio Misc 9, 36 Ohio Ops 2d 237, 10 ALR3d 974. Since Murphy was not physically restrained and could have left the office, any compulsion he might have felt from the possibility that terminating the meeting would have led to revocation of probation was not comparable to the pressure on a suspect who is painfully aware that he literally cannot escape a persistent custodial interrogator.

[14f] We conclude, therefore, that Murphy cannot claim the benefit of the first exception to the general rule that the Fifth Amendment privilege is not self-executing.

II

[16] The general rule that the privilege must be claimed when self-incrimination is threatened has also been deemed inapplicable in cases where the assertion of the privilege is penalized so as to "foreclos[e] a free choice to remain silent, and . . . compe[l] . . . incriminating testimony." Garner v United States, 424 US, at 661, 47 L Ed 2d 370, 96 S Ct 1178. Because revocation of his probation was threatened if he was untruthful with his probation officer, Murphy argues that he was compelled to make incriminating disclosures instead of claiming the privilege. Although this contention is not without force, we find it unpersuasive on close examination.

In each of the so-called "penalty" cases, the state not only compelled an individual to appear and testify, but also sought to induce him to forgo the Fifth Amendment privilege by threatening to impose economic or other sanctions "capable of forcing the self-incrimination which the Amendment forbids." Lefkowitz v Cunningham, 431 US 801, 806, 53 L Ed 2d 1, 97 S Ct 2132 (1977). In most of the cases, the attempt to override the witnesses' privilege proved unsuccessful, and the Court ruled that the state could not constitutionally make good on its prior threat. Lefkowitz v Turley, 414 US, at 79–84, 38 L Ed 2d 274, 94 S Ct 316; Sanitation Men v Commissioner of Sanitation, 392 US 280, 283–284, 20 L Ed 2d 1089, 88 S Ct 1917 (1968); Gardner v Broderick, 392 US 273, 278–279, 20 L Ed 2d 1082, 88 S Ct 1913 (1968). These cases make clear that "a State may not impose substantial penalties because a witness elects to exercise his Fifth Amendment right not to give incriminating testimony against himself." Lefkowitz v Cunningham, supra, at 805, 53 L Ed 2d 1, 97 S Ct 2132. Occasionally, however, an individual succumbed to the pressure placed upon him, failed to assert the privilege, and disclosed incriminating information, which the state later sought to use against him in a criminal prosecution. Garrity v New Jersey, 385 US 493, 17 L Ed 2d 562, 87 S Ct 616 (1967), was such a case, and the Court held that an individual threatened with discharge from employment for exercising the privilege had not waived it by responding to questions rather than standing on his right to remain silent. Id., at 498–499, 17 L Ed 2d 562, 87 S Ct 616.

[17] The threat of punishment for reliance on the privilege distinguishes cases of this sort from the ordinary case in which a witness is merely required to appear and give testimony. A state may require a probationer to appear and discuss matters that affect his probationary status; such a requirement, without more, does not give rise to a self-executing privilege. The result may be different if the questions put to the probationer, however relevant to his probationary status, call for answers that would incriminate him in a pending or later criminal prosecution. There is thus a substantial basis in our cases for concluding that if the state, either expressly or by implication, asserts that invocation of the privilege would lead to revocation of probation, it would have created the classic penalty situation, the failure to assert the privilege would be excused, and the probationer's answers would be deemed compelled and inadmissible in a criminal prosecution.

Even so we must inquire whether Murphy's probation conditions merely required him to appear and give testimony about matters relevant to his probationary status or whether they went farther and required him to choose between making incriminating statements and jeopardizing his conditional liberty by remaining silent. Because we conclude that Minnesota did not attempt to take the extra, impermissible step, we hold that Murphy's Fifth Amendment privilege was not self-executing.

As we have already indicated, Murphy was informed that he was required to be truthful with his probation officer in all matters and that failure to do so could result in revocation of probation. The opinion of the Minnesota Supreme Court made clear that this was indeed the case, but its conclusion that the probation officer's failure to give Murphy adequate warnings barred the use of his incriminating statements in the criminal trial did not rest on the ground that a refusal to furnish incriminating information would have justified revocation of probation. Although the court recognized that imposing a penalty for a valid exercise of the Fifth Amendment privilege could impermissibly foreclose a free choice to remain silent, 324 NW2d, at 342–343, it did not purport to find that Minnesota's probation revocation statute had such an effect. The court relied instead on the fact that Murphy was under legal compulsion to attend the meeting and to answer truthfully the questions of a probation officer who anticipated incriminating answers. Id., at 344. Such compulsion, however, is indistinguishable from that felt by any witness who is required to appear and give testimony, and, as we have already made clear, it is insufficient to excuse Murphy's failure to exercise the privilege in a timely manner.

The State court did not attempt to define the precise contours of Murphy's obligation to respond to questions. On its face, Murphy's probation condition proscribed only false statements; it said nothing about his freedom to decline to answer particular questions and certainly contained no suggestion that his probation was conditional on his waiving his Fifth Amendment privilege with respect to further criminal prosecution. "At this point in our history virtually every schoolboy is familiar with the concept, if not the language, of the [Fifth Amendment]." Michigan v Tucker, 417 US 433, 439, 41 L Ed 2d 182, 94 S Ct 2357 (1974). Yet Murphy, although he had a right to do so, see State v Austin, 295 NW2d 246 (Minn 1980), did not seek clarification of the condition. Without the benefit of an authoritative state-court construction of the condition, we are hesitant to read into the truthfulness requirement an additional obligation that Murphy refrain from raising legitimate objections to furnishing information that might lead to his conviction for another crime.

Whether we employ a subjective or an objective test, there is no reasonable basis for concluding that Minnesota attempted to attach an impermissible penalty to the exercise of the privilege against self-incrimination. There is no direct evidence that Murphy confessed because he feared that his probation would be revoked if he remained silent. Unlike the police officers in Garrity v New Jersey, 385 US 493, 17 L Ed 2d 562, 87 S Ct 616 (1967), Murphy was not expressly informed during the crucial meeting with his probation officer that an assertion of the privilege would result in the imposition of a penalty. And the fact that Murphy apparently felt no compunction about adamantly denying the false imprisonment charge on which he had been convicted before admitting to the rape and murder strongly suggests that the "threat" of revocation did not overwhelm his resistance.

[18] If Murphy did harbor a belief that his probation might be revoked for exercising the Fifth Amendment privilege, that belief would not have been reasonable. Our decisions have made clear that the State could not constitutionally carry out a threat to revoke probation for the legitimate exercise of the Fifth Amendment privilege. It is not surprising, then, that neither the State court nor any State officer has suggested otherwise. Indeed, in its brief in this

Court, the State submits that it would not, and legally could not, revoke probation for refusing to answer questions calling for information that would incriminate in separate criminal proceedings. Brief for Petitioner 36–39, and n 7. See also Tr of Oral Arg 7–8, 10–14.

Minnesota's revocation statute, which was accurately summarized in Murphy's notice of probation, see App to Pet for Cert C33–C34, authorizes revocation "[w]hen it appears that the defendant has violated any of the conditions of his probation or has otherwise been guilty of misconduct which warrants the imposing or execution of sentence." Minn Stat § 609.14 (1982). Revocation is not automatic under this provision. Even if the probation officer desires revocation, a probationer must be afforded a hearing, Pearson v State, 308 Minn 287, 289–290, 241 NW2d 490, 492–493 (1976); State ex rel. Halverson v Young, 278 Minn 381, 386–387, 154 NW2d 699, 702–703 (1967), and the court must find that he violated a specific condition, that the violation was intentional or inexcusable, and that the need for confinement outweighs the policies favoring probation. State v Austin, supra, at 250. We have not been advised of any case in which Minnesota has attempted to revoke probation merely because a probationer refused to make nonimmunized disclosures concerning his own criminal conduct; and, in light of our decisions proscribing threats of penalties for the exercise of Fifth Amendment rights, Murphy could not reasonably have feared that the assertion of the privilege would have led to revocation.

Accordingly, we cannot conclude that Murphy was deterred from claiming the privilege by a reasonably perceived threat of revocation.

III

[19] A third exception to the general requirement of a timely assertion of the Fifth Amendment privilege, closely related to the penalty exception, has been developed in the context of the federal occupational and excise taxes on gamblers. In recognition of the pervasive criminal regulation of gambling activities and the fact that claiming the privilege in lieu of filing a return would tend to incriminate, the Court has held that the privilege may be exercised by failing to file. Marchetti v United States, 390 US 39, 19 L Ed 2d 889, 88 S Ct 697, 43 Ohio Ops 2d 215 (1968); Grosso v United States, 390 US 62, 19 L Ed 2d 906, 88 S Ct 709, 43 Ohio Ops 2d 226 (1968). See also Mackey v United States, 401 US 667, 28 L Ed 2d 404, 91 S Ct 1160 (1971).

> "[M]aking a claim of privilege when the disclosures were requested, i.e., when the returns were due, would have identified the claimant as a gambler. The Court therefore forgave the usual requirement that the claim of privilege be presented for evaluation in favor of a 'claim' by silence. . . . If a particular gambler would not have incriminated himself by filing the tax returns, the privilege would not justify a failure to file." Garner v United States, 424 US, at 658–659, n 11, 47 L Ed 2d 370, 96 S Ct 1178.

But, while a taxpayer who claims the privilege instead of filing gambling tax returns necessarily identifies himself as a gambler, a probationer confronted with incriminating questions ordinarily will have no problem effectively claiming the privilege at the time disclosures are requested. There exists, therefore, no reason to forgive the requirement that the claim be presented for evaluation in a timely manner.

IV

[1c] We conclude, in summary, that since Murphy revealed incriminating information instead of timely asserting his Fifth Amendment privilege, his disclosures were not compelled incriminations. Because he had not been compelled to incriminate himself, Murphy could not successfully invoke the privilege to prevent the information he volunteered to his probation officer from being used against him in a criminal prosecution.

The judgment of the Minnesota Supreme Court is reversed.

CHAPTER 9

Contents

Eighth Amendment—Prohibitions against Government

§ 9.1 Introduction

It has been noted earlier in this text that the Constitution of the United States grants powers to the government and then limits those powers. The Bill of Rights portion (the first ten amendments) is a portion of the Constitution which limits the powers of the federal government. The Supreme Court, under the Due Process Clause of the Fourteenth Amendment, has made most of the Bill of Rights applicable to state government. As has been demonstrated, this has taken place over a long span of years. Decisions of the Court, one by one, have caused their absorption into the guarantees of state justice rights.

The Eighth Amendment has come before the Court for interpretation several times. The Eighth Amendment as adopted in 1791 reads as follows:

> *Excessive bail shall not be required, nor excessive fines imposed, nor cruel and unusual punishments inflicted.*

The excessive bail provision has not been specifically absorbed into state government limitations by the Court. However, it did mention, in passing upon the constitutionality of a small administrative charge that Illinois placed upon defendants when the state handled bail deposits, that "... Bail, of course, is basic to our system of law, and the Eighth Amendment's proscription of excessive bail has been assumed to have application to the States through the Fourteenth Amendment." Schilb v. Kuebel, 404 U.S. 357, 92 S.Ct. 479, 30 L.Ed.2d 502 (1971).

§ 9.2 Excessive Bail

The phrase "excessive bail" is one that may have a different meaning to different people. It is therefore very difficult for an appellate court to criticize a lower court judge who fixed bail in what the defendant claims is an excessive amount. The cases that come before appellate judges or courts for bail review, where the original jurist's decision on bail is modified downward, are those where there is an obvious arbitrary, capricious, and unreasonable amount set as the bail requirement.

If we are to consider that every defendant is presumed to be innocent until proven guilty beyond a reasonable doubt, we must give the defendant every opportunity to an unfettered opportunity to prepare a defense.

The reader should imagine him/herself as being arrested for a robbery committed several days before the arrest. Let us further imagine that the reader is innocent and at the time of the robbery, s/he was in a crowded bar located on the other side of town from the robbery location, imbibing in some spirits with some newfound acquaintances of the night. The reader is processed in the usual police procedure and comes before a magistrate who is determined that no robbers will be tolerated in his/her town. Bail is fixed at $25,000 and you do not have more than $50 to your name and on your person; you have no friends or relatives who have any assets that can be used as collateral for your bail. A lawyer is assigned to defend you and you protest that you are innocent. The lawyer asks you if you have any witnesses and you answer that if you could only get out of jail, you could locate some of the people who were at the bar on the night of the robbery who would testify that you were at the bar with them when the robbery took place. This is the dilemma many defendants find themselves in. On the other hand, if bail conditions were too lenient, many defendants would forfeit bail and they would defeat the ends of justice.

In Stack v. Boyle, 342 U.S. 1, 72 S.Ct. 1, 96 L.Ed. 3 (1951), bail was fixed for $50,000 in Federal District Court for each defendant who was charged with violating the Smith Act. The case reached the Supreme Court where Chief Justice Vinson wrote the opinion. He said, "From the passage of the Judiciary Act of 1789 to the present Federal Rules of Criminal Procedure Rule 46(a)(1), federal law has unequivocably provided that a person arrested for a noncapital offense SHALL be admitted to bail. This traditional right to freedom before conviction permits the unhampered preparation of a defense, and serves to prevent the infliction of punishment prior to conviction. Unless this right to bail before trial is preserved, the presumption of innocence, secured only after centuries of struggle would lose its meaning ... To infer from the fact of indictment alone a need for bail in a unusually high amount is an arbitrary act ...." Justice Jackson, in a concurring opinion, wrote inter alia, "The question when application for bail is made relates to each one's trustworthiness to appear for trial and what security will supply reasonable assurance of his appearance."

Bail conditions should not be set so high that it is tantamount to punishment. A judge should take the following into consideration in setting bail:

1. The nature and circumstances of the offense charged;
2. The weight of the evidence against the accused;

3. The accused's family ties;
4. Employment;
5. Financial resources;
6. Character and mental condition;
7. The length of his residence;
8. The prior convictions of accused;
9. The record of appearance at court proceedings or flight or failure to appear at court proceedings.
   (See Bail Reform Act of 1966, Section 3146b)

Many states have provisions in their constitutions limiting the right to bail in capital cases when the proof is evident or the presumption is great. In light of the more recent pronouncement of the Court with respect to imposition of the death penalty in certain situations as being a violation of the Fourteenth Amendment and Eighth Amendment Cruel and Unusual Punishment Clause, there may be newer views with respect to bail conditions in "capital" offenses. Future courts will have to tell us which path to take. See Furman v. Georgia, 408 U.S. 238, 92 S.Ct. 2726, 33 L.Ed.2d 346 (1972); Gregg v. Georgia, 428 U.S. 242, 96 S.Ct. 2960, 49 L.Ed.2d 859 (1976).

§ 9.3 Excessive Fines

The issue of an excessive fine has surfaced where a mayor-judge sat in a court which raised a substantial portion of the expenses of running the village through the imposition of fines. The Court held where a substantial portion of a municipality's funds are raised in a mayor's court, the mayor, having wide executive powers, cannot be an impartial judge to determine the law and facts on a not guilty plea. This would not be a fair trial and would be a deprivation of the right of due process as contained in the Fourteenth Amendment. Ward v. Village of Monroeville, Ohio, 409 U.S. 57, 93 S.Ct. 80, 34 L.Ed.2d 267 (1973).

Fines for violation of statutes are fixed by the legislature. This could be the legislature of the state, the county, the city, the town, the village or any other duly constituted entity established by the state. A fine might be so high that it becomes confiscatory and a violation of the Due Process Clause of the Fourteenth Amendment. Similarly, statutes which require forfeiture of personal or real property might be violations of due process under certain conditions. For example, it was held that a statute providing for the confiscation or forfeiture of vehicles used to transport contraband may be unconstitutional on the ground of denial of due process of law if provision is not made for notice of the proceedings to the owner of the vehicle and to all persons having an interest in it, and an opportunity afforded them to be heard. N.Y.—Cohen v. City of New York, 69 Misc.2d 189, 329 N.Y.S.2d 596 (1972); Cal.—People v. Broad, 216 Cal. 1, 12 P.2d 941, cert.den. 287 U.S. 661, 53 S.Ct. 220, 77 L.Ed. 570.

§ 9.4 Cruel and Unusual Punishment

There are some countries which even to this day punish persons convicted of crimes by cutting off their hands, castration, beheading in a public ceremony, and other similar procedures. The history of Anglo-Saxon law is not free from such punishments. Even in America, we find in village restorations that there were whipping posts erected in the center of the village. We also can see the stocks where malefactors were shackled in the village square to be mocked and taunted by the citizenry. Some even were known to be stoned while they were so confined.

The English Declaration of Rights of 1688 had a provision forbidding the infliction of cruel and unusual punishment. This was the forerunner of the constitutional mandate against cruel and unusual punishment as contained in the Eighth Amendment. The command was addressed initially to legislative action but by interpretations of the Court, it has also been directed towards executive action as the following sections will reveal. This provision of the Eighth Amendment has been made applicable to state action as well as federal action by Trop v. Dulles, 356 U.S. 86, 78 S.Ct. 590, 2 L.Ed.2d 630 (1958), but more specifically in Robinson v. California, 370 U.S. 660, 82 S.Ct. 1417, 8 L.Ed.2d 758 (1962).

The issue still remains as to what constitutes cruel and unusual punishment. At the time of the adoption of the constitution, retribution was accepted as a biblical command. Surely the taking of a life would call for the life of the malefactor. The Court has treated this and similar problems as will be explained in the sections which follow.

§ 9.5 Punishment for Capital Crimes

There are some crimes that many people believe require the most severe retribution against the perpetrator. Even moderate thinking people will be heard to say, "There is no punishment that can fit this outrageous act." Criminologists argue that the function of punishment inflicted upon convicted criminals should only be severe enough to rehabilitate the offender and act as a deterrent to others not to commit the act.

The divergence of opinion is great. Notwithstanding this, the Eighth Amendment prescribes that no cruel and unusual punishments can be imposed. The issue then reverts to what constitutes cruel and unusual punishment. Surely the framers of the Constitution did not envisage the abolition of the death penalty. Yet the Supreme Court in nine separate opinions in Furman v. Georgia, 408 U.S. 238, 92 S.Ct. 2726, 33 L.Ed.2d 346 (1972), held that the conviction of the defendant should be reversed. Five justices agreed, for different reasons, that the death sentences in three cases that were heard simultaneously before the Court should be reversed. The other four dissented, each with a different reason. Great difficulty is encountered in attempting to get one common ground for all of the decisions. An educated guess is that if the sanction of death penalty was provided without discrimination based on race, financial condition, or intelligence, the punishment may not be considered as violative of the Due Process of Law Clause and might be upheld as constitutional.

In Gregg v. Georgia, 428 U.S. 242, 96 S.Ct. 2960, 49 L.Ed.2d 859 (1976), a 7–2 majority decision delivered by Mr. Justice Stewart upheld the post Furman-Georgia capital sentencing procedures; thereby it rejected the basic idea that "the punishment of death always, regardless of the enormity of the offense or the procedure followed in imposing the sentence, is cruel and unusual punishment in violation of the Constitution." The Gregg case was decided along with its companion cases of Proffit v. Florida, 428 U.S. 242, 96 S.Ct. 2960, 50 L.Ed.2d 30 (1976), and Jurek v. Texas, 428 U.S. 262, 96 S.Ct. 2950, 50 L.Ed.2d 30 (1976), wherein the Court divided in the same way but different justices wrote the Court's decision in each case. In Proffit, Powell, J., wrote the decision and in Jurek, Stevens, J., was the Justice writing the decision.

In Gregg v. Georgia (supra) the petitioner had been sentenced to death after being convicted of murder under a post Furman-Georgia procedure wherein the death penalty was retained for six categories of crime: murder, kidnapping for ransom or where the victim is harmed, armed robbery, rape, treason, and aircraft hijacking. "The capital defendant's guilt or innocence is determined in the traditional manner, either by a trial judge or a jury, in the first stage . . . If the trial is by jury, the trial judge is required to charge lesser included offenses when they are supported by any view of the evidence. After a verdict, finding, or plea of guilty to a capital crime, a presentence hearing is conducted before whomever made the determination of guilt. . . . the judge (or jury) shall hear additional evidence in extenuation, mitigation, and aggravation of punishment, including the record of any prior criminal convictions and pleas of guilty or pleas of nolo contendere of the defendant, or the absence of any prior conviction and pleas: Provided however, that only such evidence in aggravation as the State has made known to the defendant prior to his trial shall be admissible. The judge (or jury) shall also hear argument by defendant or his counsel and the prosecuting attorney. . . ."

Evidence submitted during the first stage may be considered during the sentencing trial without being resubmitted. The judge is required to consider or to charge in the sentencing trial "any mitigating circumstances or aggravating circumstances otherwise authorized by law and any of the statutory aggravating circumstances which may be supported by the evidence . . . . Before a convicted defendant may be sentenced to death, however, except in cases of treason or aircraft hijacking, the jury, or the trial judge in cases tried without a jury, must find beyond a reasonable doubt, one of the statutory aggravating circumstances and then elects to impose that sentence. If the verdict is death the jury or judge must specify the aggravating circumstance(s) found. In jury cases, the trial judge is bound by the jury's recommended sentence. In addition to the conventional appellate process available in all criminal cases, provision is made for special expedited direct review by the Supreme Court of Georgia of the appropriateness of imposing the sentence of death in the particular case . . . ."

The Court held that "the punishment of death does not invariably violate the Constitution . . . We hold that the death penalty is not a form of punishment that may never be imposed, regardless of the circumstances of the offense, regardless of the character of the offender, and regardless of the procedure followed in reaching the decision to impose it . . . we hold that the statutory system under which Gregg was sentenced to death does not violate the Constitution."

The Court reasoned that the legislatures of thirty-five states expressed the will of the people in enacting new statutes providing for the death penalty after the Furman decision. The Court further states "that a heavy burden rests on those who would attack the judgment of the representatives of the people." It studied the procedures of the Georgia statute and found that the death penalty in this case was pursuant to due process and was not arrived at capriciously and arbitrarily.

In Coker v. Georgia, 433 U.S. 584, 97 S.Ct. 2861, 53 L.Ed.2d 982, 21 Cr.L. 3199 (1977), the Court held for the principle that the death penalty for the crime of rape is grossly disproportionate punishment when the perpetrator raped an adult woman, if the rapist does not himself take the life of his victim, and the penalty is in violation of the Eighth Amendment's prohibition against cruel and unusual punishment. However, the Court during the same term decided Dobbert v. Florida, 432 U.S. 282, 97 S.Ct. 2290, 53 L.Ed.2d 344, 21 Cr.L. 3159 (1977). In that case the Court followed the holding in Proffit v. Florida (supra) of Florida's death penalty statute, which provided for a bifurcated trial wherein guilt or innocence was determined, and if the defendant was found guilty, another trial ensued wherein the jury rendered an advisory decision, relating to the punishment. The judge is not bound by the jury's decision. In this case the jury recommended a life sentence for a conviction, inter alia, of first degree murder. The judge imposed the death penalty. The case came to the Court and the petitioner argued that the law changing the role of the judge and jury was ex post facto since there was no death penalty in Florida at the time of the murder because the statute on the books at that time was declared unconstitutional and the current statute requires anyone sentenced to life imprisonment to serve at least twenty-five years before becoming eligible for parole, whereas the prior statute contained no such limitation. The Court held that there was no ex post facto violation of Article I, § 10, in these circumstances.

In GODFREY v. GEORGIA, 446 U.S. 420, 100 S.Ct. 1759, 64 L.Ed.2d 398, 27 Cr.L. 3115 (1980) the death sentence imposed on the petitioner under the hitherto declared constitutional death sentence statute was held to be improperly applied and the case was reversed insofar as the death penalty for convictions of murder when, as the Georgia Supreme Court concluded that "(i) the evidence that the offense was "outrageously or wantonly vile, horrible or inhuman" and must demonstrate "torture, depravity of mind or an aggravated battery to the victim," (ii) the phrase "depravity of mind" comprehended only the kind of mental state that led the murderer to torture or to commit an aggravated battery before killing his victim and (iii) the word "torture" must be construed in PARI MATERIA with "aggravated battery" so as to require evidence of serious physical abuse of the victim before death."

In the instant case, the petitioner, in an unsuccessful attempt to reconcile with his wife shot through a trailer window, killing her instantly, then struck and injured his fleeing daughter and then shot and killed his mother-in-law, all of whom were in the trailer. He then called the Sheriff's office and when they arrived, he acknowledged what he had done and expressed remorse.

The Court held that petitioner's crimes cannot be said to have reflected a consciousness materially more "depraved" than that of any person guilty of murder. Therefore the Court remanded it with respect to the death sentence portion of the judgement.

Where the jury was not instructed to consider a lesser included offense, a defendant, in a capital case who was found guilty of a capital crime, was denied due process in violation of his constitutional rights. BECK v. ALABAMA, 447 U.S. 625, 100 S.Ct. 2392, 65 L.Ed.2d. 392, 27 Cr.L. 3181 (1980).

The question of a mitigating circumstance involving a defendant's unhappy upbringing and emotional disturbance was not considered, in EDDINGS v. OKLAHOMA as a matter of law, —U.S.—, 102 S.Ct. 869, 71 L.Ed.2d. 1, 30 Cr.L. 3047 (1982) in the sentencing of a 16-year-old for the first degree murder for killing a police officer in Oklahoma. The case came on to be heard in the United States Supreme Court where it was held that the death sentence must be vacated as it was imposed without the type of individualized considerations of mitigating factors . . . "required by the Eighth and Fourteenth Amendments in capital cases," citing LOCKETT v. OHIO, 438 U.S. 586, 600.

In ENMUND v. FLORIDA, —U.S.—, 102 S.Ct. 3368, 73 L.Ed.2d. 1140, 31 Cr.L. 3149 (1982) the Court held that the Eighth Amendment prohibits the imposition of the death penalty on defendants who aid and abet felonies during which murders occur, but who do not themselves kill, or intend that a killing take place.

§ 9.6 Solitary Confinement as Punishment

It is often said that one does not appreciate good health until one loses it. So too with the unrestrained freedom to go where one wishes to go and to talk with people of one's own choice. Anyone who has been incarcerated in a prison either as an inmate or as a prison guard in an isolated assignment, such as a "turnkey" or tower post, can understand the emotions that one endures when deprived of the freedom of movement and conversation. It sometimes becomes necessary either for the physical protection of the prisoner or for disciplinary reasons to place the prisoner in solitary confinement where s/he has no contact with anyone other than the person who might feed the prisoner or supply the inmate with other personal necessities. There may or may not be a bed or mattress in the cell, fresh air, light, or sanitary facilities. If the reader can conjure up in his/her mind such intolerable conditions that the animal humane societies would go to court over, these are the conditions that could exist in a prison where the guards and administration have an almost dictatorial power over the prison population. There have been attempts to unionize prisoners and these have met with some results. The inmates soon learn to adjust, if they are lucky, to the society and governance of the prison. However, to leave to the prison keepers the unfettered right to do as they wish with their charges is alien to a democratic society. The Court has been setting up constitutional guidelines within which the prison administrators must perform.

Mental cruelty has been included as constitutionally prohibited as well as physical cruelty. Trop v. Dulles, 356 U.S. 86, 78 S.Ct. 590, 2 L.Ed.2d 630 (1958). It has been decided that unreasonably harsh treatment of a prisoner which is not necessary for his safe confinement is an unconstitutional deprivation of rights. C.A. Pa. 465 F.2d 179, on remand 376 F.Supp. 675. The Court has, however, permitted prison officials to place a prisoner in solitary confinement. Trezza v. Brush, 142 U.S. 160, 12 S.Ct. 158, 35 L.Ed. 974 (1891). Isolated confinement on "death row" does not constitute cruel and unusual punishment. Rosenberg v. Carroll, S.D.N.Y. 99 F.Supp. 630 (1951); Adams v. Pate (7th Cir.C.A.) 445 F.2d 105 (1971); Ind.—Shack v. State, 288 N.E.2d 155. Recoveries are available to prisoners in tort or pursuant to federal civil rights laws if they are subjected to cruel and unusual punishment. Prisoners can also avail themselves of injunctive relief over the warden or jailer which could be additionally reinforced by the warden or jailer being required to post a bond to be forfeited upon proof of violation of the injunction.

A term known as "administrative segregation" is being used sometimes interchangeably with the term "solitary confinement." Sometimes it consists of the placing of a prisoner in a more sheltered environment to protect the prisoner from injury that may be inflicted on the subject by other inmates. Sometimes it is used as a form of punishment by prison administrators. This procedure was used against Aaron Helms following a riot in the Pennsylvania State Prison. Helms was thought to be a leader of the riot and when the authorities regained control, Helms was confined to administrative segregation pending an investigation into his role in the riot. He was given written notice of misconduct charges against him. He had an opportunity to have his version of the events reported. A Hearing Committee reviewed the evidence but no finding of guilt was made. Later criminal charges were lodged against him and a Review Committee ruled that he should remain in administrative segregation as posing a threat to the safety of other inmates and to prison officials, and the security of the prison. Subsequently the Hearing Committee found him guilty of misconduct and ordered him confined in administrative segregation for six months. He sued in Federal Court—He petitioned the U.S. District Court for Habeas Corpus. The Court granted it but was reversed by the Court of Appeals. The U.S. Supreme Court held that prison officials have broad administrative powers and discretionary authority over the institutions they manage, and lawfully incarcerated persons retain only a narrow range of protected liberty interests. Administrative segregation is the sort of confinement that inmates should reasonably anticipate receiving at some point in their incarceration, and does not involve an interest independently protected by the Due Process Clause. The process afforded respondent satisfied the minimum requirements of the due process clause. HEWITT ET AL. PETITIONERS v. ARRON HELMS, —U.S.—, 103 S.Ct. 864, L.Ed.2d. 675, 32 Cr.L. 3037 (1983).

§ 9.7 Prisoners' Access to the Courts

The Court has recognized the right of a prisoner to have access to the courts. It has held unconstitutional a prison rule that restricted access of prisoners to lawyers, investigators, law students, and paraprofessionals. Procunier v. Martinez, 416 U.S. 396, 94 S.Ct. 1800, 40 L.Ed.2d 224 (1974).

However in U.S. v. GOUVEIA, —U.S.—, 104 S.Ct. 2292, L.Ed.2d. 140 (1984) the Court held that the Sixth Amendment does not require the appointment of counsel prior to the initiation of adversary judicial proceedings against indigent inmates who were confined in administrative detention for 19 months before their indictment on federal criminal charges for a murder of an inmate in the prison. Therefore, in effect, they did not have counsel during that time to assist in their access to the court and it was held not to be a violation of the Eighth Amendment.

§ 9.8 Confinement with Hostile Co-Prisoner

When a former police officer or an informant is incarcerated, his/her life is constantly in danger within the prison walls because of the possibility of being killed by co-prisoners. Young, good-looking prisoners are sometimes adopted as the homosexual mates of more domineering prisoners and are forced into committing perverted homosexual acts. Gang rapes and other physical assaults occur all too frequently. In the case of New York State Assoc. for Retarded Children Inc. v. Rockefeller, D.C.N.Y., 357 F.Supp. 752 (1973), it was held that "One of the basic rights of a person in confinement is protection from assaults by fellow inmates or staff . . . Prisoners may not be denied medical care . . . they are entitled to adequate heat during cold weather and to the necessary elements of basic hygiene."

§ 9.9 Incarceration of Sick Persons and Status Offenses

There have been instances where a statute declares a person to be a narcotic addict, an alcoholic, a prostitute, a gambler, or a vagrant. The statutes prescribe sanctions against those who would fall into those categories. These are known to be status offenses. The Court has held status offenses to be unconstitutional under the Fourteenth Amendment due process clause and violative of the prohibition against cruel and unusual punishment.

California made it a crime for a person to "be addicted to the use of narcotics." The Court reversed a ninety-day sentence saying, "We hold that a state law which imprisons a person thus afflicted as a criminal, even though he has never touched a narcotic within the State or been guilty of any irregular behavior there, inflicts a cruel and unusual punishment in violation of the Fourteenth Amendment." Robinson v. California, 370 U.S. 660, 82 S.Ct. 1417, 8 L.Ed.2d 758 (1962) reh.den. 371 U.S. 905, 83 S.Ct. 202, 19 L.Ed.2d 166 (1962).

§ 9.10 Corporal Punishment of Prisoners

It was not uncommon in Anglo-Saxon history to subject a prisoner to all sorts of physical and mental torture. Often a prison sentence in reality was a sentence of slow death through ill treatment of the prisoner. The modern concept of punishment is designed toward an effort to rehabilitate the inmate to aid him/her to be integrated into the main stream of society when released. This desired result is not always obtained for various reasons such as shortage of qualified staff, shortage of funds, shortsightedness of prison officials and state legislatures, and presence of the "members of the old guard" still in command of prison policy with their resistance to change, etc.

The courts have accepted fines, imprisonment, and execution as acceptable modes to punish convicted criminals. In United States v. Jones, 207 F.2d 785, 5th Cir. (1953), it was held that corporal punishment used against a prisoner is unconstitutional as cruel and unusual punishment. This case was followed by Jackson v. Bishop, 404 F.2d 511 (8th Cir.) (1968), to the same import. Most jurisdictions have abolished corporal punishment by statute. Cal. Penal Code § 2652 (1970), N.D. Cent. Code § 12-47-26 (1960). It was held as early as 1918 in a Federal District Court decision that sterilization of a prisoner is unconstitutional as cruel and unusual punishment. Mickle v. Hendricks, 262 Fed. 687 (D.Nev.) (1918).

§ 9.11 Deprivation of Sexual Contact for Prisoners

It is paradoxical for lawyers and law to protect the defendant prior to conviction and then ignore the inadequacy of corrections. Many correction administrators are attempting to humanize their institutions but because of citizen apathy it has been an uphill struggle. Chief Justice Burger, in writing about prison conditions in the *American Bar Association Journal,* 56 A.B.A.J. 325 (1970), indicated that "It is here that the success or failure of our society will make itself known." In response to this, the American Bar Association, Criminal Justice Section, in the winter of 1977 drafted a Tentative Draft of Standards Relating to the Legal Status of Prisoners which suggests the extension of prisoner rights beyond those previously afforded by statute, rule, or court decision.

Thus far, no court known to the author has characterized the lack of sexual contact with one's spouse, legal or common-law, for convicted inmates a deprivation of the constitutional right to be free from cruel and unusual punishment. However, it is thought that the day is not too far distant when the Court will interpret this abstinance as a deprivation of a constitutional right. Conjugal visits have been ordered for pretrial detainees. See Inmates v. Eisenstadt, 360 F.Supp. 676 (D.Mass.) (1973); Jones v. Wittenberg, 330 F.Supp. 707 (1971); Miller v. Carson, 401 F.Supp. 835 (M.D.Fla.) (1975).

§ 9.12 Deprivation of Contact Visits for Prisoners

I again ask the reader to imagine him/herself in a situation where absolutely no physical contact is permitted with a loved one. No handshaking, no kissing, no embracing are permitted. These freedoms are accepted by each of us without much thought about what emotional impact would be the result of their deprivation.

For security reasons, correctional administrators have limited or eliminated entirely any body-contact between their prisoners and the loved ones or friends of the prisoners. Is this cruel and unusual punishment? The United States Court for the Southern District of New York treated this problem in Rhem v. Malcolm, 371 F.Supp. 594 (S.D. of N.Y.) (1974), wherein no contact visiting was permitted and ordered such visiting except in unique situations, particularly for pretrial detainees.

California had the first experiment in "family visiting" in this country, although many other countries have been practicing this method of correction. This concept involves the purchase of private facilities such as trailers or houses in medium and minimum security prisons; "... family visits range from 19 to 72 hours." California Department of Corrections Newscam, May 24, 1976, p. 3.

§ 9.13 Firearms—Used in Crime

Sentencing has always been a problem in the past but the future argues for some improvement. It is customary for one judge to be characterized as an easy judge and another to be a tough judge. The "easy" designation is given to the judge who metes out lenient sentences to the guilty whereas the "tough" judge is the one who is known to give long sentences of imprisonment. Most state statutes give the judge discretionary limits within which he/she must use as a guide to decide on the sentence to be given to the convicted person standing before the court. Often, persons who stand convicted of similar offenses, get to know each other in prison where they learn about the disparity of the sentencing for similar offenses. Many states are establishing a judicial review panel of several judges to second guess the sentences imposed on convicted persons. These review panels usually have the power to reduce a sentence but not to increase it.

Some states, and the federal government, in response to an ever increasing use of firearms in the commission of crime, have enacted legislation, increasing the penalties if the defendant is found to use or carry a firearm while in the commission of a crime. In BUSIC v. UNITED STATES, 446 U.S. 398, 100 S.Ct. 1747, 64 L.Ed.2d. 381, 27 Cr.L. 3109 (1980) the petitioner was convicted of, inter alia, armed assault on federal officers. The statute that they were indicted under, 18 USC 111 makes it unlawful to assault a federal officer and provides for more punishment when the perpetrator uses a deadly weapon. The petitioner was also charged with 18 USC 924(i) which makes it illegal to carry a firearm in the commission of the armed assault and authorizes the imposition of enhanced penalties for such a defendant.

The Court held that the latter charge may not be applied to a defendant who uses a firearm in the course of a felony that is proscribed by a statute which itself authorizes enhancement if a dangerous weapon is used.

Judicial Decisions Relating to Chapter 9

Schilb et al. *v.* Kuebel et al.

404 U.S. 357, 92 S.Ct. 479, 30 L.Ed. 2d. 502 (1971)

APPEAL FROM THE SUPREME COURT OF ILLINOIS

Argued October 12, 1971—Decided December 20, 1971

. . .

MR. JUSTICE BLACKMUN delivered the opinion of the Court.

John Schilb, of Belleville, Illinois, was arrested on January 16, 1969, and charged (a) with leaving the scene of an automobile accident and (b) with obstructing traffic. In order to gain his liberty pending trial, and in accord with the Illinois bail statutes hereinafter described, Schilb deposited $75 in cash with the clerk of the court. This amount was 10% of the aggregate bail fixed on the two charges ($500 on the first and $250 on the second). At his ensuing trial Schilb was acquitted of the charge of leaving the scene, but was convicted of traffic obstruction. When he paid his fine, the amount Schilb had deposited was returned to him decreased, however, by $7.50 retained as "bail bond costs" by the court clerk pursuant to the statute. The amount so retained was 1% of the specified bail and 10% of the amount actually deposited.

Schilb, by this purported state class action against the court clerk, the county, and the county treasurer, attacks the statutory 1% charge on Fourteenth Amendment due process and equal protection grounds. The Circuit Court of St. Clair County upheld the statute and dismissed the complaint. The Supreme Court of Illinois affirmed, with two justices dissenting. 46 Ill. 2d 538, 264 N.E. 2d 377 (1970). We noted probable jurisdiction. 402 U.S. 928 (1971).

I

The Illinois bail statutes compose Article 110 of the State's Code of Criminal Procedure of 1963, made effective January 1, 1964. This Code complemented Illinois' then new and revised Criminal Code of 1961, made effective January 1, 1962. The work of revision of the theretofore existing statutes was that of a Joint Committee of the Illinois State and Chicago Bar Associations. See 1 Ill. Rev. Stat. 1963, p. 1629.

Prior to 1964 the professional bail bondsman system with all its abuses was in full and odorous bloom in Illinois. Under that system the bail bondsman customarily collected the maximum fee (10% of the amount of the bond) permitted by statute, House Bill No. 734, approved July 17, 1959, Ill. Laws 1959, pp. 1372, 1376, and retained that entire amount even though the accused fully satisfied the conditions of the bond. See People ex rel. Gendron v. Ingram, 34 Ill. 2d 623, 626, 217 N. E. 2d 803, 805 (1966). Payment of this substantial "premium" was required of the good risk as well as of the bad. The results were that a heavy and irretrievable burden fell upon the accused, to the excellent profit of the bondsman, and that professional bondsmen, and not the courts, exercised significant control over the actual workings of the bail system.

One of the stated purposes of the new bail provisions in the 1963 Code was to rectify this offensive situation. The purpose appears to have been accomplished. It is said that the bail bondsman abruptly disappeared in Illinois "due primarily to the success of the ten percent bail deposit provision." Boyle, Bail Under the Judicial Article, 17 De Paul L. Rev. 267, 272 (1968). See Kamin, Bail Administration in Illinois, 53 Ill. B.J. 674, 680 (1965).

II

Article 110 of the 1963 Code, as it read at the time Schilb was arrested and charged, provided that an eligible accused could obtain pretrial release in one of three ways:

(1) Under § 110–2 he may be released on his personal recognizance.

(2) Under § 110–7 he may execute a bail bond and deposit with the clerk cash equal to only 10% of the bail or $25, whichever is the greater. When bail is made in this way and the conditions of the bond have been performed, the clerk returns to the accused 90% of the sum deposited. The remaining 10% (1% of the bail) is retained by the clerk "as bail bond costs."

(3) Under § 110–8 he may execute a bail bond and secure it by a deposit with the clerk of the full amount of the bail in cash, or in stocks and bonds authorized for trust funds in Illinois, or by unencumbered nonexempt Illinois real estate worth double the amount of the bail. When bail is made in this way and the conditions of the bond have been performed, the clerk returns the deposit of cash or stocks or bonds, or releases the real estate, as the case may be, without charge or retention of any amount.

In each case bail is fixed by a judicial officer. Section 110–5 prescribes factors to be considered in fixing the amount of bail. Under § 110–6 either the State or the defendant may apply to the court for an increase or for a reduction in the amount of bail or for alteration of the bond's conditions.

The choice between § 110–7 and § 110–8 is reserved to the accused.

The thinking and intentions of the Joint Committee revisers are apparent from the Committee's comments, as revised by its Chairman, Professor Charles H. Bowman, and reproduced in Ill. Ann. Stat., c. 38 (Smith-Hurd ed. 1970).

The parties have stipulated that when bail in a particular case is fixed, the judge's "discretion in such respect is not guided by statute, rule of court or any definite, fixed standard; various and divers judges in fact fix the amount of bail for the same types of offenses at various and divers amounts, without relationship as to guilt or innocence of the particular defendant in a criminal charge, and without relationship of the particular offense charged and the bail fixed." They have also stipulated, "The actual cost of administering the provisions of said Sections 110–7 and 110–8 are substantially the same but there may probably be a slightly greater cost in the administration of Section 110–8."

III

The Court more than once has said that state legislative reform by way of classification is not to be invalidated merely because the legislature moves one step at a time. "The prohibition of the Equal Protection Clause goes no further than the invidious discrimination." Williamson v. Lee Optical Co., 348 U.S. 483, 489 (1955). "Legislatures are presumed to have acted constitutionally . . . and their statutory classifications will be set aside only if no grounds can be conceived to justify them. . . . With this much discretion, a legislature traditionally has been allowed to take reform 'one step at a time, addressing itself to the phase of the problem which seems most acute to the legislative mind.'" McDonald v. Board of Election Commissioners, 394 U.S. 802, 809 (1969). The measure of equal protection has been described variously as whether "the distinctions drawn have some basis in practical experience," South Carolina v. Katzenbach, 383 U.S. 301, 331 (1966), or whether the legislature's action falls short of "the invidious discrimination," Williamson v. Lee Optical Co., 348 U.S., at 489, or whether "any state of facts reasonably may be conceived to justify" the statutory discrimination, McGowan v. Maryland, 366 U.S. 420, 426 (1961); see United States v. Maryland Savings-Share Ins. Corp., 400 U.S. 4, 6 (1970), or whether the classification is "on the basis of criteria wholly unrelated to the objective of [the] statute," Reed v. Reed, ante, p. 71, at 76. But the Court also has refined this traditional test and has said that a statutory classification based upon suspect criteria or affecting "fundamental rights" will encounter equal protection difficulties unless justified by a "*compelling* governmental interest." Shapiro v. Thompson, 394 U.S. 618, 634, 638 (1969); Oregon v. Mitchell, 400 U.S. 112, 247 n. 30 (1970) (opinion of BRENNAN, WHITE, and MARSHALL, JJ.).

Bail, of course, is basic to our system of law, Stack v. Boyle, 342 U.S. 1 (1951); Herzog v. United States, 75 S. Ct. 349, 351, 99 L. Ed. 1299, 1301 (1955) (opinion of DOUGLAS, J.), and the Eighth Amendment's proscription of excessive bail has been assumed to have application to the States through the Fourteenth Amendment. Pilkinton v. Circuit Court, 324 F. 2d 45, 46 (CA8 1963); see Robinson v. California, 370 U.S. 660, 666 (1962), and id., at 675 (DOUGLAS, J., concurring). But we are not at all concerned here with any fundamental right to bail or with any Eighth Amendment–Fourteenth Amendment question of bail excessiveness. Our concern, instead, is with the 1% cost-retention provision. This smacks of administrative detail and of procedure and is hardly to be classified as a "fundamental" right or as based upon any suspect criterion. The applicable measure, therefore, must be the traditional one: Is the distinction drawn by the statutes invidious and without rational basis? Dandridge v. Williams, 397 U.S. 471, 483–487 (1970). See Richardson v. Belcher, ante, p. 78, at 81.

IV

With this background, we turn to the appellants' primary argument. It is threefold: (1) that the 1% retention charge under § 110–7 (f) is imposed on only one segment of the class gaining pretrial release; (2) that it is imposed on the poor and nonaffluent and not on the rich and affluent; and (3) that its imposition with respect to an accused found innocent amounts to a court cost assessed against the not-guilty person.

We are compelled to note preliminarily that the attack on the Illinois bail statutes, in a very distinct sense, is paradoxical. The benefits of the new system, as compared with the old, are conceded. And the appellants recognize that under the pre-1964 system Schilb's particular bail bond cost would have been 10% of his bail, or $75; that this premium price for his pretrial freedom, once paid, was irretrievable; and that, if he could not have raised the $75, he would have been consigned to jail until his trial. Thus, under the old system the cost of Schilb's pretrial freedom was $75, but under the new it was only $7.50. While acknowledging this obvious benefit of the statutory reform, Schilb and his co-appellants decry the classification the statutes make and present the usual argument that the legislation must be struck down because it does not reform enough.

A. It is true that no charge is made to the accused who is released on his personal recognizance. We are advised, however, that this was also true under the old (pre-1964) system and that "Illinois has never charged people out on recognizance." Thus, the burden on the State with respect to a personal recognizance is no more under the new system than what the State had assumed under the old. Also, with a recognizance, there is nothing the State holds for safekeeping, with resulting responsibility and additional paperwork. All this provides a rational basis for distinguishing between the personal recognizance and the deposit situations.

There is also, however, no retention charge to the accused who deposits the full amount of cash bail or securities or real estate. Yet the administrative cost attendant upon the 10% deposit and that upon the full deposit are, by the stipulation, "substantially the same" with, indeed, any higher cost incurred with respect to the full deposit.

This perhaps is a more tenuous distinction, but we cannot conclude that it is constitutionally vulnerable. One who deposits securities or encumbers his real estate precludes the use of that property for other purposes. And one who deposits the full amount of his bail in cash is dispossessed of a productive asset throughout the period of the deposit; presumably, at least, its interim possession by the State accrues to the benefit of the State. Further, the State's protection against the expenses that inevitably are incurred when bail is jumped is greater when 100% cash or securities or real estate is deposited or obligated than when only 10% of the bail amount is advanced. The Joint Committee's and the State Legislature's decision in balancing these opposing considerations in the way that they did cannot be described as lacking in rationality to the point where equal protection considerations require that they be struck down.

Rinaldi v. Yeager, 384 U.S. 305 (1966), lends no support to the appellants here. In that case a New Jersey statute imposed the cost of a transcript upon the indigent appellant who had been convicted of a crime and was sentenced to prison and who then was unsuccessful on his appeal. The statute, however, did not impose that cost upon the indigent appellant who likewise was convicted of a crime, and was unsuccessful on his appeal, but who had received a suspended sentence or who had been placed on probation or who had been fined rather than sentenced to prison. The distinction the New Jersey statute drew between appellants was based only upon the nature of their punishment, and the burden was imposed only upon those who were confined. The Court held, and rightly so, that a punishment distinction had no rational connection with a transcript cost and served to deny equal protection to the convicted appellant whose liberty was at issue on the appeal. MR. JUSTICE STEWART, in speaking for the Court, said,

> "The Equal Protection Clause requires more of a state law than nondiscriminatory application within the class it establishes. It also imposes a requirement of some rationality in the nature of the class singled out. To be sure, the constitutional demand is not a demand that a statute necessarily apply to all persons. 'The Constitution does not require things which are different in fact . . . to be treated in law as though they were the same.' Hence, legislation may impose special burdens upon defined classes in order to achieve permissible ends. But the Equal Protection Clause does require that, in defining a class subject to legislation, the distinctions that are drawn have 'some relevance to the purpose for which the classification is made.'" 384 U.S., at 308–309 (citations omitted).

The New Jersey distinction thus was invidious and without rationality for it was not related to the fiscal objectives of the statute and rested on no administrative convenience.

B. The poor-man–affluent-man argument centers, of course, in Griffin v. Illinois, 351 U.S. 12 (1956), and in the many later cases that "reaffirm allegiance to the basic command that justice be applied equally to all persons." Williams v. Illinois, 399 U.S. 235, 241 (1970).

In no way do we withdraw today from the Griffin principle. That remains steadfast. But it is by no means certain, as the appellants suggest, that the 10% deposit provision under § 110–7 is a provision for the benefit of the poor and the less affluent and that the full-deposit provision of § 110–8 is one for the rich and the more affluent. It should be obvious that the poor man's real hope and avenue for relief is the personal recognizance provision of § 110–2. We do not presume to say, as the appellants in their brief intimate, that § 110–2 is not utilized by Illinois judges and made available for the poor and the less affluent.

Neither is it assured, as the appellants also suggest, that the affluent will take advantage of the full-deposit provision of § 110–8, with no retention charge, and that the less affluent are relegated to the 10% deposit provision of § 110–7 and the 1% retention charge. The record is silent, but the flow indeed may be the other way. The affluent, more aware of and more experienced in the marketplace, may see the advantage, in these days of high interest rates, in retaining the use of 90% of the bail amount. A 5% or greater return on this 90% in a short period of time more than offsets the 1% retention charge. In other words, it is by no means clear that the route of §110–8 is more attractive to the affluent defendant than the § 110–7 route. The situation, therefore, wholly apart from the fact that appellant Schilb himself has not pleaded indigency, is not one where we may assume that the Illinois plan works to deny relief to the poor man merely because of his poverty.

C. The court-cost argument is that the person found innocent but already "put to the expense, disgrace and anguish of a trial" is "then assessed a cost for exercising his right to release pending trial." Giaccio v. Pennsylvania, 382 U.S. 399 (1966), is cited. Giaccio was a holding that an ancient Pennsylvania statute that permitted the jury to impose court costs upon an acquitted defendant, in order to offset the expenses of prosecution, violated the Due Process Clause because of vagueness and the absence of any standards preventing the arbitrary imposition of costs. The Court thus did not reach the merits, although MR. JUSTICE STEWART and MR. JUSTICE FORTAS, each separately concurring, 382 U.S., at 405, felt that the very imposition of costs upon an acquitted defendant was violative of due process.

Giaccio is not dispositive precedent for the appellants here. Certainly § 110-7 is not subject to attack for vagueness or for lack of standards. Neither is it a vehicle for the imposition of costs of prosecution as was the Pennsylvania statute. Instead, § 110-7 authorizes retention of the 1% as "bail bond costs." This is what that description implies, namely, an administrative cost imposed upon all those, guilty and innocent alike, who seek the benefit of § 110-7. This conclusion is supported by the presence of the long-established Illinois rule against the imposition of costs of prosecution upon an acquitted or discharged criminal defendant, Wells v. McCullock, 13 Ill. 606 (1852), and by the Illinois court's own determination, 46 Ill. 2d, at 551-552, 264 N.E. 2d, at 384, that the charge under § 110-7 (f) is an administrative fee and not a cost of prosecution imposed under Ill. Rev. Stat., c. 38, § 180-3 (1969), only upon the convicted defendant.

V

Finally, the appellants would point out that Article 110 has its federal counterpart in § 3 (a) of the Bail Reform Act of 1966, Pub. L. 89-465, 89th Cong., 2d Sess., 80 Stat. 214, and in particular in that portion now codified as 18 U.S.C. § 3146 (a) (3). They note that S. 2840, 88th Cong., 2d Sess., contained a 1% retention provision "to defray bail bond costs" but that a parallel bill, S. 1357, 89th Cong., 1st Sess., as it progressed through Congress, at no time had a provision of that kind. It was S. 1357 that was enacted as Pub. L. 89-465.

The committee reports, S. Rep. No. 750, 89th Cong., 1st Sess., and H.R. Rep. No. 1541, 89th Cong., 2d Sess., accompanying the 1966 Act, and the debates, 112 Cong. Rec. 12488-12504, 12841-12843, make no reference to this change from the earlier S. 2840. In the face of this silence, and without more, and being cognizant of the fact that the federal act, unlike the Illinois one, was not directed against the professional bail bondsman, we are not inclined to read constitutional implications into the absence of the retention provision in the Bail Reform Act of 1966.

Neither are we inclined to read constitutional implications into either the presence or the absence of a retention provision in corresponding statutes of States other than Illinois. See N.Y. Laws 1936, c. 518, N.Y. Code Crim. Proc. § 586.3 (Supp. 1970-1971), having a 2% fee provision, now replaced by §§ 520.10-520.30 of New York's new Criminal Procedure Law, effective September 1, 1971, without the provision. See Wis. Stat. §§ 969.02 (5) and 969.03 (1) (c) (1969), where a 1% fee is specified but not upon dismissal or acquittal. See Alaska Stat. § 12.30.020 (b) (4) (Supp. 1971); D.C. Code Ann. § 23-1321 (a) (3) (Supp. 1971); and Iowa Code Ann. § 763.16.1c. (Supp. 1971), in each of which a 10% deposit is authorized with no fee-retention provision.

VI

We refrain from nullifying this Illinois statute that, with its companion sections, has brought reform and needed relief to the State's bail system. The judgment of the Supreme Court of Illinois is

Affirmed.

Ward *v.* Village of Monroeville

409 U.S. 57, 93 S.Ct. 80, 34 L.Ed. 2d. 267 (1972)

CERTIORARI TO THE SUPREME COURT OF OHIO

Argued October 17, 1972—Decided November 14, 1972

. . .

MR. JUSTICE BRENNAN delivered the opinion of the Court.

Pursuant to Ohio Rev. Code Ann. § 1905.01 et seq. (1968), which authorizes mayors to sit as judges in cases of ordinance violations and certain traffic offenses, the Mayor of Monroeville, Ohio, convicted petitioner of two traffic offenses and fined him $50 on each. The Ohio Court of Appeals for Huron County, 21 Ohio App. 2d 17, 254 N.E. 2d 375 (1969), and the Ohio Supreme Court, 27 Ohio St. 2d 179, 271 N.E. 2d 757 (1971), three justices dissenting, sustained the conviction, rejecting petitioner's objection that trial before a mayor who also had responsibilities for revenue production and law enforcement denied him a trial before a disinterested and impartial judicial officer as guaranteed by the Due Process Clause of the Fourteenth Amendment. We granted certiorari. 404 U.S. 1058 (1972).

The Mayor of Monroeville has wide executive powers and is the chief conservator of the peace. He is president of the village council, presides at all meetings, votes in case of a tie, accounts annually to the council respecting village finances, fills vacancies in village offices and has general overall supervision of village affairs. A major part of village income is derived from the fines, forfeitures, costs, and fees imposed by him in his mayor's court. Thus, in 1964 this income contributed $23,589.50 of total village revenues of $46,355.38; in 1965 it was $18,508.95 of $46,752.60; in 1966 it was $16,085 of $43,585.13; in 1967 it was $20,060.65 of $53,931.43; and in 1968 it was $23,439.42 of $52,995.95. This revenue was of such importance to the village that when legislation threatened its loss, the village retained a management consultant for advice upon the problem.

Conceding that "the revenue produced from a mayor's court provides a substantial portion of a municipality's funds," the Supreme Court of Ohio held nonetheless that "such fact does not mean that a mayor's impartiality is so diminished thereby that he cannot act in a disinterested fashion in a judicial capacity." 27 Ohio St. 2d, at 185, 271 N.E. 2d, at 761. We disagree with that conclusion.

The issue turns, as the Ohio court acknowledged, on whether the Mayor can be regarded as an impartial judge under the principles laid down by this Court in Tumey v. Ohio, 273 U.S. 510 (1927). There, convictions for prohibition law violations rendered by the Mayor of North College Hill, Ohio, were reversed when it appeared that, in addition to his regular salary, the Mayor received $696.35 from the fees and costs levied by him against alleged violators. This Court held that "it certainly violates the Fourteenth Amendment, and deprives a defendant in a criminal case of due process of law, to subject his liberty or property to the judgment of a court the judge of which has a direct, personal, substantial, pecuniary interest in reaching a conclusion against him in his case." Id., at 523.

The fact that the mayor there shared directly in the fees and costs did not define the limits of the principle. Although "the mere union of the executive power and the judicial power in him can not be said to violate due process of law," id., at 534, the test is whether the mayor's situation is one "which would offer a possible temptation to the average man as a judge to forget the burden of proof required to convict the defendant, or which might lead him not to hold the balance nice, clear and true between the State and the accused...." Id., at 532. Plainly that "possible temptation" may also exist when the mayor's executive responsibilities for village finances may make him partisan to maintain the high level of contribution from the mayor's court. This, too, is a "situation in which an official perforce occupies two practically and seriously inconsistent positions, one partisan and the other judicial, [and] necessarily involves a lack of due process of law in the trial of defendants charged with crimes before him." Id., at 534.

This situation is wholly unlike that in Dugan v. Ohio, 277 U.S. 61 (1928), which the Ohio Supreme Court deemed controlling here. There the Mayor of Xenia, Ohio, had judicial functions but only very limited executive authority. The city was governed by a commission of five members, including the Mayor, which exercised all legislative powers. A city manager, together with the commission, exercised all executive powers. In those circumstances, this Court held that the Mayor's relationship to the finances and financial policy of the city was too remote to warrant a presumption of bias toward conviction in prosecutions before him as judge.

Respondent urges that Ohio's statutory provision, Ohio Rev. Code Ann. § 2937.20 (Supp. 1971), for the disqualification of interested, biased, or prejudiced judges is a sufficient safeguard to protect petitioner's rights. This argument is not persuasive. First, it is highly dubious that this provision was available to raise petitioner's broad challenge to the mayor's court of this village in respect to all prosecutions there in which fines may be imposed. The provision is apparently designed only for objection to a particular mayor "*in a specific case* where the circumstances in that municipality might warrant a finding of *prejudice in that case*."

27 Ohio St. 2d, at 184, 271 N.E. 2d, at 760 (emphasis added). If this means that an accused must show special prejudice in his particular case, the statute requires too much and protects too little. But even if petitioner might have utilized the procedure to make his objection, the Ohio Supreme Court passed upon his constitutional contention despite petitioner's failure to invoke the procedure. In that circumstance, see Raley v. Ohio, 360 U.S. 423, 436 (1959), he may be heard in this Court to urge that the Ohio Supreme Court erred in holding that he had not established his Fourteenth Amendment claim.

Respondent also argues that any unfairness at the trial level can be corrected on appeal and trial de novo in the County Court of Common Pleas. We disagree. This "procedural safeguard" does not guarantee a fair trial in the mayor's court; there is nothing to suggest that the incentive to convict would be diminished by the possibility of reversal on appeal. Nor, in any event, may the State's trial court procedure be deemed constitutionally acceptable simply because the State eventually offers a defendant an impartial adjudication. Petitioner is entitled to a neutral and detached judge in the first instance. Accordingly, the judgment of the Supreme Court of Ohio is reversed and the case is remanded for further proceedings not inconsistent with this opinion.

It is so ordered.

Gregg *v.* Georgia

428 U.S. 242, 96 S.Ct. 2909, 49 L.Ed. 2d. 859 (1976)

. . .

MR. JUSTICE STEWART, MR. JUSTICE POWELL, and MR. JUSTICE STEVENS announced the judgment of the Court and filed an opinion delivered by MR. JUSTICE STEWART.

The issue in this case is whether the imposition of the sentence of death for the crime of murder under the law of Georgia violates the Eighth and Fourteenth Amendments.

I

The petitioner, Troy Gregg, was charged with committing armed robbery and murder. In accordance with Georgia procedure in capital cases, the trial was in two stages, a guilt stage and a sentencing stage. The evidence at the guilt trial established that on November 21, 1973, the petitioner and a traveling companion, Floyd Allen, while hitchhiking north in Florida were picked up by Fred Simmons and Bob Moore. Their was some of the cash he was carrying. While still in Florida, they picked up another hitchhiker, Dennis Weaver, who rode with them to Atlanta, where he was let out about 11 p.m. A short time later the four men interrupted their journey for a rest stop along the highway. The next morning the bodies of Simmons and Moore were discovered in a ditch nearby.

On November 23, after reading about the shootings in an Atlanta newspaper, Weaver communicated with the Gwinnett County police and related information concerning the journey with the victims, including a description of the car. The next afternoon, the petitioner and Allen, while in Simmons' car, were arrested in Asheville, N.C. In the search incident to the arrest a .25-caliber pistol, later shown to be that used to kill Simmons and Moore, was found in the petitioner's pocket. After receiving the warnings required by Miranda v. United States, 384 U.S. 436, 86 S.Ct. 1602, 16 L.Ed.2d 694 (1966), and signing a written waiver of his rights, the petitioner signed a statement in which he admitted shooting, then robbing Simmons and Moore. He justified the slayings on grounds of self-defense. The next day, while being transferred to Lawrenceville, Ga., the petitioner and Allen were taken to the scene of the shootings. Upon arriving there, Allen recounted the events leading to the slayings. His version of these events was as follows: After Simmons and Moore left the car, the petitioner stated that he intended to rob them. The petitioner then took his pistol in hand and positioned himself on the car to improve his aim. As Simmons and Moore came up an embankment towards the car, the petitioner fired three shots and the two men fell near a ditch. The petitioner, at close range, then fired a shot into the head of each. He robbed them of valuables and drove away with Allen.

A medical examiner testified that Simmons died from a bullet wound in the eye and that Moore died from bullet wounds in the cheek and in the back of the head. He further testified that both men had several bruises and abrasions about the face and head which probably were sustained either from the fall into the ditch or from being dragged or pushed along the embankment. Although Allen did not testify, a police detective recounted the substance of Allen's statements about the slayings and indicated that directly after Allen had made these statements the petitioner had admitted that Allen's account was accurate. The petitioner testified in his own defense. He confirmed that Allen had made the statements described by the detective, but denied their truth or ever having admitted to their accuracy. He indicated that he had shot Simmons and Moore because of fear and in self-defense, testifying they had attacked Allen and him, one wielding a pipe and the other a knife.

The trial judge submitted the murder charges to the jury on both felony-murder and nonfelony-murder theories. He also instructed on the issue of self-defense but declined to instruct on manslaughter. He submitted the robbery case to the jury on both an armed-robbery theory and on the lesser included offense of robbery by intimidation. The jury found the petitioner guilty of two counts of armed robbery and two counts of murder.

At the penalty stage, which took place before the same jury, neither the prosecutor nor the petitioner's lawyer offered any additional evidence. Both counsel, however, made lengthy arguments dealing generally with the propriety of capital punishment under the circumstances and with the weight of the evidence of guilt. The trial judge instructed the jury that it could recommend either a death sentence or a life prison sentence on each count. The judge further charged the jury that in determining what sentence was appropriate the jury was free to consider the facts and circumstances, if any, presented by the parties in mitigation or aggravation.

Finally, the judge instructed the jury that it "would not be authorized to consider [imposing] the penalty of death" unless it first found beyond a reasonable doubt one of these aggravating circumstances:

> "One—That the offense of murder was committed while the offender was engaged in the commission of two other capital felonies, to-wit the armed robbery of [Simmons and Moore].
> "Two—That the offender committed the offense of murder for the purpose of receiving money and the automobile described in the indictment.
> "Three—The offense of murder was outrageously and wantonly vile, horrible and inhuman, in that they [sic] involved the depravity of [the] mind of the defendant." Tr. 476–477.

Finding the first and second of these circumstances, the jury returned verdicts of death on each count.

The Supreme Court of Georgia affirmed the convictions and the imposition of the death sentences for murder. 233 Ga. 117, 210 S.E.2d 659 (1974). After reviewing the trial transcript and the record, including the evidence, and comparing the evidence and sentence in similar cases in accordance with the requirements of Georgia law, the court concluded that, considering the nature of the crime and the defendant, the sentences of death had not resulted from prejudice or any other arbitrary factor and were not excessive or disproportionate to the penalty applied in similar cases.

. . .

We granted the petitioner's application for a writ of certiorari challenging the imposition of the death sentences in this case as "cruel and unusual" punishment in violation of the Eighth and the Fourteenth Amendments. ___ U.S. ___, 96 S.Ct. 1090, 47 L.Ed.2d 93 (1976).

II

Before considering the issues presented it is necessary to understand the Georgia statutory scheme for the imposition of the death penalty. The Georgia statute, as amended after our decision in Furman v. Georgia, 408 U.S. 238, 92 S.Ct. 2726, 33 L.Ed.2d 346 (1972), retains the death penalty for six categories of crime: murder, kidnapping for ransom or where the victim is harmed, armed robbery, rape, treason, and aircraft hijacking. Ga.Code Ann. §§ 26–1101, 26–1311, 26–1902, 26–2001, 26–2201, 26–3301 (1972). The capital defendant's guilt or innocence is determined in the traditional manner, either by a trial judge or a jury, in the first stage of a bifurcated trial.

If trial is by jury, the trial judge is required to charge lesser included offenses when they are supported by any view of the evidence. Sims v. State, 203 Ga. 668, 47 S.E.2d 862 (1948). See Linder v. State, 132 Ga.App. 624, 625, 208 S.E.2d 630, 631

(1974). After a verdict, finding, or plea of guilty to a capital crime, a presentence hearing is conducted before whomever made the determination of guilt. The sentencing procedures are essentially the same in both bench and jury trials. At the hearing,

> "the judge [or jury] shall hear additional evidence in extenuation, mitigation, and aggravation of punishment, including the record of any prior criminal convictions and pleas of guilty or pleas of nolo contendere of the defendant, or the absence of any prior conviction and pleas: Provided, however, that only such evidence in aggravation as the State has made known to the defendant prior to his trial shall be admissible. The judge [or jury] shall also hear argument by defendant or his counsel and the prosecuting attorney... regarding the punishment to be imposed." § 27-2503. (Supp. 1975.)

The defendant is accorded substantial latitude as to the types of evidence that he may introduce. See Brown v. State, 235 Ga. 644, 647–650, 220 S.Ed.2d 925 (1975). Evidence considered during the guilt stage may be considered during the sentencing stage without being resubmitted. Eberheart v. State, 232 Ga. 247, 253, 206 S.E.2d 12, 17 (1974).

In the assessment of the appropriate sentence to be imposed the judge is also required to consider or to include in his instructions to the jury "any mitigating circumstances or aggravating circumstances otherwise authorized by law and any of [10] statutory aggravating circumstances which may be supported by the evidence..." § 27–2534.1(b) (Supp.1975). The scope of the nonstatutory aggravating or mitigating circumstances is not delineated in the statute. Before a convicted defendant may be sentenced to death, however, except in cases of treason or aircraft hijacking, the jury, or the trial judge in cases tried without a jury, must find beyond a reasonable doubt one of the 10 aggravating circumstances specified in the statute. The sentence of death may be imposed only if the jury (or judge) finds one of the statutory aggravating circumstances and then elects to impose that sentence. § 26–3102 (Supp. 1975). If the verdict is death the jury or judge must specify the aggravating circumstance(s) found. § 27–2534.1(c). (Supp.1975.) In jury cases, the trial judge is bound by the jury's recommended sentence. §§ 26–3102, 27–2514 (Supp.1975).

In addition to the conventional appellate process available in all criminal cases, provision is made for special expedited direct review by the Supreme Court of Georgia of the appropriateness of imposing the sentence of death in the particular case. The court is directed to consider "the punishment as well as any errors enumerated by way of appeal," and to determine:

> "(1) Whether the sentence of death was imposed under the influence of passion, prejudice, or any other arbitrary factor, and
>
> "(2) Whether, in cases other than treason or aircraft hijacking, the evidence supports the jury's or judge's finding of a statutory aggravating circumstance as enumerated in section 27.2534.1(b), and

"(3) Whether the sentence of death is excessive or disproportionate to the penalty imposed in similar cases, considering both the crime and the defendant." § 27-2537 (Supp.1975).

If the court affirms a death sentence, it is required to include in its decision reference to similar cases that it has taken into consideration. § 27-2537(e).

A transcript and complete record of the trial, as well as a separate report by the trial judge, are transmitted to the court for its use in reviewing the sentence. § 27-2537(a) (1972). The report is in the form of a six and one half page questionnaire, designed to elicit information about the defendant, the crime, and the circumstances of the trial. It requires the trial judge to characterize the trial in several ways designed to test for arbitrariness and disproportionality of sentence. Included in the report are responses to detailed questions concerning the quality of the defendant's representation, whether race played a role in the trial, and, whether, in the trial court's judgment, there was any doubt about the defendant's guilt or the appropriateness of the sentence. A copy of the report is served upon defense counsel. Under its special review authority, the court may either affirm the death sentence or remand the case for resentencing. In cases in which the death sentence is affirmed there remains the possibility of executive clemency.

III

We address initially the basic contention that the punishment of death for the crime of murder is, under all circumstances, "cruel and unusual" in violation of the Eighth and Fourteenth Amendments of the Constitution. In Part IV of this opinion, we will consider the sentence of death imposed under the Georgia statutes at issue in this case.

The Court on a number of occasions has both assumed and asserted the constitutionality of capital punishment. In several cases that assumption provided a necessary foundation for the decision, as the Court was asked to decide whether a particular method of carrying out a capital sentence would be allowed to stand under the Eighth Amendment. But until Furman v. Georgia, 408 U.S. 238, 92 S.Ct. 2726, 33 L.Ed.2d 346 (1972), the Court never confronted squarely the fundamental claim that the punishment of death always, regardless of the enormity of the offense or the procedure followed in imposing the sentence, is cruel and unusual punishment in violation of the Constitution. Although this issue was presented and addressed in Furman, it was not resolved by the Court. Four Justices would have held that capital punishment is not unconstitutional per se; two Justices would have reached the opposite conclusion; and three Justices, while agreeing that the statutes then before the Court were invalid as applied, left open the question whether such punishment may ever be imposed. We now hold that the punishment of death does not invariably violate the Constitution.

A

The history of the prohibition of "cruel and unusual" punishment already has been reviewed by this Court at length. The phrase first appeared in the English Bill of Rights of 1689, which was drafted by Parliament at the accession of William and Mary. See Granucci, "Nor Cruel and Unusual Punishments Inflicted:" The Original Meaning, 57 Cal.L.Rev. 839, 852–853 (1969). The English version appears to have been directed against punishments unauthorized by statute and beyond the jurisdiction of the sentencing court, as well as those disproportionate to the offense involved. Id., at 860. The American draftsmen, who adopted the English phrasing in drafting the Eighth Amendment, were primarily concerned, however, with proscribing "tortures" and other "barbarous" methods of punishment." Id., at 842.

In the earliest cases raising Eighth Amendment claims, the Court focused on particular methods of execution to determine whether they were too cruel to pass constitutional muster. The constitutionality of the sentence of death itself was not at issue, and the criterion used to evaluate the mode of execution was its similarity to "torture" and other "barbarous" methods. See Wilkerson v. Utah, 99 U.S., at 136 ("[I]t is safe to affirm that punishments of torture, . . . and all others in the same line of unnecessary cruelty, are forbidden by that amendment . . . ."); In re Kemmler, 136 U.S., at 447, 10 S.Ct., at 933 ("Punishments are cruel when they involve torture or a lingering death. . . ."). See also Louisiana ex rel. Francis v. Resweber, 329 U.S. 459, 464, 67 S.Ct. 374, 376, 91 L.Ed. 422 (1947) (A second attempt at electrocution found not to violate the Eighth Amendment, since the failure of the initial execution attempt was "an unforeseeable accident" and "[t]here [was] no purpose to inflict unnecessary pain nor any unnecessary pain involved in the proposed execution.").

But the Court has not confined the prohibition embodied in the Eighth Amendment to "barbarous" methods that were generally outlawed in the 18th century. Instead, the Amendment has been interpreted in a flexible and dynamic manner. The Court early recognized that "a principle to be vital, must be capable of wider application than the mischief which gave it birth." Weems v. United States, 217 U.S. 349, 373, 30 S.Ct. 544, 551, 54 L.Ed. 793 (1910). Thus the clause forbidding "cruel and unusual" punishments "is not fastened to the obsolete but may acquire meaning as public opinion becomes enlightened by a humane justice." Id., at 378, 30 S.Ct., at 553. See also Furman v. Georgia, 408 U.S., at 429–430, 92 S.Ct., at 2823–2824 (POWELL, J., dissenting); Trop v. Dulles, 356 U.S., at 100–101, 78 S.Ct., at 597–598 (plurality opinion).

In Weems the Court addressed the constitutionality of the Philippine punishment of cadena temporal for the crime of falsifying an official document. That punishment included imprisonment for at least 12 years and one day, in chains, at hard and painful labor; the loss of many basic civil rights; and subjection to lifetime surveillance. Although the Court acknowledged the possibility that "the cruelty of pain" may be present in the challenged punishment, 217 U.S., at 366, 30 S.Ct., at 549, it did not rely on that factor, for it rejected the proposition that the Eighth Amendment reaches only punishments that are "inhuman and barbarous, torture and the like." Id., at 368, 30 S.Ct., at 549. Rather, the Court focused on the lack of proportion between the crime and the offense:

"Such penalties for such offenses amaze those who have formed their conception of the relation of a state to even its offending citizens from the practice of the American commonwealths, and believe that it is a precept of justice that punishment for crime should be graduated and proportioned to offense." Id., at 366–367, 30 S.Ct., at 549.

Later, in Trop v. Dulles, 356 U.S. 86, 78 S.Ct. 590, 2 L.Ed.2d 630 (1958), the Court reviewed the constitutionality of the punishment of denationalization imposed upon a soldier who escaped from an Army stockade and became a deserter for one day. Although the concept of proportionality was not the basis of the holding, the plurality observed in dicta that "[f]ines, imprisonment and even execution may be imposed depending upon the enormity of the crime." Id., at 100, 78 S.Ct., at 598.

The substantive limits imposed by the Eighth Amendment on what can be made criminal and punished were discussed in Robinson v. California, 370 U.S. 660, 82 S.Ct. 1417, 8 L.Ed.2d 758 (1962). The Court found unconstitutional a state statute that made the status of being addicted to a narcotic drug a criminal offense. It held, in effect, that it is "cruel and unusual" to impose any punishment at all for the mere status of addiction. The cruelty in the abstract of the actual sentence imposed was irrelevant: "Even one day in prison would be cruel and unusual punishment for the 'crime' of having a common cold." Id., at 667, 82 S.Ct. at 1421. Most recently, in Furman v. Georgia, 408 U.S. 238, 92 S.Ct. 2726, 33 L.Ed.2d 346 (1972), three Justices in separate concurring opinions found the Eighth Amendment applicable to procedures employed to select convicted defendants for the sentence of death.

It is clear from the foregoing precedents that the Eighth Amendment has not been regarded as a static concept. As Chief Justice Warren said, in an oft-quoted phrase, "[t]he Amendment must draw its meaning from the evolving standards of decency that mark the progress of a maturing society." Trop v. Dulles, supra, 356 U.S., at 101, 78 S.Ct., at 598. See also Jackson v. Bishop, 404 F.2d 571, 579 (CA 8 1968). Cf. Robinson v. California, supra, 370 U.S., at 666, 82 S.Ct., at 1420. Thus, an assessment of contemporary values concerning the infliction of a challenged sanction is relevant to the application of the Eighth Amendment. As we develop below more fully, see pp. 2926–2927, infra, this assessment does not call for a subjective judgment. It requires, rather, that we look to objective indicia that reflect the public attitude toward a given sanction.

But our cases also make clear that public perceptions of standards of decency with respect to criminal sanctions are not conclusive. A penalty also must accord with "the dignity of man," which is the "basic concept underlying the Eighth Amendment." Trop v. Dulles, supra, 356 U.S., at 100, 78 S.Ct., at 597 (plurality opinion). This means, at least, that the punishment not be "excessive." When a form of punishment in the abstract (in this case, whether capital punishment may ever be imposed as a sanction for murder) rather than in the particular (the propriety of death as a penalty to be applied to a specific defendant for a specific crime) is under consideration, the inquiry into "excessiveness" has two aspects. First, the punishment must not involve the unnecessary and wanton infliction of pain. Furman v. Georgia, supra, 408 U.S., at 392–393, 92 S.Ct., at 2805–2806 (Burger,

C. J., dissenting). See Wilkerson v. Utah, 99 U.S., at 136; Weems v. United States, 217 U.S., at 381, 30 S.Ct., at 554. Second, the punishment must not be grossly out of proportion to the severity of the crime. Trop v. Dulles, supra, 356 U.S., at 100, 78 S.Ct., at 597 (plurality opinion) (dictum); Weems v. United States, supra, 217 U.S., at 367, 30 S.Ct., at 549.

B

Of course, the requirements of the Eighth Amendment must be applied with an awareness of the limited role to be played by the courts. This does not mean that judges have no role to play, for the Eighth Amendment is a restraint upon the exercise of legislative power.

> "Judicial review by definition, often involves a conflict between judicial and legislative judgment as to what the Constitution means or requires. In this respect, Eighth Amendment cases come to us in no different posture. It seems conceded by all that the Amendment imposes some obligations on the judiciary to judge the constitutionality of punishment and that there are punishments that the Amendment would bar whether legislatively approved or not." Furman v. Georgia, supra, 408 U.S., at 313–314, 92 S.Ct., at 2764 (WHITE, J., concurring).

But, while we have an obligation to insure that constitutional bounds are not overreached, we may not act as judges as we might as legislators.

> "Courts are not representative bodies. They are not designed to be a good reflex of a democratic society. Their judgment is best informed, and therefore most dependable, within narrow limits. Their essential quality is detachment, founded on independence. History teaches that the independence of the judiciary is jeopardized when courts become embroiled in the passions of the day and assume primary responsibility in choosing between competing political, economic and social pressures." Dennis v. United States, 341 U.S. 494, 525, 71 S.Ct. 857, 875, 95 L.Ed. 1137 (1951) (FRANKFURTER, J., concurring in affirmance).

Therefore, in assessing a punishment selected by a democratically elected legislature against the constitutional measure, we presume its validity. We may not require the legislature to select the least severe penalty possible so long as the penalty selected is not cruelly inhumane or disproportionate to the crime involved. And a heavy burden rests on those who would attack the judgment of the representatives of the people.

This is true in part because the constitutional test is intertwined with an assessment of contemporary standards and the legislative judgment weighs heavily in ascertaining such standards. "[I]n a democratic society legislatures, not courts, are constituted to respond to the will and consequently the moral values of the people." Furman v. Georgia, 408 U.S., at 383, 92 S.Ct., at 2800 (BURGER, C. J., dissenting). The deference we owe to the decisions of the state legislatures under our federal system, id., at 465–470, 92 S.Ct., at 2842–2844 (REHNQUIST, J., dissenting), is enhanced where the specification of punishments is concerned, for "these are peculiarly questions of legislative policy." Gore v. United States, 357 U.S. 386, 393, 78 S.Ct. 1280, 1285, 2 L.Ed.2d 1405 (1958). Cf. Robinson v. California, 370 U.S., at 664–665, 82 S.Ct., at 1419–1420; Trop v. Dulles, 356 U.S., at 103, 78 S.Ct., at 599 (plurality opinion); In re Kemmler, 136 U.S., at 447, 10 S.Ct., at 933. Caution is necessary lest this Court become, "under the aegis of the Cruel and Unusual Punishment Clause, the ultimate arbiter of the standards of criminal responsibility . . . throughout the country." Powell v. Texas, 392 U.S. 514, 533, 88 S.Ct. 2145, 2154, 20 L.Ed.2d 1254 (1968). A decision that a given punishment is impermissible under the Eighth Amendment cannot be reversed short of a constitutional amendment. The ability of the people to express their preference through the normal democratic processes, as well as through ballot referenda, is shut off. Revisions cannot be made in the light of further experience. See Furman v. Georgia, supra, 408 U.S., at 461–462, 92 S.Ct., at 2839–2840 (POWELL, J., dissenting).

C

In the discussion to this point we have sought to identify the principles and considerations that guide a court in addressing an Eighth Amendment claim. We now consider specifically whether the sentence of death for the crime of murder is a per se violation of the Eighth and Fourteenth Amendments to the Constitution. We note first that history and precedent strongly support a negative answer to this question.

1

The imposition of the death penalty for the crime of murder has a long history of acceptance both in the United States and in England. The common-law rule imposed a mandatory death sentence on all convicted murderers. McGautha v. California, 402 U.S., at 197–198, 91 S.Ct., at 1462–1463. And the penalty continued to be used into the 20th century by most American States, although the breadth of the common-law rule was diminished, initially by narrowing the class of murders to be punished by death and subsequently by widespread adoption of laws expressly granting juries the discretion to recommend mercy. Id., at 199–200, 91 S.Ct., at 1463–1464. See Woodson v. North Carolina, ___ U.S. ___ , 96 S.Ct. 2978, 48 L.Ed.2d ___ .

It is apparent from the text of the Constitution itself that the existence of capital punishment was accepted by the Framers. At the time the Eighth Amendment was ratified, capital punishment was a common sanction in every State. Indeed, the First Congress of the United States enacted legislation providing death as the penalty for specified crimes. 1 Stat. 112 (1790). The Fifth Amendment, adopted at the same time as the Eighth, contemplated the continued existence of the capital sanction by imposing certain limits on the prosecution of capital cases:

> "No person shall be held to answer for a capital, or otherwise infamous crime, unless on a presentment or indictment of a Grand Jury . . . ; nor shall any person be subject for the same offense to be twice put in jeopardy of life or limb; . . . nor be deprived of life, liberty, or property, without due process of law . . . ."

And the Fourteenth Amendment, adopted over three-quarters of a century later, similarly contemplates the existence of the capital sanction in providing that no State shall deprive any person of "life, liberty, or property" without due process of law.

For nearly two centuries, this Court, repeatedly and often expressly, has recognized that capital punishment is not invalid per se. In Wilkerson v. Utah, 99 U.S., at 134–135, where the Court found no constitutional violation in inflicting death by public shooting, it said:

> "Cruel and unusual punishments are forbidden by the Constitution, but the authorities referred to are quite sufficient to show that the punishment of shooting as a mode of executing the death penalty for the crime of murder in the first degree is not included in that category, within the meaning of the eighth amendment."

Rejecting the contention that death by electrocution was "cruel and unusual," the Court in In re Kemmler, 136 U.S., at 447, 10 S.Ct., at 933 reiterated:

> ". . . the punishment of death is not cruel, within the meaning of that word as used in the Constitution. It implies there something inhuman and barbarous, something more than the mere extinguishment of life."

Again, in Louisiana ex rel. Francis v. Resweber, 329 U.S., at 464, 67 S.Ct., at 376, the Court remarked: "The cruelty against which the Constitution protects a convicted man is cruelty inherent in the method of punishment, not the necessary suffering involved in any method employed to extinguish life humanely." And in Trop v. Dulles, 356 U.S., at 99, 78 S.Ct., at 597, Chief Justice Warren, for four Justices, wrote:

> "Whatever the arguments may be against capital punishment, both on moral grounds and in terms of accomplishing the purposes of punishment . . . the death penalty has been employed throughout our history, and, in a day when it is still widely accepted, it cannot be said to violate the constitutional concept of cruelty."

Four years ago, the petitioners in Furman and its companion cases predicated their argument primarily upon the asserted proposition that standards of decency had evolved to the point where capital punishment no longer could be tolerated. The petitioners in those cases said, in effect, that the evolutionary process had come to an end, and that standards of decency required that the Eighth Amendment be construed finally as prohibiting capital punishment for any crime regardless of its depravity and impact on society. This view was accepted by two Justices. Three other Justices were unwilling to go so far; focusing on the procedures by which convicted defendants were selected for the death penalty rather than on the actual punishment inflicted, they joined in the conclusion that the statutes before the Court were constitutionally invalid.

The petitioners in the capital cases before the Court today renew the "standards of decency" argument, but developments during the four years since Furman have undercut substantially the assumptions upon which their argument rested. Despite the continuing debate, dating back to the 19th century, over the morality and utility of capital punishment, it is now evident that a large proportion of American society continues to regard it as an appropriate and necessary criminal sanction.

The most marked indication of society's endorsement of the death penalty for murder is the legislative response to Furman. The legislatures of at least 35 States have enacted new statutes that provide for the death penalty for at least some crimes that result in the death of another person. And the Congress of the United States, in 1974, enacted a statute providing the death penalty for aircraft piracy that results in death. These recently adopted statutes have attempted to address the concerns expressed by the Court in Furman primarily (i) by specifying the factors to be weighed and the procedures to be followed in deciding when to impose a capital sentence, or (ii) by making the death penalty mandatory for specified crimes. But all of the post-Furman statutes make clear that capital punishment itself has not been rejected by the elected representatives of the people.

In the only statewide referendum occurring since Furman and brought to our attention, the people of California adopted a constitutional amendment that authorized capital punishment, in effect negating a prior ruling by the Supreme Court of California in People v. Anderson, 6 Cal.3d 628, 100 Cal.Rptr. 152, 493 P.2d 880, cert. denied, 406 U.S. 958, 92 S.Ct. 2060, 32 L.Ed.2d 344 (1972), that the death penalty violated the California Constitution.

The jury also is a significant and reliable objective index of contemporary values because it is so directly involved. See Furman v. Georgia, 408 U.S., at 439–440, 92 S.Ct., at 2828–2829 (POWELL, J., dissenting). See generally Powell, Jury Trial of Crimes, 23 Wash. & Lee L.Rev. 1 (1966). The Court has said that "one of the most important functions any jury can perform in making . . . a selection [between life imprisonment and death for a defendant convicted in a capital case] is to maintain a link between contemporary community values and the penal system." Witherspoon v. Illinois, 391 U.S. 510, 519 n. 15, 88 S.Ct. 1770, 1775, 20 L.Ed.2d 776 (1968). It may be true that evolving standards have influenced juries in recent decades to be more discriminating in imposing the sentence of death. But the relative infrequency of jury verdicts imposing the death sentence does not indicate rejection of capital punishment per se. Rather, the reluctance of juries in many cases to impose the sentence may well reflect the humane feeling that this most irrevocable of sanctions should be reserved for a small number of extreme cases. See Furman v. Georgia, supra, 408 U.S., at 388, 92 S.Ct., at 2803 (BURGER, C. J., dissenting). Indeed, the actions of juries in many States since Furman is fully compatible with the legislative judgments, reflected in the new statutes, as to the continued utility and necessity of capital punishment in appropriate cases. At the close of 1974 at least 254 persons had been sentenced to death since Furman, and by the end of March 1976, more than 460 persons were subject to death sentences.

As we have seen, however, the Eighth Amendment demands more than that a challenged punishment be acceptable to contemporary society. The Court also must ask whether it comports with the basic concept of human dignity at the core of the Amendment. Trop v. Dulles, 356 U.S., at 100, 78 S.Ct., at 597 (plurality opinion). Although we cannot "invalidate a category of penalties because we deem less severe penalties adequate to serve the ends of penology," Furman v. Georgia, supra, 408 U.S., at 451, 92 S.Ct., at 2834 (POWELL, J., dissenting), the sanction imposed cannot be so totally without penological justification that it results in the gratuitous infliction of suffering. Cf. Wilkerson v. Utah, 99 U.S., at 135–136; In re Kemmler, 136 U.S., at 447, 10 S.Ct., at 933.

The death penalty is said to serve two principal social purposes: retribution and deterrence of capital crimes by prospective offenders.

In part, capital punishment is an expression of society's moral outrage at particularly offensive conduct. This function may be unappealing to many, but it is essential in an ordered society that asks its citizens to rely on legal processes rather than self-help to vindicate their wrongs.

> "The instinct for retribution is part of the nature of man, and channeling that instinct in the administration of criminal justice serves an important purpose in promoting the stability of a society governed by law. When people begin to believe that organized society is unwilling or unable to impose upon criminal offenders the punishment they 'deserve,' then there are sown the seeds of anarchy—of self-help, vigilante justice, and lynch law." Furman v. Georgia, supra, 408 U.S., at 308, 92 S.Ct., at 2761 (STEWART, J., concurring).

"Retribution is no longer the dominant objective of the criminal law," Williams v. New York, 337 U.S. 241, 248, 69 S.Ct. 1079, 1084, 93 L.Ed. 1337 (1949), but neither is it a forbidden objective nor one inconsistent with our respect for the dignity of men. Furman v. Georgia, supra, 408 U.S., at 394–395, 92 S.Ct., at 2806–2807 (BURGER, C. J., dissenting), 452–454, 92 S.Ct. 2835–2836 (POWELL, J., dissenting); Powell v. Texas, 392 U.S., at 531, 535–536, 88 S.Ct., at 2153, 2155–2156. Indeed, the decision that capital punishment may be the appropriate sanction in extreme cases is an expression of the community's belief that certain crimes are themselves so grievous an affront to humanity that the only adequate response may be the penalty of death.

Statistical attempts to evaluate the worth of the death penalty as a deterrent to crimes by potential offenders have occasioned a great deal of debate. The results simply have been inconclusive. As one opponent of capital punishment has said:

> "... after all possible inquiry, including the probing of all possible methods of inquiry, we do not know, and for systematic and easily visible reasons cannot know, what the truth about this 'deterrent' effect may be ....
>
> The inescapable flaw is ... that social conditions in any state are not constant through time, and that social conditions are not the same in any two states. If an effect were observed (and the observed effects one way or another, are not large) then one could not at all tell whether any of this effect is attributable to the presence or absence of capital punishment. A 'scientific'—that is to say, a soundly based—conclusion is simply impossible, and no methodological path out of this tangle suggests itself." C. Black, Capital Punishment: The Inevitability of Caprice and Mistake 25–26 (1974).

Although some of the studies suggest that the death penalty may not function as a significantly greater deterrent than lesser penalties, there is no convincing empirical evidence either supporting or refuting this view. We may nevertheless assume safely that there are murderers, such as those who act in passion, for whom the threat of death has little or no deterrent effect. But for many others, the death penalty undoubtedly is a significant deterrent. There are carefully contemplated murders, such as murder for hire, where the possible penalty of death may well enter into the cold calculus that precedes the decision to act. And there are some categories of murder, such as murder by a life prisoner, where other sanctions may not be adequate.

The value of capital punishment as a deterrent of crime is a complex factual issue the resolution of which properly rests with the legislatures, which can evaluate the results of statistical studies in terms of their own local conditions and with a flexibility of approach that is not available to the courts. Furman v. Georgia, 408 U.S., at 403–405, 92 S.Ct., at 2810–2812 (BURGER, C. J., dissenting). Indeed, many of the post-Furman statutes reflect just such a responsible effort to define those crimes and those criminals for which capital punishment is most probably an effective deterrent.

In sum, we cannot say that the judgment of the Georgia legislature that capital punishment may be necessary in some cases is clearly wrong. Considerations of federalism, as well as respect for the ability of a legislature to evaluate, in terms of its particular state the moral consensus concerning the death penalty and its social utility as a sanction, require us to conclude, in the absence of more convincing evidence, that the infliction of death as a punishment for murder is not without justification and thus is not unconstitutionally severe.

Finally, we must consider whether the punishment of death is disproportionate in relation to the crime for which it is imposed. There is no question that death as a punishment is unique in its severity and irrevocability. Furman v. Georgia, supra, at 286–291, 92 S.Ct. at 2750–2753 (BRENNAN, J., concurring), 306, 92 S.Ct. 2760 (STEWART, J., concurring). When a defendant's life is at stake, the Court has been particularly sensitive to insure that every safeguard is observed. Powell v. State of Alabama, 287 U.S. 45, 71, 53 S.Ct. 55, 65, 77 L.Ed. 158 (1932); Reid v. Covert, 354 U.S. 1, 77, 77 S.Ct. 1222, 1262, 1 L.Ed.2d 1148 (1957) (HARLAN, J., concurring in the result). But we are concerned here only with the imposition of capital punishment for the crime of murder, and when a life has been taken deliberately by the offender, we cannot say that the punishment is invariably disproportionate to the crime. It is an extreme sanction, suitable to the most extreme of crimes.

We hold that the death penalty is not a form of punishment that may never be imposed, regardless of the circumstances of the offense, regardless of the character of the offender, and regardless of the procedure followed in reaching the decision to impose it.

IV

We now consider whether Georgia may impose the death penalty on the petitioner in this case.

A

While Furman did not hold that the infliction of the death penalty per se violates the Constitution's ban on cruel and unusual punishments, it did recognize that the penalty of death is different in kind from any other punishment imposed under our system of criminal justice. Because of the uniqueness of the death penalty, Furman held that it could not be imposed under sentencing procedures that created a substantial risk that it would be inflicted in an arbitrary and capricious manner. MR. JUSTICE WHITE concluded that "the death penalty is exacted with great infrequency even for the most atrocious crimes and ... there is no meaningful basis for distinguishing the few cases in which it is imposed from the many cases in which it is not." 408 U.S., at 313, 92 S.Ct., at 2764. Indeed, the death sentences examined by the Court in Furman were "cruel and unusual in the same way that being struck by lightening is cruel and unusual. For, of all the people convicted of [capital crimes], many just as reprehensible as these, the petitioners [in Furman were] among a capriciously selected random handful upon which the sentence of death has in fact been imposed.... [T]he Eighth and Fourteenth Amendments cannot tolerate the infliction of a sentence of death under legal systems that permit this unique penalty to be so wantonly and so freakishly imposed." Id., at 309–310, 92 S.Ct., at 2762 (STEWART, J., concurring).

Furman mandates that where discretion is afforded a sentencing body on a matter so grave as the determination of whether a human life should be taken or spared, that discretion must be suitably directed and limited so as to minimize the risk of wholly arbitrary and capricious action.

It is certainly not a novel proposition that discretion in the area of sentencing be exercised in an informed manner. We have long recognized that "[f]or the determination of sentences, justice generally requires ... that there be taken into account the circumstances of the offense together with the character and propensities of the offender." Pennsylvania v. Ashe, 302 U.S. 51, 55, 58 S.Ct. 59, 61, 82 L.Ed. 43 (1937). See also Williams v. Oklahoma, 358 U.S. 576, 585, 79 S.Ct. 421, 426, 3 L.Ed.2d 516 (1959); Williams v. New York, 337 U.S. 241, 247, 69 S.Ct. 1079, 1083, 93 L.Ed. 1337 (1949). Otherwise, "the system cannot function in a consistent and rational manner." ABA Standards Relating to Sentencing Alternatives and Procedures § 4.1(a), Commentary, p. 201. See also President's Comm'n on Law Enforcement & Administration of Justice, The Challenge of Crime in a Free Society 144 (1967); Model Penal Code § 7.07, Comment 1, pp. 52–53 (Tent. Draft No. 2, 1954).

The cited studies assumed that the trial judge would be the sentencing authority. If an experienced trial judge, who daily faces the difficult task of imposing sentences, has a vital need for accurate information about a defendant and the crime he committed in order to be able to impose a rational sentence in the typical criminal case, then accurate sentencing information is an indispensable prerequisite to a reasoned determination of whether a defendant shall live or die by a jury of people who may never before have made a sentencing decision.

Jury sentencing has been considered desirable in capital cases in order "to maintain a link between contemporary community values and the penal system—a link without which the determination of punishment could hardly reflect 'the evolving standards of decency that mark the progress of a maturing society.'" But it creates special problems. Much of the information that is relevant to the sentencing decision may have no relevance to the question of guilt, or may even be extremely prejudicial to a fair determination of that question. This problem, however, is scarcely insurmountable. Those who have studied the question suggest that a bifurcated procedure—one in which the question of sentence is not considered until the determination of guilt has been made—is the best answer. The drafters of the Model Penal Code concluded that if a unitary proceeding is used

> "the determination of punishment must be based on less than all the evidence that has a bearing on that issue, such for example as a previous criminal record of the accused, or evidence must be admitted on the ground that it is relevant to sentence, though it would be excluded as irrelevant or prejudicial with respect to guilt or innocence alone. Trial lawyers understandably have little confidence in a solution that admits the evidence and trusts to an instruction to the jury that it should be considered only in determining the penalty and disregarded in assessing guilt.
>
> "... The obvious solution ... is to bifurcate the proceeding, abiding strictly by the rules of evidence until and unless there is a conviction, but once guilt has been determined opening the record to further information that is relevant to sentence. This is the analogue of the procedure in the ordinary case when capital punishment is not in issue; the court conducts a separate inquiry before imposing sentence." Model Penal Code § 201.6, Comment 5, pp. 75–75 (Tent. Draft No. 9, 1959).

See also Spencer v. Texas, 385 U.S. 554, 567–569, 87 S.Ct. 648, 655–657, 17 L.Ed.2d 606; Report of the Royal Commission on Capital Punishment, 1949–1953, Cmd. 8932, ¶¶ 555, 574; Knowlton, Problems of Jury Discretion in Capital Cases, 101 U.Pa.L.Rev. 1099, 1135–1136 (1953). When a human life is at stake and when the jury must have information prejudicial to the question of guilt but relevant to the question of penalty in order to impose a rational sentence, a bifurcated system is more likely to ensure elimination of the constitutional deficiencies identified in Furman.

But the provision of relevant information under fair procedural rules is not alone sufficient to guarantee that the information will be properly used in the imposition of punishment, especially if sentencing is performed by a jury. Since the members of a jury will have had little, if any, previous experience in sentencing, they are unlikely to be skilled in dealing with the information they are given. See ABA Standards Relating to Sentencing Alternatives & Procedures, § 1.1(b), Commentary, pp. 46–47; President's Comm'n on Law Enforcement & Administration of Justice: The Challenge of Crime in a Free Society, Task Force Report: The Courts 26 (1967). To the extent that this problem is inherent in jury sentencing, it may not be totally correctible. It seems clear, however, that the problem will be alleviated if the jury is given guidance regarding the factors about the crime and the defendant that the State, representing organized society, deems particularly relevant to the sentencing decision.

The idea that a jury should be given guidance in its decisionmaking is also hardly a novel proposition. Juries are invariably given careful instructions on the law and how to apply it before they are authorized to decide the merits of a lawsuit. It would be virtually unthinkable to follow any other course in a legal system that has traditionally operated by following prior precedents and fixed rules of law. See Gasoline Products Co. v. Champlin Refining Co., 283 U.S. 494, 498, 51 S.Ct. 513, 514, 75 L.Ed. 1188, Fed.Rule Civ.Proc. 51. When erroneous instructions are given, retrial is often required. It is quite simply a hallmark of our legal system that juries be carefully and adequately guided in their deliberations.

While some have suggested that standards to guide a capital jury's sentencing deliberations are impossible to formulate, the fact is that such standards have been developed. When the drafters of the Model Penal Code faced this problem, they concluded "that it is within the realm of possibility to point to the main circumstances of aggravation and of mitigation that should be weighed *and weighed against each other*, when they are presented in a concrete case." Model Penal Code § 201.6, Comment 3, p. 71 (Tent. Draft No. 9, 1959) (emphasis original). While such standards are by necessity somewhat general, they do provide guidance to the sentencing authority and thereby reduce the likelihood that it will impose a sentence that fairly can be called capricious or arbitrary. Where the sentencing authority is required to specify the factors it relied upon in reaching its decision, the further safeguard of meaningful appellate review is available to ensure that death sentences are not imposed capriciously or in a freakish manner.

In summary, the concerns expressed in Furman that the penalty of death not be imposed in an arbitrary or capricious manner can be met by a carefully drafted statute that ensures that the sentencing authority is given adequate information and guidance. As a general proposition these concerns are best met by a system that provides for a bifurcated proceeding at which the sentencing authority is apprised of the information relevant to the imposition of sentence and provided with standards to guide its use of the information.

We do not intend to suggest that only the above-described procedures would be permissible under Furman or that any sentencing system constructed along these general lines would inevitably satisfy the concerns of Furman, for each distinct system must be examined on an individual basis. Rather, we have embarked upon this general exposition to make clear that it is possible to construct capital-sentencing systems capable of meeting Furman's constitutional concerns.

B

We now turn to consideration of the constitutionality of Georgia's capital-sentencing procedures. In the wake of Furman, Georgia amended its capital punishment statute, but chose not to narrow the scope of its murder provisions. See Part II, supra. Thus, now as before Furman, in Georgia "[a] person commits murder when he unlawfully and with malice aforethought, either express or implied, causes the death of another human being." Ga. Code Ann., § 26-1101(a) (1972). All persons convicted of murder "shall be punished by death or by imprisonment for life." § 26-1101(c) (1972).

Georgia did act, however, to narrow the class of murderers subject to capital punishment by specifying 10 statutory aggravating circumstances, one of which must be found by the jury to exist beyond a reasonable doubt before a death sentence can ever be imposed. In addition, the jury is authorized to consider any other appropriate aggravating or mitigating circumstances. § 27–2534.1(b) (Supp.1975). The jury is not required to find any mitigating circumstance in order to make a recommendation of mercy that is binding on the trial court, see § 27–2302 (Supp.1975), but it must find a *statutory* aggravating circumstance before recommending a sentence of death.

These procedures require the jury to consider the circumstances of the crime and the criminal before it recommends sentence. No longer can a Georgia jury do as Furman's jury did: reach a finding of the defendant's guilt and then, without guidance or direction, decide whether he should live or die. Instead, the jury's attention is directed to the specific circumstances of the crime: Was it committed in the course of another capital felony? Was it committed for money? Was it committed upon a peace officer or judicial officer? Was it committed in a particularly heinous way or in a manner that endangered the lives of many persons? In addition, the jury's attention is focused on the characteristics of the person who committed the crime: Does he have a record of prior convictions for capital offenses? Are there any special facts about this defendant that mitigate against imposing capital punishment (e.g., his youth, the extent of his cooperation with the police, his emotional state at the time of the crime)? As a result, while some jury discretion still exists, "the discretion to be exercised is controlled by clear and objective standards so as to produce non-discriminatory application." Coley v. State, 231 Ga. 829, 834, 204 S.E.2d 612, 615.

As an important additional safeguard against arbitrariness and caprice, the Georgia statutory scheme provides for automatic appeal of all death sentences to the State's supreme court. That court is required by statute to review each sentence of death and determine whether it was imposed under the influence of passion or prejudice, whether the evidence supports the jury's finding of a statutory aggravating circumstance, and whether the sentence is disproportionate compared to those sentences imposed in similar cases. § 27–2537(c) (Supp. 1975).

In short, Georgia's new sentencing procedures require as a prerequisite to the imposition of the death penalty, specific jury findings as to the circumstances of the crime or the character of the defendant. Moreover to guard further against a situation comparable to that presented in Furman, the Supreme Court of Georgia compares each death sentence with the sentences imposed on similarly situated defendants to ensure that the sentence of death in a particular case is not disproportionate. On their face these procedures seem to satisfy the concerns of Furman. No longer should there be "no meaningful basis for distinguishing the few cases in which [the death penalty] is imposed from the many cases in which it is not." 408 U.S., at 313, 92 S.Ct., at 2764 (WHITE, J., concurring).

The petitioner contends, however, that the changes in the Georgia sentencing procedures are only cosmetic, that the arbitrariness and capriciousness condemned by Furman continue to exist in Georgia—both in traditional practices that still remain and in the new sentencing procedures adopted in response to Furman.

1

First, the petitioner focuses on the opportunities for discretionary action that are inherent in the processing of any murder case under Georgia law. He notes that the state prosecutor has unfettered authority to select those persons whom he wishes to prosecute for a capital offense and to plea bargain with them. Further, at the trial the jury may choose to convict a defendant of a lesser included offense rather than find him guilty of a crime punishable by death, even if the evidence would support a capital verdict. And finally, a defendant who is convicted and sentenced to die may have his sentence commuted by the Governor of the State and the Georgia Board of Pardons and Paroles.

The existence of these discretionary stages is not determinative of the issues before us. At each of these stages an actor in the criminal justice system makes a decision which may remove a defendant from consideration as a candidate for the death penalty. Furman, in contrast, dealt with the decision to impose the death sentence on a specific individual who had been convicted of a capital offense. Nothing in any of our cases suggests that the decision to afford an individual defendant mercy violates the Constitution. Furman held only that, in order to minimize the risk that the death penalty would be imposed on a capriciously selected group of offenders, the decision to impose it had to be guided by standards so that the sentencing authority would focus on the particularized circumstances of the crime and the defendant.

2

The petitioner further contends that the capital-sentencing procedures adopted by Georgia in response to Furman do not eliminate the dangers of arbitrariness and caprice in jury sentencing that were held in Furman to be violative of the Eighth and Fourteenth Amendments. He claims that the statute is so broad and vague as to leave juries free to act as arbitrarily and capriciously as they wish in deciding whether to impose the death penalty. While there is no claim that the jury in this case relied upon a vague or overbroad provision to establish the existence of a statutory aggravating circumstance, the petitioner looks to the sentencing system as a whole (as the Court did in Furman and we do today) and argues that it fails to reduce sufficiently the risk of arbitrary infliction of death sentences. Specifically, Gregg urges that the statutory aggravating circumstances are too broad and too vague, that the sentencing procedure allows for arbitrary grants of mercy, and that the scope of the evidence and argument that can be considered at the presentence hearing is too wide.

The petitioner attacks the seventh statutory aggravating circumstance, which authorizes imposition of the death penalty if the murder was "outrageously or wantonly vile, horrible or inhuman in that it involved torture, depravity of mind, or an aggravated battery to the victim," contending that it is so broad that capital punishment could be imposed in any murder case. It is, of course, arguable that any murder involves depravity of mind or an aggravated battery. But this language need not be construed in this way, and there is no reason to assume that the Supreme Court of Georgia will adopt such an open-ended construction. In only one case has it upheld a jury's decision to sentence a defendant to death when the only statutory aggravating circumstance found was that of § 7, see McCorquodale v. State, 233 Ga. 369, 211 S.E.2d 577 (1974), and that homicide was a horrifying torture-murder.

The petitioner also argues that two of the statutory aggravating circumstances are vague and therefore susceptible to widely differing interpretations, thus creating a substantial risk that the death penalty will be arbitrarily inflicted by Georgia juries. In light of the decisions of the Supreme Court of Georgia we must disagree. First, the petitioner attacks that part of § 1 that authorizes a jury to consider whether a defendant has a "substantial history of serious assaultive criminal convictions." The Supreme Court of Georgia, however, has demonstrated a concern that the new sentencing procedures provide guidance to juries. It held this provision to be impermissibly vague in Arnold v. State, 236 Ga. 534, 540, 224 S.E.2d 386, 391 (1976), because it did not provide the jury with "sufficiently 'clear and objective standards.'" Second, the petitioner points to § 3 which speaks of creating a "great risk of death to more than one person." While such a phrase might be susceptible to an overly broad interpretation, the Supreme Court of Georgia has not so construed it. The only case in which the court upheld a conviction in reliance on this aggravating circumstance involved a man who stood up in a church and fired a gun indiscriminately into the audience. See Chenault v. State, 234 Ga. 216, 215 S.E.2d 223 (1975). On the other hand, the court expressly reversed a finding of great risk when the victim was simply kidnapped in a parking lot. See Jarrell v. State, 234 Ga. 410, 424, 216 S.E.2d 258, 269 (1975).

The petitioner next argues that the requirements of Furman are not met here because the jury has the power to decline to impose the death penalty even if it finds that one or more statutory aggravating circumstances is present in the case. This contention misinterprets Furman. See p. 418, supra. Moreover, it ignores the role of the Supreme Court of Georgia which reviews each death sentence to determine whether it is proportional to other sentences imposed for similar crimes. Since the proportionality requirement on review is intended to prevent caprice in the decision to inflict the penalty, the isolated decision of a jury to afford mercy does not render unconstitutional death sentences imposed on defendants who were sentenced under a system that does not create a substantial risk of arbitrariness or caprice.

The petitioner objects, finally, to the wide scope of evidence and argument allowed at presentence hearings. We think that the Georgia court wisely has chosen not to impose unnecessary restrictions on the evidence that can be offered at such a hearing and to approve open and far-ranging argument. See, e.g., Brown v. State, 235 Ga. 644, 220 S.E.2d 922 (1975). So long as the evidence introduced and the arguments made at the presentence hearing do not prejudice a defendant, it is preferable not to impose restrictions. We think it desirable for the jury to have as much information before it as possible when it makes the sentencing decision. See p. 414, supra.

3

Finally, the Georgia statute has an additional provision designed to assure that the death penalty will not be imposed on a capriciously selected group of convicted defendants. The new sentencing procedures require that the state supreme court review every death sentence to determine whether it was imposed under the influence of passion, prejudice, or any other arbitrary factor, whether the evidence supports the findings of a statutory aggravating circumstance, and "[w]hether the sentence of death is excessive or disproportionate to the penalty imposed in similar cases, considering both the crime and the defendant." § 27-2537(c)(3) (Supp.1975). In performing its sentence review function, the Georgia court has held that "if the death penalty is only rarely imposed for an act or it is substantially out of line with sentences imposed for other acts it will be set aside as excessive." Coley v. State, 231 Ga. 829, 834, 204 S.E.2d 612, 616 (1974). The court on another occasion stated that "we view it to be our duty under the similarity standard to assure that no death sentence is affirmed unless in similar cases throughout the state the death penalty has been imposed generally..." Moore v. State, 233 Ga. 861, 864, 213 S.E.2d 829, 832 (1975). See also Jarrell v. State, 234 Ga. 410, 425, 216 S.E.2d 258, 270 (1975) (standard is whether "juries generally throughout the state have imposed the death penalty"); Smith v. State, 236 Ga. 12, 24, 222 S.E.2d 308 (1976) (found "a clear pattern" of jury behavior).

It is apparent that the Supreme Court of Georgia has taken its review responsibilities seriously. In Coley, it held that "[t]he prior cases indicate that the past practice among juries faced with similar factual situations and like aggravating circumstances has been to impose only the sentence of life imprisonment for the offense of rape, rather than death." 231 Ga., at 835, 204 S.E.2d at, 617. It thereupon reduced Coley's sentence from death to life imprisonment. Similarly, although armed robbery is a capital offense under Georgia law, § 26-1902 (1972), the Georgia court concluded that the death sentences imposed in this case for that crime were "unusual in that they are rarely imposed for [armed robbery]. Thus, under the test provided by statute,... they must be considered to be excessive or disproportionate to the penalties imposed in similar cases." Gregg v. State, 233 Ga. 117, 127, 210 S.E.2d 659, 667 (1974). The court therefore vacated Gregg's death sentences for armed robbery and has followed a similar course in every other armed robbery death penalty case to come before it. See Floyd v. State, 233 Ga. 280, 285, 210 S.E.2d 810, 814 (1974); Jarrell v. State, 234 Ga. 410, 424-425, 216 S.E.2d 258, 270 (1975). See Dorsey v. State, 236 Ga. 591, 225 S.E.2d 418 (1976).

The provision for appellate review in the Georgia capital-sentencing system serves as a check against the random or arbitrary imposition of the death penalty. In particular, the proportionality review substantially eliminates the possibility that a person will be sentenced to die by the action of an aberrant jury. If a time comes when juries generally do not impose the death sentence in a certain kind of murder case, the appellate review procedures assures that no defendant convicted under such circumstances will suffer a sentence of death.

V

The basic concern of Furman centered on those defendants who were being condemned to death capriciously and arbitrarily. Under the procedures before the Court in that case, sentencing authorities were not directed to give attention to the nature or circumstances of the crime committed or to the character or record of the defendant. Left unguided, juries imposed the death sentence in a way that could only be called freakish. The new Georgia sentencing procedures, by contrast, focus the jury's attention on the particularized nature of the crime and the particularized characteristics of the individual defendant. While the jury is permitted to consider any aggravating or mitigating circumstances, it must find and identify at least one statutory aggravating factor before it may impose a penalty of death. In this way the jury's discretion is channeled. No longer can a jury wantonly and freakishly impose the death sentence; it is always circumscribed by the legislative guidelines. In addition, the review function of the Supreme Court of Georgia affords additional assurance that the concerns that prompted our decision in Furman are not present to any significant degree in the Georgia procedure applied here.

For the reasons expressed in this opinion, we hold that the statutory system under which Gregg was sentenced to death does not violate the Constitution. Accordingly, the judgment of the Georgia Supreme Court is affirmed.

It is so ordered.

Ehrlich Anthony Coker, Petitioner, *v.* State of Georgia

433 U.S. 584, 97 S.Ct. 2861, 53 L.Ed. 2d. 982, 21 Cr.L. 3199 (1977)

Argued March 28, 1977.—Decided June 29, 1977.

. . .

MR. JUSTICE WHITE announced the judgment of the Court and filed an opinion in which MR. JUSTICE STEWART, MR. JUSTICE BLACKMUN, and MR. JUSTICE STEVENS, joined.

Georgia Code Ann § 26–2001 (1972) provides that "[a] person convicted of rape shall be punished by death or by imprisonment for life, or by imprisonment for not less than 20 years." Punishment is determined by a jury in a separate sentencing proceeding in which at least one of the statutory aggravating circumstances must be found before the death penalty may be imposed. Petitioner Coker was convicted of rape and sentenced to death. Both conviction and sentence were affirmed by the Georgia Supreme Court. Coker was granted a writ of certiorari, 429 US 815, 50 L Ed 2d 75, 97 S Ct 56, limited to the single claim, rejected by the Georgia court, that the punishment of death for rape violates the Eighth Amendment, which proscribes "cruel and unusual punishments" and which must be observed by the States as well as the Federal Government. Robinson v California, 370 US 660, 8 L Ed 2d 758, 82 S Ct 1417 (1962).

I

While serving various sentences for murder, rape, kidnapping, and aggravated assault, petitioner escaped from the Ware Correctional Institution near Waycross, Ga., on September 2, 1974. At approximately 11 p.m. that night, petitioner entered the house of Allen and Elnita Carver through an unlocked kitchen door. Threatening the couple with a "board," he tied up Mr. Carver in the bathroom, obtained a knife from the kitchen, and took Mr. Carver's money and the keys to the family car. Brandishing the knife and saying "you know what's going to happen to you if you try anything, don't you," Coker then raped Mrs. Carver. Soon thereafter, petitioner drove away in the Carver car, taking Mrs. Carver with him. Mr. Carver, freeing himself, notified the police; and not long thereafter petitioner was apprehended. Mrs. Carver was unharmed.

Petitioner was charged with escape, armed robbery, motor vehicle theft, kidnapping, and rape. Counsel was appointed to represent him. Having been found competent to stand trial, he was tried. The jury returned a verdict of guilty, rejecting his general plea of insanity. A sentencing hearing was then conducted in accordance with the procedures dealt with at length in Gregg v Georgia, 428 US 153, 49 L Ed 2d 859, 96 S Ct 2909 (1976), where this Court sustained the death penalty for murder when imposed pursuant to the statutory procedures. The jury was instructed that it could consider as aggravating circumstances whether the rape had been committed by a person with a prior record of conviction for a capital felony and whether the rape had been committed in the course of committing another capital felony, namely, the armed robbery of Allen Carver. The court also instructed, pursuant to statute, that even if aggravating circumstances were present, the death penalty need not be imposed if the jury found they were outweighed by mitigating circumstances, that is, circumstances not constituting justification or excuse for the offense in question, "but which, in fairness and mercy, may be considered as extenuating or reducing the degree" of moral culpability or punishment. App 300. The jury's verdict on the rape count was death by electrocution. Both aggravating circumstances on which the court instructed were found to be present by the jury.

II

Furman v Georgia, 408 US 238, 33 L Ed 2d 346, 92 S Ct 2726 (1972), and the Court's decisions last Term in Gregg v Georgia, supra; Proffitt v Florida, 428 US 242, 49 L Ed 2d 913, 96 S Ct 2960 (1976); Jurek v Texas, 428 US 262, 49 L Ed 2d 929, 96 S Ct 2950 (1976); Woodson v North Carolina, 428 US 280, 49 L Ed 2d 944, 96 S Ct 2978 (1976); and Roberts v Louisiana, 428 US 325, 49 L Ed 2d 974, 96 S Ct 3001 (1976), make unnecessary the recanvassing of certain critical aspects of the controversy about the constitutionality of capital punishment. It is now settled that the death penalty is not invariably cruel and unusual punishment within the meaning of the Eighth Amendment; it is not inherently barbaric or an unacceptable mode of punishment for crime; neither is it always disproportionate to the crime for which it is imposed. It is also established that imposing capital punishment, at least for murder, in accordance with the procedures provided under the Georgia statutes saves the sentence from the infirmities which led the Court to invalidate the prior Georgia capital punishment statute in Furman v Georgia, supra.

In sustaining the imposition of the death penalty in Gregg, however, the Court firmly embraced the holdings and dicta from prior cases, Furman v Georgia, supra; Robinson v California, 370 US 660, 8 L Ed 2d 758, 82 S Ct 1417 (1962); Trop v Dulles, 356 US 86, 2 L Ed 2d 630, 78 S Ct 590 (1958); and Weems v United States, 217 US 349, 54 L Ed 793, 30 S Ct 544 (1910), to the effect that the Eighth Amendment bars not only those punishments that are "barbaric" but also those that are "excessive" in relation to the crime committed. Under Gregg, a punishment is "excessive" and unconstitutional if it (1) makes no measurable contribution to acceptable goals of punishment and hence is nothing more than the purposeless and needless imposition of pain and suffering; or (2) is grossly out of proportion to the severity of the crime. A punishment might fail the test on either ground. Furthermore, these Eighth Amendment judgments should not be, or appear to be, merely the subjective views of individual Justices; judgment should be informed by objective factors to the maximum possible extent. To this end, attention must be given to the public attitudes concerning a particular sentence—history and precedent, legislative attitudes, and the response of juries reflected in their sentencing decisions are to be consulted. In Gregg, after giving due regard to such sources, the Court's judgment was that the death penalty for deliberate murder was neither the purposeless imposition of severe punishment nor a punishment grossly disproportionate to the crime. But the Court reserved the question of the constitutionality of the death penalty when imposed for other crimes. 428 US, at 187, n 35, 49 L Ed 2d 859, 96 S Ct 2909.

III

That question, with respect to rape of an adult woman, is now before us. We have concluded that a sentence of death is grossly disproportionate and excessive punishment for the crime of rape and is therefore forbidden by the Eighth Amendment as cruel and unusual punishment.

A

As advised by recent cases, we seek guidance in history and from the objective evidence of the country's present judgment concerning the acceptability of death as a penalty for rape of an adult woman. At no time in the last 50 years has a majority of the States authorized death as a punishment for rape. In 1925, 18 States, the District of Columbia, and the Federal Government authorized capital punishment for the rape of an adult female. By 1971 just prior to the decision in Furman v Georgia, that number had declined, but not substantially, to 16 States plus the Federal Government. Furman then invalidated most of the capital punishment statutes in this country, including the rape statutes, because, among other reasons, of the manner in which the death penalty was imposed and utilized under those laws.

With their death penalty statutes for the most part invalidated, the States were faced with the choice of enacting modified capital punishment laws in an attempt to satisfy the requirements of Furman or of being satisfied with life imprisonment as the ultimate punishment for *any* offense. Thirty-five States immediately reinstituted the death penalty for at least limited kinds of crime. Gregg v Georgia, supra, at 179 n 23, 49 L Ed 2d 859, 96 S Ct 2909. This public judgment as to the acceptability of capital punishment, evidenced by the immediate, post-Furman legislative reaction in a large majority of the States, heavily influenced the Court to sustain the death penalty for murder in Gregg v Georgia. 428 US, at 179–182, 49 L Ed 2d 859, 96 S Ct 2909.

But if the "most marked indication of a society's endorsement of the death penalty for murder is the legislative response to Furman," Gregg v Georgia, supra, at 179–180, 49 L Ed 2d 859, 96 S Ct 2909, it should also be a telling datum that the public judgment with respect to rape, as reflected in the statutes providing the punishment for that crime, has been dramatically different. In reviving death penalty laws to satisfy Furman's mandate, none of the States that had not previously authorized death for rape chose to include rape among capital felonies. Of the 16 States in which rape had been a capital offense, only three provided the death penalty for rape of an adult woman in their revised statutes—Georgia, North Carolina, and Louisiana. In the latter two States, the death penalty was mandatory for those found guilty, and those laws were invalidated by Woodson and Roberts. When Louisiana and North Carolina, responding to those decisions, again revised their capital punishment laws, they reenacted the death penalty for murder but not for rape; none of the seven other legislatures that to our knowledge have amended or replaced their death penalty statutes since July 2, 1976, including four States (in addition to Louisiana and North Carolina) that had authorized the death sentence for rape prior to 1972 and had reacted to Furman with mandatory statutes, included rape among the crimes for which death was an authorized punishment.

Georgia argues that 11 of the 16 States that authorized death for rape in 1972 attempted to comply with Furman by enacting arguably mandatory death penalty legislation and that it is very likely that aside from Louisiana and North Carolina, these States simply chose to eliminate rape as a capital offense rather than to *require* death for *each* and *every* instance of rape. The argument is not without force; but four of the 16 States did not take the mandatory course and also did *not* continue rape of an adult woman as a capital offense. Further, as we have indicated, the legislatures of six of the 11 arguably mandatory States have revised their death penalty laws since Woodson and Roberts without enacting a new death penalty for rape. And this is to say nothing of 19 other States that enacted nonmandatory, post-Furman statutes and chose not to sentence rapists to death.

It should be noted that Florida, Mississippi, and Tennessee also authorized the death penalty in some rape cases, but only where the victim was a child and the rapist an adult. The Tennessee statute has since been invalidated because the death sentence was mandatory. Collins v State, ___ US ___ , (1977). The upshot is that Georgia is the sole jurisdiction in the United States at the present time that authorizes a sentence of death when the rape victim is an adult woman, and only two other jurisdictions provide capital punishment when the victim is a child.

The current judgment with respect to the death penalty for rape is not wholly unanimous among state legislatures, but it obviously weighs very heavily on the side of rejecting capital punishment as a suitable penalty for raping an adult woman.

B

It was also observed in Gregg that "[t]he jury . . . is a significant and reliable index of contemporary values because it is so directly involved," 428 US, at 181, 49 L Ed 2d 859, 96 S Ct 2909, and that it is thus important to look to the sentencing decisions that juries have made in the course of assessing whether capital punishment is an appropriate penalty for the crime being tried. Of course, the jury's judgment is meaningful only where the jury has an appropriate measure of choice as to whether the death penalty is to be imposed. As far as execution for rape is concerned, this is now true only in Georgia and in Florida; and in the latter State, capital punishment is authorized only for the rape of children.

According to the factual submissions in this Court, out of all rape convictions in Georgia since 1973—and that total number has not been tendered—63 cases had been reviewed by the Georgia Supreme Court as of the time of oral argument; and of these, six involved a death sentence, one of which was set aside, leaving five convicted rapists now under sentence of death in the State of Georgia. Georgia juries have thus sentenced rapists to death six times since 1973. This obviously is not a negligible number; and the State argues that as a practical matter juries simply reserve the extreme sanction for extreme cases of rape and that recent experience surely does not prove that jurors consider the death penalty to be a disproportionate punishment for every conceivable instance of rape, no matter how aggravated. Nevertheless, it is true that in the vast majority of cases, at least nine out of 10, juries have not imposed the death sentence.

IV

These recent events evidencing the attitude of state legislatures and sentencing juries do not wholly determine this controversy, for the Constitution contemplates that in the end our own judgment will be brought to bear on the question of the acceptability of the death penalty under the Eighth Amendment. Nevertheless, the legislative rejection of capital punishment for rape strongly confirms our own judgment, which is that death is indeed a disproportionate penalty for the crime of raping an adult woman.

We do not discount the seriousness of rape as a crime. It is highly reprehensible, both in a moral sense and in its almost total contempt for the personal integrity and autonomy of the female victim and for the latter's privilege of choosing those with whom intimate relationships are to be established. Short of homicide, it is the "ultimate violation of self." It is also a violent crime because it normally involves force, or the threat of force or intimidation, to overcome the will and the capacity of the victim to resist. Rape is very often accompanied by physical injury to the female and can also inflict mental and psychological damage. Because it undermines the community's sense of security, there is public injury as well.

Rape is without doubt deserving of serious punishment; but in terms of moral depravity and of the injury to the person and to the public, it does not compare with murder, which does involve the unjustified taking of human life. Although it may be accompanied by another crime, rape by definition does not include the death or even the serious injury to another person. The murderer kills; the rapist, if no more than that, does not. Life is over for the victim of the murderers; for the rape victim, life may not be nearly so happy as it was, but it is not over and normally is not beyond repair. We have the abiding conviction that the death penalty, which "is unique in its severity and revocability," 428 US 187, 49 L Ed 2d 859, 96 S Ct 2909, is an excessive penalty for the rapist who, as such, does not take human life.

This does not end the matter; for under Georgia law, death may not be imposed for any capital offense, including rape, unless the jury or judge finds one of the statutory aggravating circumstances and then elects to impose that sentence. Section 26-3102 (supp 1975); Gregg v Georgia, supra, at 165-166, 49 L Ed 2d 859, 96 S Ct 2909. For the rapist to be executed in Georgia, it must therefore be found not only that he committed rape but also that one or more of the following aggravating circumstances were present: (1) that the rape was committed by a person with a prior record of conviction for a capital felony; (2) that the rape was committed while the offender was engaged in the commission of another capital felony, or aggravated battery; or (3) the rape "was outrageously or wantonly vile, horrible or inhuman in that it involved torture, depravity of mind, or aggravated battery to the victim." Here, the first two of these aggravating circumstances were alleged and found by the jury.

Neither of these circumstances, nor both of them together, change our conclusion that the death sentence imposed on Coker is a disproportionate punishment for rape. Coker had prior convictions for capital felonies—rape, murder and kidnapping—but these prior convictions do not change the fact that the instant crime being punished is a rape not involving the taking of life.

It is also true that the present rape occurred while Coker was committing armed robbery, a felony for which the Georgia statutes authorize the death penalty. But Coker was tried for the robbery offense as well as for rape and received a separate life sentence for this crime; the jury did not deem the robbery itself deserving of the death penalty, even though accompanied by the aggravating circumstance, which was stipulated, that Coker had been convicted of a prior capital crime.

We note finally that in Georgia a person commits murder when he unlawfully and with malice aforethought, either express or implied, causes the death of another human being. He also commits that crime when in the commission of a felony he causes the death of another human being, irrespective of malice. But even where the killing is deliberate, it is not punishable by death absent proof of aggravating circumstances. It is difficult to accept the notion, and we do not, that the rape, with or without aggravating circumstances, should be punished more heavily than the deliberate killer as long as the rapist does not himself take the life of his victim. The judgment of the Georgia Supreme Court upholding the death sentence is reversed and the case is remanded to that court for further proceedings not inconsistent with this opinion.

So ordered.

Ernest John Dobbert, Jr., Petitioner, *v.* State of Florida

432 U.S. 282, 98 S.Ct. 246, 53 L.Ed. 2d. 344 (1977)

Argued March 28, 1977.—Decided June 17, 1977.

. . .

MR. JUSTICE REHNQUIST delivered the opinion of the Court.

Petitioner was convicted of murder in the first degree, murder in the second degree, child abuse, and child torture. The victims were his children. Under the Florida death penalty statute then in effect he was sentenced by the trial judge to death. The Florida Supreme Court affirmed and we granted certiorari to consider whether changes in the Florida death penalty statutes subjected him to trial under an ex post facto law or denied him equal protection of the laws, and whether the significant amount of pretrial publicity concerning the crime deprived petitioner of his right to a fair trial. We conclude that petitioner has not shown the deprivation of any federal constitutional right, and affirm the judgment of the Florida Supreme Court.

I

Petitioner was convicted of murdering his daughter Kelly Ann, age 9, and his son Ryder Scott, age 7. He was also found guilty of torturing his son Ernest John, age 11, and of abusing his daughter Honore Elizabeth, age 5. The brutality and heinousness of these crimes are relevant both to petitioner's motion for a change of venue due to pretrial publicity and to the trial judge's imposition of the sentence of death. The trial judge, in his factual findings at the sentencing phase of the trial, summarized petitioner's treatment of his own offspring as follows:

> "The evidence and testimony showed premeditated and continuous torture, brutality, sadism and unspeakable horrors committed against all of the children over a period of time." App 47.

The judge then detailed some of the horrors inflicted upon young Kelly Ann, upon which he relied to meet the statutory requirement that aggravating circumstances be found:

> "Over the period of time of the latter portion of Kelly Ann's short, tortuous life the defendant did these things to her on one or many occasions:

"1. Beat her in the head until it was swollen.
"2. Burned her hands.
"3. Poked his fingers in her eyes.
"4. Beat her in the abdomen until 'it was swollen like she was pregnant.'
"5. Knocked her against a wall and 'when she fell, kicked her in the lower part of the body.'
"6. Held her under water in both the bath tub and toilet.
"7. Kicked her against a table which cut her head—then defendant sewed up her wound with needle and thread.
"8. Scarred her head and body by beating her with a belt and board—causing marks from her cheek, across the neck and down her back—which injuries worsened without treatment 'until the body juices came out.'
"9. On one occasion beat her continuously for 45 minutes.
"10. On many occasions kicked her in the stomach with his shoes on, and on the night she died he kicked her a number of times.
"11. Kept her out of school so that the many scars, cuts and bruises on her body would not be seen by others.
"12. Defendant made no effort to get professional medical care and attention for the child and in fact actively prevented any out-siders from discovering her condition.
"13. Choked her on the night she died and when she stopped breathing he placed her body in a plastic garbage bag and buried her in an unmarked and unknown grave." App 47.

This sordid tale began to unravel in early 1972 when Ernest John III was found battered and wandering in Jacksonville, Fla. An arrest warrant was issued for petitioner, who evidently fled the area. About a year later, Honore Elizabeth was found in a Ft. Lauderdale hospital with a note pinned to her clothing asking that she be sent to her mother in Wisconsin. Shortly thereafter petitioner's abandoned automobile was found near a bridge with a suicide note on the front seat. Petitioner, however, had fled to Texas, where he was eventually arrested and extradited to Florida.

Prior to trial, petitioner applied to the Supreme Court of Florida for a Constitutional Stay of Trial, alleging the application of an ex post facto law and a violation of equal protection. App 81–86. The application was denied. Petitioner also moved in the lower court for a change of venue, alleging that he was charged with "inherently odious" acts, App 17, and that extensive publicity regarding his flight, extradition, and arrest, as well as a search for bodies by the Jacksonville Police Department, had rendered impossible a fair and impartial trial in Duval County. App 17–18. The trial judge took the motion under advisement and issued an order enjoining anyone connected with the trial from releasing any statement about the case to the news media. App 25–26. The motion was later denied.

Trial was had and the jury found petitioner guilty of, inter alia, murder in the first degree. Pursuant to the Florida death penalty statute then in effect, a sentencing hearing was held before the judge and jury. The jury by a 10-to-2 majority found sufficient mitigating circumstances to outweigh any aggravating circumstances and recommended a sentence of life imprisonment. The trial judge, pursuant to his authority under the amended Florida statute, overruled the jury's recommendation and sentenced petitioner to death. The Florida Supreme Court affirmed over two dissents.

II

Petitioner makes three separate claims based on the prohibition against ex post facto laws, and a related claim based upon the Equal Protection Clause of the Fourteenth Amendment. His first ex post facto claim is addressed to the change in the function of judge and jury in the imposition of death sentences in Florida between the time he committed the acts charged and the time he was tried for them. The second ex post facto claim is grounded on his contention that at the time he acted there was no valid death penalty statute in effect in Florida. The third claim relates to the more stringent parole requirements attached to a life sentence under the new law. A discussion of the relevant changes in Florida death sentencing procedures brings these claims into focus.

The murders for which petitioner was convicted were alleged to have occurred on December 31, 1971 (Kelly Ann) and between January 1 and April 8, 1972 (Ryder Scott). During that period of time, FSA §§ 775.082 (1971) and 921.141 (1971), as then written, provided that a person convicted of a capital felony was to be punished by death unless the verdict included a recommendation of mercy by a majority of the jury.

On June 22, 1972, this Court struck down a Georgia death penalty statute as violative of the Eighth and Fourteenth Amendments. Furman v Georgia, 408 US 238, 33 L Ed 2d 346, 92 S Ct 2726 (1972). Shortly thereafter, on July 17, 1972, in Donaldson v Sack, 265 So 2d 499 (Fla 1972), the Florida Supreme Court found the 1971 Florida death penalty statutes inconsistent with Furman. Late in 1972 Florida enacted a new death penalty procedure, Chap 72-724, Laws of Florida (1972), amending, inter alia, §§ 775.082 and 921.141.

The opinion of Mr. Justice Stewart, Mr. Justice Powell, and Mr. Justice Stevens in Proffitt v Florida, 428 US 242, 49 L Ed 2d 913, 96 S Ct 2960 (1976), in which the constitutionality of this statute was upheld, details at length the operation of the revised § 921.141. Id., at ___, 49 L Ed 2d 913, 96 S Ct 2960. After a defendant is found guilty of a capital felony, a separate sentencing hearing is held before the trial judge and the trial jury. Any evidence that the judge deems relevant to sentencing may be admitted, and certain evidence relating to aggravating or mitigating circumstances must be admitted. The jury, by a majority vote, then renders an advisory decision, not binding on the court, based upon these aggravating and mitigating circumstances. The court must then also weigh the aggravating and mitigating circumstances. If the court imposes a sentence of death, it must set forth written findings of fact regarding the aggravating and mitigating circumstances. A judgment of conviction and sentence of death is then subject to an automatic, priority review by the Florida Supreme Court. It is in the light of these changes that we must adjudge petitioner's ex post facto claims.

A

Petitioner argues that the change in the role of the judge and jury in the imposition of the death sentence in Florida between the time of the murders and the time of the trial constitutes an ex post facto violation. Petitioner views the change in the Florida death sentencing procedure as depriving him of a substantial right to have the jury determine, without review by the trial judge, whether that penalty should be imposed. We conclude that the changes in the law are procedural, and on the whole ameliorative, and that there is no ex post facto violation.

Article I, § 10, of the United States Constitution prohibits a State from passing any "ex post facto Law." Our cases have not attempted to precisely delimit the scope of this Latin phrase, but have instead given it substance by an accretion of case law. In Beazell v Ohio, 269 US 167, 169, 70 L Ed 216, 46 S Ct 68 (1925), MR. JUSTICE STONE summarized for the Court the characteristics of an ex post facto law:

> "It is settled, by decisions of this Court so well known that their citation may be dispensed with, that any statute which punishes as a crime an act previously committed, which was innocent when done; which makes more burdensome the punishment for a crime after its commission, or which deprives one charged with crime of any defense available according to law at the time when the act was committed, is prohibited as ex post facto."

It is equally well settled, however, that "the inhibition upon the passage of ex post facto laws does not give a criminal a right to be tried, in all respects, by the law in force when the crime charged was committed." Gibson v Mississippi, 162 US 565, 590, 40 L Ed 1075, 16 S Ct 904 (1896). "[T]he constitutional provision was intended to secure substantial personal rights against arbitrary and oppressive legislation, see Malloy v South Carolina, 237 US 180, 183, 59 L Ed 905, 35 S Ct 507], and not to limit the legislative control of remedies and modes of procedure which do not affect matters of substance." Beazell v Ohio, supra, at 171, 70 L Ed 216, 46 S Ct 68.

Even though it may work to the disadvantage of a defendant, a procedural change is not ex post facto. For example, in Hopt v Utah, 110 US 574, 28 L Ed 262, 4 S Ct 202 (1884), as of the date of the alleged homicide a convicted felon could not have been called as a witness. Subsequent to that date, but prior to the trial of the case, this law was changed; a convicted felon was called to the stand and testified, implicating Hopt in the crime charged against him. Even though this change in the law obviously had a detrimental impact upon the defendant, the Court found that the law was not ex post facto because it neither made criminal a theretofore innocent act, nor aggravated a crime previously committed, nor provided greater punishment, nor changed the proof necessary to convict. Id., at 589, 28 L Ed 262, 4 S Ct 202.

In Thompson v Missouri, 171 US 380, 43 L Ed 204, 18 S Ct 922 (1898), a defendant was convicted of murder solely upon circumstantial evidence. His conviction was reversed by the Missouri Supreme Court because of the inadmissibility of certain evidence. Prior to the second trial, the law was changed to make the evidence admissible and defendant was again convicted. Nonetheless, the Court held that this change was procedural and not violative of the ex post facto clause.

In the case at hand, the change in the statute was clearly procedural. The new statute simply altered the methods employed in determining whether the death penalty was to be imposed; there was no change in the quantum of punishment attached to the crime. In Hopt v Utah, supra, the following language, applicable with equal force to the case at hand, summarized our conclusion that the change was procedural and not a violation of the ex post facto clause:

> "The crime for which the present defendant was indicted, the punishment prescribed therefor, and the quantity or the degree of proof necessary to establish his guilt, all remained unaffected by the subsequent statute." Id., at 589–590. 28 L Ed 262, 4 S Ct 202.

In this case, not only was the change in the law procedural, it was ameliorative. It is axiomatic that for a law to be ex post facto it must be more onerous than the prior law. Petitioner argues that the change in the law harmed him because the jury's recommendation of life imprisonment would not have been subject to review by the trial judge under the prior law. But it certainly cannot be said with assurance that, had his trial been conducted under the old statute, the jury would have returned a verdict of life.

Hence, petitioner's speculation that the jury would have recommended life were the prior procedure in effect is not compelling. We must compare the two statutory procedures in toto to determine if the new may be fairly characterized as more onerous. Under the old procedure, the death penalty was "presumed" unless the jury, in its unbridled discretion, made a recommendation for mercy. The Florida Legislature enacted the new procedure specifically to provide the constitutional procedural protections required by Furman, thus providing capital defendants with more, rather than less, judicial protection. These protections, upheld by this Court in Proffitt, provided are substantial. A separate hearing is held; the defendant is allowed to present any relevant mitigating evidence. The jury renders an advisory verdict based upon its perception of aggravating and mitigating factors in the case. The court makes the final determination, but may impose death only after making a written finding that there are insufficient mitigating circumstances to outweigh the aggravating circumstances.

Finally, in what may be termed a tripartite review, the Florida Supreme Court is required to review each sentence of death. This required review, not present under the old procedure, is by no means perfunctory; as we noted in Proffitt, as of that time the Florida Supreme Court had vacated eight of the 21 death sentences that it had reviewed to that date. 428 US 242, 49 L Ed 2d 913, 96 S Ct 2960. Perhaps most importantly, the Florida Supreme Court has held that the following standard must be used to review a trial court's rejection of a jury's recommendation of life:

> "In order to sustain a sentence of death following a jury recommendation of life, the facts suggesting a sentence of death should be so *clear and convincing that virtually no reasonable person could differ*." Tedder v State, 322 So 2d 908, 910 (1975) (emphasis added). Cited with approbation in Proffitt v Florida, 428 US 242, at ___, 49 L Ed 2d 913, 96 S Ct 2960.

This crucial protection demonstrates that the new statute affords significantly more safeguards to the defendant than did the old. Death is not automatic, absent a jury recommendation of mercy, as it was under the old procedure. A jury recommendation of life may be overridden by the trial judge only under the exacting standards of Tedder. Hence, defendants are not significantly disadvantaged vis-à-vis the recommendation of life by the jury; on the other hand, unlike the old statute, a jury determination of death is not binding. Under the new statute, defendants have a second chance for life with the trial judge and a third, if necessary, with the Florida Supreme Court. No such protection was afforded by the old statute. Hence, viewing the totality of the procedural changes wrought by the new statute, we conclude that the new statute did not work an onerous application of an ex post facto change in the law. Perhaps the ultimate proof of this fact is that this old statute was held to be violative of the United States Constitution in Donaldson, supra, while the new law was upheld by this Court in Proffitt, supra.

B

Petitioner's second ex post facto claim is based on the contention that at the time he murdered his children there was no death penalty "in effect" in Florida. This is so, he contends, because the earlier statute enacted by the legislature was, after the time he acted, found by the Supreme Court of Florida to be invalid under our decision in Furman v Georgia, supra. Therefore, argues petitioner, there was no "valid" death penalty in effect in Florida as of the date of his actions. But this sophistic argument mocks the substance of the ex post facto clause. Whether or not the old statute would, in the future, withstand constitutional attack, it clearly indicated Florida's view of the severity of murder and of the degree of punishment that the legislature wished to impose upon murderers. The statute was intended to provide maximum deterrence, and its existence on the statute books provided fair warning as to the degree of culpability which the State ascribed to the act of murder.

Petitioner's highly technical argument is at odds with the statement of this Court in Chicot County District v Bank, 308 US 371, 375, 84 L Ed 329, 60 S Ct 317:

> "The courts below have proceeded on the theory that the Act of Congress, having been found to be unconstitutional, was not a law; that it was inoperative, conferring no rights and imposing no duties, and hence affording no basis for the challenged decree. Norton v. Shelby County, 118 US 425, 442, [30 L Ed 178, 6 S Ct 1121]; Chicago, I. & L. Ry. Co. v Hackett, 228 US 559, 566, [57 L Ed 966, 33 S Ct 581]. It is quite clear, however, that such broad statements as to the effect of a determination of unconstitutionality must be taken with qualifications. The actual existence of a statute, prior to such a determination, is an operative fact and may have consequences which cannot justly be ignored." 308 U.S., at 374, 84 L Ed 329, 60 S Ct 317.

Here the existence of the statute served as an "operative fact" to warn the petitioner of the penalty which Florida would seek to impose on him if he were convicted of first-degree murder. This was sufficient compliance with the ex post facto provision of the United States Constitution.

C

Petitioner's third ex post facto contention is based on the fact that the new Florida statute provides that anyone sentenced to life imprisonment under that section must serve at least 25 years before becoming eligible for parole. The prior section contained no such limitation. The Florida Supreme Court in Lee v State, 294 So 2d 305 (1974), found that this provision restricting parole could not constitutionally be applied to crimes committed prior to its effective date. Petitioner contends that nonetheless its enactment by the Florida Legislature amounts to an ex post facto law, and that because of this he may successfully challenge the death sentence imposed upon him.

Petitioner, of course, did not receive a life sentence, and so any added onus attaching to it as a result of the change in Florida law had no effect on him. In Lindsey v Washington, 301 US 397, 400–401, 81 L Ed 1182, 57 S Ct 797, the Court stated:

> "The effect of the new statute is to make mandatory what was before only the maximum sentence. Under it the prisoners may be held to confinement during the entire fifteen year period. Even if they are admitted to parole, to which they become eligible after the expiration of the terms fixed by the board, they remain subject to its surveillance and the parole may until the expiration of the fifteen years, be revoked at the discretion of the board or cancelled at the will of the governor. *It is true that petitioners might have been sentenced to fifteen years under the old statute. But the ex post facto clause looks to the standard of punishment prescribed by a statute, rather than to the sentence actually imposed.* The Constitution forbids the application of any new punitive measure to a crime already consummated, to the detriment or material disadvantage of the wrongdoer. Kring v Missouri, supra, 228–229, [27 L Ed 506, 2 S Ct 443]; In re Medley, 134 US 160, 171, [33 L Ed 835, 10 S Ct 384]; Thompson v Utah, 170 US 343, 351, [42 L Ed 1061, 18 S Ct 620]. *It is for this reason that an increase in the possible penalty is ex post facto,* Calder v Bull, 3 Dall 386, 390, [1 L Ed 648]; Cummings v Missouri, supra, 326, [18 L Ed 356]; Malloy v South Carolina, 237 US 180, 184, [59 L Ed 905, 35 S Ct 507]; *regardless of the length of the sentence actually imposed, since the measure of punishment prescribed by the later statute is more severe than that of the earlier* State v Callahan, 109 La 946; 33 So 931; State v Smith, 56 Ore 21; 107 Pac 980." (Emphasis added.)

Lifted from their context and read expansively, the italicized portions of the quoted language would lend some support to petitioner's claim. But we think that consideration of the Lindsey language in the factual context in which that case was decided does not lead to the result sought by petitioner.

Lindsey came here from the Supreme Court of Washington on a claim that a change in the state law respecting the sentence to be imposed upon one convicted of the felony of grand larceny violated the ex post facto clause. At the time Lindsey committed the larceny, the law provided for a maximum sentence of 15 years, and a minimum sentence of not less than six months. At the time Lindsey was sentenced, the law had been changed to provide for a mandatory 15 year sentence. Even though under the new statute a convict could be admitted to parole at a time far short of the expiration of his mandatory sentence, the Court observed that even on parole he would remain "subject to the surveillance" of the parole board and that his parole itself was subject to revocation.

Lindsey, then, had received a sentence under the new law which was within permissible bounds under the old law, albeit at the outer limits of those bounds. But under the new law it was the *only* sentence he could have received, while under the old law the sentencing judge could in his discretion have imposed a much shorter sentence. In contrast to the petitioner here, Lindsey was not complaining in the abstract about some change in the law, which as events proved, would have no applicability to his case. His complaint was that the new law totally eliminated any sentence of less than 15 years once he was convicted of larceny, and thereby assured that he would receive what was only the discretionary maximum sentence under the old law.

We think the excerpted language from Lindsey must be read in the light of these facts to mean that one is not barred from challenging a change in the penal code on ex post facto grounds simply because the sentence he received under the new law was not more onerous than that which he might have received under the old. It is one thing to find an ex post facto violation where under the new law a defendant *must* receive a sentence which was under the old law only the maximum in a discretionary spectrum of length; it would be quite another to do so in a case, such as this, where the change has had no effect on the defendant in the proceedings of which he complains.

Petitioner here can make no claim comparable to Lindsey's. Under the new law, both life imprisonment and death remain as possible alternative sentences. Only if we were to read the excerpted portion of the quoted language from Lindsey to confer standing on the defendant to complain of an added burden newly attached to a sentence which was never imposed on him would that language assist him. But we hold that petitioner, having been sentenced to death, may not complain of burdens attached to the life sentence under the new law which may not have attached to it under the old.

D

After our Furman decision and its own decision in Donaldson v Sack, the Florida Supreme Court resentenced all prisoners under sentence of death pursuant to the old statute to life imprisonment. Anderson v Florida, 267 So 2d 8 (Fla 1972); In re Baker, 267 So 2d 331 (Fla 1972). Petitioner argues that since his crimes were committed before our decision in Furman, the imposition of the death sentence upon him pursuant to the new statute which was in effect at the time of his trial denies him equal protection of the laws.

But petitioner is simply not similarly situated to those whose sentences were commuted. He was neither tried nor sentenced prior to Furman, as were they, and the only effect of the former statute was to provide sufficient warning of the gravity Florida attached to first-degree murder so as to make the application of this new statute to him consistent with the ex post facto clause of the United States Constitution. Florida obviously had to draw the line at some point between those whose cases which had progressed sufficiently far in the legal process so as to be governed solely by the old statute, with the concomitant unconstitutionality of its death penalty provision, and those whose involving acts which could properly be subjected to punishment under the new statute. There is nothing irrational about Florida's decision to relegate petitioner to the latter class, since the new statute was in effect at the time of his trial and sentence.

III

There was, understandably, extensive pre-trial publicity concerning several aspects of this case. We accept petitioner's assertion, Brief for Petitioner, at 38–48, that there was substantial media coverage, including a number of television and radio stories regarding the various aspects of the case.

In Murphy v Florida, 421 US 794, 44 L Ed 2d 589, 95 S Ct 2031 (1975), we reviewed a trial in which many jurors had heard of the defendant through extensive news coverage. Characterizing our previous cases in which we had overturned a state court conviction on these grounds as involving "a trial atmosphere that had been utterly corrupted by press coverage," id., at 798, 44 L Ed 2d 589, 95 S Ct 2031, we recognized that:

> "Qualified jurors need not, however, be totally ignorant of the facts and issues involved.
>
> "'To hold that the mere existence of any preconceived notion as to the guilt or innocence of an accused, without more, is sufficient to rebut the presumption of a prospective juror's impartiality would be to establish an impossible standard. It is sufficient if the juror can lay aside his impression or opinion and render a verdict based on the evidence presented in court. [Irvin v Dowd, 366 US 717, 723, [6 L Ed 2d 751, 81 S Ct 1639] (1961).]'" Id., at 799–800, 44 L Ed 2d 589, 95 S Ct 2031.

We concluded that the petitioner in Murphy had failed to show that the trial setting was inherently prejudicial or that the jury selection process permitted an inference of actual prejudice. Id., at 803, 44 L Ed 2d 589, 95 S Ct 2031.

The Florida Supreme Court in this case noted that 78 prospective jurors were interviewed, and that petitioner exercised only 27 of his 32 peremptory challenges. Specifically referring to our decision in Murphy, that court concluded:

> ". . . [W]e find from the record that the trial judge did everything possible to insure an impartial trial for the defendant. The jurors, carefully and extensively examined by defense counsel to determine that they could be fair and impartial, were sequestered and comprehensive gag order was placed on all participants of the trial. . . .

> "Appellant has failed to show that he did not receive a fair and impartial trial, that the setting of his trial was inherently prejudicial." 328 So 2d, at 439–440.

Petitioner's argument that the extensive coverage by the media denied him a fair trial rests almost entirely upon the quantum of publicity which the events received. He has directed us to no specific portions of the record, in particular the voir dire examination of the jurors, which would require a finding of constitutional unfairness as to the method of jury selection or as to the character of the jurors actually selected. But under Murphy, extensive knowledge in the community of neither the crimes nor the putative criminal is sufficient by itself to render a trial constitutionally unfair. Petitioner in this case has simply shown that the community was made well aware of the charges against him and asks us on that basis to presume unfairness of constitutional magnitude at his trial. This we will not do in the absence of a "trial atmosphere utterly corrupted by press coverage," Murphy v Florida, supra. One who is reasonably suspected of murdering his children cannot expect to remain anonymous. Petitioner has failed to convince us that under the "totality of circumstances," Murphy, supra, the Florida Supreme Court was wrong in finding no constitutional violation with respect to the pretrial publicity. The judgment of the Supreme Court of Florida is therefore

Affirmed.

ROBERT BULLINGTON, Petitioner, *v.* STATE OF MISSOURI

451 U.S. 430, 68 L.Ed.2d 270, 101 S.Ct. 1852 (1981)

Justice Blackmun delivered the opinion of the Court. *Stroud* v. *United States,* 251 U.S. 15 (1919), concerned a defendant who was convicted of first-degree murder and sentenced to life imprisonment, and who then obtained, upon confession of error by the Solicitor General, a reversal of his conviction and a new trial. This Court, by a unanimous vote in that case, held that the Double Jeopardy Clause of the Fifth Amendment did not bar the imposition of the death penalty when Stroud at his new trial was again convicted.

The issue in the present case is whether the reasoning of *Stroud* is also to apply under a system where a jury's sentencing decision is made at a bifurcated proceeding's second stage at which the prosecution has the burden of proving certain elements beyond a reasonable doubt before the death penalty may be imposed.

I

Missouri law provides two, and only two, possible sentences for a defendant convicted of capital murder: (a) death, or (b) life imprisonment without eligibility for probation or parole for 50 years. Mo. Rev. Stat. § 565.008.1 (1978).

Like most death penalty legislation enacted after this Court's decision in *Furman* v. *Georgia,* 408 U.S. 238 (1972), the Missouri statutes contain substantive standards to guide the discretion of the sentencer. The statutes also afford procedural safeguards to the convicted defendant. Section 565.006 provides that the trial court shall conduct a separate presentence hearing for the defendant who is convicted by a jury of capital murder. The hearing must be held before the same jury that found the defendant guilty, and "additional evidence in extenuation, mitigation, and aggravation of punishment" shall be heard. "Only such evidence in aggravation as the prosecution has made known to the defendant prior to his trial shall be admissible." The jury must consider whether the evidence shows that there exist any of the 10 aggravating circumstances or the 7 mitigating circumstances specified by the statute, see §§ 565.012.2 and 565.012.3; whether any other mitigating or aggravating circumstances authorized by law exist; whether any aggravating circumstances that do exist are sufficient to warrant the imposition of the death penalty; and whether any mitigating circumstances that exist outweigh the aggravating circumstances. § 565.012.1. A jury that imposes the death penalty must designate in writing the aggravating circumstance or circumstances that it finds beyond a reasonable doubt. § 565.012.4. It also must be convinced beyond a reasonable doubt that any aggravating circumstance or circumstances that it finds to exist are sufficient to warrant the imposition of the death penalty. Missouri Approved Instructions—Criminal (MAI–Cr) § 15.42 (1979). A Missouri jury is instructed that it is not compelled to impose the death penalty, even if it decides that a sufficient aggravating circumstance or circumstances exist and that it or they are not outweighed by any mitigating circumstance or circumstances. MAI–Cr. § 15.46. A jury's decision to impose the death penalty must be unanimous. If the jury is unable to agree, the defendant receives the alternative sentence of life imprisonment described above. § 565.006.2; MAI–Cr. § 15.48.

II

In December 1977, petitioner Robert Bullington was indicted in St. Louis County, Mo., for capital murder and other crimes arising out of the abduction of a young woman and her subsequent death by drowning.

The Circuit Court of St. Louis County granted petitioner's pretrial motion for a change of venue to Jackson County in the western part of the State. The prosecution, by letter, informed the defense that the State would seek the death penalty if the jury convicted the defendant of capital murder. App. 12. The letter-notice stated that the prosecution would present evidence of two aggravating circumstances specified by the statute: that "[t]he offense was committed by a person . . . who has a substantial history of serious assaultive criminal convictions," § 565.012.2 (1), and that "[t]he offense was outrageously or wantonly vile, horrible or inhuman in that it involved torture, or depravity of mind," § 565.012.2 (7).

At the guilt-or-innocence phase of petitioner's trial, the jury returned a verdict of guilty of capital murder. App. 21. On the following day, the trial court proceeded to hold the presentence hearing required by § 565.006.2. Evidence submitted by the prosecution was received. None was offered by the defense. After argument by counsel, instructions from the judge, and deliberation, the jury returned its additional verdict fixing petitioner's punishment not at death, but at imprisonment for life without eligibility for probation or parole for 50 years. App. 27.

Petitioner then moved, on various grounds, for judgment of acquittal or in the alternative for a new trial. While that motion was pending, *Duren* v. *Missouri,* 439 U.S. 357 (1979), was decided. In that case this Court held that Missouri's constitutional and statutory provisions allowing women to claim automatic exemption from jury service deprived a defendant of his Sixth and Fourteenth Amendments right to a jury drawn from a fair cross-section of the community. The trial court overruled petitioner's motion for acquittal but, relying upon *Duren,* granted his motion for a new trial. App. 44.

Soon thereafter, the prosecution served and filed a formal "Notice of Evidence in Aggravation," stating that it intended again to seek the death penalty. The notice specified the same aggravating circumstances the State sought to prove at the first trial, see also Tr. of Oral Arg. 36, and asserted that it would introduce the evidence that was previously disclosed to defense counsel. App. 45–46. The defense moved to strike the notice, *id.,* at 47, arguing that the Double Jeopardy Clause of the Fifth Amendment (as made applicable to the States through the Fourteenth Amendment, *Benton* v. *Maryland,* 395 U.S. 784, 794 (1969)) barred the imposition of the penalty of death when the first jury had declined to impose the death sentence.

The trial court announced that it would grant that motion and would not permit the State to seek the death penalty. Before the court issued a formal order to this effect, the prosecution sought a writ of prohibition or mandamus from the Missouri Court of Appeals for the Western District. After granting a temporary "stop order," App. 56, the Court of Appeals without opinion denied the State's request and dissolved the stop order. *Id.,* at 57. The Supreme Court of Missouri, however, granted the prosecution's motion for transfer of the case to that court and issued a preliminary writ of prohibition. After argument, the court, sitting en banc and by a divided vote, sustained the State's position and made the writ absolute. *State ex rel. Westfall* v. *Mason,* 594 S. W. 2d 908 (1980). It held that neither the Double Jeopardy Clause, nor the Eighth Amendment, nor the Due Process Clause barred the imposition of the death penalty upon petitioner at his new trial, and that allowing the prosecution to seek capital punishment would not impermissibly chill a defendant's effort to seek redress for any constitutional violation committed at his initial trial.

We granted certiorari, 449 U.S. 819 (1980), in order to consider the important issues raised by petitioner regarding the administration of the death penalty.

III

It is well established that the Double Jeopardy Clause forbids the retrial of a defendant who has been *acquitted* of the crime charged. *United States* v. *DiFrancesco,* 449 U.S. 117, 129–130 (1980); *Burks* v. *United States,* 437 U.S. 1, 16 (1978); *United States* v. *Martin Linen Supply Co.,* 430 U.S. 564, 571 (1977); *Fong Foo* v. *United States,* 369 U.S. 141, 143 (1962); *Green* v. *United States,* 355 U.S. 184 (1957). This Court, however, has resisted attempts to extend that principle to sentencing. The imposition of a particular sentence usually is not regarded as an "acquittal" of any more severe sentence that could have been imposed. The Court generally has concluded, therefore, that the Double Jeopardy Clause imposes no absolute prohibition against the imposition of a harsher sentence at retrial after a defendant has succeeded in having his original conviction set aside. See *North Carolina* v. *Pearce,* 395 U.S. 711 (1969). See also *United States* v. *DiFrancesco,* 449 U.S., at 133, 137–138; *Chaffin* v. *Stynchcombe,* 412 U.S. 17, 23–24 (1973); *Stroud* v. *United States,* 251 U.S. 15 (1919).

The procedure that resulted in the imposition of the sentence of life imprisonment upon petitioner Bullington at his first trial, however, differs significantly from those employed in any of the Court's cases where the Double Jeopardy Clause has been held inapplicable to sentencing. The jury in this case was not given unbounded discretion to select an appropriate punishment from a wide range authorized by statute. Rather, a separate hearing was required and was held, and the jury was presented both a choice between two alternatives and standards to guide the making of that choice. Nor did the prosecution simply recommend what it felt to be an appropriate punishment. It undertook the burden of establishing certain facts beyond a reasonable doubt in its quest to obtain the harsher of the two alternative verdicts. The presentence hearing resembled and, indeed, in all relevant respects was like the immediately preceding trial on the issue of guilt or innocence. It was itself a trial on the issue of punishment so precisely defined by the Missouri statutes.

In contrast, the sentencing procedures considered in the Court's previous cases did not have the hallmarks of the trial on guilt or innocence. In *Pearce, Chaffin,* and *Stroud,* there was no separate sentencing proceeding at which the prosecution was required to prove—beyond a reasonable doubt or otherwise—additional facts in order to justify the particular sentence. In each of those cases, moreover, the sentencer's discretion was essentially unfettered. In *Stroud,* no standards had been enacted to guide the jury's discretion. In *Pearce,* the judge had a wide range of punishments from which to choose with no explicit standards imposed to guide him. And in *Chaffin,* the discretion given to the jury was extremely broad. That defendant, convicted in Georgia of robbery, could have been sentenced to death, to life imprisonment, or to a prison term of between 4 and 20 years. 412 U.S., at 18, and n. 1. The statute contained no standards to guide the jury's exercise of its discretion.

In only one prior case, *United States* v. *DiFrancesco,* has this Court considered a separate or bifurcated sentencing procedure at which it was necessary for the prosecution to prove additional facts. The federal statute under consideration there, the "dangerous special offender" provision of the Organized Crime Control Act of 1970, 18 U. S. C. §§ 3575 and 3576, requires a separate presentence hearing. The Government must prove the additional fact that the defendant is a "dangerous special offender," as defined in the statute, in order for the court to impose an enhanced sentence. But there are highly pertinent differences between the Missouri procedures controlling the present case and those found constitutional in *DiFrancesco.* The federal procedures at issue in *DiFrancesco* include appellate review of a sentence "on the record of the sentencing court," § 3576, not a *de novo* proceeding that gives the Government the opportunity to convince a second factfinder of its view of the facts. Moreover, the choice presented to the federal judge under § 3575 is far broader than that faced by the state jury at the present petitioner's trial. Bullington's Missouri jury was given—and under the State's statutes could be given—only two choices, death or life imprisonment. On the other hand, if the Federal Government proves that a person convicted of a felony is a dangerous special offender, the judge may sentence that person to "an appropriate term not to exceed twenty-five years and not disproportionate in severity to the maximum term otherwise authorized by law for such felony." § 3575 (b). Finally, although the statute requires the Government to prove the additional fact that the defendant is a "dangerous special offender," it need do so only by a preponderance of the evidence. *Ibid.* This stands in contrast to the reasonable-doubt standard of the Missouri statute, the same standard required to be used at the trial on the issue of guilt or innocence. *Jackson* v. *Virginia,* 443 U.S. 307 (1979); *In re Winship,* 397 U.S. 358 (1970). The State's use of this standard indicates that, as has been said generally of the criminal case, "the interests of the defendant are of such magnitude that . . . they have been protected by standards of proof designed to exclude as nearly as possible the likelihood of an erroneous judgment. . . . [O]ur society imposes almost the entire risk of error upon itself." *Addington* v. *Texas,* 441 U.S. 418, 423–424 (1979).

IV

These procedural differences become important when the underlying rationale of the cases is considered. The State here relies principally upon *North Carolina* v. *Pearce.* The Court's starting point in that case, 395 U.S., at 719–720, was the established rule that there is no double jeopardy bar to retrying a defendant who has succeeded in overturning his conviction. See, *e. g., United States* v. *Tateo,* 377 U.S. 463 (1964); *United States* v. *Ball,* 163 U.S. 662, 672 (1896). The Court stated that this rule rests on the premise that the original conviction has been nullified and "the slate wiped clean." 395 U.S., at 721. Therefore, if the defendant is convicted again, he constitutionally may be subjected to whatever punishment is lawful, subject only to the limitation that he receive credit for time served.

There is an important exception, however, to the rule recognized in *Pearce.*

A defendant may not be retried if he obtains a reversal of his conviction on the ground that the evidence was insufficient to convict. *Burks* v. *United States,* 437 U.S. 1 (1978). The reasons for this exception are relevant here:

> "[R]eversal for trial error, as distinguished from evidentiary insufficiency, does not constitute a decision to the effect that the government has failed to prove its cases. As such, it implies nothing with respect to the guilt or innocence of the defendant. . . .
> "The same cannot be said when a defendant's conviction has been overturned due to a failure of proof at trial, in which case the prosecution cannot complain of prejudice, for it has been given one fair opportunity to offer whatever proof it can assemble. . . . Since we necessarily accord absolute finality to a jury's *verdict* of acquittal—no matter how erroneous its decision—it is difficult to conceive how society has any greater interest in retrying a defendant when, on review, it is decided as a matter of law that the jury could not properly have returned a verdict of guilty." *Id.,* at 15–16 (emphasis in original).

The decision in *Burks* was foreshadowed by *Green* v. *United States,* 355 U.S. 184 (1957). In that case, the defendant had been indicted for first-degree murder, and the trial court instructed the jury that it could convict him either of that crime or of the lesser included offense of second-degree murder. The jury convicted him of second-degree murder, but the conviction was reversed on appeal. The Court held that a retrial on the first-degree murder charge was barred by the Double Jeopardy Clause, because the defendant "was forced to run the gantlet once on that charge and the jury refused to convict him." *Id.,* at 190. See also *Price* v. *Georgia,* 398 U.S. 323 (1970).

Thus, the "clean slate" rationale recognized in *Pearce* is inapplicable whenever a jury agrees or an appellate court decides that the prosecution has not proved its case.

In the usual sentencing proceeding, however, it is impossible to conclude that a sentence less than the statutory maximum "constitute[s] a decision to the effect that the government has failed to prove its case." In the normal process of sentencing, "there are virtually no rules or tests or standards—and thus no issues to resolve. . . ." M. Frankel, Criminal Sentences: Law Without Order 38 (1973). Thus, "[t]he discretion of the judge . . . in [sentencing] matters is virtually free of substantive control or guidance. Where the judge has power to select a term of imprisonment within a range the exercise of that authority is left fairly at large." Kadish, Legal Norm and Discretion in the Police and Sentencing Processes, 75 Harv. L. Rev. 904, 916 (1962).

The Court's cases that have considered the role of the Double Jeopardy Clause in sentencing have noted this absence of sentencing standards. In *DiFrancesco,* for example, we observed: "[A] sentence is characteristically determined in large part on the basis of information, such as the presentence report, developed outside the courtroom. It is purely a judicial determination, and much that goes into it is the result of inquiry that is nonadversary in nature." 449 U.S., at 136–137. And even if it is the jury that imposes the sentence, "[n]ormally, there would be no way for the jury to place on the record the reasons for its collective sentencing determination. . . ." *Chaffin* v. *Stynchcombe,* 412 U.S., at 28, n. 15.

By enacting a capital sentencing procedure that resembles a trial on the issue of guilt or innocence, however, Missouri *explicitly requires* the jury to determine whether the prosecution has "proved its case." Both *Burks* and *Green,* as has been noted, state an exception to the general rule relied upon in *North Carolina* v. *Pearce.* That exception is applicable here, and we therefore refrain from extending the rationale of *Pearce* to the very different facts of the present case. Chief Justice Bardgett, in his dissent from the ruling of the Missouri Supreme Court majority, observed that the sentence of life imprisonment which petitioner received at his first trial meant that "the jury has already acquitted the defendant of whatever was necessary to impose the death sentence." 594 S. W. 2d, at 922. We agree.

A verdict of acquittal on the issue of guilt or innocence is, of course, absolutely final. The values that underlie this principle, stated for the Court by Justice Black, are equally applicable when a jury has rejected the State's claim that the defendant deserves to die:

> "The underlying idea, one that is deeply ingrained in at least the Anglo-American system of jurisprudence, is that the State with all its resources and power should not be allowed to make repeated attempts to convict an individual for an alleged offense, thereby subjecting him to embarrassment, expense and ordeal and compelling him to live in a continuing state of anxiety and insecurity, as well as enhancing the possibility that even though innocent he may be found guilty." *Green* v. *United States,* 355 U.S., at 187–188.

See also *United States* v. *DiFrancesco,* 449 U.S., at 136. The "embarrassment, expense and ordeal" and the "anxiety and insecurity" faced by a defendant at the penalty phase of a Missouri capital murder trial surely are at least equivalent to that faced by any defendant at the guilt phase of a criminal trial. The "unacceptably high risk that the [prosecution], with its superior resources, would wear down a defendant," *id.,* at 130, thereby leading to an erroneously imposed death sentence, would exist if the State were to have a further opportunity to convince a jury to impose the ultimate punishment. Missouri's use of the reasonable-doubt standard indicates that in a capital sentencing proceeding, it is the State, not the defendant, that should bear "almost the entire risk of error." *Addington* v. *Texas,* 441 U.S., at 424. Given these considerations, our decision today does not at all depend upon the State's announced intention to rely only upon the same aggravating circumstances it sought to prove at petitioner's first trial or upon its statement that it would introduce no new evidence in support of its contention that petitioner deserves the death penalty. Having received "one fair opportunity to offer whatever proof it could assemble," *Burks* v. *United States,* 437 U.S., at 16, the State is not entitled to another.

V

The Court already has held that many of the protections available to a defendant at a criminal trial also are available at a sentencing hearing similar to that required by Missouri in a capital case. See, *e. g., Specht* v. *Patterson,* 386 U.S. 605 (1967) (due process protections such as right to counsel, right to confront witnesses, and right to present favorable evidence are available at hearing at which sentence may be imposed based upon "a new finding of fact . . . that was not an ingredient of the offense charged," *id.,* at 608). Because the sentencing proceeding at petitioner's first trial was like the trial on the question of guilt or innocence, the protection afforded by the Double Jeopardy Clause to one acquitted by a jury also is available to him, with respect to the death penalty, at his retrial. We therefore refrain from extending the reasoning of *Stroud* v. *United States,* 251 U.S. 15 (1919), to this very different situation.

The judgment of the Supreme Court of Missouri is reversed, and the case is remanded to that court for further proceedings not inconsistent with this opinion.

It is so ordered.

JUSTICE POWELL, with whom THE CHIEF JUSTICE, JUSTICE WHITE, and JUSTICE REHNQUIST join, dissenting.

R. PULLEY, WARDEN, Petitioner *v.* ROBERT ALTON HARRIS

—US—, 104 S Ct 871 79 L Ed 2d 29,(1984)

OPINION OF THE COURT

Justice **White,** delivered the opinion of the Court.

Respondent Harris was convicted of a capital crime in a California court and was sentenced to death. Along with many other challenges to the conviction and sentence, Harris claimed on appeal that the California capital punishment statute was invalid under the United States Constitution because it failed to require the California Supreme Court to compare Harris's sentence with the sentences imposed in similar capital cases and thereby to determine whether they were proportionate. Rejecting the constitutional claims by citation to earlier cases, the California Supreme Court affirmed. People v Harris, 28 Cal 3d 935, 623 P2d 240 (1981). We denied certiorari. 454 US 882, 70 L Ed 2d 192, 102 S Ct 365 (1981).

[1a] Harris then sought a writ of habeas corpus in the state courts. He again complained of the failure to provide him with comparative proportionality review. The writ was denied without opinion, and we denied certiorari. 457 US 1111, 73 L Ed 2d 1322, 102 S Ct 2915 (1982). Harris next sought habeas corpus in the United States District Court for the Southern District of California, pressing the claim, among others, that he had been denied the comparative proportionality review assertedly required by the United States Constitution.

The District Court denied the writ and refused to stay Harris's execution, but issued a certificate of probable cause. The Court of Appeals, after holding that the proportionality review demanded by Harris was constitutionally required, vacated the judgment of the District Court and ordered that the writ issue relieving Harris of the death sentence unless within 120 days the California Supreme Court undertook to determine whether the penalty imposed on Harris is proportionate to sentences imposed for similar crimes. 692 F2d 1189 (1982). We granted the State's petition for certiorari presenting the question whether the proportionality review mandated by the Court of Appeals is required by the United States Constitution. —— US ——, 75 L Ed 2d 787, 103 S Ct 1425 (1983).

I

[2] Harris concedes that the Court of Appeals' judgment rested on a federal constitutional ground. He nonetheless contends that we should affirm the judgment, which has the effect of returning the case to the state courts, because state law may entitle him to the comparative proportionality review that he has unsuccessfully demanded. We are unimpressed with the submission. Under 28 USC § 2241 [28 USCS § 2241], a writ of habeas corpus disturbing a state-court judgment may issue only if it is found that a prisoner is in custody "in violation of the Constitution or laws or treaties of the United States." 28 USC § 2241(c)(3) [28 USCS § 2241(c)(3)] (1976). A federal court may not issue the writ on the basis of a perceived error of state law.

Even if an error of state law could be sufficiently egregious to amount to a denial of equal protection or of due process of law guaranteed by the Fourteenth Amendment, Harris's submission is not persuasive. He relies on People v Frierson, 25 Cal 3d 142 (1979), and People v Jackson, 28 Cal 3d 264 (1981), for the proposition that proportionality review should have been extended to him as matter of state law. But since deciding those cases, the California Supreme Court has twice rejected Harris's demand for proportionality review without suggesting that it was in any way departing from precedent. Indeed, on direct review, it indicated that Harris's constitutional claims had been adversely decided in those very cases.

Finally, if Harris's claim is that because of an evolution of state law he would now enjoy the kind of proportionality review that has so far been denied him, that claim, even if accurate, would not warrant issuing a writ of habeas corpus. Rather it would appear to be a matter that the state courts should consider, if they are so inclined, free of the constraints of the federal writ. Accordingly, we deem it necessary to reach the constitutional question on which certiorari was granted.

II

[3] At the outset, we should more clearly identify the issue before us. Traditionally, "proportionality" has been used with reference to an abstract evaluation of the appropriateness of a sentence for a particular crime. Looking to the gravity of the offense and the severity of the penalty, to sentences imposed for other crimes, and to sentencing practices in other jurisdictions, this Court has occasionally struck down punishments as inherently disproportionate, and therefore cruel and unusual, when imposed for a particular crime or category of crime. See, e.g., Solem v Helm, —— US ——, 77 L Ed 2d 637, 103 S Ct 3001 (1983); Enmund v Florida, 458 US 782, 73 L Ed 2d 1140, 102 S Ct 3368 (1982); Coker v Georgia, 433 US 584, 53 L Ed 2d 982, 97 S Ct 2861, (1977). The death penalty is not in all cases a disproportionate penalty in this sense. Gregg v Georgia, 428 US 153, 187, 49 L Ed 2d 859, 96 S Ct 2909 (1976) (opinion of Justices Stewart, Powell, and Stevens); id., at 226, 49 L Ed 2d 859, 96 S Ct 2909 (White, J., concurring).

[1b] The proportionality review sought by Harris, required by the Court of Appeals, and provided for in numerous state statutes is of a different sort. This sort of proportionality review presumes that the death sentence is not disproportionate to the crime in the traditional sense. It purports to inquire instead whether the penalty is nonetheless unacceptable in a particular case because disproportionate to the punishment imposed on others convicted of the same crime. The issue in this case, therefore, is whether the Eighth Amendment, applicable to the States through the Fourteenth Amendment, requires a state appellate court, before it affirms a death sentence, to compare the sentence in the case before it with the penalties imposed in similar cases if requested to do so by the prisoner. Harris insists that it does and that this is the invariable rule in every case. Apparently, the Court of Appeals was of the same view. We do not agree.

III

Harris's submission is rooted in Furman v Georgia, 408 US 238, 33 L Ed 2d 346, 92 S Ct 2726 (1972). In Furman, the Court concluded that capital punishment, as then administered under statutes vesting unguided sentencing discretion in juries and trial judges, had become unconstitutionally cruel and unusual punishment. The death penalty was being imposed so discriminatorily, 408 US, at 240, 33 L Ed 2d 346, 92 S Ct 2726 (Douglas, J., concurring), so wantonly and freakishly, id., at 306, 33 L Ed 2d 346, 92 S Ct 2726 (Stewart, J., concurring), and so infrequently, id., at 310, 33 L Ed 2d 346, 92 S Ct 2726 (White, J., concurring), that any given death sentence was cruel and unusual. In response to that decision, roughly two-thirds of the States promptly redrafted their capital sentencing statutes in an effort to limit jury discretion and avoid arbitrary and inconsistent results. All of the new statutes provide for automatic appeal of death sentences. Most, such as Georgia's, require the reviewing court, to some extent at least, to determine whether, considering both the crime and the defendant, the sentence is disproportionate to that imposed in similar cases. Not every State has adopted such a procedure. In some States, such as Florida, the appellate court performs proportionality review despite the absence of a statutory requirement; in others, such as California and Texas, it does not.

Four years after Furman, this Court examined several of the new state statutes. We upheld one of each of the three sorts mentioned above. See Gregg v Georgia, supra; Proffitt v Florida, 428 US 242, 49 L Ed 2d 913, 96 S Ct 2960 (1976); Jurek v Texas, 428 US 262, 49 L Ed 2d 929, 96 S Ct 2950 (1976). Needless to say, that some schemes providing proportionality review are constitutional does not mean that such review is indispensable. We take statutes as we find them. To endorse the statute as a whole is not to say that anything different is unacceptable. As was said in Gregg, "[w]e do not intend to suggest that only the above-described procedures would be permissible under Furman or that any sentencing system constructed along these general lines would inevitably satisfy the concerns of Furman, for each distinct system must be examined on an individual basis." 428 US, at 195, 49 L Ed 2d 859, 96 S Ct 2909 (footnote omitted). Examination of our 1976 cases makes clear that they do not establish proportionality review as a constitutional requirement.

In Gregg, six Justices concluded that the Georgia system adequately directed and limited the jury's discretion. The bifurcated proceedings, the limited number of capital crimes, the requirement that at least one aggravating circumstance be present, and the consideration of mitigating circumstances minimized the risk of wholly arbitrary, capricious, or freakish sentences. In the opinion announcing the judgment of the Court, three Justices concluded that sentencing discretion under the statute was sufficiently controlled by clear and objective standards. 428 US, at 197–198, 49 L Ed 2d 859, 96 S Ct 2909. In a separate concurrence, three other Justices found sufficient reason to expect that the death penalty would not be imposed so wantonly, freakishly, or infrequently as to be invalid under Furman. Id., at 222, 49 L Ed 2d 859, 96 S Ct 2909.

Both opinions made much of the statutorily-required comparative proportionality review. Id., at 198, 204–206, 222–223, 49 L Ed 2d 859, 96 S Ct 2909. This was considered an additional safeguard against arbitrary or capricious sentencing. While the opinion of Justices Stewart, Powell and Stevens suggested that some form of meaningful appellate review is required, id., at 153, 198, 204–206, 49 L Ed 2d 859, 96 S Ct 2909, those Justices did not declare that comparative review was so critical that without it the Georgia statute would not have passed constitutional muster. Indeed, in summarizing the components of an adequate capital sentencing scheme, Justices Stewart, Powell, and Stevens did not mention comparative review:

> "[T]he concerns expressed in Furman . . . can be met by a carefully drafted statute that ensures that the sentencing authority be given adequate information and guidance. As a general proposition, these concerns are best met by a system that provides for a bifurcated proceeding at which the sentencing authority is apprised of the information relevant to the imposition of sentence and provided with standards to guide its use of the information." Id., at 195, 49 L Ed 2d 859, 96 S Ct 2909.

In short, the Court of Appeals erred in concluding that Gregg required proportionality review.

There is even less basis for reliance on Proffitt v Florida, supra. The Florida statute provides for a bifurcated procedure and forecloses the death penalty unless the sentencing authority finds that at least one of eight statutory aggravating circumstances is present and is not outweighed by any mitigating circumstances. The joint opinion of Justices Stewart, Powell, and Stevens observed that the Florida scheme, like its Georgia counterpart, requires the sentencer to focus on the individual circumstances of each homicide and each defendant. Id., at 251, 49 L Ed 2d 913, 96 S Ct 2960. Also, by vesting ultimate sentencing authority in the judge rather than the jury, the statute was expected to yield more consistent sentencing at the trial court level. Id., at 252, 49 L Ed 2d 913, 96 S Ct 2960. Only after concluding that trial judges are given specific and detailed guidance to assist them in deciding whether to impose the death penalty did the opinion observe that death sentences are reviewed to ensure that they are consistent with the sentences imposed in similar cases. Id., at 250–251, 49 L Ed 2d 913, 96 S Ct 2960. The concurring opinion filed by three other Justices approved the Florida statute without even mentioning appellate review. Id., at 260–261,

That Gregg and Proffitt did not establish a constitutional requirement of proportionality review is made clearer by Jurek v Texas, 428 US 262, 49 L Ed 2d 929, 96 S Ct 2950 (1976), decided the same day. In Jurek we upheld a death sentence even though neither the statute, as in Georgia, nor state caselaw, as in Florida, provided for comparative proportionality review. Justices Stewart, Powell, and Stevens, after emphasizing the limits on the jury's discretion, concluded that:

> "Texas' capital sentencing procedures, like those of Georgia and Florida, do not violate the Eighth and Fourteenth Amendments. By narrowing its definition of capital murder, Texas has essentially said that there must be at least one statutory aggravating circumstance in a first-degree murder case before a death sentence may even be considered. By authorizing the defense to bring before the jury at the separate sentencing hearing whatever mitigating circumstances relating to the individual defendant can be adduced, Texas has ensured that the sentencing jury will have adequate guidance to enable it to perform its sentencing function. By providing prompt judicial review of the jury's decision in a court with statewide jurisdiction, Texas has provided a means to promote the evenhanded, rational, and consistent imposition of death sentences under law. Because this system serves to assure that sentences of death will not be 'wantonly' or 'freakishly' imposed, it does not violate the Constitution." Id., at 276, 49 L Ed 2d 929, 96 S Ct 2950.

That the three Justices considered such appellate review as Texas provided "a means to promote the even-handed, rational, and consistent imposition of death sentences," ibid., is revealing. First, it makes plain that, at least in light of the other safeguards in the Texas statute, proportionality review would have been constitutionally superfluous. Second, it suggests that the similarly-worded references to appellate review in Gregg and Proffitt were focused not on proportionality review as such, but only on the provision of some sort of prompt and automatic appellate review. The concurring opinion expressing the views of three other Justices sustained the Texas statute by focusing solely on the limitations on the jury's discretion, without even mentioning appellate review. In view of Jurek, we are quite sure that at that juncture the Court had not mandated comparative proportionality review whenever a death sentence was imposed.

Harris also relies on Zant v Stephens, —— US ——, 77 L Ed 2d 235, 103 S Ct 2733 (1983), which was announced after the Court of Appeals' decision in this case. Zant did not depart from Gregg and did not question Jurek. Indeed, Jurek was cited in support of the decision. Id., at ——, n 13, 77 L Ed 2d 235, 103 S Ct 2733. While emphasizing the importance of mandatory appellate review under the Georgia statute, id., at ——, 77 L Ed 2d 235, 103 S Ct 2733, we did not hold that without comparative proportionality review the statute would be unconstitutional. To the contrary, we relied on the jury's finding of aggravating circumstances, not the State Supreme Court's finding of proportionality, as rationalizing the sentence. Thus, the emphasis was on the constitutionally necessary narrowing function of statutory aggravating circumstances. Proportionality review was considered to be an additional safeguard against arbitrarily imposed death sentences, but we certainly did not hold that comparative review was constitutionally required.

[1c] There is thus no basis in our cases for holding that comparative proportionality review by an appellate court is required in every case in which the death penalty is imposed and the defendant requests it. Indeed, to so hold would effectively overrule Jurek and would substantially depart from the sense of Gregg and Proffitt. We are not persuaded that the Eighth Amendment requires us to take that course.

IV

Assuming that there could be a capital sentencing system so lacking in other checks on arbitrariness that it would not pass constitutional muster without comparative proportionality review, the 1977 California statute is not of that sort. Under this scheme, a person convicted of first degree murder is sentenced to life imprisonment unless one or more "special circumstances" are found, in which case the punishment is either death or life imprisonment without parole. Cal Penal Code Ann §§ 190, 190.2 (West 1977). Special circumstances are alleged in the charging paper and tried with the issue of guilt at the initial phase of the trial. At the close of evidence, the jury decides guilt or innocence and determines whether the special circumstances alleged are present. Each special circumstance must be proved beyond a reasonable doubt. § 190.4(a). If the jury finds the defendant guilty of first degree murder and finds at least one special circumstance, the trial proceeds to a second phase to determine the appropriate penalty. Additional evidence may be offered and the jury is given a list of relevant factors. § 190.3. "After having heard all the evidence, the trier of fact shall consider, take into account and be guided by the aggravating and mitigating circumstances referred to in this section, and shall determine whether the penalty shall be death or life imprisonment without the possibility of parole." Ibid. If the jury returns a verdict of death, the defendant is deemed to move to modify the verdict. § 190.4(e). The trial judge then reviews the evidence and, in light of the statutory factors, makes an "independent determination as to whether the weight of the evidence supports the jury's findings and verdicts." Ibid. The judge is required to state on the record the reasons for his findings. Ibid. If the trial judge denies the motion for modification, there is an automatic appeal. §§ 190.4(e), 1239(b). The statute does not require comparative proportionality review or otherwise describe the nature of the appeal. It does state that the trial judge's refusal to modify the sentence "shall be reviewed." § 190.4(e). This would seem to include review of the evidence relied on by the judge. As the California Supreme Court has said, "the statutory requirements that the jury specify the special circumstances which permit imposition of the death penalty, and that the trial judge specify his reasons for denying modification of the death penalty, serve to assure thoughtful and effective appellate review, focusing upon the circumstances present in each particular case." People v Frierson, 25 Cal 3d 142, 179, 599 P2d 587, 609 (1979). That court has reduced a death sentence to life imprisonment because the evidence did not support the findings of special circumstances. People v Thompson, 27 Cal 3d 303, 611 P2d 883 (1980).

By requiring the jury to find at least one special circumstance beyond a reasonable doubt, the statute limits the death sentence to a small sub-class of capital-eligible cases. The statutory list of relevant factors, applied to defendants within this sub-class, "provide[s] jury guidance and lessen[s] the chance of arbitrary application of the death penalty," Harris v Pulley, 692 F2d, at 1194, "guarantee[ing] that the jury's discretion will be guided and its consideration deliberate," id., at 1195. The jury's "discretion is suitably directed and limited so as to minimize the risk of wholly arbitrary and capricious action." Gregg, 428 US, at 189, 49 L Ed 2d 859, 96 S Ct 2909. Its decision is reviewed by the trial judge and the State Supreme Court. On its face, this system, without any requirement or practice of comparative proportionality review, cannot be successfully challenged under Furman and our subsequent cases.

[4] Any capital sentencing scheme may occasionally produce aberrational outcomes. Such inconsistencies are a far cry from the major systemic defects identified in Furman. As we have acknowledged in the past, "there can be 'no perfect procedure for deciding in which cases governmental authority should be used to impose death.'" Zant v Stephens, —— US, at ——, 77 L Ed 2d 235, 103 S Ct 2733, quoting Lockett v Ohio, 438 US 586, 605, 57 L Ed 2d 973, 98 S Ct 2954 (1977) (plurality opinion). As we are presently informed, we cannot say that the California procedures provided Harris inadequate protection against the evil identified in Furman. The Court of Appeals therefore erred in ordering the writ of habeas corpus to issue. Its judgment is reversed and the case remanded for further proceedings consistent with this opinion.

It is so ordered.

CHAPTER 10

Contents

Reserved Powers of the Tenth Amendment

§ 10.1 Introduction

The Tenth Amendment reads as follows:

> *The powers not delegated to the United States by the Constitution, nor prohibited by it to the states, are reserved to the States respectively, or to the people.*

This amendment has come to be known as the reserved powers amendment. You will recall that the Constitution of the United States was referred to as an instrument which delegated governmental powers to the federal government. If the power was not specifically delegated, it is argued that it was meant to be retained by the states to exercise that power. The police power of government, i.e., protection of the health, welfare, and morals of the people, was never specifically delegated to the federal government and hence these powers have been the subject of local authority.

The Court and legislation have gradually whittled away at local authority and power in the criminal justice area by Court interpretations of the due process clause of the Fourteenth Amendment and by legislation granting funds to state agencies providing the agencies accept some federal control. In effect, an agency is waiving a constitutional right to manage its own police problems if it accepts federal funds under these conditions. Taxpayer suits have been initiated to prevent similar practices on the grounds that Congress exceeds the powers granted to it under Article I of the Constitution. See Frothingham v. Mellon, 262 U.S. 447, 43 S.Ct. 597, 67 L.Ed. 1078 (1923). This petitioner was unsuccessful because the Court found that the petitioner did not have a substantial taxpayer interest; but see Flast v. Cohen, 392 U.S. 83, 88 S.Ct. 1942, 20 L.Ed.2d 947 (1968), where the Court held that taxpayer could be a proper party to seek review of federal statutes where there is an allegation of unconstitutional exercise of the taxing and spending clause of the Constitution, but the Court did not rule on the merits of the constitutionality of the statute.

§ 10.2 Authority and Responsibility of States in Law Enforcement

The Attorney General's First Annual Report to the Congress dated September 1, 1972, above the signature of Richard G. Kleindienst, Attorney General of the United States, presented a very understandable exposition of the respective functions of federal and state law enforcement and it is reprinted below.

Scope of Federal Jurisdiction

At the time of the founding of the Republic, the States exercised virtually exclusive jurisdiction over all crimes. That was altogether appropriate to the conditions of the time. The Federal Government exercised jurisdiction over such crimes as treason, piracy, revenue violations, customs offenses, and postal crimes, but little more.

As the Nation grew in population and complexity, as it grew geographically, as the economy developed, and as opportunity for abuses increased, so State jurisdiction was seen to need an increased but still complementary effort by the Federal Government.

During the latter part of the 18th Century and all of the 19th Century, this dual approach to criminal conduct developed and matured. The present posture of criminal law in the United States is consistent with that intended by the Founding Fathers: the States retain jurisdiction over crimes committed within the State which are local in nature; the Federal Government has jurisdiction over certain crimes that involve interstate commerce, taxes, assaults on Federal and foreign officials, and the like.

The Federal Government traditionally has fulfilled the function of assisting States in their efforts to prevent and control crime. This assistance began with such activities as the aid given by the Armed Services to the States, faced with civil disorders. It now includes, for example, the funding program of the Law Enforcement Assistance Administration and the unique laboratory facilities of the Federal Bureau of Investigation, and the Bureau of Narcotics and Dangerous Drugs, all within the Department of Justice, and the Bureau of Alcohol, Tobacco, and Firearms of the Department of the Treasury.

Yet, Federal efforts remain auxiliary to State efforts in combating the crime problem. The common crimes, such as murder, rape, robbery, burglary, fraud, prostitution, obscenity, extortion, and usury, remain largely State crimes.

Even where Federal jurisdiction exists, the Congress may have limited Federal involvement. Thus, the Congress has enacted such provisions as that requiring that at least $5,000 worth of certain kinds of stolen property be involved before it is a Federal offense to transport that property in interstate commerce (18 U.S.C. 2314).

The Federal Government has jurisdiction over crimes which are national in nature, such as crimes involving national security, immigration and naturalization, operations of the Government itself, internal revenue and customs matters, civil rights, and regulatory matters. The Federal Government also complements State law where common crimes such as theft, inciting to riot, and kidnapping may involve interstate commerce; there,

Federal power is brought to bear to apprehend and punish the violator where no State could effectively extend its jurisdiction to do so.

Powers of the Congress

Since there are no common law crimes against the United States, only those acts which the Congress forbids and punishes are Federal crimes. These acts now number in the many hundreds, and most legislation relating to them is found in title 18 of the United States Code.

The powers of the Congress to forbid and punish conduct derive from several sources in the Constitution. Only three clauses, however, other than the impeachment clause, actually mention crimes which the Congress may enact legislation to punish.

Two of these are in Article 1, Section 8. The first, Clause 6, empowers the Congress "... To provide for the Punishment of counterfeiting the Securities and current Coin of the United States..."

The second, Clause 10, empowers the Congress "... To define and punish Piracies and Felonies committed on the high Seas, and Offences against the Laws of Nations...." This clause contains the only specific grant of constitutional power to the Congress to prohibit and punish offenses committed outside the territorial limits of the United States.

The third reference is found in Article III, Section 3, defining treason:

> "Treason against the United States, shall consist only in levying War against them, or in adhering to their Enemies, giving them Aid and Comfort. No Person shall be convicted of Treason unless on the Testimony of two Witnesses to the same overt Act, or on Confession in open Court.
>
> "The Congress shall have Power to declare the Punishment of Treason, but no Attainder of Treason shall work Corruption of Blood, or Forfeiture except during the Life of the Person attainted."

Coefficient clause. The broad sweep of the power of the Congress to prohibit and punish certain acts derives from Article I, Section 8, Clause 18 of the Constitution, which states that the Congress shall have power:

> "To make all Laws which shall be necessary and proper for carrying into Execution the foregoing Powers, and all other Powers vested by this Constitution in the Government of the United States, or in any Department or Officer thereof."

This clause is referred to variously as the "necessary and proper" clause or the "coefficient" clause. It constitutes a broad grant of power from the people to the Congress to carry out its responsibilities, which include providing for the collection of taxes and duties, the regulation of interstate and foreign commerce, rules of naturalization and laws on bankruptcies, the coinage of money, the establishment of post offices, and the calling forth of Armed Forces to suppress insurrection.

That this clause is a broad grant of power, and not a limiting restraint, was established in McCulloch v. Maryland, 4 Wheat. 316 (1819), in which Chief Justice Marshall said of the powers of the Congress under this clause:

> "Let the end be legitimate, let it be within the scope of the Constitution, and all means which are appropriate, which are plainly adapted to that end, which are not prohibited, but consist with the letter and spirit of the Constitution, are constitutional." (4 Wheat. at 421)

It has long been universally conceded that the Congress has the power to create, define, and punish crimes and offenses when necessary to carry out its constitutional duties and responsibilities.

Powers of the President

The law enforcement power of the President is found in Article II, Section 3, of the Constitution, which requires that the President "... shall take Care that the Laws be faithfully executed...."

As it has in regard to the "necessary and proper" clause, the Supreme Court has read this clause as a broad grant of authority. It has said that the reference to laws in this clause encompasses not only statutes enacted by the Congress but also "... the rights, duties, and obligations growing out of the Constitution itself, our international relations, and all the protection implied by the nature of government under the Constitution." In re Neagle, 135 U.S. 1, 64 (1890).

This duty of the President is taken to include, therefore, the powers of investigation and prosecution of violations of Federal criminal law and the power to take appropriate steps to prevent the violation of Federal law.

Judicial Decisions Relating to Chapter 10

Commonwealth of Massachusetts *v.* Mellon, Secretary of the Treasury, et al.
In Equity.
Frothingham *v.* Mellon, Secretary of the Treasury, et al.

262 U.S. 447, 43 S.Ct. 597, 67 L.Ed. 1078 (1923)

APPEAL FROM THE COURT OF APPEALS OF THE DISTRICT OF COLUMBIA.

Argued May 3, 4, 1923.—Decided June 4, 1923.

. . .

MR. JUSTICE SUTHERLAND delivered the opinion of the Court.

These cases were argued and will be considered and disposed of together. The first is an original suit in this Court. The other was brought in the Supreme Court of the District of Columbia. That court dismissed the bill and its decree was affirmed by the District Court of Appeals. Thereupon the case was brought here by appeal. Both cases challenge the constitutionality of the Act of November 23, 1921, c. 135, 42 Stat. 224, commonly called the Maternity Act. Briefly, it provides for an initial appropriation and thereafter annual appropriations for a period of five years, to be apportioned among such of the several States as shall accept and comply with its provisions, for the purpose of coöperating with them to reduce maternal and infant mortality and protect the health of mothers and infants. It creates a bureau to administer the act in coöperation with state agencies, which are required to make such reports concerning their operations and expenditures as may be prescribed by the federal bureau. Whenever that bureau shall determine that funds have not been properly expended in respect of any State, payments may be withheld.

It is asserted that these appropriations are for purposes not national, but local to the States, and together with numerous similar appropriations constitute an effective means of inducing the States to yield a portion of their sovereign rights. It is further alleged that the burden of the appropriations provided by this act and similar legislation falls unequally upon the several States, and rests largely upon the industrial States, such as Massachusetts; that the act is a usurpation of power not granted to Congress by the Constitution—an attempted exercise of the power of local self-government reserved to the States by the Tenth Amendment; and that the defendants are proceeding to carry the act into operation. In the Massachusetts case it is alleged that the plaintiff's rights and powers as a sovereign State and the rights of its citizens have been invaded and usurped by these expenditures and acts; and that, although the State has not accepted the act, its constitutional rights are infringed by the passage thereof and the imposition upon the State of an illegal and unconstitutional option either to yield to the Federal Government a part of its reserved rights or lose the share that it would otherwise be entitled to receive of the moneys appropriated. In the Frothingham case plaintiff alleges that the effect of the statute will be to take her property, under the guise of taxation, without due process of law.

We have reached the conclusion that the cases must be disposed of for want of jurisdiction without considering the merits of the constitutional questions.

In the first case, the State of Massachusetts presents no justiciable controversy either in its own behalf or as the representative of its citizens. The appellant in the second suit has no such interest in the subject-matter, nor is any such injury inflicted or threatened, as will enable her to sue.

First. The State of Massachusetts in its own behalf, in effect, complains that the act in question invades the local concerns of the State, and is a usurpation of power, viz: the power of local self-government reserved to the States.

Probably, it would be sufficient to point out that the powers of the State are not invaded, since the statute imposes no obligation but simply extends an option which the State is free to accept or reject. But we do not rest here. Under Article III, § 2, of the Constitution, the judicial power of this Court extends "to controversies . . . between a State and citizens of another State" and the Court has original jurisdiction "in all cases . . . in which a State shall be party." The effect of this is not to confer jurisdiction upon the Court merely because a State is a party, but only where it is a party to a proceeding of judicial cognizance. Proceedings not of a justiciable character are outside the contemplation of the constitutional grant. In Wisconsin v. Pelican Insurance Co., 127 U.S. 265, 289, MR. JUSTICE GRAY, speaking for the Court, said:

> "As to 'controversies between a State and citizens of another State.' The object of vesting in the courts of the United States jurisdiction of suits by one State against the citizens of another was to enable such controversies to be determined by a national tribunal, and thereby to avoid the partiality, or suspicion of partiality, which might exist if the plaintiff State were compelled to resort to the courts of the State of which the defendants were citizens. Federalist No. 80; CHIEF JUSTICE JAY, in Chisholm v. Georgia, 2 Dall. 419, 475; Story on the Constitution, §§ 1638, 1682. The grant is of 'judicial power,' and was not intended to confer upon the courts of the United States jurisdiction of a suit or prosecution by the one State, of such a nature that it could not, on the settled principles of public and international law, be entertained by the judiciary of the other State at all."

That was an action brought by the State of Wisconsin to enforce a judgment of one of its own courts for a penalty against a resident of another State, and, in pursuance of the doctrine announced by the language just quoted, this Court declined to assume jurisdiction upon the ground that the courts of no country will execute the penal laws of another.

In an earlier case it was held that a proceeding by mandamus by one State to compel the Governor of another to surrender a fugitive from justice was not within the powers of the judicial department, since the duty of the Governor in the premises was in the nature of a moral rather than a legal obligation. Kentucky v. Dennison, 24 How. 66, 109. In New Hampshire v. Louisiana; New York v. Louisiana, 108 U.S. 76, this Court declined to take jurisdiction of actions to enforce payment of the bonds of another State for the benefit of the assignors, citizens of the plaintiff States. In Georgia v. Stanton, 6 Wall. 50, 75, and kindred cases, to which we shall presently refer, jurisdiction was denied in respect of questions of a political or governmental character. On the other hand, jurisdiction was maintained in Texas v. White, 7 Wall. 700; Florida v. Anderson, 91 U.S. 667; and Alabama v. Burr, 115 U.S. 413, because proprietary rights were involved; in Georgia v. Tennessee Copper Co., 206 U.S. 230, 237, because the right of dominion of the State over the air and soil within its domain was affected; in Missouri v. Holland, 252 U.S. 416, because, as asserted, there was an invasion, by acts done and threatened, of the quasi-sovereign right of the State to regulate the taking of wild game within its borders; and in other cases because boundaries were in dispute. It is not necessary to cite additional cases. The foregoing, for present purposes, sufficiently indicate the jurisdictional line of demarcation.

What, then, is the nature of the right of the State here asserted and how is it affected by this statute? Reduced to its simplest terms, it is alleged that the statute constitutes an attempt to legislate outside the powers granted to Congress by the Constitution and within the field of local powers exclusively reserved to the States. Nothing is added to the force or effect of this assertion by the further incidental allegations that the ulterior purpose of Congress thereby was to induce the States to yield a portion of their sovereign rights; that the burden of the appropriations falls unequally upon the several States; and that there is imposed upon the States an illegal and unconstitutional option either to yield to the Federal Government a part of their reserved rights or lose their share of the moneys appropriated. But what burden is imposed upon the States, unequally or otherwise? Certainly there is none, unless it be the burden of taxation, and that falls upon their inhabitants, who are within the taxing power of Congress as well as that of the States where they reside. Nor does the statute require the States to do or to yield anything. If Congress enacted it with the ulterior purpose of tempting them to yield, that purpose may be effectively frustrated by the simple expedient of not yielding.

In the last analysis, the complaint of the plaintiff State is brought to the naked contention that Congress has usurped the reserved powers of the several States by the mere enactment of the statute, though nothing has been done and nothing is to be done without their consent; and it is plain that that question, as it is thus presented, is political and not judicial in character, and therefore is not a matter which admits of the exercise of the judicial power.

In Georgia v. Stanton, supra, this Court held that a bill to enjoin the Secretary of War, and other officers, from carrying into execution certain acts of Congress, which it was asserted would annul and abolish the existing state government and establish another and different one in its place, called for a judgment upon a political question and presented no case within the jurisdiction of the Court. MR. JUSTICE NELSON, speaking for the Court, said (6 Wall. 77):

> "That these matters, both as stated in the body of the bill, and, in the prayers for relief, call for the judgment of the court upon political questions, and, upon rights, not of persons or property, but of a political character, will hardly be denied. For the rights for the protection of which our authority is invoked, are the rights of sovereignty, of political jurisdiction, of government, of corporate existence as a State, with all its constitutional powers and privileges. No case of private rights or private property infringed, or in danger of actual or threatened infringement, is presented by the bill, in a judicial form, for the judgment of the court."

In Cherokee Nation v. Georgia, 5 Pet. 1, an injunction was sought to prevent certain acts of legislation from being carried into execution within the territory of the Cherokee Nation of Indians, the original jurisdiction of this Court being invoked on the ground that plaintiff was a foreign nation. It was asserted that the acts in question, if executed, would have the effect of subverting the tribal government and subjecting the Indians to the jurisdiction of the State of Georgia. It was held that the Cherokee Nation could not be regarded as a foreign nation, within the meaning of the Judiciary Act, but CHIEF JUSTICE MARSHALL, delivering the opinion for the majority, said, further (p. 20):

> "That part of the bill which respects the land occupied by the Indians, and prays the aid of the court to protect their possession, may be more doubtful. The mere question of right might, perhaps, be decided by this court, in a proper case, with proper parties. But the court is asked to do more than decide on the title. The bill requires us to control the legislature of Georgia, and to restrain the exertion of its physical force. The propriety of such an interposition by the court may be well questioned; it savors too much of the exercise of political power, to be within the proper province of the judicial department."

And MR. JUSTICE THOMPSON, with whom MR. JUSTICE STORY concurred, in the course of an opinion, said (p. 75):

> "It is only where the rights of persons or property are involved, and when such rights can be presented under some judicial form of proceedings, that courts of justice can interpose relief. This court can have no right to pronounce an abstract opinion upon the constitutionality of a state law. Such law must be brought into actual or threatened operation, upon rights properly falling under judicial cognizance, or a remedy is not to be had here."

See also Luther v. Borden, 7 How. 1; Mississippi v. Johnson, 4 Wall. 475, 500; Pacific Telephone Co. v. Oregon, 223 U.S. 118; Louisiana v. Texas, 176 U.S. 1, 23; Fairchild v. Hughes, 258 U.S. 126.

It follows that in so far as the case depends upon the assertion of a right on the part of the State to sue in its own behalf we are without jurisdiction. In that aspect of the case we are called upon to adjudicate, not rights of person or property, not rights of dominion over physical domain, not quasi-sovereign rights actually invaded or threatened, but abstract questions of political power, of sovereignty, of government. No rights of the State falling within the scope of the judicial power have been brought within the actual or threatened operation of the statute and this Court is as much without authority to pass abstract opinions upon the constitutionality of acts of Congress as it was held to be, in Cherokee Nation v. Georgia, supra, of state statutes. If an alleged attempt by congressional action to annul and abolish an existing state government "with all its constitutional powers and privileges," presents no justiciable issue, as was ruled in Georgia v. Stanton, supra, no reason can be suggested why it should be otherwise where the attempt goes no farther, as it is here alleged, than to propose to share with the State the field of state power.

We come next to consider whether the suit may be maintained by the State as the representative of its citizens. To this the answer is not doubtful. We need not go so far as to say that a State may never intervene by suit to protect its citizens against any form of enforcement of unconstitutional acts of Congress; but we are clear that the right to do so does not arise here. Ordinarily, at least, the only way in which a State may afford protection to its citizens in such cases is through the enforcement of its own criminal statutes, where that is appropriate, or by opening its courts to the injured persons for the maintenance of civil suits or actions. But the citizens of Massachusetts are also citizens of the United States. It cannot be conceded that a State, as parens patriae, may institute judicial proceedings to protect citizens of the United States from the operation of the statutes thereof. While the State, under some circumstances, may sue in that capacity for the protection of its citizens, Missouri v. Illinois, 180 U.S. 208, 241, it is no part of its duty or power to enforce their rights in respect of their relations with the Federal Government. In that field it is the United States, and not the State, which represents them as parens patriae, when such representation becomes appropriate; and to the former, and not to the latter, they must look for such protective measures as flow from that status.

Second. The attack upon the statute in the Frothingham case is, generally, the same, but this plaintiff alleges in addition that she is a taxpayer of the United States; and her contention, though not clear, seems to be that the effect of the appropriations complained of will be to increase the burden of future taxation and thereby take her property without due process of law. The right of a taxpayer to enjoin the execution of a federal appropriation act, on the ground that it is invalid and will result in taxation for illegal purposes, has never been passed upon by this Court. In cases where it was presented, the question has either been allowed to pass sub silentio or the determination of it expressly withheld. Millard v. Roberts, 202 U.S. 429, 438; Wilson v. Shaw, 204 U.S. 24, 31; Bradfield v. Roberts, 175 U.S. 291, 295. The case last cited came here from the Court of Appeals of the District of Columbia, and that court sustained the right of the plaintiff to sue by treating the case as one directed against the District of Columbia, and therefore subject to the rule frequently stated by this Court, that resident taxpayers may sue to enjoin an illegal use of the moneys of a municipal corporation. Roberts v. Bradfield, 12 App. D.C. 453, 459–460. The interest of a taxpayer of a municipality in the application of its moneys is direct and immediate and the remedy by injunction to prevent their misuse is not inappropriate. It is upheld by a large number of state cases and is the rule of this Court. Crampton v. Zabriskie, 101 U.S. 601, 609. Nevertheless, there are decisions to the contrary. See, for example, Miller v. Grandy, 13 Mich. 540, 550. The reasons which support the extension of the equitable remedy to a single taxpayer in such cases are based upon the peculiar relation of the corporate taxpayer to the corporation, which is not without some resemblance to that subsisting between stockholder and private corporation. IV Dillon Municipal Corporations, 5th ed., § 1580, et seq. But the relation of a taxpayer of the United States to the Federal Government is very different. His interest in the moneys of the Treasury—partly realized from taxation and partly from other sources—is shared with millions of others; is comparatively minute and indeterminable; and the effect upon future taxation, of any payment out of the funds, so remote, fluctuating and uncertain, that no basis is afforded for an appeal to the preventive powers of a court of equity.

The administration of any statute, likely to produce additional taxation to be imposed upon a vast number of taxpayers, the extent of whose several liability is indefinite and constantly changing, is essentially a matter of public and not of individual concern. If one taxpayer may champion and litigate such a cause, then every other taxpayer may do the same, not only in respect of the statute here under review but also in respect of every other appropriation act and statute whose administration requires the outlay of public money, and whose validity may be questioned. The bare suggestion of such a result, with its attendant inconveniences, goes far to sustain the conclusion which we have reached, that a suit of this character cannot be maintained. It is of much significance that no precedent sustaining the right to maintain suits like this has been called to our attention, although, since the formation of the government, as an examination of the acts of Congress will disclose, a large number of statutes appropriating or involving the expenditure of moneys for non-federal purposes have been enacted and carried into effect.

The functions of government under our system are apportioned. To the legislative department has been committed the duty of making laws; to the executive the duty of executing them; and to the judiciary the duty of interpreting and applying them in cases properly brought before the courts. The general rule is that neither department may invade the province of the other and neither may control, direct or restrain the action of the other. We are not now speaking of the merely ministerial duties of officials. Gaines v. Thompson, 7 Wall. 347. We have no power per se to review and annul acts of Congress on the ground that they are unconstitutional. That question may be considered only when the justification for some direct injury suffered or threatened, presenting a justiciable issue, is made to rest upon such an act. Then the power exercised is that of ascertaining and declaring the law applicable to the controversy. It amounts to little more than the negative power to disregard an unconstitutional enactment, which otherwise would stand in the way of the enforcement of a legal right. The party who invokes the power must be able to show not only that the statute is invalid but that he has sustained or is immediately in danger of sustaining some direct injury as the result of its enforcement, and not merely that he suffers in some indefinite way in common with people generally. If a case for preventive relief be presented the court enjoins, in effect, not the execution of the statute, but the acts of the official, the statute notwithstanding. Here the parties plaintiff have no such case. Looking through forms of words to the substance of their complaint, it is merely that officials of the executive department of the government are executing and will execute an act of Congress asserted to be unconstitutional; and this we are asked to prevent. To do so would be not to decide a judicial controversy, but to assume a position of authority over the governmental acts of another and co-equal department, an authority which plainly we do not possess.

No. 24, Original, dismissed.
No. 962 affirmed.

Flast et al. *v.* Cohen, Secretary of Health, Education, and Welfare, et al.

392 U.S. 83, 88 S.Ct. 1942, 20 L.Ed. 2d 947 (1968)

APPEAL FROM THE UNITED STATES DISTRICT COURT FOR THE SOUTHERN DISTRICT OF NEW YORK.

Argued March 12, 1968.—Decided June 10, 1968.

. . .

MR. CHIEF JUSTICE WARREN delivered the opinion of the Court.

In Frothingham v. Mellon, 262 U.S. 447 (1923), this Court ruled that a federal taxpayer is without standing to challenge the constitutionality of a federal statute. That ruling has stood for 45 years as an impenetrable barrier to suits against Acts of Congress brought by individuals who can assert only the interest of federal taxpayers. In this case, we must decide whether the Frothingham barrier should be lowered when a taxpayer attacks a federal statute on the ground that it violates the Establishment and Free Exercise Clauses of the First Amendment.

Appellants filed suit in the United States District Court for the Southern District of New York to enjoin the allegedly unconstitutional expenditure of federal funds under Titles I and II of the Elementary and Secondary Education Act of 1965, 79 Stat. 27, 20 U.S.C. §§ 241a et seq., 821 et seq. (1964 ed., Supp. II). The complaint alleged that the seven appellants had as a common attribute that "each pay[s] income taxes of the United States," and it is clear from the complaint that the appellants were resting their standing to maintain the action solely on their status as federal taxpayers. The appellees, who are charged by Congress with administering the Elementary and Secondary Education Act of 1965, were sued in their official capacities.

The gravamen of the appellants' complaint was that federal funds appropriated under the Act were being used to finance instruction in reading, arithmetic, and other subjects in religious schools, and to purchase textbooks and other instructional materials for use in such schools. Such expenditures were alleged to be in contravention of the Establishment and Free Exercise Clauses of the First Amendment. Appellants' constitutional attack focused on the statutory criteria which state and local authorities must meet to be eligible for federal grants under the Act. Title I of the Act establishes a program for financial assistance to local educational agencies for the education of low-income families. Federal payments are made to state educational agencies, which pass the payments on in the form of grants to local educational agencies. Under § 205 of the Act, 20 U.S.C. § 241e, a local educational agency wishing to have a plan or program funded by a grant must submit the plan or program to the appropriate state educational agency for approval. The plan or program must be "consistent with such basic criteria as the [appellee United States Commissioner of Education] may establish." The specific criterion of that section attacked by the appellants is the requirement

> "that, to the extent consistent with the number of educationally deprived children in the school district of the local educational agency who are enrolled in private

> elementary and secondary schools, such agency has made provision for including special educational services and arrangements (such as dual enrollment, educational radio and television, and mobile educational services and equipment) in which such children can participate. . . ." 20 U.S.C. § 241e (a) (2).

Under § 206 of the Act, 20 U.S.C. § 241f, the Commissioner of Education is given broad powers to supervise a State's participation in Title I programs and grants. Title II of the Act establishes a program of federal grants for the acquisition of school library resources, textbooks, and other printed and published instructional materials "for the use of children and teachers in public and private elementary and secondary schools." 20 U.S.C. § 821. A State wishing to participate in the program must submit a plan to the Commissioner for approval, and the plan must

> "provide assurance that to the extent consistent with law such library resources, textbooks, and other instructional materials will be provided on an equitable basis for the use of children and teachers in private elementary and secondary schools in the State. . . ." 20 U.S.C. § 823 (a) (3) (B).

While disclaiming any intent to challenge as unconstitutional all programs under Title I of the Act, the complaint alleges that federal funds have been disbursed under the Act, "with the consent and approval of the [appellees]," and that such funds have been used and will continue to be used to finance "instruction in reading, arithmetic and other subjects and for guidance in religious and sectarian schools" and "the purchase of textbooks and instructional and library materials for use in religious and sectarian schools." Such expenditures of federal tax funds, appellants alleged, violate the First Amendment because "they constitute a law respecting an establishment of religion" and because "they prohibit the free exercise of religion on the part of the [appellants]. . . by reason of the fact that they constitute compulsory taxation for religious purposes." The complaint asked for a declaration that appellees' actions in approving the expenditure of federal funds for the alleged purposes were not authorized by the Act or, in the alternative, that if appellees' actions are deemed within the authority and intent of the Act, "the Act is to that extent unconstitutional and void." The complaint also prayed for an injunction to enjoin appellees from approving any expenditure of federal funds for the allegedly unconstitutional purposes. The complaint further requested that a three-judge court be convened as provided in 28 U.S.C. §§ 2282, 2284.

The Government moved to dismiss the complaint on the ground that appellants lacked standing to maintain the action. District Judge Frankel, who considered the motion, recognized that Frothingham v. Mellon, supra, provided "powerful" support for the Government's position, but he ruled that the standing question was of sufficient substance to warrant the convening of a three-judge court to decide the question. 267 F. Supp. 351 (1967). The three-judge court received briefs and heard arguments limited to the standing question, and the court ruled on the authority of Frothingham that appellants lacked standing. Judge Frankel dissented. 271 F. Supp. 1 (1967). From the dismissal of their complaint on that ground, appellants appealed directly to this Court, 28 U.S.C. § 1253, and we noted probable jurisdiction. 389 U.S. 895 (1967). For reasons explained at length below, we hold that appellants do have standing as federal taxpayers to maintain this action, and the judgment below must be reversed.

I

We must deal first with the Government's contention that this Court lacks jurisdiction on direct appeal because a three-judge court was improperly convened below. Under 28 U.S.C. § 1253, direct appeal to this Court from a district court lies only "from an order granting or denying . . . an interlocutory or permanent injunction in any civil action, suit or proceeding required by any Act of Congress to be heard and determined by a district court of three judges." Thus, if the Government is correct, we lack jurisdiction over this direct appeal.

The Government's argument on this question is two-pronged. First, noting that appellants have conceded that the case should be deemed one limited to the practices of the New York City Board of Education, the Government contends that appellants wish only to forbid specific local programs which they find objectionable and not to enjoin the operation of the broad range of programs under the statutory scheme. Only if the latter relief is sought, the Government argues, can a three-judge court properly be convened under 28 U.S.C. § 2282. We cannot accept the Government's argument in the context of this case. It is true that the appellants' complaint makes specific reference to the New York City Board of Education's programs which are funded under the challenged statute, and we can assume that appellants' proof at trial would focus on those New York City programs. However, we view these allegations of the complaint as imparting specificity and focus to the issues in the lawsuit and not as limiting the impact of the constitutional challenge made in this case. The injunctive relief sought by appellants is not limited to programs in operation in New York City but extends to *any* program that would have the unconstitutional features alleged in the complaint. Congress enacted § 2282 "to prevent a single federal judge from being able to paralyze totally the operation of an entire regulatory scheme . . . by issuance of a broad injunctive order." Kennedy v. Mendoza-Martinez, 372 U.S. 144, 154 (1963). If the District Court in this case were to rule for appellants on the merits of their constitutional attack on New York City's federally funded programs, that decision would cast sufficient doubt on similar programs elsewhere as to cause confusion approaching paralysis to surround the challenged statute. Therefore, even if the injunction which might issue in this case were narrower than that sought by appellants, we are satisfied that the legislative policy underlying § 2282 was served by the convening of a three-judge court, despite appellants' focus on New York City's programs.

Secondly, the Government argues that a three-judge court should not have been convened because appellants question not the constitutionality of the Elementary and Secondary Education Act of 1965 but its administration. The decision in Zemel v. Rusk, 381 U.S. 1 (1965), is dispositive on this issue. It is true that appellants' complaint states a nonconstitutional ground for relief namely, that appellees' actions in approving the expenditure of federal funds for allegedly unconstitutional programs are in excess of their authority under the Act. However, the complaint also requests an alternative and constitutional ground for relief, namely, a declaration that, if appellees' actions "are within the authority and intent of the Act, the Act is to that extent unconstitutional and void." The Court noted in Zemel v. Rusk, supra, "[W]e have often held that a litigant need not abandon his nonconstitutional arguments in order to obtain a three-judge court." 381 U.S., at 5–6. See also Florida Lime Growers v. Jacobsen, 362 U.S. 73 (1960); Allen v. Grand Central Aircraft Co., 347 U.S. 535 (1954). The complaint in this case falls within that rule.

Thus, since the three-judge court was properly convened below, direct appeal to this Court is proper. We turn now to the standing question presented by this case.

II

This Court first faced squarely the question whether a litigant asserting only his status as a taxpayer has standing to maintain a suit in a federal court in Frothingham v. Mellon, supra, and that decision must be the starting point for analysis in this case. The taxpayer in Frothingham attacked as unconstitutional the Maternity Act of 1921, 42 Stat. 224, which established a federal program of grants to those States which would undertake programs to reduce maternal and infant mortality. The taxpayer alleged that Congress, in enacting the challenged statute, had exceeded the powers delegated to it under Article I of the Constitution and had invaded the legislative province reserved to the several States by the Tenth Amendment. The taxpayer complained that the result of the allegedly unconstitutional enactment would be to increase her future federal tax liability and "thereby take her property without due process of law." 262 U.S., at 486. The Court noted that a federal taxpayer's "interest in the moneys of the Treasury . . . is comparatively minute and indeterminable" and that "the effect upon future taxation, of any payment out of the [Treasury's] funds, . . . [is] remote, fluctuating and uncertain." Id., at 487. As a result, the Court ruled that the taxpayer had failed to allege the type of "direct injury" necessary to confer standing. Id., at 488.

Although the barrier Frothingham erected against federal taxpayer suits has never been breached, the decision has been the source of some confusion and the object of considerable criticism. The confusion has developed as commentators have tried to determine whether Frothingham establishes a constitutional bar to taxpayer suits or whether the Court was simply imposing a rule of self-restraint which was not constitutionally compelled. The conflicting viewpoints are reflected in the arguments made to this Court by the parties in this case. The Government has pressed upon us the view that Frothingham announced a constitutional rule, compelled by the Article III limitations on federal-court jurisdiction and grounded in considerations of the doctrine of separation of powers. Appellants, however, insist that Frothingham expressed no more than a policy of judicial self-restraint which can be disregarded when compelling reasons for assuming jurisdiction over a taxpayer's suit exist. The opinion delivered in Frothingham can be read to support either position. The concluding sentence of the opinion states that, to take jurisdiction of the taxpayer's suit, "would be not to decide a judicial controversy, but to assume a position of authority over the governmental acts of another and co-equal department, an authority which plainly we do not possess." 262 U.S., at 489. Yet the concrete reasons given for denying standing to a federal taxpayer suggest that the Court's holding rests on something less than a constitutional foundation. For example, the Court conceded that standing had previously been conferred on municipal taxpayers to sue in that capacity. However, the Court viewed the interest of a federal taxpayer in total federal tax revenues as "comparatively minute and indeterminable" when measured against a municipal taxpayer's interest in a smaller city treasury. Id., at 486–487. This suggests that the petitioner in Frothingham was denied standing not because she was a taxpayer but because her tax bill was not large enough. In addition, the Court spoke of the "attendant inconveniences" of entertaining that taxpayer's suit because it might open the door of federal courts to countless such suits "in respect of every other appropriation act and statute whose administration requires the outlay of public money, and whose validity may be questioned." Id., at 487. Such a statement suggests pure policy considerations.

To the extent that Frothingham has been viewed as resting on policy considerations, it has been criticized as depending on assumptions not consistent with modern conditions. For example, some commentators have pointed out that a number of corporate taxpayers today have a federal tax liability running into hundreds of millions of dollars, and such taxpayers have a far greater monetary stake in the Federal Treasury than they do in any municipal treasury. To some degree, the fear expressed in Frothingham that allowing one taxpayer to sue would inundate the federal courts with countless similar suits has been mitigated by the ready availability of the devices of class actions and joinder under the Federal Rules of Civil Procedure, adopted subsequent to the decision in Frothingham. Whatever the merits of the current debate over Frothingham, its very existence suggests that we should undertake a fresh examination of the limitations upon standing to sue in a federal court and the application of those limitations to taxpayer suits.

III

The jurisdiction of federal courts is defined and limited by Article III of the Constitution. In terms relevant to the question for decision in this case, the judicial power of federal courts is constitutionally restricted to "cases" and "controversies." As is so often the situation in constitutional adjudication, those two words have an iceberg quality, containing beneath their surface simplicity submerged complexities which go to the very heart of our constitutional form of government. Embodied in the words "cases" and "controversies" are two complementary but somewhat different limitations. In part those words limit the business of federal courts to questions presented in an adversary context and in a form historically viewed as capable of resolution through the judicial process. And in part those words define the role assigned to the judiciary in a tripartite allocation of power to assure that the federal courts will not intrude into areas committed to the other branches of government.

Justiciability is the term of art employed to give expression to this dual limitation placed upon federal courts by the case-and-controversy doctrine.

Justiciability is itself a concept of uncertain meaning and scope. Its reach is illustrated by the various grounds upon which questions sought to be adjudicated in federal courts have been held not to be justiciable. Thus, no justiciable controversy is presented when the parties seek adjudication of only a political question, when the parties are asking for an advisory opinion, when the question sought to be adjudicated has been mooted by subsequent developments, and when there is no standing to maintain the action. Yet it remains true that "[j]usticiability is . . . not a legal concept with a fixed content or susceptible of scientific verification. Its utilization is the resultant of many subtle pressures. . . ." Poe v. Ullman, 367 U.S. 497, 508 (1961).

Part of the difficulty in giving precise meaning and form to the concept of justiciability stems from the uncertain historical antecedents of the case-and-controversy doctrine. For example, MR. JUSTICE FRANKFURTER twice suggested that historical meaning could be imparted to the concepts of justiciability and case and controversy by reference to the practices of the courts of Westminster when the Constitution was adopted. Joint Anti-Fascist Committee v. McGrath, 341 U.S. 123, 150 (1951) (concurring opinion); Coleman v. Miller, 307 U.S. 433, 460 (1939) (separate opinion). However, the power of English judges to deliver advisory opinions was well established at the time the Constitution was drafted. 3 K. Davis, Administrative Law Treatise 127–128 (1958). And it is quite clear that "the oldest and most consistent thread in the federal law of justiciability is that the federal courts will not give advisory opinions." C. Wright, Federal Courts 34 (1963). Thus, the implicit policies embodied in Article III, and not history alone, impose the rule against advisory opinions on federal courts. When the federal judicial power is invoked to pass upon the validity of actions by the Legislative and Executive Branches of the Government, the rule against advisory opinions implements the separation of powers prescribed by the Constitution and confines federal courts to the role assigned them by Article III. See Muskrat v. United States, 219 U.S. 346 (1911); 3 H. Johnston, Correspondence and Public Papers of John Jay 486–489 (1891) (correspondence between Secretary of State Jefferson and CHIEF JUSTICE JAY). However, the rule against advisory opinions also recognizes that such suits often "are not pressed before the Court with that clear concreteness provided when a question emerges precisely framed and necessary for decision from a clash of adversary argument exploring every aspect of a multifaced situation embracing conflicting and demanding interests." United States v. Fruehauf, 365 U.S. 146, 157 (1961). Consequently, the Article III prohibition against advisory opinions reflects the complementary constitutional considerations expressed by the justiciability doctrine: Federal judicial power is limited to those disputes which confine federal courts to a role consistent with a system of separated powers and which are traditionally thought to be capable of resolution through the judicial process.

Additional uncertainty exists in the doctrine of justiciability because that doctrine has become a blend of constitutional requirements and policy considerations. And a policy limitation is "not always clearly distinguished from the constitutional limitation." Barrows v. Jackson, 346 U.S. 249, 255 (1953). For example, in his concurring opinion in Ashwander v. Tennessee Valley Authority, 297 U.S. 288, 345–348 (1936), MR. JUSTICE BRANDEIS listed seven rules developed by this Court "for its own governance" to avoid passing prematurely on constitutional questions. Because the rules operate in "cases confessedly within [the Court's] jurisdiction," id., at 346, they find their source in policy, rather than purely constitutional, considerations. However, several of the cases cited by MR. JUSTICE BRANDEIS in illustrating the rules of self-governance articulated purely constitutional grounds for decision. See, e.g., Massachusetts v. Mellon, 262 U.S. 447 (1923); Fairchild v. Hughes, 258 U.S. 126 (1922); Chicago & Grand Trunk R. Co. v. Wellman, 143 U.S. 339 (1892). The "many subtle pressures" which cause policy considerations to blend into the constitutional limitations of Article III make the justiciability doctrine one of uncertain and shifting contours.

It is in this context that the standing question presented by this case must be viewed and that the Government's argument on that question must be evaluated. As we understand it, the Government's position is that the constitutional scheme of separation of powers, and the deference owed by the federal judiciary to the other two branches of government within that scheme, present an absolute bar to taxpayer suits challenging the validity of federal spending programs. The Government views such suits as involving no more than the mere disagreement by the taxpayer "with the uses to which tax money is put." According to the Government, the resolution of such disagreements is committed to other branches of the Federal Government and not to the judiciary. Consequently, the Government contends that, under no circumstances, should standing be conferred on federal taxpayers to challenge a federal taxing or spending program. An analysis of the function served by standing limitations compels a rejection of the Government's position.

Standing is an aspect of justiciability and, as such, the problem of standing is surrounded by the same complexities and vagaries that inhere in justiciability. Standing has been called one of "the most amorphous [concepts] in the entire domain of public law." Some of the complexities peculiar to standing problems result because standing "serves, on occasion, as a shorthand expression for all the various elements of justiciability." In addition, there are at work in the standing doctrine the many subtle pressures which tend to cause policy considerations to blend into constitutional limitations.

Despite the complexities and uncertainties, some meaningful form can be given to the jurisdictional limitations placed on federal court power by the concept of standing. The fundamental aspect of standing is that it focuses on the party seeking to get his complaint before a federal court and not on the issues he wishes to have adjudicated. The "gist of the question of standing" is whether the party seeking relief has "alleged such a personal stake in the outcome of the controversy as to assure that concrete adverseness which sharpens the presentation of issues upon which the court so largely depends for illumination of difficult constitutional questions." Baker v. Carr, 369 U.S. 186, 204 (1962). In other words, when standing is placed in issue in a case, the question is whether the person whose standing is challenged is a proper party to request an adjudication of a particular issue and not whether the issue itself is justiciable. Thus, a party may have standing in a particular case, but the federal court may nevertheless decline to pass on the merits of the case because, for example, it presents a political question. A proper party is demanded so that federal courts will not be asked to decide "ill-defined controversies over constitutional issues," United Public Workers v. Mitchell, 330 U.S. 75, 90 (1947), or a case which is of "a hypothetical or abstract character," Aetna Life Insurance Co. v. Haworth, 300 U.S. 227, 240 (1937). So stated, the standing requirement is closely related to, although more general than, the rule that federal courts will not entertain friendly suits, Chicago & Grand Trunk R. Co. v. Wellman, supra, or those which are feigned or collusive in nature, United States v. Johnson, 319 U.S. 302 (1943); Lord v. Veazie, 8 How. 251 (1850).

When the emphasis in the standing problem is placed on whether the person invoking a federal court's jurisdiction is a proper party to maintain the action, the weakness of the Government's argument in this case becomes apparent. The question whether a particular person is a proper party to maintain the action does not, by its own force, raise separation of powers problems related to improper judicial interference in areas committed to other branches of the Federal Government. Such problems arise, if at all, only from the substantive issues the individual seeks to have adjudicated. Thus, in terms of Article III limitations on federal court jurisdiction, the question of standing is related only to whether the dispute sought to be adjudicated will be presented in an adversary context and in a form historically viewed as capable of judicial resolution. It is for that reason that the emphasis in standing problems is on whether the party invoking federal court jurisdiction has "a personal stake in the outcome of the controversy," Baker v. Carr, supra, at 204, and whether the dispute touches upon "the legal relations of parties having adverse legal interests." Aetna Life Insurance Co. v. Haworth, supra, at 240–241. A taxpayer may or may not have the requisite personal stake in the outcome, depending upon the circumstances of the particular case. Therefore, we find no absolute bar in Article III to suits by federal taxpayers challenging allegedly unconstitutional federal taxing and spending programs. There remains, however, the problem of determining the circumstances under which a federal taxpayer will be deemed to have the personal stake and interest that impart the necessary concrete adverseness to such litigation so that standing can be conferred on the taxpayer qua taxpayer consistent with the constitutional limitations of Article III.

IV

The various rules of standing applied by federal courts have not been developed in the abstract. Rather, they have been fashioned with specific reference to the status asserted by the party whose standing is challenged and to the type of question he wishes to have adjudicated. We have noted that, in deciding the question of standing, it is not relevant that the substantive issues in the litigation might be nonjusticiable. However, our decisions establish that, in ruling on standing, it is both appropriate and necessary to look to the substantive issues for another purpose, namely, to determine whether there is a logical nexus between the status asserted and the claim sought to be adjudicated. For example, standing requirements will vary in First Amendment religion cases depending upon whether the party raises an Establishment Clause claim or a claim under the Free Exercise Clause. See McGowan v. Maryland, 366 U.S. 420, 429–430 (1961). Such inquiries into the nexus between the status asserted by the litigant and the claim he presents are essential to assure that he is a proper and appropriate party to invoke federal judicial power. Thus, our point of reference in this case is the standing of individuals who assert only the status of federal taxpayers and who challenge the constitutionality of a federal spending program. Whether such individuals have standing to maintain that form of action turns on whether they can demonstrate the necessary stake as taxpayers in the outcome of the litigation to satisfy Article III requirements.

The nexus demanded of federal taxpayers has two aspects to it. First, the taxpayer must establish a logical link between that status and the type of legislative enactment attacked. Thus, a taxpayer will be a proper party to allege the unconstitutionality only of exercises of congressional power under the taxing and spending clause of Art. I, § 8, of the Constitution. It will not be sufficient to allege an incidental expenditure of tax funds in the administration of an essentially regulatory statute. This requirement is consistent with the limitation imposed upon state-taxpayer standing in federal courts in Doremus v. Board of Education, 342 U.S. 429 (1952). Secondly, the taxpayer must establish a nexus between that status and the precise nature of the constitutional infringement alleged. Under this requirement, the taxpayer must show that the challenged enactment exceeds specific constitutional limitations imposed upon the exercise of the congressional taxing and spending power and not simply that the enactment is generally beyond the powers delegated to Congress by Art. I, § 8. When both nexuses are established, the litigant will have shown a taxpayer's stake in the outcome of the controversy and will be a proper and appropriate party to invoke a federal court's jurisdiction.

The taxpayer-appellants in this case have satisfied both nexuses to support their claim of standing under the test we announce today. Their constitutional challenge is made to an exercise by Congress of its power under Art. I, § 8, to spend for the general welfare, and the challenged program involves a substantial expenditure of federal tax funds. In addition, appellants have alleged that the challenged expenditures violate the Establishment and Free Exercise Clauses of the First Amendment. Our history vividly illustrates that one of the specific evils feared by those who drafted the Establishment Clause and fought for its adoption was that the taxing and spending power would be used to favor one religion over another or to support religion in general. James Madison, who is generally recognized as the leading architect of the religion clauses of the First Amendment, observed in his famous Memorial and Remonstrance Against Religious Assessments that "the same authority which can force a citizen to contribute three pence only of his property for the support of any one establishment, may force him to conform to any other establishment in all cases whatsoever." 2 Writings of James Madison 183, 186 (Hunt ed. 1901). The concern of Madison and his supporters was quite clearly that religious liberty ultimately would be the victim if government could employ its taxing and spending powers to aid one religion over another or to aid religion in general. The Establishment Clause was designed as a specific bulwark against such potential abuses of governmental power, and that clause of the First Amendment operates as a specific constitutional limitation upon the exercise by Congress of the taxing and spending power conferred by Art. I, § 8.

The allegations of the taxpayer in Frothingham v. Mellon, supra, were quite different from those made in this case, and the result in Frothingham is consistent with the test of taxpayer standing announced today. The taxpayer in Frothingham attacked a federal spending program and she, therefore, established the first nexus required. However, she lacked standing because her constitutional attack was not based on an allegation that Congress, in enacting the Maternity Act of 1921, had breached a specific limitation upon its taxing and spending power. The taxpayer in Frothingham alleged essentially that Congress, by enacting the challenged statute, had exceeded the general powers delegated to it by Art. I, § 8, and that Congress had thereby invaded the legislative province reserved to the States by the Tenth Amendment. To be sure, Mrs. Frothingham made the additional allegation that her tax liability would be increased as a result of the allegedly unconstitutional enactment, and she framed that allegation in terms of a deprivation of property without due process of law. However, the Due Process Clause of the Fifth Amendment does not protect taxpayers against increases in tax liability, and the taxpayer in Frothingham failed to make any additional claim that the harm she alleged resulted from a breach by Congress of the specific constitutional limitations imposed upon an exercise of the taxing and spending power. In essence, Mrs. Frothingham was attempting to assert the States' interest in their legislative prerogatives and not a federal taxpayer's interest in being free of taxing and spending in contravention of specific constitutional limitations imposed upon Congress' taxing and spending power.

We have noted that the Establishment Clause of the First Amendment does specifically limit the taxing and spending power conferred by Art. I, § 8. Whether the Constitution contains other specific limitations can be determined only in the context of future cases. However, whenever such specific limitations are found, we believe a taxpayer will have a clear stake as a taxpayer in assuring that they are not breached by Congress. Consequently, we hold that a taxpayer will have standing consistent with Article III to invoke federal judicial power when he alleges that congressional action under the taxing and spending clause is in derogation of those constitutional provisions which operate to restrict the exercise of the taxing and spending power. The taxpayer's allegation in such cases would be that his tax money is being extracted and spent in violation of specific constitutional protections against such abuses of legislative power. Such an injury is appropriate for judicial redress, and the taxpayer has established the necessary nexus between his status and the nature of the allegedly unconstitutional action to support his claim of standing to secure judicial review. Under such circumstances, we feel confident that the questions will be framed with the necessary specificity, that the issues will be contested with the necessary adverseness and that the litigation will be pursued with the necessary vigor to assure that the constitutional challenge will be made in a form traditionally thought to be capable of judicial resolution. We lack that confidence in cases such as Frothingham where a taxpayer seeks to employ a federal court as a forum in which to air his generalized grievances about the conduct of government or the allocation of power in the Federal System.

While we express no view at all on the merits of appellants' claims in this case, their complaint contains sufficient allegations under the criteria we have outlined to give them standing to invoke a federal court's jurisdiction for an adjudication on the merits.

Reversed.

CHAPTER 11

Contents

Civil Rights in the Constitution

§ 11.1 Civil Rights Defined

Many attempts have been made to precisely define what is meant by the phrase "civil rights" but it almost defies definition. It might be said that it is analogous to a two-pronged pitchfork which is stuck in the ground to make two holes. One hole could be used to plant seeds for a plant which we will call political rights. In the other hole we could plant seeds from which a plant will grow, which will grow branches to control many areas of individual or private freedom of action into which the government may not intrude.

§ 11.2 Historical Significance of Federal and State Citizenship

A cursory look at American history reveals that the framers of the Constitution were experts at the art of compromise. Varied sectional economic and social differences were required to meet in a common area of agreement. There was great distrust of a strong central government and only delegated powers were given to the central government, as more fully described in Chapter 10 (supra). There was a question as to which citizenship was paramount, i.e., that of citizenship of a state or citizenship of the national government. In the case of Dred Scott v. Sanford, 19 How. 393, 15 L.Ed. 69 (1857), this issue was resolved in favor of state citizenship preeminence. In that case, a slave owned by a surgeon of the United States Army moved with him from state to state. Some of this time he was assigned to military posts above latitude 36°30′ and therefore was in an area where slavery was forbidden by the terms of the Missouri Compromise of 1820. Scott, with the aid of abolitionists, brought suit in a federal court after arranging for his purchase by the brother of the widow of his deceased master, Dr. Emerson. The defendant in this case, John Sanford, was a citizen of New York and the case was initiated in a federal court in Missouri after the Supreme Court of Missouri had reversed a lower Missouri court which had granted the petitioner his freedom. The Court, speaking through Mr. Justice Taney, held that "...it cannot be believed that the large slaveholding States regarded them [slaves] as included in the word citizens, or would have consented to a Constitution which might compel them to receive them in that character from another state.... No one, we presume, supposes that any change in public opinion or feeling, in relation to this unfortunate race, in the civilized nations of Europe or in this country, should induce the court to give to the words of the Constitution a more liberal construction in their favor than they were intended to bear when the instrument was framed and adopted.... If any of its provisions are deemed unjust, there is a mode prescribed in the instrument itself by which it may be amended... Any other rule of construction would abrogate the judicial character of this court and make it the mere reflex of the popular opinion or passion of the day."

In an effort to protect the former slaves after the end of the War between the States, the Federal Government intervened by adopting the Thirteenth, Fourteenth, and Fifteenth Amendments to the United States Constitution.

After this war, the southern states were in serious economic disarray. Many freed black people were totally unprepared to fend for themselves in a competitive economic environment. Some of them resented the fact that they had to work. When the crop had to be picked, many left their homes and lived off the land as they went. Others were reported to have left their families, and still others left to attempt to find the families from which they had been separated by their sale or otherwise.

Various mechanisms were established by government to combat these problems in an attempt to get the economy moving. The most onerous of these were called the "Black Codes," which every ex-Confederate state except Tennessee had adopted by 1866. These laws attempted to define the legal position of the newly created freedman. They gave blacks the right to sue, to give evidence in courts, to sanctify marriage relationships, to attend school and gave protection of the state to apprenticed children. However, there were prohibitions to blacks' from holding political office, serving on juries, voting, and bearing arms. Most states also limited their employment to farming in that they were prohibited from working as mechanics or artisans. What was most disturbing was that they could not leave their jobs except under prescribed conditions. Vagrancy laws were also very oppressive. Many states enacted statutes giving the state the right to pick up and try a black person who had no visible means of support, and after conviction, they could be made to work on chain gangs or contracted out to planters and other employers who would pay the fines that had been imposed and any expenses that the state had incurred for their upkeep.

In effect, the "Black Codes" reestablished slavery in the affected states. In response to these measures, the Fourteenth Amendment was adopted, Section 1 of which reads as follows:

> *All persons born or naturalized in the United States, and subject to the jurisdiction thereof, are citizens of the United States and of the State wherein they reside. No State shall make or enforce any law which shall abridge the privileges or immunities of citizens of the United States; nor shall any*

State deprive any person of life, liberty, or property, without due process of law; nor deny to any person within its jurisdiction the equal protection of the laws.

With the adoption of the Fourteenth Amendment, the former slave effectively came under a greater protection of the Federal government. Except for the opening sentences, the interpretation of the purpose and intent of the Fourteenth Amendment has been litigated often. It has been argued that it was designed to include a limitation of state governmental powers to grant the individual rights of each of the first eight amendments to state action. Others have argued that its proponents only intended to effect the rights of blacks and that the Federal Bill of Rights was not to be incorporated as a limitation upon the states.

§ 11.3 Equal Privileges and Immunities Clause

A test of the meaning of the equal privileges and immunities clause found its way to the Court in the Slaughter House Cases, 83 U.S. 36, 21 L.Ed. 394 (1873). In these cases, a number of butchers made a challenge to a state law which created a monopoly of slaughtering animals for a named company for a period of twenty-five years. The challenge was founded on the equal protection and privileges and immunities clauses of the Fourteenth Amendment. The Court rejected the petitioners' claim but in so doing, the Court only dealt with the privileges and immunities clause, neglecting the arguments of equal protection. It held that the right to follow a profession or trade without state interference was not a "privilege or immunity" of citizens of the United States. It explained that the privilege and immunity clause extended to the right of the people to come to the seat of their government to assert claims against the government, the right to seek the protection of government, the right to hold office and to perform the administrative function of government, as well as the right to use the navigable waters of the United States. Infringement by the states upon these privileges would constitute a violation of the Fourteenth Amendment. However, there was no privilege which United States citizens possessed to operate a business where the state had granted a monopoly to another.

Since the Slaughter House Cases, the litigation concerning the interpretation of the Fourteenth Amendment has concerned itself with the due process and equal protection clauses. By constantly "pounding at the door of the Court" inroads were made on a selective basis to absorb the Bill of Rights into state action based on the theory of "substantive due process." This theory refers to the process of declaring unconstitutional regulatory laws of legislative bodies because they were thought on their face to constitute unreasonable schemes of regulation.

§ 11.4 Historical Significance of Due Process Clause

The provision in the Fifth Amendment which reads "... nor be deprived of life, liberty, or property without due process of law ..." was meant to apply only to the federal government and not to the states. There was a great fear of a central government and many states conditioned their ratification of the Constitution on the insertion of this language. Yet, the term due process has not been precisely defined by the framers of the Constitution or the Court. This, as has been explained earlier, was the result of intention rather than oversight.

The Fourteenth Amendment, however, was intended to apply to state action but as has been indicated in the Slaughter House Cases (supra), the privileges and immunities clause was held not to apply to the states where its own citizens were involved. The due process clause of the Fourteenth Amendment has had a more interesting history which made inroads into the action of state governments.

The application of this clause to the First, Fourth, Fifth, Sixth, and Eighth Amendments to state action has been discussed in earlier chapters of this book. What follows in this chapter is an amplification of the historical changes as it relates to the incorporation or absorptions of these rights into state action.

§ 11.5 Freedom of Press and Speech

The First Amendment's commands with respect to the prohibition against Congress from making a law which abridged the freedom of speech or of the press was considered to be so fundamental that this prohibition extended to state action. In 1925, the Court placed to rest several confusing decisions when it decided Gitlow v. New York, 268 U.S. 652, 45 S.Ct. 625, 69 L.Ed. 1138 (1923). The Court said, "... For present purposes we may and do assume that freedom of speech and of the press—which are protected by the First Amendment from abridgment by Congress—are among the fundamental personal rights and liberties protected by the Due Process Clause of the Fourteenth Amendment from impairment by the states...."

It should be noted that freedom of speech and press is not an unfettered freedom. In Schenk v. United States, 249 U.S. 47, 39 S.Ct. 247, 63 L.Ed. 470 (1919), the Court held, "The question in every case is whether the words used are used in such circumstances and are of such a nature as to create a CLEAR AND PRESENT DANGER that they will bring about substantive evil that evil that Congress has a right to prevent. It is a question of proximity and degree."

§ 11.6 Freedom of Religion

The immediate objective of the framers of the Constitution in separating the church from the state was to separate the new state from the established church as it had been known in England and in most of the colonies. However, because of their foresight, the prohibition of "Congress shall make no law respecting an establishment of religion," as found in the First Amendment, did not limit this proscription to any particular form of state supported theology.

State-church conflicts have arisen over compulsory bible reading in a state supported public school, Abington School District v. Schemp, 374 U.S. 203 (1961); compulsory prayer in a state supported public school, Engel v. Vitale, 370 U.S. 421, 82 S.Ct. 1261, 8 L.Ed.2d 601 (1962); distribution of religious literature or personal visitations, Murdock v. Commonwealth of Pennsylvania, 319 U.S. 105, 63 S.Ct. 870, 87 L.Ed. 1292, 146 A.L.R. 81 (1943); compelling persons to salute the flag in contravention of their religious beliefs, Taylor v. State of Mississippi, 319 U.S. 583, 63 S.Ct. 1200, 87 L.Ed. 1600 (1943); being compelled to close a store on a Sunday because of state "Blue Laws"; and a denial of a claim for unemployment compensation because the petitioner was unable to get a job which did not require her to work on a Saturday, her sabbath day.

In Braunfeld v. Brown, 366 U.S. 599, 81 S.Ct. 1144, 6 L.Ed.2d 563 (1961), the appellants were Orthodox Jewish merchants in Philadelphia who engaged in the retail sale of clothing and home furnishings. They alleged that Sunday closing would impair their ability to earn a livelihood and would cause at least one of them to discontinue in business. They contended that the Sunday closing legislation prohibited the exercise of their religion because they would lose substantial business to their non-Sabbatarian competitors if they continued their Sabbath observance. The Court held that "the statute at bar does not make unlawful any religious practice of appellants; the Sunday law simply regulates a secular activity and, as applied to appellants, operates so as to make the practice of their religious beliefs more expensive. Furthermore, the law's effect does not inconvenience all members of the Orthodox Jewish faith but only those who, believe it necessary to work on Sunday." In a concurring opinion, Justices Frankfurter and Harlan wrote, "The general principles of church separation were found to be included in the (Fourteenth) Amendment's Due

Process Clause in view of the meaning which the presuppositions of our society infuse into the concept of 'liberty' protected by the clause. This is the source of limitation imposed upon the States. To the extent that those limitations are akin to the restrictions which the First Amendment places upon the action of the central government, it is because—as with freedom of thought and speech of which Mr. Justice Cardoza spoke in Palko v. State of Connecticut, 302 U.S. 319—it is accurate to say concerning the principle that a government must neither establish nor suppress religious belief...."

§ 11.7 Freedom from Unreasonable Search and Seizure

We have already alluded to the case of Mapp v. Ohio, 367 U.S. 643, 81 S.Ct. 1684, 6 L.Ed.2d 108 (1961), in Section 6.1 (supra). In that section we traced the history of the exclusionary rule wherein evidence obtained by state law enforcement officers which is in violation of a defendant's constitutional rights will not be admissible in evidence at that person's trial. At this juncture, it is to be emphasized that the Supreme Court in making the federal rules of exclusion applicable to state courts did so by virtue of the Due Process Clause of the Fourteenth Amendment. However, the Court's first mention of this theory of exclusion of evidence secured by state authorities in violation of the Fourth Amendment appeared in Wolf v. Colorado, 338 U.S. 25, 69 S.Ct. 1359, 93 L.Ed. 1782 (1949), where the Court said, "The security of one's privacy against arbitrary intrusion by the police—which is at the core of the Fourth Amendment—is basic to a free society. It is therefore implicit in 'the concept of ordered liberty' and as such enforceable against the States through the Due Process Clause (Fourteenth Amendment)... Accordingly, we have no hesitation in saying that were a State affirmatively to sanction such police incursion into privacy it would run counter to the guaranty of the Fourteenth Amendment."

In the Wolf case the State of Colorado did not affirmatively sanction arbitrary intrusion by the police and hence the Court did not reverse the conviction of the petitioner. In the Mapp case, notwithstanding the fact that the State of Ohio did not affirmatively sanction police incursion into privacy, the Court said, "The ignoble shortcut to conviction left open to the State tends to destroy the entire system of constitutional restraints on which the liberties of the people rest. Having once recognized that the right of privacy embodied in the Fourth Amendment is enforceable against the States, and the right to be secure against rude invasions of privacy by state officers is, therefore, constitutional in origin, we can no longer permit that right to remain an empty promise. Because it is enforceable in the same manner and to like effect as other basic rights secured by the Due Process Clause, we can no longer permit it to be revocable at the whim of any police officer who, in the name of law enforcement itself, chooses to suspend its enjoyment."

§ 11.8 Protection against Double Jeopardy

Evidence has been found in ancient canon law and in the early laws of Greece and Rome that it was unacceptable pursuant to moral and legal standards to try a person twice for the same offense. This concept became so entrenched in the common law that it was incorporated into the language of the Fifth Amendment. Similar provisions were found in the constitutions of all of the states except Connecticut, Maryland, Massachusetts, North Carolina, and Vermont. (Brock v. North Carolina, 344 U.S. 424, 435, 73 S.Ct. 349, 97 L.Ed. 436 [1953].) The Magna Carta (1215) did not contain any reference to it but the concept was so implanted in the common law that it was apparently thought that it need not appear in the Magna Carta.

The issue of state application of the Fifth Amendment double jeopardy clause was tested in Palko v. Connecticut, 302 U.S. 319, 58 S.Ct. 149, 82 L.Ed. 288 (1937). In the Palko case, the State of Connecticut had tried the petitioner for murder, first degree, and the jury found him guilty of murder in the second degree with life imprisonment as the sanction. The State of Connecticut appealed on the grounds of substantial errors committed at the trial and the first conviction was reversed and the case remanded for a new trial. He was tried again for murder, first degree. At the outset of the trial, he raised the objection that he was denied his constitutional right of Fifth Amendment double jeopardy clause as made applicable to the states through the Fourteenth Amendment Due Process Clause. His objection was overruled by the Connecticut Courts and he was convicted on the second trial of the crime of murder, first degree, carrying a punishment of death. The case came before the United States Supreme Court and, in a decision written by Mr. Justice Benjamin Cardoza, the Court held, "... Is that kind of double jeopardy to which the statute has subjected him a hardship so acute and shocking that our policy will not endure it? Does it violate those 'fundamental principles of liberty and justice which lie at the base of all our civil and political institutions'? The answer surely must be 'no'. What the answer would have to be if the state were permitted after a trial free from error to try the accused over again or to bring another case against him, we have no occasion to consider. We deal with the statute before us and no other. The state is not attempting to wear the accused out by a multitude of cases with accumulated trials. It asks no more than this, that the case against him shall go on free from the corrosion of substantial legal error.... If the trial had been infected with error adverse to the accused, there might have been review at his instance, and as often as necessary to purge the vicious taint."

Thus, the Palko case set a precedent that if the defendant in a state action had a trial with substantial errors and he was found guilty, or if he was acquitted, the state could correct the errors through appeal and retrial. The defendant had no recourse to the Fifth Amendment through the Fourteenth Amendment Due Process Clause.

The Palko case, however, was not the final word in the absorption of the double jeopardy protection against state actions. In Benton v. Maryland, 395 U.S. 784, 89 S.Ct. 2056, 23 L.Ed.2d 707 (1969), the petitioner was tried in a Maryland court on charges of burglary and larceny. The jury convicted him of burglary but acquitted him of larceny. It turned out later that the grand jury and the petty jury had been invalidly selected. He was given the option of reindictment and retrial. He accepted this but after the second trial he was found guilty of both burglary and larceny. He challenged the second conviction on the basis of the Fourteenth Amendment Due Process Clause, making the Fifth Amendment applicable to state action. The Court in a 7–2 decision reversed Palko v. Connecticut (supra) stating, "... the double jeopardy prohibition of the Fifth Amendment represents a fundamental ideal in our constitutional heritage, and that it should apply to the States through the Fourteenth Amendment." It held further "that the petitioner's larceny conviction cannot stand once federal double jeopardy standards are applied." Thus the Palko case was reversed and a new right was absorbed into state action.

§ 11.9 Protection against Self-Incrimination

The Fifth Amendment self-incrimination clause was discussed in Chapter 7 (infra), but in that section, the emphasis was not on the Due Process Clause of the Fourteenth Amendment.

It was in 1964 when the Fifth Amendment privilege against self-incrimination became applicable to state action. In that year the Court decided Malloy v. Hogan, 378 U.S. 1, 84 S.Ct. 1489, 12 L.Ed.2d 653. It held that "the Fourteenth Amendment secures against state invasion the same privilege that the Fifth Amendment guarantees against federal infringement—the right of a person to remain silent unless he chooses to speak in the unfettered exercise of his own will, and to suffer no penalty as held in Twining for such silence."

In a companion case of Murphy v. Waterfront Commission, 378 U.S. 52, 84 S.Ct. 1594, 12 L.Ed.2d. 678 (1964), the petitioners had been held in contempt of court because they refused to respond to certain questions presented to them at a hearing conducted by the Waterfront Commission of New York Harbor, even though they were granted immunity from state prosecution, on the ground that their answers might tend to incriminate them under federal law. The Court, in a unanimous decision but through several concurring opinions, overturned the established rule "that a constitutional privilege against self-incrimination does not protect a witness in one jurisdiction against being compelled to give testimony which could be used to convict him in another jurisdiction." The Court speaking through Mr. Justice Goldberg said, "Most if not all, of (the) policies and purposes (of the privilege against self-incrimination) are defeated when a witness 'can be whipsawed into incriminating himself under both state and federal law even though' the constitutional privilege against self-incrimination is applicable."

§ 11.10 Right to a Speedy and Public Trial

North Carolina had a statute which permitted the prosecutor to bring a case to trial at any time on his motion. This gave the prosecutor great latitude in the prosecution of defendants. If a defendant was unable to get bail or other forms of release, he would languish in a detention facility until the prosecutor decided that the trial should go on. This practice led to many abuses where persons who were later found to be innocent were incarcerated for extensive periods of time. The issue of the constitutionality of this statute was presented to the Court in Klopfer v. North Carolina, 386 U.S. 213, 87 S.Ct. 988, 18 L.Ed.2d 1 (1967), where it was held "... that the right to a speedy trial is as fundamental as any of the rights secured by the Sixth Amendment." In so doing, the Court made the fundamental fairness doctrine of the Fourteenth Amendment Due Process Clause applicable to the Sixth Amendment speedy trial proscription and thus made it refer to the action of the states against its own citizens.

In Estas v. Texas, 381 U.S. 532, 85 S.Ct. 1628, 14 L.Ed.2d 543 (1965), the Court said, "We start with the proposition that it is a 'public trial' that the Sixth Amendment guarantees to the 'accused.'" In effect, without expressly stating that a public trial is guaranteed to state citizens by their state courts, it assumed that a public trial was one of the fundamental rights afforded all citizens whether the trial took place in state or federal courts. This had been decided earlier in In Re Oliver, 333 U.S. 257, 68 S.Ct. 499, 92 L.Ed.

682 (1948), where a "one man grand jury" was permitted under Michigan law. In that case a judge told the petitioner that his story did not "jell," then immediately charged him with contempt immediately convicted him, and sentenced him to sixty days in jail. No public or private counsel was present. It was not considered to be a public trial.

§ 11.11 Right to a Jury Trial

The Sixth Amendment guarantee of a jury trial was not absorbed into the state procedural constitutional rights until 1968 when in Duncan v. Louisiana, 391 U.S. 145, 88 S.Ct. 1444, 20 L.Ed.2d 491 (1968), the Court held, "Because we believe that trial by jury in criminal cases is fundamental to the American scheme of justice, we hold that the Fourteenth Amendment guarantees a right of jury trial in all criminal cases which—were they to be tried in a federal court—would come within the Sixth Amendment's guarantee." In that case the appellant had been convicted of simple battery which under Louisiana law was a misdemeanor, punishable by two years imprisonment and a $300 fine. Louisiana only granted jury trials in cases where capital punishment or imprisonment at hard labor may be imposed. While the Court did not rule in that case that a state must provide for a jury trial in every case, it did say, "We need not, however, settle in this case the exact location of the line between petty offenses and serious crimes. It is sufficient for our purposes to hold that a crime punishable by two years in prison is, based on past and contemporary standards in this country, a serious crime and not a petty offense." Consequently, appellant was entitled to a jury trial and it was error to deny it.

In Baldwin v. New York, 399 U.S. 66, 90 S.Ct. 1886, 26 L.Ed.2d 437 (1970), the Court said, "no offense can be deemed 'petty' for purposes of right to trial by jury where imprisonment for more than six months is authorized."

§ 11.12 Right to Notice of Charge

The Sixth Amendment proscription that a defendant ". . . be informed of the nature and cause of the accusation . . ." was absorbed into state procedure as a constitutional right in Cole v. Arkansas, 333 U.S. 196, 68 S.Ct. 514, 92 L.Ed. 644 (1948), where the Court said, "No principle of procedural due process is more clearly established than that notice of the specific charge, and a chance to be heard in a trial of the issues raised by that charge, if desired, are among the constitutional rights of every accused in a criminal proceeding in all courts, state or federal." In that same term of the Court, In Re Oliver, 333 U.S. 257, 68 S.Ct. 499, 92 L.Ed. 682 (1948), was decided and the Court said, "... A person's right to reasonable notice of charge against him, and an opportunity to be heard in his defense—a right to his day in court—are basic in our system of jurisprudence; and these rights include as a minimum, a right to examine witnesses against him, to offer testimony, and to be represented by counsel." The reader will remember that In Re Oliver was a Michigan case where the judge after hearing testimony before a "one man Grand Jury," convicted the petitioner immediately for contempt and sentenced him to sixty days, all without a public trial and with no counsel being present. (§ 11.10, supra.)

In 1967, In Re Gault, 387 U.S. 1, 87 S.Ct. 1428, 18 L.Ed.2d 527, was decided by the Court. This case involved the Juvenile Court system which prevailed in many states where the judge of the children's court had almost unbridled authority over the juvenile in a parens patriae relationship. The juvenile was supposedly not incarcerated; he was sent to a training school which by whatever name the state chose to call it, was incarceration without benefit of due process of law. The Court said that "... Due Process of law requires notice of the sort we have described—that is, notice which would be deemed constitutionally adequate in a civil or criminal proceeding." The Court also ruled that the juvenile is to be afforded the right of counsel and the rights of confrontation, freedom from self-incrimination, and the right to cross-examine witnesses testifying against him.

§ 11.13 Right to Confront the Witnesses

The right to confront witnesses against a defendant was incorporated into state action when in 1965, the Court decided Pointer v. Texas, 380 U.S. 400, 85 S.Ct. 1065, 13 L.Ed.2d 923, where the Court reversed petitioner's conviction when he demonstrated that he did not have a fair opportunity to cross-examine a witness against him at his trial. The Court said, "We hold today that the Sixth Amendment's right of an accused to confront the witnesses against him is likewise a fundamental right made obligatory on the states by the Fourteenth Amendment."

§ 11.14 Right to Compulsory Process for Obtaining Witnesses

The right to compulsory process in state criminal actions was decided in Washington v. Texas, 388 U.S. 14, 87 S.Ct. 1920, 18 L.Ed.2d 1019 (1967).

This case tested the constitutionality of a Texas statute which prohibited persons charged as principles, accomplices, or accessories in the same crime to be witnesses for each other. The Court said, "The right of an accused to have compulsory process for obtaining witnesses in his favor stands on lesser footing than other Sixth Amendment rights that we have previously held applicable to the States."

§ 11.15 Right to Assistance of Counsel

The defendant's right to assistance of counsel in state criminal trials and its evolution have been described rather fully in Section 8.10 et seq. (supra), and its repetition here is deemed unnecessary.

§ 11.16 Bail Provisions

The bail provisions of the Eighth Amendment have not, to this date, been incorporated into the constitutional rights of state citizens by state courts. The issue was raised in New York v. Oneil, 359 U.S. 1, 79 S.Ct. 564, 3 L.Ed.2d 585 (1959), but it was not decided by the Court.

§ 11.17 Cruel and Unusual Punishment

The Due Process Clause of the Fourteenth Amendment was discussed in Robinson v. California, 370 U.S. 660, 82 S.Ct. 1417, 8 L.Ed.2d 758 (1962). The statute upon which the petitioner was convicted made it a misdemeanor for a person either to use narcotics or to be addicted to the use of narcotics. The judge charged the jury, "All that the People must show is either that the defendant did use a narcotic in Los Angeles County, or that while in the City of Los Angeles he was addicted to the use of narcotics. . . ." The Court held ". . . that a state which imprisons a person thus afflicted as a criminal, even though he has never touched any narcotic drug within the State or been guilty of any irregular behavior there, inflicts a cruel and unusual punishment in violation of the Fourteenth Amendment. . . . Even one day in prison would be cruel and unusual punishment for the 'crime' of having a common cold."

The reader will recall that § 9.5 introduced the constitutional problem of the death penalty. What follows is an elaboration of the major decisions in that area of law as it concerns the Fourteenth Amendment. The first case dealing with this problem to come before the Court was Furman v. Georgia, 408 U.S. 238, 92 S.Ct. 2726, 33 L.Ed.2d 346 (1972). This case was decided simultaneously with Jackson v. Georgia and Branch v. Texas. In the Furman case the petitioner was convicted of murder in Georgia and sentenced to death. In the Jackson case, the petitioner was convicted of rape in Georgia and was sentenced to death; and in the Branch case, the petitioner was also convicted of rape and sentenced to death.

Certiorari was granted in each of these cases but it was limited to the question, "Does the imposition and carrying out of the death penalty (in these cases) constitute cruel and unusual punishment in violation of the Eighth and Fourteenth Amendments?" In a 5–4 decision the death penalty in the cases before the Court was struck down as being unconstitutional and in violation of the Eighth Amendment proscription against cruel and unusual punishment. The majority agreed on the constitutional grounds of it being cruel and unusual punishment but they failed to agree on the reasons for their conclusion. Mr. Justice Douglas, Mr. Justice Brennan, Mr. Justice Stewart, Mr. Justice White, and Mr. Justice Marshall, while agreeing in principle, wrote separate opinions supporting their conclusions.

Mr. Justice Douglas attacked the uncontrolled discretion of judges and juries as to what defendants should live or die. Under these laws, he said, no standards govern the selection of the penalty.

Mr. Justice Brennan, while agreeing with Mr. Justice Douglas, added that the state may not arbitrarily inflict an unusually severe punishment and that the death penalty, although to be found to be of long-standing usage and accepted in this country, was seldom used and was unnecessary. He held that a punishment is excessive if it is unnecessary. He further said that "when a country of over 200 million people inflicts an unusually severe punishment no more than fifty times a year, the inference is strong that the punishment is not being regularly and fairly applied."

Mr. Justice Stewart wrote another concurring but separate opinion. He said, "In the first place, it is clear that these sentences are 'cruel' in the sense that they excessively go beyond, not in degree but in kind, the punishments that the state legislatures have determined to be necessary. In the second place, it is equally clear that these sentences are 'unusual' in the sense that the penalty of death is infrequently imposed for murder, and that its imposition for rape is extraordinarily rare." While hinting that racial discrimination was at the basis of the selection of subjects for the death penalty, he said that this was not proved. He ended his decision by saying, "I simply conclude that the Eighth and Fourteenth Amendments cannot tolerate the infliction of a sentence of death under legal systems that permit this unique penalty to be so wantonly and so freakishly imposed."

Mr. Justice White, in a separate concurring opinion wrote, "... In joining the Court's judgment, I do not at all intimate that the death penalty is unconstitutional per se or that there is no system of capital punishment that would comport with the Eighth Amendment.... The narrower question to which I address myself concerns the constitutionality of capital punishment statutes under which (1) the legislature authorizes the imposition of a death penalty for murder or rape; (2) the legislature does not itself mandate the penalty in any particular class or kind of case (that is legislative will is not frustrated if the penalty is never imposed) but delegates to judges or juries the decision as to those cases, if any, in which the penalty will be utilized; and (3) judges and juries have ordered the death penalty with such infrequency that the odds are now very much against imposition and execution of the penalty with respect to any convicted murderer or rapist... I cannot avoid the conclusion that as the statutes before us are now administered, the penalty is so infrequently imposed that the threat of execution is too attenuated to be of substantial service to criminal justice."

Mr. Justice Marshall wrote an additional concurring opinion for the majority. He traced the historical significance of the use of capital punishment and said, "The fact, therefore, that the Court, or individual Justices, may have in the past expressed an opinion that the death penalty is constitutional is not now binding on us.... It is not improper at this point to take judicial notice of the fact that for more than 200 years men have labored to demonstrate that capital punishment serves no purpose that life imprisonment could not serve equally as well.... even if capital punishment is not excessive, it nonetheless violates the Eighth Amendment because it is morally unacceptable to the people of the United States at this time in their history."

Thus we see that the Court, for various reasons, held that the imposition of the death penalty in the cases before it was a violation of the Eighth and Fourteenth Amendments, but the issue of whether the imposition of the death penalty per se was a violation of these amendments was yet to be decided. There was a great public debate on this issue and depending upon whose public opinion poll one wished to believe, the statistics went either way as to what the public opinion really was. If the public opinion were to be in favor of the death penalty, then, of course, the opinion of Mr. Justice Marshall would not be valid because it would be morally acceptable to the people of the United States at this time in their history. The issue was once again presented to the Court in Gregg v. Georgia, 428 U.S. 242, 96 S.Ct. 2960, 49 L.Ed.2d 859 (1976).

In the Gregg case, the issue presented to the Court was whether the imposition of the sentence of death for the crime of murder under the law of

Georgia violates the Eighth and Fourteenth Amendments. The petitioner was convicted of armed robbery and murder. The post Furman Georgia statute retained the death penalty for six categories of crimes which were murder, kidnapping for ransom or where the victim is harmed, armed robbery, rape, treason, and aircraft hijacking. The defendant's guilt in these cases was determined either by a trial judge or a jury in a traditional manner in a bifurcated trial. If the trial was by jury, the trial judge was required to charge lesser included offenses when they are supported by any view of the evidence. If the defendant was found guilty, a hearing ensued before whomever made the determination of guilt. At this hearing, the judge or jury would hear evidence in extenuation, mitigation, and aggravation of punishment, including prior criminal convictions and pleas of guilty or pleas of nolo contendere of the defendant, or the absence of any prior conviction and pleas. Only such evidence which the state may produce to aggravate the sanction was admissible if it was made known to the defendant prior to the trial. Argument was to be heard by the defendant's attorney and by the prosecutor regarding the punishment to be imposed.

Before a convicted defendant was sentenced to death, except in cases of treason or aircraft hijacking, the jury, or the trial judge in cases tried without a jury, had to find beyond a reasonable doubt one of ten aggravating circumstances specified in a statute which indicated certain conditions which would warrant the imposition of the death penalty, if the judge or the jury (depending on whether it was a jury trial) elected to impose the death penalty. If that sentence was imposed, the aggravating circumstance had to be specified. In jury cases, the judge was bound by the jury's "recommendation."

Appellate processes were available to the defendant which reviewed not only enumerated errors but also to review the imposition of the death sentence with certain specific guidelines.

Here, Justices Stewart, Powell, and Stevens held that the punishment of death does not invariably violate the Constitution. The Court said, "(I)n a democratic society i.e. legislatures, not courts, are constituted to respond to the will and consequently the moral value of the people." The Court noted that since Furman (supra) the legislatures of thirty-five states have enacted new statutes that provide for the death penalty for at least some crimes that result in the death of another person. They further stated, "The basic concern of Furman centered on those defendants who were being condemned to death capriciously and arbitrarily.... The new Georgia sentencing procedures, by contrast, focus the jury's attention on the particularized nature of the crime and the particularized characteristics of the individual defendant.... No longer can a jury wantonly and freakishly impose the death sentence; it is always circumscribed by the legislative guidelines. In addition, the review function of the Supreme Court of Georgia affords additional assurance that the concerns that prompted our decision in Furman are not present to any significant degree in the Georgia procedure applied here.

"For the reasons expressed in this opinion, we hold that the statutory system under which Gregg was sentenced to death does not violate the Constitution."

Mr. Justice White, Chief Justice Burger, and Mr. Justice Rehnquist joined in a concurring opinion in which they said, ". . . one of society's most basic tasks is that of protecting the lives of its citizens and one of the most basic ways in which it achieves the task is through criminal laws against murder. I decline to interfere with the manner in which Georgia has chosen to enforce such laws on what is simply an assertion of lack of faith in the ability of the system of justice to operate in a fundamentally fair manner."

Mr. Justice Blackman concurred in the judgment.

Thus we have what might be termed a democratic influence on the thinking of a majority of the Court when after Furman, thirty-five states enacted death penalty statutes which each believed conformed to the thinking of the diffused majority in Furman. All of the states, however, were not that successful. However, in Proffitt v. Florida, 428 U.S. 242, 96 S.Ct. 2960, 50 L.Ed.2d 30 (1976), the Court considered the Florida death penalty statute. In Florida the statute provided for the trial judge to determine the sentence rather than the jury. The Court found that Florida's capital sentencing procedure sought to assure that the death penalty would not be imposed in an arbitrary or capricious manner. Moreover, to the extent that any risk to the contrary exists, it is minimized by Florida's appellate review system, under which the evidence of the aggravating and mitigating circumstances is reviewed and reweighed by the Supreme Court of Florida "to determine independently whether the imposition of the ultimate penalty is warranted." The Court held that the Florida procedure satisfied the constitutional deficiencies identified in Furman.

In the case of Jurek v. Texas, 428 U.S. 262, 96 S.Ct. 2950, 50 L.Ed.2d 30 (1976), dealing with a Texas statute imposing the death sentence, the Court held that although the Texas statute did not adopt a list of statutory aggravating circumstances, the existence of which can justify the imposition of the death penalty, its action in narrowing the categories of murders for which a death sentence may ever be imposed serves much the same purpose. The Court said, "Thus, in order to meet the requirements of the Eighth and Fourteenth Amendments, a capital-sentencing system must allow the sentencing authority to consider mitigating circumstances."

The Texas statute did not speak of specific mitigating circumstances, but it directed the jury to answer three questions which the Court concluded were similar in import to mitigating circumstances and hence held the Texas statute as not violative of the Eighth and Fourteenth Amendments.

North Carolina and Louisiana, however, were not that lucky. In Woodson v. North Carolina, 428 U.S. 280, 96 S.Ct. 2978, 49 L.Ed.2d 944 (1976), the state legislature had made the death penalty mandatory in murder, first degree, convictions. Murder first degree was spelled out to have specific aggravating factors. No provision was made for mitigating factors to avoid the imposition of the death penalty. This omission caused the Court to reverse the conviction and to find the statute a violation of the Eighth and Fourteenth Amendments. Roberts v. Louisiana, 428 U.S. 325, 96 S.Ct. 3001, 49 L.Ed.2d 974 (1976), decided the same day as Woodson (supra), held that a mandatory death sentence procedure similar to North Carolina's was a violation of the Eighth and Fourteenth Amendments.

In Coker v. Georgia, 433 U.S. 584, 97 S.Ct. 2861, 53 L.Ed.2d 982, 21 Cr.L. 3199 (1977), a highly divided Court appears to have agreed on the concept that the death penalty for the rape of an adult woman, with or without aggravating circumstances, is cruel and unusual punishment in violation of the Eighth and Fourteenth Amendments, so long as the rapist did not take the life of his victim.

There are state statutes presently in effect which have not yet been tested by the Court. Some eminent jurists are accepting pleas to a lesser included offense when the defendant is indicted for a capital offense because they believe that the state statute under which they are conducting their courts is unconstitutional.

In the United States, it is common knowledge that the jails and prisons have been "bursting at their seams." There is developing an awareness that confinement, as punishment, is not necessarily indicated in every case. Alternatives to confinement are being proposed for non-violent, non-recidivist convicted persons. Community Service, Probation and Parole as well as substantial fines tailored to the individual defendant have been proposed. Nevertheless, as of this writing, overcrowding in the places of confinement is a problem to be dealt with. Ohio had dealt with the problem by double celling prisoners in Southern Ohio Correctional Facility, a maximum-security state prison. The District Court was the first court to deal with an action under Title 42 Section 1983 brought by two prisoners on behalf of themselves and others similarly situated. The District Court made a surprise visit to the facility and found the physical plant to be "unquestionably a top flight, first class facility." All parties agreed to these findings. The United States Supreme Court held that double celling in this institution is not cruel and unusual punishment. There were no deprivations of essential food, medical care, or sanitation. Nor were there any other intolerable conditions. No pain was inflicted. RHODES v. CHAPMAN, 452 U.S. 337, 101 S.Ct. 2392, 69 L.Ed.2d. 59, 29 Cr.L. 3061 (1981).

The ingenuity of the mind of man is amazing. Just when it was thought that the death penalty arguments had ceased to exist, Robert Alton Harris, or his attorneys, advanced a new argument, but they were not successful. In the case of PULLEY, WARDEN v. HARRIS, —U.S.—, 104 S.Ct. 871, 79 L.Ed.2d. 29 (1984) the argument was presented that this California death sentence should have been subjected to a "proportionality review" where the sentence was to be compared with similar cases. The appellant contended that the California Supreme Court had that duty pursuant to California case law and did not do it in this case. The respondent claimed that this resulted in a denial of the Eighth Amendment right prohibiting cruel and unusual punishment. The Court held that it was not a denial of the Eighth Amendment prohibition because there was no such requirement in the Eighth Amendment nor in the cases in the United States Supreme Court upholding capital punishment.

§ 11.18 Burden of Proof

The burden of proof in a criminal action rests upon the prosecution because Anglo-Saxon law presumes a defendant to be innocent. A presumption, in the law of evidence, determines from whom the proof must come. A New York statute requires that if a defendant is charged with a homicide, the defendant must go forward with the evidence as an affirmative defense and prove by a preponderance of the credible evidence that the homicide was committed while the defendant was under extreme emotional upset. If the defendant can prove this to the satisfaction of the trier of the facts, the defendant is entitled to be convicted of manslaughter, which carries with it a lesser punishment than murder, first or second degree.

In Patterson v. New York, 432 U.S. 197, 97 S.Ct. 2319, 53 L.Ed.2d 281, 21 Cr.L. 3146 (1977), the petitioner contested the constitutionality of the statute as a deprivation of the right of due process under the Fourteenth Amendment. The Court held that this statute did not violate the due process clause of that amendment.

Judicial Decisions Relating to Chapter 11

Schenck *v.* United States. Baer *v.* United States.

249 U.S. 47, 39 S.Ct. 247, 63 L.Ed. 470 (1919)

ERROR TO THE DISTRICT COURT OF THE UNITED STATES FOR THE EASTERN DISTRICT OF PENNSYLVANIA.

Argued January 9, 10, 1919.—Decided March 3, 1919.

. . .

MR. JUSTICE HOLMES delivered the opinion of the Court.

This is an indictment in three counts. The first charges a conspiracy to violate the Espionage Act of June 15, 1917, c. 30, § 3, 40 Stat. 217, 219, by causing and attempting to cause insubordination, &c., in the military and naval forces of the United States, and to obstruct the recruiting and enlistment service of the United States, when the United States was at war with the German Empire, to-wit, that the defendants wilfully conspired to have printed and circulated to men who had been called and accepted for military service under the Act of May 18, 1917, a document set forth and alleged to be calculated to cause such insubordination and obstruction. The count alleges overt acts in pursuance of the conspiracy, ending in the distribution of the document set forth. The second count alleges a conspiracy to commit an offence against the United States, to-wit, to use the mails for the transmission of matter declared to be non-mailable by Title XII, § 2 of the Act of June 15, 1917, to-wit, the above mentioned document, with an averment of the same overt acts. The third count charges an unlawful use of the mails for the transmission of the same matter and otherwise as above. The defendants were found guilty on all the counts. They set up the First Amendment to the Constitution forbidding Congress to make any law abridging the freedom of speech, or of the press, and bringing the case here on that ground have argued some other points also of which we must dispose.

It is argued that the evidence, if admissible, was not sufficient to prove that the defendant Schenck was concerned in sending the documents. According to the testimony Schenck said he was general secretary of the Socialist party and had charge of the Socialist headquarters from which the documents were sent. He identified a book found there as the minutes of the Executive Committee of the party. The book showed a resolution of August 13, 1917, that 15,000 leaflets should be printed on the other side of one of them in use, to be mailed to men who had passed exemption boards, and for distribution. Schenck personally attended to the printing. On August 20 the general secretary's report said "Obtained new leaflets from printer and started work addressing envelopes" &c.; and there was a resolve that Comrade Schenck be allowed $125 for sending leaflets through the mail. He said that he had about fifteen or sixteen thousand printed. There were files of the circular in question in the inner office which he said were printed on the other side of the one-sided circular and were there for distribution. Other copies were proved to have been sent through the mails to drafted men. Without going into confirmatory details that were proved, no reasonable man could doubt that the defendant Schenck was largely instrumental in sending the circulars about. As to the defendant Baer there was evidence that she was a member of the Executive Board and that the minutes of its transactions were hers. The argument as to the sufficiency of the evidence that the defendants conspired to send the documents only impairs the seriousness of the real defence.

It is objected that the documentary evidence was not admissible because obtained upon a search warrant, valid so far as appears. The contrary is established. Adams v. New York, 192 U.S. 585; Weeks v. United States, 232 U.S. 383, 395, 396. The search warrant did not issue against the defendant but against the Socialist headquarters at 1326 Arch Street and it would seem that the documents technically were not even in the defendants' possession. See Johnson v. United States, 228 U.S. 457. Notwithstanding some protest in argument the notion that evidence even directly proceeding from the defendant in a criminal proceeding is excluded in all cases by the Fifth Amendment is plainly unsound. Holt v. United States, 218 U.S. 245, 252, 253.

The document in question upon its first printed side recited the first section of the Thirteenth Amendment, said that the idea embodied in it was violated by the Conscription Act and that a conscript is little better than a convict. In impassioned language it intimated that conscription was despotism in its worst form and a monstrous wrong against humanity in the interest of Wall Street's chosen few. It said "Do not submit to intimidation," but in form at least confined itself to peaceful measures such as a petition for the repeal of the act. The other and later printed side of the sheet was headed "Assert Your Rights." It stated reasons for alleging that any one violated the Constitution when he refused to recognize "your right to assert your opposition to the draft," and went on "If you do not assert and support your rights, you are helping to deny or disparage rights which it is the solemn duty of all citizens and residents of the United States to retain." It described the arguments on the other side as coming from cunning politicians and a mercenary capitalist press, and even silent consent to the conscription law as helping to support an infamous conspiracy. It denied the power to send our citizens away to foreign shores to shoot up the people of other lands, and added that words could not express the condemnation such cold-blooded ruthlessness deserves, &c., &c., winding up "You must do your share to maintain, support and uphold the rights of the people of this country." Of course the document would not have been sent unless it had been intended to have some effect, and we do not see what effect it could be expected to have upon persons subject to the draft except to influence them to obstruct the carrying of it out. The defendants do not deny that the jury might find against them on this point.

But it is said, suppose that that was the tendency of this circular, it is protected by the First Amendment to the Constitution. Two of the strongest expressions are said to be quoted respectively from well-known public men. It well may be that the prohibition of laws abridging the freedom of speech is not confined to previous restraints, although to prevent them may have been the main purpose, as intimated in Patterson v. Colorado, 205 U.S. 454, 462. We admit that in many places and in ordinary times the defendants in saying all that was said in the circular would have been within their constitutional rights. But the character of every act depends upon the circumstances in which it is done. Aikens v. Wisconsin, 195 U.S. 194, 205, 206. The most stringent protection of free speech would not protect a man in falsely shouting fire in a theatre and causing a panic. It does not even protect a man from an injunction against uttering words that may have all the effect of force. Gompers v. Bucks Stove & Range Co., 221 U.S. 418, 439. The question in every case is whether the words used are used in such circumstances and are of such a nature as to create a clear and present danger that they will bring about the substantive evils that Congress has a right to prevent. It is a question of proximity and degree. When a nation is at war many things that might be said in time of peace are such a hindrance to its effort that this utterance will not be endured so long as men fight and that no Court could regard them as protected by any constitutional right. It seems to be admitted that if an actual obstruction of the recruiting service were proved, liability for words that produced that effect might be enforced. The statute of 1917 in § 4 punishes conspiracies to obstruct as well as actual obstruction. If the act, (speaking, or circulating a paper,) its tendency and the intent with which it is done are the same, we perceive no ground for saying that success alone warrants making the act a crime. Goldman v. United States, 245 U.S. 474, 477. Indeed that case might be said to dispose of the present contention if the precedent covers all media concludendi. But as the right to free speech was not referred to specially, we have thought fit to add a few words.

It was not argued that a conspiracy to obstruct the draft was not within the words of the Act of 1917. The words are "obstruct the recruiting or enlistment service," and it might be suggested that they refer only to making it hard to get volunteers. Recruiting heretofore usually having been accomplished by getting volunteers the word is apt to call up that method only in our minds. But recruiting is gaining fresh supplies for the forces, as well by draft as otherwise. It is put as an alternative to enlistment or voluntary enrollment in this act. The fact that the Act of 1917 was enlarged by the amending Act of May 16, 1918, c. 75, 40 Stat. 553, of course, does not affect the present indictment and would not, even if the former act had been repealed. Rev. Stats., § 13.

Judgments affirmed.

Gitlow *v.* People of New York.

268 U.S. 652, 45 S.Ct. 625, 69 L.Ed. 1138 (1925)

ERROR TO THE SUPREME COURT OF THE STATE OF NEW YORK.

Argued April 12, 1923; reargued November 23, 1923.—Decided June 8, 1925.

. . .

MR JUSTICE SANFORD delivered the opinion of the Court.

Benjamin Gitlow was indicted in the Supreme Court of New York, with three others, for the statutory crime of criminal anarchy. New York Penal Laws, §§ 160, 161. He was separately tried, convicted, and sentenced to imprisonment. The judgment was affirmed by the Appellate Division and by the Court of Appeals. 195 App. Div. 773; 234 N.Y. 132 and 539. The case is here on writ of error to the Supreme Court, to which the record was remitted. 260 U.S. 703.

The contention here is that the statute, by its terms and as applied in this case, is repugnant to the due process clause of the Fourteenth Amendment. Its material provisions are:

> "§ 160. *Criminal anarchy defined.* Criminal anarchy is the doctrine that organized government should be overthrown by force or violence, or by assassination of the executive head or of any of the executive officials of government, or by any unlawful means. The advocacy of such doctrine either by word of mouth or writing is a felony.
>
> "§ 161. *Advocacy of criminal anarchy.* Any person who:
>
> "1. By word of mouth or writing advocates, advises or teaches the duty, necessity or propriety of overthrowing or overturning organized government by force or violence, or by assassination of the executive head or of any of the executive officials of government, or by any unlawful means; or,
>
> "2. Prints, publishes, edits, issues or knowingly circulates, sells, distributes or publicly displays any book, paper, document, or written or printed matter in any form, containing or advocating, advising or teaching the doctrine that organized government should be overthrown by force, violence or any unlawful means...
>
> "Is guilty of a felony and punishable" by imprisonment or fine, or both.

The indictment was in two counts. The first charged that the defendant had advocated, advised and taught the duty, necessity and propriety of overthrowing and overturning organized government by force, violence and unlawful means, by certain writings therein set forth entitled "The Left Wing Manifesto"; the second that he had printed, published and knowingly circulated and distributed a certain paper called "The Revolutionary Age," containing the writings set forth in the first count advocating, advising and teaching the doctrine that organized government should be overthrown by force, violence and unlawful means.

The following facts were established on the trial by undisputed evidence and admissions: The defendant is a member of the Left Wing Section of the Socialist Party, a dissenting branch or faction of that party formed in opposition to its dominant policy of "moderate Socialism." Membership in both is open to aliens as well as citizens. The Left Wing Section was organized nationally at a conference in New York City in June, 1919, attended by ninety delegates from twenty different States. The conference elected a National Council, of which the defendant was a member, and left to it the adoption of a "Manifesto." This was published in The Revolutionary Age, the official organ of the Left Wing. The defendant was on the board of managers of the paper and was its business manager. He arranged for the printing of the paper and took to the printer the manuscript of the first issue which contained the Left Wing Manifesto, and also a Communist Program and a Program of the Left Wing that had been adopted by the conference. Sixteen thousand copies were printed, which were delivered at the premises in New York City used as the office of the Revolutionary Age and the headquarters of the Left Wing, and occupied by the defendant and other officials. These copies were paid for by the defendant, as business manager of the paper. Employees at this office wrapped and mailed out copies of the paper under the defendant's direction; and copies were sold from this office. It was admitted that the defendant signed a card subscribing to the Manifesto and Program of the Left Wing, which all applicants were required to sign before being admitted to membership; that he went to different parts of the State to speak to branches of the Socialist Party about the principles of the Left Wing and advocated their adoption; and that he was responsible for the Manifesto as it appeared, that "he knew of the publication, in a general way and he knew of its publication afterwards, and is responsible for its circulation."

There was no evidence of any effect resulting from the publication and circulation of the Manifesto.

No witnesses were offered in behalf of the defendant.

Extracts from the Manifesto are set forth in the margin. Coupled with a review of the rise of Socialism, it condemned the dominant "moderate Socialism" for its recognition of the necessity of the democratic parliamentary state; repudiated its policy of introducing Socialism by legislative measures; and advocated, in plain and unequivocal language, the necessity of accomplishing the "Communist Revolution" by a militant and "revolutionary Socialism", based on "the class struggle" and mobilizing the "power of the proletariat in action," through mass industrial revolts developing into mass political strikes and "revolutionary mass action", for the purpose of conquering and destroying the parliamentary state and establishing in its place, through a "revolutionary dictatorship of the proletariat", the system of Communist Socialism. The then recent strikes in Seattle and Winnipeg were cited as instances of a development already verging on revolutionary action and suggestive of proletarian dictatorship, in which the strike-workers were "trying to usurp the functions of municipal government"; and revolutionary Socialism, it was urged, must use these mass industrial revolts to broaden the strike, make it general and militant, and develop it into mass political strikes and revolutionary mass action for the annihilation of the parliamentary state.

At the outset of the trial the defendant's counsel objected to the introduction of any evidence under the indictment on the grounds that, as a matter of law, the Manifesto "is not in contravention of the statute," and that "the statute is in contravention of" the due process clause of the Fourteenth Amendment. This objection was denied. They also moved, at the close of the evidence, to dismiss the indictment and direct an acquittal "on the grounds stated in the first objection to evidence", and again on the grounds that "the indictment does not charge an offense" and the evidence "does not show an offense." These motions were also denied.

The court, among other things, charged the jury, in substance, that they must determine what was the intent, purpose and fair meaning of the Manifesto; that its words must be taken in their ordinary meaning, as they would be understood by people whom it might reach; that a mere statement or analysis of social and economic facts and historical incidents, in the nature of an essay, accompanied by prophecy as to the future course of events, but with no teaching, advice or advocacy of action, would not constitute the advocacy, advice or teaching of a doctrine for the overthrow of government within the meaning of the statute; that a mere statement that unlawful acts might accomplish such a purpose would be insufficient, unless there was a teaching, advising and advocacy of employing such unlawful acts for the purpose of overthrowing government; and that if the jury had a reasonable doubt that the Manifesto did teach, advocate or advise the duty, necessity, or propriety of using unlawful means for the overthrowing of organized government, the defendant was entitled to an acquittal.

The defendant's counsel submitted two requests to charge which embodied in substance the statement that to constitute criminal anarchy within the meaning of the statute it was necessary that the language used or published should advocate, teach or advise the duty, necessity or propriety of doing "some definite or immediate act or acts" of force, violence or unlawfulness directed toward the overthrowing of organized government. These were denied further than had been charged. Two other requests to charge embodied in substance the statement that to constitute guilt the language used or published must be "reasonably and ordinarily calculated to incite certain persons" to acts of force, violence or unlawfulness, with the object of overthrowing organized government. These were also denied.

The Appellate Division, after setting forth extracts from the Manifesto and referring to the Left Wing and Communist Programs published in the same issue of the Revolutionary Age, said: "It is perfectly plain that the plan and purpose advocated... contemplate the overthrow and destruction of the governments of the United States and of all the States, not by the free action of the majority of the people through the ballot box in electing representatives to authorize a change of government by amending or changing the Constitution,... but by immediately organizing the industrial proletariat into militant Socialist unions and at the earliest opportunity through mass strike and force and violence, if necessary, compelling the government to cease to function, and then through a proletarian dictatorship, taking charge of and appropriating all property and administering it and governing through such dictatorship until such time as the proletariat is permitted to administer and govern it.... The articles in question are not a discussion of ideas and theories. They advocate a doctrine deliberately determined upon and planned for militantly disseminating a propaganda advocating that it is the duty and necessity of the proletariat engaged in industrial pursuits to organize to such an extent that, by massed strike, the wheels of government may ultimately be stopped and the government overthrown..."

The Court of Appeals held that the Manifesto "advocated the overthrow of this government by violence, or by unlawful means." In one of the opinions representing the views of a majority of the court, it was said: "It will be seen... that this defendant through the manifesto... advocated the destruction of the state and the establishment of the dictatorship of the proletariat.... To advocate... the commission of this conspiracy or action by mass strike whereby government is crippled, the administration of justice paralyzed, and the health, morals and welfare of a community endangered, and this for the purpose of bringing about a revolution in the state, is to advocate the overthrow of organized government by unlawful means." In the other it was said: "As we read this manifesto . . . we feel entirely clear that the jury were justified in rejecting the view that it was a mere academic and harmless discussion of the advantages of communism and advanced socialism" and "in regarding it as a justification and advocacy of action by one class which would destroy the rights of all other classes and overthrow the state itself by use of revolutionary mass strikes. It is true that there is no advocacy in specific terms of the use of . . . force or violence. There was no need to be. Some things are so commonly incident to others that they do not need to be mentioned when the underlying purpose is described."

And both the Appellate Division and the Court of Appeals held the statute constitutional.

The specification of the errors relied on relates solely to the specific rulings of the trial court in the matters hereinbefore set out. The correctness of the verdict is not questioned, as the case was submitted to the jury. The sole contention here is, essentially, that as there was no evidence of any concrete result flowing from the publication of the Manifesto or of circumstances showing the likelihood of such result, the statute as construed and applied by the trial court penalizes the mere utterance, as such, of "doctrine" having no quality of incitement, without regard either to the circumstances of its utterance or to the likelihocd of unlawful sequences; and that, as to the exercise of the right of free expression with relation to government is only punishable "in circumstances involving likelihood of substantive evil," the statute contravenes the due process clause of the Fourteenth Amendment. The argument in support of this contention rests primarily upon the following propositions: 1st, That the "liberty" protected by the Fourteenth Amendment includes the liberty of speech and of the press; and 2nd, That while liberty o expression "is not absolute," it may be restrained "only in circumstances where its exercise bears a causal relation with some substantive evil, consummated, attempted or likely," and as the statute "takes no account of circumstances," it unduly restrains this liberty and is therefore unconstitutional.

The precise question presented, and the only question which we can consider under this writ of error, then is, whether the statute, as construed and applied in this case by the state courts, deprived the defendant of his liberty of expression in violation of the due process clause of the Fourteenth Amendment.

The statute does not penalize the utterance or publication of abstract "doctrine" or academic discussion having no quality of incitement to any concrete action. It is not aimed against mere historical or philosophical essays. It does not restrain the advocacy of changes in the form of government by constitutional and lawful means. What it prohibits is language advocating, advising or teaching the overthrow of organized government by unlawful means. These words imply urging to action. Advocacy is defined in the Century Dictionary as: "1. The act of pleading for, supporting, or recommending; active espousal." It is not the abstract "doctrine" of overthrowing organized government by unlawful means which is denounced by the statute, but the advocacy of action for the accomplishment of that purpose. It was so construed and applied by the trial judge, who specifically charged the jury that: "A mere grouping of historical events and a prophetic deduction from them would neither constitute advocacy, advice or teaching of a doctrine for the overthrow of government by force, violence or unlawful means. [And] if it were a mere essay on the subject, as suggested by counsel, based upon deductions from alleged historical events, with no teaching, advice or advocacy of action, it would not constitute a violation of the statute...."

The Manifesto, plainly, is neither the statement of abstract doctrine nor, as suggested by counsel, mere prediction that industrial disturbances and revolutionary mass strikes will result spontaneously in an inevitable process of evolution in the economic system. It advocates and urges in fervent language mass action which shall progressively foment industrial disturbances and through political mass strikes and revolutionary mass action overthrow and destroy organized parliamentary government. It concludes with a call to action in these words: "The proletariat revolution and the Communist reconstruction of society—*the struggle for these*—is now indispensable.... The Communist International calls the proletariat of the world to the final struggle!" This is not the expression of philosophical abstraction, the mere prediction of future events; it is the language of direct incitement.

The means advocated for bringing about the destruction of organized parliamentary government, namely, mass industrial revolts usurping the functions of municipal government, political mass strikes directed against the parliamentary state, and revolutionary mass action for its final destruction, necessarily imply the use of force and violence, and in their essential nature are inherently unlawful in a constitutional government of law and order. That the jury were warranted in finding that the Manifesto advocated not merely the abstract doctrine of overthrowing organized government by force, violence and unlawful means, but action to that end, is clear.

For present purposes we may and do assume that freedom of speech and of the press—which are protected by the First Amendment from abridgment by Congress—are among the fundamental personal rights and "liberties" protected by the due process clause of the Fourteenth Amendment from impairment by the States. We do not regard the incidental statement in Prudential Ins. Co. v. Cheek, 259 U.S. 530, 543, that the Fourteenth Amendment imposes no restrictions on the States concerning freedom of speech, as determinative of this question.

It is a fundamental principle, long established, that the freedom of speech and of the press which is secured by the Constitution, does not confer an absolute right to speak or publish, without responsibility, whatever one may choose, or an unrestricted and unbridled license that gives immunity for every possible use of language and prevents the punishment of those who abuse this freedom. 2 Story on the Constitution, 5th ed., § 1580, p. 634; Robertson v. Baldwin, 165 U.S. 275, 281; Patterson v. Colorado, 205 U.S. 454, 462; Fox v. Washington, 236 U.S. 273, 276; Schenck v. United States, 249 U.S. 47, 52; Frohwerk v. United States, 249 U.S. 204, 206; Debs v. United States, 249 U.S. 211, 213; Schaefer v. United States, 251 U.S. 466,

474; Gilbert v. Minnesota, 254 U.S. 325, 332; Warren v. United States, (C.C.A.) 183 Fed. 718, 721. Reasonably limited, it was said by Story in the passage cited, this freedom is an inestimable privilege in a free government; without such limitation, it might become the scourge of the republic.

That a State in the exercise of its police power may punish those who abuse this freedom by utterances inimical to the public welfare, tending to corrupt public morals, incite to crime, or disturb the public peace, is not open to question. Robertson v. Baldwin, supra, p. 281; Patterson v. Colorado, supra, p. 462; Fox v. Washington, supra, p. 277; Gilbert v. Minnesota, supra, p. 339; People v. Most, 171 N.Y. 423, 431; State v. Holm, 139 Minn. 267, 275; State v. Hennessy, 114 Wash. 351, 359; State v. Boyd, 86 N.J.L. 75, 79; State v. McKee, 73 Conn. 18, 27. Thus it was held by this Court in the Fox Case, that a State may punish publications advocating and encouraging a breach of its criminal laws; and, in the Gilbert Case, that a State may punish utterances teaching or advocating that its citizens should not assist the United States in prosecuting or carrying on war with its public enemies.

And, for yet more imperative reasons, a State may punish utterances endangering the foundations of organized government and threatening its overthrow by unlawful means. These imperil its own existence as a constitutional State. Freedom of speech and press, said Story (supra) does not protect disturbances to the public peace or the attempt to subvert the government. It does not protect publications or teachings which tend to subvert or imperil the government or to impede or hinder it in the performance of its governmental duties. State v. Holm, supra, p. 275. It does not protect publications prompting the overthrow of government by force; the punishment of those who publish articles which tend to destroy organized society being essential to the security of freedom and the stability of the State. People v. Most, supra, pp. 431, 432. And a State may penalize utterances which openly advocate the overthrow of the representative and constitutional form of government of the United States and the several States, by violence or other unlawful means. People v. Lloyd, 304 Ill. 23, 34. See also, State v. Tachin, 92 N.J.L. 269, 274; and People v. Steelik, 187 Cal. 361, 375. In short this freedom does not deprive a State of the primary and essential right of self preservation; which, so long as human governments endure, they cannot be denied. Turner v. Williams, 194 U.S. 279, 294. In Toledo Newspaper Co. v. United States, 247 U.S. 402, 419, it was said: "The safeguarding and fructification of free and constitutional institutions is the very basis and mainstay upon which the freedom of the press rests, and that freedom, therefore, does not and cannot be held to include the right virtually to destroy such institutions."

By enacting the present statute the State has determined, through its legislative body, that utterances advocating the overthrow of organized government by force, violence and unlawful means, are so inimical to the general welfare and involve such danger of substantive evil that they may be penalized in the exercise of its police power. That determination must be given great weight. Every presumption is to be indulged in favor of the validity of the statute. Mugler v. Kansas, 123 U.S. 623, 661. And the case is to be considered "in the light of the principle that the State is primarily the judge of regulations required in the interest of public safety and welfare;" and that its police "statutes may only be declared unconstitutional where they are arbitrary or unreasonable attempts to exercise authority vested in the State in the public interest." Great Northern Ry. v. Clara City, 246 U.S. 434, 439. That utterances inciting to the overthrow of organized government by unlawful means, present a sufficient danger of substantive evil to bring their punishment within the range of legislative discretion, is clear. Such utterances, by their very nature, involve danger to the public peace and to the security of the State. They threaten breaches of the peace and ultimate revolution. And the immediate danger is none the less real and substantial, because the effect of a given utterance cannot be accurately foreseen. The State cannot reasonably be required to measure the danger from every such utterance in the nice balance of a jeweler's scale. A single revolutionary spark may kindle a fire that, smouldering for a time, may burst into a sweeping and destructive conflagration. It cannot be said that the State is acting arbitrarily or unreasonably when in the exercise of its judgment as to the measures necessary to protect the public peace and safety, it seeks to extinguish the spark without waiting until it has enkindled the flame or blazed into the conflagration. It cannot reasonably be required to defer the adoption of measures for its own peace and safety until the revolutionary utterances lead to actual disturbances of the public peace or imminent and immediate danger of its own destruction; but it may, in the exercise of its judgment, suppress the threatened danger in its incipiency. In People v. Lloyd, supra, p. 35, it was aptly said: "Manifestly, the legislature has authority to forbid the advocacy of a doctrine designed and intended to overthrow the government without waiting until there is a present and imminent danger of the success of the plan advocated. If the State were compelled to wait until the apprehended danger became certain, then its right to protect itself would come into being simultaneously with the overthrow of the government, when there would be neither prosecuting officers nor courts for the enforcement of the law."

We cannot hold that the present statute is an arbitrary or unreasonable exercise of the police power of the State unwarrantably infringing the freedom of speech or press; and we must and do sustain its constitutionality.

This being so it may be applied to every utterance—not too trivial to be beneath the notice of the law—which is of such a character and used with such intent and purpose as to bring it within the prohibition of the statute. This principle is illustrated in Fox v. Washington, supra, p. 277; Abrams v. United States, 250 U.S. 616, 624; Schaefer v. United States, supra, pp. 479, 480; Pierce v. United States, 252 U.S. 239, 250, 251; and Gilbert v. Minnesota, supra, p. 333. In other words, when the legislative body has determined generally, in the constitutional exercise of its discretion, that utterances of a certain kind involve such danger of substantive evil that they may be punished, the question whether any specific utterance coming within the prohibited class is likely, in and of itself, to bring about the substantive evil, is not open to consideration. It is sufficient that the statute itself be constitutional and that the use of the language comes within its prohibition.

It is clear that the question in such cases is entirely different from that involved in those cases where the statute merely prohibits certain acts involving the danger of substantive evil, without any reference to language itself, and it is sought to apply its provisions to language used by the defendant for the purpose of bringing about the prohibited results. There, if it be contended that the statute cannot be applied to the language used by the defendant because of its protection by the freedom of speech or press, it must necessarily be found, as an original question, without any previous determination by the legislative body, whether the specific language used involved such likelihood of bringing about the substantive evil as to deprive it of the constitutional protection. In such cases it has been held that the general provisions of the statute may be constitutionally applied to the specific utterance of the defendant if its natural tendency and probable effect was to bring about the substantive evil which the legislative body might prevent. Schenck v. United States, supra, p. 51; Debs v. United States, supra, pp. 215, 216. And the general statement in the Schenck Case (p. 52) that the "question in every case is whether the words are used in such circumstances and are of such a nature as to create a clear and present danger that they will bring about the substantive evils,"—upon which great reliance is placed in the defendant's argument—was manifestly intended, as shown by the context, to apply only in cases of this class, and has no application to those like the present, where the legislative body itself has previously determined the danger of substantive evil arising from utterances of a specified character.

The defendant's brief does not separately discuss any of the rulings of the trial court. It is only necessary to say that, applying the general rules already stated, we find that none of them involved any invasion of the constitutional rights of the defendant. It was not necessary, within the meaning of the statute, that the defendant should have advocated "some definite or immediate act or acts" of force, violence or unlawfulness. It was sufficient if such acts were advocated in general terms; and it was not essential that their immediate execution should have been advocated. Nor was it necessary that the language should have been "reasonably and ordinarily calculated to incite certain persons" to acts of force, violence, or unlawfulness. The advocacy need not be addressed to specific persons. Thus, the publication and circulation of a newspaper article may be an encouragement or endeavor to persuade to murder, although not addressed to any person in particular. Queen v. Most, L.R., 7 Q.B.D. 244.

We need not enter upon a consideration of the English common law rule of seditious libel or the Federal Sedition Act of 1798, to which reference is made in the defendant's brief. These are so unlike the present statute, that we think the decisions under them cast no helpful light upon the questions here.

And finding, for the reasons stated, that the statute is not in itself unconstitutional, and that it has not been applied in the present case in derogation of any constitutional right, the judgment of the Court of Appeals is

Affirmed.

Taylor *v.* Mississippi

319 U.S. 583, 63 S.Ct. 1200, 87 L.Ed. 1600 (1943)

APPEAL FROM THE SUPREME COURT OF MISSISSIPPI.

Argued April 15, 16, 1943.—Decided June 14, 1943.

. . .

MR. JUSTICE ROBERTS delivered the opinion of the Court.

March 20, 1942, the State of Mississippi enacted a statute the title of which declares that it is intended to secure the peace and safety of the United States and of the State of Mississippi during war and to prohibit acts detrimental to public peace and safety. The first section, with which alone we are here concerned, provides:

> "That any person who individually, or as a member of any organization, association, or otherwise, shall intentionally preach, teach, or disseminate any teachings, creed, theory, or set of alleged principles, orally, or by means of a phonograph or other contrivance of any kind of nature, or by any other means or method, or by the distribution of any sort of literature, or written or printed matter, designed and calculated to encourage violence, sabotage, or disloyalty to the government of the United States, or the state of Mississippi, or who by action or speech, advocates the cause of the enemies of the United States or who gives information as to the military operations, or plans of defense or military secrets of the nation or this state, by speech, letter, map or picture which would incite any sort of racial distrust, disorder, prejudices or hatreds, or which reasonably tends to create an attitude of stubborn refusal to salute, honor or respect the flag or government of the United States, or of the state of Mississippi, shall be guilty of a felony and punished by imprisonment in the state penitentiary until treaty of peace be declared by the United States but such imprisonment shall not exceed ten years."

At the June 1942 term of the Madison County Circuit Court, Taylor, the appellant in No. 826, was indicted for orally disseminating teachings designed and calculated to encourage disloyalty to the government of the United States and that of the State of Mississippi; and for orally disseminating teachings and distributing literature and printed matter reasonably tending to create an attitude of stubborn refusal to salute, honor, and respect the flag and government of the United States and of the State of Mississippi, and designed and calculated to encourage disloyalty to the government of the United States.

At the June 1942 term of the Marion County Circuit Court, Betty Benoit, the appellant in No. 827, was indicted for disseminating and distributing literature and printed matter designed and calculated, and which reasonably tended, to create an attitude of stubborn refusal to salute, honor, and respect the flag and government of the United States.

At the July 1942 term of the Warren County Circuit Court, Cummings, the appellant in No. 828, was indicted for distributing printed matter designed and calculated to encourage disloyalty to the United States Government and to the State of Mississippi, and tending to create an attitude of stubborn refusal to salute, honor or respect the flag or the government of the United States and the State of Mississippi.

Demurrers and motions to quash, challenging the constitutional validity of the statute, were overruled. The defendants pleaded to the indictments and, after trial, were convicted. Each was sentenced to imprisonment in the state penitentiary for a term to expire at the end of the existing war, but not to exceed ten years. Appeals were perfected to the Supreme Court of Mississippi which, by an evenly divided court, affirmed the convictions.

The appellants maintained below, and assert here, that their convictions denied them the rights guaranteed by the Fourteenth and First Amendments, in that, as construed and applied to them, the Act abridges freedom of press and of speech and is so vague, indefinite, and uncertain as to furnish no reasonably ascertainable standard of guilt.

The evidence was contradictory and conflicting but the juries resolved the conflicts against the appellants. We must, therefore, examine the questions presented on the basis of the proofs submitted by the State.

In No. 826 the prosecution offered evidence to show that Taylor, in the course of interviews with several women, the sons of two of whom had been killed in battle overseas, stated that it was wrong for our President to send our boys across in uniform to fight our enemies; that it was wrong to fight our enemies; that these boys were being shot down for no purpose at all; that the two women's sons may have thought they were doing the right thing to fight our enemies, but it was wrong; that Hitler would rule but would not have to come here to rule; that the quicker people here quit bowing down and worshiping and saluting our flag and Government the sooner we would have peace. Books and pamphlets distributed by Taylor were placed in evidence. Certain statements in these books, said by the Supreme Court of Mississippi to be typical, are copied in the margin.

In No. 827 it was proved that the appellant Betty Benoit distributed Volume XXIII, No. 583, of a publication entitled "Consolation," which contained a reprint of an editorial from a Lewiston, Maine, newspaper commenting adversely upon the decision in Minersville School District v. Gobitis, 310 U.S. 586, and vigorously asserting that the salute of the national flag amounted to a contemptible form of primitive idol worship. The publication also contained an alleged foreign dispatch which stated that the flag salute ceremony, a daily event in French schools, originated in the Catholic schools of France; commented that the type of mind which finds satisfaction in worshiping images would also be most inclined towards various kinds of emblem worship, and added that the dispatch confirms the claim that the flag salute in the United States has been covertly pushed by the Catholic hierarchy here.

In No. 828 the State proved that the appellant Cummings distributed a book called "Children." The volume was placed in evidence. Long excerpts were read to the jury most of which seem irrelevant to the charges in the indictment. One passage, however, appears to be that on which the prosecution especially relied. It is copied in the margin.

The appellants are all members of Jehovah's Witnesses. There is nothing in the records to indicate that, in making the statements and distributing the printed matter in question, they were communicating and teaching any doctrine in which they did not sincerely believe.

Section 1 of the Act defines six offenses. The indictments in Nos. 826 and 828 charge the commission of two of them in a single count,—(1) teaching and dissemination of printed matter designed and calculated to encourage disloyalty to the national and state governments, and (2) distribution of printed matter reasonably tending to create an attitude of stubborn refusal to honor or respect the flag or government of the United States or of the State of Mississippi. In No. 827 the single offense charged is the dissemination of literature reasonably tending to create the denounced attitude towards the flag and Government.

In West Virginia State Board of Education v. Barnette, post, p. 624, the court has decided that a state may not enforce a regulation requiring children in the public schools to salute the national emblem. The statute here in question seeks to punish as a criminal one who teaches resistance to governmental compulsion to salute. If the Fourteenth Amendment bans enforcement of the school regulation, a fortiori it prohibits the imposition of punishment for urging and advising that, on religious grounds, citizens refrain from saluting the flag. If the state cannot constrain one to violate his conscientious religious conviction by saluting the national emblem, then certainly it cannot punish him for imparting his views on the subject to his fellows and exhorting them to accept those views.

Inasmuch as Betty Benoit was charged only with disseminating literature reasonably tending to create an attitude of stubborn refusal to salute, honor, or respect the national and state flags and governments, her conviction denies her the liberty guaranteed by the Fourteenth Amendment. Her conviction and the convictions of Taylor and Cummings, for advocating and teaching refusal to salute the flag, cannot be sustained.

The last-mentioned appellants were also charged with oral teachings and the dissemination of literature calculated to encourage disloyalty to the state and national governments. Their convictions on this charge must also be set aside.

The statute as construed in these cases makes it a criminal offense to communicate to others views and opinions respecting governmental policies, and prophecies concerning the future of our own and other nations. As applied to the appellants, it punishes them although what they communicated is not claimed or shown to have been done with an evil or sinister purpose, to have advocated or incited subversive action against the nation or state, or to have threatened any clear and present danger to our institutions or our Government. What these appellants communicated were their beliefs and opinions concerning domestic measures and trends in national and world affairs.

Under our decisions criminal sanctions cannot be imposed for such communication.

The judgments are

Reversed.

Benton *v.* Maryland

395 U.S. 784, 89 S.Ct. 2056, 23 L.Ed. 2d. 707 (1969)

CERTIORARI TO THE COURT OF SPECIAL APPEALS OF MARYLAND.

Argued December 21, 1968.—Reargued March 24, 1969.—Decided June 23, 1969.

. . .

MR. JUSTICE MARSHALL delivered the opinion of the Court.

In August 1965, petitioner was tried in a Maryland state court on charges of burglary and larceny. The jury found petitioner not guilty of larceny but convicted him on the burglary count. He was sentenced to 10 years in prison. Shortly after his notice of appeal was filed in the Maryland Court of Appeals, that court handed down its decision in the case of Schowgurow v. State, 240 Md. 121, 213 A. 2d 475 (1965). In Schowgurow the Maryland Court of Appeals struck down a section of the state constitution which required jurors to swear their belief in the existence of God. As a result of this decision, petitioner's case was remanded to the trial court. Because both the grand and petit juries in petitioner's case had been selected under the invalid constitutional provision, petitioner was given the option of demanding re-indictment and retrial. He chose to have his conviction set aside, and a new indictment and new trial followed. At this second trial, petitioner was again charged with both larceny and burglary. Petitioner objected to retrial on the larceny count, arguing that because the first jury found him not guilty of larceny, retrial would violate the constitutional prohibition against subjecting persons to double jeopardy for the same offense. The trial judge denied petitioner's motion to dismiss the larceny charge, and petitioner was tried for both larceny and burglary. This time the jury found petitioner guilty of both offenses, and the judge sentenced him to 15 years on the burglary count and 5 years for larceny, the sentences to run concurrently. On appeal to the newly created Maryland Court of Special Appeals, petitioner's double jeopardy claim was rejected on the merits. 1 Md. App. 647, 232 A. 2d. 541 (1967). The Court of Appeals denied discretionary review.

On the last day of last Term, we granted certiorari, 392 U.S. 925 (1968), but limited the writ to the consideration of two issues:

> "(1) Is the double jeopardy clause of the Fifth Amendment applicable to the States through the Fourteenth Amendment?
> "(2) If so, was the petitioner 'twice put in jeopardy' in this case?"

After oral argument, it became clear that the existence of a concurrent sentence on the burglary count might prevent the Court from reaching the double jeopardy issue, at least if we found that any error affected only petitioner's larceny conviction. Therefore, we scheduled the case for reargument, 393 U.S. 994 (1968), limited to the following additional question not included in the original writ:

> "Does the 'concurrent sentence doctrine,' enunciated in Hirabayashi v. United States, 320 U.S. 81, 105, and subsequent cases, have continuing validity in light of

such decisions as Ginsberg v. New York, 390 U.S. 629, 633, n. 2, Peyton v. Rowe, 391 U.S. 54, Carafas v. LaVallee, 391 U.S. 234, 237–238, and Sibron v. New York, 392 U.S. 40, 50–58?"

The Solicitor General was invited to file a brief expressing the views of the United States and to participate in oral argument.

After consideration of all the questions before us, we find no bar to our decision of the double jeopardy issue. On the merits, we hold that the Double Jeopardy Clause of the Fifth Amendment is applicable to the States through the Fourteenth Amendment, and we reverse petitioner's conviction for larceny.

I

At the outset of this case we are confronted with a jurisdictional problem. If the error specified in the original writ of certiorari were found to affect only petitioner's larceny conviction, reversal of that conviction would not require the State to change the terms of petitioner's confinement. Whatever the status of his sentence on the larceny conviction, petitioner would probably stay in prison until he had served out his sentence for burglary. Is there, in these circumstances, a live "case" or "controversy" suitable for resolution by this Court, or is the issue moot? Is petitioner asking for an advisory opinion on an abstract or hypothetical question? The answer to these questions is crucial, for it is well settled that federal courts may act only in the context of a justiciable case or controversy. Muskrat v. United States, 219 U.S. 346 (1911); see Flast v. Cohen, 392 U.S. 83, 94–97 (1968).

The language used in a number of this Court's opinions might be read to indicate that the existence of a valid concurrent sentence removes the necessary elements of a justiciable controversy. The "concurrent sentence doctrine" took root in this country quite early, although its earliest manifestations occurred in slightly different contexts. In Locke v. United States, 7 Cranch 339 (1813), a cargo belonging to the plaintiff in error had been condemned under a libel containing 11 counts. CHIEF JUSTICE JOHN MARSHALL, speaking for the Court, found it unnecessary to consider Locke's challenges to all 11 counts. He declared, simply enough, "The Court however, is of opinion, that the 4th count is good, and this renders it unnecessary to decide on the others." Id., at 344. Similar reasoning was later applied in a case where a single general sentence rested on convictions under several counts of an indictment. Drawing upon some English cases and some dicta from Lord Mansfield, the Court in Claassen v. United States, 142 U.S. 140, 146 (1891), held that if the defendant had validly been convicted on any one count "the other counts need not be considered." The most widely cited application of this approach to cases where concurrent sentences, rather than a single sentence, have been imposed is Hirabayashi v. United States, 320 U.S. 81 (1943). In that case the defendant had been found guilty of two different offenses and had received concurrent three-month sentences. He challenged the constitutionality of both convictions, but this Court affirmed the lower court's judgment after considering and rejecting only one of his challenges. Since the conviction on the second count was valid, the Court found it "unnecessary" to consider the challenge to the first count. Id., at 85, 105.

The concurrent sentence doctrine has been widely, if somewhat haphazardly, applied in this Court's decisions. At times the Court has seemed to say that the doctrine raises a jurisdictional bar to the consideration of counts under concurrent sentences. Some opinions have baldly declared that judgments of conviction "must be upheld" if any one count was good. Barenblatt v. United States, 360 U.S. 109, 115 (1959); see United States v. Gainey, 380 U.S. 63, 65 (1965). In other cases the Court has chosen somewhat weaker language, indicating only that a judgment "may be affirmed if the conviction on either count is valid." Roviaro v. United States, 353 U.S. 53, 59, n. 6 (1957). And on at least one occasion, the Court has ignored the rule entirely and decided an issue that affected only one count, even though there were concurrent sentences. Putnam v. United States, 162 U.S. 687 (1896).

One can search through these cases, and related ones, without finding any satisfactory explanation for the concurrent sentence doctrine. See United States v. Hines, 256 F. 2d 561, 562–563 (C.A. 2d Cir. 1958). But whatever the underlying justifications for the doctrine, it seems clear to us that it cannot be taken to state a jurisdictional rule. See Yates v. United States, 355 U.S. 66, 75–76 (1957); Putnam v. United States, supra. Moreover, whatever may have been the approach in the past, our recent decisions on the question of mootness in criminal cases make it perfectly clear that the existence of concurrent sentences does not remove the elements necessary to create a justiciable case or controversy.

In Sibron v. New York, 392 U.S. 40 (1968), we held that a criminal case did not become moot upon the expiration of the sentence imposed. We noted "the obvious fact of life that most criminal convictions do in fact entail adverse collateral legal consequences." Id., at 55. We concluded that the mere possibility of such collateral consequences was enough to give the case the "impact of actuality" which was necessary to make it a justiciable case or controversy. Sibron and a number of other recent cases have canvassed the possible adverse collateral effects of criminal convictions, and we need not repeat that analysis here. It is enough to say that there are such possibilities in this case. For example, there are a few States which consider all prior felony convictions for the purpose of enhancing sentence under habitual criminal statutes, even if the convictions actually constituted only separate counts in a single indictment tried on the same day. Petitioner might some day in one of these States have both his larceny and burglary convictions counted against him. Although this possibility may well be a remote one, it is enough to give this case an adversary cast and make it justiciable. Moreover, as in Sibron, both of petitioner's convictions might some day be used to impeach his character if put in issue at a future trial. Although petitioner could explain that both convictions arose out of the same transaction, a jury might not be able to appreciate this subtlety.

We cannot, therefore, say that this Court lacks jurisdiction to decide petitioner's challenge to his larceny conviction. It may be that in certain circumstances a federal appellate court, as a matter of discretion, might decide (as in Hirabayashi) that it is "unnecessary" to consider all the allegations made by a particular party. The concurrent sentence rule may have some continuing validity as a rule of judicial convenience. That is not a subject we must canvass today, however. It is sufficient for present purposes to hold that there is no jurisdictional bar to consideration of challenges to multiple convictions, even though concurrent sentences were imposed.

II

While Maryland apparently agrees that there is no jurisdictional bar to consideration of petitioner's larceny conviction, it argues that the possibility of collateral consequences is so remote in this case that any double jeopardy violation should be treated as a species of "harmless error." The Solicitor General, while not commenting at length on the facts of this particular case, suggests that we treat the concurrent sentence doctrine as a principle of judicial efficiency which permits judges to avoid decision of issues which have no appreciable impact on the rights of any party. Both Maryland and the Solicitor General argue that the defendant should bear the burden of convincing the appellate court of the need to review all his concurrent sentences. Petitioner, on the other hand, sees in Sibron a command that federal appellate courts treat all errors which may possibly affect a defendant's rights, and he argues that the concurrent sentence rule therefore has no continuing validity, even as a rule of convenience.

Because of the special circumstances in this case, we find it unnecessary to resolve this dispute. For even if the concurrent sentence doctrine survives as a rule of judicial convenience, we find good reason not to apply it here. On direct appeal from petitioner's conviction, the Maryland Court of Special Appeals did in fact rule on his double jeopardy challenge to the larceny count. 1 Md. App., at 650–651, 232 A. 2d, at 542–543. It is unclear whether Maryland courts always consider all challenges raised on direct appeal, notwithstanding the existence of concurrent sentences, but at least in this case the State decided not to apply the concurrent sentence rule. This may well indicate that the State has some interest in keeping the larceny conviction alive; if, as Maryland argues here, the larceny conviction is of no importance to either party, one wonders why the state courts found it necessary to pass on it. Since the future importance of the conviction may well turn on issues of state law about which we are not well informed, we propose, on direct appeal from the Maryland courts, to accept their judgment on this question. Since they decided this federal constitutional question, we see no reason why we should not do so as well. Moreover, the status of petitioner's burglary conviction and the eventual length of his sentence are both still in some doubt. Should any attack on the burglary conviction be successful, or should the length of the burglary sentence be reduced to less than five years, petitioner would then clearly have a right to have his larceny conviction reviewed. As we said in Sibron v. New York, supra, at 56–57, it is certainly preferable to have that review now on direct appeal, rather than later. For these reasons, and because there is no jurisdictional bar, we find it appropriate to reach the questions specified in our original writ of certiorari.

III

In 1937, this Court decided the landmark case of Palko v. Connecticut, 302 U.S. 319. Palko, although indicted for first-degree murder, had been convicted of murder in the second degree after a jury trial in a Connecticut state court. The State appealed and won a new trial. Palko argued that the Fourteenth Amendment incorporated, as against the States, the Fifth Amendment requirement that no person "be subject for the same offence to be twice put in jeopardy of life or limb." The Court disagreed. Federal double jeopardy standards were not applicable against the States. Only when a kind of jeopardy subjected a defendant to "a hardship so acute and shocking that our polity will not endure it," id., at 328, did the Fourteenth Amendment apply. The order for a new trial was affirmed. In subsequent appeals from state courts, the Court continued to apply this lesser Palko standard. See, e.g., Brock v. North Carolina, 344 U.S. 424 (1953).

Recently, however, this Court has "increasingly looked to the specific guarantees of the [Bill of Rights] to determine whether a state criminal trial was conducted with due process of law." Washington v. Texas, 388 U.S. 14, 18 (1967). In an increasing number of cases, the Court "has rejected the notion that the Fourteenth Amendment applies to the States only a 'watered-down, subjective version of the individual guarantees of the Bill of Rights....'" Malloy v. Hogan, 378 U.S. 1, 10–11 (1964). Only last Term we found that the right to trial by jury in criminal cases was "fundamental to the American scheme of justice," Duncan v. Louisiana, 391 U.S. 145, 149 (1968), and held that the Sixth Amendment right to a jury trial was applicable to the States through the Fourteenth Amendment. For the same reasons, we today find that the double jeopardy prohibition of the Fifth Amendment represents a fundamental ideal in our constitutional heritage, and that it should apply to the States through the Fourteenth Amendment. Insofar as it is inconsistent with this holding, Palko v. Connecticut is overruled.

Palko represented an approach to basic constitutional rights which this Court's recent decisions have rejected. It was cut of the same cloth as Betts v. Brady, 316 U.S. 455 (1942), the case which held that a criminal defendant's right to counsel was to be determined by deciding in each case whether the denial of that right was "shocking to the universal sense of justice." Id., at 462. It relied upon Twining v. New Jersey, 211 U.S. 78 (1908), which held that the right against compulsory self-incrimination was not an element of Fourteenth Amendment due process. Betts was overruled by Gideon v. Wainwright, 372 U.S. 335 (1963); Twining, by Malloy v. Hogan, 378 U.S. 1 (1964). Our recent cases have thoroughly rejected the Palko notion that basic constitutional rights can be denied by the States as long as the totality of the circumstances does not disclose a denial of "fundamental fairness." Once it is decided that a particular Bill of Rights guarantee is "fundamental to the American scheme of justice," Duncan v. Louisiana, supra, at 149, the same constitutional standards apply against both the State and Federal Governments. Palko's roots had thus been cut away years ago. We today only recognize the inevitable.

The fundamental nature of the guarantee against double jeopardy can hardly be doubted. Its origins can be traced to Greek and Roman times, and it became established in the common law of England long before this Nation's independence. See Bartkus v. Illinois, 359 U.S. 121, 151–155 (1959) (Black, J., dissenting). As with many other elements of the common law, it was carried into the jurisprudence of this Country through the medium of Blackstone, who codified the doctrine in his Commentaries. "[T]he plea of autrefoits acquit, or a former acquittal," he wrote, "is grounded on this universal maxim of the common law of England, that no man is to be brought into jeopardy of his life more than once for the same offence." Today, every State incorporates some form of the prohibition in its constitution or common law. As this Court put it in Green v. United States, 355 U.S. 184, 187–188 (1957), "[t]he underlying idea, one that is deeply ingrained in at least the Anglo-American system of jurisprudence, is that the State with all its resources and power should not be allowed to make repeated attempts to convict an individual for an alleged offense, thereby subjecting him to embarrassment, expense and ordeal and compelling him to live in a continuing state of anxiety and insecurity, as well as enhancing the possibility that even though innocent he may be found guilty." This underlying notion has from the very beginning been part of our constitutional tradition. Like the right to trial by jury, it is clearly "fundamental to the American scheme of justice." The validity of petitioner's larceny conviction must be judged, not by the watered-down standard enunciated in Palko, but under this Court's interpretations of the Fifth Amendment double jeopardy provision.

IV

It is clear that petitioner's larceny conviction cannot stand once federal double jeopardy standards are applied. Petitioner was acquitted of larceny in his first trial. Because he decided to appeal his burglary conviction, he is forced to suffer retrial on the larceny count as well. As this Court held in Green v. United States, supra, at 193–194, "[c]onditioning an appeal of one offense on a coerced surrender of a valid plea of former jeopardy on another offense exacts a forfeiture in plain conflict with the constitutional bar against double jeopardy."

Maryland argues that Green does not apply to this case because petitioner's original indictment was absolutely void. One cannot be placed in "jeopardy" by a void indictment, the State argues. This argument sounds a bit strange, however, since petitioner could quietly have served out his sentence under this "void" indictment had he not appealed his burglary conviction. Only by accepting the option of a new trial could the indictment be set aside; at worst the indictment would seem only voidable at the defendant's option, not absolutely void. In any case, this argument was answered here over 70 years ago in United States v. Ball, 163 U.S. 662 (1896). In that case Millard Fillmore Ball was indicted, together with two other men, for the murder of one William T. Box in the Indian Territory. He was acquitted and his codefendants were convicted. They appealed and won a reversal on the ground that the indictment erroneously failed to aver the time or place of Box's death. All three defendants were retried, and this time Ball was convicted. This Court sustained his double jeopardy claim, notwithstanding the technical invalidity of the indictment upon which he was first tried. The Court refused to allow the Government to allege its own error to deprive the defendant of the benefit of an acquittal by a jury. Id., at 667–668. "[A]lthough the indictment was fatally defective, yet, if the court had jurisdiction of the cause and of the party, its judgment is not void, but only voidable by writ of error . . . ," and the Government could not have the acquittal set aside over the defendant's objections. Id., at 669–670. This case is totally indistinguishable. Petitioner was acquitted of larceny. He has, under Green, a valid double jeopardy plea which he cannot be forced to waive. Yet Maryland wants the earlier acquittal set aside, over petitioner's objections, because of a defect in the indictment. This it cannot do. Petitioner's larceny conviction cannot stand.

V

Petitioner argues that his burglary conviction should be set aside as well. He contends that some evidence, inadmissible under state law in a trial for burglary alone, was introduced in the joint trial for both burglary and larceny, and that the jury was prejudiced by this evidence. This question was not decided by the Maryland Court of Special Appeals because it found no double jeopardy violation at all. It is not obvious on the face of the record that the burglary conviction was affected by the double jeopardy violation. To determine whether there is in fact any such evidentiary error, we would have to explore the Maryland law of evidence and the Maryland definitions of larceny and burglary, and then examine the record in detail. We do not think that this is the kind of determination we should make unaided by prior consideration by the state courts. Accordingly, we think it "just under the circumstances," 28 U.S.C. § 2106, to vacate the judgment below and remand for consideration of this question. The judgment is vacated and the case is remanded for further proceedings not inconsistent with this opinion.

It is so ordered.

CHAPTER 12

Contents

Plea Bargaining

§ 12.1 Introduction

There is hardly a student of criminal justice who has not heard of the term "plea bargaining." However it has come to the attention of the author that too many of these students do not understand how this procedure operates but are embarrassed to ask about it. For this reason the process will be explained in the following pages.

§ 12.2 Plea Bargaining Defined and Justified

By the use of the words "plea" and "bargain," we can analogize this to the situation when one is attempting to purchase a home. The person who wishes to purchase will make an offer of a stated amount of money to purchase the residence. The seller may reject that offer but may make a counteroffer in excess of the prospective purchaser's offer. The purchaser may then raise the original offer to an amount of money somewhere between the purchaser's original offer and the seller's counteroffer. Sometimes the seller will accept the purchaser's second offer and the deal is consummated if other conditions of the contract are met, such as financing, occupancy date, etc.

In the plea-bargaining process, the seriousness of the charge to which the defendant agrees to plead guilty is substituted for the amount of money that a person agrees to pay for the house. Thus a defendant, usually through his/her attorney, will bargain with the prosecutor to induce the prosecutor to accept a plea of guilty to the least serious charge that the attorney can get the prosecutor to accept in satisfaction for all charges pending against the client in that county.

Some jurisdictions permit this prosecutorial discretion provided the defendant pleads guilty to a lesser included offense. That is to say that a larceny may be the lesser included offense of robbery because the elements of the crime of larceny are included in the crime of robbery but robbery has additional required elements.

Other jurisdictions will permit the prosecutor to accept one count of an indictment in satisfaction of all other counts to the same indictment, or the prosecutor will withdraw from prosecution the other counts of the indictment.

The prosecutor has the discretion to prosecute or not to prosecute malefactors for crimes which allegedly have been perpetrated. This prosecutorial discretion in plea bargaining is embodied in the concept that in the interest of justice it would be better for the people of the state (commonwealth) to accept a plea carrying with it a lesser punishment than the charge the defendant was originally facing.

In effect, the defendant, in agreeing to such a bargain, barters away constitutional rights of a trial by jury, privilege against self-incrimination, confrontation of witnesses, and proof beyond a reasonable doubt in exchange for a lighter sentence. The inferred concomitant of this is that those who exercise their constitutional rights will most likely receive a more severe sentence if, after trial, they are found guilty. The justification for this process has been that the defendants prefer plea bargaining over a trial, and that it is less expensive to government, for without plea bargaining the cost of more courtrooms, judges, court personnel, and attorneys for prosecutions, as well as defense attorneys for indigent defendants, would be astronomical. Somehow, it is thought that the public benefits from plea bargaining.

§ 12.3 Plea Bargain in Operation

The plea bargain operates as follows. The defendant, through his/her counsel, finds out from the prosecutor what charges will be dropped and/or what lesser sentence s/he will receive, should the defendant plead guilty. The defendant's counsel, after learning of the prosecutor's deal, should s/he plead guilty, relays the information back to the defendant for a counteroffer. When an agreement is reached it is usually subject to approval of the court (presiding judge) to make sure that the court is agreeable to the "bargain," and if this arrangement is satisfactory to all parties, the defendant is then called before the bench and a colloquy usually ensues wherein the prosecutor may move to amend the complaint to include the crime to which the defendant will plead guilty if it be an offense based upon an information (usually a misdemeanor), or the prosecutor may move to dismiss certain counts of an indictment, all in the interest of justice. Some jurisdictions require the prosecutor to move the court to hold in abeyance the prosecution of certain counts to an indictment with the understanding that the prosecution will not move those counts of the indictment to trial at a future date.

The recommendation of the prosecutor's role in plea negotiation is spelled out as follows in ABA Standards, Pleas of Guilty, § 3.1 (1968):

> *3.1 Propriety of plea discussions and plea agreements.*
>
> (a) In cases in which it appears that the interest of the public in the effective administration of criminal justice (as stated in section 1.8) would thereby be served, the prosecuting attorney may engage in plea discussions

for the purpose of reaching a plea agreement. He should engage in plea discussions or reach a plea agreement with the defendant only through defense counsel, except when the defendant is not eligible for or does not desire appointment of counsel and has not retained counsel.

(b) The prosecuting attorney, in reaching a plea agreement, may agree to one or more of the following, as dictated by the circumstances of the individual case:

(i) to make or not to oppose favorable recommendations as to the sentence which should be imposed if the defendant enters a plea of guilty or nolo contendere;

(ii) to seek or not to oppose dismissal of the offense charged if the defendant enters a plea of guilty or nolo contendere to another offense reasonably related to defendant's conduct; or

(iii) to seek or not to oppose dismissal of other charges or potential charges against the defendant if the defendant enters a plea of guilty or nolo contendere.

(c) Similarly situated defendants should be afforded equal plea agreement opportunities.

The approval by the court is usually obtained initially in the chambers of the judge where a discussion may take place with respect to the sanction that the court will impose if the bargain is consummated. Many jurists will not make any commitment with respect to the sentence that will be imposed. This frequently causes a defendant to elect to go to trial because s/he does not want to take the chance of lengthy imprisonment by pleading guilty to a lesser included offense only to be severely punished anyway. The defendant may take the position that if s/he is to be severely punished, s/he should have a trial and perhaps, after trial, the verdict may be "not guilty."

On the other hand, other jurists may give a conditional commitment that a designated sanction will be imposed on the condition that a presentence investigation report reveals that the defendant has a good criminal record or that the criminal record is no more than that which the defendant's counsel has indicated it to be at the plea bargaining discussion. If, after the presentence investigation is completed, the judge finds that the previous record has been misrepresented, the judge may allow the defendant to withdraw his/her plea of guilty in lieu of receiving a more severe sentence than the one originally promised.

There is some authority to permit a defendant to withdraw a plea if the judge does not give the sentence that was promised in pretrial plea bargaining or where the prosecutor fails to honor the agreement. U.S.—Shelton v. United States, 242 F.2d 101 (C.C.A.5th Circ.). Accordingly, it has been recommended that the defendant be entitled as of right to withdraw his guilty plea if the court finds the prosecutor has breached the plea agreement. ABA Standards, Pleas of Guilty, § 2.1 (1968). The prosecutor may find that s/he is unable to fulfill the agreement previously made either because the agreement exceeded the power of the prosecutor who made it or because new facts show that it was inappropriate. N.Y.—Peo. v. Pagano, 282 App.Div. 1075, 131 N.Y.S.2d 167 (1954).

In U.S. v. Herman, D.C.S.N.Y. 76-Cr-1013 (1977), an attorney was refused permission to withdraw his plea of guilty to an information charging him with selling unregistered stock. He sought to withdraw his plea because he might face automatic disbarment. The judge noted that in the United States Supreme Court case of Brady v. U.S., 397 U.S. 742, 90 S.Ct. 1463, 25 L.Ed.2d 747 (1970), "A defendant is not entitled to withdraw his plea merely because he discovers . . . that his calculus misapprehended the quality of the state's case or the likely penalties attached to alternative courses of action. More particularly, absent misrepresentation or other impermissible conduct . . . a voluntary plea of guilty intelligently made in the light of the then applicable law does not become vulnerable because later judicial decisions indicate that the plea rested on a faulty premise."

In one case, the defendant entered a plea of guilty to Murder 2nd degree. Later it was determined that he was not aware that intent to kill was a necessary element of the crime and that an evidentiary hearing in a United States District Court determined that the defendant was never informed that intent to kill was a necessary element of Murder 2nd degree. The Court found the plea of guilty involuntary. Henderson v. Morgan, 426 U.S. 638, 96 S.Ct. 2253, 49 L.Ed.2d 108 (1976).

However, where a plea is withdrawn with permission of the trial court and the defendant has confessed to the commission of the crime even though it was not a precondition of the acceptance of the plea, the confession may not be suppressed and may be used at the trial of the defendant. Hutto v. Ross, 429 U.S. 28, 97 S.Ct. 202, 50 L.Ed.2d 194 (1976).

An unusual situation is found in MARBY v. JOHNSON, —U.S.—, 104 S.Ct. 1411, 79 L.Ed.2d. 437 (1984) where a prosecutor offered the defendant in exchange for a guilty plea to a charge of accessory after a felony murder, that he would recommend a 21 year sentence to be served concurrently with a concurrent burglary and assault sentence. The defendant's attorney telephoned the prosecutor 3 days later to accept the offer. The prosecutor replied that the offer was a mistake and made another offer that was less desirable to the defendant. Initially, the defendant rejected the new offer but later accepted it. After exhausting state remedies, the case came before the United States Supreme Court. It held that respondent's acceptance of the prosecutor's first proposed plea bargain did not create a constitutional right to have the bargain specifically enforced and he may not successfully attack his subsequent guilty plea.

§ 12.4 Arguments for and against Plea Bargaining

It is not the function of this text to take a position on the advantages and disadvantages of plea bargaining. However, it should be pointed out that the defendant who engages in plea bargaining is giving up constitutional rights which have been won by the efforts of many people. The defendant is often effectively coerced into taking a plea for fear of greater punishment, if after a trial, the defendant, having taken up the time of the court and its personnel, is given a very severe sentence for exercising the constitutional rights to which s/he was entitled.

Some other cases on plea bargaining which have found their way to the United States Supreme Court are as follows: Moore v. Michigan, 355 U.S. 155, 78 S.Ct. 191, 2 L.Ed.2d 167 (1957), where the Court held that the right to legal representation at trial was included in plea bargaining discussions; a fortiore Argersinger v. Hamlin, 407 U.S. 25, 92 S.Ct. 2006, 32 L.Ed.2d 530 (1972), where it was considered a critical stage of a criminal proceeding; Boykin v. Alabama, 395 U.S. 238, 89 S.Ct. 1709, 23 L.Ed.2d 274 (1969); and McCarthy v. United States, 394 U.S. 459, 89 S.Ct. 1166, 22 L.Ed.2d 418 (1969), where it was held that a plea of guilty is valid only if the trial court affirmatively shows that the plea was intelligent and voluntary. In Moore, Boykin, McCarthy, and Santabello, the Court held that a plea of guilty is clearly involuntary and therefore invalid—if it is the result of "actual or theatened physical harm or . . . mental coercion overbearing the will of the defendant." However, in McMann v. Richardson, 397 U.S. 759, 90 S.Ct. 1441, 25 L.Ed.2d 763 (1970), the Court held that a plea is "intelligent" and valid even if it was entered upon an attorney's erroneous advice that a confession was admissible.

The Court has legitimized a plea of guilty where the defendant so pleaded to avoid a death penalty if he would be tried and found guilty. In this case the defendant stated that he did not do the act for which he was charged but was fearful of a trial because of his prior record. U.S.—North Carolina v. Alford, 400 U.S. 25, 91 S.Ct. 160, 27 L.Ed.2d 162 (1970). In Santobello v. New York, 404 U.S. 257, 92 S.Ct. 495, 30 L.Ed.2d 427 (1971), the Court said in a case where the prosecutor's office failed to honor a sentence recommendation in a plea negotiation, "The disposition of criminal charges by agreement between the prosecutor and the accused, sometimes loosely called 'plea bargaining' is an essential component of the administration of justice."

Challenges to the plea bargaining process were made in Bordenkircher v. Hayes, 434 U.S. 357, 98 S.Ct. 663, 54 L.Ed.2d 604 (1978), and Corbitt v. New Jersey, U.S. , 99 S.Ct. 492, 58 L.Ed.2d 146 (1978). In Bordenkircher v. Hayes, during plea bargaining negotiations, the prosecutor threatened that if defendant did not accept a plea offered by the prosecutor, the government threatened to seek an indictment under the Habitual Criminal Act. The prosecutor was aware of a prior felony conviction at the time of the original indictment. The Supreme Court rejected defendant's argument that this was a denial of due process of law.

In Corbitt v. New Jersey, we find that under a New Jersey statute defendants who are convicted of first-degree murder by a jury receive a mandatory life sentence while a term of not more than thirty years is imposed for second-degree murder. Nonjury trials are not permitted in murder cases but a plea of non vult is allowed. If a non vult plea is accepted, the judge need not decide the degree of murder but the punishment could be life imprisonment or the same as is imposed for second-degree murder. Corbitt was convicted of first-degree murder after pleading not guilty and was sentenced to life imprisonment. He then contended that his Fifth, Sixth, and Fourteenth Amendment rights were violated. The Court rejected his contentions saying, inter alia, that there is no per se rule against encouraging guilty pleas and the statute is not a violation of due process of law.

If the student is interested in a detailed study of the advantages and disadvantages of the use of plea bargaining in the criminal justice system, reference is made to the following studies: The Challenge of Crime in a Free Society 135 (1967); President's Commission on Law Enforcement and Administration of Justice, Task Force Reports; The Courts 10 (1969); American Bar Association Project on Minimum Standards for Criminal Justice, Standards Relating to Pleas of Guilty (approved Draft 1968); the Unconstitutionality of Plea Bargaining 83, Harv. L. Rev. 1387 (1970).

There is movement away from plea bargaining. The National Advisory Commission on Criminal Justice Standards and Goals on January 23, 1973 recommended that plea bargaining be abolished by 1978. While this goal has not been accomplished throughout the land, there are some innovations taking place to discontinue the procedure.

The prosecutor of Maricopa County, Arizona, eliminated plea bargaining for a number of felonies in recent years and the courts of that county have not been congested. The prosecutor of that county, M. Berger, has said that "It also should be pointed out that although our office prohibits plea bargaining, it recognizes the exceptional case when plea bargaining is still necessary. For example, a case may be so weak that a plea to some other charge may be preferable to going to trial and losing the entire case. This could happen when, for example, a critical witness has died or is unavailable. Another situation justifying the plea bargain is when the defendant has been used by the police as an informer or when he is needed as a witness to convict another defendant who is more deeply involved in crime." It therefore appears that the abolition of plea bargaining is not an inflexible rule. Notwithstanding this, Alaska has abolished plea negotiations and other states are initiating legislation to follow Alaska's lead.

During most of the history of the common law, pleas of guilty were actively discouraged by English and American courts. For centuries litigation was thought to be the "safest test of justice." Indeed, as recently as the 1920s, the legal profession was largely united in its opposition to plea bargaining. Even after it was solidly established, there lingered a strong distrust of plea bargaining. In an article written in 1942, based on data pertaining to the operation of what is now Manhattan Supreme Court in 1939, R. Weintraub and R. Though, two sociologists from Hunter College, expressed their surprise to find plea bargaining flourishing under the reform prosecutor Thomas E. Dewey. A sense of alarm over the prevalence of plea bargaining pervades this early appraisal.[1]

The speedy trial requirement of the Constitution may come directly in conflict with those who advocate the abolition of plea bargaining for, if defense counsel join in demanding trials for every case, the courts' calendars may be so clogged that motions for dismissal for lack of speedy prosecutions may be granted to open up the jailhouse doors. It is a question of priorities. Some say that a nation that can spend so much money to send men to the moon and to erect roads of concrete across the nation should be able to staff sufficient criminal justice agencies to effectively deal with the initial shock of the transition to a no-plea-bargaining criminal justice system.

---

[1]Federal Probation. September 1974, Vol. XXXVIII, p. 19.

Judicial Decisions Relating to Chapter 12

Moore *v.* Michigan

355 U.S. 155, 78 S.Ct. 191, 2 L.Ed. 2d 167 (1957)

CERTIORARI TO THE SUPREME COURT OF MICHIGAN.

Argued October 15–16, 1957.—Decided December 9, 1957.

. . .

MR. JUSTICE BRENNAN delivered the opinion of the Court.

On October 29, 1938, the Circuit Court of Kalamazoo County, Michigan, accepted the petitioner's plea of guilty to an information charging him with the murder of an elderly white lady. He was sentenced to solitary confinement at hard labor for life in Michigan's Jackson Prison, where he has since been confined. Petitioner, a Negro with a seventh-grade education, was 17 years old at the time. On May 26, 1950, he filed a delayed motion for a new trial in the Circuit Court. He asserted constitutional invalidity in his conviction and sentence because he did not have the assistance of counsel at the time of his plea and sentence. The Circuit Court, after hearing, denied the motion, and the Supreme Court of Michigan affirmed. We granted certiorari to decide the important question raised involving a plea of guilty to a charge of murder where the accused was without the benefit of counsel.

The petitioner was arrested during the afternoon of October 26, 1938, a few hours after the murder was committed. He was confined in a Kalamazoo jail and was questioned by local law authorities from time to time until the afternoon of October 28, when he orally confessed to the crime. On Saturday morning, October 29, 1938, he was arraigned in the Circuit Court where he pleaded guilty, was adjudged guilty of murder in the first degree, and, after sentence, was transferred from the Kalamazoo jail to the Jackson Prison.

In accordance with the then prevailing procedure no stenographic transcript was taken of the proceedings in the Circuit Court at the time of the arraignment and plea. However, at the hearing held on the delayed motion for a new trial, two witnesses, who were present in the courtroom on October 29, 1938, testified as to what then transpired. On the basis of their testimony the Circuit Court in denying the motion for new trial found as a fact—which finding is, of course, accepted by us—that before the petitioner tendered the plea of guilty the trial judge asked the petitioner "whether he had a lawyer and whether he desired to have a lawyer, and that [the petitioner] gave a negative reply to both of these inquiries, and stated that he wanted to get the matter over with."

The record further discloses that at the arraignment the trial judge, acting in conformity with Michigan procedure, which required him to conduct an investigation into the voluntariness of any plea of guilty, conferred privately with petitioner for "some five to ten minutes" in chambers. Upon the return of the judge and petitioner to the courtroom, the judge stated that the plea would be accepted and proceeded to conduct the hearing required by Michigan law to determine the degree of the offense of murder. At this hearing several witnesses testified to the details of the crime. The petitioner took no part in the examination of these witnesses nor did he testify. At the conclusion of the testimony, the trial judge pronounced judgment that the petitioner was guilty of murder in the first degree, and imposed sentence.

The judge made a statement, stenographically transcribed, that, over the previous three years, the petitioner had "been in trouble four or five times, consisting of breaking and entering and unlawful taking of automobiles" and had been handled as a juvenile offender on such occasions. He also stated that the petitioner had "discussed the whole affair [the murder] very freely with me in all its revolting details" and that "in my private interview with respondent, I assured him that he must not plead guilty unless he really is guilty; that he was not required to plead guilty; that he could have a trial by jury if he desired it. He assured me freely and voluntarily that he is guilty and that his one desire is to have it all over, to get to the institution to which he is to be committed, and to be under observation and to be examined...." The judge at this point recited the details of the crime as told to him by the petitioner and then stated: "Such is his story to me in private, told very calmly; without any compulsion whatever. He insists that there is something wrong with his head; that he has had something akin to queer sensations before this."

We may reasonably infer from the record that neither the trial judge nor the Michigan courts which considered the delayed motion thought that the petitioner's plight required the assistance of counsel to satisfy the requisites of the fair hearing secured by the Due Process Clause of the Fourteenth Amendment in a state prosecution. The principles determining the extent to which this constitutional right to counsel is secured in a state prosecution have been discussed in a long series of decisions of this Court. We hold that the petitioner's case falls within that class in which the intervention of counsel, unless intelligently waived by the accused, is an essential element of a fair hearing.

The petitioner was 17 years of age and had a seventh-grade education. Cf. De Meerleer v. Michigan, 329 U.S. 663; Wade v. Mayo, 334 U.S. 672; Williams v. Huff, 79 U.S. App. D.C. 326, 146 F. 2d 867. He was charged with a crime carrying Michigan's maximum penalty, viz., solitary confinement at hard labor for life without possibility of parole. Mich. Stat. Ann., 1954, §§ 28.548, 28.2304. Cf. Powell v. Alabama, 287 U.S. 45. The record shows possible defenses which might reasonably have been asserted at trial, but the extent of their availability raised questions of considerable technical difficulty obviously beyond his capacity to comprehend. For instance, one possible defense was insanity, suggested by the trial judge's statements that "his one desire is to have it all over, to get to the institution to which he is to be committed, and to be under observation and to be examined..."; "he insists that there is something wrong with his head; that he has had something akin to queer sensations before this." Another possible defense was mistaken identity, suggested by the fact that the evidence pointing to him as the perpetrator of the crime was entirely circumstantial. Cf. Pennsylvania ex rel. Herman v. Claudy, 350 U.S. 116; Rice v. Olson, 324 U.S. 786. Moreover, the proceedings to determine the degree of murder, the outcome of which determined the extent of punishment, introduced their own complexities. With the aid of counsel, the petitioner, who, as we have said, neither testified himself in the proceeding nor cross-examined the prosecution's witnesses, might have done much to establish a lesser degree of the substantive crime, or to establish facts and make arguments which would have mitigated the sentence. The right to counsel is not a right confined to representation during the trial on the merits. Reece v. Georgia, 350 U.S. 85. The circumstances compel the conclusion that the petitioner's rights could not have been fairly protected without the assistance of counsel to help him with his defense.

However, we may also infer from the record that the Michigan courts held that even if petitioner was constitutionally entitled to the assistance of counsel he waived this right when he told the trial judge that "he didn't want one, didn't have one, he wanted to get it over with." The constitutional right, of course, does not justify forcing counsel upon an accused who wants none. See Carter v. Illinois, 329 U.S. 173, 174. But, "where a person convicted in a state court has not intelligently and understandingly waived the benefit of counsel and where the circumstances show that his rights could not have been fairly protected without counsel, the Due Process Clause invalidates his conviction...." Pennsylvania ex rel. Herman v. Claudy, 350 U.S. 116, 118. Where the right to counsel is of such critical importance as to be an element of Due Process under the Fourteenth Amendment, a finding of waiver is not lightly to be made. Cf. Johnson v. Zerbst, 304 U.S. 458, 464; Glasser v. United States, 315 U.S. 60, 70; Von Moltke v. Gillies, 332 U.S. 708, 723.

This Court held in Johnson v. Zerbst, supra, that when a judgment of conviction entered in a federal court is collaterally attacked upon the ground that the defendant did not have the benefit of counsel, he has the burden of showing, by a preponderance of the evidence, that he did not have counsel and did not competently and intelligently waive his constitutional right to the assistance of counsel. We have found that the petitioner was entitled to the benefit of counsel to secure the fair hearing guaranteed to him by the Due Process Clause of the Fourteenth Amendment. Whatever may be the differences in the substantive right to counsel in federal and state cases, when the defendant in a state case has established his constitutional right to the benefit of counsel, he should carry the same burden of proving non-waiver as is required of a defendant in a federal case. We therefore hold that the rule of Johnson v. Zerbst applies in this case and that the petitioner had the burden of showing, by a preponderance of the evidence, that he did not intelligently and understandingly waive his right to counsel.

Notwithstanding the petitioner's express disavowal, before his plea, of a desire for counsel, the petitioner developed evidence at the hearing on the delayed motion which sustained his burden of showing that the disavowal was not intelligently and understandingly made and hence was not a waiver. Williams v. Huff, 79 U.S. App. D.C. 326, 146 F. 2d 867. This crucial evidence, apparently not known to the trial judge, was brought out on the cross-examination of the Sheriff of Kalamazoo County at the hearing on the delayed motion, and concerned conversations between the Sheriff and the petitioner before the petitioner orally confessed on the afternoon of October 28, 1938:

"*Question:* You didn't advise him it would probably be best to plead guilty?

"*Answer:* Well, the only way I could answer that right is just to give you a little of the conversation there, perhaps, if you wish me to.

"*Question:* Relate that, that will probably be helpful.

"*Answer:* In talking with Willie Moore—that was before he had made any statement—I told him that if he was guilty of it he might better own up on it because I says there could be trouble. Tension is very high outside and there could be trouble. If you are not guilty of it, why then, I says, I would stand pat forever after. Then I told—I spoke to him about what would be required of him and I would have to take him to the Municipal Court for his arraignment in the lower court and then back over there, and I told him he would be entitled to a hearing in lower court and I says, 'There you will have the Judge read to you and you can waive or demand an examination. You are entitled to an examination over there. It is my duty, and it is up to me, to protect you, to use every effort at my command to protect you,' but I says, '*tension is high out there and I am just telling you what could happen if it was started by someone.*' I don't know the language I used.

. . .

"*Question:* Did you also tell him if he plead guilty he would be sent to Jackson immediately? Do you remember saying anything like that?

"*Answer:* I don't know as I come out and said at any time for him to plead one way or the other, *but what I was putting over to him was the fact that if you are guilty and will be sent away you might better be getting away before trouble* because I had had information there was certain colored fellows, a group of them, that was going to interfere with me, and also that there was a bunch of Holland fellows going to meet me when I go to Jackson, they would meet me there at Galesburg there, and, therefore, when he was sentenced I avoided the main route and went way through by Gull Lake and across over in the hills there." (Emphasis supplied.)

Although the trial judge rejected the petitioner's testimony as not worthy of belief, in this instance the Sheriff corroborated the petitioner's testimony, given before the Sheriff took the stand, that the Sheriff had told him "that if I didn't plead guilty to this crime, they couldn't protect me, under those conditions, they says, during the riot, that they didn't know what people they would do, and that they couldn't protect me." Petitioner further testified that he pleaded guilty because of that statement of the Sheriff: "After the man tell me he couldn't protect me then there wasn't nothing I could do. I was mostly scared than anything else."

The Circuit Court found the Sheriff's testimony insignificant because other evidence showed that there was in fact "no threat of mob violence, no congregation of anything that could by any stretch of reasoning be considered a mob or a riotous gathering, and that while the Sheriff felt inclined to take certain precautions and did take certain precautions to avoid any trouble, there was nothing in the situation then existing to indicate that the Respondent had been coerced into a false plea, or that he had been placed in fear of insisting upon his constitutional rights." But plainly it is of no moment to the inquiry that the situation described to the petitioner by the Sheriff did not exist. The petitioner saw only law officers while being held continuously in close confinement from a time just hours after the murder until he orally confessed, and was hardly in a position to know or test the accuracy of what the Sheriff told him. The Sheriff's statement must be evaluated for its effect upon the capacity of this 17-year-old Negro youth of limited education and mental capacity to make an intelligent, understanding waiver of constitutional rights of supreme importance to him in his situation.

We believe that the expectation of mob violence, planted by the Sheriff in the mind of this then 17-year-old Negro youth, raises an inference of fact that his refusal of counsel was motivated to a significant extent by the desire to be removed from the Kalamazoo jail at the earliest possible moment. The trial judge's report of his interview with the petitioner is consistent with this inference in that the report states that the petitioner told the judge that "his one desire is to have it all over, to get to the institution to which he is to be committed, and to be under observation and to be examined." A rejection of federal constitutional rights motivated by fear cannot, in the circumstances of this case, constitute an intelligent waiver. This conclusion against an intelligent waiver is fortified by the inferences which may be drawn from the age of petitioner, Williams v. Huff, 79 U.S. App. D.C. 326, 146 F. 2d 867, and the evidence of emotional disturbance, Hallowell v. United States, 197 F. 2d 926.

We thus conclude that the petitioner had sustained his ultimate burden of proving that his plea of guilty was invalidly accepted as obtained without the benefit of counsel and that he did not waive his right to counsel.

The judgment is reversed, and the cause is remanded for proceedings not inconsistent with this opinion.

Reversed and remanded.

North Carolina *v.* Alford

400 U.S. 25, 91 S.Ct. 160, 27 L.Ed. 2d 162 (1970)

APPEAL FROM THE UNITED STATES COURT OF APPEALS FOR THE FOURTH CIRCUIT

Argued November 17, 1969—Reargued October 14, 1970—Decided November 23, 1970

. . .

MR. JUSTICE WHITE delivered the opinion of the Court.

On December 2, 1963, Alford was indicted for first-degree murder, a capital offense under North Carolina law. The court appointed an attorney to represent him, and this attorney questioned all but one of the various witnesses who appellee said would substantiate his claim of innocence. The witnesses, however, did not support Alford's story but gave statements that strongly indicated his guilt. Faced with strong evidence of guilt and no substantial evidentiary support for the claim of innocence, Alford's attorney recommended that he plead guilty, but left the ultimate decision to Alford himself. The prosecutor agreed to accept a plea of guilty to a charge of second-degree murder, and on December 10, 1963, Alford pleaded guilty to the reduced charge.

Before the plea was finally accepted by the trial court, the court heard the sworn testimony of a police officer who summarized the State's case. Two other witnesses besides Alford were also heard. Although there was no eyewitness to the crime, the testimony indicated that shortly before the killing Alford took his gun from his house, stated his intention to kill the victim, and returned home with the declaration that he had carried out the killing. After the summary presentation of the State's case, Alford took the stand and testified that he had not committed the murder but that he was pleading guilty because he faced the threat of the death penalty if he did not do so. In response to the questions of his counsel, he acknowledged that his counsel had informed him of the difference between second- and first-degree murder and of his rights in case he chose to go to trial. The trial court then asked appellee if, in light of his denial of guilt, he still desired to plead guilty to second-degree murder and appellee answered, "Yes, sir. I plead guilty on—from the circumstances that he [Alford's attorney] told me." After eliciting information about Alford's prior criminal record, which was a long one, the trial court sentenced him to 30 years' imprisonment, the maximum penalty for second-degree murder.

Alford sought post-conviction relief in the state court. Among the claims raised was the claim that his plea of guilty was invalid because it was the product of fear and coercion. After a hearing, the state court in 1965 found that the plea was "willingly, knowingly, and understandingly" made on the advice of competent counsel and in the face of a strong prosecution case. Subsequently, Alford petitioned for a writ of habeas corpus, first in the United States District Court for the Middle District of North Carolina, and then in the Court of Appeals for the Fourth Circuit. Both courts denied the writ on the basis of the state court's findings that Alford voluntarily and knowingly agreed to plead guilty. In 1967, Alford again petitioned for a writ of habeas corpus in the District Court for the Middle District of North Carolina. That court, without an evidentiary hearing, again denied relief on the grounds that the guilty plea was voluntary and waived all defenses and non-jurisdictional defects in any prior stage of the proceedings, and that the findings of the state court in 1965 clearly required rejection of Alford's claim that he was denied effective assistance of counsel prior to pleading guilty. On appeal, a divided panel of the Court of Appeals for the Fourth Circuit reversed on the ground that Alford's guilty plea was made involuntarily. 405 F. 2d 340 (1968). In reaching its conclusion, the Court of Appeals relied heavily on United States v. Jackson, 390 U.S. 570 (1968), which the court read to require invalidation of the North Carolina statutory framework for the imposition of the death penalty because North Carolina statutes encouraged defendants to waive constitutional rights by the promise of no more than life imprisonment if a guilty plea was offered and accepted. Conceding that Jackson did not require the automatic invalidation of pleas of guilty entered under the North Carolina statutes, the Court of Appeals ruled that Alford's guilty plea was involuntary because its principal motivation was fear of the death penalty. By this standard, even if both the judge and the jury had possessed the power to impose the death penalty for first-degree murder or if guilty pleas to capital charges had not been permitted, Alford's plea of guilty to second-degree murder should still have been rejected because impermissibly induced by his desire to eliminate the possibility of a death sentence. We noted probable jurisdiction. 394 U.S. 956 (1969). We vacate the judgment of the Court of Appeals and remand the case for further proceedings.

We held in Brady v. United States, 397 U.S. 742 (1970), that a plea of guilty which would not have been entered except for the defendant's desire to avoid a possible death penalty and to limit the maximum penalty to life imprisonment or a term of years was not for that reason compelled within the meaning of the Fifth Amendment. Jackson established no new test for determining the validity of guilty pleas. The standard was and remains whether the plea represents a voluntary and intelligent choice among the alternative courses of action open to the defendant. See Boykin v. Alabama, 395 U.S. 238, 242 (1969); Machibroda v. United States, 368 U.S. 487, 493 (1962); Kercheval v. United States, 274 U.S. 220, 223 (1927). That he would not have pleaded except for the opportunity to limit the possible penalty does not necessarily demonstrate that the plea of guilty was not the product of a free and rational choice, especially where the defendant was represented by competent counsel whose advice was that the plea would be to the defendant's advantage. The standard fashioned and applied by the Court of Appeals was therefore erroneous and we would, without more, vacate and remand the case for further proceedings with respect to any other claims of Alford which are properly before that court, if it were not for other circumstances appearing in the record which might seem to warrant an affirmance of the Court of Appeals.

As previously recounted, after Alford's plea of guilty was offered and the State's case was placed before the judge, Alford denied that he had committed the murder but reaffirmed his desire to plead guilty to avoid a possible death sentence and to limit the penalty to the 30-year maximum provided for second-degree murder. Ordinarily, a judgment of conviction resting on a plea of guilty is justified by the defendant's admission that he committed the crime charged against him and his consent that judgment be entered without a trial of any kind. The plea usually subsumes both elements, and justifiably so, even though there is no separate, express admission by the defendant that he committed the particular acts claimed to constitute the crime charged in the indictment. See Brady v. United States, supra, at 748; McCarthy v. United States, 394 U.S. 459, 466 (1969). Here Alford entered his plea but accompanied it with the statement that he had not shot the victim.

If Alford's statements were to be credited as sincere assertions of his innocence, there obviously existed a factual and legal dispute between him and the State. Without more, it might be argued that the conviction entered on his guilty plea was invalid, since his assertion of innocence negatived any admission of guilt, which, as we observed last Term in Brady, is normally "[c]entral to the plea and the foundation for entering judgment against the defendant. . . ." 397 U.S., at 748.

In addition to Alford's statement, however, the court had heard an account of the events on the night of the murder, including information from Alford's acquaintances that he had departed from his home with his gun stating his intention to kill and that he had later declared that he had carried out his intention. Nor had Alford wavered in his desire to have the trial court determine his guilt without a jury trial. Although denying the charge against him, he nevertheless preferred the dispute between him and the State to be settled by the judge in the context of a guilty plea proceeding rather than by a formal trial. Thereupon, with the State's telling evidence and Alford's denial before it, the trial court proceeded to convict and sentence Alford for second-degree murder.

State and lower federal courts are divided upon whether a guilty plea can be accepted when it is accompanied by protestations of innocence and hence contains only a waiver of trial but no admission of guilt. Some courts, giving expression to the principle that "[o]ur law only authorizes a conviction where guilt is shown," Harris v. State, 76 Tex. Cr. R. 126, 131, 172 S.W. 975, 977 (1915), require that trial judges reject such pleas. See, e.g., Hulsey v. United States, 369 F. 2d 284, 287 (CA5 1966); United States ex rel. Elksnis v. Gilligan, 256 F. Supp. 244, 255–257 (SDNY 1966); People v. Morrison, 348 Mich. 88, 81 N.W. 2d 667 (1957); State v. Reali, 26 N.J. 222, 139 A. 2d 300 (1958); State v. Leyba, 80 N.M. 190, 193, 453 P. 2d 211, 214 (1969); State v. Stacy, 43 Wash. 2d 358, 361–364, 261 P. 2d 400, 402–403 (1953). But others have concluded that they should not "force any defense on a defendant in a criminal case," particularly when advancement of the defense might "end in disaster...." Tremblay v. Overholser, 199 F. Supp. 569, 570 (DC 1961). They have argued that, since "guilt, or the degree of guilt, is at times uncertain and elusive," "[a]n accused, though believing in or entertaining doubts respecting his innocence, might reasonably conclude a jury would be convinced of his guilt and that he would fare better in the sentence by pleading guilty...." McCoy v. United States, 124 U.S. App. D.C. 177, 179, 363 F. 2d 306, 308 (1966). As one state court observed nearly a century ago, "[r]easons other than the fact that he is guilty may induce a defendant to so plead,... [and] [h]e must be permitted to judge for himself in this respect." State v. Kaufman, 51 Iowa 578, 580, 2 N.W. 275, 276 (1879) (dictum). Accord, e.g., Griffin v. United States, 132 U.S. App. D.C. 108, 405 F. 2d 1378 (1968); Bruce v. United States, 126 U.S. App. D.C. 336, 342–343, 379 F. 2d 113, 119–120 (1967); City of Burbank v. General Electric Co., 329 F. 2d 825, 835 (CA9 1964) (dictum); State v. Martinez, 89 Idaho 129, 138, 403 P. 2d 597, 602–603 (1965); People v. Hetherington, 379 Ill. 71, 39 N.E. 2d 361 (1942); State ex rel. Crossley v. Tahash, 263 Minn. 299, 307–308, 116 N.W. 2d 666, 672 (1962); Commonwealth v. Cottrell, 433 Pa. 177, 249 A. 2d 294 (1969). Cf. United States ex rel. Brown v. LaVallee, 424 F. 2d 457 (CA2 1970).

This Court has not confronted this precise issue, but prior decisions do yield relevant principles. In Lynch v. Overholser, 369 U.S. 705 (1962), Lynch, who had been charged in the Municipal Court of the District of Columbia with drawing and negotiating bad checks, a misdemeanor punishable by a maximum of one year in jail, sought to enter a plea of guilty, but the trial judge refused to accept the plea since a psychiatric report in the judge's possession indicated that Lynch had been suffering from "a manic depressive psychosis, at the time of the crime charged," and hence might have been not guilty by reason of insanity. Although at the subsequent trial Lynch did not rely on the insanity defense, he was found not guilty by reason of insanity and committed for an indeterminate period to a mental institution. On habeas corpus, the Court ordered his release, construing the congressional legislation seemingly authorizing the commitment as not reaching a case where the accused preferred a guilty plea to a plea of insanity. The Court expressly refused to rule that Lynch had an absolute right to have his guilty plea accepted, see id., at 719, but implied that there would have been no constitutional error had his plea been accepted even though evidence before the judge indicated that there was a valid defense.

The issue in Hudson v. United States, 272 U.S. 451 (1926), was whether a federal court has power to impose a prison sentence after accepting a plea of nolo contendere, a plea by which a defendant does not expressly admit his guilt, but nonetheless waives his right to a trial and authorizes the court for purposes of the case to treat him as if he were guilty. The Court held that a trial court does have such power, and, except for the cases which were rejected in Hudson, the federal courts have uniformly followed this rule, even in cases involving moral turpitude. Bruce v. United States, supra, at 343, n. 20, 379 F. 2d, at 120 n. 20 (dictum). See, e.g., Lott v. United States, 367 U.S. 421 (1961) (fraudulent evasion of income tax); Sullivan v. United States, 348 U.S. 170 (1954) (ibid.); Farnsworth v. Zerbst, 98 F. 2d 541 (CA5 1938) (espionage); Pharr v. United States, 48 F. 2d 767 (CA6 1931) (misapplication of bank funds); United States v. Bagliore, 182 F. Supp. 714 (EDNY 1960) (receiving stolen property). Implicit in the nolo contendere cases is a recognition that the Constitution does not bar imposition of a prison sentence upon an accused who is unwilling expressly to admit his guilt but who, faced with grim alternatives, is willing to waive his trial and accept the sentence.

These cases would be directly in point if Alford had simply insisted on his plea but refused to admit the crime. The fact that his plea was denominated a plea of guilty rather than a plea of nolo contendere is of no constitutional significance with respect to the issue now before us, for the Constitution is concerned with the practical consequences, not the formal categorizations, of state law. See Smith v. Bennett, 365 U.S. 708, 712 (1961); Jones v. United States, 362 U.S. 257, 266 (1960). Cf. Kermarec v. Compagnie Generale Transatlantique, 358 U.S. 625, 630–632 (1959). Thus, while most pleas of guilty consist of both a waiver of trial and an express admission of guilt, the latter element is not a constitutional requisite to the imposition of criminal penalty. An individual accused of crime may voluntarily, knowingly, and understandingly consent to the imposition of a prison sentence even if he is unwilling or unable to admit his participation in the acts constituting the crime.

Nor can we perceive any material difference between a plea that refuses to admit commission of the criminal act and a plea containing a protestation of innocence when, as in the instant case, a defendant intelligently concludes that his interests require entry of a guilty plea and the record before the judge contains strong evidence of actual guilt. Here the State had a strong case of first-degree murder against Alford. Whether he realized or disbelieved his guilt, he insisted on his plea because in his view he had absolutely nothing to gain by a trial and much to gain by pleading. Because of the overwhelming evidence against him, a trial was precisely what neither Alford nor his attorney desired. Confronted with the choice between a trial for first-degree murder, on the one hand, and a plea of guilty to second-degree murder, on the other, Alford quite reasonably chose the latter and thereby limited the maximum penalty to a 30-year term. When his plea is viewed in light of the evidence against him, which substantially negated his claim of innocence and which further provided a means by which the judge could test whether the plea was being intelligently entered, see McCarthy v. United States, supra, at 466–467 (1969), its validity cannot be seriously questioned. In view of the strong factual basis for the plea demonstrated by the State and Alford's clearly expressed desire to enter it despite his professed belief in his innocence, we hold that the trial judge did not commit constitutional error in accepting it.

Relying on United States v. Jackson, supra, Alford now argues in effect that the State should not have allowed him this choice but should have insisted on proving him guilty of murder in the first degree. The States in their wisdom may take this course by statute or otherwise and may prohibit the practice of accepting pleas to lesser included offenses under any circumstances. But this is not the mandate of the Fourteenth Amendment and the Bill of Rights. The prohibitions against involuntary or unintelligent pleas should not be relaxed, but neither should an exercise in arid logic render those constitutional guarantees counterproductive and put in jeopardy the very human values they were meant to preserve.

The Court of Appeals for the Fourth Circuit was in error to find Alford's plea of guilty invalid because it was made to avoid the possibility of the death penalty. That court's judgment directing the issuance of the writ of habeas corpus is vacated and the case is remanded to the Court of Appeals for further proceedings consistent with this opinion.

It is so ordered.

Santobello *v.* New York

404 U.S. 257, 92 S.Ct. 495, 30 L.Ed. 2d. 427 (1971)

CERTIORARI TO APPELLATE DIVISION OF THE SUPREME COURT OF NEW YORK, FIRST JUDICIAL DEPARTMENT

Argued November 15, 1971—Decided December 20, 1971

. . .

MR. CHIEF JUSTICE BURGER delivered the opinion of the Court.

We granted certiorari in this case to determine whether the State's failure to keep a commitment concerning the sentence recommendation on a guilty plea required a new trial.

The facts are not in dispute. The State of New York indicted petitioner in 1969 on two felony counts, Promoting Gambling in the First Degree, and Possession of Gambling Records in the First Degree, N.Y. Penal Law §§ 225.10, 225.20.

Petitioner first entered a plea of not guilty to both counts. After negotiations, the Assistant District Attorney in charge of the case agreed to permit petitioner to plead guilty to a lesser-included offense, Possession of Gambling Records in the Second Degree, N.Y. Penal Law § 225.15, conviction of which would carry a maximum prison sentence of one year. The prosecutor agreed to make no recommendation as to the sentence.

On June 16, 1969, petitioner accordingly withdrew his plea of not guilty and entered a plea of guilty to the lesser charge. Petitioner represented to the sentencing judge that the plea was voluntary and that the facts of the case, as described by the Assistant District Attorney, were true. The court accepted the plea and set a date for sentencing. A series of delays followed, owing primarily to the absence of a presentence report, so that by September 23, 1969, petitioner had still not been sentenced. By that date petitioner acquired new defense counsel.

Petitioner's new counsel moved immediately to withdraw the guilty plea. In an accompanying affidavit, petitioner alleged that he did not know at the time of his plea that crucial evidence against him had been obtained as a result of an illegal search. The accuracy of this affidavit is subject to challenge since petitioner had filed and withdrawn a motion to suppress, before pleading guilty. In addition to his motion to withdraw his guilty plea, petitioner renewed the motion to suppress and filed a motion to inspect the grand jury minutes.

These three motions in turn caused further delay until November 26, 1969, when the court denied all three and set January 9, 1970, as the date for sentencing. On January 9 petitioner appeared before a different judge, the judge who had presided over the case to this juncture having retired. Petitioner renewed his motions, and the court again rejected them. The court then turned to consideration of the sentence.

At this appearance, another prosecutor had replaced the prosecutor who had negotiated the plea. The new prosecutor recommended the maximum one-year sentence. In making this recommendation, he cited petitioner's criminal record and alleged links with organized crime. Defense counsel immediately objected on the ground that the State had promised petitioner before the plea was entered that there would be no sentence recommendation by the prosecution. He sought to adjourn the sentence hearing in order to have time to prepare proof of the first prosecutor's promise. The second prosecutor, apparently ignorant of his colleague's commitment, argued that there was nothing in the record to support petitioner's claim of a promise, but the State, in subsequent proceedings, has not contested that such a promise was made.

The sentencing judge ended discussion, with the following statement, quoting extensively from the presentence report:

> "Mr. Aronstein [Defense Counsel], I am not at all influenced by what the District Attorney says, so that there is no need to adjourn the sentence, and there is no need to have any testimony. It doesn't make a particle of difference what the District Attorney says he will do, or what he doesn't do.
>
> "I have here, Mr. Aronstein, a probation report. I have here a history of a long,

> long serious criminal record. I have here a picture of the life history of this man. . . .
>
> "'He is unamenable to supervision in the community. He is a professional criminal.' This is in quotes. 'And a recidivist. Institutionalization—'; that means in plain language, just putting him away, 'is the only means of halting his anti-social activities,' and protecting you, your family, me, my family, protecting society. 'Institutionalization.' Plain language, put him behind bars.
>
> "Under the plea, I can only send him to the New York City Correctional Institution for men for one year, which I am hereby doing."

The judge then imposed the maximum sentence of one year.

Petitioner sought and obtained a certificate of reasonable doubt and was admitted to bail pending an appeal. The Supreme Court of the State of New York, Appellate Division, First Department, unanimously affirmed petitioner's conviction, 35 App. Div. 2d 1084, 316 N.Y.S. 2d 194 (1970), and petitioner was denied leave to appeal to the New York Court of Appeals. Petitioner then sought certiorari in this Court. MR. JUSTICE HARLAN granted bail pending our disposition of the case.

This record represents another example of an unfortunate lapse in orderly prosecutorial procedures, in part, no doubt, because of the enormous increase in the workload of the often understaffed prosecutor's offices. The heavy workload may well explain these episodes, but it does not excuse them. The disposition of criminal charges by agreement between the prosecutor and the accused, sometimes loosely called "plea bargaining," is an essential component of the administration of justice. Properly administered, it is to be encouraged. If every criminal charge were subjected to a full-scale trial, the States and the Federal Government would need to multiply by many times the number of judges and court facilities.

Disposition of charges after plea discussions is not only an essential part of the process but a highly desirable part for many reasons. It leads to prompt and largely final disposition of most criminal cases; it avoids much of the corrosive impact of enforced idleness during pretrial confinement for those who are denied release pending trial; it protects the public from those accused persons who are prone to continue criminal conduct even while on pretrial release; and, by shortening the time between charge and disposition, it enhances whatever may be the rehabilitative prospects of the guilty when they are ultimately imprisoned. See Brady v. United States, 397 U.S. 742, 751–752 (1970).

However, all of these considerations presuppose fairness in securing agreement between an accused and a prosecutor. It is now clear, for example, that the accused pleading guilty must be counseled, absent a waiver. Moore v. Michigan, 355 U.S. 155 (1957). Fed. Rule Crim. Proc. 11, governing pleas in federal courts, now makes clear that the sentencing judge must develop, *on the record,* the factual basis for the plea, as, for example, by having the accused describe the conduct that gave rise to the charge. The plea must, of course, be voluntary and knowing and if it was induced by promises, the essence of those promises must in some way be made known. There is, of course, no absolute right to have a guilty plea accepted. Lynch v. Overholser, 369 U.S. 705, 719 (1962); Fed. Rule Crim. Proc. 11. A court may reject a plea in exercise of sound judicial discretion.

This phase of the process of criminal justice, and the adjudicative element inherent in accepting a plea of guilty, must be attended by safeguards to insure the defendant what is reasonably due in the circumstances. Those circumstances will vary, but a constant factor is that when a plea rests in any significant degree on a promise or agreement of the prosecutor, so that it can be said to be part of the inducement or consideration, such promise must be fulfilled.

On this record, petitioner "bargained" and negotiated for a particular plea in order to secure dismissal of more serious charges, but also on condition that no sentence recommendation would be made by the prosecutor. It is now conceded that the promise to abstain from a recommendation was made, and at this stage the prosecution is not in a good position to argue that its inadvertent breach of agreement is immaterial. The staff lawyers in a prosecutor's office have the burden of "letting the left hand know what the right hand is doing" or has done. That the breach of agreement was inadvertent does not lessen its impact.

We need not reach the question whether the sentencing judge would or would not have been influenced had he known all the details of the negotiations for the plea. He stated that the prosecutor's recommendation did not influence him and we have no reason to doubt that. Nevertheless, we conclude that the interests of justice and appropriate recognition of the duties of the prosecution in relation to promises made in the negotiation of pleas of guilty will be best served by remanding the case to the state courts for further consideration. The ultimate relief to which petitioner is entitled we leave to the discretion of the state court, which is in a better position to decide whether the circumstances of this case require only that there be specific performance of the agreement on the plea, in which case petitioner should be resentenced by a different judge, or whether, in the view of the state court, the circumstances require granting the relief sought by petitioner, i.e., the opportunity to withdraw his plea of guilty. We emphasize that this is in no sense to question the fairness of the sentencing judge; the fault here rests on the prosecutor, not on the sentencing judge.

The judgment is vacated and the case is remanded for reconsideration not inconsistent with this opinion.

It is so ordered.

Henderson, Correctional Superintendent *v.* Morgan

426 U.S. 638, 96 S.Ct. 2253, 49 L.Ed. 2d. 108 (1976)

CERTIORARI TO THE UNITED STATES COURT OF APPEALS FOR THE SECOND CIRCUIT

Argued February 24, 1976—Decided June 17, 1976

. . .

MR. JUSTICE STEVENS delivered the opinion of the Court.

The question presented is whether a defendant may enter a voluntary plea of guilty to a charge of second-degree murder without being informed that intent to cause the death of his victim was an element of the offense.

The case arises out of a collateral attack on a judgment entered by a state trial court in Fulton County, N.Y., in 1965. Respondent, having been indicted on a charge of first-degree murder, pleaded guilty to second-degree murder and was sentenced to an indeterminate term of imprisonment of 25 years to life. He did not appeal.

In 1970, respondent initiated proceedings in the New York courts seeking to have his conviction vacated on the ground that his plea of guilty was involuntary. The state courts denied relief on the basis of the written record. Having exhausted his state remedies, in 1973, respondent filed a petition for writ of habeas corpus in the United States District Court for the Northern District of New York. He alleged that his guilty plea was involuntary because he was not aware (1) of the sentence that might be imposed upon conviction of second-degree murder, or (2) that intent to cause death was an element of the offense. Based on the state-court record, the Federal District Court denied relief. The Court of Appeals reversed summarily and directed the District Court "to conduct an evidentiary hearing on the issues raised by petitioner, including whether, at the time of his entry of his guilty plea, he was aware that intent was an essential element of the crime and was advised of the scope of the punishment that might be imposed."

Upon remand the District Judge heard the testimony of several witnesses including respondent, the two lawyers who had represented him in 1965, the prosecutor, and respondent's mother. In addition, the transcript of the relevant state-court proceedings and certain psychological evaluations of respondent were made a part of the record.

At the conclusion of the hearing, the District Court made only two specific findings of fact. First, contrary to respondent's testimony, the court expressly found that he was advised that a 25-year sentence would be imposed if he pleaded guilty. Second, the court found that respondent "was not advised by counsel or court, at any time, that an intent to cause the death or a design to effect the death of the victim was an essential element of Murder 2nd degree." On the basis of the latter finding, the District Court held "as a matter of law" that the plea of guilty was involuntary and had to be set aside. This holding was affirmed, without opinion, by the Court of Appeals.

Before addressing the question whether the District Court correctly held the plea invalid as a matter of law, we review some of the facts developed at the evidentiary hearing.

I

On April 6, 1965, respondent killed Mrs. Ada Francisco in her home.

When he was in seventh grade, respondent was committed to the Rome State School for Mental Defectives where he was classified as "retarded." He was released to become a farm laborer and ultimately went to work on Mrs. Francisco's farm.

Following an argument, she threatened to return him to state custody. He then decided to abscond. During the night he entered Mrs. Francisco's bedroom with a knife, intending to collect his earned wages before leaving; she awoke, began to scream, and he stabbed her. He took a small amount of money, fled in her car, and became involved in an accident about 80 miles away. The knife was found in the glove compartment of her car. He was promptly arrested and made a statement to the police. He was then 19 years old and substantially below average intelligence.

Respondent was indicted for first-degree murder and arraigned on April 15, 1965. Two concededly competent attorneys were appointed to represent him. The indictment, which charged that he "willfully" stabbed his victim, was read in open court. His lawyers requested, and were granted, access to his written statement and to earlier psychiatric reports. A new psychiatric examination was requested and ordered.

Respondent was found competent to stand trial. Defense counsel held a series of conferences with the prosecutors, with the respondent, and with members of his family. The lawyers "thought manslaughter first would satisfy the needs of justice." They therefore endeavored to have the charge reduced to manslaughter, but the prosecution would agree to nothing less than second-degree murder and a minimum sentence of 25 years. The lawyers gave respondent advice about the different sentences which could be imposed for the different offenses, but, as the District Court found, did not explain the required element of intent.

On June 8, 1965, respondent appeared in court with his attorneys and entered a plea of guilty to murder in the second degree in full satisfaction of the first-degree murder charge made in the indictment. In direct colloquy with the trial judge respondent stated that his plea was based on the advice of his attorneys, that he understood he was accused of killing Mrs. Francisco in Fulton County, that he was waiving his right to a jury trial and that he would be sent to prison. There was no discussion of the elements of the offense of second-degree murder, no indication that the nature of the offense had ever been discussed with respondent, and no reference of any kind to the requirement of intent to cause the death of the victim.

At the sentencing hearing a week later his lawyers made a statement explaining his version of the offense, particularly noting that respondent "meant no harm to that lady" when he entered her room with the knife. The prosecutor disputed defense counsel's version of the matter, but did not discuss it in detail. After studying the probation officer's report, the trial judge pronounced sentence.

At the evidentiary hearing in the Federal District Court, respondent testified that he would not have pleaded guilty if he had known that an intent to cause the death of his victim was an element of the offense of second-degree murder. The District Judge did not indicate whether or not he credited this testimony.

II

Petitioner contends that the District Court applied an unrealistically rigid rule of law. Instead of testing the voluntariness of a plea by determining whether a ritualistic litany of the formal legal elements of an offense was read to the defendant, petitioner argues that the court should examine the totality of the circumstances and determine whether the substance of the charge, as opposed to its technical elements, was conveyed to the accused. We do not disagree with the thrust of petitioner's argument, but we are persuaded that even under the test which he espouses, this judgment finding respondent guilty of second-degree murder was defective.

We assume, as petitioner argues, that the prosecutor had overwhelming evidence of guilt available. We also accept petitioner's characterization of the competence of respondent's counsel and of the wisdom of their advice to plead guilty to a charge of second-degree murder. Nevertheless, such a plea cannot support a judgment of guilt unless it was voluntary in a constitutional sense. And clearly the plea could not be voluntary in the sense that it constituted an intelligent admission that he committed the offense unless the defendant received "real notice of the true nature of the charge against him, the first and most universally recognized requirement of due process." Smith v. O'Grady, 312 U.S. 329, 334.

The charge of second-degree murder was never formally made. Had it been made, it necessarily would have included a charge that respondent's assault was "committed with a design to effect the death of the person killed." That element of the offense might have been proved by the objective evidence even if respondent's actual state of mind was consistent with innocence or manslaughter. But even if such a design to effect death would almost inevitably have been inferred from evidence that respondent repeatedly stabbed Mrs. Francisco, it is nevertheless also true that a jury would not have been required to draw that inference. The jury would have been entitled to accept defense counsel's appraisal of the incident as involving only manslaughter in the first degree. Therefore, an admission by respondent that he killed Mrs. Francisco does not necessarily also admit that he was guilty of second-degree murder.

There is nothing in this record that can serve as a substitute for either a finding after trial, or a voluntary admission, that respondent had the requisite intent. Defense counsel did not purport to stipulate to that fact; they did not explain to him that his plea would be an admission of that fact; and he made no factual statement or admission necessarily implying that he had such intent. In these circumstances it is impossible to conclude that his plea to the unexplained charge of second-degree murder was voluntary.

Petitioner argues that affirmance of the Court of Appeals will invite countless collateral attacks on judgments entered on pleas of guilty, since frequently the record will not contain a complete enumeration of the elements of the offense to which an accused person pleads guilty. We think petitioner's fears are exaggerated.

Normally the record contains either an explanation of the charge by the trial judge, or at least a representation by defense counsel that the nature of the offense has been explained to the accused. Moreover, even without such an express representation, it may be appropriate to presume that in most cases defense counsel routinely explain the nature of the offense in sufficient detail to give the accused notice of what he is being asked to admit. This case is unique because the trial judge found as a fact that the element of intent was not explained to respondent. Moreover, respondent's unusually low mental capacity provides a reasonable explanation for counsel's oversight; it also forecloses the conclusion that the error was harmless beyond a reasonable doubt, for it lends at least a modicum of credibility to defense counsel's appraisal of the homicide as a manslaughter rather than a murder.

Since respondent did not receive adequate notice of the offense to which he pleaded guilty, his plea was involuntary and the judgment of conviction was entered without due process of law.

Affirmed.

Hutto, Arkansas Department of Correction Commissioner *v.* Ross

429 U.S. 28, 97 S.Ct. 202, 50 L.Ed. 2d. 194 (1976)

ON PETITION FOR WRIT OF CERTIORARI TO THE UNITED STATES COURT OF APPEALS FOR THE EIGHTH CIRCUIT

Decided November 1, 1976

. . .

PER CURIAM.

In March 1972, in Johnson County, Ark., respondent was charged by information with the crime of embezzlement. With the assistance of counsel, respondent entered into plea negotiations with the prosecuting attorney, and the parties reached an agreement that respondent would enter a plea of guilty on the understanding that the prosecutor would recommend a 15-year prison sentence, with 10 years suspended. Approximately two weeks later, the prosecuting attorney asked respondent's counsel whether respondent would be willing to make a statement concerning the crimes. Although counsel advised respondent of his Fifth Amendment privilege and informed him that the terms of the negotiated plea bargain were available regardless of his willingness to comply with the prosecuting attorney's request, the respondent agreed to make a statement confessing to the crime charged. The record discloses that the statement was made under oath in the office of respondent's counsel, with counsel present, and after respondent had been advised of his rights under Miranda v. Arizona, 384 U.S. 436 (1966).

Respondent subsequently withdrew from the plea bargain, retained new counsel, and demanded a jury trial. The trial court ruled, after hearing evidence outside the presence of the jury, that respondent had confessed voluntarily. The statement was admitted at trial, and respondent was convicted and sentenced to 21 years' imprisonment. On appeal, the Arkansas Supreme Court affirmed. Ross v. State, 257 Ark. 44, 514 S.W. 2d 409 (1974). This Court denied certiorari. 421 U.S. 931 (1975).

Respondent then filed a petition for a writ of habeas corpus in the United States District Court for the Western District of Arkansas challenging the state court's finding of voluntariness. 28 U.S.C. § 2254. The District Court held an evidentiary hearing, and on May 23, 1975, denied the petition, agreeing with the state court that the confession was voluntary and therefore admissible. Mobley ex rel. Ross v. Meek, 394 F. Supp. 1219.

The Court of Appeals for the Eighth Circuit reversed, finding the statement inadmissible because "it... was made in connection with an offer to plead guilty and after a [plea] bargain had been agreed upon." 531 F. 2d 924, 926 (1976). It made no difference, in the court's view, that the confession was not an express precondition of the plea bargain; the confession became "part and parcel" of the plea bargain because "[the] confession would [not] have been made at the request of the prosecution *but for* the plea bargain." Ibid. (emphasis added). Since the plea bargain had not been executed, the court found the confession involuntary and therefore inadmissible.

The only question in this case is whether a confession is per se inadmissible in a criminal trial because it was made subsequent to an agreed upon plea bargain that did not call for such a confession. We conclude that the Court of Appeals erred when it held that *any* statement made as a result of a plea bargain is inadmissible.

The Court of Appeals reasoned that respondent's confession was involuntary because it was made "as a result of the plea bargain" and would not have been made "but for the plea bargain." Id., at 927, 926. But causation in that sense has never been the test of voluntariness. See Brady v. United States, 397 U.S. 742, 749–750 (1970). The test is whether the confession was "'extracted by any sort of threats or violence, [or] obtained by any direct or implied promises, however slight, [or] by the exertion of any improper influence.'" Bram v. United States, 168 U.S. 532, 542–543 (1897); see Brady v. United States, supra, at 753. The existence of the bargain may well have entered into respondent's decision to give a statement, but counsel made it clear to respondent that he could enforce the terms of the plea bargain whether or not he confessed. The confession thus does not appear to have been the result of "'any direct or implied promises'" or any coercion on the part of the prosecution, and was not involuntary. Bram v. United States, supra, at 542–543.

The petition for a writ of certiorari is granted, the judgment of the Court of Appeals is reversed, and the case is remanded for further proceedings consistent with this opinion.

It is so ordered.

CHAPTER 13

Contents

Entrapment

§ 13.1 Entrapment Defined

There is a popular misconception as to the meaning of entrapment. The layman feels that any government encouragement to a person to commit a crime constitutes entrapment. We hear of speed traps along our highways where police are known to give traffic summonses or arrest drivers who exceed the posted speed limit. These officers may be engaged in a revenue producing activity, but presumably they are enforcing the law as enacted by local legislative bodies. The problem sometimes arises when there is little or no warning of a speed limit. In those cases, a due process of law claim becomes a viable defense. The person who is so accosted by a police officer usually will not contest such a deprivation of constitutional rights because the expense of litigation will far exceed the fine which is imposed. Hence, constitutional rights of due process of law are deprived to these people and little is done about it. Sometimes, organizations such as the American Automobile Association or the American Civil Liberties Union will undertake class actions to correct these wrongs but the faster and most direct way at present to remedy this situation is to publicize a travelers' advisory to urge travelers to avoid passing through affected communities and to appeal to the state officials to remedy the situation by all means at their disposal. Perhaps the better approach to prevent abuses of this sort is to bring an action for damages under Title 42, Section 1983, of the United States Code, where the offending parties might be held personally liable for their deprivation of rights to United States citizens. This will be discussed in greater detail in Chapter 14 (infra).

Persons who have a predisposition to commit a crime cannot be entrapped. It is only those persons who were led into the criminal activity by law enforcement officers and who had no predisposition to commit the offense who can raise a valid defense of entrapment. Perhaps an illustration may explain this better.

Let us suppose that a policeman is assigned to plain-clothes duty and is attempting to arrest a prostitute for the offense of prostitution. Let us further assume that the policeman enters a bar-and-grill and steps up to the bar where there is a pretty young female already seated at the bar. He engages her in conversation and they appear to be enjoying each other's company. After about an hour of this, the following conversation takes place:

Officer: How would you like to go to the hotel down the block with me? I'll give you $50 for a good time.

Female: I'm not that kind of girl. I enjoy talking with you here. Let's continue this way.
Officer: I'll give you $100.
Female: I told you that I'm not that kind of girl. Please let's keep our friendship and forget about your proposition.
Officer: I want you badly. I'll give you $1,000.
Female: You must be crazy but if you want me that badly, I'll accept the $1,000 and go with you and do what you want to do.

Here we have a clear case of entrapment. The female was obviously not trying to raise the price for her performance. She was not interested in the proposition until the officer made it so attractive that she just could not refuse his offer.

§ 13.2 Model Penal Code Entrapment Provisions

The Federal Criminal Code and the American Law Institute Model Penal Code, § 2.13, provide as follows:

1. A public law enforcement official or a person acting in cooperation with such an official perpetrates an entrapment if for the purpose of obtaining evidence of the commission of an offense, he induces or encourages another person to engage in conduct constituting such offense by either:
   (a) making knowingly false representations designed to induce the belief that such conduct is not prohibited; or
   (b) employing methods of persuasion or inducement which create a substantial risk that such an offense will be committed by persons other than those who are ready to commit it.
2. Except as provided in Subsection (3) of this Section, a person prosecuted for an offense shall be acquitted if he proves by a preponderance of evidence that his conduct occurred in response to an entrapment. The issue of entrapment shall be tried by the Court in the absence of the jury.
3. The defense afforded by this Section is unavailable when causing or threatening bodily injury is an element of the offense charged and the prosecution is based on conduct causing or threatening such injury to a person other than the person perpetrating the entrapment.

Section 702 of the proposed new federal code, which represents the first federal codification of the judicially developed defense of entrapment, provides:

(1) Affirmative Defense. It is an affirmative defense that the defendant was entrapped into committing the offense.
(2) Entrapment Defined. Entrapment occurs when a law enforcement agent induces the commission of an offense, using persuasion or other means likely to cause normally law-abiding persons to commit the offense. Conduct merely affording a person an opportunity to commit an offense does not constitute entrapment.
(3) Law Enforcement Agent Defined. In this section "law enforcement agent" includes personnel of state and local enforcement agencies as well as the United States, and any person cooperating with such an agency.

§ 13.3 Supreme Court Supervision over Entrapment Defense

In § 2.9 (supra), the supervisory powers of the Supreme Court were explained. The Court invoked these supervisory powers in the problem of entrapment to ascertain whether there was general fairness by undercover law enforcement officers in assisting a malefactor to commit a crime. That issue was met in United States v. Russell, 411 U.S. 423, 93 S.Ct. 1637, 36 L.Ed.2d 366 (1973), where an undercover agent of the Federal Bureau of Narcotics and Dangerous Drugs provided phenyl-2-propanone, an essential ingredient in the manufacture of methamphetamine in return for one-half of the drug produced. The phenyl-2-propanone was generally difficult to obtain but it was obtainable. The respondent (Russell) argued that the extent of the undercover man's involvement in this case was so great that a criminal prosecution for the drug's manufacture violated the fundamental principles of due process.

The Court did not agree. The Court said, "The illicit manufacture of drugs is not a sporadic, isolated criminal incident, but a continuing, though illegal, business enterprise. In order to obtain convictions for illegally manufacturing drugs, the gathering of evidence of past unlawful conduct frequently proves to be an all but impossible task. Thus in drug related offenses law enforcement personnel have turned to one of the only practicable means of detection: the infiltration of drug rings and a limited participation in their unlawful present practices. Such infiltration is a recognized and permissible means of apprehension .... (The defendant) was an active participant in an illegal drug manufacturing enterprise which began before the government agent appeared on the scene, and continued after the government agent had left the scene. He was ... not an 'unwary innocent' but an 'unwary criminal.'"

In Hampton v. United States, 425 U.S. 484, 96 S.Ct. 1646, 48 L.Ed.2d 113 (1976), the Court sustained a conviction where the undercover man supplied a substance that was illegal to be held by the government agent. However two of the five-justice majority would not rule out the possibility that, in some future case, the conduct of government agents might be so unfair that the defendant would be able to prevail on a due process claim in spite of his predisposition to commit the crime.

Judicial Decisions Relating to Chapter 13

United States *v.* Russell

411 U.S. 423, 93 S.Ct. 1637, 36 L.Ed.2d 366 (1973)

CERTIORARI TO THE UNITED STATES COURT OF APPEALS FOR THE NINTH CIRCUIT

Argued February 27, 1973.—Decided April 24, 1973.

. . .

MR. JUSTICE REHNQUIST delivered the opinion of the Court.

Respondent Richard Russell was charged in three counts of a five-count indictment returned against him and codefendants John and Patrick Connolly. After a jury trial in the District Court, in which his sole defense was entrapment, respondent was convicted on all three counts of having unlawfully manufactured and processed methamphetamine ("speed") and of having unlawfully sold and delivered that drug in violation of 21 U.S.C. §§ 331 (q) (1), (2), 360a (a), (b) (1964 ed., Supp. V). He was sentenced to concurrent terms of two years in prison for each offense, the terms to be suspended on the condition that he spend six months in prison and be placed on probation for the following three years. On appeal, the United States Court of Appeals for the Ninth Circuit, one judge dissenting, reversed the conviction solely for the reason that an undercover agent supplied an essential chemical for manufacturing the methamphetamine which formed the basis of respondent's conviction. The court concluded that as a matter of law "a defense to a criminal charge may be founded upon an intolerable degree of governmental participation in the criminal enterprise." 459 F. 2d 671, 673 (1972). We granted certiorari, 409 U.S. 911 (1972), and now reverse that judgment.

There is little dispute concerning the essential facts in this case. On December 7, 1969, Joe Shapiro, an undercover agent for the Federal Bureau of Narcotics and Dangerous Drugs, went to respondent's home on Whidbey Island in the State of Washington where he met with respondent and his two codefendants, John and Patrick Connolly. Shapiro's assignment was to locate a laboratory where it was believed that methamphetamine was being manufactured illicitly. He told the respondent and the Connollys that he represented an organization in the Pacific Northwest that was interested in controlling the manufacture and distribution of methamphetamine. He then made an offer to supply the defendants with the chemical phenyl-2-propanone, an essential ingredient in the manufacture of methamphetamine, in return for one-half of the drug produced. This offer was made on the condition that Agent Shapiro be shown a sample of the drug which they were making and the laboratory where it was being produced.

During the conversation, Patrick Connolly revealed that he had been making the drug since May 1969 and since then had produced three pounds of it. John Connolly gave the agent a bag containing a quantity of methamphetamine that he represented as being from "the last batch that we made." Shortly thereafter, Shapiro and Patrick Connolly left respondent's house to view the laboratory which was located in the Connolly house on Whidbey Island. At the house, Shapiro observed an empty bottle bearing the chemical label phenyl-2-propanone.

By prearrangement, Shapiro returned to the Connolly house on December 9, 1969, to supply 100 grams of propanone and observe the manufacturing process. When he arrived he observed Patrick Connolly and the respondent cutting up pieces of aluminum foil and placing them in a large flask. There was testimony that some of the foil pieces accidentally fell on the floor and were picked up by the respondent and Shapiro and put into the flask. Thereafter, Patrick Connolly added all of the necessary chemicals, including the propanone brought by Shapiro, to make two batches of methamphetamine. The manufacturing process having been completed the following morning, Shapiro was given one-half of the drug and respondent kept the remainder. Shapiro offered to buy, and the respondent agreed to sell, part of the remainder for $60.

About a month later, Shapiro returned to the Connolly house and met with Patrick Connolly to ask if he was still interested in their "business arrangement." Connolly replied that he was interested but that he had recently obtained two additional bottles of phenyl-2-propanone and would not be finished with them for a couple of days. He provided some additional methamphetamine to Shapiro at that time. Three days later Shapiro returned to the Connolly house with a search warrant and, among other items, seized an empty 500-gram bottle of propanone and a 100-gram bottle, not the one he had provided, that was partially filled with the chemical.

There was testimony at the trial of respondent and Patrick Connolly that phenyl-2-propanone was generally difficult to obtain. At the request of the Bureau of Narcotics and Dangerous Drugs, some chemical supply firms had voluntarily ceased selling the chemical.

At the close of the evidence, and after receiving the District Judge's standard entrapment instruction, the jury found the respondent guilty on all counts charged. On appeal, the respondent conceded that the jury could have found him predisposed to commit the offenses, 459 F. 2d, at 672, but argued that on the facts presented there was entrapment as a matter of law. The Court of Appeals agreed, although it did not find the District Court had misconstrued or misapplied the traditional standards governing the entrapment defense. Rather, the court in effect expanded the traditional notion of entrapment, which focuses on the predisposition of the defendant, to mandate dismissal of a criminal prosecution whenever the court determines that there has been "an intolerable degree of governmental participation in the criminal enterprise." In this case the court decided that the conduct of the agent in supplying a scarce ingredient essential for the manufacture of a controlled substance established that defense.

This new defense was held to rest on either of two alternative theories. One theory is based on two lower court decisions which have found entrapment, regardless of predisposition, whenever the government supplies contraband to the defendants. United States v. Bueno, 447 F. 2d 903 (CA5 1971); United States v. Chisum, 312 F. Supp. 1307 (CD Cal. 1970). The second theory, a nonentrapment rationale, is based on a recent Ninth Circuit decision that reversed a conviction because a government investigator was so enmeshed in the criminal activity that the prosecution of the defendants was held to be repugnant to the American criminal justice system. Greene v. United States, 454 F. 2d 783 (CA9 1971). The court below held that these two rationales constitute the same defense, and that only the label distinguishes them. In any event, it held that "[b]oth theories are premised on fundamental concepts of due process and evince the reluctance of the judiciary to countenance 'overzealous law enforcement.'" 459 F. 2d, at 674, quoting Sherman v. United States, 356 U.S. 369, 381 (1958) (FRANKFURTER, J., concurring in result).

This Court first recognized and applied the entrapment defense in Sorrells v. United States, 287 U.S. 435 (1932). In Sorrells, a federal prohibition agent visited the defendant while posing as a tourist and engaged him in conversation about their common war experiences. After gaining the defendant's confidence, the agent asked for some liquor, was twice refused, but upon asking a third time the defendant finally capitulated, and was subsequently prosecuted for violating the National Prohibition Act.

MR. CHIEF JUSTICE HUGHES, speaking for the Court, held that as a matter of statutory construction the defense of entrapment should have been available to the defendant. Under the theory propounded by the Chief Justice, the entrapment defense prohibits law enforcement officers from instigating a criminal act by persons "otherwise innocent in order to lure them to its commission and to punish them." 287 U.S., at 448. Thus, the thrust of the entrapment defense was held to focus on the intent or predisposition of the defendant to commit the crime. "[I]f the defendant seeks acquittal by reason of entrapment he cannot complain of an appropriate and searching inquiry into his own conduct and predisposition as bearing upon that issue." Id., at 451.

MR. JUSTICE ROBERTS concurred but was of the view "that courts must be closed to the trial of a crime instigated by the government's own agents." Id., at 459. The difference in the view of the majority and the concurring opinions is that in the former the inquiry focuses on the predisposition of the defendant, whereas in the latter the inquiry focuses on whether the government "instigated the crime."

In 1958 the Court again considered the theory underlying the entrapment defense and expressly reaffirmed the view expressed by the Sorrells majority. Sherman v. United States, supra. In Sherman the defendant was convicted of selling narcotics to a Government informer. As in Sorrells, it appears that the Government agent gained the confidence of the defendant and, despite initial reluctance, the defendant finally acceded to the repeated importunings of the agent to commit the criminal act. On the basis of Sorrells, this Court reversed the affirmance of the defendant's conviction.

In affirming the theory underlying Sorrells, MR. CHIEF JUSTICE WARREN for the Court, held that "[t]o determine whether entrapment has been established, a line must be drawn between the trap for the unwary innocent and the trap for the unwary criminal." 356 U.S., at 372. MR. JUSTICE FRANKFURTER stated in an opinion concurring in the result that he believed MR. JUSTICE ROBERTS had the better view in Sorrells and would have framed the question to be asked in an entrapment defense in terms of "whether the police conduct revealed in the particular case falls below standards... for the proper use of governmental power." Id., at 382.

In the instant case, respondent asks us to reconsider the theory of the entrapment defense as it is set forth in the majority opinions in Sorrells and Sherman. His principal contention is that the defense should rest on constitutional grounds. He argues that the level of Shapiro's involvement in the manufacture of the methamphetamine was so high that a criminal prosecution for the drug's manufacture violates the fundamental principles of due process. The respondent contends that the same factors that led this Court to apply the exclusionary rule to illegal searches and seizures, Weeks v. United States, 232 U.S. 383 (1914); Mapp v. Ohio, 367 U.S. 643 (1961), and confessions, Miranda v. Arizona, 384 U.S. 436 (1966), should be considered here. But he would have the Court go further in deterring undesirable official conduct by requiring that any prosecution be barred absolutely because of the police involvement in criminal activity. The analogy is imperfect in any event, for the principal reason behind the adoption of the exclusionary rule was the Government's "failure to observe its own laws." Mapp v. Ohio, supra, at 659. Unlike the situations giving rise to the holdings in Mapp and Miranda, the Government's conduct here violated no independent constitutional right of the respondent. Nor did Shapiro violate any federal statute or rule or commit any crime in infiltrating the respondent's drug enterprise.

Respondent would overcome this basic weakness in his analogy to the exclusionary rule cases by having the Court adopt a rigid constitutional rule that would preclude any prosecution when it is shown that the criminal conduct would not have been possible had not an undercover agent "supplied an indispensable means to the commission of the crime that could not have been obtained otherwise, through legal or illegal channels." Even if we were to surmount the difficulties attending the notion that due process of law can be embodied in fixed rules, and those attending respondent's particular formulation, the rule he proposes would not appear to be of significant benefit to him. For, on the record presented, it appears that he cannot fit within the terms of the very rule he proposes.

The record discloses that although the propanone was difficult to obtain, it was by no means impossible. The defendants admitted making the drug both before and after those batches made with the propanone supplied by Shapiro. Shapiro testified that he saw an empty bottle labeled phenyl-2-propanone on his first visit to the laboratory on December 7, 1969. And when the laboratory was searched pursuant to a search warrant on January 10, 1970, two additional bottles labeled phenyl-2-propanone were seized. Thus, the facts in the record amply demonstrate that the propanone used in the illicit manufacture of methamphetamine not only *could* have been obtained without the intervention of Shapiro but was in fact obtained by these defendants.

While we may some day be presented with a situation in which the conduct of law enforcement agents is so outrageous that due process principles would absolutely bar the government from invoking judicial processes to obtain a conviction, cf. Rochin v. California, 342 U.S. 165 (1952), the instant case is distinctly not of that breed. Shapiro's contribution of propanone to the criminal enterprise already in process was scarcely objectionable. The chemical is by itself a harmless substance and its possession is legal. While the Government may have been seeking to make it more difficult for drug rings, such as that of which respondent was a member, to obtain the chemical, the evidence described above shows that it nonetheless was obtainable. The law enforcement conduct here stops far short of violating that "fundamental fairness, shocking to the universal sense of justice," mandated by the Due Process Clause of the Fifth Amendment. Kinsella v. United States ex rel. Singleton, 361 U.S. 234, 246 (1960).

The illicit manufacture of drugs is not a sporadic, isolated criminal incident, but a continuing, though illegal, business enterprise. In order to obtain convictions for illegally manufacturing drugs, the gathering of evidence of past unlawful conduct frequently proves to be an all but impossible task. Thus in drug-related offenses law enforcement personnel have turned to one of the only practicable means of detection: the infiltration of drug rings and a limited participation in their unlawful present practices. Such infiltration is a recognized and permissible means of investigation; if that be so, then the supply of some item of value that the drug ring requires must, as a general rule, also be permissible. For an agent will not be taken into the confidence of the illegal entrepreneurs unless he has something of value to offer them. Law enforcement tactics such as this can hardly be said to violate "fundamental fairness" or "shocking to the universal sense of justice," Kinsella, supra.

Respondent also urges, as an alternative to his constitutional argument, that we broaden the nonconstitutional defense of entrapment in order to sustain the judgment of the Court of Appeals. This Court's opinions in Sorrells v. United States, supra, and Sherman v. United States, supra, held that the principal element in the defense of entrapment was the defendant's predisposition to commit the crime. Respondent conceded in the Court of Appeals, as well he might, "that he may have harbored a predisposition to commit the charged offenses." 459 F. 2d, at 672. Yet he argues that the jury's refusal to find entrapment under the charge submitted to it by the trial court should be overturned and the views of JUSTICES ROBERTS and FRANKFURTER, in Sorrells and Sherman, respectively, which make the essential element of the defense turn on the type and degree of governmental conduct, be adopted as the law.

We decline to overrule these cases. Sorrells is a precedent of long standing that has already been once reexamined in Sherman and implicitly there reaffirmed. Since the defense is not of a constitutional dimension, Congress may address itself to the question and adopt any substantive definition of the defense that it may find desirable.

Critics of the rule laid down in Sorrells and Sherman have suggested that its basis in the implied intent of Congress is largely fictitious, and have pointed to what they conceive to be the anomalous difference between the treatment of a defendant who is solicited by a private individual and one who is entrapped by a government agent. Questions have been likewise raised as to whether "predisposition" can be factually established with the requisite degree of certainty. Arguments such as these, while not devoid of appeal, have been twice previously made to this Court, and twice rejected by it, first in Sorrells and then in Sherman.

We believe that at least equally cogent criticism has been made of the concurring views in these cases. Commenting in Sherman on MR. JUSTICE ROBERTS' position in Sorrells that "although the defendant could claim that the Government had induced him to commit the crime, the Government could not reply by showing that the defendant's criminal conduct was due to his own readiness and not to the persuasion of government agents," Sherman v. United States, 356 U.S., at 376–377, MR. CHIEF JUSTICE WARREN quoted the observation of JUDGE LEARNED HAND in an earlier stage of that proceeding:

> "'Indeed, it would seem probable that, if there were no reply [to the claim of inducement], it would be impossible ever to secure convictions of any offences which consist of transactions that are carried on in secret.' United States v. Sherman, 200 F. 2d 880, 882." Sherman v. United States, 356 U.S., at 377, n. 7.

Nor does it seem particularly desirable for the law to grant complete immunity from prosecution to one who himself planned to commit a crime, and then committed it, simply because government undercover agents subjected him to inducements which might have seduced a hypothetical individual who was not so predisposed. We are content to leave the matter where it was left by the Court in Sherman:

> "The function of law enforcement is the prevention of crime and the apprehension of criminals. Manifestly, that function does not include the manufacturing of crime. Criminal activity is such that stealth and strategy are necessary weapons in the arsenal of the police officer. However, 'A different question is presented when the criminal design originates with the officials of the Government, and they implant in the mind of an innocent person the disposition to commit the alleged offense and induce its commission in order that they may prosecute.'" Id., at 372, quoting Sorrells v. United States, 287 U.S., at 442.

Several decisions of the United States district courts and courts of appeals have undoubtedly gone beyond this Court's opinions in Sorrells and Sherman in order to bar prosecutions because of what they thought to be, for want of a better term, "overzealous law enforcement." But the defense of entrapment enunciated in those opinions was not intended to give the federal judiciary a "chancellor's foot" veto over law enforcement practices of which it did not approve. The execution of the federal laws under our Constitution is confided primarily to the Executive Branch of the Government subject to applicable constitutional and statutory limitations and to judicially fashioned rules to enforce those limitations. We think that the decision of the Court of Appeals in this case quite unnecessarily introduces an unmanageably subjective standard which is contrary to the holdings of this Court in Sorrells and Sherman.

Those cases establish that entrapment is a relatively limited defense. It is rooted, not in any authority of the Judicial Branch to dismiss prosecutions for what it feels to have been "overzealous law enforcement," but instead in the notion that Congress could not have intended criminal punishment for a defendant who has committed all the elements of a proscribed offense, but was induced to commit them by the Government.

Sorrells and Sherman both recognize "that the fact that officers or employees of the Government merely afford opportunities or facilities for the commission of the offense does not defeat the prosecution," 287 U.S., at 441; 356 U.S., at 372. Nor will the mere fact of deceit defeat a prosecution, see, e.g., Lewis v. United States, 385 U.S. 206, 208–209 (1966), for there are circumstances when the use of deceit is the only practicable law enforcement technique available. It is only when the Government's deception actually implants the criminal design in the mind of the defendant that the defense of entrapment comes into play.

Respondent's concession in the Court of Appeals that the jury finding as to predisposition was supported by the evidence is, therefore, fatal to his claim of entrapment. He was an active participant in an illegal drug manufacturing enterprise which began before the Government agent appeared on the scene, and continued after the Government agent had left the scene. He was, in the words of Sherman, supra, not an "unwary innocent" but an "unwary criminal." The Court of Appeals was wrong, we believe, when it sought to broaden the principle laid down in Sorrells and Sherman. Its judgment is therefore

Reversed.

Hampton, aka Byers *v.* United States

425 U.S. 484, 96 S.Ct. 1646, 48 L.Ed. 2d. 113 (1976)

CERTIORARI TO THE UNITED STATES COURT OF APPEALS FOR THE EIGHTH CIRCUIT

Argued December 1, 1975—Decided April 27, 1976

. . .

MR. JUSTICE REHNQUIST announced the judgment of the Court in an opinion in which THE CHIEF JUSTICE and MR. JUSTICE WHITE join.

This case presents the question of whether a defendant may be convicted for the sale of contraband which he procured from a Government informant or agent. The Court of Appeals for the Eighth Circuit held he could be, and we agree.

I

Petitioner was convicted of two counts of distributing heroin in violation of 21 U.S.C. § 841 (a) (1) in the United States District Court for the Eastern District of Missouri and sentenced to concurrent terms of five years' imprisonment (suspended). The case arose from two sales of heroin by petitioner to agents of the Federal Drug Enforcement Administration (DEA) in St. Louis on February 25 and 26, 1974. The sales were arranged by one Hutton, who was a pool-playing acquaintance of petitioner at the Pud bar in St. Louis and also a DEA informant.

According to the Government's witnesses in late February 1974, Hutton and petitioner were shooting pool at the Pud when petitioner, after observing "track" (needle) marks on Hutton's arms told Hutton that he needed money and knew where he could get some heroin. Hutton responded that he could find a buyer and petitioner suggested that he "get in touch with those people." Hutton then called DEA Agent Terry Sawyer and arranged a sale for 10 p.m. on February 25.

At the appointed time, Hutton and petitioner went to a prearranged meeting place and were met by Agent Sawyer and DEA Agent McDowell, posing as narcotics dealers. Petitioner produced a tinfoil packet from his cap and turned it over to the agents who tested it, pronounced it "okay," and negotiated a price of $145 which was paid to petitioner. Before they parted, petitioner told Sawyer that he could obtain larger quantities of heroin and gave Sawyer a phone number where he could be reached.

The next day Sawyer called petitioner and arranged for another "buy" that afternoon. Petitioner got Hutton to go along and they met the agents again near where they had been the previous night.

They all entered the agents' car, and petitioner again produced a tinfoil packet from his cap. The agents again field-tested it and pronounced it satisfactory. Petitioner then asked for $500 which Agent Sawyer said he would get from the trunk. Sawyer got out and opened the trunk which was a signal to other agents to move in and arrest petitioner, which they did.

Petitioner's version of events was quite different. According to him, in response to his statement that he was short of cash, Hutton said that he had a friend who was a pharmacist who could produce a nonnarcotic counterfeit drug which would give the same reaction as heroin. Hutton proposed selling this drug to gullible acquaintances who would be led to believe they were buying heroin. Petitioner testified that they successfully duped one buyer with this fake drug and that the sales which led to the arrest were solicited by petitioner in an effort to profit further from this ploy.

Petitioner contended that he neither intended to sell, nor knew that he was dealing in heroin and that all of the drugs he sold were supplied by Hutton. His account was at least partially disbelieved by the jury which was instructed that in order to convict petitioner they must find that the Government proved "that the defendant knowingly did an act which the law forbids, purposely intending to violate the law." Thus the guilty verdict necessarily implies that the jury rejected petitioner's claim that he did not know the substance was heroin, and petitioner himself admitted both soliciting and carrying out sales. The only relevance of his version of the facts, then, lies in his having requested an instruction embodying that version. He did not request a standard entrapment instruction but he did request the following:

> "The defendant asserts that he was the victim of entrapment as to the crimes charged in the indictment.
>
> "If you find that the defendant's sales of narcotics were sales of narcotics supplied to him by an informer in the employ of or acting on behalf of the government, then you must acquit the defendant because the law as a matter of policy forbids his conviction in such a case.

> "Furthermore, under this particular defense, you need not consider the predisposition of the defendant to commit the offense charged, because if the governmental involvement through its informer reached the point that I have just defined in your own minds, then the predisposition of the defendant would not matter." Brief for Petitioner 9.

The trial court refused the instruction and petitioner was found guilty. He appealed to the United States Court of Appeals for the Eighth Circuit, claiming that if the jury had believed that the drug was supplied by Hutton he should have been acquitted. The Court of Appeals rejected this argument and affirmed the conviction, relying on our opinion in United States v. Russell, 411 U.S. 423 (1973). 507 F. 2d 832 (1974).

II

In Russell we held that the statutory defense of entrapment was not available where it was conceded that a Government agent supplied a necessary ingredient in the manufacture of an illicit drug. We reaffirmed the principle of Sorrells v. United States, 287 U.S. 435 (1932), and Sherman v. United States, 356 U.S. 369 (1958), that the entrapment defense "focus[es] on the intent or predisposition of the defendant to commit the crime," Russell, supra, at 429, rather than upon the conduct of the Government's agents. We ruled out the possibility that the defense of entrapment could ever be based upon governmental misconduct in a case, such as this one, where the predisposition of the defendant to commit the crime was established.

In holding that "[i]t is only when the Government's deception actually implants the criminal design in the mind of the defendant that the defense of entrapment comes into play," 411 U.S., at 436, we, of course, rejected the contrary view of the dissents in that case and the concurrences in Sorrells and Sherman. In view of these holdings, petitioner correctly recognizes that his case does not qualify as one involving "entrapment" at all. He instead relies on the language in Russell that "we may some day be presented with a situation in which the conduct of law enforcement agents is so outrageous that due process principles would absolutely bar the government from invoking judicial processes to obtain a conviction, cf. Rochin v. California, 342 U.S. 165 (1952)...." 411 U.S., at 431–432.

In urging that this case involves a violation of his due process rights, petitioner misapprehends the meaning of the quoted language in Russell, supra. Admittedly petitioner's case is different from Russell's but the difference is one of degree, not of kind. In Russell the ingredient supplied by the Government agent was a legal drug which the defendants demonstrably could have obtained from other sources besides the Government. Here the drug which the Government informant allegedly supplied to petitioner both was illegal and constituted the corpus delicti for the sale of which the petitioner was convicted. The Government obviously played a more significant role in enabling petitioner to sell contraband in this case than it did in Russell.

But in each case the Government agents were acting in concert with the defendant, and in each case either the jury found or the defendant conceded that he was predisposed to commit the crime for which he was convicted. The remedy of the criminal defendant with respect to the acts of Government agents, which, far from being resisted, are encouraged by him, lies solely in the defense of entrapment. But, as noted, petitioner's conceded predisposition rendered this defense unavailable to him.

To sustain petitioner's contention here would run directly contrary to our statement in Russell that the defense of entrapment is not intended "to give the federal judiciary a 'chancellor's foot' veto over law enforcement practices of which it did not approve. The execution of the federal laws under our Constitution is confided primarily to the Executive Branch of the Government, subject to applicable constitutional and statutory limitations and to judicially fashioned rules to enforce those limitations." 411 U.S., at 435.

The limitations of the Due Process Clause of the Fifth Amendment come into play only when the Government activity in question violates some protected right of the *defendant*. Here, as we have noted, the police, the Government informer, and the defendant acted in concert with one another. If the result of the governmental activity is to "implant in the mind of an innocent person the disposition to commit the alleged offense and induce its commission . . . ," Sorrells, supra, at 442, the defendant is protected by the defense of entrapment. If the police engage in illegal activity in concert with a defendant beyond the scope of their duties the remedy lies, not in freeing the equally culpable defendant, but in prosecuting the police under the applicable provisions of state or federal law. See O'Shea v. Littleton, 414 U.S. 488, 503 (1974); Imbler v. Pachtman, 424 U.S. 409, 428–429 (1976). But the police conduct here no more deprived defendant of any right secured to him by the United States Constitution than did the police conduct in Russell deprive Russell of any rights.

Affirmed.

CHAPTER 14

Contents

Civil Rights Cases and Legislation

§ 14.1 Introduction

As has been mentioned in Section 11.1, the phrase "civil rights" is very difficult to define. It is perhaps an abbreviation of many relationships among individuals and among groups of individuals. Generally, one might say that civil rights in the United States refer to freedom of action that government cannot take away from a person. Another way that it might be expressed is that certain rights are so fundamental that government may not interfere with them.

The reader will remember Section 1.19 (supra) where it was pointed out that many states refused to ratify the Constitution unless a bill of rights was to be included in the document. They demanded that there be a guarantee of freedom of religion, speech, jury trials, freedom from unreasonable searches and seizures, and a guarantee to life, liberty, and property as well as a protection against excessive bail. Many states ratified the Constitution upon the understanding that a bill of rights be adopted containing the aforementioned basic principles.

The basic document of the Constitution had limitations against the government which were included to prevent abuses of individual freedom. Most fundamental of these is found in Article 1, Section 9, second paragraph:

> *The Privilege of the Writ of Habeas Corpus shall not be suspended unless in Cases of Rebellion or Invasion the public Safety may require it.*

The writ of habeas corpus is a court order directed against a person who has another person in the first person's custody and control. It orders the controlling person to bring the controlled person before a court so that the court may determine the legality of the second person's detention. It is usually directed against a keeper or principal officer of a correctional facility, such as a warden of a prison or a commissioner of correction. It is also used in family law where one parent has custody of an infant and the other parent wants a court determination as to whether the infant shall remain in the custody of the custodian parent. It is a highly valued writ and some states levy large sanctions against jurists who refuse to issue such a writ where the legality of the confinement has not been previously determined by habeas corpus. N.Y.—Civil Practice Law & Rules § 7003.

If, after the issuance of a habeas corpus writ, a judge determines that the detainee is being held in violation of law, the person is released from custody immediately. On the other hand, if it is determined that the detention is lawful, the detained person may be retained in custody to await a trial, or to finish his/her sentence, or bail conditions may be ordered.

Article 1, Section 9, Paragraph 3, of the United States Constitution reads:

> *No Bill of Attainder or ex post facto Law shall be passed.*

A Bill of Attainder has been defined as a legislative act in any form, that applies "either to named individuals or to easily ascertained members of a group in such a way as to inflict punishment on them without a judicial trial." United States v. Brown, 381 U.S. 437, 448, 85 S.Ct. 1707, 14 L.Ed. 484 (1965).

An ex post facto Law has been defined as:

> ...every law that makes an action done before the passing of the law and which was innocent when done to be criminal and punishable; every law that aggravates a crime or makes it greater than when it was committed; every law that changes and inflicts a greater punishment; and every law that alters the legal rules of evidence, and requires less, or different testimony than the law required at the time of the commission of the offense in order to convict the offender. [Cardwell v. State (Tex.), 171 S.W.2d 880.]

Ex post facto laws have been held to be applicable only to criminal statutes. Calder v. Bull, 3 U.S.(Dall.) 386, 3 S.Ct. 386, 1 L.Ed. 648 (1798).

Accordingly, if a government taxed a person for engaging in a business after the person had been engaged in this business tax free for six months, it could conceivably be no violation of the constitutional mandate of the proscription against an ex post facto law because this law is not directed to criminal behavior. There may be other remedies available to the taxpayer.

A case that reached the Court dealing with the ex post facto principle occurred in United States v. Lovett, 328 U.S. 303, 66 S.Ct. 1073, 90 L.Ed. 1252 (1946). In that case three government employees were found to have subversive affiliations by the House Un-American Activities Committee. Congress attached a provision to an appropriation bill which stopped salary payments to the three employees and barred them from future employment with the federal government. The Court declared this action unconstitutional as a violation of the Bill of Attainder proscription. It held that this act was an infliction of punishment without a judicial trial. In the instant case, the House of Representatives acted as accuser, trier of the facts, and lastly, as the legislative arm of government, thereby circumventing the checks and balances concept written into the Constitution.

Another ex-post facto case occurred when the Court found a Florida statute unconstitutional where it altered the method that a state's "gain time" for good conduct was applied to inmates who were committed for incarceration before enactment. In WEAVER v. GRAHAM, 450 U.S. 24, 101 S.Ct. 960, 67 L.Ed.2d. 17, 28 Cr.L. 3077 (1981) a state statute reduced gain time that had been available to the petitioner when he was first incarcerated. The Court said that the statute making the punishment more onerous is in violation of the ex-post facto clauses of the Constitution. Article 1 Section 9 and Article 1 Section 10, citing KRING v. MISSOURI, 107 U.S. 221 where the Court said, "So much importance did the Convention attach to [the ex-post facto prohibition] that it is found twice in the Constitution.

As we continue to look at the main body of the Constitution, we see Article III, Section 2, Paragraph 3 where we find:

The trial of all Crimes, except in Cases of Impeachment, shall be by Jury, and such trial shall be held in the State where the said Crimes shall have been committed; but when not committed within any State, the Trial shall be at such Place or Places as the Congress may by Law have directed.

Trials by judges are more likely to be unfair than those which have been tried by a jury of a defendant's peers. It is presumed that the collective reasoning of a group of people listening to arguments of the court adversaries as well as those jurors who might take a position contrary to the colleagues on the jury will result in a higher degree of fairness than the reasoning and judgment of one judge.

In Article IV, Section 2, we find:

The Citizens of each State shall be entitled to all Privileges and Immunities of Citizens in the several States.

This means that a state cannot discriminate against citizens of other states in favor of its own citizens.

Article VI, Section 3, states in part:

...but no religious Test shall ever be required as a Qualification to any Office or public Trust under the United States.

§ 14.2 The Black Person's American Heritage

The early history of the United States with its high theoretical goals of religious freedom, freedom of speech, and the other basic freedoms already alluded to, closed its eyes to the lack of freedom and personal rights afforded to its black inhabitants who were historically referred to as negroes.

The northern industrial states did not require slave labor. On the other hand, the south with its agricultural economic base, devoid of mechanical means of tilling the soil, claimed that its economic existence depended on a slave labor force. Article IV, Section 2, of the Constitution guaranteed the property right of a slaveholder in his slave.

The atrocities committed on the black people during their period of slavery are well known and do not need repeating here. It should be pointed out, however, that there were slave owners who were not despotic and who did care for and treat their charges well.

The political significance of slavery was also treated in Article I, Section 2, Paragraph 3, where each slave was to be counted as three-fifths of a white person for the purpose of apportioning representation in the House of Representatives. The Supreme Court gave approval of slavery in the decision of Dred Scott v. Sandford, 60 U.S. (19 How.) 393, 15 L.Ed. 1222 (1856), where Chief Justice Taney wrote that "... the dark race was a subordinate and inferior class of beings. . . ." It took a war between the states to finally resolve the cleavage of a half-free and half-slave nation.

§ 14.3 Civil Rights Legislation during Reconstruction

Following the Civil War, the task of restoring the nation fell upon Congress. The plight of the black was of greatest priority because southern legislators were passing the "Black Codes" (Section 11.2 supra) which effectively restored the black to his former position as a slave, notwithstanding the passage of the Thirteenth Amendment which was expected to discontinue slavery and involuntary servitude.

With the passage of the Fifteenth Amendment, providing for the right of citizens of the United States to vote regardless of race, color, or previous condition of servitude, along with enforcement powers for this amendment delegated to Congress, the die had been set for equal rights of black and white persons. While, in principle, equal rights were the law of the nation, it is not yet fully realized. Equal opportunities for voting, living conditions, job opportunities, education, and the like have had a long and stormy history.

Although it is not the author's intention to trace the long struggle of the black person in the United States for true emancipation, certain legislative acts are of such importance that to omit them from consideration in a text of this nature would be a disservice to those who labored diligently for their passage and to the black persons of our nation who still are struggling to gain equal rights in all facets of their lives.

§ 14.4 Civil Rights Act of 1875

The Civil Rights Act of 1875 was passed by Congress in an effort to give blacks equal treatment in private accommodations. Section 1 of that law reads as follows:

> That all persons within . . . the United States shall be entitled to the full and equal enjoyment of the accommodations, advantages, facilities, and privileges of inns, public conveyances on land or water, theatres and other places of public amusement; subject only to conditions and limitations established by law, and applicable alike to citizens of every race and color, regardless of any previous condition of servitude.

Section 2 provided for civil and criminal remedies against a person who violated Section 1 of this law.

It was not long after its passage that the Court was called upon to rule on its constitutionality. In 1883 the case of Robinson and wife against the Memphis & Charleston Railroad Co., 109 U.S. 3, 3 S.Ct. 18, 27 L.Ed. 835, came before the Court. It was decided that the law was unconstitutional because the Court said that the act was passed in conformity with the enforcement provision of the Thirteenth Amendment (prohibition of slavery or involuntary servitude) and that the mere inn owner, etc. cannot be justly regarded as imposing any badge of slavery. Thus it is beyond the power of Congress to enact such a law. If any right is violated, the Court said, the aggrieved person should seek his redress under the laws of the state. Naturally, the aggrieved person was thus without any remedy.

§ 14.5 Civil Rights Act of 1964

The civil rights gains of the 1950s and early 1960s were won in the Court by virtue of the Court's new interpretation of the Fourteenth Amendment. The sit-ins of the early 1960s were a successful publicity campaign that shocked the nation. While the Fourteenth Amendment had been directed at government interference with a person's civil rights, it was left to Congress to advance the cause further by the enactment of the Civil Rights Act of 1964. It contained eleven sections which dealt with such categories as voting rights, school desegregation, use of public facilities, equal employment opportunities, nondiscrimination in federally assisted programs, and other items directed to the extinguishment of segregation in the life of the nation.

Title II created a new federal right which had been declared unconstitutional in Robinson and wife v. Memphis & Charleston Railroad Co. (Section 14.4 supra), i.e., the right of all persons to enjoy full and equal use of certain places of public accommodations without discriminating on the ground of race, color, religion, or national origin. (42 U.S.C. § 2000a.)

The act did not cover the admission policies of privately run swimming pools, golf courses, skating rinks, tennis facilities unless it was an integral part of a hotel or other covered establishment, or it maintained on the premises a snack bar or refreshment stand serving food which had traveled in interstate commerce, or leased or sold to patrons sporting equipment which originated out of state, nor did it cover many other types of private businesses unless it was located in an area where segregation codes were still law. For a more detailed analysis, the student is referred to 42 U.S.C. 2000 et seq.

It is noteworthy that the act was not a criminal statute and deference is given to state or local remedy, if it is available. If it was not available, the aggrieved could file suit immediately for injunctive relief in a federal court. The District Court would have the option to first refer the complaint to a community relations service in an effort to secure voluntary compliance. Failing this, an injunction could be issued with contempt of court remedy available for noncompliance with the injunction.

The 1964 Civil Rights Law did not provide for damages to be awarded to an aggrieved person. The most retribution that one might expect under that law was a fine and jail sentence to the offending party. However, there was a remedy available to these people. 42 U.S.C. 1983 turned out to be that remedy.

§ 14.6 Voting Rights Act of 1965

The Voting Rights Act of 1965 was designed to eliminate voting discrimination where it had been most flagrant. There was a widespread practice in some states to require an applicant to pass literacy and other tests in order to be qualified to vote. The areas covered "for which there was evidence of actual voting discrimination"—Alabama, Louisiana, Mississippi, Georgia, South Carolina and much of North Carolina—shared "two characteristics incorporated by Congress into the coverage formula." The Court held that it was permissible to impose the new remedies on the few remaining states and political subdivisions covered by the formula, at least in the absence of proof that they have been free of substantial voting discrimination in recent years. South Carolina v. Katzenbach, 383 U.S. 301, 86 S.Ct. 803, 15 L.Ed.2d 769 (1966).

§ 14.7 Civil Weapon Available for Violations of Civil Rights

As the Due Process Clause of the Fourteenth Amendment continues to be interpreted by the Court in a way that almost every violation of the Bill of Rights has been incorporated into state law, it becomes increasingly necessary for state personnel and especially state law enforcement persons to be aware of the laws to prevent a devastating damage action against them. One of the weapons which is being used by aggrieved persons is a civil action instituted in the federal court under authority of 42 U.S.C. 1983.

This statute reads as follows:

> Every person who, under color of any statute, ordinance, regulation, custom, or usage, of any State or Territory, subjects, or causes to be subjected, any citizen of the United States or any other person within the jurisdiction thereof to the deprivation of any rights, privileges, or immunities secured by the Constitution and laws, shall be liable to the party injured in any action at law, suit in equity, or other proper proceeding for redress.

The phrase "under color of any statute, ordinance, regulation, custom or usage" has been applied to police officers who misuse their authority. A state could not be expected to violate the statute in the present-day setting. However, a police officer acting on his/her own could do so while acting under the guise of a police officer.

The statute, along with 18 U.S.C. 241 and 18 U.S.C. 242, was adopted in 1871. It was initially known as the Ku Klux Klan Act and was designed to afford a federal remedy to aggrieved persons who suffered constitutional deprivations at the hands of the Ku Klux Klan. The Klan claimed as its members the leading citizens of the community as well as the lowest and, hence, state law enforcement was not interested in protecting persons who were the subject of Klan action. Nevertheless, the law was rarely invoked successfully until 1941 when the Court decided United States v. Classic, 313 U.S. 299, 61 S.Ct. 1031, 85 L.Ed. 1368, wherein the Court said, "Misuse of power, possessed by virtue of a state law and made possible only because the wrongdoer is clothed with authority of state law, is action taken 'under color of state law.'" Accordingly, the stage was set for a meaningful redress of an aggrieved person's claim. A line of cases then developed to hold the officer accountable in attempts of circumvention of the law. For example, an officer cannot escape liability by being dressed in plain clothes and while riding in an unmarked car. Catlette v. United States, 132 F.2d 902 (4th Circ. 1943). Of utmost importance to the officer should be the knowledge that the Court has held that neither the city (employer) nor the police department of which he is a member is liable in damages for the officer's behavior. The officer is the one who must pay the judgment if it is found that there is liability.

Federal law enforcement agents are not subject to this statute.

It was not until the 1960s, however, that this law was rediscovered and it became popular to sue state law enforcement persons. In Monroe v. Pape, 365 U.S. 167, 81 S.Ct. 473, 5 L.Ed.2d 492 (1963), the plaintiffs, husband and wife along with their children, had gone to bed foı the night when thirteen Chicago policemen broke into their apartment during the early morning hours. The plaintiffs were caused to get out of bed and to stand naked while the officers ransacked every room, ripping mattress covers and emptying drawers. The husband was then taken to the police station and held on open charges for ten hours during which time he was questioned about a murder which had taken place two days prior to the arrest. He was not taken before a magistrate even though one was available and he was denied contact with his family or an attorney. The policemen had no search warrant for the initial intrusion and no written charges were lodged against him. He was released after the long interrogation. His action against the thirteen officers was successful.

If, however, an officer acts in good faith and a law under which he acted is later declared to be unconstitutional, the officer cannot be held liable for damages. Pierson v. Ray, 386 U.S. 547, 87 S.Ct. 1213, 18 L.Ed.2d 288 (1967).

In a case brought under 42 U.S.C. 1983, the petitioners sought pecuniary as well as injunctive relief. The Court held that the responsible authorities were not found to have affirmatively sanctioned any constitutional deprivations, and thus no equitable relief would be granted. Rizzo v. Goode, 423 U.S. 362, 96 S.Ct. 598, 46 L.Ed.2d 561 (1976).

It should be noted that pursuant to Imbler v. Pachtman, 424 U.S. 409, 94 S.Ct. 984, 47 L.Ed.2d 128 (1975), the court held that prosecutors and judges are not subject to suits under this statute but they are liable under 18 U.S.C. 241 and 18 U.S.C. 242.

Later, Monell v. Department of Social Services, 436 U.S. 658, 98 S.Ct. 2018, 56 L.Ed.2d 611 (1978), overruled Monroe v. Pape, 365 U.S. 167, 81 S.Ct. 473, 5 L.Ed.2d 492 (1961). In the Monell case, the Court permitted plaintiffs to sue local government for monetary, declaratory, or injunctive relief where the action was grounded on allegations of an unconstitutional policy, statement, ordinance, regulation, or decision officially adopted by the body's officers or where constitutional deprivation was visited on the plaintiffs pursuant to governmental "custom" even though such custom had not received formal approval through the body's decision-making channel. It further held that local governmental officials were "persons" under Section 1983 in those cases where local government would be able to be sued in its own name. A municipality could not be held liable under Section 1983 solely on a respondeat superior theory and stare decisis did not bar overruling of Monroe v. Pape.

In SMITH v. WADE, —U.S.—, —S.Ct.—, —L.Ed.2d.—, 33 Cr.L. 3013 (1983), a prison guard was found liable for punitive damages where he was found to be guilty of gross negligence, or egregarious failure to protect a youthful inmate from harassment, beating and sexual assault.

An interesting case involving a police officer's liability arose in HARING v. PROSISE, 462 U.S. 306, 103 S.Ct. 2368, 76 L.Ed.2d. 595, (1983). In that case a defendant pleaded guilty to a charge of manufacturing a controlled substance. At the hearing, one of the arresting officers testified regarding the search of the defendant's apartment that led to the discovery of the contraband material prior to their obtaining a search warrant. No objection was made at the time of trial to the search but while defendant was confined, he filed a pro se action for damages under 42 USC 1983. The Court held that even though the defendant made no objection to the search at the time of trial or sentencing, he was not barred from prosecuting the action later if it was not previously litigated, even though Virginia had a collateral estoppel policy which would bar his subsequent civil challenge to police conduct. The author recommends that in cases where a plea is negotiated, if there is any possible civil liability on the part of law enforcement personnel, that an agreed statement be recorded in open court that the state, city, county and village, its officers employees and/or agents are to be relieved of any civil or criminal liability in connection with the search, arrest and/or confinement of the defendant, as a condition for the acceptance of the plea by the presiding judge.

BRANDON v. HOLT, —U.S.—, 105 S.Ct. 873, 83 L.Ed.2d. 878 (1985) appears to have modified MONELL (supra). In the BRANDON v. HOLT case, the Director of Police of the Memphis Police Department was named as a defendant in a civil rights action under 42 U.S.C. 1983. The lower courts rejected plaintiff's contention that the suit against the Director of Police was being brought against him in his representative capacity. However, the United States Supreme Court held. The City was not named as a defendant because the complaint was filed before MONELL v. PAPE (supra). There is a distinction between suing a government official in his individual capacity and suing him in a representative capacity. In this case he was being sued in a representative capacity and thus a judgment against a public servant "in his official capacity" imposes liability on the entity that he represents.

In OKLAHOMA CITY v. TUTTLE, 37 Cr.L. 3067 (1985) the Court held that a city could not be held liable for a 42 U.S.C. 1983 violation by a single incident of unusual excessive use of force by a police officer.

Municipalities sued for damages under 42 U.S.C. 1983 for constitutional violations are not entitled to qualified immunity on the good faith of their officials. OWENS v. CITY OF INDEPENDENCE, 445 U.S. 622, 100 S.Ct. 1398, 63 L.Ed.2d. 673, reh den, 446 U.S. 993, 100 S.Ct. 2979, 64 L.Ed.2d. 850, 27 Cr.L. 3047 (1980). This was a case where the petitioner, a Chief of Police of Independence, Missouri was dismissed by the City Manager without notice of reasons, charged, that his dismissal was without a hearing in violation of his constitutional rights to procedural and substantive due process in violation of his constitutional rights. The petitioner brought an action under 42 USC 1983 against city officials and the City. The District Court entered judgement for respondents. The Court of Appeals affirmed saying although the petitioner's Fourteenth Amendment rights were violated all respondents were entitled to qualified immunity from liability based on the good faith of the officials involved. The Supreme Court reversed.

In CARLSON v. GREEN, 454 U.S. 944, 102 S.Ct. 484, 70 L.Ed.2d. 254, reh den 454 U.S. 1093, 102 S.Ct. 661, 70 L.Ed.2d. 633. (1980) Same case below, 649 F.2d. 285 the Court held that a BIVENS v. SIX UNKNOWN FEDERAL NARCOTICS AGENTS, 403 U.S. 388, remedy was available to a mother whose son had died in a federal prison in Indiana after he had suffered personal injuries while in prison and petitioner claimed that her son's Eighth Amendment rights were violated by prison officials by failing to give him proper medical attention. She asserted jurisdiction under 28 USC Section 1331(a). In this case, there were additional jurisdiction problems in that the damages were limited to that provided by Indiana's survivorship and wrongful death laws which the trial court said was insufficient to meet Section 1331(a)'s $10,000 jurisdictional amount requirement. The Court of Appeals reversed, saying that the federal common law (Bivens) allows survival of the action. The Supreme Court affirmed.

The case of STONE v. POWELL, 428 U.S. 465, 96 S.Ct. 3037, 49 L.Ed.2d. 1067, 19 Cr.L. 3333 (1976) prevented a state prisoner from bringing a federal habeas corpus challenge to an adverse state court ruling on a motion to suppress unconstitutionally seized evidence when the state courts had a full and fair hearing.

In ALLEN v. CURRY, 452 U.S. 965, 101 S.Ct. 3118, 69 L.Ed.2d. 977, 28 Cr.L. 3009 (1980) the defendant had made a motion in a Missouri court to suppress evidence. The motion was denied and he was later convicted. No assertion was made that he was denied a full and fair hearing in state court and he was thus barred from federal habeas corpus relief. He brought an action for damages under Title 42 Section 1983 and the defense claimed that the matter of constitutionality was res judicata in the state court and that the Federal District Court should dismiss the case based on the theory of collateral estopple. The two lower courts disagreed on this issue. The Supreme Court granted certiorari and agreed with the prosecution.

Punitive damages are usually incorporated into a statute to cause the potential wrongdoer to think at least a second time when the perpetrator is about to commit an offense. It is used as an additional deterrent to prevent violations of law. Title 42 Section 1983 of the United States Code provides for punitive damages against an offender with the deterrent effect in mind. The question then arose as to whether this was to apply to a Municipality as well as an individual who had been found liable under this statute.

In the case of CITY OF NEWPORT ET AL v. FACT CONCERTS, INC. and MARVIN LERMAN, 453 U.S. 247, 101 S.Ct. 2748, 69 L.Ed.2d. 616, 29 Cr.L. 3105 (1981) after disposing of procedural questions, which are not relevant to our studies, the Court held that considerations of public policy do not support exposing municipalities to punitive damages for malicious or reckless conduct of its officials.

The state is obligated to provide counsel for indigents charged with a crime pursuant to the constitution and to case law more fully explained in section 11.15 supra. States vary in the methods that they use to implement this requirement. Some use what is called a public defender system or a county advocate office whereby the state pays the salaries and expenses of the public defenders who may or may not be full time employees of the state. Others utilize legal aid societies that are partially supported by private contributions and partially by government subsidy. Where two or more defendants are involved in the same crime, there is always a possibility of a conflict of interest, if one attorney represents both or all defendants. In such a case, the usual procedure is to provide by statute for the appointment of a member of the private bar to represent one of the defendants and the public defender or legal aid attorney will represent one defendant. If there are more than two defendants, a member of the private bar will be appointed to represent each defendant except the one which the public defender or the legal aid society lawyer will represent. The private bar attorney, so appointed, will be paid for the representation out of state funds. These, however, are usually at minimum rates and often almost represent pro bono representation.

There was a serious question as to the civil liability of such counsel as to whether they were liable under Title 42 Section 1983 of the United States Code. Many members of the private bar, not wishing to expose themselves to potential civil liability under this statute, were refusing to represent these clients. The matter was finally determined when on December 14, 1981 the Supreme Court handed down its decision in POLK COUNTY ET AL PETITIONERS v. RUSSEL RICHARD DODSON, 454 U.S. 312, 102 S.Ct. 445, 70 L.Ed.2d. 509, 30 Cr.L. 3033 (1981) where the court held that a public defender does not act "under color of state law" when performing a lawyer's traditional functions as counsel to an indigent defendant in a state criminal proceeding.

In that case, Martha Shepard, an attorney in the Polk County, Iowa, Offender Advocate's Office, moved for permission to withdraw as counsel on the ground that respondent's claims were legally frivolous. The respondent brought suit under Title 42 Section 1983 for damages on the grounds that the attorney had failed to represent him adequately in an appeal to the Iowa Supreme Court. The United States Supreme Court dismissed the action on the theory indicated above. The attorney is however still liable under a common law malpractice claim but there are certain limitations on that claim, not relevant to a study of constitutional law.

Mentally retarded persons who are involuntarily committed in a state institution, have a Title 42 Section 1983 cause of action for failure of those in charge of the institution to provide safe conditions of confinement, freedom from unreasonable bodily restraints, and such minimally adequate training as reasonably required of such interests but the proper standard for determining whether the state has adequately protected such interests and rights is whether professional judgement was exercised. This can be established by proof of a qualified professional's judgement that is entitled to a presumption of correctness. MILLS v. ROGERS, —U.S.—, 102 S.Ct. 2442, 73 L.Ed.2d. 2616, 31 Cr.L. 3071 (1982).

Ordinarily it is incumbent upon a litigant seeking redress against a state for violations of a federal constitutional right to exhaust state remedies before the Federal Court is authorized to entertain jurisdiction. However in PATSY v. FLORIDA BOARD OF REGENTS, —U.S.—, 102 S.Ct. 2557, 73 L.Ed.2d. 172, 31 Cr.L. 3089 (1982) the United States

Supreme Court held that in a Title 42 Section 1983 case, there is no exhaustion requirement except in the case of adult prisoners bringing actions pursuant to that law.

Police officers have thought themselves to be highly vulnerable to an 1983 civil rights action. Judges have been held immune to this cause of action in PIERSON v. RAY, 386 U.S. 547; prosecutors in IMBLER v. PACHTMAN, 424 U.S. 409; legal aid attorneys in POLK COUNTY, ET AL, v. DODSON, —U.S.—, 102 S.Ct. 445, 70 L.Ed.2d. 509, 30 Cr.L. 3033 (1981); and in 1983 in the case of BRISCOE v. LAHUE, —U.S.—, 103 S.Ct. 1108, 75 L.Ed.2d. 96, 32 Cr.L. 3073 (1982) the Court held that a police officer is immune from suit for damages under 42 USC 1983 brought by a former criminal defendant on the basis, as alleged, that the officer perjured his testimony at the defendant's criminal trial.

§ 14.8 Criminal Weapon Available for Violations of Civil Rights

Under the common law, if one is aggrieved, the injured party may elect his remedy either at civil law or criminal law. Both remedies were not simultaneously available. However, most states have enacted legislation making both remedies available for one injury. These statutes are said to be in derogation of the common law. So, too, has Congress made simultaneous criminal statutes available to an aggrieved who under color of state law has been deprived of a federal constitutional or statutory right. The remedy is to be found in 18 U.S.C. 241 and 18 U.S.C. 242.

It is to be noted that a criminal action requires proof beyond a reasonable doubt whereas a civil action merely requires a preponderance of the credible evidence, i.e., mere tipping of the scale of justice, for the action to be successful. Accordingly, a conviction under the criminal remedy of Sections 241 and 242 infra is more difficult to accomplish than a recovery under Section 1983 supra. If the officer violates a local law as well as the federal law, s/he may be prosecuted in both jurisdictions.

18 U.S.C. 241 provides as follows:

> If two or more persons conspire to injure, oppress, threaten or intimidate any citizen in the free exercise or enjoyment of any right or privilege secured to him by the Constitution or laws of the United States, or because of his having so exercised the same; or
>
> If two or more persons go in disguise on the highway, or on the premises of another, with intent to prevent or hinder his free exercise or enjoyment of any right or privilege so secured—

> They shall be fined not more than $5,000.00 or imprisonment not more than ten years or both.

Prior to 1966, this statute was thought to apply to private persons not connected with the government. However, the Court decided otherwise in that year in the case of United States v. Price, 383 U.S. 787, 86 S.Ct. 1152, 16 L.Ed.2d 267. This case grew out of the murder of three civil rights workers, Andrew Goodman, Michael Schwerner and James Chaney, in Mississippi. They were intercepted by a deputy sheriff, taken to a lonely, dark road and the deputy was there joined by two other law enforcement officers and fifteen private persons who collectively arranged to kill the young workers. The Federal Justice Department instituted the procedure for indictments under Section 241 for conspiring to "injure, oppress, threaten and intimidate" the three victims "in the free exercise and enjoyment of the right... not to be deprived of life or liberty without due process of law...." The United States District Court dismissed the indictments reasoning that § 241 did not embrace conspiracies to deprive an individual of due process of law. However, the United States Supreme Court held that to act under color of law does not require that the accused be an officer of the state. "It is enough that he is a willing participant in joint activity with the State or its agents. Those who took advantage of participation by state officers in accomplishment of the foul purpose alleged must suffer the consequences of that participation." The Court further held that the rights covered in the statute included those rights of the Fourteenth Amendment.

18 U.S.C. 242 reads as follows:

> Whoever, under color of any law, statute, ordinance, regulation or custom, wilfully subjects any inhabitant of any State, Territory or District to the deprivation of any rights, privileges, or immunities, secured or protected by the Constitution or Laws of the United States... shall be fined not more than $1,000 or imprisoned not more than one year, or both.

The Court interpreted the word "wilful" as requiring a specific intent to deprive a person of a right which had been made clear and definite either by express terms of the Constitution or by laws of the United States, or by decisions interpreting them. Screws v. United States, 325 U.S. 91, 65 S.Ct. 1031, 89 L.Ed. 1495 (1945).

§ 14.9 Separate but Equal Concept Regarding Civil Rights

Plessy v. Ferguson, 163 U.S. 537, 16 S.Ct. 1138, 41 L.Ed. 256 (1896), gave the force of law to Jim Crow segregationist policies in many southern states. Plessy, a black man, refused to leave a coach reserved for whites only. The case was decided by an 8–1 majority in favor of the state legislation requiring segregation as long as equivalent facilities were provided for both races. The lone dissent of Mr. Justice John M. Harlan, who came from Kentucky, read in part:

> Our Constitution is color blind, and neither knows nor tolerates classes among citizens. In respect of civil rights, all citizens are equal before the law. The humblest is the peer of the most powerful. The law regards man as man, and takes no account of his surroundings or his color when his civil rights as guaranteed by the supreme law of the land are involved.

Mr. Justice Harlan's dissent later became the law of the land in Brown v. Board of Education, 347 U.S. 483, 74 S.Ct. 686, 98 L.Ed. 873 (1954), when Mr. Chief Justice Earl Warren spoke for a unanimous court and said that the doctrine of Plessy v. Ferguson no longer satisfied the Constitution. Other cases of similar import followed such as desegregation of hospitals, Simkins v. Moses H. Cone Memorial Hospital, 323 F.2d 959 (4th Circ. 1963); transportation facilities, Gale v. Browder, 352 U.S. 903, 77 S.Ct. 144, 1 L.Ed.2d 114 (1956); and golf courses, Holmes v. Atlanta, 350 U.S. 879, 76 S.Ct. 141, 100 L.Ed. 721 (1955).

With the advent of the equal rights for women movement, a male defendant in a statutory rape case tried to turn the table on women but was not successful. He, a 17½ year old male was convicted of having sexual intercourse with a female under the age of 18 years. He contended that the statute under which he was convicted was unconstitutional in that it discriminated against males and that a female of his age engaging in sexual intercourse with a male under 18 years of age would not be held liable under the statute. The Court did not agree with his argument, saying "Gender based classification are not inherently suspect" so as to be subject to so called "strict scrutiny" but will be upheld if they bear a "fair and reasonable relationship to legitimate state ends." The court felt that the fact that men could walk away from such an experience while females might become pregnant established a reasonable state interest in protecting the female. MICHAEL M. PETITIONER v. SUPERIOR COURT OF SONOMA COUNTY, 450 U.S. 464, 101 S.Ct. 1200, 67 L.Ed.2d. 437, 28 Cr.L. 3121 (1981).

§ 14.10 Civil Rights of Women

Like slavery of old, women were thought to be mere chattels of a man. Like so many struggles for freedom, women have had a difficult time achieving their goal of complete equality with men. Part of the problem appears to be because a large segment of the female population enjoys the protected status of women and these people often hinder the women's movement for equal rights. Notwithstanding this "fifth column," women have been achieving equal rights but the rate of speed has been at a snail's pace.

In 1873, the Court unanimously denied Myra Bradwell, in the case of Bradwell v. Illinois, the right to become a member of the bar of the State of Illinois. Justice Joseph P. Bradley, writing for the Court, rejected her argument, holding that the Fourteenth Amendment left the power to grant or withhold licenses in the hands of the states. He said "... the paramount destiny and mission of woman are (sic) to fulfill the noble and benign offices of wife and mother. This is the law of the Creator. And the rules of civil society cannot be based on exceptional cases." Thus we can understand the reasoning of that era.

In Muller v. Oregon, 208 U.S. 412, 28 S.Ct. 324, 52 L.Ed. 551 (1908), Louis Brandeis, then a young lawyer, later to become a Justice of the Supreme Court, argued the "Brandeis Brief" which relied on facts and statutes as well as legal arguments to show that women needed protection from excessive hours of labor and the Court accepted his argument to uphold maximum hour legislation for women.

However, in 1923, the Court rejected a similar concept in Adkins v. Children's Hospital, 261 U.S. 525, 41 S.Ct. 394, 67 L.Ed. 785 (1923), where the Court rejected an argument that women occupied a unique societal position sufficient to justify governmental fixing of minimum wages for those who were employed.

The position of the Court appeared to be waivering in favor of equal treatment of women. However, apparently the Court and the people of the United States were not fully ready to accept this because in 1937, the case of West Coast Hotel Co. v. Parish, 300 U.S. 379, 57 S.Ct. 578, 81 L.Ed. 703 (1937), was decided by the Court. It held that government did have power to regulate women's minimum wages.

It soon became evident to those who were seeking equal rights for women that they must relinquish protective laws for, if they are to have equal rights, they should have equal responsibilities.

Several cases found their way to the Court, such as Goesaert v. Cleary, 335 U.S. 464, 69 S.Ct. 198, 93 L.Ed. 163 (1948), where a Michigan statute preventing women, other than wives and daughters, from being licensed bartenders was upheld; Hoyt v. Florida, 368 U.S. 57, 82 S.Ct. 159, 7 L.Ed.2d 118 (1961), where a female defendant challenged a jury verdict of guilty to second degree murder because Florida law did not make jury service obligatory on females; and Reed v. Reed, 404 U.S. 71, 92 S.Ct. 351, 30 L.Ed.2d 43 (1971), where a female successfully invalidated an Idaho statute which gave preference to males in the granting of administration papers for the estate of a deceased. This case represents the first time that the Court condemned sexual discrimination as a violation of the equal protection clause of the Fourteenth Amendment. Chief Justice Burger said, "The question presented by this case, then, is whether a difference in the sex of competing applicants for letters of administration bears a rational relationship to a state objective that is sought to be advanced by the operation of (the Idaho statute)." He held that the Idaho statute violated the equal protection clause.

There have been several other meaningful cases in this area, but this chapter of American Constitutional Law is being made on a day-by-day basis. The student is urged to read Title VII of the Civil Rights Act of 1964, the Equal Pay Act of 1963, and Title IX of the Educational Amendments Act of 1972.

The Court, to the date of this writing, has refused to hold that sex is an inherently suspect classification similar to race and national origin. Probably the next step in this struggle will be the eventual passage of the ERA (Equal Rights Amendment). The reader will probably see the passage of this amendment in his/her lifetime and thus will participate in a major change in the society in which we live.

§ 14.11 Conclusion

The author has attempted in this book to make the student aware that the changes in the way in which we conduct our government and consequently our personal lives did not occur overnight. Many valiant persons clinging steadfastly to their ideals brought about change in the United States. While perfection is as elusive as a dummy rabbit in a race of greyhound dogs, the goal is there. Each of us should be motivated to do our little "thing" to make history so that our descendants will have a better place to live and work.

Naturally, in a work of this type, size of the book was an important consideration and much of constitutional law has been omitted. Notwithstanding this, it is hoped that the student will have a greater appreciation of our constitutional development. If the student is engaged in the law enforcement profession, s/he will have a greater understanding of the constitutional rights which are afforded citizens and others within our borders. In this way, job performance and job satisfaction will be immeasurably increased. To deny a person his/her constitutional rights is only a way of teaching disrespect for the law and simultaneously causing the jailhouse doors to be opened when, after appeal, the defendant is set free because of the actions of the law enforcement officer. When the officer has thus deprived a person of constitutional rights, the actions of this officer materially contribute to an increase in the crime rate as the prisoner goes free to once again ply his/her nefarious trade.

§ 14.12 Institutionalized Persons—Injunctive Relief

It is well known that many persons confined in prisons, jails, hospitals for the mentally ill, disabled or retarded, or for those chronically ill or handicapped or similar institutions housing adults and/or juveniles are treated in a cruel and inhuman manner in violation of their constitutional rights, privileges and immunities. Congress had supplied a criminal and civil remedy to them as indicated in sections 14.7 and 14.8 (supra) but it was not until May 23, 1980 did Congress get around to approving equitable relief to these people where a court may enjoin further violations. Congress did this when it passed the Civil Rights of Institutionalized Persons Act by Public Law 96–247 in the 96th Congress. Generally, the act provides authority for the Attorney General to initiate actions against public institutions, i.e. owned, operated or managed by, or provided services on behalf of a state or political subdivision of the state. Most private institutions were exempted from the operation of the act even though they were licensed to operate by the state.

Judicial Decisions Relating to Chapter 14

Brown et al. *v.* Board of Education of Topeka et al

347 U.S. 483, 74 S.Ct. 686, 98 L.Ed. 873 (1954)

APPEAL FROM THE UNITED STATES DISTRICT COURT FOR THE DISTRICT OF KANSAS.

Argued December 9, 1952.—Reargued December 8, 1953.—Decided May 17, 1954.

. . .

MR. CHIEF JUSTICE WARREN delivered the opinion of the Court.

These cases come to us from the States of Kansas, South Carolina, Virginia, and Delaware. They are premised on different facts and different local conditions, but a common legal question justifies their consideration together in this consolidated opinion.

In each of the cases, minors of the Negro race, through their legal representatives, seek the aid of the courts in obtaining admission to the public schools of their community on a nonsegregated basis. In each instance, they had been denied admission to schools attended by white children under laws requiring or permitting segregation according to race. This segregation was alleged to deprive the plaintiffs of the equal protection of the laws under the Fourteenth Amendment. In each of the cases other than the Delaware case, a three-judge federal district court denied relief to the plaintiffs on the so-called "separate but equal" doctrine announced by this Court in Plessy v. Ferguson, 163 U.S. 537. Under that doctrine, equality of treatment is accorded when the races are provided substantially equal facilities, even though these facilities be separate. In the Delaware case, the Supreme Court of Delaware adhered to that doctrine, but ordered that the plaintiffs be admitted to the white schools because of their superiority to the Negro schools.

The plaintiffs contend that segregated public schools are not "equal" and cannot be made "equal," and that hence they are deprived of the equal protection of the laws. Because of the obvious importance of the question presented, the Court took jurisdiction. Argument was heard in the 1952 Term, and reargument was heard this Term on certain questions propounded by the Court.

Reargument was largely devoted to the circumstances surrounding the adoption of the Fourteenth Amendment in 1868. It covered exhaustively consideration of the Amendment in Congress, ratification by the states, then existing practices in racial segregation, and the views of proponents and opponents of the Amendment. This discussion and our own investigation convince us that, although these sources cast some light, it is not enough to resolve the problem with which we are faced. At best, they are inconclusive. The most avid proponents of the post-War Amendments undoubtedly intended them to remove all legal distinctions among "all persons born or naturalized in the United States." Their opponents, just as certainly, were antagonistic to both the letter and the spirit of the Amendments and wished them to have the most limited effect. What others in Congress and the state legislatures had in mind cannot be determined with any degree of certainty.

An additional reason for the inconclusive nature of the Amendment's history, with respect to segregated schools, is the status of public education at that time. In the South, the movement toward free common schools, supported by general taxation, had not yet taken hold. Education of white children was largely in the hands of private groups. Education of Negroes was almost nonexistent, and practically all of the race were illiterate. In fact, any education of Negroes was forbidden by law in some states. Today, in contrast, many Negroes have achieved outstanding success in the arts and sciences as well as in the business and professional world. It is true that public school education at the time of the Amendment had advanced further in the North, but the effect of the Amendment on Northern States was generally ignored in the congressional debates. Even in the North, the conditions of public education did not approximate those existing today. The curriculum was usually rudimentary; ungraded schools were common in rural areas; the school term was but three months a year in many states; and compulsory school attendance was virtually unknown. As a consequence, it is not surprising that there should be so little in the history of the Fourteenth Amendment relating to its intended effect on public education.

In the first cases in this Court construing the Fourteenth Amendment, decided shortly after its adoption, the Court interpreted it as proscribing all state-imposed discriminations against the Negro race. The doctrine of "separate but equal" did not make its appearance in this Court until 1896 in the case of Plessy v. Ferguson, supra, involving not education but transportation. American courts have since labored with the doctrine for over half a century. In this Court, there have been six cases involving the "separate but equal" doctrine in the field of public education. In Cumming v. County Board of Education, 175 U.S. 528, and Gong Lum v. Rice, 275 U.S. 78, the validity of the doctrine itself was not challenged. In more recent cases, all on the graduate school level, inequality was found in that specific benefits enjoyed by white students were denied to Negro students of the same educational qualifications. Missouri ex rel. Gaines v. Canada, 305 U.S. 337; Sipuel v. Oklahoma, 332 U.S. 631; Sweatt v. Painter, 339 U.S. 629; McLaurin v. Oklahoma State Regents, 339 U.S. 637. In none of these cases was it necessary to re-examine the doctrine to grant relief to the Negro plaintiff. And in Sweatt v. Painter, supra, the Court expressly reserved decision on the question whether Plessy v. Ferguson should be held inapplicable to public education.

In the instant cases, that question is directly presented. Here, unlike Sweatt v. Painter, there are findings below that the Negro and white schools involved have been equalized, or are being equalized, with respect to buildings, curricula, qualifications and salaries of teachers, and other "tangible" factors. Our decision, therefore, cannot turn on merely a comparison of these tangible factors in the Negro and white schools involved in each of the cases. We must look instead to the effect of segregation itself on public education.

In approaching this problem, we cannot turn the clock back to 1868 when the Amendment was adopted, or even to 1896 when Plessy v. Ferguson was written.

We must consider public education in the light of its full development and its present place in American life throughout the Nation. Only in this way can it be determined if segregation in public schools deprives these plaintiffs of the equal protection of the laws.

Today, education is perhaps the most important function of state and local governments. Compulsory school attendance laws and the great expenditures for education both demonstrate our recognition of the importance of education to our democratic society. It is required in the performance of our most basic public responsibilities, even service in the armed forces. It is the very foundation of good citizenship. Today it is a principal instrument in awakening the child to cultural values, in preparing him for later professional training, and in helping him to adjust normally to his environment. In these days, it is doubtful that any child may reasonably be expected to succeed in life if he is denied the opportunity of an education. Such an opportunity, where the state has undertaken to provide it, is a right which must be made available to all on equal terms.

We come then to the question presented: Does segregation of children in public schools solely on the basis of race, even though the physical facilities and other "tangible" factors may be equal, deprive the children of the minority group of equal educational opportunities? We believe that it does.

In Sweatt v. Painter, supra, in finding that a segregated law school for Negroes could not provide them equal educational opportunities, this Court relied in large part on "those qualities which are incapable of objective measurement but which make for greatness in a law school." In McLaurin v. Oklahoma State Regents, supra, the Court, in requiring that a Negro admitted to a white graduate school be treated like all other students, again resorted to intangible considerations: "... his ability to study, to engage in discussions and exchange views with other students, and, in general, to learn his profession." Such considerations apply with added force to children in grade and high schools. To separate them from others of similar age and qualifications solely because of their race generates a feeling of inferiority as to their status in the community that may affect their hearts and minds in a way unlikely ever to be undone. The effect of this separation on their educational opportunities was well stated by a finding in the Kansas case by a court which nevertheless felt compelled to rule against the Negro plaintiffs:

> "Segregation of white and colored children in public schools has a detrimental effect upon the colored children. The impact is greater when it has the sanction of the law; for the policy of separating the races is usually interpreted as denoting the inferiority of the negro group. A sense of inferiority affects the motivation of a child to learn. Segregation with the sanction of law, therefore, has a tendency to [retard] the educational and mental development of negro children and to deprive them of some of the benefits they would receive in a racial[ly] integrated school system."

Whatever may have been the extent of psychological knowledge at the time of Plessy v. Ferguson, this finding is amply supported by modern authority. Any language in Plessy v. Ferguson contrary to this finding is rejected.

We conclude that in the field of public education the doctrine of "separate but equal" has no place. Separate educational facilities are inherently unequal. Therefore, we hold that the plaintiffs and others similarly situated for whom the actions have been brought are, by reason of the segregation complained of, deprived of the equal protection of the laws guaranteed by the Fourteenth Amendment. This disposition makes unnecessary any discussion whether such segregation also violates the Due Process Clause of the Fourteenth Amendment.

Because these are class actions, because of the wide applicability of this decision, and because of the great variety of local conditions, the formulation of decrees in these cases presents problems of considerable complexity. On reargument, the consideration of appropriate relief was necessarily subordinated to the primary question—the constitutionality of segregation in public education. We have now announced that such segregation is a denial of the equal protection of the laws. In order that we may have the full assistance of the parties in formulating decrees, the cases will be restored to the docket, and the parties are requested to present further argument on Questions 4 and 5 previously propounded by the Court for the reargument this Term. The Attorney General of the United States is again invited to participate. The Attorneys General of the states requiring or permitting segregation in public education will also be permitted to appear as amici curiae upon request to do so by September 15, 1954, and submission of briefs by October 1, 1954.

It is so ordered.

Reed *v.* Reed, Administrator

404 U.S. 71, 92 S.Ct. 351, 30 L.Ed. 2d. 225 (1971)

APPEAL FROM THE SUPREME COURT OF IDAHO

Argued October 19, 1971—Decided November 22, 1971

. . .

MR. CHIEF JUSTICE BURGER delivered the opinion of the Court.

Richard Lynn Reed, a minor, died intestate in Ada County, Idaho, on March 29, 1967. His adoptive parents, who had separated sometime prior to his death, are the parties to this appeal. Approximately seven months after Richard's death, his mother, appellant Sally Reed, filed a petition in the Probate Court of Ada County, seeking appointment as administratrix of her son's estate. Prior to the date set for a hearing on the mother's petition, appellee Cecil Reed, the father of the decedent, filed a competing petition seeking to have himself appointed administrator of the son's estate. The probate court held a joint hearing on the two petitions and thereafter ordered that letters of administration be issued to appellee Cecil Reed upon his taking the oath and filing the bond required by law. The court treated §§ 15–312 and

15–314 of the Idaho Code as the controlling statutes and read those sections as compelling a preference for Cecil Reed because he was a male.

Section 15–312 designates the persons who are entitled to administer the estate of one who dies intestate. In making these designations, that section lists 11 classes of persons who are so entitled and provides, in substance, that the order in which those classes are listed in the section shall be determinative of the relative rights of competing applicants for letters of administration. One of the 11 classes so enumerated is "[t]he father or mother" of the person dying intestate. Under this section, then, appellant and appellee, being members of the same entitlement class, would seem to have been equally entitled to administer their son's estate. Section 15–314 provides, however, that

> "[o]f several persons claiming and equally entitled [under § 15–312] to administer, males must be preferred to females, and relatives of the whole to those of the half blood."

In issuing its order, the probate court implicitly recognized the equality of entitlement of the two applicants under § 15–312 and noted that neither of the applicants was under any legal disability; the court ruled, however, that appellee, being a male, was to be preferred to the female appellant "by reason of Section 15–314 of the Idaho Code." In stating this conclusion, the probate judge gave no indication that he had attempted to determine the relative capabilities of the competing applicants to perform the functions incident to the administration of an estate. It seems clear the probate judge considered himself bound by statute to give preference to the male candidate over the female, each being otherwise "equally entitled."

Sally Reed appealed from the probate court order, and her appeal was treated by the District Court of the Fourth Judicial District of Idaho as a constitutional attack on § 15–314. In dealing with the attack, that court held that the challenged section violated the Equal Protection Clause of the Fourteenth Amendment and was, therefore, void; the matter was ordered "returned to the Probate Court for its determination of which of the two parties" was better qualified to administer the estate.

This order was never carried out, however, for Cecil Reed took a further appeal to the Idaho Supreme Court, which reversed the District Court and reinstated the original order naming the father administrator of the estate. In reaching this result, the Idaho Supreme Court first dealt with the governing statutory law and held that under § 15–312 "a father and mother are 'equally entitled' to letters of administration," but the preference given to males by § 15–314 is "mandatory" and leaves no room for the exercise of a probate court's discretion in the appointment of administrators. Having thus definitely and authoritatively interpreted the statutory provisions involved, the Idaho Supreme Court then proceeded to examine, and reject, Sally Reed's contention that § 15–314 violates the Equal Protection Clause by giving a mandatory preference to males over females, without regard to their individual qualifications as potential estate administrators. 93 Idaho 511, 465 P. 2d 635.

Sally Reed thereupon appealed for review by this Court pursuant to 28 U.S.C. § 1257 (2), and we noted probable jurisdiction. 401 U.S. 934. Having examined the record and considered the briefs and oral arguments of the parties, we have concluded that the arbitrary preference established in favor of males by § 15–314 of the Idaho Code cannot stand in the face of the Fourteenth Amendment's command that no State deny the equal protection of the laws to any person within its jurisdiction.

Idaho does not, of course, deny letters of administration to women altogether. Indeed, under § 15–312, a woman whose spouse dies intestate has a preference over a son, father, brother, or any other male relative of the decedent. Moreover, we can judicially notice that in this country, presumably due to the greater longevity of women, a large proportion of estates, both intestate and under wills of decedents, are administered by surviving widows.

Section 15–314 is restricted in its operation to those situations where competing applications for letters of administration have been filed by both male and female members of the same entitlement class established by § 15–312. In such situations, § 15–314 provides that different treatment be accorded to the applicants on the basis of their sex; it thus establishes a classification subject to scrutiny under the Equal Protection Clause.

In applying that clause, this Court has consistently recognized that the Fourteenth Amendment does not deny to States the power to treat different classes of persons in different ways. Barbier v. Connolly, 113 U.S. 27 (1885); Lindsley v. Natural Carbonic Gas Co., 220 U.S. 61 (1911); Railway Express Agency v. New York, 336 U.S. 106 (1949); McDonald v. Board of Election Commissioners, 394 U.S. 802 (1969). The Equal Protection Clause of that amendment does, however, deny to States the power to legislate that different treatment be accorded to persons placed by a statute into different classes on the basis of criteria wholly unrelated to the objective of that statute. A classification "must be reasonable, not arbitrary, and must rest upon some ground of difference having a fair and substantial relation to the object of the legislation, so that all persons similarly circumstanced shall be treated alike." Royster Guano Co. v. Virginia, 253 U.S. 412, 415 (1920). The question presented by this case, then, is whether a difference in the sex of competing applicants for letters of administration bears a rational relationship to a state objective that is sought to be advanced by the operation of §§ 15–312 and 15–314.

In upholding the latter section, the Idaho Supreme Court concluded that its objective was to eliminate one area of controversy when two or more persons, equally entitled under § 15–312, seek letters of administration and thereby present the probate court "with the issue of which one should be named." The court also concluded that where such persons are not of the same sex, the elimination of females from consideration "is neither an illogical nor arbitrary method devised by the legislature to resolve an issue that would otherwise require a hearing as to the relative merits . . . of the two or more petitioning relatives . . . ." 93 Idaho, at 514, 465 P. 2d, at 638.

Clearly the objective of reducing the workload on probate courts by eliminating one class of contests is not without some legitimacy. The crucial question, however, is whether § 15–314 advances that objective in a manner consistent with the command of the Equal Protection Clause. We hold that it does not. To give a mandatory preference to members of either sex over members of the other, merely to accomplish the elimination of hearings on the merits, is to make the very kind of arbitrary legislative choice forbidden by the Equal Protection Clause of the Fourteenth Amendment; and whatever may be said as to the positive values of avoiding intrafamily controversy, the choice in this context may not lawfully be mandated solely on the basis of sex.

We note finally that if § 15–314 is viewed merely as a modifying appendage to § 15–312 and as aimed at the same objective, its constitutionality is not thereby saved. The objective of § 15–312 clearly is to establish degrees of entitlement of various classes of persons in accordance with their varying degrees and kinds of relationship to the intestate. Regardless of their sex, persons within any one of the enumerated classes of that section are similarly situated with respect to that objective. By providing dissimilar treatment for men and women who are thus similarly situated, the challenged section violates the Equal Protection Clause. Royster Guano Co. v. Virginia, supra.

The judgment of the Idaho Supreme Court is reversed and the case remanded for further proceedings not inconsistent with this opinion.

Reversed and remanded.

Monell et al. *v.* Department of Social Services of the City of New York et al.

438 U.S. 658, 98 S.Ct. 2018, 56 L.Ed. 2d. 611 (1978)

CERTIORARI TO THE UNITED STATES COURT OF APPEALS FOR THE SECOND CIRCUIT

Argued November 2, 1977—Decided June 6, 1978

. . .

MR. JUSTICE BRENNAN delivered the opinion of the Court.

Petitioners, a class of female employees of the Department of Social Services and of the Board of Education of the City of New York, commenced this action under 42 U.S.C. § 1983 in July 1971. The gravamen of the complaint was that the Board and the Department had as a matter of official policy compelled pregnant employees to take unpaid leaves of absence before such leaves were required for medical reasons. Cf. Cleveland Board of Education v. LaFleur, 414 U.S. 632 (1974). The suit sought injunctive relief and backpay for periods of unlawful forced leave. Named as defendants in the action were the Department and its Commissioner, the Board and its Chancellor, and the city of New York and its Mayor. In each case, the individual defendants were sued solely in their official capacities.

On cross-motions for summary judgment, the District Court for the Southern District of New York held moot petitioners' claims for injunctive and declaratory relief since the city of New York and the Board, after the filing of the complaint, had changed their policies relating to maternity leaves so that no pregnant employee would have to take leave unless she was medically unable to continue to perform her job. 394 F. Supp. 853, 855 (1975). No one now challenges this conclusion. The court did conclude, however, that the acts complained of were unconstitutional under LaFleur, supra. 394 F. Supp., at 855. Nonetheless plaintiffs' prayers for backpay were denied because any such damages would come ultimately from the City of New York and, therefore, to hold otherwise would be to "circumven[t]" the immunity conferred on municipalities by Monroe v. Pape, 365 U.S. 167 (1961). See 394 F. Supp., at 855.

On appeal, petitioners renewed their arguments that the Board of Education was not a "municipality" within the meaning of Monroe v. Pape, supra, and that, in any event, the District Court had erred in barring a damages award against the individual defendants. The Court of Appeals for the Second Circuit rejected both contentions. The court first held that the Board of Education was not a "person" under § 1983 because "it performs a vital governmental function . . . , and, significantly, while it has the right to determine how the funds appropriated to it shall be spent . . . , it has no final say in deciding what its appropriations shall be." 532 F. 2d 259, 263 (1976). The individual defendants, however, were "persons" under § 1983, even when sued solely in their official capacities. 532 F. 2d, at 264. Yet, because a damages award would "have to be paid by a city that was held not to be amenable to such an action in Monroe v. Pape," a damages action against officials sued in their official capacities could not proceed. Id., at 265.

We granted certiorari in this case, 429 U.S. 1071, to consider

> "Whether local governmental officials and/or local independent school boards are 'persons' within the meaning of 42 U.S.C. § 1983 when equitable relief in the nature of back pay is sought against them in their official capacities?" Pet. for Cert. 8.

Although, after plenary consideration, we have decided merits of over a score of cases brought under § 1983 which the principal defendant was a school board—and indeed, in some of which § 1983 and its jurisdictional counterpart, 28 U.S.C. § 1343, provided the only basis for jurisdiction—we indicated in Mt. Healthy City Board of Education v. Doyle, 429 U.S. 274, 279 (1977), last Term that the question presented here was open and would be decided "another day." That other day has come and we now overrule Monroe v. Pape, supra, insofar as it holds that local governments are wholly immune from suit under § 1983.

I

In Monroe v. Pape, we held that "Congress did not undertake to bring municipal corporations within the ambit of [§ 1983]." 365 U.S., at 187. The sole basis for this conclusion was an inference drawn from Congress' rejection of the "Sherman amendment" to the bill which became the Civil Rights Act of 1871, 17 Stat. 13—the precursor of § 1983—which would have held a municipal corporation liable for damage done to the person or property of its inhabitants by *private* persons "riotously and tumultuously assembled." Cong. Globe, 42d Cong., 1st Sess., 749 (1871) (hereinafter Globe). Although the Sherman amendments did not seek to amend § 1 of the Act, which is now § 1983, and although the nature of the obligation created by that amendment was vastly different from that created by § 1, the Court nonetheless concluded in Monroe that Congress must have meant to exclude municipal corporations from the coverage of § 1 because "'the House [in voting against the Sherman amendment] had solemnly decided that in their judgment Congress had no constitutional power to impose any *obligation* upon county and town organizations, the mere instrumentality for the administration of state law.'" 365 U.S., at 190 (emphasis added), quoting Globe 804 (Rep. Poland). This statement, we thought, showed that Congress doubted its "constitutional power... to impose *civil liability* on municipalities," 365 U.S., at 190 (emphasis added), and that such doubt would have extended to any type of civil liability.

A fresh analysis of debate on the Civil Rights Act of 1871, and particularly of the case law which each side mustered in its support, shows, however, that Monroe incorrectly equated the "obligation" of which Representative Poland spoke with "civil liability."

A. An Overview

There are three distinct stages in the legislative consideration of the bill which became the Civil Rights Act of 1871. On March 28, 1871, Representative Shellabarger, acting for a House select committee, reported H.R. 320, a bill "to enforce the provisions of the fourteenth amendment to the Constitution of the United States, and for other purposes." H.R. 320 contained four sections. Section 1, now codified as 42 U.S.C. § 1983, was the subject of only limited debate and was passed without amendment. Sections 2 through 4 dealt primarily with the "other purpose" of suppressing Ku Klux Klan violence in the Southern States. The wisdom and constitutionality of these sections—not § 1, now § 1983—were the subject of almost all congressional debate and each of these sections was amended. The House finished its initial debates on H.R. 320 on April 7, 1871, and one week later the Senate also voted out a bill. Again, debate on § 1 of the bill was limited and that section was passed as introduced.

Immediately prior to the vote on H.R. 320 in the Senate, Senator Sherman introduced his amendment. This was *not* an amendment to § 1 of the bill, but was to be added as § 7 at the end of the bill. Under the Senate rules, no discussion of the amendment was allowed and, although attempts were made to amend the amendment, it was passed as introduced. In this form, the amendment did *not* place liability on municipal corporations, but made any inhabitant of a municipality liable for damage inflicted by persons "riotously and tumultuously assembled."

The House refused to acquiesce in a number of amendments made by the Senate, including the Sherman amendment, and the respective versions of H.R. 320 were therefore sent to a conference committee. Section 1 of the bill, however, was not a subject of this conference since, as noted, it was passed verbatim as introduced in both Houses of Congress.

On April 18, 1871, the first conference committee completed its work on H.R. 320. The main features of the conference committee draft of the Sherman amendment were these: First, a cause of action was given to persons injured by

> "any persons riotously and tumultuously assembled together . . . with intent to deprive any person of any right conferred upon him by the Constitution and laws of the United States, or to deter him or punish him for exercising such right, or by reason of his race, color, or previous condition of servitude . . . ."

Second, the bill provided that the action would be against the county, city, or parish in which the riot had occurred and that it could be maintained by either the person injured or his legal representative. Third, unlike the amendment as proposed, the conference substitute made the government defendant liable on the judgment if it was not satisfied against individual defendants who had committed the violence. If a municipality were liable, the judgment against it could be collected

> "by execution, attachment, mandamus, garnishment, or any other proceeding in aid of execution or applicable to the enforcement of judgments against municipal corporations; and such judgment [would become] a lien as well upon all moneys in the treasury of such county, city, or parish, as upon the other property thereof."

In the ensuing debate on the first conference report, which was the first debate of any kind on the Sherman amendment, Senator Sherman explained that the purpose of his amendment was to enlist the aid of persons of property in the enforcement of the civil rights laws by making their property "responsible" for Ku Klux Klan damage. Statutes drafted on a similar theory, he stated, had long been in force in England and were in force in 1871 in a number of States. Nonetheless there were critical differences between the conference substitute and extant state and English statutes: The conference substitute, unlike most state riot statutes, lacked a short statute of limitations and imposed liability on the government defendant whether or not it had notice of the impending riot, whether or not the municipality was authorized to exercise a police power, whether or not it exerted all reasonable efforts to stop the riot, and whether or not the rioters were caught and punished.

The first conference substitute passed the Senate but was rejected by the House. House opponents, within whose ranks were some who had supported § 1, thought the Federal Government could not, consistent with the Constitution, obligate municipal corporations to keep the peace if those corporations were neither so obligated nor so authorized by their state charters. And, because of this constitutional objection, opponents of the Sherman amendment were unwilling to impose damages liability for nonperformance of a duty which Congress could not require municipalities to perform. This position is reflected in Representative Poland's statement that is quoted in Monroe.

Because the House rejected the first conference report a second conference was called and it duly issued its report. The second conference substitute for the Sherman amendment abandoned municipal liability and, instead, made "any person or persons having knowledge [that a conspiracy to violate civil rights was afoot], and having power to prevent or aid in preventing the same," who did not attempt to stop the same, liable to any person injured by the conspiracy. The amendment in this form was adopted by both Houses of Congress and is now codified as 42 U.S.C. § 1986.

The meaning of the legislative history sketched above can most readily be developed by first considering the debate on the report of the first conference committee. This debate shows conclusively that the constitutional objections raised against the Sherman amendment—on which our holding in Monroe was based, see supra, at 664—would not have prohibited congressional creation of a civil remedy against state municipal corporations that infringed federal rights. Because § 1 of the Civil Rights Act does not state expressly that municipal corporations come within its ambit, it is finally necessary to interpret § 1 to confirm that such corporations were indeed intended to be included within the "persons" to whom that section applies.

B. Debate on the First Conference Report

The style of argument adopted by both proponents and opponents of the Sherman amendment in both Houses of Congress was largely legal, with frequent references to cases decided by this Court and the Supreme Courts of the several States. Proponents of the Sherman amendment did not, however, discuss in detail the argument in favor of its constitutionality. Nonetheless, it is possible to piece together such an argument from the debates on the first conference report and those on § 2 of the civil rights bill, which, because it allowed the Federal Government to prosecute crimes "in the States," had also raised questions of federal power. The account of Representative Shellabarger, the House sponsor of H.R. 320, is the most complete.

Shellabarger began his discussion of H.R. 320 by stating that "there is a domain of constitutional law involved in the right consideration of this measure which is wholly unexplored." Cong. Globe, 42d Cong., 1st Sess., App. 67 (1871) (hereinafter Globe App.). There were analogies, however. With respect to the meaning of § 1 of the Fourteenth Amendment, and particularly its Privileges or Immunities Clause, Shellabarger relied on the statement of Mr. Justice Washington in Corfield v. Coryell, 4 Wash. C.C. 371 (CC ED Pa. 1825), which defined the privileges protected by Art. IV:

> "'What these fundamental privileges are[,] it would perhaps be more tedious than difficult to enumerate. They may, however, be all comprehended under the following general heads: protection by the Government;'—
>
> "*Mark that*—
>
> "'*protection by the Government;* the enjoyment of life and liberty, with the right to acquire and possess property of every kind, and to pursue and obtain happiness and safety....'" Globe App. 69 (emphasis added), quoting 4 Wash. C.C., at 380–381.

Building on his conclusion that citizens were owed protection—a conclusion not disputed by opponents of the Sherman Amendment—Shellabarger then considered Congress' role in providing that protection. Here again there were precedents:

> "[Congress has always] assumed to enforce, as against the States, and also persons, every one of the provisions of the Constitution. Most of the provisions of the Constitution which restrain and directly relate to the States, such as those in [Art. I,

§ 10,] relate to the divisions of the political powers of the State and General Governments.... These prohibitions upon political powers of the States are all of such nature that they can be, and even have been... enforced by the courts of the United States declaring void all State acts of encroachment on Federal powers. Thus, and thus sufficiently, has the United States 'enforced' these provisions of the Constitution. But there are some that are not of this class. These are where the court secures the rights or the liabilities of persons within the States, as between such persons and the States.

"These three are: first, that as to fugitives from justice; second, that as to fugitives from service, (or slaves); third, that declaring that the 'citizens of each State shall be entitled to all the privileges and immunities of citizens in the several States.'

"And, sir, every one of these—the only provisions where it was deemed that legislation was required to enforce the constitutional provisions—the only three where the rights or liabilities of persons in the States, as between these persons and the States, are directly provided for, Congress has by legislation affirmatively interfered to protect... such persons." Globe App. 69–70.

Of legislation mentioned by Shellabarger, the closest analog of the Sherman amendment, ironically, was the statute implementing the fugitives from justice and fugitive slave provisions of Art. IV—the Act of Feb. 12, 1793, 1 Stat. 302—the constitutionality of which had been sustained in 1842, in Prigg v. Pennsylvania, 16 Pet. 539. There, Mr. Justice Story, writing for the Court, held that Art. IV gave slaveowners a federal right to the unhindered possession of their slaves in whatever State such slaves might be found. 16 Pet., at 612. Because state process for recovering runaway slaves might be inadequate or even hostile to the rights of the slaveowner, the right intended to be conferred could be negated if left to state implementation. Id., at 614. Thus, since the Constitution guaranteed the right and this in turn required a remedy, Story held it to be a "natural inference" that Congress had the power itself to ensure an appropriate (in the Necessary and Proper Clause sense) remedy for the right. Id., at 615.

Building on Prigg, Shellabarger argued that a remedy against municipalities and counties was an appropriate—and hence constitutional—method for ensuring the protection which the Fourteenth Amendment made every citizen's federal right. This much was clear from the adoption of such statutes by the several States as devices for suppressing riot. Thus, said Shellabarger, the only serious question remaining was "whether, since a county is an integer or part of a State, the United States can impose upon it, as such, *any obligations to keep the peace* in obedience to United States laws." This he answered affirmatively, citing Board of Commissioners v. Aspinwall, 24 How. 376 (1861), the first of many cases upholding the power of federal courts to enforce the Contract Clause against municipalities.

House opponents of the Sherman amendment—whose views are particularly important since only the House voted down the amendment—did not dispute Shellabarger's claim that the Fourteenth Amendment created a federal right to protection, see n. 21, supra, but they argued that the local units of government upon which the amendment fastened liability were not obligated to keep the peace at state law and further that the Federal Government could not constitutionally require local governments to create police forces, whether this requirement was levied directly, or indirectly by imposing damages for breach of the peace on municipalities. The most complete statement of this position is that of Representative Blair:

> "The proposition known as the Sherman amendment... is entirely new. It is altogether without a precedent in this country.... That amendment claims the power in the General Government to go into the States of this Union and lay such obligations as it may please upon the municipalities, which are the creations of the States alone....
>
> "...[H]ere it is proposed, not to carry into effect an obligation which rests upon the municipality, but to create that obligation, and that is the provision I am unable to assent to. The parallel of the hundred does not in the least meet the case. The power that laid the obligation upon the hundred first put the duty upon the hundred that it should perform in that regard, and failing to meet the obligation which had been laid upon it, it was very proper that it should suffer damage for its neglect....
>
> "...[T]here are certain rights and duties that belong to the States,... there are certain powers that inhere in the State governments. They create these municipalities, they say what their powers shall be and what their obligations shall be. If the Government of the United States can step in and add to those obligations, may it not utterly destroy the municipality? If it can say that it shall be liable for damages occurring from a riot,... where [will] its power... stop and what obligations... might [it] not lay upon a municipality....
>
> "Now, only the other day, the Supreme Court... decided [in Collector v. Day, 11 Wall. 113 (1871)] that there is no power in the Government of the United States, under its authority to tax, to tax the salary of a State officer. Why? Simply because the power to tax involves the power to destroy, and it was not the intent to give the Government of the United States power to destroy the government of the States in any respect. It was held also in the case of Prigg vs. Pennsylvania [16 Pet. 539 (1842)] that it is not within the power of the Congress of the United States to lay duties upon a State officer; that we cannot command a State officer to do any duty whatever, as such; and I ask... the difference between that and commanding a municipality, which is equally the creature of the State, to perform a duty." Globe 795.

Any attempt to impute a unitary constitutional theory to opponents of the Sherman amendment is, of course, fraught with difficulties, not the least of which is that most Members of Congress did not speak to the issue of the constitutionality of the amendment. Nonetheless, two considerations lead us to conclude that opponents of the Sherman amendment found it unconstitutional substantially because of the reasons stated by Representative Blair: First, Blair's analysis is precisely that of Poland, whose views were quoted as authoritative in Monroe, see supra, at 664, and that analysis was shared in large part by all House opponents who addressed the constitutionality of the Sherman amendment. Second, Blair's exegesis of the reigning constitutional theory of his day, as we shall explain, was clearly supported by precedent—albeit precedent that has not survived, see Ex parte Virginia, 100 U.S. 339, 347–348 (1880); Graves v. New York ex rel. O'Keefe, 306 U.S. 466, 486 (1939)—and no other constitutional formula was advanced by participants in the House debates.

Collector v. Day, cited by Blair, was the clearest and, at the time of the debates, the most recent pronouncement of a doctrine of coordinate sovereignty that, as Blair stated, placed limits on even the enumerated powers of the National Government in favor of protecting state prerogatives. There, the Court held that the United States could not tax the income of Day, a Massachusetts state judge, because the independence of the States within their legitimate spheres would be imperiled if the instrumentalities through which States executed their powers were "subject to the control of another and distinct government." 11 Wall., at 127. Although the Court in Day apparently rested this holding in part on the proposition that the taxing "power acknowledges no limits but the will of the legislative body imposing the tax," id., at 125–126; cf. McCulloch v. Maryland, 4 Wheat. 316 (1819), the Court had in other cases limited other national powers in order to avoid interference with the States.

In Prigg v. Pennsylvania, for example, MR. JUSTICE STORY, in addition to confirming a broad national power to legislate under the Fugitive Slave Clause, see supra, at 672, held that Congress could not "insist that states . . . provide means to carry into effect the duties of the national government." 16 Pet., at 615–616. And MR. JUSTICE MCLEAN agreed that, "[a]s a general principle," it was true "that Congress had no power to impose duties on state officers, as provided in the [Act of Feb. 12, 1793]." Nonetheless he wondered whether Congress might not impose "positive" duties on state officers where a clause of the Constitution, like the Fugitive Slave Clause, seemed to require affirmative government assistance, rather than restraint of government, to secure federal rights. See id., at 664–665.

Had MR. JUSTICE MCLEAN been correct in his suggestion that, where the Constitution envisioned affirmative government assistance, the States or their officers or instrumentalities could be required to provide it, there would have been little doubt that Congress could have insisted that municipalities afford by "positive" action the protection owed individuals under § 1 of the Fourteenth Amendment whether or not municipalities were obligated by state law to keep the peace. However, any such argument, largely foreclosed by Prigg, was made impossible by the Court's holding in Kentucky v. Dennison, 24 How. 66 (1861). There, the Court was asked to require Dennison, the Governor of Ohio, to hand over Lago, a fugitive from justice wanted in Kentucky, as required by § 1 of the Act of Feb. 12, 1793, which implemented Art. IV, § 2, cl. 2, of the Constitution. MR. CHIEF JUSTICE TANEY, writing for a unanimous Court, refused to enforce that section of the Act:

> "[W]e think it clear, that the Federal Government, under the Constitution, has no power to impose on a State officer, as such, any duty whatever, and compel him to perform it; for if it possessed this power, it might overload the officer with duties which would fill up all his time, and disable him from performing his obligations to the State, and might impose on him duties of a character incompatible with the rank and dignity to which he was elevated by the State." 24 How., at 107–108.

The rationale of Dennison—that the Nation could not impose duties on state officers since that might impede States in their legitimate activities—is obviously identical to that which animated the decision in Collector v. Day. See supra, at 676. And, as Blair indicated, municipalities as instrumentalities through which States executed their policies could be equally disabled from carrying out state policies if they were also obligated to carry out federally imposed duties. Although no one cited Dennison by name, the principle for which it stands was well known to Members of Congress, many of whom discussed Day as well as a series of State Supreme Court cases in the mid-1860's which had invalidated a federal tax on the process of state courts on the ground that the tax threatened the independence of a vital state function. Thus, there was ample support for Blair's view that the Sherman amendment, by putting municipalities to the Hobson's choice of keeping the peace or paying civil damages, attempted to impose obligations on municipalities by indirection that could not be imposed directly, thereby threatening to "destroy the government of the States." Globe 795.

If municipal liability under § 1 of the Civil Rights Act of 1871 created a similar Hobson's choice, we might conclude, as Monroe did, that Congress could not have intended municipalities to be among the "persons" to which that section applied. But this is not the case.

First, opponents expressly distinguished between imposing an obligation to keep the peace and merely imposing civil liability for damages on a municipality that was obligated by state law to keep the peace, but which had not in violation of the Fourteenth Amendment. Representative Poland, for example, reasoning from Contract Clause precedents, indicated that Congress could constitutionally confer jurisdiction on the federal courts to entertain suits seeking to hold municipalities liable for using their authorized powers in violation of the Constitution—which is as far as § 1 of the Civil Rights Act went:

> "I presume . . . that where a State had imposed a duty [to keep the peace] upon [a] municipality . . . an action would be allowed to be maintained against them in the courts of the United States under the ordinary restrictions as to jurisdiction. But the enforcing a liability, existing by their own contract, or by a State law, in the courts, is a very widely different thing from devolving a new duty or liability upon them by the national Government, which has no power either to create or destroy them, and no power or control over them whatever." Globe 794.

Representative Burchard agreed:

> "[T]here is no duty imposed by the Constitution of the United States, or usually by State laws, upon a county to protect the people of that county against the commission of the offenses herein enumerated, such as the burning of buildings or any other injury to property or injury to person. Police powers are not conferred upon counties as corporations; they are conferred upon cities that have qualified legislative power. And so far as cities are concerned, where the equal protection required to be afforded by a State is imposed upon a city by State laws, perhaps the United States courts could enforce its performance. But counties . . . do not have any control of the police . . . ." Id., at 795.

See also the views of Rep. Willard, discussed at n. 30, supra.

Second, the doctrine of dual sovereignty apparently put no limit on the power of federal courts to enforce the Constitution against municipalities that violated it. Under the theory of dual sovereignty set out in Prigg, this is quite understandable. So long as federal courts were vindicating the Federal Constitution, they were providing the "positive" government action required to protect federal constitutional rights and no question was raised of enlisting the States in "positive" action. The limits of the principles announced in Dennison and Day are not so well defined in logic, but are clear as a matter of history. It must be remembered that the same Court which rendered Day also vigorously enforced the Contract Clause against municipalities—an enforcement effort which included various forms of "positive" relief, such as ordering that taxes be levied and collected to discharge federal-court judgments, once a constitutional infraction was found. Thus, federal judicial enforcement of the Constitution's express limits on state power, since it was done so frequently, must, notwithstanding anything said in Dennison or Day, have been permissible, at least so long as the interpretation of the Constitution was left in the hands of the judiciary. Since § 1 of the Civil Rights Act simply conferred jurisdiction on the federal courts to enforce § 1 of the Fourteenth Amendment—a situation precisely analogous to the grant of diversity jurisdiction under which the Contract Clause was enforced against municipalities—there is no reason to suppose that opponents of the Sherman amendment would have found any constitutional barrier to § 1 suits against municipalities.

Finally, the very votes of those Members of Congress, who opposed the Sherman amendment but who had voted for § 1, confirm that the liability imposed by § 1 was something very different from that imposed by the amendment. Section 1 without question could be used to obtain a damages judgment against state or municipal *officials* who violated federal constitutional rights while acting under color of law. However, for Prigg-Dennison-Day purposes, as Blair and others recognized, there was no distinction of constitutional magnitude between officers and agents—including corporate agents—of the State: Both were state instrumentalities and the State could be impeded no matter over which sort of instrumentality the Federal Government sought to assert its power. Dennison and Day, after all, were not suits against municipalities but against *officers*, and Blair was quite conscious that he was extending these cases by applying them to municipal corporations. Nonetheless, Senator Thurman, who gave the most exhaustive critique of § 1—inter alia complaining that it would be applied to state officers, see Globe App. 217—and who opposed both § 1 and the Sherman amendment, the latter on Prigg grounds, agreed unequivocally that § 1 was constitutional. Those who voted for § 1 must similarly have believed in its constitutionality despite Prigg, Dennison, and Day.

C. Debate on § 1 of the Civil Rights Bill

From the foregoing discussion, it is readily apparent that nothing said in debate on the Sherman amendment would have prevented holding a municipality liable under § 1 of the Civil Rights Act for its own violations of the Fourteenth Amendment. The question remains, however, whether the general language describing those to be liable under § 1—"any person"—covers more than natural persons. An examination of the debate on § 1 and application of appropriate rules of construction show unequivocally that § 1 was intended to cover legal as well as natural persons.

Representative Shellabarger was the first to explain the function of § 1:

> "[Section 1] not only provides a civil remedy for persons whose former condition may have been that of slaves, but also to all people where, under color of State law, they or any of them may be deprived of rights to which they are entitled under the Constitution by reason and virtue of their national citizenship." Globe App. 68.

By extending a remedy to all people, including whites, § 1 went beyond the mischief to which the remaining sections of the 1871 Act were addressed. Representative Shellabarger also stated without reservation that the constitutionality of § 2 of the Civil Rights Act of 1866 controlled the constitutionality of § 1 of the 1871 Act, and that the former had been approved by "the supreme courts of at least three States of this Union" and by Mr. Justice Swayne, sitting on circuit, who had concluded: "'We have no doubt of the constitutionality of every provision of this act.'" Globe App. 68. He then went on to describe how the courts would and should interpret § 1:

> "This act is remedial, and in aid of the preservation of human liberty and human rights. All statutes and constitutional provisions authorizing such statutes are liberally and beneficently construed. It would be most strange and, in civilized law, monstrous were this not the rule of interpretation. As has been again and again decided by your own Supreme Court of the United States, and everywhere else where there is wise judicial interpretation, the largest latitude consistent with the words employed is uniformly given in construing such statutes and constitutional provisions as are meant to protect and defend and give remedies for their wrongs to all the people.... Chief Justice Jay and also Story say:
>
> "'Where a power is remedial in its nature there is much reason to contend that it ought to be construed liberally, and it is generally adopted in the interpretation of laws.'—1 Story on Constitution, sec. 429." Globe App., at 68.

The sentiments expressed in Representative Shellabarger's opening speech were echoed by Senator Edmunds, the manager of H.R. 320 in the Senate:

> "The first section is one that I believe nobody objects to, as defining the rights secured by the Constitution of the United States when they are assailed by any State law or under color of any State law, and it is merely carrying out the principles of the civil rights bill [of 1866], which have since become a part of the Constitution." Globe 568.
>
> "[Section 1 is] so very simple and really reenacting the Constitution." Id., at 569.

And he agreed that the bill "secure[d] the rights of white men as much as of colored men." Id., at 696.

In both Houses, statements of the supporters of § 1 corroborated that Congress, in enacting § 1, intended to give a broad remedy for violations of federally protected civil rights. Moreover, since municipalities through their official acts could, equally with natural persons create the harms intended to be remedied by § 1, and, further, since Congress intended § 1 to be broadly construed, there is no reason to suppose that municipal corporations would have been excluded from the sweep of § 1. Cf., e.g., Ex parte Virginia, 100 U.S. 339, 346–347 (1880); Home Tel. & Tel. Co. v. Los Angeles, 227 U.S. 278, 286–287, 294–296 (1913). One need not rely on this inference alone, however, for the debates show that Members of Congress understood "persons" to include municipal corporations.

Representative Bingham, for example, in discussing § 1 of the bill, explained that he had drafted § 1 of the Fourteenth Amendment with the case of Barron v. Mayor of Baltimore, 7 Pet. 243 (1833), especially in mind. "In [that] case the *city* had taken private property for public use, without compensation . . . , and there was no redress for the wrong . . . ." Globe App. 84 (emphasis added). Bingham's further remarks clearly indicate his view that such takings by cities, as had occurred in Barron, would be redressable under § 1 of the bill. See Globe App. 85. More generally, and as Bingham's remarks confirm, § 1 of the bill would logically be the vehicle by which Congress provided redress for takings, since that section provided the only civil remedy for Fourteenth Amendment violations and that Amendment unequivocally prohibited uncompensated takings. Given this purpose, it beggars reason to suppose that Congress would have exempted municipalities from suit, insisting instead that compensation for a taking come from an officer in his individual capacity rather than from the government unit that had the benefit of the property taken.

In addition, by 1871, it was well understood that corporations should be treated as natural persons for virtually all purposes of constitutional and statutory analysis. This had not always been so. When this Court first considered the question of the status of corporations, Mr. Chief Justice Marshall, writing for the Court, denied that corporations "as such" were persons as that term was used in Art. III and the Judiciary Act of 1789. See Bank of the United States v. Deveaux, 5 Cranch 61, 86 (1809). By 1844, however, the Deveaux doctrine was unhesitatingly abandoned:

> "[A] corporation created by and doing business in a particular state, is to be deemed *to all intents and purposes as a person,* although an artificial person, . . . capable of being treated as a citizen of that state, as much as a natural person." Louisville R. Co. v. Letson, 2 How. 497, 558 (1844) (emphasis added), discussed in Globe 752.

And only two years before the debates on the Civil Rights Act, in Cowles v. Mercer County, 7 Wall. 118, 121 (1869), the Letson principle was automatically and without discussion extended to municipal corporations. Under this doctrine, municipal corporations were routinely sued in the federal courts and this fact was well known to Members of Congress.

That the "usual" meaning of the word "person" would extend to municipal corporations is also evidenced by an Act of Congress which had been passed only months before the Civil Rights Act was passed. This Act provided that "in all acts hereafter passed . . . the word 'person' may extend and be applied to bodies politic and corporate . . . unless the context shows that such words were intended to be used in a more limited sense." Act of Feb. 25, 1871, § 2, 16 Stat. 431.

Municipal corporations in 1871 were included within the phrase "bodies politic and corporate" and, accordingly, the "plain meaning" of § 1 is that local government bodies were to be included within the ambit of the persons who could be sued under § 1 of the Civil Rights Act. Indeed, a Circuit Judge, writing in 1873 in what is apparently the first reported case under § 1, read the Dictionary Act in precisely this way in a case involving a corporate plaintiff and a municipal defendant. See Northwestern Fertilizing Co. v. Hyde Park, 18 F. Cas. 393, 394 (No. 10,336) (CC ND Ill. 1873).

II

Our analysis of the legislative history of the Civil Rights Act of 1871 compels the conclusion that Congress *did* intend municipalities and other local government units to be included among those persons to whom § 1983 applies. Local governing bodies, therefore, can be sued directly under § 1983 for monetary, declaratory, or injunctive relief where, as here, the action that is alleged to be unconstitutional implements or executes a policy statement, ordinance, regulation, or decision officially adopted and promulgated by that body's officers. Moreover, although the touchstone of the § 1983 action against a government body is an allegation that official policy is responsible for a deprivation of rights protected by the Constitution, local governments, like every other § 1983 "person," by the very terms of the statute, may be sued for constitutional deprivations visited pursuant to governmental "custom" even though such a custom has not received formal approval through the body's official decisionmaking channels. As MR. JUSTICE HARLAN, writing for the Court, said in Adickes v. S. H. Kress & Co., 398 U.S. 144, 167–168 (1970): "Congress included customs and usages [in § 1983] because of the persistent and widespread discriminatory practices of state officials . . . . Although not authorized by written law, such practices of state officials could well be so permanent and well settled as to constitute a 'custom or usage' with the force of law."

On the other hand, the language of § 1983, read against the background of the same legislative history, compels the conclusion that Congress did not intend municipalities to be held liable unless action pursuant to official municipal policy of some nature caused a constitutional tort. In particular, we conclude that a municipality cannot be held liable *solely* because it employs a tortfeasor—or, in other words, a municipality cannot be held liable under § 1983 on a respondeat superior theory.

We begin with the language of § 1983 as passed:

"[*A*]*ny person who,* under color of any law, statute, ordinance, regulation, custom, or usage of any State, *shall subject, or cause to be subjected,* any person . . . to the deprivation of any rights, privileges, or immunities secured by the Constitution of the United States, shall, any such law, statute, ordinance, regulation, custom, or

> usage of the State to the contrary notwithstanding, be liable to the party injured in any action at law, suit in equity, or other proper proceeding for redress. . . ." 17 Stat. 13 (emphasis added).

The italicized language plainly imposes liability on a government that, under color of some official policy, "causes" an employee to violate another's constitutional rights. At the same time, that language cannot be easily read to impose liability vicariously on governing bodies solely on the basis of the existence of an employer-employee relationship with a tortfeasor. Indeed, the fact that Congress did specifically provide that A's tort became B's liability if B "caused" A to subject another to a tort suggests that Congress did not intend § 1983 liability to attach where such causation was absent. See Rizzo v. Goode, 423 U.S. 362, 370–371 (1976).

Equally important, creation of a federal law of *respondeat superior* would have raised all the constitutional problems associated with the obligation to keep the peace, an obligation Congress chose not to impose because it thought imposition of such an obligation unconstitutional. To this day, there is disagreement about the basis for imposing liability on an employer for the torts of an employee when the sole nexus between the employer and the tort is the fact of the employer-employee relationship. See W. Prosser, Law of Torts, § 69, p. 459 (4th ed. 1971). Nonetheless, two justifications tend to stand out. First is the common-sense notion that no matter how blameless an employer appears to be in an individual case, accidents might nonetheless be reduced if employers had to bear the cost of accidents. See, e.g., ibid.; 2 F. Harper & F. James, The Law of Torts, § 26.3, pp. 1368–1369 (1956). Second is the argument that the cost of accidents should be spread to the community as a whole on an insurance theory. See, e.g., id., § 26.5; Prosser, supra, at 459.

The first justification is of the same sort that was offered for statutes like the Sherman amendment: "The obligation to make compensation for injury resulting from riot is, by arbitrary enactment of statutes, affirmatory law, and the reason of passing the statute is to secure a more perfect police regulation." Globe 777 (Sen. Frelinghuysen). This justification was obviously insufficient to sustain the amendment against perceived constitutional difficulties and there is no reason to suppose that a more general liability imposed for a similar reason would have been thought less constitutionally objectionable. The second justification was similarly put forward as a justification for the Sherman amendment: "we do not look upon [the Sherman amendment] as a punishment. . . . It is a mutual insurance." Id., at 792 (Rep. Butler). Again, this justification was insufficient to sustain the amendment.

We conclude, therefore, that a local government may not be sued under § 1983 for an injury inflicted solely by its employees or agents. Instead, it is when execution of a government's policy or custom, whether made by its lawmakers or by those whose edicts or acts may fairly be said to represent official policy, inflicts the injury that the government as an entity is responsible under § 1983. Since this case unquestionably involves official policy as the moving force of the constitutional violation found by the District Court, see supra, at 600–662, and n. 2, we must reverse the judgment below. In so doing, we have no occasion to address, and do not address, what the full contours of municipal liability under § 1983 may be. We have attempted only to sketch so much of the § 1983 cause of action against a local government as is apparent from the history of the 1871 Act and our prior cases, and we expressly leave further development of this action to another day.

III

Although we have stated that stare decisis has more force in statutory analysis than in constitutional adjudication because, in the former situation, Congress can correct our mistakes through legislation, see, e.g., Edelman v. Jordan, 415 U.S. 651, 671, and n. 14 (1974), we have never applied stare decisis mechanically to prohibit overruling our earlier decisions determining the meaning of statutes. See, e.g., Continental T.V., Inc. v. GTE Sylvania Inc., 433 U.S. 36, 47–49 (1977); Burnet v. Coronado Oil & Gas Co., 285 U.S. 393, 406 n. 1 (1932) (Brandeis, J., dissenting) (collecting cases). Nor is this a case where we should "place on the shoulders of Congress the burden of the Court's own error." Girouard v. United States, 328 U.S. 61, 70 (1946).

First, Monroe v. Pape, insofar as it completely immunizes municipalities from suit under § 1983, was a departure from prior practice. See, e.g., Northwestern Fertilizing Co. v. Hyde Park, 18 F. Cas. 393 (No. 10,336) (CC ND Ill. 1873); City of Manchester v. Leroy, 117 F. 2d 661 (CA1 1941); Hannan v. City of Haverhill, 120 F. 2d 87 (CA1 1941); Douglas v. City of Jeannette, 319 U.S. 157 (1943); Holmes v. Atlanta, 350 U.S. 879 (1955), in each of which municipalities were defendants in § 1983 suits. Moreover, the constitutional defect that led to the rejection of the Sherman amendment would not have distinguished between municipalities and school boards, each of which is an instrumentality of state administration. See supra, at 673–682. For this reason, our cases—decided both before and after Monroe, see n. 5, supra—holding school boards liable in § 1983 actions are inconsistent with Monroe, especially as Monroe's immunizing principle was extended to suits for injunctive relief in City of Kenosha v. Bruno, 412 U.S. 507 (1973). And although in many of these cases jurisdiction was not questioned, we ought not "disregard the implications of an exercise of judicial authority assumed to be proper for [100] years." Brown Shoe Co. v. United States, 370 U.S. 294, 307 (1962); see Bank of the United States v. Deveaux, 5 Cranch, at 88 (Marshall, C.J.) ("Those decisions are not cited as authority . . . but they have much weight, as they show that this point neither occurred to the bar or the bench"). Thus, while we have reaffirmed Monroe without further examination on three occasions, it can scarcely be said that Monroe is so consistent with the warp and woof of civil rights law as to be beyond question.

Second, the principle of blanket immunity established in Monroe cannot be cabined short of school boards. Yet such an extension would itself be inconsistent with recent expressions of congressional intent. In the wake of our decisions, Congress not only has shown no hostility to federal-court decisions against school boards, but it has indeed rejected efforts to strip the federal courts of jurisdiction over school boards. Moreover, recognizing that school boards are often defendants in school desegregation suits, which have almost without exception been § 1983 suits, Congress has twice passed legislation authorizing grants to school boards to assist them in complying with federal-court decrees. Finally, in the Civil Rights

Attorney's Fees Awards Act of 1976, 90 Stat. 2641, 42 U.S.C.A. § 1988 (Supp. 1977), which allows prevailing parties (in the discretion of the court) in § 1983 suits to obtain attorney's fees from the losing parties, the Senate stated:

> "[D]efendants in these cases are often State or local *bodies* or State or local officials. In such cases it is intended that the attorneys' fees, like other items of costs, will be collected either directly from the official, *in his official capacity*, from funds of his agency or under his control, or *from the State or local government (whether or not the agency or government is a named party)*." S. Rep. No. 94-1011, p. 5 (1976) (emphasis added; footnotes omitted).

Far from showing that Congress has relied on Monroe, therefore, events since 1961 show that Congress has refused to extend the benefits of Monroe to school boards and has attempted to allow awards of attorney's fees against local governments even though Monroe, City of Kenosha v. Bruno, and Aldinger v. Howard, 427 U.S. 1 (1976), have made the joinder of such governments impossible.

Third, municipalities can assert no reliance claim which can support an absolute immunity. As Mr. Justice Frankfurter said in Monroe, "[t]his is not an area of commercial law in which, presumably, individuals may have arranged their affairs in reliance on the expected stability of decision." 365 U.S. at 221–222 (dissenting in part). Indeed, municipalities simply cannot "arrange their affairs" on an assumption that they can violate constitutional rights indefinitely since injunctive suits against local officials under § 1983 would prohibit any such arrangement. And it scarcely need be mentioned that nothing in Monroe encourages municipalities to violate constitutional rights or even suggests that such violations are anything other than completely wrong.

Finally, even under the most stringent test for the propriety of overruling a statutory decision proposed by Mr. Justice Harlan in Monroe—"that it appear beyond doubt from the legislative history of the 1871 statute that [Monroe] misapprehended the meaning of the [section]," 365 U.S., at 192 (concurring opinion)—the overruling of Monroe insofar as it holds that local governments are not "persons" who may be defendants in § 1983 suits is clearly proper. It is simply beyond doubt that, under the 1871 Congress' view of the law, were § 1983 liability unconstitutional as to local governments, it would have been equally unconstitutional as to state officers. Yet everyone—proponents and opponents alike—knew § 1983 would be applied to state officers and nonetheless stated that § 1983 was constitutional. See supra, at 680–682. And, moreover, there can be no doubt that § 1 of the Civil Rights Act was intended to provide a remedy, to be broadly construed, against all forms of official violation of federally protected rights. Therefore, absent a clear statement in the legislative history supporting the conclusion that § 1 was not to apply to the official acts of a municipal corporation—which simply is not present—there is no justification for excluding municipalities from the "persons" covered by § 1.

For the reasons stated above, therefore, we hold that stare decisis does not bar our overruling of Monroe insofar as it is inconsistent with Parts I and II of this opinion.

IV

Since the question whether local government bodies should be afforded some form of official immunity was not presented as a question to be decided on this petition and was not briefed by the parties or addressed by the courts below, we express no views on the scope of any municipal immunity beyond holding that municipal bodies sued under § 1983 cannot be entitled to an absolute immunity, lest our decision that such bodies are subject to suit under § 1983 "be drained of meaning," Scheuer v. Rhodes, 416 U.S. 232, 248 (1974). Cf. Bivens v. Six Unknown Fed. Narcotics Agents, 403 U.S. 388, 397–398 (1971).

V

For the reasons stated above, the judgment of the Court of Appeals is

Reversed.

Rizzo *v.* Goode

423 U.S. 362, 96 S.Ct. 598, 46 L.Ed. 2d. 561 (1976)

. . .

MR. JUSTICE REHNQUIST delivered the opinion of the Court.

The District Court for the Eastern District of Pennsylvania, after parallel trials of separate actions filed in 1970, entered an order in 1973 requiring petitioners "to submit to [the District] Court for its approval a comprehensive program for improving the handling of citizen complaints alleging police misconduct" in accordance with a comprehensive opinion filed together with the order. The proposed program, negotiated between petitioners and respondents for the purpose of complying with the order, was incorporated six months later into a final judgment. Petitioner City Police Commissioner was thereby required, inter alia, to put into force a directive governing the manner by which citizens' complaints against police officers should henceforth be handled by the Department. The Court of Appeals for the Third Circuit, upholding the District Court's finding that the existing procedures for handling citizen complaints were "inadequate," affirmed the District Court's choice of equitable relief: "The revisions were ... ordered because they appeared to have the potential for prevention of future police misconduct." Goode v. Rizzo, 506 F.2d 542, 548 (CA3 1974). We granted certiorari to consider petitioners' claims that the judgment of the District Court represents an unwarranted intrusion by the federal judiciary into the discretionary authority committed to them by state and local law to perform their official functions. We find ourselves substantially in agreement with these claims, and we therefore reverse the judgment of the Court of Appeals.

I

The central thrust of respondents' efforts in the two trials was to lay a foundation for equitable intervention, in one degree or another, because of an assertedly pervasive pattern of illegal and unconstitutional mistreatment by police officers. This mistreatment was said to have been directed against minority citizens in particular and against all Philadelphia residents in general. The named individual and group respondents (hereafter individual respondents) were certified to represent these two classes. The principal petitioners here—the Mayor, the City Managing Director, and the Police Commissioner—were charged with conduct ranging from express authorization or encouragement of this mistreatment to failure to act in a manner so as to assure that it would not recur in the future.

Hearing some 250 witnesses during 21 days of hearings, the District Court was faced with a staggering amount of evidence; each of the 40-odd incidents might alone have been the pièce de résistance of a short separate trial. The District Court carefully and conscientiously resolved often sharply conflicting testimony, and made detailed findings of fact, which both sides now accept, with respect to eight of the incidents presented by the Goode respondents and with respect to 28 of those presented by COPPAR.*

The principal antagonists in the eight incidents recounted in Goode were officers De Fazio and D'Amico, members of the city's "Highway Patrol" force. They were not named as parties to the action. The District Court found the conduct of these officers to be violative of the constitutional rights of the citizen complainants in three of the incidents, and further found that complaints to the police Board of Inquiry had resulted in one case in a relatively mild five-day suspension and in another case a conclusion that there was no basis for disciplinary action.

In only two of the 28 incidents recounted in COPPAR (which ranged in time from October 1969 to October 1970) did the District Court draw an explicit conclusion that the police conduct amounted to a deprivation of a federally secured right; it expressly found no police misconduct whatsoever in four of the incidents; and in one other the departmental policy complained of was subsequently changed. As to the remaining 21, the District Court did not proffer a comment on the degree of misconduct that had occurred: whether simply improvident, illegal under police regulations or state law, or actually violative of the individual's constitutional rights. Respondents' brief asserts that of this latter group, the facts as found in fourteen of them "reveal [federal] violations." While we think that somewhat of an overstatement, we accept it arguendo, and thus take it as established that, insofar as the COPPAR record reveals, there were 16 incidents occurring in the city of Philadelphia over a year's time in which numbers of police officers violated citizens' constitutional rights. Additionally, the District Court made reference to citizens' complaints to the police in seven of those 16; in four of which, involving conduct of constitutional dimension, the police department received complaints but ultimately took no action against the offending officers.

---

*The Council of Organizations on Philadelphia Police Accountability and Responsibility.

The District Court made a number of conclusions of law, not all of which are relevant to our analysis. It found that the evidence did not establish the existence of any policy on the part of the named petitioners to violate the legal and constitutional rights of the plaintiff classes, but it did find that evidence of departmental procedure indicated a tendency to discourage the filing of civilian complaints and to minimize the consequences of police misconduct. It found that as to the larger plaintiff class, the residents of Philadelphia, only a small percentage of policemen commit violations of their legal and constitutional rights, but that the frequency with which such violations occur is such that "they cannot be dismissed as rare, isolated instances." 357 F.Supp., at 1319. In the course of its opinion, the District Court commented that:

> "In the course of these proceedings, much of the argument has been directed toward the proposition that courts should not attempt to supervise the functioning of the police department. Although, contrary to the defendants' assertions, the Court's legal power to do just that is firmly established, . . . I am not persuaded that any such drastic remedy is called for, at least initially, in the present cases." Id., at 1320.

The District Court concluded by directing petitioners to draft, for the approval of the District Court, "a comprehensive program for dealing adequately with civilian complaints", to be formulated along the following "guidelines" suggested by the Court:

> "(1) Appropriate revision of police manuals and rules of procedure spelling out in some detail, in simple language, the 'dos and don'ts' of permissible conduct in dealing with civilians (for example, manifestations of racial bias, derogatory remarks, offensive language, etc.; unnecessary damage to property and other unreasonable conduct in executing search warrants; limitations on pursuit of persons charged only with summary offenses; recording and processing civilian complaints, etc.). (2) Revision of procedures for processing complaints against police, including (a) ready availability of forms for use by civilians in lodging complaints against police officers; (b) a screening procedure for eliminating frivolous complaints; (c) prompt and adequate investigation of complaints; (d) adjudication of nonfrivolous complaints by an impartial individual or body, insulated so far as practicable from chain of command pressures, with a fair opportunity afforded the complainant to present his complaint, and to the police officer to present his defense; and (3) prompt notification to the concerned parties, informing them of the outcome." Id., at 1321.

While noting that the "guidelines" were consistent with "generally recognized minimum standards" and imposed "no substantial burdens" on the police department, the District Court emphasized that Respondents had no constitutional *right* to improved police procedures for handling civilian complaints. But given that violations of constitutional rights of citizens occur in "unacceptably" high numbers, and are likely to continue to occur, the Court-mandated revision was a "necessary first step" in attempting to prevent future abuses. Id., at 1321. On petitioner's appeal the Court of Appeals affirmed.

II

These actions were brought, and the affirmative equitable relief fashioned, under the Civil Rights Act of 1871, 42 U.S.C. § 1983. It provides that "[e]very person who, under color of [law] subjects, or causes to be subjected, any . . . person [within the jurisdiction of the United States] to the deprivation of any rights . . . secured by the Constitution and laws, shall be liable to the party injured in an action at law [or] suit in equity . . ." The plain words of the statute impose liability—whether in the form of payment of redressive damages or being placed under an injunction—only for conduct which "subjects or causes to be subjected" the complainant to a deprivation of a right secured by the Constitution.

The findings of fact made by the District Court at the conclusion of these two parallel trials—in sharp contrast to that which respondents sought to prove with respect to petitioners—disclose a central paradox which permeates that Court's legal conclusions. Individual police officers *not named as parties* to the action were found to have violated the constitutional rights of particular individuals only a few of whom were parties plaintiff. As the facts developed, there was no affirmative link between the occurrence of the various incidents of police misconduct and the adoption of any plan or policy by petitioners—express or otherwise—showing their authorization or approval of such misconduct. Instead, the *sole* causal connection found by the District Court between petitioners and the individual respondents was that in the absence of a change in police disciplinary procedures, the incidents were likely to continue to occur, *not* with respect to them but as to the members of the classes they represented. In sum, the genesis of this lawsuit—a heated dispute between individual citizens and certain policemen—has evolved into an attempt by the federal judiciary to resolve a "controversy" between the entire citizenry of Philadelphia and the petitioning elected and appointed officials over what steps might, in the Court of Appeals' words, "appeared to have the potential for prevention of future police misconduct." 506 F.2d, at 548. The lower courts have, we think, overlooked several significant decisions of this Court in validating this type of litigation and the relief ultimately granted.

A

We first of all entertain serious doubts whether on the facts as found there was made out the requisite Art. III case or controversy between the individually named respondents and petitioners. In O'Shea v. Littleton, 414 U.S. 488, 94 S.Ct. 669, 38 L.Ed.2d 674 (1974), the individual respondents, plaintiffs in the District Court, alleged that petitioners, a county magistrate and judge, had embarked on a continuing, intentional practice of racially discriminatory bond-setting, sentencing, and assessing jury fees. No specific instances involving the individual respondents were set forth in the prayer for injunctive relief against the judicial officers. And even though respondents' counsel at oral argument had stated that some of the named respondents had in fact "suffered from the alleged unconstitutional practices," the Court concluded that "[p]ast exposure to illegal conduct does not in itself show a present case or controversy regarding injunctive relief, however, if unaccompanied by any continuing, present adverse effects." Id., at 495–496, 94 S.Ct., at 676. The Court further recognized that while "past wrongs are evidence bearing [up]on whether there is a real and immediate threat of repeated injury", the attempt to anticipate under what circumstances the respondents there would be made to appear in the future before petitioners "takes us into the area of speculation and conjecture." Id., at 496–497, 94 S.Ct., at 676. These observations apply here with even more force, for the individual respondents' claim to "real and immediate" injury rests not upon what the named petitioners might do to them in the future—such as set a bond on the basis of race—but upon what one of a small, unnamed minority of policemen might do to them in the future because of that unknown policeman's perception of departmental disciplinary procedures. This hypothetical is even more attenuated than those allegations of future injury found insufficient in O'Shea to warrant invocation of federal jurisdiction. Thus, insofar as the individual respondents were concerned, we think they lacked the requisite "personal stake in the outcome," Baker v. Carr, 369 U.S. 186, 204, 82 S.Ct. 691, 703, 7 L.Ed.2d 663 (1962), i.e., the order overhauling police disciplinary procedures.

B

That conclusion alone might appear to end the matter, for O'Shea also noted that "if none of the named plaintiffs . . . establishes the requisite of a case or controversy with the defendants, none may seek relief on behalf of himself or any other member of the class" which they purport to represent. Id., 414 U.S. at 494, 94 S.Ct. at 675. But, unlike O'Shea, this case did not arise on the pleadings. The District Court, having certified the plaintiff classes, bridged the gap between the facts shown at trial and the classwide relief sought with an unprecedented theory of § 1983 liability. It held that the classes' § 1983 action for equitable relief against petitioners was made out on a showing of an "unacceptably high" number of those incidents of constitutional dimension—some 20 in all—occurring at large in a city of three million inhabitants, with 7,500 policemen.

Nothing in Hague v. CIO, 307 U.S. 496, 59 S.Ct. 954, 83 L.Ed. 1423 (1939), the only decision of this Court cited by the District Court, or any other case from this Court, supports such an open-ended construction of § 1983. In Hague, the pattern of police misconduct upon which liability and injunctive relief were grounded was the adoption and enforcement of deliberate policies by the defendants there (including the Mayor and the Chief of Police) of excluding and removing the plaintiff's labor organizers and forbidding peaceful communication of their views to the citizens of Jersey City. These policies were implemented "by force and violence" on the part of individual policemen. There was no mistaking that the defendants proposed to continue their unconstitutional policies against the members of this discrete group.

Likewise, in Allee v. Medrano, 416 U.S. 802, 94 S.Ct. 2191, 40 L.Ed.2d 566 (1974), relied upon by the Court of Appeals and respondents here, we noted that

> "[t]he complaint charged that the enjoined conduct was but one part of a *single plan* by the defendants, and the District Court found a *pervasive pattern of intimi-*

> *dation* in which the law enforcement authorities sought to suppress appellees' constitutional rights. In this blunderbuss effort the police not only relied on statutes . . . found constitutionally deficient, but concurrently exercised their authority under valid laws in an unconstitutional manner." Id., at 812, 94 S.Ct., at 2198 (emphasis added).

The numerous incidents of misconduct on the part of the *named* Texas Rangers, as found by the District Court and summarized in this Court's opinion, established beyond peradventure not only a "persistent pattern" but one which flowed from an intentional, concerted, and indeed conspiratorial effort to deprive the organizers of their First Amendment rights and place them in fear of coming back. Id., 814–815, 94 S.Ct. 2199–2200.

Respondents stress that the District Court not only found an "unacceptably high" number of incidents but held, as did the Court of Appeals, that "when a *pattern* of frequent police violations of rights is shown, the law is clear that injunctive relief may be granted." 357 F.Supp., at 1318 (emphasis added). However, there was no showing that the behavior of the Philadelphia police was different in kind or degree from that which exists elsewhere; indeed, the District Court found "that the problems disclosed by the record . . . are fairly typical of [those] afflicting police departments in major urban areas." Ibid. Thus, invocation of the word "pattern" in a case where, unlike Hague and Medrano, the defendants are not causally linked to it, is but a distant echo of the findings in those cases. The focus in Hague and Medrano was not simply on the number of violations which occurred but on the common thread running through them: a "pervasive pattern of intimidation" flowing from a deliberate plan by the *named* defendants to crush the nascent labor organizations. Medrano, 416 U.S., at 812, 94 S.Ct., at 2198. The District Court's unadorned finding of a statistical pattern is quite dissimilar to the factual settings of these two cases.

The theory of liability underlying the District Court's opinion, and urged upon us by respondents, is that even without a showing of direct responsibility for the actions of a small percentage of the police force, petitioners' *failure* to act in the face of a statistical pattern is indistinguishable from the active conduct enjoined in Hague and Medrano. Respondents posit a constitutional "duty" on the part of petitioners (and a corresponding "right" of the citizens of Philadelphia) to "eliminate" future police misconduct; a "default" of that affirmative duty being shown by the statistical pattern, the District Court is empowered to act in petitioners' stead and take whatever preventive measures are necessary, within its discretion, to secure the "right" at issue. Such reasoning, however, blurs accepted usages and meanings in the English language in a way which would be quite inconsistent with the words Congress chose in § 1983. We have never subscribed to these amorphous propositions, and we decline to do so now.

Respondents claim that the theory of liability embodied in the District Court's opinion is supported by desegregation cases such as Swann v. Charlotte-Mecklenburg Board of Education, 402 U.S. 1, 91 S.Ct. 1267, 28 L.Ed.2d 554 (1971). But this case, and the long line of precedents cited therein, simply reaffirmed the body of law originally enunciated in Brown v. Board of Education, 347 U.S. 483, 74 S.Ct. 686, 98 L.Ed. 873 (1954):

> "Nearly seventeen years ago this Court held, in explicit terms, that state-imposed segregation by race in public schools denies equal protection of the laws. At no time has the Court deviated in the slightest degree from that holding or its constitutional underpinnings.
>
> . . .
>
> "Once a right and a violation have been shown, the scope of a district court's equitable power to remedy past wrongs is broad, for breadth and flexibility are inherent in equitable remedies." Swann, 402 U.S., at 11, 15, 91 S.Ct., at 1274.

Respondents, in their effort to bring themselves within the language of Swann, ignore a critical factual distinction between their case and the desegregation cases decided by this Court. In the latter, segregation imposed by law had been implemented by state authorities for varying periods of time, whereas in the instant case the District Court found that the responsible authorities had played no affirmative part in depriving any members of the two respondent classes of any constitutional rights. Those against whom injunctive relief was directed in cases such as Swann and Brown were not administrators and school board members who had in their employ a small number of individuals, which latter on their own deprived black students of their constitutional rights to a unitary school system. They were administrators and school board members who were found by their *own* conduct in the administration of the school system to have denied those rights. Here, the District Court found that none of the petitioners had deprived the respondent classes of any rights secured under the Constitution. Under the well-established rule that federal "judicial powers may be exercised only on the basis of a constitutional violation," Swann, 402 U.S., at 16, 91 S.Ct., at 1276, this case presented no occasion for the District Court to grant equitable relief against petitioners.

C

Going beyond considerations concerning the existence of a live controversy and threshold statutory liability, we must address an additional and novel claim advanced by respondent classes. They assert that given the citizenry's "right" to be protected from unconstitutional exercises of police power, and the "need for protection from such abuses," respondents have a right to mandatory equitable relief in some form when those in supervisory positions do not institute steps to reduce the incidence of unconstitutional police misconduct. The scope of federal equity power, it is proposed, should be extended to the fashioning of prophylactic procedures for a state agency designed to minimize this kind of misconduct on the part of a handful of its employees. But on the facts of this case, not only is this novel claim quite at odds with the settled rule that in federal equity cases "the nature of the violation determines the scope of the remedy," Swann, 402 U.S., at 16, 91 S.Ct., at 1276, important considerations of federalism are additional factors weighing against it. Where, as here, the exercise of authority by state officials is attacked, federal courts must be constantly mindful of the "special delicacy of the adjustment to be preserved between federal equitable power and State administration of its own law." Stefanelli v. Minard, 342 U.S. 117, 120, 72 S.Ct. 118, 120, 96 L.Ed. 138 (1951), quoted in O'Shea v. Littleton, supra, 414 U.S., at 500, 94 S.Ct., at 678.

Section 1983 by its terms confers authority to grant equitable relief as well as damages, but its words "allow a suit in equity only when that is the proper proceeding for redress, and they refer to existing standards to determine what is a proper proceeding." Giles v. Harris, 189 U.S. 475, 486, 23 S.Ct. 639, 642, 47 L.Ed. 909 (1903) (HOLMES, J.). Even in an action between private individuals, it has long been held that an injunction is "to be used sparingly, and only in a clear and plain case." Irwin v. Dixion, 9 How. 10, 33, 13 L.Ed. 25 (1850). When a plaintiff seeks to enjoin the activity of a government agency, even within a unitary court system, his case must contend with "the well-established rule that the Government has traditionally been granted the widest latitude in the 'dispatch of its own internal affairs,' Cafeteria and Restaurant Workers Union Local 473 A.F.L.-C.I.O. v. McElroy, 367 U.S. 886, 896, 81 S.Ct. 1743, 1749, 6 L.Ed.2d 1230 (1961)," quoted in Sampson v. Murray, 415 U.S. 61, 83, 94 S.Ct. 937, 950, 39 L.Ed.2d 166 (1974). The District Court's injunctive order here, significantly revising the internal procedures of the Philadelphia police department, was indisputably a sharp limitation on the department's "latitude in the 'dispatch of its own internal affairs.'"

When the frame of reference moves from a unitary court system, governed by the principles just stated, to a system of federal courts representing the Nation, subsisting side by side with 50 state judicial, legislative, and executive branches, appropriate consideration must be given to principles of federalism in determining the availability and scope of equitable relief. Doran v. Salem Inn, Inc., 422 U.S. 922, 928, 95 S.Ct. 2561, 2566, 45 L.Ed.2d 648 (1975).

So strongly has Congress weighted this factor of federalism in the case of a state criminal proceeding that it has enacted 28 U.S.C. § 2283 to actually deny to the District Courts the authority to issue injunctions against such proceedings unless the proceedings come with narrowly specified exceptions. Even though an action brought under § 1983, as this was, is within those exceptions, Mitchum v. Foster, 407 U.S. 225, 92 S.Ct. 2151, 32 L.Ed.2d 705 (1972), the underlying notions of federalism which Congress has recognized in dealing with the relationships between federal and state courts still have weight. Where an injunction against a criminal proceeding is sought under § 1983, "the principles of equity, comity, and federalism" must nonetheless restrain a federal court. Id., at 243, 92 S.Ct., at 2162.

But even where the prayer for injunctive relief does not seek to enjoin the state criminal proceedings themselves, we have held that the principles of equity nonetheless militate heavily against the grant of an injunction except in the most extraordinary circumstances. In O'Shea v. Littleton, supra, 414 U.S., at 502, 94 S.Ct., at 679, we held that "a major continuing intrusion of the equitable power of the federal courts into the daily conduct of state criminal proceedings is in sharp conflict with the principles of equitable restraint which this Court has recognized in the decisions previously noted." And the same principles of federalism may prevent the injunction by a federal court of a state civil proceeding once begun. Huffman v. Pursue, Ltd., 420 U.S. 592, 95 S.Ct. 1200, 43 L.Ed.2d 482 (1975).

Thus the principles of federalism which play such an important part in governing the relationship between federal courts and state governments, though initially expounded and perhaps entitled to their greatest weight in cases where it was sought to enjoin a criminal prosecution in progress, have not been limited either to that situation or indeed to a criminal proceeding itself. We think these principles likewise have applicability where injunctive relief is sought not against the judicial branch of the state government, but against those in charge of an executive branch of an agency of state or local governments such as respondents here. Indeed, in the recent case of Mayor v. Educational Equality League, 415 U.S. 605, 94 S.Ct. 1323, 39 L.Ed.2d 630 (1974), in which private individuals sought injunctive relief against the Mayor of Philadelphia, we expressly noted the existence of such considerations, saying "[t]here are also delicate issues of federal-state relationships underlying this case." Id., at 615, 94 S.Ct., at 1331.

Contrary to the District Court's flat pronouncement that a federal court's legal power to "supervise the functioning of the police department . . . is firmly established," it is the foregoing cases and principles that must govern consideration of the type of injunctive relief granted here. When it injected itself by injunctive decree into the internal disciplinary affairs of this state agency, the District Court departed from these precepts.

For the foregoing reasons the judgment of the Court of Appeals which affirmed the decree of the District Court is

Reversed.

Constitution of the United States of America—1787[1]

WE THE PEOPLE of the United States, in Order to form a more perfect Union, establish Justice, insure domestic Tranquility, provide for the common defence, promote the general Welfare, and secure the Blessings of Liberty to ourselves and our posterity, do ordain and establish this Constitution for the United States of America.

---

[1]In May, 1785, a committee of Congress made a report recommending an alteration in the Articles of Confederation, but no action was taken on it, and it was left to the State Legislatures to próceed in the matter. In January, 1786, the Legislature of Virginia passed a resolution providing for the appointment of five commissioners, who, or any three of them, should meet such commissioners as might be appointed in the other States of the Union, at a time and place to be agreed upon, to take into consideration the trade of the United States; to consider how far a uniform system in their commercial regulations may be necessary to their common interest and their permanent harmony; and to report to the several States such an act, relative to this great object, as, when ratified by them, will enable the United States in Congress effectually to provide for the same. The Virginia commissioners, after some correspondence, fixed the first Monday in September as the time, and the city of Annapolis as the place for the meeting, but only four other States were represented, viz: Delaware, New York, New Jersey, and Pennsylvania; the commissioners appointed by Massachusetts, New Hampshire, North Carolina, and Rhode Island failed to attend. Under the circumstances of so partial a representation, the commissioners present agreed upon a report, (drawn by Mr. Hamilton, of New York,) expressing their unanimous conviction that it might essentially tend to advance the interests of the Union if the States by which they were respectively delegated would concur, and use their endeavors to procure the concurrence of the other States, in the appointment of commissioners to meet at Philadelphia on the Second Monday of May following, to take into consideration the situation of the United States; to devise such further provisions as should appear to them necessary to render the Constitution of the Federal Government adequate to the exigencies of the Union; and to report such an act for that purpose to the United States in Congress assembled as, when agreed to by them and afterwards confirmed by the Legislatures of every State, would effectually provide for the same.

Congress, on the 21st of February, 1787, adopted a resolution in favor of a convention, and the Legislatures of those States which had not already done so (with the exception of Rhode Island) promptly appointed delegates. On the 25th of May, seven States having convened, George Washington, of Virginia, was unanimously elected President, and the consideration of the proposed constitution was commenced. On the 17th of September, 1787, the Constitution as engrossed and agreed upon was signed by all the members present, except Mr. Gerry of Massachusetts, and Messrs. Mason and Randolph, of Virginia. The president of the convention transmitted it to Congress, with a resolution stating how the proposed Federal Government should be put in operation, and an explanatory letter. Congress, on the 28th of September, 1787, directed the Constitution so framed, with the resolutions and letter concerning the same, to "be transmitted to the several Legislatures in order to be submitted to a convention of delegates chosen in each State by the people thereof, in conformity to the resolves of the convention."

On the 4th of March, 1789, the day which had been fixed for commencing the operations of Government under the new Constitution, it had been ratified by the conventions chosen in each State to consider it, as follows: Delaware, December 7, 1787; Pennsylvania, December 12, 1787; New Jersey, December 18, 1787; Georgia, January 2, 1788; Connecticut, January 9, 1788; Massachusetts, February 6, 1788; Maryland, April 28, 1788; South Carolina, May 23, 1788; New Hampshire, June 21, 1788; Virginia, June 25, 1788; and New York, July 26, 1788.

The President informed Congress, on the 28th of January, 1790, that North Carolina had ratified the Constitution November 21, 1789; and he informed Congress on the 1st of June, 1790, that Rhode Island had ratified the Constitution May 29, 1790. Vermont, in convention, ratified the Constitution January 10, 1791, and was, by an act of Congress approved February 18, 1791, "received and admitted into this Union as a new and entire member of the United States."

Article I.

SECTION 1. All legislative Powers herein granted shall be vested in a Congress of the United States, which shall consist of a Senate and House of Representatives.

SECTION 2. The House of Representatives shall be composed of Members chosen every second Year by the People of the several States, and the Electors in each State shall have the Qualifications requisite for Electors of the most numerous Branch of the State Legislature.

No person shall be a Representative who shall not have attained to the Age of twenty five Years, and been seven Years a Citizen of the United States, and who shall not, when elected, be an Inhabitant of that State in which he shall be chosen.

[2]Representatives and direct Taxes shall be apportioned among the several States which may be included within this Union, according to their respective Numbers, which shall be determined by adding to the whole Number of free Persons, including those bound to Service for a Term of Years, and excluding Indians not taxes, three fifths of all other Persons. The actual Enumeration shall be made within three Years after the first Meeting of the Congress of the United States, and within every subsequent Term of ten Years, in such Manner as they shall be Law direct. The Number of Representatives shall not exceed one for every thirty Thousand, but each State shall have at Least one Representative; and until such enumeration shall be made, the State of New Hampshire shall be entitled to chuse three, Massachusetts eight, Rhode-Island and Providence Plantations one, Connecticut five, New-York six, New Jersey four, Pennsylvania eight, Delaware one, Maryland six, Virginia ten, North Carolina five, South Carolina five, and Georgia three.

When vacancies happen in the Representation from any State, the Executive Authority thereof shall issue Writs of Election to fill such Vacancies.

The House of Representatives shall chuse their Speaker and other Officers; and shall have the sole Power of Impeachment.

[3]SECTION 3. The Senate of the United States shall be composed of two Senators from each State, chosen by the Legislature thereof, for six Years; and each Senator shall have one Vote.

Immediately after they shall be assembled in Consequence of the first Election, they shall be divided as equally as may be into three Classes. The Seats of the Senators of the first Class shall be vacated at the Expiration of the second year, of the second Class at the Expiration of the fourth Year, and of the third Class at the Expiration of the sixth Year, so that one third may be chosen every second Year; and if Vacancies happen by Resignation, or otherwise, during the Recess of the Legislature of any State, the Executive thereof may make temporary Appointments until the next Meeting of the Legislature, which shall then fill such Vacancies.

No Person shall be a Senator who shall not have attained to the Age of thirty Years, and been nine Years a Citizen of the United States, and who shall not, when elected, be an Inhabitant of that State for which he shall be chosen.

The Vice President of the United States shall be President of the Senate, but shall have no Vote, unless they be equally divided.

The Senate shall chuse their other Officers, and also a President pro tempore, in the Absence of the Vice President, or when he shall exercise the Office of President of the United States.

The Senate shall have the sole Power to try all Impeachments. When sitting for that Purpose, they shall be on Oath or Affirmation. When the President of the United States is

---

[2]This clause has been affected by the 14th and 16th amendments.

[3]This section has been affected by the 17th amendment.

tried, the Chief Justice shall preside: And no Person shall be convicted without the Concurrence of two thirds of the Members present.

Judgment in Cases of Impeachment shall not extend further than to removal from Office, and disqualification to hold and enjoy any Office of honor, Trust or Profit under the United States: but the Party convicted shall nevertheless be liable and subject to Indictment, Trial, Judgment and Punishment, according to Law.

[4]SECTION 4. The Times, Places and Manner of holding Elections for Senators and Representatives, shall be prescribed in each State by the Legislature thereof; but the Congress may at any time by Law make or alter such Regulations, except as to the Places of chusing Senators.

The Congress shall assemble at least once in every Year, and such Meeting shall be on the first Monday in December, unless they shall by Law appoint a different Day.

SECTION 5. Each House shall be the Judge of the Elections, Returns and Qualifications of its own Members, and a Majority of each shall constitute a Quorum to do Business; but a smaller Number may adjourn from day to day, and may be authorized to compel the Attendance of absent Members, in such Manner, and under such Penalties as each House may provide.

Each House may determine the Rules of its Proceedings, punish its Members for disorderly Behaviour, and, with the Concurrence of two thirds, expel a Member.

Each House shall keep a Journal of its Proceedings, and from time to time publish the same, excepting such Parts as may in their Judgment require Secrecy; and the Yeas and Nays of the Members of either House on any question shall, at the Desire of one fifth of those present, be entered on the Journal.

Neither House, during the Session of Congress, shall, without the Consent of the other, adjourn for more than three days, nor to any other Place than that in which the two Houses shall be sitting.

SECTION 6. The Senators and Representatives shall receive a Compensation for their Services, to be ascertained by Law, and paid out of the Treasury of the United States. They shall in all Cases, except Treason, Felony and Breach of the Peace, be privileged from Arrest during their Attendance at the Session of their respective Houses, and in going to and returning from the same; and for any Speech or Debate in either House, they shall not be questioned in any other Place.

No Senator or Representative shall, during the Time for which he was elected, be appointed to any civil Office under the Authority of the United States, which shall have been created, or the Emoluments whereof shall have been encreased during such time; and no Person holding any Office under the United States, shall be a Member of either House during his Continuance in Office.

SECTION 7. All Bills for raising Revenue shall originate in the House of Representatives; but the Senate may propose or concur with Amendments as on other Bills.

Every Bill which shall have passed the House of Representatives and the Senate, shall, before it become a Law, be presented to the President of the United States; If he approves he shall sign it, but if not he shall return it, with his Objections to that House in which it shall have originated, who shall enter the Objections at large on their Journal, and proceed to reconsider it. If after such Reconsideration two thirds of that House shall agree to pass the Bill, it shall be sent, together with the Objections, to the other House, by which it shall likewise be reconsidered, and if approved by two thirds of that House, it shall become a Law. But in all such Cases the Votes of both Houses shall be determined by yeas and Nays, and the Names of the Persons voting for and against the Bill shall be entered on the Journal of each

[4]This section has been affected by the 20th amendment.

House respectively. If any Bill shall not be returned by the President within ten Days (Sundays excepted) after it shall have been presented to him, the Same shall be a Law, in like Manner as if he had signed it, unless the Congress by their Adjournment prevent its Return, in which Case it shall not be a Law.

Every Order, Resolution, or Vote to which the Concurrence of the Senate and House of Representatives may be necessary (except on a question of Adjournment) shall be presented to the President of the United States; and before the Same shall take Effect, shall be approved by him, or being disapproved by him, shall be repassed by two thirds of the Senate and House of Representatives, according to the Rules and Limitations prescribed in the Case of a Bill.

SECTION 8. The Congress shall have Power To lay and collect Taxes, Duties, Imposts and Excises, to pay the Debts and provide for the common Defence and general Welfare of the United States; but all Duties, Imposts and Excises shall be uniform throughout the United States;

To borrow Money on the credit of the United States;

To regulate Commerce with foreign Nations, and among the several States, and with the Indian Tribes;

To establish a uniform Rule of Naturalization, and uniform Laws on the subject of Bankruptcies throughout the United States;

To coin Money, regulate the Value thereof, and of foreign Coin, and fix the Standard of Weights and Measures;

To provide for the Punishment of counterfeiting the Securities and current Coin of the United States;

To establish Post Offices and post Roads;

To promote the Progress of Science and useful Arts, by securing for limited Times to Authors and Inventors the exclusive Right to their respective writings and Discoveries;

To constitute Tribunals inferior to the supreme Court;

To define and punish Piracies and Felonies committed on the high Seas, and Offences against the Law of Nations;

To declare War, grant Letters of Marque and Reprisal, and make Rules concerning Captures on Land and Water;

To raise and support Armies, but no Appropriation of Money to that Use shall be for a longer Term than two Years;

To provide and maintain a Navy;

To make Rules for the Government and Regulation of the land and naval Forces;

To provide for calling forth the Militia to execute the Laws of the Union, suppress Insurrections and repel Invasions;

To provide for organizing, arming, and disciplining, the Militia, and for governing such Part of them as may be employed in the Service of the United States, reserving to the States respectively, the Appointment of the Officers, and the Authority of training the Militia according to the discipline prescribed by Congress;

To exercise exclusive Legislation in all Cases whatsoever, over such District (not exceeding ten Miles square) as may, by Cession of particular States, and the Acceptance of Congress, become the Seat of the Government of the United States, and to exercise like Authority over all Places purchased by the Consent of the Legislature of the State in which the Same shall be, for the Erection of Forts, Magazines, Arsenals, dock-Yards, and other needful Buildings;—And

To make all Laws which shall be necessary and proper for carrying into Execution the foregoing Powers, and all other Powers vested by this Constitution in the Government of the United States, or in any Department or Officer thereof.

SECTION 9. The Migration or Importation of such Persons as any of the States now existing shall think proper to admit, shall not be prohibited by the Congress prior to the Year one thousand eight hundred and eight, but a Tax or duty may be imposed on such Importation, not exceeding ten dollars for each Person.

The Privilege of the Writ of Habeas Corpus shall not be suspended, unless when in Cases of Rebellion or Invasion the public Safety may require it.

No Bill of Attainder or ex post facto Law shall be passed.

No Capitation, or other direct, Tax shall be laid, unless in Proportion to the Census or Enumeration herein before directed to be taken.[5]

No Tax or Duty shall be laid on Articles exported from any State.

No Preference shall be given by any Regulation of Commerce or Revenue to the Ports of one State over those of another: nor shall Vessels bound to, or from, one State, be obliged to enter, clear, or pay Duties in another.

No Money shall be drawn from the Treasury, but in Consequence of Appropriations made by Law; and a regular Statement and Account of the Receipts and Expenditures of all public Money shall be published from time to time.

No Title of Nobility shall be granted by the United States: And no Person holding any Office of Profit or Trust under them, shall, without the Consent of the Congress, accept of any present, Emolument, Office, or Title, of any kind whatever, from any King, Prince, or foreign State.

SECTION 10. No State shall enter into any Treaty, Alliance, or Confederation; grant Letters of Marque and Reprisal; coin Money; emit Bills of Credit; make any Thing but gold and silver Coin a Tender in Payment of Debts; pass any Bill of Attainder, ex post facto Law, or Law impairing the Obligation of Contracts, or grant any Title of Nobility.

No State shall, without the Consent of the Congress, lay any Imposts or Duties on Imports or Exports, except what may be absolutely necessary for executing it's inspection Laws: and the net Produce of all Duties and Imposts, laid by any State on Imports or Exports, shall be for the Use of the Treasury of the United States; and all such Laws shall be subject to the Revision and Controul of the Congress.

No State shall, without the Consent of Congress, lay any Duty of Tonnage, keep Troops, or Ships of War in time of Peace, enter into any Agreement or Compact with another State, or with a foreign Power, or engage in War, unless actually invaded, or in such imminent Danger as will not admit of delay.

Article II.

SECTION 1. The executive Power shall be vested in a President of the United States of America. He shall hold his Office during the Term of four Years, and, together with the Vice President, chosen for the Same Term, be elected as follows

Each State shall appoint, in such Manner as the Legislature thereof may direct, a Number of Electors, equal to the whole Number of Senators and Representatives to which the State may be entitled in the Congress: but no Senator or Representative, or Person holding an Office of Trust or Profit under the United States, shall be appointed an Elector.

[6]The Electors shall meet in their respective States, and vote by Ballot for two Persons of whom one at least shall not be an Inhabitant of the same State with themselves. And they shall make a List of all the Persons voted for, and of the Number of Votes for each; which List they shall sign and certify, and transmit sealed to the Seat of the Government of the United States, directed to the President of the Senate. The President of the Senate shall, in the Presence of the Senate and House of Representatives, open all the Certificates, and the Votes shall then be counted. The Person having the greatest Number of Votes shall be the

[5]This clause has been affected by the 16th amendment.

[6]This clause has been affected by the 12th amendment.

President, if such Number be a Majority of the whole Number of Electors appointed; and if there be more than one who have such Majority, and have an equal Number of Votes, then the House of Representatives shall immediately chuse by Ballot one of them for President; and if no Person have a Majority, then from the five highest on the List the said House shall in like Manner chuse the President. But in chusing the President, the Votes shall be taken by States, the Representation from each State having one Vote; A quorum for this Purpose shall consist of a Member or Members from two thirds of the States, and a Majority of all the States shall be necessary to a Choice. In every Case, after the Choice of the President, the Person having the greatest Number of Votes of the Electors shall be the Vice President. But if there should remain two or more who have equal Votes, the Senate shall chuse from them by Ballot the Vice President.

The Congress may determine the Time of chusing the Electors, and the Day on which they shall give their Votes; which Day shall be the same throughout the United States.

No Person except a natural born Citizen, or a Citizen of the United States, at the time of the Adoption of this Constitution, shall be eligible to the Office of President; neither shall any Person be eligible to that Office who shall not have attained to the Age of thirty five Years, and been fourteen Years a Resident within the United States.

In Case of the Removal of the President from Office, or of his Death, Resignation, or Inability to discharge the Powers and Duties of the said Office, the same shall devolve on the Vice President, and the Congress may by Law provide for the Case of Removal, Death, Resignation or Inability, both of the President and Vice President, declaring what Officer shall then act as President, and such Officer shall act accordingly, until the Disability be removed, or a President shall be elected.

The President shall, at stated Times, receive for his Services, a Compensation, which shall neither be encreased nor diminished during the Period for which he shall have been elected, and he shall not receive within that Period any other Emolument from the United States, or any of them.

Before he enter on the Execution of his Office, he shall take the following Oath or Affirmation:—"I do solemnly swear (or affirm) that I will faithfully execute the Office of President of the United States, and will to the best of my Ability, preserve, protect and defend the Constitution of the United States."

SECTION 2. The President shall be Commander in Chief of the Army and Navy of the United States, and of the Militia of the several States, when called into the actual Service of the United States; he may require the Opinion, in writing, of the principal Officer in each of the executive Departments, upon any Subject relating to the Duties of their respective Offices, and he shall have Power to grant Reprieves and Pardons for Offences against the United States, except in Cases of Impeachment.

He shall have Power, by and with the Advice and Consent of the Senate, to make Treaties, provided two thirds of the Senators present concur; and he shall nominate, and by and with the Advice and Consent of the Senate, shall appoint Ambassadors, other public Ministers and Consuls, Judges of the supreme Court, and all other Officers of the United States, whose Appointments are not herein otherwise provided for, and which shall be established by Law: but the Congress may by Law vest the Appointment of such inferior Officers, as they think proper, in the President alone, in the Courts of Law, or in the Heads of Departments.

The President shall have Power to fill up all Vacancies that may happen during the Recess of the Senate, by granting Commissions which shall expire at the End of their next Session.

SECTION 3. He shall from time to time give to the Congress Information of the State of the Union, and recommend to their Consideration such Measures as he shall judge necessary and expedient; he may, on extraordinary Occasions, convene both Houses, or either of them, and in Case of Disagreement between them, with Respect to the Time of Adjournment, he may adjourn them to such Time as he shall think proper; he shall receive Ambassadors and other public Ministers; he shall take Care that the Laws be faithfully executed, and shall Commission all the Officers of the United States.

SECTION 4. The President, Vice President and all civil Officers of the United States, shall be removed from Office on Impeachment for, and Conviction of, Treason, Bribery, or other high Crimes and Misdemeanors.

Article III.

SECTION 1. The judicial Power of the United States, shall be vested in one supreme Court, and in such inferior Courts as the Congress may from time to time ordain and establish. The Judges, both of the supreme and inferior Courts, shall hold their Offices during good Behaviour, and shall, at stated Times, receive for their Services, a Compensation, which shall not be diminished during their Continuance in Office.

[7]SECTION 2. The judicial Power shall extend to all Cases, in Law and Equity, arising under this Constitution, the Laws of the United States, and Treaties made, or which shall be made, under their Authority;—to all Cases affecting Ambassadors, other public Ministers and Consuls;—to all Cases of admiralty and maritime Jurisdiction;—to Controversies to which the United States shall be a party;—to Controversies between two or more States;—between a State and Citizens of another State;—between Citizens of different States,—between Citizens of the same State claiming Lands under Grants of different States, and between a State, or the Citizens thereof, and foreign States, Citizens or Subjects.

In all Cases affecting Ambassadors, other public Ministers and Consuls, and those in which a State shall be Party, the supreme Court shall have original Jurisdiction. In all the other Cases before mentioned, the supreme Court shall have appellate Jurisdiction, both as to Law and Fact, with such Exceptions, and under such Regulations as the Congress shall make.

The Trial of all Crimes, except in Cases of Impeachment, shall be by Jury; and such Trial shall be held in the State where the said Crimes shall have been committed; but when not committed within any State, the Trial shall be at such Place or Places as the Congress may by Law have directed.

SECTION 3. Treason against the United States, shall consist only in levying War against them, or in adhering to their Enemies, giving them Aid and Comfort. No Person shall be convicted of Treason unless on the Testimony of two Witnesses to the same overt Act, or on Confession in open Court.

The Congress shall have Power to declare the Punishment of Treason, but no Attainder of Treason shall work Corruption of Blood, or Forfeiture except during the Life of the Person attainted.

Article IV.

SECTION 1. Full Faith and Credit shall be given in each State to the public Acts, Records, and judicial Proceedings of every other State. And the Congress may by general Laws prescribe the Manner in which such Acts, Records and Proceedings shall be proved, and the Effect thereof.

SECTION 2. The Citizens of each State shall be entitled to all Privileges and Immunities of Citizens in the several States.

A Person charged in any State with Treason, Felony, or other Crime, who shall flee from Justice, and be found in another State, shall on Demand of the executive Authority of

---

[7]This section has been affected by the 11th amendment.

the State from which he fled, be delivered up, to be removed to the State having Jurisdiction of the Crime.

No Person held to Service or Labour in one State, under the Laws thereof, escaping into another, shall, in Consequence of any Law or Regulation therein, be discharged from such Service or Labour, but shall be delivered up on Claim of the Party to whom such Service or Labour may be due.[8]

SECTION 3. New States may be admitted by the Congress into this Union; but no new State shall be formed or erected within the Jurisdiction of any other State; nor any State be formed by the Junction of two or more States, or Parts of States, without the Consent of the Legislatures of the States concerned as well as of the Congress.

The Congress shall have Power to dispose of and make all needful Rules and Regulations respecting the Territory or other Property belonging to the United States; and nothing in this Constitution shall be so construed as to Prejudice any Claims of the United States, or of any particular State.

SECTION 4. The United States shall guarantee to every State in this Union a Republican Form of Government, and shall protect each of them against Invasion; and on Application of the Legislature, or of the Executive (when the Legislature cannot be convened) against domestic Violence.

Article V.

The Congress, whenever two thirds of both Houses shall deem it necessary, shall propose Amendments to this Constitution, or on the Application of the Legislatures of two thirds of the several States, shall call a Convention for proposing Amendments, which, in either Case, shall be valid to all Intents and Purposes, as Part of this Constitution, when ratified by the Legislatures of three fourths of the several States, or by Conventions in three fourths thereof, as the one or the other Mode of Ratification may be proposed by the Congress; Provided that no Amendment which may be made prior to the Year One thousand eight hundred and eight shall in any Manner affect the first and fourth Clauses in the Ninth Section of the first Article; and that no State, without its Consent, shall be deprived of its equal Suffrage in the Senate.

Article VI.

All Debts contracted and Engagements entered into, before the Adoption of this Constitution, shall be as valid against the United States under this Constitution, as under the Confederation.

This Constitution, and the laws of the United States which shall be made in Pursuance thereof; and all Treaties made, or which shall be made, under the Authority of the United States, shall be the supreme Law of the Land; and the Judges in every State shall be bound thereby, any Thing in the Constitution or Laws of any State to the Contrary notwithstanding.

The Senators and Representatives before mentioned, and the Members of the several State Legislatures, and all executive and judicial Officers, both of the United States and of the several States, shall be bound by Oath or Affirmation, to support this Constitution; but no religious Test shall ever be required as a Qualification to any Office or public Trust under the United States.

Article VII.

The Ratification of the Conventions of nine States, shall be sufficient for the Establishment of this Constitution between the States so ratifying the Same.

---

[8]This clause was affected by the 13th amendment.

DONE in Convention by the Unanimous Consent of the States present the Seventeenth Day of September in the Year of our Lord one thousand seven hundred and Eighty seven and of the Independence of the United States of America the Twelfth. IN WITNESS whereof we have hereunto subscribed our Names,

GO. WASHINGTON—*Presid't. and deputy from Virginia*

Attest WILLIAM JACKSON *Secretary*

New Hampshire

JOHN LANGDON
NICHOLAS GILMAN

Massachusetts

NATHANIEL GORHAM
RUFUS KING

Connecticut

WM. SAML. JOHNSON
ROGER SHERMAN

New York

ALEXANDER HAMILTON

New Jersey

WIL. LIVINGSTON
DAVID BREARLEY.
WM. PATERSON.
JONA. DAYTON

Pennsylvania

B. FRANKLIN
THOMAS MIFFLIN
ROBT. MORRIS
GEO. CLYMER
THOS. FITZSIMONS
JARED INGERSOLL
JAMES WILSON.
GOUV. MORRIS

Delaware

GEO. READ
GUNNING BEDFORD jun
JOHN DICKINSON
RICHARD BASSETT
JACO. BROOM

Maryland

JAMES MCHENRY
DAN OF ST. THOS. JENIFER
DANL. CARROLL.

Virginia

JOHN BLAIR—
JAMES MADISON Jr.

North Carolina

WM. BLOUNT
RICHD. DOBBS SPAIGHT.
HU. WILLIAMSON

South Carolina

J. Rutledge	Charles Pinckney
Charles Cotesworth Pinckney	Pierce Butler.

Georgia

William Few	Abr. Baldwin

ARTICLES IN ADDITION TO, AND AMENDMENT OF THE CONSTITUTION OF THE UNITED STATES OF AMERICA, PROPOSED BY CONGRESS, AND RATIFIED BY THE LEGISLATURES OF THE SEVERAL STATES, PURSUANT TO THE FIFTH ARTICLE OF THE ORIGINAL CONSTITUTION.

Article [I.][9]

Congress shall make no law respecting an establishment of religion, or prohibiting the free exercise thereof; or abridging the freedom of speech, or of the press; or the right of the people peaceably to assemble, and to petition the Government for a redress of grievances.

Article [II.]

A well regulated militia, being necessary to the security of a free State, the right of the people to keep and bear arms, shall not be infringed.

Article [III.]

No Soldier shall, in time of peace be quartered in any house, without the consent of the owner, nor in time of war, but in a manner to be prescribed by law.

Article [IV.]

The right of the people to be secure in their persons, houses, papers, and effects, against unreasonable searches and seizures, shall not be violated, and no warrants shall issue, but upon probable cause, supported by oath or affirmation, and particularly describing the place to be searched, and the persons or things to be seized.

Article [V.]

No person shall be held to answer for a capital, or otherwise infamous crime, unless on a presentment or indictment of a Grand Jury, except in cases arising in the land or naval forces, or in the militia, when in actual service in time of war or public danger; nor shall any person be subject for the same offence to be twice put in jeopardy of life or limb; nor shall be compelled in any criminal case to be a witness against himself, nor be deprived of life, liberty, or property, without due process of law; nor shall private property be taken for public use, without just compensation.

---

[9]The first ten amendments to the Constitution of the United States were proposed to the legislatures of the several States by the First Congress, on the 25th of September, 1789. They were ratified by the following States, and the notifications of ratification by the governors thereof were successfully communicated by the President to Congress: New Jersey, November 20, 1789; Maryland, December 19, 1789; North Carolina, December 22, 1789; South Carolina, January 19, 1790; New Hampshire, January 25, 1790; Delaware, January 28, 1790; New York, February 24, 1790; Pennsylvania, March 10, 1790; Rhode Island, June 7, 1790; Vermont, November 3, 1791, and Virginia, December 15, 1791. The amendments were subsequently ratified by the legislatures of Massachusetts, March 2, 1939; Georgia, March 18, 1939; and Connecticut, April 19, 1939.

Article [VI.]

In all criminal prosecutions, the accused shall enjoy the right to a speedy and public trial, by an impartial jury of the State and district wherein the crime shall have been committed, which district shall have been previously ascertained by law, and to be informed of the nature and cause of the accusation; to be confronted with the witnesses against him; to have compulsory process for obtaining witnesses in his favor, and to have the assistance of counsel for his defence.

Article [VII.]

In Suits at common law, where the value in controversy shall exceed twenty dollars, the right of trial by jury shall be preserved, and no fact tried by a jury, shall be otherwise reexamined in any Court of the United States, than according to the rules of the common law.

Article [VIII.]

Excessive bail shall not be required, nor excessive fines imposed, nor cruel and unusual punishments inflicted.

Article [IX.]

The enumeration in the Constitution, of certain rights, shall not be construed to deny or disparage others retained by the people.

Article [X.]

The powers not delegated to the United States by the Constitution, nor prohibited by it to the States, are reserved to the States respectively, or to the people.

[Article XI.]

The Judicial power of the United States shall not be construed to extend to any suit in law or equity, commenced or prosecuted against one of the United States by Citizens of another State, or by Citizens or Subjects of any Foreign State.

Proposal and Ratification

The eleventh amendment to the Constitution of the United States was proposed to the legislatures of the several States by the Third Congress, on the 4th of March 1794; and was declared in a message from the President to Congress, dated the 8th of January, 1798, to have been ratified by the legislatures of three-fourths of the States. The dates of ratification were: New York, March 27, 1794; Rhode Island, March 31, 1794; Connecticut, May 8, 1794; New Hampshire, June 16, 1794; Massachusetts, June 26, 1794; Vermont, between October 9, 1794 and November 9, 1794; Virginia, November 18, 1794; Georgia, November 29, 1794; Kentucky, December 7, 1794; Maryland, December 26, 1794; Delaware, January 23, 1795; North Carolina, February 7, 1795.

Ratification was completed on February 7, 1795.

The amendment was subsequently ratified by South Carolina on December 4, 1797. New Jersey and Pennsylvania did not take action on the amendment.

[Article XII.][10]

The Electors shall meet in their respective states, and vote by ballot for President and Vice-President, one of whom, at least, shall not be an inhabitant of the same state with themselves; they shall name in their ballots the person voted for as President, and in distinct

[10]This amendment was affected by the 20th amendment, § 3.

ballots the person voted for as Vice-President, and they shall make distinct lists of all persons voted for as President, and of all persons voted for as Vice-President, and of the number of votes for each, which lists they shall sign and certify, and transmit sealed to the seat of the government of the United States, directed to the President of the Senate;—The President of the Senate shall, in the presence of the Senate and House of Representatives, open all the certificates and the votes shall then be counted;—The person having the greatest number of votes for President, shall be the President, if such number be a majority of the whole number of Electors appointed; and if no person have such majority, then from the persons having the highest numbers not exceeding three on the list of those voted for as President, the House of Representatives shall choose immediately, by ballot, the President. But in choosing the President, the votes shall be taken by states, the representation from each state having one vote; a quorum for this purpose shall consist of a member or members from two-thirds of the states, and a majority of all the states shall be necessary to a choice. And if the House of Representatives shall not choose a President whenever the right of choice shall devolve upon them, before the fourth day of March next following, then the Vice-President shall act as President, as in the case of the death or other constitutional disability of the President.—The person having the greatest number of votes as Vice-President, shall be the Vice-President, if such number be a majority of the whole number of Electors appointed, and if no person have a majority, then from the two highest numbers on the list, the Senate shall choose the Vice-President; a quorum for the purpose shall consist of two-thirds of the whole number of Senators, and a majority of the whole number shall be necessary to a choice. But no person constitutionally ineligible to the office of President shall be eligible to that of Vice-President of the United States.

Proposal and Ratification

The twelfth amendment to the Constitution of the United States was proposed to the legislatures of the several States by the Eighth Congress, on the 9th of December, 1803, in lieu of the original third paragraph of the first section of the second article; and was declared in a proclamation of the Secretary of State, dated the 25th of September, 1804, to have been ratified by the legislatures of 13 of the 17 States. The dates of ratification were: North Carolina, December 21, 1803; Maryland, December 24, 1803; Kentucky, December 27, 1803; Ohio, December 30, 1803; Pennsylvania, January 5, 1804; Vermont, January 30, 1804; Virginia, February 3, 1804; New York, February 10, 1804; New Jersey, February 22, 1804; Rhode Island, March 12, 1804; South Carolina, May 15, 1804; Georgia, May 19, 1804; New Hampshire, June 15, 1804.

Ratification was completed on June 15, 1804.

The amendment was subsequently ratified by Tennessee, July 27, 1804.

The amendment was rejected by Delaware, January 18, 1804; Massachusetts, February 3, 1804; Connecticut, at its session begun May 10, 1804.

Article XIII.

SECTION 1. Neither slavery nor involuntary servitude, except as a punishment for crime whereof the party shall have been duly convicted, shall exist within the United States, or any place subject to their jurisdiction.

SECTION 2. Congress shall have power to enforce this article by appropriate legislation.

Proposal and Ratification

The thirteenth amendment to the Constitution of the United States was proposed to the legislatures of the several States by the Thirty-eighth Congress, on the 31st day of

January, 1865, and was declared, in a proclamation of the Secretary of State, dated the 18th of December, 1865, to have been ratified by the legislatures of twenty-seven of the thirty-six States. The dates of ratification were: Illinois, February 1, 1865; Rhode Island, February 2, 1865; Michigan, February 2, 1865; Maryland, February 3, 1865; New York, February 3, 1865; Pennsylvania, February 3, 1865; West Virginia, February 3, 1865; Missouri, February 6, 1865; Maine, February 7, 1865; Kansas, February 7, 1865; Massachusetts, February 7, 1865; Virginia, February 9, 1865; Ohio, February 10, 1865; Indiana, February 13, 1865; Nevada, February 16, 1865; Louisiana, February 17, 1865; Minnesota, February 23, 1865; Wisconsin, February 24, 1865; Vermont, March 9, 1865; Tennessee, April 7, 1865; Arkansas, April 14, 1865; Connecticut, May 4, 1865; New Hampshire, July 1, 1865; South Carolina, November 13, 1865; Alabama, December 2, 1865; North Carolina, December 4, 1865; Georgia, December 6, 1865.

Ratification was completed on December 6, 1865.

The amendment was subsequently ratified by Oregon, December 8, 1865; California, December 19, 1865; Florida, December 28, 1865 (Florida again ratified on June 9, 1868, upon its adoption of a new constitution); Iowa, January 15, 1866; New Jersey, January 23, 1866 (after having rejected the amendment on March 16, 1865); Texas, February 18, 1870; Delaware, February 12, 1901 (after having rejected the amendment on February 8, 1865); Kentucky, March 18, 1976 (after having rejected it on February 24, 1865).

The amendment was rejected (and not subsequently ratified) by Mississippi, December 4, 1865.

Article XIV.

SECTION 1. All persons born or naturalized in the United States, and subject to the jurisdiction thereof, are citizens of the United States and of the State wherein they reside. No State shall make or enforce any law which shall abridge the privileges or immunities of citizens of the United States; nor shall any State deprive any person of life, liberty, or property, without due process of law; nor deny to any person within its jurisdiction the equal protection of the laws.

SECTION 2. Representatives shall be apportioned among the several States according to their respective numbers, counting the whole number of persons in each State, excluding Indians not taxed. But when the right to vote at any election for the choice of electors for President and Vice President of the United States, Representatives in Congress, the Executive and Judicial officers of a State, or the members of the Legislature thereof, is denied to any of the male inhabitants of such State, being twenty-one years of age, and citizens of the United States, or in any way abridged, except for participation in rebellion, or other crime, the basis of representation therein shall be reduced in the proportion which the number of such male citizens shall bear to the whole number of male citizens twenty-one years of age in such State.

SECTION 3. No person shall be a Senator or Representative in Congress, or elector of President and Vice President, or hold any office, civil or military, under the United States, or under any State, who, having previously taken an oath, as a member of Congress, or as an officer of the United States, or as a member of any State legislature, or as an executive or judicial officer of any State, to support the Constitution of the United States, shall have engaged in insurrection or rebellion against the same, or given aid or comfort to the enemies thereof. But Congress may by a vote of two-thirds of each House, remove such disability.

SECTION 4. The validity of the public debt of the United States, authorized by law, including debts incurred for payment of pensions and bounties for services in suppressing insurrection or rebellion, shall not be questioned. But neither the United States nor any State shall assume or pay any debt or obligation incurred in aid of insurrection or rebellion against the United States, or any claim for the loss or emancipation of any slave; but all such debts, obligations and claims shall be held illegal and void.

SECTION 5. The Congress shall have power to enforce, by appropriate legislation, the provisions of this article.

Proposal and Ratification

The fourteenth amendment to the Constitution of the United States was proposed to the legislatures of the several States by the Thirty-ninth Congress, on the 13th of June, 1866. It was declared, in a certificate of the Secretary of State dated July 28, 1868 to have been ratified by the legislatures of 28 of the 37 States. The dates of ratification were: Connecticut, June 25, 1866; New Hampshire, July 6, 1866; Tennessee, July 19, 1866; New Jersey, September 11, 1866 (subsequently the legislature rescinded its ratification, and on March 5, 1868, readopted its resolution of rescission over the Governor's veto); Oregon, September 19, 1866 (and rescinded its ratification on October 15, 1868); Vermont, October 30, 1866; Ohio, January 4, 1867 (and rescinded its ratification on January 15, 1868); New York, January 10, 1867; Kansas, January 11, 1867; Illinois, January 15, 1867; West Virginia, January 16, 1867; Michigan, January 16, 1867; Minnesota, January 16, 1867; Maine, January 19, 1867; Nevada, January 22, 1867; Indiana, January 23, 1867; Missouri, January 25, 1867; Rhode Island, February 7, 1867; Wisconsin, February 7, 1867; Pennsylvania, February 12, 1867; Massachusetts, March 20, 1867; Nebraska, June 15, 1867; Iowa, March 16, 1868; Arkansas, April 6, 1868; Florida, June 9, 1868; North Carolina, July 4, 1868 (after having rejected it on December 14, 1866); Louisiana, July 9, 1868 (after having rejected it on February 6, 1867); South Carolina, July 9, 1868 (after having rejected it on December 20, 1866).

Ratification was completed on July 9, 1868.

The amendment was subsequently ratified by Alabama, July 13, 1868; Georgia, July 21, 1868 (after having rejected it on November 9, 1866); Virginia, October 8, 1869 (after having rejected it on January 9, 1867); Mississippi, January 17, 1870; Texas, February 18, 1870 (after having rejected it on October 27, 1866); Delaware, February 12, 1901 (after having rejected it on February 8, 1867); Maryland, April 4, 1959 (after having rejected it on March 23, 1867); California, May 6, 1959; Kentucky, March 18, 1976 (after having rejected it on January 8, 1867).

Article XV.

SECTION 1. The right of citizens of the United States to vote shall not be denied or abridged by the United States or by any State on account of race, color, or previous condition of servitude.

SECTION 2. The Congress shall have power to enforce this article by appropriate legislation.

Proposal and Ratification

The fifteenth amendment to the Constitution of the United States was proposed to the legislatures of the several States by the Fortieth Congress, on the 26th of February, 1869, and was declared, in a proclamation of the Secretary of State, dated March 30, 1870, to have been ratified by the legislatures of twenty-nine of the thirty-seven States. The dates of ratification were: Nevada, March 1, 1869; West Virginia, March 3, 1869; Illinois, March 5, 1869; Louisiana, March 5, 1869; North Carolina, March 5, 1869; Michigan, March 8, 1869; Wisconsin, March 9, 1869; Maine, March 11, 1869; Massachusetts, March 12, 1869; Arkansas, March 15, 1869; South Carolina, March 15, 1869; Pennsylvania, March 25, 1869; New York, April 14, 1869 (and the legislature of the same State passed a resolution January 5, 1870, to withdraw its consent to it, which action it rescinded on March 30, 1970); Indiana, May 14, 1869; Connecticut, May 19, 1869; Florida, June 14, 1869; New Hampshire, July 1, 1869; Virginia, October 8, 1869; Vermont, October 20, 1869; Missouri, January 7, 1870; Minnesota, January 13, 1870; Mississippi, January 17, 1870; Rhode Island, January 18, 1870; Kansas, January 19,

1870; Ohio, January 27, 1870 (after having rejected it on April 30, 1869); Georgia, February 2, 1870; Iowa, February 3, 1870.

Ratification was completed on February 3, 1870, unless the withdrawal of ratification by New York was effective; in which event ratification was completed on February 17, 1870, when Nebraska ratified.

The amendment was subsequently ratified by Texas, February 18, 1870; New Jersey, February 15, 1871 (after having rejected it on February 7, 1870); Delaware, February 12, 1901 (after having rejected it on March 18, 1869); Oregon, February 24, 1959; California, April 3, 1962 (after having rejected it on January 28, 1870); Kentucky, March 18, 1976 (after having rejected it on March 12, 1869).

The amendment was approved by the Governor of Maryland, May 7, 1973; Maryland having previously rejected it on February 26, 1870.

The amendment was rejected (and not subsequently ratified) by Tennessee, November 16, 1869.

Article XVI.

The Congress shall have power to lay and collect taxes on incomes, from whatever source derived, without apportionment among the several States, and without regard to any census or enumeration.

Proposal and Ratification

The sixteenth amendment to the Constitution of the United States was proposed to the legislatures of the several States by the Sixty-first Congress on the 12th of July, 1909, and was declared, in a proclamation of the Secretary of State, dated the 25th of February, 1913, to have been ratified by 36 of the 48 States. The dates of ratification were: Alabama, August 10, 1909; Kentucky, February 8, 1910; South Carolina, February 19, 1910; Illinois, March 1, 1910; Mississippi, March 7, 1910; Oklahoma, March 10, 1910; Maryland, April 8, 1910; Georgia, August 3, 1910; Texas, August 16, 1910; Ohio, January 19, 1911; Idaho, January 20, 1911; Oregon, January 23, 1911; Washington, January 26, 1911; Montana, January 30, 1911; Indiana, January 30, 1911; California, January 31, 1911; Nevada, January 31, 1911; South Dakota, February 3, 1911; Nebraska, February 9, 1911; North Carolina, February 11, 1911; Colorado, February 15, 1911; North Dakota, February 17, 1911; Kansas, February 18, 1911; Michigan, February 23, 1911; Iowa, February 24, 1911; Missouri, March 16, 1911; Maine, March 31, 1911; Tennessee, April 7, 1911; Arkansas, April 22, 1911 (after having rejected it earlier); Wisconsin, May 26, 1911; New York, July 12, 1911; Arizona, April 6, 1912; Minnesota, June 11, 1912; Louisiana, June 28, 1912; West Virginia, January 31, 1913; New Mexico, February 3, 1913.

Ratification was completed on February 3, 1913.

The amendment was subsequently ratified by Massachusetts, March 4, 1913; New Hampshire, March 7, 1913 (after having rejected it on March 2, 1911).

The amendment was rejected (and not subsequently ratified) by Connecticut, Rhode Island, and Utah.

Article [XVII.]

The Senate of the United States shall be composed of two Senators from each State, elected by the people thereof, for six years; and each Senator shall have one vote. The electors in each State shall have the qualifications requisite for electors of the most numerous branch of the State legislatures.

When vacancies happen in the representation of any State in the Senate, the executive authority of such State shall issue writs of election to fill such vacancies: *Provided,* That the legislature of any State may empower the executive thereof to make temporary appointments until the people fill the vacancies by election as the legislature may direct.

This amendment shall not be so construed as to affect the election or term of any Senator chosen before it becomes valid as part of the Constitution.

Proposal and Ratification

The seventeenth amendment to the Constitution of the United States was proposed to the legislatures of the several States by the Sixty-second Congress on the 13th of May, 1912, and was declared, in a proclamation of the Secretary of State, dated the 31st of May, 1913, to have been ratified by the legislatures of 36 of the 48 States. The dates of ratification were: Massachusetts, May 22, 1912; Arizona, June 3, 1912; Minnesota, June 10, 1912; New York, January 15, 1913; Kansas, January 17, 1913; Oregon, January 23, 1913; North Carolina, January 25, 1913; California, January 28, 1913; Michigan, January 28, 1913; Iowa, January 30, 1913; Montana, January 30, 1913; Idaho, January 31, 1913; West Virginia, February 4, 1913; Colorado, February 5, 1913; Nevada, February 6, 1913; Texas, February 7, 1913; Washington, February 7, 1913; Wyoming, February 8, 1913; Arkansas, February 11, 1913; Maine, February 11, 1913; Illinois, February 13, 1913; North Dakota, February 14, 1913; Wisconsin, February 18, 1913; Indiana, February 19, 1913; New Hampshire, February 19, 1913; Vermont, February 19, 1913; South Dakota, February 19, 1913; Oklahoma, February 24, 1913; Ohio, February 25, 1913; Missouri, March 7, 1913; New Mexico, March 13, 1913; Nebraska, March 14, 1913; New Jersey, March 17, 1913; Tennessee, April 1, 1913; Pennsylvania, April 2, 1913; Connecticut, April 8, 1913.

Ratification was completed on April 8, 1913.

The amendment was subsequently ratified by Louisiana, June 11, 1914.

The amendment was rejected by Utah (and not subsequently ratified) on February 26, 1913.

Article [XVIII.][11]

SECTION 1. After one year from the ratification of this article the manufacture, sale, or transportation of intoxicating liquors within, the importation thereof into, or the exportation thereof from the United States and all territory subject to the jurisdiction thereof for beverage purposes is hereby prohibited.

SEC. 2. The Congress and the several States shall have concurrent power to enforce this article by appropriate legislation.

SEC. 3. This article shall be inoperative unless it shall have been ratified as an amendment to the Constitution by the legislatures of the several States, as provided in the Constitution, within seven years from the date of the submission hereof to the States by the Congress.

Proposal and Ratification

The eighteenth amendment to the Constitution of the United States was proposed to the legislatures of the several States by the Sixty-fifth Congress, on the 18th of December, 1917, and was declared, in a proclamation of the Secretary of State, dated the 29th of January, 1919, to have been ratified by the legislatures of 36 of the 48 States. The dates of ratification were: Mississippi, January 8, 1918; Virginia, January 11, 1918; Kentucky, January 14, 1918; North Dakota, January 25, 1918; South Carolina, January 29, 1918; Maryland, February 13, 1918; Montana, February 19, 1918; Texas, March 4, 1918; Delaware, March 18, 1918; South

---

[11]Repealed. See Article [XXI.]

Dakota, March 20, 1918; Massachusetts, April 2, 1918; Arizona, May 24, 1918; Georgia, June 26, 1918; Louisiana, August 3, 1918; Florida, December 3, 1918; Michigan, January 2, 1919; Ohio, January 7, 1919; Oklahoma, January 7, 1919; Idaho, January 8, 1919; Maine, January, 8, 1919; West Virginia, January 9, 1919; California, January 13, 1919; Tennessee, January 13, 1919; Washington, January 13, 1919; Arkansas, January 14, 1919; Kansas, January 14, 1919; Alabama, January 15, 1919; Colorado, January 15, 1919; Iowa, January 15, 1919; New Hampshire, January 15, 1919; Oregon, January 15, 1919; Nebraska, January 16, 1919; North Carolina, January 16, 1919; Utah, January 16, 1919; Missouri, January 16, 1919; Wyoming, January 16, 1919.

Ratification was completed on January 16, 1919.

The amendment was subsequently ratified by Minnesota on January 17, 1917; Wisconsin, January 17, 1919; New Mexico, January 20, 1919; Nevada, January 21, 1919; New York, January 29, 1919; Vermont, January 29, 1919; Pennsylvania, February 25, 1919; Connecticut, May 6, 1919; and New Jersey, March 9, 1922.

The amendment was rejected (and not subsequently ratified) by Rhode Island.

Article [XIX.]

The right of citizens of the United States to vote shall not be denied or abridged by the United States or by any State on account of sex.

Congress shall have power to enforce this article by appropriate legislation.

Proposal and Ratification

The nineteenth amendment to the Constitution of the United States was proposed to the legislatures of the several States by the Sixty-sixth Congress, on the 4th of June, 1919, and was declared, in a proclamation of the Secretary of State, dated the 26th of August, 1920, to have been ratified by the legislatures of 36 of the 48 States. The dates of ratification were: Illinois, June 10, 1919 (and that State readopted its resolution of ratification June 17, 1919); Michigan, June 10, 1919; Wisconsin, June 10, 1919; Kansas, June 16, 1919; New York, June 16, 1919; Ohio, June 16, 1919; Pennsylvania, June 24, 1919; Massachusetts, June 25, 1919; Texas, June 28, 1919; Iowa, July 2, 1919; Missouri, July 3, 1919; Arkansas, July 28, 1919; Montana, August 2, 1919; Nebraska, August 2, 1919; Minnesota, September 8, 1919; New Hampshire, September 10, 1919; Utah, October 2, 1919; California, November 1, 1919; Maine, November 5, 1919; North Dakota, December 1, 1919; South Dakota, December 4, 1919; Colorado, December 15, 1919; Kentucky, January 6, 1920; Rhode Island, January 6, 1920; Oregon, January 13, 1920; Indiana, January 16, 1920; Wyoming, January 27, 1920; Nevada, February 7, 1920; New Jersey, February 9, 1920; Idaho, February 11, 1920; Arizona, February 12, 1920; New Mexico, February 21, 1920; Oklahoma, February 28, 1920; West Virginia, March 10, 1920; Washington, March 22, 1920; Tennessee, August 18, 1920.

Ratification was completed on August 18, 1920.

The amendment was subsequently ratified by Connecticut on September 14, 1920 (and that State reaffirmed on September 21, 1920); Vermont, February 8, 1921; Maryland, March 29, 1941 (after having rejected it on February 24, 1920; ratification certified on February 25, 1958); Virginia, February 21, 1952 (after rejecting it on February 12, 1920); Alabama, September 8, 1953 (after rejecting it on September 22, 1919); Florida, May 13, 1969; South Carolina, July 1, 1969 (after rejecting it on January 28, 1920; ratification certified on August 22, 1973); Georgia, February 20, 1970 (after rejecting it on July 24, 1919); Louisiana, June 11, 1970 (after rejecting it on July 1, 1920); North Carolina, May 6, 1971.

The amendment was rejected (and not subsequently ratified) by Mississippi, March 29, 1920; Delaware, June 2, 1920.

Article [XX.]

SECTION 1. The terms of the President and Vice President shall end at noon on the 20th day of January, and the terms of Senators and Representatives at noon on the 3d day of January, of the years in which such terms would have ended if this article had not been ratified; and the terms of their successors shall then begin.

SEC. 2. The Congress shall assemble at least once in every year, and such meeting shall begin at noon on the 3d day of January, unless they shall by law appoint a different day.

SEC. 3. If, at the time fixed for the beginning of the term of the President, the President elect shall have died, the Vice President elect shall become President. If a President shall not have been chosen before the time fixed for the beginning of his term, or if the President elect shall have failed to qualify, then the Vice President elect shall act as President until a President shall have qualified; and the Congress may by law provide for the case wherein neither a President elect nor a Vice President elect shall have qualified, declaring who shall then act as President, or the manner in which one who is to act shall be selected, and such person shall act accordingly until a President or Vice President shall have qualified.

SEC. 4. The Congress may by law provide for the case of the death of any of the persons from whom the House of Representatives may choose a President whenever the rights of choice shall have devolved upon them, and for the case of the death of any of the persons from whom the Senate may choose a Vice President whenever the right of choice shall have devolved upon them.

SEC. 5. Sections 1 and 2 shall take effect on the 15th day of October following the ratification of this article.

SEC. 6. This article shall be inoperative unless it shall have been ratified as an amendment to the Constitution by the legislatures of three-fourths of the several States within seven years from the date of its submission.

Proposal and Ratification

The twentieth amendment to the Constitution was proposed to the legislatures of the several states by the Seventy-Second Congress, on the 2d day of March, 1932, and was declared, in a proclamation by the Secretary of State, dated on the 6th day of February, 1933, to have been ratified by the legislatures of 36 of the 48 States. The dates of ratification were: Virginia, March 4, 1932; New York, March 11, 1932; Mississippi, March 16, 1932; Arkansas, March 17, 1932; Kentucky, March 17, 1932; New Jersey, March 21, 1932; South Carolina, March 25, 1932; Michigan, March 31, 1932; Maine, April 1, 1932; Rhode Island, April 14, 1932; Illinois, April 21, 1932; Louisiana, June 22, 1932; West Virginia, July 30, 1932; Pennsylvania, August 11, 1932; Indiana, August 15, 1932; Texas, September 7, 1932; Alabama, September 13, 1932; California, January 4, 1933; North Carolina, January 5, 1933; North Dakota, January 9, 1933; Minnesota, January 12, 1933; Arizona, January 13, 1933; Montana, January 13, 1933; Nebraska, January 13, 1933; Oklahoma, January 13, 1933; Kansas, January 16, 1933; Oregon, January 16, 1933; Delaware, January 19, 1933; Washington, January 19, 1933; Wyoming, January 19, 1933; Iowa, January 20, 1933; South Dakota, January 20, 1933; Tennessee, January 20, 1933; Idaho, January 21, 1933; New Mexico, January 21, 1933; Georgia, January 23, 1933; Missouri, January 23, 1933; Ohio, January 23, 1933; Utah, January 23, 1933.

Ratification was completed on January 23, 1933.

The amendment was subsequently ratified by Massachusetts on January 24, 1933; Wisconsin, January 24, 1933; Colorado, January 24, 1933; Nevada, January 26, 1933; Connecticut, January 27, 1933; New Hampshire, January 31, 1933; Vermont, February 2, 1933; Maryland, March 24, 1933; Florida, April 26, 1933.

Article [XXI.]

SECTION 1. The eighteenth article of amendment to the Constitution of the United States is hereby repealed.

SEC. 2. The transportation or importation into any State, Territory, or possession of the United States for delivery or use therein of intoxicating liquors, in violation of the laws thereof, is hereby prohibited.

SEC. 3. This article shall be inoperative unless it shall have been ratified as an amendment to the Constitution by conventions in the several States, as provided in the Constitution, within seven years from the date of the submission hereof to the States by the Congress.

Proposal and Ratification

The twenty-first amendment to the Constitution was proposed to the several states by the Seventy-Second Congress, on the 20th day of February, 1933, and was declared, in a proclamation by the Secretary of State, dated on the 5th day of December, 1933, to have been ratified by 36 of the 48 States. The dates of ratification were: Michigan, April 10, 1933; Wisconsin, April 25, 1933; Rhode Island, May 8, 1933; Wyoming, May 25, 1933; New Jersey, June 1, 1933; Delaware, June 24, 1933; Indiana, June 26, 1933; Massachusetts, June 26, 1933; New York, June 27, 1933; Illinois, July 10, 1933; Iowa, July 10, 1933; Connecticut, July 11, 1933; New Hampshire, July 11, 1933; California, July 24, 1933; West Virginia, July 25, 1933; Arkansas, August 1, 1933; Oregon, August 7, 1933; Alabama, August 8, 1933; Tennessee, August 11, 1933; Missouri, August 29, 1933; Arizona, September 5, 1933; Nevada, September 5, 1933; Vermont, September 23, 1933; Colorado, September 26, 1933; Washington, October 3, 1933; Minnesota, October 10, 1933; Idaho, October 17, 1933; Maryland, October 18, 1933; Virginia, October 25, 1933; New Mexico, November 2, 1933; Florida, November 14, 1933; Texas, November 24, 1933; Kentucky, November 27, 1933; Ohio, December 5, 1933; Pennsylvania, December 5, 1933; Utah, December 5, 1933.

Ratification was completed on December 5, 1933.

The amendment was subsequently ratified by Maine, on December 6, 1933, and by Montana, on August 6, 1934.

The amendment was rejected (and not subsequently ratified) by South Carolina, on December 4, 1933.

Article [XXII.]

SECTION 1. No person shall be elected to the office of the President more than twice, and no person who has held the office of President, or acted as President, for more than two years of a term to which some other person was elected President shall be elected to the office of the President more than once. But this Article shall not apply to any person holding the office of President when this Article was proposed by the Congress, and shall not prevent any person who may be holding the office of President, or acting as President, during the term within which this Article becomes operative from holding the office of President or acting as President during the remainder of such term.

SEC. 2. This article shall be inoperative unless it shall have been ratified as an amendment to the Constitution by the legislatures of three-fourths of the several States within seven years from the date of its submission to the States by the Congress.

Proposal and Ratification

This amendment was proposed to the legislatures of the several States by the Eightieth Congress on Mar. 21, 1947 by House Joint Res. No. 27, and was declared by the Administrator of General Services, on Mar. 1, 1951, to have been ratified by the legislatures of 36 of the 48 States. The dates of ratification were: Maine, March 31, 1947; Michigan, March 31, 1947; Iowa, April 1, 1947; Kansas, April 1, 1947; New Hampshire, April 1, 1947; Delaware, April 2, 1947; Illinois, April 3, 1947; Oregon, April 3, 1947; Colorado, April 12, 1947; California, April 15, 1947; New Jersey, April 15, 1947; Vermont, April 15, 1947; Ohio, April 16, 1947; Wisconsin, April 16, 1947; Pennsylvania, April 29, 1947; Connecticut, May 21, 1947; Missouri, May 22, 1947; Nebraska, May 23, 1947; Virginia, January 28, 1948; Mississippi, February 12, 1948; New York, March 9, 1948; South Dakota, January 21, 1949; North Dakota, February 25, 1949; Louisiana, May 17, 1950; Montana, January 25, 1951; Indiana, January 29, 1951; Idaho, January 30, 1951; New Mexico, February 12, 1951; Wyoming, February 12, 1951; Arkansas, February 15, 1951; Georgia, February 17, 1951; Tennessee, February 20, 1951; Texas, February 22, 1951; Nevada, February 26, 1951; Utah, February 26, 1951; Minnesota, February 27, 1951.

Ratification was completed on February 27, 1951.

The amendment was subsequently ratified by North Carolina on February 28, 1951; South Carolina, March 13, 1951; Maryland, March 14, 1951; Florida, April 16, 1951; Alabama, May 4, 1951.

The amendment was rejected (and not subsequently ratified) by Oklahoma in June 1947, and Massachusetts on June 9, 1949.

Certification of Validity

Publication of the certifying statement of the Administrator of General Services that the Amendment had become valid was made on Mar. 1, 1951, F.R. Doc. 51-2940, 16 F.R. 2019.

Article [XXIII.]

SECTION 1. The District constituting the seat of Government of the United States shall appoint in such manner as the Congress may direct:

A number of electors of President and Vice President equal to the whole number of Senators and Representatives in Congress to which the District would be entitled if it were a State, but in no event more than the least populous State; they shall be in addition to those appointed by the States, but they shall be considered, for the purposes of the election of President and Vice President, to be electors appointed by a State; and they shall meet in the District and perform such duties as provided by the twelfth article of amendment.

SEC. 2. The Congress shall have power to enforce this article by appropriate legislation.

Proposal and Ratification

This amendment was proposed by the Eighty-sixth Congress on June 17, 1960 and was declared by the Administrator of General Services on Apr. 3, 1961, to have been ratified by 38 of the 50 States. The dates of ratification were: Hawaii, June 23, 1960 (and that State made a technical correction to its resolution on June 30, 1960); Massachusetts, August 22, 1960; New Jersey, December 19, 1960; New York, January 17, 1961; California, January 19, 1961; Oregon, January 27, 1961; Maryland, January 30, 1961; Idaho, January 31, 1961; Maine, January 31, 1961; Minnesota, January 31, 1961; New Mexico, February 1, 1961; Nevada, February 2, 1961; Montana, February 6, 1961; South Dakota, February 6, 1961; Colorado, February 8, 1961; Washington, February 9, 1961; West Virginia, February 9, 1961; Alaska, February 10, 1961; Wyoming, February 13, 1961; Delaware, February 20, 1961; Utah, February 21, 1961; Wisconsin, February 21, 1961; Pennsylvania, February 28, 1961; Indiana, March 3, 1961; North Dakota, March 3, 1961; Tennessee, March 6, 1961; Michigan, March 8, 1961; Connecticut, March 9, 1961; Arizona, March 10, 1961; Illinois, March 14, 1961; Nebraska, March 15, 1961; Vermont, March 15, 1961; Iowa, March 16, 1961; Missouri, March 20, 1961; Oklahoma, March 21, 1961; Rhode Island, March 22, 1961; Kansas, March 29, 1961; Ohio, March 29, 1961.

Ratification was completed on March 29, 1961.

The amendment was subsequently ratified by New Hampshire on March 30, 1961 (when that State annulled and then repeated its ratification of March 29, 1961).

The amendment was rejected (and not subsequently ratified) by Arkansas on January 24, 1961.

Certification of Validity

Publication of the certifying statement of the Administrator of General Services that the Amendment had become valid was made on Apr. 3, 1961, F.R. Doc. 61-3017, 26 F.R. 2808.

Article [XXIV.]

SECTION 1. The right of citizens of the United States to vote in any primary or other election for President or Vice President, for electors for President or Vice President, or for Senator or Representative in Congress, shall not be denied or abridged by the United States or any State by reason of failure to pay any poll tax or other tax.

SEC. 2. The Congress shall have power to enforce this article by appropriate legislation.

Proposal and Ratification

This amendment was proposed by the Eighty-seventh Congress by Senate Joint Resolution No. 29, which was approved by the Senate on Mar. 27, 1962, and by the House of Representatives on Aug. 27, 1962. It was declared by the Administrator of General Services on Feb. 4, 1964, to have been ratified by the legislatures of 38 of the 50 States.

This amendment was ratified by the following States:

Illinois, Nov. 14, 1962; New Jersey, Dec. 3, 1962; Oregon, Jan. 25, 1963; Montana, Jan. 28, 1963; West Virginia, Feb. 1, 1963; New York, Feb. 4, 1963; Maryland, Feb. 6, 1963; California, Feb. 7, 1963; Alaska, Feb. 11, 1963; Rhode Island, Feb. 14, 1963; Indiana, Feb. 19, 1963; Utah, Feb. 20, 1963; Michigan, Feb. 20, 1963; Colorado, Feb. 21, 1963; Ohio, Feb. 27, 1963; Minnesota, Feb. 27, 1963; New Mexico, Mar. 5, 1963; Hawaii, Mar. 6, 1963; North Dakota, Mar. 7, 1963; Idaho, Mar. 8, 1963; Washington, Mar. 14, 1963; Vermont, Mar. 15, 1963; Nevada, Mar. 19, 1963; Connecticut, Mar. 20, 1963; Tennessee, Mar. 21, 1963; Pennsylvania, Mar. 25, 1963; Wisconsin, Mar. 26, 1963; Kansas, Mar. 28, 1963; Massachusetts, Mar. 28, 1963; Nebraska, Apr. 4, 1963; Florida, Apr. 18, 1963; Iowa, Apr. 24, 1963; Delaware, May 1, 1963; Missouri, May 13, 1963; New Hampshire, June 12, 1963; Kentucky, June 27, 1963; Maine, Jan. 16, 1964; South Dakota, Jan. 23, 1964; Virginia, Feb. 25, 1977.

Ratification was completed on January 23, 1964.

The amendment was rejected by Mississippi (and not subsequently ratified) on December 20, 1962.

Certification of Validity

Publication of the certifying statement of the Administrator of General Services that the Amendment had become valid was made on Feb. 5, 1964, F.R. Doc. 64-1229, 29 F.R. 1715.

Article [XXV.]

SECTION 1. In case of the removal of the President from office or of his death or resignation, the Vice President shall become President.

SEC. 2. Whenever there is a vacancy in the office of the Vice President, the President shall nominate a Vice President who shall take office upon confirmation by a majority vote of both Houses of Congress.

SEC. 3. Whenever the President transmits to the President pro tempore of the Senate and the Speaker of the House of Representatives his written declaration that he is unable to discharge the powers and duties of his office, and until he transmits to them a written declaration to the contrary, such powers and duties shall be discharged by the Vice President as Acting President.

SEC. 4. Whenever the Vice President and a majority of either the principal officers of the executive departments or of such other body as Congress may by law provide, transmit to the President pro tempore of the Senate and the Speaker of the House of Representatives their written declaration that the President is unable to discharge the powers and duties of his office, the Vice President shall immediately assume the powers and duties of the office as Acting President.

Thereafter, when the President transmits to the President pro tempore of the Senate and the Speaker of the House of Representatives his written declaration that no inability exists, he shall resume the powers and duties of his office unless the Vice President and a majority of either the principal officers of the executive department or of such other body as Congress may by law provide, transmit within four days to the President pro tempore of the Senate and the Speaker of the House of Representatives their written declaration that the President is unable to discharge the powers and duties of his office. Thereupon Congress shall decide the issue, assembling within forty-eight hours for that purpose if not in session. If the Congress, within twenty-one days after receipt of the latter written declaration, or, if Congress is not in session, within twenty-one days after Congress is required to assemble, determines by two-thirds vote of both Houses that the President is unable to discharge the powers and duties of his office, the Vice President shall continue to discharge the same as Acting President; otherwise, the President shall resume the powers and duties of his office.

Proposal and Ratification

This amendment was proposed by the Eighty-ninth Congress by Senate Joint Resolution No. 1, which was approved by the Senate on Feb. 19, 1965, and by the House of Representatives, in amended form, on Apr. 13, 1965. The House of Representatives agreed to a Conference Report on June 30, 1965, and the Senate agreed to the Conference Report on July 6, 1965. It was declared by the Administrator of General Services, on Feb. 23, 1967, to have been ratified by the legislatures of 39 of the 50 States.

This amendment was ratified by the following States:

Nebraska, July 12, 1965; Wisconsin, July 13, 1965; Oklahoma, July 16, 1965; Massachusetts, Aug. 9, 1965; Pennsylvania, Aug. 18, 1965; Kentucky, Sept. 15, 1965; Arizona, Sept. 22, 1965; Michigan, Oct. 5, 1965; Indiana, Oct. 20, 1965; California, Oct. 21, 1965; Arkansas, Nov. 4, 1965; New Jersey, Nov. 29, 1965; Delaware, Dec. 7, 1965; Utah, Jan. 17, 1966; West Virginia, Jan. 20, 1966; Maine, Jan. 24, 1966; Rhode Island, Jan. 28, 1966; Colorado, Feb. 3, 1966; New Mexico, Feb. 3, 1966; Kansas, Feb. 8, 1966; Vermont, Feb. 10, 1966; Alaska, Feb. 18, 1966; Idaho, Mar. 2, 1966; Hawaii, Mar. 3, 1966; Virginia, Mar. 8, 1966; Mississippi, Mar. 10, 1966; New York, Mar. 14, 1966; Maryland, Mar. 23, 1966; Missouri, Mar. 30, 1966; New Hampshire, June 13, 1966; Louisiana, July 5, 1966; Tennessee, Jan. 12, 1967; Wyoming, Jan. 25, 1967; Washington, Jan. 26, 1967; Iowa, Jan. 26, 1967; Oregon, Feb. 2, 1967; Minnesota, Feb. 10, 1967; Nevada, Feb. 10, 1967.

Ratification was completed on Feb. 10, 1967.

The amendment was subsequently ratified by Connecticut, Feb. 14, 1967; Montana, Feb. 15, 1967; South Dakota, Mar. 6, 1967; Ohio, Mar. 7, 1967; Alabama, Mar. 14, 1967; North Carolina, Mar. 22, 1967; Illinois, Mar. 22, 1967; Texas, April 25, 1967; Florida, May 25, 1967.

Certification of Validity

Publication of the certifying statement of the Administrator of General Services that the Amendment had become valid was made on Feb. 25, 1967, F.R. Doc. 67-2208, 32 F.R. 3287.

Article [XXVI.]

SECTION 1. The right of citizens of the United States, who are eighteen years of age or older, to vote shall not be denied or abridged by the United States or by any State on account of age.

SEC. 2. The Congress shall have power to enforce this article by appropriate legislation.

Proposal and Ratification

This amendment was proposed by the Ninety-second Congress by Senate Joint Resolution No. 7, which was approved by the Senate on Mar. 10, 1971, and by the House of Representatives on Mar. 23, 1971. It was declared by the Administrator of General Services on July 5, 1971, to have been ratified by the legislatures of 39 of the 50 States.

This amendment was ratified by the following States: Connecticut, March 23, 1971; Delaware, March 23, 1971; Minnesota, March 23, 1971; Tennessee, March 23, 1971; Washington, March 23, 1971; Hawaii, March 24, 1971; Massachusetts, March 24, 1971; Montana, March 29, 1971; Arkansas, March 30, 1971; Idaho, March 30, 1971; Iowa, March 30, 1971; Nebraska, April 2, 1971; New Jersey, April 3, 1971; Kansas, April 7, 1971; Michigan, April 7, 1971; Alaska, April 8, 1971; Maryland, April 8, 1971; Indiana, April 8, 1971; Maine, April 9, 1971; Vermont, April 16, 1971; Louisiana, April 17, 1971; California, April 19, 1971; Colorado, April 27, 1971; Pennsylvania, April 27, 1971; Texas, April 27, 1971; South Carolina, April 28, 1971; West Virginia, April 28, 1971; New Hampshire, May 13, 1971; Arizona, May 14, 1971; Rhode Island, May 27, 1971; New York, June 2, 1971; Oregon, June 4, 1971; Missouri, June 14, 1971; Wisconsin, June 22, 1971; Illinois, June 29, 1971; Alabama, June 30, 1971; Ohio, June 30, 1971; North Carolina, July 1, 1971; Oklahoma, July 1, 1971.

Ratification was completed on July 1, 1971.

The amendment was subsequently ratified by Virginia, July 8, 1971; Wyoming, July 8, 1971; Georgia, October 4, 1971.

Certification of Validity

Publication of the certifying statement of the Administrator of General Services that the Amendment had become valid was made on July 7, 1971, F.R. Doc. 71-9691, 36 F.R. 12725.

PROPOSED AMENDMENTS

Resolved by the Senate and House of Representatives of the United States of America in Congress assembled (two-thirds of each House concurring therein), That the following article is proposed as an amendment to the Constitution of the United States, which shall be valid to all intents and purposes as part of the Constitution when ratified by the legislatures of three-fourths of the several States within seven years from the date of its submission by the Congress:

PROPOSED AMENDMENT
TO THE
CONSTITUTION OF THE UNITED STATES
SECOND SESSION, NINETY-SECOND CONGRESS

JOINT RESOLUTION

Proposing an amendment to the Constitution of the United States relative to equal rights for men and women. [H. J. Res. 208]

Resolved by the Senate and House of Representatives of the United States of America in Congress assembled (two-thirds of each House concurring therein), That the following article is proposed as an amendment to the Constitution of the United States, which shall be valid to all intents and purposes as part of the Constitution when ratified by the legislatures of three-fourths of the several States within seven years from the date of its submission by the Congress:

"ARTICLE —

"SECTION 1. Equality of rights under the law shall not be denied or abridged by the United States or by any State on account of sex.

"SEC. 2. The Congress shall have the power to enforce, by appropriate legislation, the provisions of this article.

"SEC. 3. This amendment shall take effect two years after the date of ratification."

CARL ALBERT
Speaker of the House of Representatives.

ALLEN J. ELLENDER
President of the Senate pro Tempore.

I certify that this Joint Resolution originated in the House of Representatives.

W. PAT JENNINGS
Clerk.

BY W. RAYMOND COLLEY

[Received by the Office of the Federal Register, National Archives and Records Service, General Services Administration, March 23, 1972.]

LEGISLATIVE HISTORY:

HOUSE REPORT No. 92–359 (Comm. on the Judiciary).
SENATE REPORT No. 92–689, also accompanying S. J. Res. 8 and S. J. Res. 9 (Comm. on the Judiciary).
CONGRESSIONAL RECORD:
Vol. 117 (1971): Aug. 6, S. J. Res. 150 considered in Senate.
Oct. 6, 12, H. J. Res. 208 considered and passed House.
Vol. 118 (1972): Mar. 15, 17, 20–22, considered and passed Senate.

Extension of Time for Ratification

H.J.Res. 638 of the Ninety-Fifth Congress, Second Session, provided: "That notwithstanding any provision of House Joint Resolution 208 of the Ninety-Second Congress, Second Session, to the contrary, the article of amendment proposed to the States in such joint resolution shall be valid to all intents and purposes as part of the Constitution when ratified by the legislatures of three-fourths of the several States not later than June 30, 1982."

The Proposed Amendment was not ratified by the legislatures of three-fourths of the States by June 30, 1982.

Ratification by the States

Hawaii	March 22, 1972
Delaware	March 23, 1972
New Hampshire	March 23, 1972
Idaho	March 24, 1972
Kansas	March 28, 1972
Nebraska	March 29, 1972
Tennessee	April 4, 1972
Alaska	April 5, 1972
Rhode Island	April 14, 1972
New Jersey	April 17, 1972
Texas	April 19, 1972
Colorado	April 21, 1972
Iowa	April 21, 1972
West Virginia	April 22, 1972
Wisconsin	April 26, 1972
New York	May 3, 1972
Michigan	May 22, 1972
Maryland	May 26, 1972
Massachusetts	June 21, 1972
Kentucky	June 26, 1972
Pennsylvania	Sept. 26, 1972
California	Nov. 13, 1972
Wyoming	Jan. 26, 1973
South Dakota	Feb. 5, 1973
Oregon	Feb. 8, 1973
Minnesota	Feb. 12, 1973
New Mexico	Feb. 28, 1973
Vermont	March 1, 1973

Connecticut	March 15, 1973
Washington	March 27, 1973
Maine	Jan. 18, 1974
Montana	Jan. 25, 1974
Ohio	Feb. 7, 1974
North Dakota	Feb. 3, 1975
Indiana	Jan. 24, 1977

Action Subsequent to Ratification

Four states have either rescinded their ratification or taken supplementary action which *might* affect their prior ratification:

Nebraska	Mar. 15, 1973
Tennessee	Apr. 23, 1974
Idaho	Feb. 8, 1977
Kentucky	Mar. 16, 1978

H. J. Res. 554

NINETY-FIFTH CONGRESS OF THE UNITED STATES OF AMERICA

AT THE SECOND SESSION

Begun and held at the City of Washington on Thursday, the nineteenth day of January, one thousand nine hundred and seventy-eight

JOINT RESOLUTION

Proposing an amendment to the Constitution to provide for representation of the District of Columbia in the Congress.

Resolved by the Senate and House of Representatives of the United States of America in Congress assembled (two-thirds of each House concurring therein), That the following article is proposed as an amendment to the Constitution of the United States, which shall be valid to all intents and purposes as part of the Constitution when ratified by the legislatures of three-fourths of the several States within seven years from the date of its submission by the Congress:

"ARTICLE —

"SECTION 1. For purposes of representation in the Congress, election of the President and Vice President, and article V of this Constitution, the District constituting the seat of government of the United States shall be treated as though it were a State.

"SEC. 2. The exercise of the rights and powers conferred under this article shall be by the people of the District constituting the seat of government, and as shall be provided by the Congress.

"SEC. 3. The twenty-third article of amendment to the Constitution of the United States is hereby repealed.

"SEC. 4. This article shall be inoperative, unless it shall have been ratified as an amendment to the Constitution by the legislatures of three-fourths of the several States within seven years from the date of its submission."

THOMAS P. O'NEILL, JR.,
Speaker of the House of Representatives.

QUENTIN BURDICK,
Acting President of the Senate-pro Tempore.

I certify that this Joint Resolution originated in the House of Representatives.

EDMUND L. HENSHAW, JR.,
Clerk.

BY W. RAYMOND COLLEY,
Deputy Clerk.

[Received by the Office of the Federal Register, National Archives and Records Service, General Services Administration, August 28, 1978]

LEGISLATIVE HISTORY:

HOUSE REPORT No. 95–886 (Comm. on the Judiciary).
CONGRESSIONAL RECORD, Vol. 124 (1978):
Mar. 1, 2, considered and passed House.
Aug. 16, 17, 21, 22, considered and passed Senate.

Ratification by the States

New Jersey	Sept. 11, 1978
Ohio	Nov. 30, 1978
Michigan	Dec. 12, 1978
Massachusetts	March 19, 1979
Minnesota	March 28, 1979
Connecticut	April 11, 1979
Wisconsin	Nov. 12, 1979
Maryland	March 19, 1980
Hawaii	April 18, 1980
Oregon	June 20, 1981
Maine	Feb. 16, 1983
West Virginia	Feb. 23, 1983
Rhode Island	May 14, 1983

Glossary of Legal Terms

The following glossary of legal terms is not intended to be exhaustive. It may be used by the student as an easily available aid to a better understanding of the text portion and the edited decisions contained in the preceding pages.

Ab Initio: From the first; from the beginning.

Abstention: In constitutional law this term is sometimes used by a federal court when it declines to exercise its jurisdiction over a matter, pending a final determination of it in the courts of a state.

Abuse of Discretion: Legal name given to a court review of the actions of a trial court or administrative officer where petitioner claims that discretion exercised was arbitrary, discriminatory, and/or unreasonable.

Abuse of Process: The use of legal papers for a purpose other than intended by law, resulting in unlawful harassment to the recipient.

Accessory: One who aids in the commission or attempted commission of an offense or in assisting a perpetrator of an offense to avoid apprehension.

Accomplice: A person who voluntarily acts with another to commit or attempt to commit an offense, both persons having a shared criminal purpose.

Accusation: A charge of wrongdoing made against a person. It may include a prosecutor's information, a grand jury indictment, or a complainant's formal affidavit of complaint.

Acquittal: A finding that a defendant is not guilty of the offense for which s/he was charged.

Actus Reus: The guilty act as opposed to the mens rea which is the guilty mind.

Ad Hoc: For this particular purpose.

Adjudication: The judicial determination of a controversy between parties wherein judgment is pronounced. May also apply to administrative tribunals.

Admissible Evidence: All means by which any alleged matter of fact is proved or disproved which is permitted into a trial record pursuant to the law of the court's jurisdiction.

Admission: In criminal law, the voluntary statement made or an act done which is contrary to a person's position on trial. It falls short of a confession which is a direct acknowledgment of guilt.

Adversary: An opponent in a legal controversy.

Affiant: The person who subscribes his/her signature to an affidavit.

Affidavit: A statement in writing subscribed by a signature of a person which was affixed under oath before a notary public, a magistrate, or a commissioner of deeds.

Affirm: To attest to the truth of a statement or the act of an appellate court indicating that the ruling or decision of the lower court was correct.

A Fortiori: All the more; a term which is used which draws a conclusion by giving a reason; to the same effect.

Aid and Abet: To intentionally assist another to attempt to or to commit a criminal offense.
Alibi: A provable account of a person's whereabouts at a particular time which negates that person's involvement in a criminal offense.
Amicus Curiae: Friend of the court. Used frequently where nonlitigants submit memoranda of law to assist the court to render a decision in a pending matter.
Arraignment: A proceeding wherein the accused is informed of the nature of the charges against him/her. This is done before a judge or a magistrate. The accused is asked how s/he pleads to the charges and bail conditions are sometimes set pending a trial at a later date.
Arrest: The initial taking into custody of a person by law enforcement authorities to answer for a criminal offense or violation of a code or ordinance.
Assault: Any unlawful attempt to inflict bodily injury upon another, accompanied by the apparent present ability to do the act.
Assignment of Error: An allegation made by appellant against a trial judge charging error which is the ground for reversal.
Attainder: In common law, a mark of infamy given to a convicted felon resulting in loss of all civil rights. *See* bill of attainder.
Attempt: An overt act, beyond mere preparation, to commit an offense.

Bail: A pecuniary or other security accepted by a court or duly authorized officer to insure the appearance of a defendant at every stage of the proceedings up to final incarceration, dismissal, payment of fine, and/or sentence of probation.
Bailiff: A court attendant or court officer.
Bar (Attorneys): Duly licensed attorneys are designated as being admitted to the bar of courts.
Bar (Procedure): A barrier to relitigating the same issue (position in court room). Defendant standing before the judge is called "prisoner at the bar" (partition in court room separating judge, court personnel and attorneys litigating the instant case from others in court room).
Barrister: English practitioner of law who functions as a trial counsel.
Battery: The touching of another person done willfully and in anger.
Bench: The place where the judge or judges sit while in a courtroom.
Bench Warrant: A court order directing a law enforcement officer to seize a named person and bring that person before the court.
Bill of Attainder: A legislative act designed to inflict punishment upon a named person or persons without the benefit of a judicial trial. A legislature however has power to quell disorder in the chamber and may punish and/or incarcerate for contempt as long as accused has opportunity to appear and respond to charges.
Brief (Court use): A written argument presented to a judge, panel of judges, or an administrative law judge to persuade that person to decide an issue presently before the tribunal in favor of one of the litigants.
Brief (Student use): An epitome of a written decision which the student writes as an aid to remembering the legal history, questions of law, facts of the case, opinion and judgment of the court.
Burden of Proof: The requirement of a litigant to persuade the trier of the facts that the allegations made against the other party to an action are true. In criminal law, the government is required to prove its case beyond any reasonable doubt. In civil cases, the party bringing the action is required to prove the allegations by a preponderance of evidence. In administrative hearings, the allegations must be proven by substantial evidence or by clear and convincing evidence.

Caveat: A warning.
Certiorari: A common law writ issued from a higher court to an inferior court, commanding the inferior court to certify and send the record of a particular case, previously decided by the inferior court, to

the higher court for review of the inferior court's actions in the case.

Circumstantial Evidence: Secondary facts from which a rational inference may be logically arrived at to prove a principal fact.

Citation: A written or printed command to a person to appear before a court on the day and time indicated. Also used as a location in a publication where a legal case may be found.

Civil Liberties: Courses of action that a person is entitled to which are immune from governmental interference. They may be limitations of governmental action, e.g., liberty of free speech guaranteed in the First Amendment of the United States Constitution.

Civil Rights: A course of action which a person is entitled to which is defined by positive laws enacted by government, e.g., right to bring a civil action against the government pursuant to statutory authority.

Clear and Convincing: A standard of proof beyond a mere preponderance but not as much as beyond a reasonable doubt. Usually that quantum of proof required of a party to prevail in an administrative tribunal. Similar to substantial evidence.

Clear and Present Danger: A limitation on the unfettered exercise of free speech such as shouting "fire" in a crowded theater when in fact there is no fire or no danger present.

Collateral Attack: A challenge to a judgment brought about indirectly and not by direct appeal, e.g., habeas corpus petition instead of appeal of a prior rendered judgment.

Collateral Estoppel: The determination of litigated facts is binding on those parties in all future proceedings against each other. The constitutional prohibition against double jeopardy enables a defendant to plead collateral estoppel if a primary issue was previously litigated and defendant's contention prevailed at former trial.

Comity: A judicial courtesy wherein one court yields to another court of concomitant jurisdiction based on the concept that a court which first asserts its jurisdiction will not be interfered with by another court, e.g., judgments of courts of competent jurisdiction of foreign nations are not interfered with by other state or federal courts based on comity.

Common Law: A system of jurisprudence which is derived from Anglo-Saxon law from principles, rather than rules, based on justice, reason, and common sense, judicially originated. The principles change with the needs of the community.

Competent (Court): One having proper jurisdiction.

Competent (Person): Capacity to understand and act reasonably.

Competent (Witness): Capacity to understand.

Confession: A direct acknowledgment of guilt.

Conjugal Visitation (Prison): Permission to engage in sexual intercourse between the inmate and his/her spouse.

Contempt of Court: An act or an omission tending to obstruct or interfere with the orderly administration of a court or to affect the dignity of a court.

Corporal Punishment: Pain inflicted upon a person as a means of correction or to prevent recidivism, e.g., whipping of a prisoner.

Crime: Any act which the government has declared to be contrary to the public good, which is declared by statute to be a crime and which is prosecuted in a criminal proceeding. In some jurisdictions crimes only include felonies and/or misdemeanors.

Crime against Nature: Deviant social behavior relevant to sexual acts, e.g., sodomy; sexual intercourse with a dead body.

Cruel and Unusual Punishment: Amorphous term which cannot be defined with specificity. Punishment which is shocking to reasonable persons. United States Supreme Court interprets this phrase on an ad hoc basis.

Custodial Interrogation: The confinement of a person by law enforcement agents/officers. The person is not free to leave and is questioned about a crime.

De Minimus: Insignificant; of no importance; not important enough to take the time and attention of a court.
Demurrer: An answer to a complaint which declares that even if all of the facts stated in the complaint are true, it does not state a cause of action. The court ruling on a demurrer may grant summary judgment for the prevailing party, thus terminating the case.
De Novo: To start for another time from the beginning.
Deposition: A statement of a person reduced to writing which is subscribed under oath or affirmation.
Dictum (Obiter dictum): A statement made by the court which is included in a judicial opinion and is not necessarily pertinent to the facts of the instant case. A dictum is not considered to be binding on future cases.
Discovery Process: Pretrial procedure whereby litigants supply information to their adversary before trial, which is necessary to the other party's position at trial.
Dismiss (Appeal): To place parties in same position as if no appeal were taken.
Dismiss (Legal): To terminate a court case without a trial.
Diversity of Citizenship: Where citizens of different states are litigants in an action. It may be cause for federal court jurisdiction if other requirements are met.
Domicile: A place of permanent residence where a person intends to return when absent. A person may have only one domicile but may have many residences.
Double Jeopardy: A person who is tried again for a crime which has been litigated to an acquittal or conviction is said to be twice placed in jeopardy if tried again for the same offense. A mistrial or appeal does not prevent a second trial unless the mistrial was the result of brash behavior by the prosecution in an obvious attempt to try the defendant at another time.
Due Process: A phrase without a fixed meaning. It has been interpreted by the U.S. Supreme Court as requiring a government to exercise fundamental fairness in the administration of criminal justice.

En Banc: By the full court.
Enjoin: A command by a court to do or refrain from doing a specific act.
Et Seq.: And the following.
Evidence: All matter of proof offered in a trial to prove or disprove an issue of fact.
Exclusionary Rule: A judicially contrived procedure which prevents evidence unconstitutionally obtained by law enforcement officers from being introduced into evidence at a criminal trial and is not to be considered by the triers of the facts of the case in arriving at a verdict.
Exculpatory: Statements or evidence which tends to prove that a person was not the perpetrator of a criminal offense.
Execute: The killing of a prisoner by authority of the government; the signing of a legal instrument.
Ex Post Facto Law: A law which declares designated behavior to be a crime which, when committed, was noncriminal; or increases the punishment after it was committed; or diminishes the requisite proof for conviction.

Fair Hearing: An extra judicial hearing usually authorized by statute to determine a controversy in an administrative tribunal. It must be conducted in a manner which includes an opportunity for all sides to present evidence, e.g., 42 U.S.C.A. Sect. 602 (a)(4) requiring fair hearing prior to termination of welfare benefits.
Felony: A crime for which a person may be imprisoned for at least a year and a day.
First Impression: The first time that a question of law has been decided by a court.
Frisk: The patting down of the outer clothing of a person who is suspected of carrying a concealed weapon.
Fruit of the Poisonous Tree Doctrine: If a law enforcement officer obtains information from a defendant in an unconstitu-

tional manner, although that evidence is not used at the defendant's trial, other evidence ascertained as a result of the illegally obtained evidence is also excludable from the trial, based on the doctrine of the fruit of the poisonous tree. Such other evidence has been held to be admissible, however, for impeachment when defendant testifies.

Full Faith and Credit: Phrase applied to the United States Constitution which requires the "public Acts, Records and Judicial Proceedings" of one state to be respected by each of the sister states, Art. 4, Sec. 1.

Grand Jury: A body of people (usually 23) who serve as part of the criminal justice system. The grand jury's function is to investigate and indict persons for crimes or render information or presentments for crimes committed in its territorial jurisdiction. It may also find that a complaint of criminal activity is not worthy of an indictment or information.

Guilty (Criminal): The finding beyond a reasonable doubt, by a jury or judge presiding without a jury, after a trial, or after a judicial confession of guilt, that a defendant committed the crime charged.

Habeas Corpus Writ: A court order requiring a person who has custody of another person to be present in court with the detainee so that the court can inquire as to the legality of the detention. Writs of Habeas Corpus may be directed to a Commissioner of Prisons and may also be used in child custody and elderly guardianship litigation.

Harmless Error: Error conducted during a trial which an appellate court has concluded does not affect a defendant's substantial right to cause a reviewing court to reverse the judgment of the trial court.

Head Note: Summary of facts, questions of law, decision and judgment of a case.

Hearing: A proceeding where evidence is taken to determine issues of fact. It may be an administrative hearing, e.g., police agency disciplinary hearing; suppression hearing (to determine whether evidence was unconstitutionally seized); prima facie hearing (to determine if allegations constitute a crime). Some hearings do not require formal rules of evidence.

Hearsay Rule: In the law of evidence hearsay is not generally admitted into evidence unless the material offered is one or more of the recognized exceptions. (See Klein's *Law of Evidence for Police*, 2nd Edition. West Publishing Co., 1978.) It is evidence of a statement made by a witness which is restating what another person either orally said or wrote, when it is offered for the truth of the assertion.

Hung Jury: A trial jury which cannot agree on a verdict according to the number set forth by law in its jurisdiction. Most criminal courts require a unanimous vote for conviction. Some require a substantial majority, e.g., 10–2. A retrial does not subject the defendant to double jeopardy.

Ibid.: In the same book or on the same page. It avoids repetition of source data.

Immunity: Usually a right of absolution from prosecution for a criminal act given to a witness to a crime in exchange for information given to a Grand Jury or prosecutor. A Grand Jury or a prosecutor has power to grant immunity.

Impeachment: Term applied to questions directed toward a witness who is testifying under cross-examination in an attempt to obtain contradictory statements to affect the credibility of the witness.

In Camera: In chambers of the judge. Chambers can mean the judge's office or it could mean the robing room adjacent to the court room.

Incriminate: To involve either one's self or another as responsible for criminal conduct.

Inculpatory: Tending to involve one's self or another as responsible for criminal conduct; incriminate.

Independent Source: Information acquired by a law enforcement agency which is not tainted by any violation of a constitutional right.

Indictment: A formal written accusation drawn up by a prosecutor and presented to a Grand Jury which then investigates the charge. If a prima facie crime is found, the foreman of the Grand Jury endorses the indictment as a "True Bill." If the charges are not substantiated, "No True Bill" is found and the indictment is so endorsed. It usually applies to felony offenses only.
Informant: A person who supplies information to a law enforcement officer referring to the commission of a crime or to some set of facts requiring the attention of the law enforcement agency.
In Loco Parentis: In the place of a parent.
Interrogation: Questioning of a person to ascertain facts.
Issue (In courtroom setting or controversy): A certain point of law or fact which is in dispute.

Judge (Trial judge): The presiding officer in a trial whose duty it is to see that a fair, impartial, and orderly trial is conducted, adhering to the Constitution of the United States, the Constitution of the State (if state jurisdiction), the laws of the court's jurisdiction and the rules of the court. The judge is an impartial arbiter who rules on the admissibility of evidence and motions of various types and instructs the fact triers as to the law of the case. Some jurisdictions give judges the title of "Justice."
Judgment: The final determination of the rights of parties to a lawsuit, whether civil or criminal, which determination is made by a judge or panel of judges, and which is entered in the clerk's records of the case.
Jury Charge (Judge's charge to jury): At the end of the testimony of a jury trial, each side indicates that it "rests." Thereupon it is the duty of the trial judge to explain the law of the case to the jury before it goes to the deliberation room. This is called "the Judge's Charge."

Lesser Included Offense: A crime or violation of law which is part of a more serious crime. A crime having less aggravating elements than a more serious crime which carries greater sanctions (punishment), e.g., larceny is a lesser included offense of robbery.
Lineup: A procedure where law enforcement officers select a number of persons to stand or sit next to each other to be viewed by witnesses or victims of crime to ascertain whether any or all of the selected persons committed a criminal offense. This is usually done before a one-way mirror with a suspect's attorney present and the proceedings are recorded.
Litigation: A controversy between parties which is brought to a court for determination of the issues.

Magistrate: A judicial officer authorized to conduct preliminary hearings, set bail conditions, administer oaths, and issue warrants. Most jurisdictions do not authorize magistrates to conduct trials of criminal offenses. A judge may also be a magistrate.
Malum in Se: Bad in itself; naturally evil, e.g., murder.
Malum Prohibitum: Bad or wrong because it is made unlawful by statute, e.g., driving a vehicle on the wrong side of the street.
Mandamus Writ: A court order wherein the court orders a designated person (governmental official or corporate officer) to perform a designated act.
Mens Rea: A mental state required in criminal law; intention; criminal negligence (gross); reckless and/or knowing.
Misdemeanor: A class of criminal deviance which is usually punished by a maximum of $1,000 fine and/or up to one year in a county or city jail. It is less serious than a felony. Different jurisdictions classify misdemeanors and sanctions for violation thereof differently.
Mistrial: Where a prejudicial error occurs, a judge, on motion or sua sponte, may declare a mistrial. This has the effect of declaring the trial a nullity and does not preclude another trial of the same parties

on the same facts. It is not a ground for a defense of double jeopardy.

Motion: An application to a judge or panel of judges requesting the relief desired, e.g., motion for a new trial.

Nisi Prius: In American law it has come to mean any court where a case is heard by a judge and jury for the first time. An appellate court is not a nisi prius court.

Nolo Contendere: From the Latin and common law courts where a defendant tells the court that he/she does not wish to interpose a defense or plea of not guilty in a criminal action. Some state courts do not permit a defendant to answer a charge in this way. The court must find a factual basis to accept this. It is not a confession of guilt. In criminal law it has the same effect as a plea of guilty.

N.O.V.: From the Latin—Non Obstante Verdicto. A motion for a judgment N.O.V., if granted, is one which reverses the conclusions reached by a jury because the court reasoned that based on the facts presented in the trial, the jury had no reasonable grounds to reach the conclusion indicated in its verdict.

Nunc pro Tunc: If a court order includes this phrase, it means that the action ordered to be taken reverts back to a specified time as if it had been taken at that time. It is frequently used to permit late filing of papers when it is in the interest of justice to permit such late filing.

Obiter Dicta: *See* dictum.

Opening Statement: This is a speech which the adversaries in a criminal trial make to the jury before any testimony is received in evidence. It is used to acquaint the jury with the facts and issues of a case which that litigant intends to prove. In criminal cases, many jurisdictions permit a defendant to waive a right to an opening statement.

Opinion: The reason that a judge gives for the court's conclusion. It differs from a decision which is the judgment of the court.

Oyer and Terminer: These were old English courts where the King would appoint a person to act as a judge to hear and determine a case forthwith, instead of waiting for the normal judicial procedure of the realm to prosecute, hear, and determine a criminal case.

Pardon: A power to forgive vested in the executive of the government, i.e., President, Governor. Its effect is to restore all rights to the defendant as if the defendant had never committed the criminal act for which s/he was pardoned.

Parole: This may be descriptive of a discretionary decision of an official or board of parole who has lawful authority to permit a prisoner to serve part of his/her sentence in the community. One who is on parole is serving part of the imposed sentence outside of confinement and in the community.

Perjury: A criminal offense where a person makes a false statement while under oath or affirmation.

Petition: A written request made to a court or governmental authority asking for an act to be done; sometimes referred to as a prayer for relief.

Plain View: This phrase is applied to items of evidence which a law enforcement officer sees without having violated a person's constitutional rights and which s/he came upon inadvertently while performing normal duties.

Plea: This is a formal answer to a charge against a defendant for a criminal offense, e.g., guilty, not guilty.

Plea Bargaining: This is a negotiation procedure where the criminal defendant's attorney discusses a possibility of the defendant's pleading guilty to a lesser included offense in return for the prosecutor's either not recommending a severe sanction or not proceeding to trial on the original charge.

Police Power: The power of the government to provide for the health, welfare, safety, morals, and general welfare of those persons within its territorial jurisdiction.

Preamble: A statement of purpose and intent which precedes the specific articles and sections of a constitution.

Preliminary Hearing: Usually a hearing held before a magistrate to determine if probable cause exists to hold a defendant for a trial or indictment. Bail conditions are sometimes set at the end of this hearing.

Presentment: An investigation and accusation of crime made by a Grand Jury, initiated by itself without the participation of the prosecutor. A prosecutor has the discretion not to sign a presentment and not to prosecute the accusation.

Prima Facie: If on the facts presented, unexplained, a defendant might be found guilty of a criminal offense in that all of the elements of a crime have been shown to exist, we say that the prosecution has proved a prima facie case.

Prison: This is a place where criminal defendants of the state or federal courts are incarcerated, usually after they have been found guilty. A jail is the term applied to City or County places of incarceration, usually used for detention while awaiting trial or incarceration for less serious offenses.

Probable Cause: The reasoning process that a reasonable person uses to conclude that (a) there is a good reason to make an arrest, and (b) there is a good reason to suspect that a person has contraband or evidence of crime in the suspect's possession.

Probation: A sanction imposed on those convicted of a crime wherein the offender is subject to conditions of behavior laid down by the judge. The defendant may be under the supervision of a probation officer to whom s/he must periodically report, or may be on a nonreporting status.

Pro Bono Publico: When attorneys represent a client without fee it is said that the representation is pro bono publico, i.e., for the public good.

Pro Se: For himself. Refers to a person arguing his/her own case instead of retaining an attorney.

Quasi: Almost; like; e.g., quasi-criminal proceeding which is almost like a criminal proceeding but not actually one; e.g., a parole revocation proceeding.

Question of Fact: An issue of what actually occurred at the time of the incident which brings the parties before the court. This issue is decided by a jury if the trial is one with a jury. If no jury is present, it is decided by the judge.

Question of Law: A dispute of what rule of law is applicable to the case at bar. The judge decides the issue of what rule of law is to determine the results in the instant case.

Quid pro Quo: Something in exchange for something, e.g., a witness may testify in behalf of the prosecution if the state will grant immunity from prosecution to the witness.

Quo Warranto: By what authority. This is an ancient common law writ.

Reasonable Doubt: Refers to the quantum of proof required to prove a defendant guilty in a criminal trial. The trier of the fact is required to come to the conclusion that a defendant is guilty beyond a reasonable doubt. This does not mean all doubt, but beyond the doubt that a reasonable person would have.

Reasonable Man (Person): This is a phrase which characterizes what a normal, average person with ordinary knowledge, intelligence, and judgment might do in a given set of circumstances. It is not necessarily what the particular judge hearing or reviewing the case might do but what a hypothetical normal person's actions might be, given the same factual situation.

Remand: To send back. Sometimes refers to a case being sent back to the court which decided it previously. Also refers to a prisoner being sent back to a prison or detention facility.

Res Judicata (Res Adjudicata): The thing decided. The issue has previously been decided by a court of competent jurisdiction and thus is not to be relitigated.

Reversible Error: An error committed at the trial which substantially affected the outcome of the trial, that mandates either a new trial or a reversal of the outcome. Also known as "substantial error" or "prejudicial error."

Revocation: Term used in connection with revocation of parole. It means that the parolee is returned to prison, usually to serve the remainder of his/her original sentence of incarceration.

Sanction: To permit one to do something. Also used to indicate punishment for violation of accepted behavior.

Search Warrant: A court order directing a law enforcement officer to search for and return to the court particular items of personal property to be used in the prosecution of a person for violation of a statute.

Selective Incorporation: This term has been used to indicate that the United States Supreme Court has absorbed most of the Bill of Rights into the minimum requirements that a state must afford to inhabitants but not every one of these rights. This has been done by the authority of the Fourteenth Amendment of the United States Constitution.

Show-up: This is to be distinguished from a lineup. In a show-up the suspect is exhibited singularly to a crime victim. This is usually done shortly after the crime has taken place where speed and the practicalities of the situation warrant this type of identification instead of a lineup.

Standing: A court's recognition of a party to a lawsuit that the party is properly before the court.

Star Chamber: An ancient English court whose jurisdiction and procedure became so onerous that it was abolished. The privilege against self-incrimination in America resulted from Star Chamber abuses.

Stare Decisis: To stand by decided cases; to decide cases based on precedent of what the courts have decided on similar issues in earlier cases.

Stop and Frisk: Refers to law enforcement's authority to stop a suspected person and pat that person's outer clothing to search for a concealed weapon. The officer must have reason to believe that the suspect is armed and dangerous.

Suppression of Evidence: When evidence is unconstitutionally obtained by law enforcement authorities, the defendant makes a motion to suppress this evidence. After a hearing before a judge, the judge will indicate that the motion is granted. This means that the prosecutor is not permitted to use the unconstitutionally obtained evidence in the trial of this defendant. Often the prosecutor is unable to proceed with the case without this evidence.

Trial: The legal proceeding where testimony is offered before a judge sitting without a jury, or a judge sitting with a jury, where issues of fact and law are determined.

True Bill: A Grand Jury finding that an indictment presented to it by the prosecutor is based on sufficient probable cause. The foreman then signs the indictment and it becomes a true bill.

Vacate: To make void; to set aside as though it never existed; to move out.

Verdict: The conclusion reached by a jury or judge deciding the facts as to the issues after the completion of other parts of a trial.

Waiver: A voluntary giving up of a known right, e.g., a waiver of jury trial wherein the defendant in a criminal action intentionally gives up his/her right to be tried by a jury.

Warrant (Criminal Law): A court order directing a law enforcement officer to perform an indicated act, e.g., search warrant, arrest warrant.

Writ: A court order directing a named person to perform a specifically indicated act.

Table of Cases

References are to sections and pages

Index

Italicized numbers refer to page numbers